Lecture Notes in Computer Science 9171

Commenced Publication in 1973
Founding and Former Series Editors:
Gerhard Goos, Juris Hartmanis, and Jan van Leeuwen

More information about this series at http://www.springer.com/series/7409

Masaaki Kurosu (Ed.)

Human-Computer Interaction

Users and Contexts

17th International Conference,
HCI International 2015
Los Angeles, CA, USA, August 2–7, 2015
Proceedings, Part III

 Springer

Editor
Masaaki Kurosu
The Open University of Japan
Chiba-shi, Chiba
Japan

ISSN 0302-9743   ISSN 1611-3349 (electronic)
Lecture Notes in Computer Science
ISBN 978-3-319-21005-6   ISBN 978-3-319-21006-3 (eBook)
DOI 10.1007/978-3-319-21006-3

Library of Congress Control Number: 2015942491

LNCS Sublibrary: SL3 – Information Systems and Applications, incl. Internet/Web, and HCI

Springer Cham Heidelberg New York Dordrecht London

Printed on acid-free paper

Springer International Publishing AG Switzerland is part of Springer Science+Business Media
(www.springer.com)

Foreword

The 17th International Conference on Human-Computer Interaction, HCI International 2015, was held in Los Angeles, CA, USA, during 2–7 August 2015. The event incorporated the 15 conferences/thematic areas listed on the following page.

A total of 4843 individuals from academia, research institutes, industry, and governmental agencies from 73 countries submitted contributions, and 1462 papers and 246 posters have been included in the proceedings. These papers address the latest research and development efforts and highlight the human aspects of design and use of computing systems. The papers thoroughly cover the entire field of Human-Computer Interaction, addressing major advances in knowledge and effective use of computers in a variety of application areas. The volumes constituting the full 28-volume set of the conference proceedings are listed on pages VII and VIII.

I would like to thank the Program Board Chairs and the members of the Program Boards of all thematic areas and affiliated conferences for their contribution to the highest scientific quality and the overall success of the HCI International 2015 conference.

This conference could not have been possible without the continuous and unwavering support and advice of the founder, Conference General Chair Emeritus and Conference Scientific Advisor, Prof. Gavriel Salvendy. For their outstanding efforts, I would like to express my appreciation to the Communications Chair and Editor of HCI International News, Dr. Abbas Moallem, and the Student Volunteer Chair, Prof. Kim-Phuong L. Vu. Finally, for their dedicated contribution towards the smooth organization of HCI International 2015, I would like to express my gratitude to Maria Pitsoulaki and George Paparoulis, General Chair Assistants.

May 2015

Constantine Stephanidis
General Chair, HCI International 2015

HCI International 2015 Thematic Areas
and Affiliated Conferences

Thematic areas:

- Human-Computer Interaction (HCI 2015)
- Human Interface and the Management of Information (HIMI 2015)

Affiliated conferences:

- 12th International Conference on Engineering Psychology and Cognitive Ergonomics (EPCE 2015)
- 9th International Conference on Universal Access in Human-Computer Interaction (UAHCI 2015)
- 7th International Conference on Virtual, Augmented and Mixed Reality (VAMR 2015)
- 7th International Conference on Cross-Cultural Design (CCD 2015)
- 7th International Conference on Social Computing and Social Media (SCSM 2015)
- 9th International Conference on Augmented Cognition (AC 2015)
- 6th International Conference on Digital Human Modeling and Applications in Health, Safety, Ergonomics and Risk Management (DHM 2015)
- 4th International Conference on Design, User Experience and Usability (DUXU 2015)
- 3rd International Conference on Distributed, Ambient and Pervasive Interactions (DAPI 2015)
- 3rd International Conference on Human Aspects of Information Security, Privacy and Trust (HAS 2015)
- 2nd International Conference on HCI in Business (HCIB 2015)
- 2nd International Conference on Learning and Collaboration Technologies (LCT 2015)
- 1st International Conference on Human Aspects of IT for the Aged Population (ITAP 2015)

Conference Proceedings Volumes Full List

1. LNCS 9169, Human-Computer Interaction: Design and Evaluation (Part I), edited by Masaaki Kurosu
2. LNCS 9170, Human-Computer Interaction: Interaction Technologies (Part II), edited by Masaaki Kurosu
3. LNCS 9171, Human-Computer Interaction: Users and Contexts (Part III), edited by Masaaki Kurosu
4. LNCS 9172, Human Interface and the Management of Information: Information and Knowledge Design (Part I), edited by Sakae Yamamoto
5. LNCS 9173, Human Interface and the Management of Information: Information and Knowledge in Context (Part II), edited by Sakae Yamamoto
6. LNAI 9174, Engineering Psychology and Cognitive Ergonomics, edited by Don Harris
7. LNCS 9175, Universal Access in Human-Computer Interaction: Access to Today's Technologies (Part I), edited by Margherita Antona and Constantine Stephanidis
8. LNCS 9176, Universal Access in Human-Computer Interaction: Access to Interaction (Part II), edited by Margherita Antona and Constantine Stephanidis
9. LNCS 9177, Universal Access in Human-Computer Interaction: Access to Learning, Health and Well-Being (Part III), edited by Margherita Antona and Constantine Stephanidis
10. LNCS 9178, Universal Access in Human-Computer Interaction: Access to the Human Environment and Culture (Part IV), edited by Margherita Antona and Constantine Stephanidis
11. LNCS 9179, Virtual, Augmented and Mixed Reality, edited by Randall Shumaker and Stephanie Lackey
12. LNCS 9180, Cross-Cultural Design: Methods, Practice and Impact (Part I), edited by P.L. Patrick Rau
13. LNCS 9181, Cross-Cultural Design: Applications in Mobile Interaction, Education, Health, Transport and Cultural Heritage (Part II), edited by P.L. Patrick Rau
14. LNCS 9182, Social Computing and Social Media, edited by Gabriele Meiselwitz
15. LNAI 9183, Foundations of Augmented Cognition, edited by Dylan D. Schmorrow and Cali M. Fidopiastis
16. LNCS 9184, Digital Human Modeling and Applications in Health, Safety, Ergonomics and Risk Management: Human Modeling (Part I), edited by Vincent G. Duffy
17. LNCS 9185, Digital Human Modeling and Applications in Health, Safety, Ergonomics and Risk Management: Ergonomics and Health (Part II), edited by Vincent G. Duffy
18. LNCS 9186, Design, User Experience, and Usability: Design Discourse (Part I), edited by Aaron Marcus
19. LNCS 9187, Design, User Experience, and Usability: Users and Interactions (Part II), edited by Aaron Marcus
20. LNCS 9188, Design, User Experience, and Usability: Interactive Experience Design (Part III), edited by Aaron Marcus

Human-Computer Interaction

Program Board Chair: Masaaki Kurosu, Japan

- Jose Abdelnour-Nocera, UK
- Sebastiano Bagnara, Italy
- Simone Barbosa, Brazil
- Kaveh Bazargan, Iran
- Thomas Berns, Sweden
- Adriana Betiol, Brazil
- Simone Borsci, UK
- Apala Lahiri Chavan, India
- Sherry Chen, Taiwan
- Kevin Clark, USA
- Torkil Clemmensen, Denmark
- Michael Craven, UK
- Henry Duh, Australia
- Achim Ebert, Germany
- Xiaowen Fang, USA
- Stefano Federici, Italy
- Sheue-Ling Hwang, Taiwan
- Wonil Hwang, Korea
- Yong Gu Ji, Korea
- Esther Jun Kim, USA
- Mitsuhiko Karashima, Japan
- Heidi Krömker, Germany
- Cecília Sík Lányi, Hungary
- Glyn Lawson, UK
- Cristiano Maciel, Brazil
- Chang S. Nam, USA
- Naoko Okuizumi, Japan
- Philippe Palanque, France
- Alberto Raposo, Brazil
- Ling Rothrock, USA
- Eunice Sari, Indonesia
- Dominique Scapin, France
- Milene Selbach Silveira, Brazil
- Guangfeng Song, USA
- Hiroshi Ujita, Japan
- Anna Wichansky, USA
- Chui Yin Wong, Malaysia
- Toshiki Yamaoka, Japan
- Kazuhiko Yamazaki, Japan
- Alvin W. Yeo, Malaysia

The full list with the Program Board Chairs and the members of the Program Boards of all thematic areas and affiliated conferences is available online at:

http://www.hci.international/2015/

HCI International 2016

The 18th International Conference on Human-Computer Interaction, HCI International 2016, will be held jointly with the affiliated conferences in Toronto, Canada, at the Westin Harbour Castle Hotel, 17–22 July 2016. It will cover a broad spectrum of themes related to Human-Computer Interaction, including theoretical issues, methods, tools, processes, and case studies in HCI design, as well as novel interaction techniques, interfaces, and applications. The proceedings will be published by Springer. More information will be available on the conference website: http://2016.hci.international/.

General Chair
Prof. Constantine Stephanidis
University of Crete and ICS-FORTH
Heraklion, Crete, Greece
Email: general_chair@hcii2016.org

http://2016.hci.international/

Contents – Part III

HCI in Business, Industry and Innovation

Societal and Cultural Impact of Technology

User Studies

Interaction and Quality for the Web and Social Media

Heuristic to Support the Sociability Evaluation in Virtual Communities of Practices

Larissa Albano Lopes[1(✉)], Daniela Freitas Guilhermino[1],
Thiago Adriano Coleti[1], Ederson Marcos Sgarbi[1],
and Thiago Fernandes de Oliveira[2]

[1] Center of Technological Sciences, State University of Paraná,
Bandeirantes, PR, Brazil
{larissa,danielaf,thiago.coleti,sgarbi}@uenp.edu.br
[2] Fiocruz Mato Grosso Do Sul, Information Technology,
Campo Grande, MS, Brazil
thiago.oliveira@fiocruz.br

Abstract. The Virtual Community of Practices (VCoPs) create collaborative spaces that promote cooperation and the construction of knowledge, because provide communication and interaction between individuals so that knowledge and experience are utilized in a coordinated manner. A significant aspect of VCoPs is sociability, because it is related to the manner that people interact in the environment. Therefore, the objective of this work is assist expert professionals in the planning and creation of VCoPs interfaces, from proposition of a heuristic evaluation of interfaces these communities in order to minimize the difficulties of users concerning the sociability. The proposed heuristic was applied in the evaluation some VCoPs aiming the construction of virtual communities that allow a higher quality interaction for participants, respecting the guidelines for good sociability.

Keywords: Heuristic · Virtual community of practices · Interface evaluation · Human-Computer interaction · Sociability

1 Introduction

The Virtual Community of Practices (VCoPs) are developed in order to allow the users to discussing about a subject and sharing experiences using the Web. The VCoPs inherent aspect is the sociability, that, according to [2] "is the human skill of establish networks, using units of individual or collective activities and makes circulate information representing the interests and opinions".

The VCoPs are also interactive systems and usually it is developed without planning and the final product does not achieve the basic user requirements such as usability and sociability. Many times, the users don't use a software because it is difficult to manipulate, has low levels of usability and does not provide appropriate sociability requirements.

This paper presents the proposition of a heuristic to support the sociability evaluation in VCoPs. The heuristic was created, mainly, based on [13], which proposed

M. Kurosu (Ed.): Human-Computer Interaction, Part III, HCII 2015, LNCS 9171, pp. 3–14, 2015.
DOI: 10.1007/978-3-319-21006-3_1

some guidelines to be used in order to achieve sociability in websites. Other researches such as [18] that presented the concepts of a CoP and their relations (community, members, competences, collaboration, decision-making and CoP resources) and the [6] research that organized the collaboration concepts in a model named Model 3C (communication, coordination and cooperation).

After the evaluations performed using the proposed heuristic, we proposed guidelines to be applied in the VCoPs in order to improve the sociability requirements such as: purpose, policies, knowledge, skills, behavior, communication and others. So, we intended to decrease the bad experiences of users, reducing the problems in the VCoPs.

This research was performed in five stages: (1) Definition of the parameters of analysis; (2) Select the evaluates according to the profile required; (3) Orientation to the evaluators as heuristic guidelines; (4) Application of heuristics in evaluating VCoPs, realized individually by each of the evaluators; and (5) Analysis of results.

2 Virtual Communities of Practices

The expression "Community of Practices" (CoP) provided by [9] is defined as a group of people that share knowledge about some subjects and aim to interacting regularly in order to improve the knowledge about this subject [22]. The community builds relationships that allow the easiest communication among their members and so, allows the all the members learn about a theme [20].

According to this concept, [6] write: "The Collaboration allows the improvement and complementation of the skills, knowledge and individual efforts".

A CoP is structured in three main components [22]:

- Domain: the knowledge that guides the community, that defines the identity and the main issues that the members should discuss about;
- Type of Community: the community of interests, the community of apprentices or goal oriented;
- Use strategy: The strategy used by users to perform their tasks.

The CoPs can be available in virtual environment such as Internet or Intranet. These CoPs are named Virtual Communities of Practices (VCoPs). This concept was defined by [16] as a group of people that share the same interests by the Internet.

A robust research in order to contribute the improvement of collaborative learning was realized by [18]. The concepts related to members, resources and knowledge were defined from the research on 12 CoPs of the Palette4 project [8]. Table 1 presents a summarize, made by [19] from research of [17, 18].

A CoP involves a series of elements (actors, resources, competence, activists, among others) and their inter-relationships, necessaries to achievement of objectives. On your work [18] presents the main elements and the semantic annotations to the learning process on CoP.

These concepts (Table 1) also are inherent to VCoPs, since that virtual communities demand similar characteristics to a real environment with relation to interaction. Thus, can be notice that a VCoP also presents the following concepts: has a motivation;

Table 1. Main CoP concepts. [20]

CoP – Main concepts		Authors
Community	Motivation, Domain, Practice	Wenger (2010)
	Area; Purpose; Structure Composition	Tifous et al. (2007)
	Cultural Diversity	Langelier (2005)
Members	Personal Characteristics; Type of involvement; Role in the CoP, Peripheral Role	Miller (1995), Tifous et al. (2007)
Competence	Type of Competence	Tifous et al. (2007)
Collaboration	Collaboration objective; Collaboration Activities; Roles; Geographic Dimension; Temporal Dimension; Collaboration Resources; Media; Type of interaction	Vidou et al. (2006)
	Engagement; Coordination	Deaudelin et al. (2003), Weiseth et al. (2006)
Decision-Making	Resources for Decision-Making; Results; Actors involved; Strategies	Tifous et al. (2007)
CoP Resources	Interactions registration; Tools CoP	

presents a domain that characterizes; has cultural diversity among its members; presents the differentiation of roles among its members; gathers different competences, needs that its members to communicate, cooperate and coordinate the group activities; among others.

3   Interaction Design on VCoPs: Collaboration and Sociability

The CoPs are collaboration environment aimed to provide the cooperation and the knowledge building due to the reason that allows the interaction among members in order to share their knowledge and experience in a coordinated way.

Due to the CoPs features, it can be related with collaborative system because both aim to meet users in order to discuss about a subject and collaborate with others to achieve a common objective. These tools allow the participants to interact among them to contribute in the collective knowledge improvement [15].

The 3C collaboration model is a model to support the collaborative tools design. The model is based on the definition that to collaborate, the participants need communication, coordination and cooperation.

According to [7] to collaborate, the people establish communication among them and during this communication, tasks are created. The tasks are created and managed by the CoPs manager. The manager organizes the group to ensure that the tasks to be performed in cooperation and in the correct order and time. The perception is essential to provide the collaboration about the subject discussed in the environment to the members.

Considering the increase of the number of VCoPs users, the developers needs to concern not only in the usability, but also in the sociability features [5]. According to [14] the sociability is the join of people in order to generate purposes and practices where the participants share the same idea and has several relations (harmonic or conflicting) allowing them always acquiring knowledge and competencies of others about the subject.

Each VCoPs user has previous knowledge about a discussed subject and due to this reason the information are distributed quickly and directly. Thus, case a problem occurs, the same problem can be solved faster [14].

Preece [13] quotes three components that support a high level of sociability: (I) Pupose: the subject shared by the community members, an interest, an information, service or support that provide a reason to a user to subscribe in a VCoPs. (II) Participants: Users that work in different tasks in the community such as manager, moderator, simple users; and (III) Policies: languages, protocols that guide the interaction among the users. Forms policies, register policies and codes of conduct can be necessary. Therefore, to promote a high quality level of sociability the VCoPs should provide a purpose and the users should be engaged in a common subject supported by policies and practices in the social interaction.

4   Heuristic for Sociability Evaluation in VCoPs

Barbosa and Silva [3] describe that the main goal of the evaluation is to enable the delivery of the product with best quality guaranteed, to fix problems and to increase the users' productivity and their satisfaction towards the product. In the long run, the evaluation may not only decrease training and support costs, but also increase the user satisfaction and minimize planning of future versions of the system, as the evaluation may call the attention of the team concerning parts that may be further explored or improved.

In order to perform the interface evaluations in the literature, mainly three methods are discussed: investigation method, inspection method and observation method. The inspection method was adopted for this paper. In this method, the evaluator examines a solution of IHC, trying to predict possible consequences of certain decisions of design upon experiences of use. Furthermore, the evaluator deals with experiences of potential use, and not actual use. There are three types of inspection evaluation: heuristic, cognitive course and inspection semiotic. In this research is proposed a heuristic to inspect VCoPs, in order to seek sociability problems involved in VCoPs.

Barbosa and Silva [3] report that heuristics for evaluation may guide the evaluators to inspect the interface, aiming to find problems that hinder its use. The heuristic is a fast and low cost alternative as opposed to empirical methods. Nielsen [12] recommended that the evaluation should involve three to five evaluators. Table 2 presents activities involved in the heuristic evaluation [3]:

Taking into account the preparation activity, the evaluators organize the screens of the system being reviewed and the heuristics list or guidelines that should be taken into consideration. The solution evaluated may be the own working system, executable prototypes or not executable. Moreover, it is recommended that the evaluator scroll the

Table 2. Heuristic Evaluation [3]

Activity	Tasks
Preparation	*All the evaluators:* to learn about the current situation: users, domain, among others. To select the parts of the interface that should be evaluated.
Collection and data interpretation	*Each evaluator, individually:* to inspect the interface to identify heuristics violations; to list problems found by the inspection, indicating location, severity, justification and recommendations for the solution.
Consolidation and Result Report	*All the evaluators:* to revise problems found, judging its relevance, severity, justification and recommendations for the solution; to generate a consolidated report.

whole interface at least two times before starting the analysis, in order to be acquainted with its ergonomic, iconographies and operational features [1].

Next, the evaluators start to the collection step and data interpretation. Each evaluator should inspect each selected screen aiming to determine whether the guidelines were respected or violated. Each violation is perceived as an IHC problem. Therefore, evaluators should note every problem, location, severity and violated guidelines.

Finally, the evaluators convene a meeting to consolidate the results. Each evaluator shares a problem list. Next, the evaluators perform a new evaluation, which each evaluator is able to assign a new severity degree for each problem. The evaluators talk and find an agreement on the final severity degree of each problem and decide what problems and suggestions should be part of the final consolidated report.

4.1 Proposal Heuristic – SVCoP

In this section, the sociability evaluation heuristic of VCoPs, named SVCoP (Sociability in Virtual Communities of Practice), is presented. SVCoP was organized, in its first level, according to the structure of [18], which defines that CoP is characterized by the following aspects: "Community", "Members", "Competence", "Collaboration", "Decision Making" and "CoP Resources". As the aspect "CoP resources" is connected to all other concepts to support them. In addition, "CoP Resources" was also eliminated from the first level of the model, but it appears in the details section of the heuristic evaluation. Figure 1 shows the structure of the heuristic proposal.

The heuristic is structured as follows:

- "Community" refers to the domain, objective, composition and cultural diversity of CoP. In addition, "Community" is aligned to the concepts of [13], "purpose" is a reason why a member would belong to VCoP and "policies" are records and codes that guide interpersonal interactions in VCoP.
- "Members" are people from CoP with your given roles and personal features, referring to the features of people from VCoP, to their different roles and positions.

Fig. 1. Heuristic Structure

- "Competency" is defined as a set of resources provided to be acquired by [18]. The resources to acquire the expected competency are "knowledge", which refers to acquiring theoretical information of a determined subject, "skills", which is the capacity of an actor to perform tasks in practice and "behavior", which is summarized by the way in which actor behaves in a group or in a particular situation.
- "Collaboration" groups concepts of "communication", "coordination", "cooperation" and "perception" as cited by [6] in Collaboration Model 3C, in the second level. This model is based on the premise of in order to have collaboration, not only communication junction, but also coordination, cooperation and perception is required.
- "Decision Making" refers to available resources for such, to the individuals involved and to the strategies utilized in the process.

From the aforementioned concepts, a set of questions has been elaborated. The questions (for each axis) comprise the proposed heuristic requisites, and are detailed in [10].

In the "Community" axis, the following items have been analyzed: Purposes and Policies. In addition, seven questions were developed aiming to analyze the community purpose, among them: Is the purpose of community in accordance with its given name? Does the community clearly transmit its intentions to its users?

To analyze the Policies, eleven questions were developed, among them: Does the community present policies of use for all developed activities (registration, publication, commercial transactions, copyrights, among others)?; Is the reliance of the community encouraged by a policy or by a procedure?; Are there any form of complaining in case the community is incorrectly utilized?

In the "Members" axis, eight questions have been elaborated, among them: Is the registration required when a person intends to either become a member of the community or leave the community?; Are anonymous users and visitants allowed?; Can a member assume a given role in VCoP (facilitator, participant, coordinator, among others)?

In the following axis, "Competence", the following items have been analyzed: "Knowledge", "Skills" and "Behavior". Five questions have been developed concerning "Knowledge", among them: Can VCoP members acquire required information on the VCoP operation?; Is information on subjects discussed in VCoP clearly transmitted?; Is the user-to-user knowledge clearly transmitted?

The "Skills" are analyzed from three questions: Is the responsibility of each member to perform tasks presented in VCoP?; Can members learn and transfer their knowledge in VCoP?; Do members assume responsibilities, risks, and consequences of their actions and, as a result, are recognized?

Finally, the "Behavior" is analysed from three questions: Does VCoP allow the evaluation of its members' satisfaction?; Does VCoP register the actions of each member aiming to be able to analyze their involvement?; Are there many ways employed in VCoP to motivate their participants?

In the next axis, "Collaboration", questions have been elaborated to analyze the following terms: Communication, Coordination, Cooperation and Perception. Seven questions have been developed in order to analyze the communication, among them: Are there several ways to communicate in the community? For instance: by written (text), by speech (audio), by pictorial (images and animations) and by gestures (video and avatar); Are there a way to read and send messages promptly (after the formulation of the message as a whole by the sender) (asynchronous communication)?; Can I express myself in the way I expect? For Instance: the type of speaking (whisper, speech, question, yell, answer, acceptance, disagreement), the type of speech (direct or indirect), and the type of emotion (happy, normal, angry).

The analysis of the "Coordination" was performed through six questions, among them: Does the community encourage empathy, confidence and cooperation?; Generally, is the community a nice place, where people are able to do what they want?; Does the community offer the availability status of the users (available, busy, away, among others)?

In order to analyze the "Cooperation", four questions were developed, among them: Are there any activities in which members depend on each other in VCoP when performing any tasks?; Are there group activities?; Does the community show any types of records to store posts that have been already published?

"Perception" was analyzed from five questions, among them: Can people see other members online in the community?; Can people see what the other members are doing in the community?; Does the community present the role of the users to other members (facilitator, participant, coordinator, among them)?

Finally, in the axis "Decision making", have been developed three questions: Does the community promote assistance for decision-making? (E.g.: Consensus - all the members decide, Majority – the majority opinion wins, Minority – a subcommittee decides, among others); Is there any specialist holding specific knowledge for decision making regarding a determined task?; Is there an authority (moderator/leader) for decision making in VCoP?

From the developed heuristic, the validation was applied, followed by the methodology described in the next section.

4.2   Heuristics Application Methodology

To perform the evaluation was created an online form containing 61 questions corresponding to heuristic guidelines. From these questions, the evaluators were able identify if the guidelines were respected or violated in VCoPs.

The form was distributed to five expert professionals that evaluated seven communities of practice. For the purpose of provide greater familiarity with VCoPs, the evaluators were able choose which would be evaluated.

To assist the evaluation process, some parameters were established to the verification of 61 questions that constitute the heuristic. The parameters vary from 0 to 2 as follows: (0) No – when there is not occurrence. The aspect is not identified in VCoP; (1) Partially - partial occurrence. The aspect is identified not satisfactorily in VCoP; (2) Yes - when the occurrence is complete. The aspect is satisfactorily in VCoP.

For instance, the area "policies" to the question that checks if "Use policies are presented?" are proposed the following options: (0) No - use policies do not presented in VCoP; (1) Partially - use policies are presented only the moment of member registration in VCOP; (2) Yes - use policies are remembered at several moments during use of VCoP.

Therefore, for each question were presented three alternatives to analyze the occurrence of sociability guidelines in VCoPs.

In order to evaluate the proposed heuristic, concerning to completeness, strengths and weaknesses, was created another online form with eight questions to be answered by the evaluators at the end of the evaluation of VCoPs. With this questionnaire, evaluators could contribute with suggestions for improvements to the proposed heuristic.

4.3   Results and Discussion

From the tests conducted through the SVCoP, we could identify the aspects of sociability which are well explored in VCoPs and aspects that present themselves poorer. Some of the issues involving the various analyzed axes (Community, Member, Competence, Collaboration, Decision Making) are highlighted in Table 3.

The best evaluated aspects are related to Community axes (Purpose and Policy), Members and Competence (knowledge, skills and behavior). It was observed that the purpose of the evaluated communities is presented very clearly and prominently, motivating its participants for their use. The policies are widely disseminated and there is a strict control for security of confidential information, bringing confidence and encouraging participants along the interaction activities. Regarding the Members, it was observed that the VCoPs well delimit the roles of each member in the community, but mostly also allow access to anonymous users. On competence, it was found that the VCoPs have several ways of sharing information contributing to the construction of knowledge.

Table 3. Some questions of heuristics - SVCoP

Heuristic - SVCoP	VCoP 1	VCoP 2	VCoP 3	VCoP 4	VCoP 5	VCoP 6	VCoP 7
Does the community clearly transmit its intentions to its users?	2	1	2	2	2	2	2
Is the reliance of the community encouraged by a policy or by a procedure?	1	0	2	1	0	0	0
Are anonymous users and visitants allowed?	0	2	1	0	2	2	2
Can a member assume a given role in VCoP?	2	2	1	2	2	2	2
Can members learn and transfer their knowledge in VCoP?	1	2	2	2	2	2	2
Does VCoP allow the evaluation of its members' satisfaction?	1	0	2	0	0	2	0
Does VCoP register the actions of each member aiming to be able to analyze their involvement?	1	1	2	2	2	2	2
Are there several ways to communicate in the community? For instance: by written, by speech, by pictorial and by gestures.	2	1	2	1	0	0	0
Does the community encourage empathy, confidence and cooperation?	2	2	2	2	2	2	2
Does the community offer the availability status of the users?	2	0	0	0	2	2	2
Are there group activities?	2	2	1	1	2	2	2
Does the community show any types of records to store posts that have been already published?	2	2	2	0	0	0	0
Does the community promote assistance for decision-making?	2	0	0	2	0	0	0
Is there an authority for decision making in VCoP?	2	2	2	0	0	0	0

The aspects that have shown a lower incidence were related to the Collaboration and Decision Making. The VCoPs demonstrated weakness with regard to communication, regarding the accessibility and forms of communication. Coordination in VCoPs is not explicit, usually because they have a more informal organization. Perception already demonstrated great deficiency in his assessment, appearing as one of the worst aspects evaluated. The lack of visibility regarding the actions of participants and roles performed are the main difficulties pointed out. The assessment indicated that the VCoPs, mostly do not have tools for Decision Making as voting arrangements, polls, among others. Two out of seven communities have a specialist for decision making. This limitation, in the view of some evaluators, makes less democratic VCoPs.

After evaluating the VCoPs, some questions about the facilities and difficulties encountered during the evaluation process were answered by the evaluators. A summary of the opinion of the evaluators is described in the following:

- All evaluators responded that: (i) the heuristic is complete with respect to the sociability aspects evaluated, however, found a very extensive evaluation, consequently tiring, (ii) the main difficulties are related to the lack of familiarity with the VCoPs, prejudicing the identifying some aspects.
- Three evaluators observed that the heuristic could include an alternative to contemplate exceptions, such as: "It is not possible to evaluate".
- Two evaluators reported that: (i) it is necessary explain the aspects that appear in the questionnaire (community members, competence, among others) to facilitate the evaluation; (ii) some questions are repetitive, then, they suggest remove it.
- One reviewer suggested adding a question to identify if the VCoP disseminates knowledge beyond its members (eg. Open videoconferences).

In general, the evaluators demonstrated satisfaction with the proposed heuristic. One very positive aspect is associated with completeness of the aspects of sociability; however, the extension was criticized by most evaluators. These suggestions have contributed to the refinement and improvement of the heuristic.

5   Conclusion

This paper proposes a heuristic model to support the designers to create VCoPs with interfaces according to sociability features.

The heuristic, called SVCoP, presents its guidelines organized by aspects which are considered intrinsic to VCoPs: Community (Purpose and Policies), Members, Competence (Knowledge, Skills and Behavior), Collaboration (communication, Coordination, Cooperation and Perception) and Decision Making. Then, were developed 61 questions to cover all aspects and their interrelationships. The questions were applied for five evaluators at the end of the reviews suggested improvements to heuristic SVCoP.

Some perceptions about Sociability were possible with the reviews, among them: Most communities makes clear the group's intent and provide information for the environment to reaffirm your purpose; Policies are present only in the registration of one member and are not remembered along the interactions in VCoPs; The VCoPs offer some forms of communication (discussion forums, chat, email), but they do not stimulate the participants to develop their own communication styles.

A relevant aspect observed is that most VCoPs not present activities that can be developed cooperatively. Another important aspect that proved absent in VCoPs is the treatment of copyright issues and protection of confidential information.

As partial result, it was identified that the instrument proposed enabled to evaluate diverse sociability aspects in VCoPs. From the suggestions of the evaluators about the model of heuristic, were made some changes, such as, the inclusion of an alternative "Can not evaluate", and the refinement of some issues, including its change, inclusion and exclusion. Included is also links with explanation of key words of the questionnaire, such as, cooperation and perception.

As future work, it is intended to perform further assessments in order to refine and improve the heuristic. In addition, it is intended apply the heuristic to other types of collaborative environments.

References

1. Andrade, A.L.L.: Usabilidade de interfaces web. Avaliação heurística no jornalismo online (2007)
2. Baechler, J.: Grupos e Sociabilidade. In: Boudon, R. (ed.) Tratado de Sociologia (Tradução de Teresa Curvelo), pp. 65–106. Zahar, Rio de Janeiro (1995)
3. Barbosa, S.D.J., Silva, B.S.: Interação Humano-Computador, 1ª edn. Campus, Rio de Janeiro (2010)
4. Deaudelin, C.: Nault, T.: Collaborer pour apprendre et faire apprendre – La place des outils technologiques, Presses de l'Université du Québec (2003)
5. Forato, B.B.A.: Heurísticas para a criação de uma comunidade online, São Paulo (2011)
6. Fuks, H., Raposo, A.B.: Gerosa, M.A.: Engenharia de *Groupware*: Desenvolvimento de Aplicações Colaborativas. In: XXI Jornada de Atualização em Informática, Anais do XXII Congresso da Sociedade Brasileira de Computação, V2, Cap.3 (2002). ISBN: 85-88442-24-8
7. Gerosa, M.A., Fuks, H., Lucena, C.J.P.: Suporte e Percepção em Ambientes de Aprendizagem Colaborativas. Revista Brasileira de Informática na Educação **11**(2), 75–85 (2003). ISSN: 1414-5685, Sociedade Brasileira de Computação
8. Henri, F.: Communities of Practice: Social Structures for the Development of Knowledge. PALETTE Kick off Meeting, Lausanne (2006)
9. Langelier, L., Wenger, E.: Work, Learning and Networked. Cefrio, Québec (2005)
10. Lopes, L.A.: Heurística de apoio à avaliação da sociabilidade em comunidades de prática virtuais (2015)
11. Miller, G.A.: WordNet: a lexical database for English. Commun. ACM **38**(11), 39–41 (1995)
12. Nielsen, J.: Heuristic Evaluation. In: Mack, R., Nielsen, J. (eds.) Usability Inspection Methods, pp. 25–62. Wiley, New York (1994)
13. Preece, J., Rogers, Y., Sharp, H.: *Design* de Interação: Além da interação humano-computador, 3ª edn. Wiley, Chichester (2013)
14. Recuero, R: *Facebook* x Orkut no Brasil: alguns apontamentos. Social Media, 24 Ago. (2009)
15. Silva, A.: Da Aprendizagem Colaborativa às Comunidades de Prática. Universidade Aberta (2010)
16. Souza, C.S., Leite, J.C., Prates, R.O., Barbosa, S.D.J.: Projeto de Interfaces de Usuário – Perspectivas Cognitivas e Semióticas, 1ª edn. Campus, Rio de Janeiro (2007)
17. Tifous, A., Dieng-Kuntz, R., Durville, P., El Ghali, A., Evangeli, C., Giboin, A., Vidou, G.: CoP- *dependent Ontologies*. Palette IST-FP6-028038 *Deliverable* D.KNO.02 (2007b)

18. Tifous, A., Ghali, A.E., Dieng-Kuntz, R., Giboin, A., Evangelou, C., Vidou, G.: Na ontology for supporting communities of practice. In: K-CAP 39–4 (2007a)
19. Trindade, D.F.G.: InCoP: Um framework conceitual para o design de ambientes colaborativos inclusivos para surdos e não surdos de cultivo a comunidade de prática (2013)
20. Vidou, G., Dieng-Kuntz, R., Ghali, A.E., Evangelou, C.E., Giboin, A., Tifous, A., Jacquemart, S.: Towards an ontology for knowledge management in communities of practice. In: Reimer, U., Karagiannis, D. (eds.) PAKM 2006. LNCS (LNAI), vol. 4333, pp. 303–314. Springer, Heidelberg (2006)
21. Weiseth, P.E., Munkvold, B.E., Tvedte, B., Larsen, S.: The Wheel of Collaboration Tools: A Typology for Analysis within a Holistic Framework. In: CSCW 2006, Banff, Canada, p. 239–248 (2006)
22. Wenger, E.: Communities of practice and social learning systems: the career of a concept. In: Blackmore, C. (ed.) Social Learning Systems and Communities of Practice, pp. 179–198. Springer, Dordrecht (2010). Ch. 11

Using a Lexical Approach to Investigate User Experience of Social Media Applications

Abdullah Azhari and Xiaowen Fang$^{(\boxtimes)}$

School of Computing College of CDM, DePaul University, 243 S. Wabash
Avenue, Chicago, IL 60604, USA
abdullah.a.azhari@gmail.com, Xfang@cdm.depaul.edu

Abstract. The objective of this research is to examine the most important issues in user experience about social media applications (SMAs) by using a lexical approach. After reviewing prior studies about user interactions with SMA, a process based on the revised lexical approach [52] is adopted to explore patterns among the adjectives in online reviews of SMAs. This process includes four stages: Stage 1: Collecting online reviews, Stage 2: Building a dictionary of SMA descriptive adjectives, Stage 3: Extracting user ratings of adjectives, and Stage 4: Factor analyses. The detailed development process is discussed.

Keywords: Social media applications · Lexical approach · Usability · User experience

1 Introduction

Social media applications (SMA) continue to grow at a fast pace. People of all generations use social media to exchange messages and share experiences of their life in a timely fashion. SMAs are not only a major form of communication but also used increasingly for entertainment, educational, therapeutic, and work-related purposes [37]. To build the best experience we need to understand what elements of using SMA that affect users most. Previous research suggests that user experience of SMA could be affected by SMA designing elements, information processing, and environment. SMA usage could also be influenced by personality, user sociality, and user needs. At the same time, SMA uses impacts user experiences of other systems, products and services in many ways. In addition, it drives user behavior toward specific actions. Furthermore, user experience and implicit feedback from SMA impact e-commerce websites on building an experience and personalization. However, what are really influencing user experiences of SMA are not well studied. Inspired by the lexical approach used in studying personality traits [1], this study attempts to approach user experience through the language used by SMA users. Similar to personality research, it is believed that SMA descriptive words (adjectives or nouns) will play a pivotal role in SMA. The objective of this research is to examine the most important issues in user experience about social media applications by analyzing the adjectives used by users in online reviews of SMAs.

M. Kurosu (Ed.): Human-Computer Interaction, Part III, HCII 2015, LNCS 9171, pp. 15–24, 2015.
DOI: 10.1007/978-3-319-21006-3_2

2 Literature Review

Experts based on different perspectives have inspected social media effects on user experience [23]. Researchers also note that one could change user experience of SMA, through SMA designing elements, information processing, and environment [25].

User personality, user sociality, and user needs could affect users experiences of SMA [1]. In addition, SMA uses could improve users experience on other systems, products and services [36]. Moreover, user experience and implicit feedback from SMA could help to build good experience and personalize products and services for users [17].

This section examines prior research on SMA interface design, role of user characteristics, marketing research, and prior SMA experience.

2.1 SMA Interface Design

Prior research suggests that the characteristics of the system of engagements and content enhance viewership of user-generated content, and that the type of background is crucial to user attitude toward the content of the page [39, 41].

Lampe, Ellison & Steinfield (2007) find that shared referents is more likely to increase the amounts of friends than the fields used to express likes and dislikes [25]. Facebook is based on four elements that lead to larger adoptions: provoke/retaliate, reveal/compare, expression, and group exchange [48]. It is also found that the influence in social networks is based on two normal and recognizable patterns, competition and deception, adopted by Facebook [48]. Borgatti and Cross [9] define the way of getting information from others as a process of (1) knowing: comprehending what that individual knows; (2) valuing: surveying what that individual knows; (3) Accessing: having the capacity to get auspicious access to that information; and (4) Costing: understanding that looking for the information from that individual is cost effective [9]. Grange and Benbasat [15] propose that getting Information from and into SMA affected by both user experience and the platform itself [15]. SMA makes information accessible and reduces the cost of sharing information between users [15]. Hutton and Fosdick [16] indicate that users motivation depends on the social media platform and how extract and process information to it. Moncur [29] states that increasing the desirability of personal social networks increases the usefulness of social networks sites. Social network environment changes its members' behavior when compared to non-members. The effect of online activities extends to affect offline events as well. Social media can also be used as lifestyle changing tool [34]. Acquisti and Gross [3] note that people concerned with privacy still join the network and they deal with their privacy concerns by trusting their capability to control the information they give and who gets access to it. It is found that an individual's privacy concerns are only a weak predictor of the membership to the network [3].

2.2 Role of User Characteristics

Social media use is not only influenced by the social media environment itself, it can also be affected by user personality, user sociality, and user needs. Ross et al. [40] indicate that personality structures, inspiration and capability can have a vital bearing on online activities. For example, the time spent on the SMA is positively connected with loneliness and shyness [2, 32]. In the meantime, shyness is negatively associated with the amount of Friends on the SMA [32]. Furthermore, highly extroverted users would have larger number of friends and would engage in more groups than those who have less extroverted characteristics, and users with higher neuroticism characteristics would be more willing to share personally-identifying information on SMA, and less likely to use private messages [6–8, 32]. In addition, user preference of specific social network platforms is associated with differences in personality and the platform design and features. For example, people with high sociability, extraversion and neuroticism have a preference for Facebook while those who have a preference for Twitter have a high need for cognition [18]. Ellison et al. [12] suggest that Facebook usage would provide greater benefits for users facing low self-esteem and low life satisfaction. Social media has the potential to be a socializing and powerful tool [26, 35]. Social network design and uses is inevitably associated with a user's social world and areas of life (work, family, and friends) [30]. The way people think about and manage communication in their social life determines future efforts in social media design. Looking to a specific tool like Facebook, Park et al. [35] show a positive relationship between the intensity of Facebook use and students' life satisfaction, social trust, civic engagement, and observed political participation. Correa et al. [11] claim that the relationship between extraversion and social media use is particularly important among the young adult cohort. McKenna et al. [28] find that users who present their true self in the Internet were more likely than others to have close online friendship and moved these relationship to a "face-to-face" basis. Users' needs and the awareness of the value of the social media can change user experience within it. This even starts from the level of adoption and how it affects the use of social media services [50, 51]. Zhao et al. [51] argue that individuals choose the identities that aid them to better situate within a given social environment depending on the characteristics of the environment in which they find themselves. People with a high need for cognition are more experienced on the Internet, use more hyperlinks, stay longer in the site and use information services in the Internet relatively more than those with a low need for cognition [5, 23]. On the other hand, it is noted that people with low need for cognition prefer interactive over linear sites [5]. Swickert et al. [43] argue that Personality is marginally related to Information Exchange (email and accessing information) and Leisure (instant messaging and playing games).

2.3 SMA Experience and Marketing Research

SMA affects e-commerce websites and its uses in many ways. Kim and Ahmad [22] find that building an experience and personalizing are two of the most effective factors in social media that have a huge impact on e-commerce websites. In fact, social media leads to both negative and positive experiences. It would be easy to spread bad experiences to a large number of users in the social media platform [22]. It is also easy to accumulate a huge number of good experiences and use word-of-mouth marketing to deliver it [22]. A huge part of the e-commerce market experiences nowadays rest on trust and distrust on SMA. With the open community in social media, users and businesses are building an experience based on this community [22]. In addition SMA is a good tool in providing personalized information and recommended products and services. SMA provides a lot of implicit feedback that could build excellent source of information about users. Thus, a common task of recommender systems is to improve customer experiences through personalized recommendations based on prior implicit feedback [36]. Recommendation system could influence consumers' decision-making [17, 49]. Burke [38] proposes that adding users' preferences to recommendation systems would make personalization more specific and accurate. Jawaheer et al. [21] show that explicit and implicit feedbacks provide different degrees of expressivity of the user's preferences. Joachims et al. [19] suggest that accuracy of implicit feedback would add more personal information to the explicit feedback of the user. Oku et al. [31] propose a recommendation system considering past /current /future users' situations and conditions that influence users expression of information and status at that time. The status of users in social media networks provides information based on: (users past actions and occurred situations at that time, current situation to obtain information from the user status, and future actions the user plan from now and expected situations) [31]. It is found that the user's action patterns depend on situations at each time [31]. It is necessary to extract the user's action patterns considering the situations at each time when the user took the actions [31]. Peska et al. [33] argue that, based on user behavior, collaborative and object rating methods are significantly better than the random method in most of the observed performance measures.

2.4   Role of Prior SMA Experiences

Sykes et al. [44] propose that improved user understanding of a system such as social media application leads to better performance within it and better explanations as to how to use it. SMA users and users who call customer service tend to report different types of performance issues [37]. In addition, Fischer and Reuber [13] state that social media interaction increases the amount of access to resources and it can expand the community [13]. They propose that this huge amount of resources and the connection with more communities makes a significant difference in decision-making and communication [13]. However, they found that investing heavily in social network interactions could lead to less productivity [13]. Also, it could be tricky without considering community orientation and community norm adherence [13]. The type of event in social media and the manner in which users engage in the social media platform changes the purpose of using the social media [10, 46]. In a study on understanding online social network usage from a network perspective, Schneider et al. [42] find that users commonly spend more than half an hour interacting with the online social networks while the byte contributions per online social network session are relatively small.

3   The Lexical Approach

The lexical approach originally used to investigate personalities is based on a lexical hypothesis. The hypothesis states that when salient individual differences are socially relevant to life, these distinctive attributes are encoded into natural languages. If many people recognize a difference, the difference is likely to be expressed by similar terms. Personality traits therefore can be identified by exploring personality descriptive adjectives in natural languages [1, 52, 53]. Zhu and Fang [52] introduced a revised lexical approach to study user experience in game play by analyzing online reviews. Four stages were involved in this revised lexical approach: (1) Stage 1: Collecting online reviews, (2) Stage 2: Building a dictionary of game descriptive adjectives, (3) Stage 3: Extracting game player ratings of adjectives, and (4) Stage 4: Factor analyses [52].

In this study, we argue that the revised lexical approach proposed by Zhu and Fang [52] can be applied to investigate user experience of SMA. It is hypothesized that SMA users will use adjectives to describe important issues/factors in online reviews as they experience SMAs. If we can aggregate a large collection of online reviews about SMAs, the most critical issues/factors related to SMAs would be reflected in the common patterns of adjectives used by users. Section 4 elaborates the detailed lexical analysis process.

4   Method

As suggested by Zhu and Fang [52], this study will employ a lexical analysis process with the following 4 stages:

- Stage 1: Collecting online reviews
- Stage 2: Building a dictionary of SMA descriptive adjectives
- Stage 3: Extracting user ratings of adjectives
- Stage 4: Factor analyses.

Stage 1 Collecting Online Reviews: The primary objective of Stage 1 is to download social media applications reviews from independent online websites and store these reviews in a structured relational database for subsequent analysis. Since the following lexical analysis focuses on the language used by SMA users, only textual information is downloaded. To ensure the quality and representativeness of online content, the following criteria are used to choose the websites where SMA reviews would be downloaded:

- A popular independent SMA review website that has attracted a significant amount of traffic. This criterion helps ensure the diversity of SMA users.
- A highly ranked SMA review websites that user trust. This criterion ensures the popularity and dominance as perceived by the SMA industry.
- A website that contains reviews of a wide variety of SMA. This criterion strives to achieve the maximal generalizability.

Table 1. Sources of online reviews about SMA

Website	Applications	Apps with users reviews	User reviews	Traffic	Alexa rank
148apps.com	7363	948	2383	934,900	21038
Theiphoneappreview.com	3857	243	1616	152,100	170251
Iphoneappreviews.net	1340	901	5024	20,100	915809
Dailyappshow.com	3880	1031	1868	214,700	115367
Appvee.com	1294306	9740	9740	59,600	447364
Whatsoniphone.com	7028	456	2210	114,600	232334
Freshapps.com	45872	1425	3164	57,800	460307
Total number of user reviews	26005				

Based on the aforementioned criteria, seven websites were chosen to download SMA reviews from: 148apps.com, Theiphoneappreview.com, Iphoneappreviews.net, Dailyappshow.com, Appvee.com, Whatsoniphone.com, and Freshapps.com. Table 1 presents the details about these websites. These websites provides us independent reviews by different users: users, developer, expert reviewers and businesses.

A special web crawler program was developed for each of the seven SMA websites using Perl. Perl was selected as the main programming language due to its powerful facility for text manipulations. It has also been used in many scientific inquiries such as bioinformatics. For this study, ActivePerl was installed on Microsoft Windows 7 system and Komodo IDE was used as the main text editor. The following issues were addressed when developing the web crawlers:

- Only texts of SMA reviews are downloaded. Any texts contained in other forms such as image, video, or advertisements are excluded.
- All of the HTML tags or any markup language tags are recognized and removed from the texts.
- Repeated contents are removed. Others might quote same reviews in forum- style content. To minimize possible bias caused by repeated contents, the web crawler programs are designed to detect such contents to the best we could and to remove them during downloading.
- The web crawler programs are developed to traverse entire hierarchical structures on the seven selected SMA Websites that might contain useful content.
- The web crawler programs are designed to resume downloading without duplicating any content if the downloading process is halted by any exceptions.
- Once the SMA reviews are downloaded, they will be stored with all relevant meta information available on the websites such as title and reviewer in a structured relational database. This database will be used as the source of information for future content analyses.

Stage 2 Building a dictionary of SMA descriptive adjective: This stage is designed to parse adjectives describing SMAs from the downloaded online reviews. Four tasks will be involved in this stage: (1) parsing individual words from original texts and checking the part of speech (PoS); (2) detecting SMA-descriptive terms; (3) filtering out stop words and retaining new jargons created by users; (4) capturing overall frequency and the number of reviews containing a word. To complete these tasks in order, a natural language processing (NLP) application will be developed using relevant Perl modules.

Stage 3 Extracting user ratings of adjective: In Stage 3, each online review will be treated as an independent observation. They will be converted to a dataset by a computer program as follows: (1) Each word on the list of adjectives produced in Stage 2, "Building a dictionary of SMA descriptive adjectives", is treated as an individual item. The list of adjectives is saved as the field names (columns) of a database table. (2) All online reviews are retrieved one at a time. Each review about one game is processed as an individual record. Adjectives used in the same review must be somehow related because they are used to describe the same application. If an adjective appears in this review, the value for this adjective (field) is set to 1. Otherwise, a zero value is registered.

Stage 4 Factor Analysis: In this stage, an exploratory factor analysis will be conducted to discover potential patterns among the SMA descriptive adjectives. The resulting patterns will reflect the most critical issues/factors concerning SMAs.

5   Current Progress and Next Step

We have completed Stage 1 and are currently working on Stage 2 to extract SMA-descriptive words. As the next step, we will convert the online reviews into a binary matrix and then conduct the factor analysis to discover patterns among the adjectives.

References

1. Ashton, M.C.: Individual Differences and Personality. Academic Press, San Diego (2007)
2. Amichai-Hamburger, Y., Ben-Artzi, E.: Loneliness and Internet use. Comput. Hum. Behav. **19**(1), 71–80 (2003)
3. Acquisti, A., Gross, R.: Imagined communities: awareness, information sharing, and privacy on the Facebook. In: Danezis, G., Golle, P. (eds.) PET 2006. LNCS, vol. 4258, pp. 36–58. Springer, Heidelberg (2006)
4. Amichai-Hamburger, Y.: Internet and personality. Comput. Hum. Behav. **18**(1), 1–10 (2002)
5. Amichai-Hamburger, Y., Kaynar, O., Fine, A.: The effects of need for cognition on Internet use. Comput. Hum. Behav. **23**(1), 880–891 (2007)
6. Amiel, T., Sargent, S.L.: Individual differences in Internet usage motives. Comput. Hum. Behav. **20**(6), 711–726 (2004)
7. Amichai-Hamburger, Y., Vinitzky, G.: Social network use and personality. Comput. Hum. Behav. **26**(6), 1289–1295 (2010)
8. Amichai-Hamburger, Y., Wainapel, G., Fox, S.: On the Internet no one knows I'm an introvert : extroversion, neuroticism, and Internet interaction. CyberPsychol. Behav. **5**(2), 125–128 (2002)

9. Borgatti, S.P., Cross, R.: A relational view of information seeking and learning in social networks. Manage. Sci. **49**(4), 432–445 (2003)

10. Cha, M., Haddadi, H., Benevenuto, F., Gummadi, P.K.: Measuring user influence in Twitter: the million follower fallacy. In: ICWSM 2010, pp. 1017 (2010)

11. Correa, T., Hinsley, A.W., De Zuniga, H.G.: Who interacts on the Web?: the intersection of users' personality and social media use. Comput. Hum. Behav. **26**(2), 247–253 (2010)

12. Ellison, N.B., Steinfield, C., Lampe, C.: The benefits of Facebook "friends:" Social capital and college students' use of online social network sites. J. Comput. Mediat. Commun. **12**(4), 1143–1168 (2007)

13. Fischer, E., Reuber, A.R.: Social interaction via new social media:(How) can interactions on Twitter affect effectual thinking and behavior? J. Bus. Ventur. **26**(1), 1–18 (2011)

14. Goldberg, L.R.: An alternative 'description of personality': The big-five factor structure. J. Pers. Soc. Psychol. **59**(6), 1216–1229 (1990)

15. Grange, C., Benbasat, I.: Information technology capabilities for digital social networks. In: International Conference on Computational Science and Engineering, CSE 2009, vol. 4, pp. 1054–1059. IEEE, August 2009

16. Hutton, G., Fosdick, M.: The globalization of social media: consumer relationships with brands evolve in the digital space. J. Advert. Res. **51**(4), 564–570 (2011). doi:10.2501/JAR-51-4-564-570

17. Hu, Y., Koren, Y., Volinsky, C.: Collaborative filtering for implicit feedback datasets. In: Eighth IEEE International Conference on Data Mining, ICDM 2008, pp. 263–272. IEEE, December 2008

18. Hughes, D.J., Rowe, M., Batey, M., Lee, A.: A tale of two sites: Twitter vs. Facebook and the personality predictors of social media usage. Comput. Hum. Behav. **28**(2), 561–569 (2012)

19. Joachims, T., Granka, L., Pan, B., Hembrooke, H., Radlinski, F., Gay, G.: Evaluating the accuracy of implicit feedback from clicks and query reformulations in web search. ACM Trans. Inf. Syst. (TOIS) **25**(2), 7 (2007)

20. Java, A., Song, X., Finin, T., Tseng, B.: Why we Twitter: understanding microblogging usage and communities. In: Proceedings of the 9th WebKDD and 1st SNA-KDD 2007 Workshop on Web Mining and Social Network Analysis, pp. 56–65. ACM, August 2007

21. Jawaheer, G., Szomszor, M., Kostkova, P.: Comparison of implicit and explicit feedback from an online music recommendation service. In: Proceedings of the 1st International Workshop on Information Heterogeneity and Fusion in Recommender Systems, pp. 47–51. ACM, September 2010

22. Kim, Y., Ahmad, M.A.: Trust, distrust and lack of confidence of users in online social media-sharing communities. Knowl.-Based Syst. **37**, 438–450 (2013)

23. Kaynar, O., Amichai-Hamburger, Y.: The effects of need for cognition on Internet use revisited. Comput. Hum. Behav. **24**(2), 361–371 (2008)

24. Kumar, N., Benbasat, I.: Para-social presence: a re-conceptualization of 'social presence' to capture the relationship between a web site and her visitors. In: Proceedings of the 35th Annual Hawaii International Conference on System Sciences, HICSS 2002, pp. 106–112. IEEE, January 2002

25. Lampe, C. A., Ellison, N., Steinfield, C.: A familiar face (book): profile elements as signals in an online social network. In: Proceedings of the SIGCHI Conference on Human Factors in Computing Systems, pp. 435–444. ACM, April 2007

26. Lee, J., Lee, H.: The computer-mediated communication network: exploring the linkage between the online community and social capital. New Media Soc. **12**(5), 711–727 (2010)

27. McKenna, K.Y., Bargh, J.A.: Plan 9 from cyberspace: the implications of the Internet for personality and social psychology. Person. Soc. Psychol. Rev. **4**(1), 57–75 (2000)

28. McKenna, K.Y., Green, A.S., Gleason, M.E.: Relationship formation on the Internet: What's the big attraction? J. Soc. Issues **58**(1), 9–31 (2002)
29. Moncur, W: Improving control of information sharing on social networking sites. In: Workshop Social Mediating Technologies: Setting the Research Agenda at CHI (2009)
30. Ozenc, F.K., Farnham, S.D.: Life modes in social media. In: Proceedings of the SIGCHI Conference on Human Factors in Computing Systems. pp. 561–570. ACM, May 2011
31. Oku, K., Nakajima, S., Miyazaki, J., Uemura, S., Kato, H., Hattori, F.: A recommendation system considering users' past/current/future contexts. In: Proceedings of CARS, September 2010
32. Orr, E.S., Sisic, M., Ross, C., Simmering, M.G., Arseneault, J.M., Orr, R.R.: The influence of shyness on the use of Facebook in an undergraduate sample. CyberPsychol. Behav. **12**(3), 337–340 (2009)
33. Peska, L., Eckhardt, A., Vojtas, P.: UPComp-a PHP component for recommendation based on user behaviour. In: 2011 IEEE/WIC/ACM International Conference on Web Intelligence and Intelligent Agent Technology (WI-IAT), vol. 3, pp. 306–309. IEEE, August 2011
34. Ploderer, B., Howard, S., Thomas, P., Reitberger, W.: Hey World, Take a Look at Me!: Appreciating the human body on social network sites. In: Oinas-Kukkonen, H., Hasle, P., Harjumaa, M., Segerståhl, K., Øhrstrøm, P. (eds.) PERSUASIVE 2008. LNCS, vol. 5033, pp. 245–248. Springer, Heidelberg (2008)
35. Park, N., Kee, K.F., Valenzuela, S.: Being immersed in social networking environment: Facebook groups, uses and gratifications, and social outcomes. CyberPsychol. Behav. **12**(6), 729–733 (2009)
36. Peška, L., Vojtáš, P.: Estimating importance of implicit factors in e-commerce recommender systems. In: Proceedings of the 2nd International Conference on Web Intelligence, Mining and Semantics, p. 62. ACM, June 2012
37. Qiu, T., Feng, J., Ge, Z., Wang, J., Xu, J., Yates, J.: Listen to me if you can: tracking user experience of mobile network on social media. In: Proceedings of the 10th ACM SIGCOMM Conference on Internet Measurement, pp. 288–293. ACM, November 2010
38. Burke, R.: Hybrid recommender systems: survey and experiments. User Model. User-Adap. Inter. **12**(4), 331–370 (2002)
39. Ransbotham, S., Kane, G.C., Lurie, N.H.: Network characteristics and the value of collaborative user-generated content. Mark. Sci. **31**(3), 387–405 (2012)
40. Ross, C., Orr, E.S., Sisic, M., Arseneault, J.M., Simmering, M.G., Orr, R.R.: Personality and motivations associated with Facebook use. Comput. Hum. Behav. **25**(2), 578–586 (2009)
41. Stevenson, J.S., Bruner, G.C., Kumar, A.: Webpage background and viewer attitudes. J. Advert. Res. **40**(1/2), 29–34 (2000)
42. Schneider, F., Feldmann, A., Krishnamurthy, B., Willinger, W.: Understanding online social network usage from a network perspective. In: Proceedings of the 9th ACM SIGCOMM Conference on Internet Measurement Conference, pp. 35–48. ACM, November 2009
43. Swickert, R.J., Hittner, J.B., Harris, J.L., Herring, J.A.: Relationships among Internet use, personality, and social support. Comput. Hum. Behav. **18**(4), 437–451 (2002)
44. Sykes, T.A., Venkatesh, V., Gosain, S.: Model of acceptance with peer support: a social network perspective to understand employees' system use. MIS Q. **33**(2), 371–394 (2009)
45. Seraj, M.: We create, we connect, we respect, therefore we are: intellectual, social, and cultural value in online communities. J. Interact. Market. **26**(4), 209–222 (2012)
46. Viswanath, B., Mislove, A., Cha, M., Gummadi, K.P.: On the evolution of user interaction in Facebook. In: Proceedings of the 2nd ACM Workshop on Online Social Networks, pp. 37–42. ACM, August 2009

47. Valenzuela, S., Park, N., Kee, K.F.: Is there social capital in a social network site?: Facebook use and college students' life satisfaction, trust, and participation1. J. Comput. Mediat. Commun. **14**(4), 875–901 (2009)
48. Weiksner, G., Fogg, B.J., Liu, X.: Six Patterns for Persuasion in Online Social Networks. In: Oinas-Kukkonen, H., Hasle, P., Harjumaa, M., Segerståhl, K., Øhrstrøm, P. (eds.) PERSUASIVE 2008. LNCS, vol. 5033, pp. 151–163. Springer, Heidelberg (2008)
49. Xiao, B., Benbasat, I.: E-commerce product recommendation agents: use, characteristics, and impact. MIS Q. **31**(1), 137–209 (2007)
50. Xu, X., Venkatesh, V., Tam, K.Y., Hong, S.J.: Model of migration and use of platforms: role of hierarchy, current generation, and complementarities in consumer settings. Manage. Sci. **56**(8), 1304–1323 (2010)
51. Zhao, S., Grasmuck, S., Martin, J.: Identity construction on Facebook: digital empowerment in anchored relationships. Comput. Hum. Behav. **24**(5), 1816–1836 (2008)
52. Zhu, M., and Fang, X.: Introducing a revised lexical approach to study user experience in game play by analyzing online reviews. In: Proceedings of the 10th Interactive Entertainment Conference (IE2014), 02-03 December 2014, 978-1-4503-2790-9/14/12. ACM, Newcastle, NSW, Australia, New York (2014). http://dx.doi.org/10.1145/2677758.2677760
53. Zhu, M., Fang, X., Chan, S.S., Brzezinski, J.: Building a dictionary of game-descriptive words to study playability. In: CHI 2013 Extended Abstracts on Human Factors in Computing Systems, pp. 1077–1082. ACM, April 2013

BETTER-Project: Web Accessibility for Persons with Mental Disorders

Renaldo Bernard[1(✉)], Carla Sabariego[1], David Baldwin[2],
Shadi Abou-Zahra[3], and Alarcos Cieza[1,4,5]

[1] Research Unit for Biopsychosocial Health, Institute for Public Health
and Health Services Research, Department of Medical Informatics, Biometry
and Epidemiology—IBE, Ludwig-Maximilians-University, Munich, Germany
{renaldo.bernard, carla.sabariego}@med.lmu.de,
ciezaa@who.int
[2] Faculty of Medicine, University of Southampton, Southampton, UK
d.s.baldwin@soton.ac.uk
[3] Web Accessibility Initiative, World Wide Web Consortium, Berlin, Germany
shadi@w3.org
[4] School of Psychology, University of Southampton,
Southampton, UK
[5] Prevention of Blindness and Deafness, Disability and Rehabilitation Unit,
World Health Organisation, Geneva, Switzerland

Abstract. The paper outlines a methodology proposed to give impetus to a collaborative effort involving integral stakeholders to determine whether Web accessibility facilitation measures must be adapted for people with depression and anxiety, and if so, in what way(s). The methodology has three-phases: (1) identification of Web accessibility barriers using two data sources: a systematic review of pertinent literature and focus group interviews with people with depression and anxiety; (2) validation of current Web accessibility facilitation measures for this population using experimental user-testing; (3) provision of expertise-based recommendations for the improvement of Web accessibility facilitation measures using a delphi method. If adopted, the study's findings are expected to herald improvements in the Web browsing experiences of people with depression and anxiety, and also everyone else who use the Web.

Keywords: Protocol · Web accessibility · Depression · Anxiety · Mental disorders

1 Introduction

The Web is an essential tool for participation within knowledge-based societies where timely and easy access to information is crucial for individual progress [1]. It is an important means by which people can gather information and learn about personally meaningful topics to make informed life choices like how best to manage one's health, what career one should pursue or even where one should live [2]. The Web is also a useful and convenient way to develop and maintain relationships with people in one's life such as life-partners, friends, family members and acquaintances among others

© Springer International Publishing Switzerland 2015
M. Kurosu (Ed.): Human-Computer Interaction, Part III, HCII 2015, LNCS 9171, pp. 25–34, 2015.
DOI: 10.1007/978-3-319-21006-3_3

[3, 4]. Additionally, it provides many opportunities to engage in recreational activities including online shopping, gaming, watching movies and listening to music [5, 6]. Understandably, those without reasonable access to the Web and its benefits are left at a disadvantage.

Facilitating access to the Web is not limited to providing the necessary technological infrastructure but also ensuring no access barriers exist that make it difficult to perceive, understand, navigate, and interact with Websites. For example, images, controls, and other structural elements on websites without equivalent text alternatives will present accessibility barriers for people with visual disabilities [7]. People with hearing impairments will experience great difficulty perceiving audio content – videos with voices and sounds – on the Web without captions or transcripts explaining what is being conveyed in media using sound [7]. It can also be especially challenging for persons with physical disabilities to use websites that do not provide full keyboard support [7].

Consequently, great effort has been put towards ensuring accessibility for those with disabilities, especially for people with sensory impairments and physical disabilities where research has been very fruitful. For instance, research surrounding accessibility for people with visual impairment focuses on conveying information via alternative sensory channels such as auditory (e.g., screen readers) and tactile means (e.g., refreshable Braille displays), along with more cutting edge efforts to develop virtual retinal displays and the customised pre-compensation of images to match the visual characteristics of individual users and produce undistorted retinal images [8]. Research into alternative input mechanisms for people with physical disabilities to gain access to systems used to navigate the Web has resulted in many special keyboards and novel pointing-based input methods operated by eye gaze tracking and other body parts (i.e., tongue, feet, elbows and head), and speech input devices [9].

People with mental disorders (PwMD) also face barriers when accessing the Web and some of these barriers may be unique to people with these disorders as well [10]. Good and Sambhanthan [11] reported several website elements that people with depression and anxiety identified as being accessibility issues: distracting design, confusing menu options, poor navigation, time limited response forms, information overload, non-perceivable icons, slow response in websites loading information, poor organisation and presentation complicated language, poor content filters, excessive advertisements, and complex purchasing processes. Ferron et al. [12] and Rotondi et al. [10] concluded that people with severe mental disorders require sites that explicitly state instructions for their use, feature a shallow hierarchy of pages, use clear and explicit labels, large navigational cues and pop-up menus to reduce clicking. Findings from Rotondi et al. [10] also reveal that these Web accessibility needs are distinct and are not covered by existing guidance and or Web-interface models.

However, improving accessibility for people with mental disorders has received little direct research attention [13]. A thorough keyword search of several databases (i.e., MEDLINE, PsycARTICLES, CINAHL, Library, Information Science and Technology Abstracts, Computers and Applied Sciences Complete, ACM Digital Library, SpringerLink, OpenGrey) for Web accessibility, mental disorders and related terms only returned 3 directly relevant results (i.e., [10–12] as discussed earlier).

It is important to identify and address the possible Web accessibility barriers people with mental disorders experience as such barriers may have a negative impact on how much they benefit from the Web due to the poor accessibility of the platform. Studies investigating several of the rapidly growing number of Web-based treatment methods including online mental health communities (e.g., [14, 15]), Web-based group therapy (e.g., [16, 17]) and self-directed therapy (e.g., [18, 19]) have presented promising results but there is also much room for improving Web-based interventions. Knowledge of how Web modifications can lead to improved access by this population will help create a more all-inclusive Web from which people with mental disorders can also benefit. The World Health Organisation reports that one in four people will be affected by a mental disorder in their lifetime [20]. This represents a very large segment of the world population that may be at a disadvantage due to barriers negatively impacting their Web usage.

A comprehensive understanding of the barriers people with mental disorders encounter on the Web is also essential for devising ways to effectively address accessibility for this population as well. The process of establishing Web accessibility facilitation measures, including standards and guidelines, should rely on evidence (e.g., research, expertise with relevant issues) about 'what' barriers exist and 'how' they could be addressed to later advise on what strategies should be employed to remove or reduce these barriers. This is why the BETTER (weB accEssibiliTy for people wiTh mEntal disoRders) project was initiated.

BETTER is a collaborative effort involving relevant stakeholders – people with mental disorders, practicing professionals in the field, regulators, policymakers and academia – to determine whether current Web accessibility facilitation measures must be adapted for people with mental disorders and if so, in what way(s). It focuses on depression and anxiety because they are the most common mental disorders [21] and account for the leading causes of disability-adjusted life years (DALYs) due to mental and substance use disorders worldwide (i.e., depressive disorders account for 40.5 % and anxiety disorders for 14.6 % of DALYs [22]). The general objective of this paper is to outline the methodology to be implemented by BETTER.

2 The Three Phases of the BETTER Project

2.1 Identification of Web Accessibility Barriers and Facilitation Measures (Phase I)

The objective of the first phase is to determine 'what' barriers people with depression and anxiety encounter when accessing the Web and 'how' those barriers can be removed or reduced. Two different methodologies will be utilised to meet this objective – a systematic review and qualitative study with people with depression and anxiety (Fig. 1).

Study 1: Current Thinking on Digital Accessibility for PwMD. The objective of this study is to identify evidence regarding accessibility barriers people with mental disorders (MD) experience when using digital technology and any corresponding facilitation measures used to address them. A systematic review of literature covering

	Phase I **Identification of Web Accessibility Barriers and Facilitation Measures**	**Phase II** **Evaluation of Web Accessibility Facilitation Measures**	**Phase III** **Improvement of Web Accessibility Facilitation Measures**
Studies	Current Thinking on Digital Accessibility for PwMD *Systematic literature review* (Study 1) Perspectives of people with depression and anxiety *Semi-structured focus groups* (Study 2)	Validating Web Accessibility Facilitation Measures for People with Depression and Anxiety *Usability-testing* (Study 3)	Developing Improvement Strategies *Delphi Consensus* (Study 4)
Expected Outcomes	Summaries of (1) digital and specifically Web accessibility barriers persons with mental disorders face; (2) facilitation measures; (3) gaps in knowledge based on a comparison and integration of findings from study 1 and 2.	Detailed description of the effectiveness of Web accessibility facilitation measures and any identified shortcomings.	Set of recommended expertise-based Web accessibility facilitation measures for depression and anxiety.

Fig. 1. Phases including studies and expected outcomes of the BETTER project.

the fields of psychology, medicine and computer science will be conducted using several databases: MEDLINE, PsycARTICLES, CINAHL, Library, Information Science and Technology Abstracts, Computers and Applied Sciences Complete, ACM Digital Library, SpringerLink, OpenGrey. A systematic review was chosen as it is especially useful for identifying, selecting, and critically evaluating relevant studies, and to collect and analyse data gathered from them [23].

Contrary to the focus in the other studies within the project, this review will not be limited to just depression and anxiety but will consider all mental disorders. This is to increase the likelihood that insight into the probable situation surrounding Web accessibility for people with depression and anxiety is gained and that the study does not suffer from the paucity of research in the area as revealed by preliminary searches. The scope of the review will also be expanded to include all digital technologies as this allows for many more opportunities to obtain relevant knowledge that a narrow focus on the Web alone will not provide.

Studies will be selected if they include participants with mental disorders, describe the difficulties that people with mental disorders encounter when using consumer information and communication technologies (ICT) or provide guidance on how to improve the accessibility of consumer ICTs for PwMD. Information about the ICTs studied, diagnoses and classifications used, barriers and corresponding facilitation measures, origin of facilitation measures, the research methodology followed and definitions for accessibility and disability will be extracted from studies where possible. A narrative synthesis [24] will then be performed to draw conclusions based on the data extracted from across the set of included studies.

Study 2: Perspectives of People with Depression and Anxiety. The objective of this study is to improve the understanding of persons with depression and anxiety's experiences using the Web from their perspective. Focus groups will be used to elicit details about participants' experiences. This method allows for a more rapid and productive way of obtaining accounts of Web usage from participants when compared to similar qualitative methodologies (e.g., ethnographic methods) [25]. It is also beneficial to participants as it gives them the opportunity to make connections with similar experiences during the group session [26].

Purposive sampling will be utilised to obtain participants for study. Participants must be: aged ≥ 18 (50 % < and ≥ 40); skilled Web users as indicated by the 10-item abbreviated Web-use skills indexes for populations with low levels of internet experiences [27]; diagnosed with depression and or anxiety as stipulated by the Diagnostic and Statistical Manual of Mental Disorders (DSM) 4/5th revision or International Classification of Diseases (ICD) 10th revision; without significant sensory or physical disabilities.

The topic guide will feature questions that provoke discussion about the difficulties participants experience when using the Web, the perceived determinants of the major difficulties experienced and ways these difficulties can be removed or reduced. Groups with young adult participants will allow the study to capture the perspective from more skilled and involved Web users [28]. Sessions with older participants (≥40) will also provide enlightening accounts about their unique experience which is known to be different from younger users' Web usage patterns [29].

Framework analysis as outlined by Ritchie and Spencer [30] will be utilised for this study. Findings in the form of emergent themes from focus group narratives will be organised around key questions posed in the topic guide [31]. A survey will be later conducted to validate these findings among a wider population of people with depression and anxiety.

Expected Outcomes of Phase I. Results from this phase will summarise (1) digital and specifically Web accessibility barriers persons with mental disorders face, (2) the strategies employed to overcome barriers and (3) identified gaps in knowledge about what barriers exist and how they could be addressed based on a comparison and integration of findings from study 1 and 2. The first and third outcomes will inform phase II by guiding the development of realistic and meaningful task scenarios for a usability testing study. Also, the second outcome will be used in phase II to determine the Web accessibility facilitation measures that are to be validated in the experimental study.

2.2   Evaluation of Web Accessibility Facilitation Measures (Phase II)

The objective of this phase is to validate all Web accessibility facilitation measures for persons with depression and anxiety identified in phase 1. It builds on phase I by testing the accessibility of websites that implemented current facilitation measures identified during that phase.

Study 3: Validating Web Accessibility Facilitation Measures for Persons with Depression and Anxiety. The objective of this study is to validate the effectiveness of facilitation measures identified in phase I that will result in the removal or reduction in Web accessibility barriers for persons with depression and anxiety. An experimental study including a control group will be used to fulfil this objective. This study design was chosen as it provides sound evidence for clear casual interpretations and delivers the strongest evidence on the effectiveness of facilitation measures [32].

Recruitment will obtain skilled Web users as indicated by the 10-item abbreviated Web-use skills indexes for populations with low levels of Internet experiences [27] who are without sensory or physical disabilities and are aged ≥ 18. The experimental group will include participants who meet criteria for a clinical diagnosis of major depression (depressive episode) and anxiety disorder as stipulated by the DSM-4/5 or ICD-10. Participants who have never been diagnosed with a mental disorder will be assigned to the control group.

Participants will complete usability testing exercises with selected webpages and be later questioned about their experience performing assigned tasks and if any, the major difficulties encountered. The webpages will be selected by a group of evaluators with similar training and years of experience that will assess a collection of webpages for their conformance to the Web accessibility facilitation measures identified in phase I. If any of these webpages do not have a high level of conformance, conforming webpages will be created for the final set of sites to be used in the study.

Results will demonstrate the effectiveness of existing facilitation measures for people with depression and anxiety. The effectiveness will be measured using the number of Web accessibility barriers and the subsequent frequency with which these barriers were encountered. Comparisons between participant groups and participants with either depression or anxiety will indicate any significant differences in their experiences. Findings will also provide critical information about how effective current facilitation measures are at removing or reducing accessibility barriers, if any changes are necessary and if so, where focus should be placed to realise improvements.

Expected Outcomes of Phase II. Phase II will detail the effectiveness of Web accessibility facilitation measures identified in phase 1. It will also provide information about barriers, if any, that persist despite the implementation of these facilitation measures. This understanding will help focus the subsequent phase on a specific set of Web accessibility barriers for people with depression and anxiety that remain after applying current facilitation measures as identified in phase 1.

2.3   Improvement of Web Accessibility Facilitation Measures (Phase III)

The objective of this phase is to work with the expertise of stakeholders to propose solutions that are likely to remove or reduce barriers that remain after the testing of Web accessibility facilitation measures for people with depression and anxiety done in phase II.

Study 4: Developing Improvement Strategies. The objective of this study is to develop expertise-based Web accessibility facilitation measures targeting the barriers for persons with depression and anxiety identified in phase II that remain after the implementation of facilitation measures revealed in phase 1. A delphi technique will be employed to achieve this objective. The technique is a well-established method for reaching consensus among subject experts about what could and should be done given a particular set of circumstances [33, 34]. The delphi method also facilitates an in-depth examination of practical issues in an anonymous environment that is not conducive to unfavourable group dynamics. For instance, respondents are freer from any pressure to express a certain perspective due to manipulation or coercion by a dominant participant [35].

Respondent selection will be mainly guided by Pill [36] and Ludwig [37] who are well-referenced researchers in delphi studies. Participants will be recruited based on their level of expertise by virtue of having over 3 years of practical experience working directly in Web accessibility.

They will be asked to offer facilitation measures that will remove or reduce the remaining barriers identified in phase II. These facilitation measures will target necessary changes at 3 levels: website authorship including design and content; design of systems, like browsers, that retrieve and render Web content; development of accessible tools that create accessible Web resources. General information about the acceptability of the recommended facilitation measures among the respondent group will be solicited using an open-ended questionnaire over several rounds until 80 % consensus is reached on which additional Web accessibility facilitation measures should be recommended for people with depression and anxiety.

Expected Outcomes of Phase III. Phase III will provide a set of expertise-based Web accessibility facilitation measures for persons with depression and anxiety targeting barriers that persist despite the implementation of Web accessibility facilitation measures identified in phase 1.

3   Practical Implications of Web Accessibility Facilitation Measures for People with Mental Disorders

BETTER, to our knowledge, is the first project involving all relevant stakeholders – people with mental disorders, practicing professionals in the field, regulators, policymakers and academia – to provide systematic documentation about the Web accessibility barriers people with depression and anxiety encounter, and how these barriers could be addressed. These findings will be shared with relevant stakeholders who can offer guidance to Web practitioners on how Web accessibility for people with depression and anxiety may be improved.

BETTER's findings will be of great value to several groups across society. People with depression and anxiety will chiefly benefit if insight from BETTER is implemented by Web managers. They will likely enjoy improved access to the Web which can enhance their participation in society and Web-based treatments as well. Governments, businesses and other organisations will be more informed about how they can better comply with article 9 of the Convention on the Rights of Persons with Disabilities with regards to accessibility on the Web and genuinely extend their reach to the large segments of the population with depression and anxiety. Depression, anxiety and other related interest groups will also be empowered to advocate for the adoption of BETTER's expertise-based Web accessibility facilitation measures when necessary.

It is anticipated that BETTER would also stimulate further Web accessibility mental disorder-specific research leading to a deeper understanding of people with mental disorders' accessibility needs when using the Web. Aspects of Web accessibility standards, education, implementation and policy can be updated to adequately accommodate the needs of people with depression and anxiety on the Web after consideration of BETTER's findings. Future research can also build on knowledge from BETTER's findings and confidently expand accessibility investigations into Web access from various devices (e.g., mobile, wearables) and into the realm of other digital technologies that are beneficial to people with depression, anxiety and other mental disorders.

Putting BETTER's recommendations into practice may likely herald improvements in the Web browsing experiences of not only people with depression and anxiety or other mental disorders but it is expected that the adoption of BETTER's findings would also result in improvements for everyone else who uses the Web.

Acknowledgements. The research leading to these results has received funding from the People Programme (Marie Curie Actions) of the European Union's Seventh Framework Programme FP7/2007 - 2013 under REA grant agreement no 316795.

References

1. van Weert, T.J.: Education of the twenty-first century: new professionalism in lifelong learning, knowledge development and knowledge sharing. Educ. Inf. Technol. **11**(3–4), 217–237 (2006)
2. Sellen, A.J., Murphy, R., Shaw, K.L.: How knowledge workers use the web. In: Proceedings of the SIGCHI Conference on Human factors in Computing Systems. ACM (2002)
3. Parks, M.R., Roberts, L.D.: Making MOOsic': the development of personal relationships on line and a comparison to their off-line counterparts. J. Soc. Person. Relat. **15**(4), 517–537 (1998)
4. Parks, M.R., Floyd, K.: Making friends in cyberspace. J. Comput. Mediat. Commun. **1**(4), 80–97 (1996)
5. Johnson, T.J., Kaye, B.K.: Around the World Wide Web in 80 ways how motives for going online are linked to Internet activities among politically interested Internet users. Soc. Sci. Comput. Rev. **21**(3), 304–325 (2003)

6. Ferguson, D.A., Perse, E.M.: The World Wide Web as a functional alternative to television. J. Broadcast. Electron. Media **44**(2), 155–174 (2000)

7. Consortium, W.W.W. Diversity of Web Users. 2008 2012 10 September 2014. http://www. w3.org/WAI/intro/people-use-web/diversity.html#visual

8. Barreto, A.: Visual impairments. In: Harpar, S., Yesilada, Y. (eds.) Web Accessibility: A Foundation For Research. Springer, London (2008)

9. Trewin, S.: Physical impairments. In: Harper, S., Yesilada, Y. (eds.) Web Accessibility: A Foundation For Research. Springer, London (2008)

10. Rotondi, A.J., et al.: Designing websites for persons with cognitive deficits: design and usability of a psychoeducational intervention for persons with severe mental illness. Psychol. Serv. **4**(3), 202–224 (2007)

11. Good, A., Sambhanthan, A.: Accessing Web based health care and resources for mental health: interface design considerations for people experiencing mental illness. In: Marcus, A. (ed.) DUXU 2014, Part III. LNCS, vol. 8519, pp. 25–33. Springer, Heidelberg (2014)

12. Ferron, J.C., et al.: Developing a quit smoking website that is usable by people with severe mental illnesses. Psychiatr. Rehabil. J. **35**(2), 111 (2011)

13. Mariger, H. Cognitive Disabilities and the Web: Where Accessibility and Usability Meet? (2006) [cited 2014 01 September 2014]. http://ncdae.org/resources/articles/cognitive/

14. Kummervold, P.F., et al.: Social support in a wired world: use of online mental health forums in Norway. Nord. J. Psychiatry **56**(1), 59–65 (2002)

15. Powell, J., McCarthy, N., Eysenbach, G.: Cross-sectional survey of users of Internet depression communities. BMC psychiatry **3**(1), 19 (2003)

16. Winzelberg, A.J., et al.: Effectiveness of an Internet-based program for reducing risk factors for eating disorders. J. Consult. Clin. Psychol. **68**(2), 346 (2000)

17. Christensen, H., Griffiths, K.M.: The prevention of depression using the Internet. Med. J. Aust. **177**, S122–S125 (2002)

18. Carlbring, P., et al.: Treatment of panic disorder via the Internet: a randomized trial of a self-help program. Behav. Ther. **32**(4), 751–764 (2001)

19. Clarke, G., et al.: Overcoming depression on the Internet (ODIN): a randomized controlled trial of an Internet depression skills intervention program. Journal of medical Internet research **4**(3), e14 (2002)

20. Organization, W.H., The World health report: 2001: Mental health: new understanding, new hope (2001)

21. Kessler, R.C., et al.: Lifetime prevalence and age-of-onset distributions of mental disorders in the World Health Organization's World Mental Health Survey Initiative. World Psychiatry **6**(3), 168 (2007)

22. Whiteford, H.A., et al.: Global burden of disease attributable to mental and substance use disorders: findings from the Global Burden of Disease Study 2010. Lancet **382**(9904), 1575–1586 (2013)

23. Collaboration, T.C. Glossary. 27 February 2015 (2004). http://community.cochrane.org/ glossary

24. Popay, J.: Guidance on the conduct of narrative synthesis in systematic reviews. A product from the ESRC methods programme. Institute of Health Research, Lancaster (2006)

25. Lloyd-Evans, S.: Focus groups. In: Desai, V., Potter, R. (eds.) Doing Development Research, pp. 153–163. SAGE Publication, London (2006)

26. Liamputtong, P.: Focus Group Methodology: Principle And Practice. Sage, Thousand Oaks (2011)

27. Hargittai, E., Hsieh, Y.P.: Succinct survey measures of web-use skills. Soc. Sci. Comput. Rev. **30**(1), 95–107 (2012)

28. Paul, G., Stegbauer, C.: Is the digital divide between young and elderly people increasing? First Monday, 2005. 10(10)

29. Morrell, R.W., Mayhorn, C.B., Bennett, J.: A survey of World Wide Web use in middle-aged and older adults. Hum Factors: J. Hum. Factor Ergono. Soc. 42(2), 175–182 (2000)

30. Ritchie, J., Spencer, L.: Qualitative data analysis for applied policy research. In: Huberman, A.M., Miles, M.B. (eds.) The Qualitative Researcher's Companion, pp. 305–329. SAGE Publication, Thousand Oaks (2002)

31. Rabiee, F.: Focus-group interview and data analysis. Proc. Nutr. Soc. 63(04), 655–660 (2004)

32. Gray, W.D., Salzman, M.C.: Damaged merchandise? A review of experiments that compare usability evaluation methods. Hum. Comput. Interact. 13(3), 203–261 (1998)

33. Hsu, C.-C., Sandford, B.A.: The Delphi technique: making sense of consensus. pract. Assess. Res. Eval. 12(10), 1–8 (2007)

34. Miller, G: Determining what could/should be: the delphi technique and its application. In: 2006 Annual Meeting of the Mid-Western Educational Research Association, Columbus, Ohio (2006)

35. Dalkey, N.C., Brown, B.B., Cochran, S.: The Delphi Method: An Experimental Study of Group Opinion, vol. 3. Rand Corporation, Santa Monica (1969)

36. Pill, J.: The Delphi method: substance, context, a critique and an annotated bibliography. Socio-Econ. Plann. Sci. 5(1), 57–71 (1971)

37. Ludwig, B.: Predicting the future: have you considered using the delphi methodology. J. Ext. 35(5), 1–4 (1997)

Short Scales of Satisfaction Assessment: A Proxy to Involve Disabled Users in the Usability Testing of Websites

Simone Borsci[1], Stefano Federici[2,3(✉)], Maria Laura Mele[2,3], and Matilde Conti[2]

[1] Human Factors Research Group, School of Mechanical, Materials and Manufacturing Engineering, The University of Nottingham, Nottingham, UK
simone.borsci@gmail.com
[2] Department of Philosophy, Social & Human Sciences and Education, University of Perugia, Perugia, Italy
stefano.federici@unipg.it, matildeconti92@hotmail.it, marialaura.mele@gmail.com
[3] ECONA, Interuniversity Centre for Research on Cognitive Processing in Natural and Artificial Systems, Sapienza University of Rome, Rome, Italy

Abstract. Short scales of user satisfaction analysis are largely applied in usability studies as part of the measures to assess the interaction experience of users. Among the traditional tools, System Usability Scale (SUS), composed of 10 items, is the most applied quick evaluation scale. Recently, researchers have proposed two new and shorter scales: the Usability Metric for User Experience (UMUX), composed of four items, and the UMUX-LITE, which consists of only the two positive items of UMUX. Despite their recent creation, researchers in human-computer interaction (HCI) have already showed that these two tools are reliable and strongly correlated to each other [1–3]. Nevertheless, there are still no studies about the use of these questionnaires with disabled users. As HCI experts claim [4–7], when disabled and elderly users are included in the assessment cohorts, they add to the overall analysis alternative and extended perspectives about the usability of a system. This is particularly relevant to those interfaces that are designed to serve a large population of end-users, such as websites of public administration or public services. Hence, for a practitioner adding to the evaluation cohorts a group of disabled people may sensibly extend number and types of errors identified during the assessment. One of the major obstacles in creating mixed cohorts is due to the increase in time and costs of the evaluation. Often, the budget does not support the inclusion of disabled users in the test. In order to overcome these hindrances, the administering to disabled users of a short questionnaire—after a period of use (expert disabled costumers) or after an interaction test performed through a set of scenario-driven tasks (novice disabled users)—permits to achieve a good trade-off between a limited effort in terms of time and costs and the advantage of evaluating the user satisfaction of disabled people in the use of websites. To date, researchers have neither analyzed the use of SUS, UMUX, and UMUX-LITE by disabled users, nor the reliability of these tools, or the relationship among those scales when administrated to disabled people.

© Springer International Publishing Switzerland 2015
M. Kurosu (Ed.): Human-Computer Interaction, Part III, HCII 2015, LNCS 9171, pp. 35–42, 2015.
DOI: 10.1007/978-3-319-21006-3_4

In this paper, we performed a usability test with 10 blind and 10 sighted users on the Italian website of public train transportation to observe the differences between the two evaluation cohorts in terms of: (i) number of identified errors, (ii) average score of the three questionnaires, and (iii) reliability and correlation of the three scales.

The outcomes confirmed that the three scales, when administered to blind or sighted users, are reliable (Cronbach's $\alpha > 0.8$), though UMUX reliability with disabled users is lower than expected (Cronbach's $\alpha < 0.5$). Moreover, all the scales are strongly correlated ($p < .001$) in line with previous studies. Nevertheless, significant differences were identified between sighed and blind participants in terms of (i) number of errors experienced during the interaction and (ii) average satisfaction rated through the three questionnaires. Our data show, in agreement with previous studies, that disabled users have divergent perspectives on satisfaction in the use of a website. The insight of disabled users could be a key factor to improve the usability of those interfaces which aim to serve a large population, such as websites of public administration and services. In sum, we argue that to preserve the budget and even incorporate disabled users' perspectives in the evaluation reports with minimal costs, practitioners may reliably test the satisfaction by administrating SUS and UMUX or UMUX-LITE to a mixed sample of users with and without disability.

Keywords: Disabled user interaction · Usability evaluation · Usability Metric for User Experience · System Usability Scale

1 Introduction

Satisfaction is one of the three main components of usability [8], along with effectiveness and efficiency. Practitioners are used to testing this component through standardized questionnaires after that people have gain some experience in the use of a website. In particular, experts are used to applying short scales of satisfaction analysis to reduce the time and the costs of the assessment of a website. Among the quick satisfaction scales, the most popular tool of assessment is SUS [9]. SUS is a free and highly reliable instrument [10–14], composed of only 10 items on a five-point scale (1: Strongly disagree; 5: Strongly agree). To compute the overall SUS score, (1) each item is converted to a 0-4 scale for which higher numbers indicate a greater amount of perceived usability, (2) the converted scores are summed, and (3) the sum is multiplied by 2.5. This process produces scores that can range from 0 to 100. Despite the fact SUS was designed to be unidimensional, since 2009, several researchers have showed that this tool has two-factor structures: Learnability (scores of items 4 and 10) and Usability (scores of items 1-3 and 5-9) [2, 3, 13, 15–17]. Moreover, the growing availability of SUS data from a large number of studies [13, 18] has led to the production of norms for the interpretation of mean SUS scores, e.g., the Curved Grading Scale (CGS) [16]. Using data from 446 studies and over 5,000 individual SUS responses, Sauro and Lewis [16] found the overall mean score of the SUS to be 68 with a standard deviation of 12.5.

The Sauro and Lewis CGS assigned grades as a function of SUS scores ranging from 'F' (absolutely unsatisfactory) to 'A+' (absolutely satisfactory), as follows:

Grade F (0–51.7); Grade D (51.8–62.6); Grade C- (62.7–64.9); Grade C (65.0–71.0); Grade C+ (71.1–72.5); Grade B- (72.6–74.0); Grade B (74.1–77.1); Grade B+ (77.2–78.8); Grade A- (78.9–80.7); Grade A (80.8-84.0); Grade A+ (84.1–100).

Recently, two new scales were proposed as shorter proxies of SUS [17]: the UMUX, a four-item tool [1, 19], and the UMUX-LITE composed of only the two positive-tone questions from the UMUX [3]. The UMUX items have seven points (1: Strongly disagree; 7: Strongly agree) and both the UMUX and its reduced version, the UMUX-LITE, are usually interpreted as unidimensional measures. The overall scales of the UMUX and UMUX-LITE range from 0 to 100. Their scoring procedures are:

UMUX: The odd items are scored as [score − 1] and even items as [7 − score]. The sum of the item scores is then divided by 24 and multiplied by 100 [1].

UMUX-LITE: The two items are scored as [score − 1], and the sum of these is divided by 12 and multiplied by 100 [3]. As researchers showed [1, 3, 19], SUS, UMUX, and UMUX-LITE are reliable (Cronbach's α between .80 and .95) and correlate significantly ($p < .001$). However, for the UMUX-LITE, it is necessary to use the following formula (1) to adjust its scores to achieve correspondence with the SUS [3].

$$UMUX - LITE = .65([\text{Item 1 score}] + [\text{Item 2 score}]) + 22.9. \qquad (1)$$

Despite the fact short scale of satisfaction analysis is quite well known and used in HCI studies, rarely have the psychometric properties of these scales been analyzed by researchers when applied to test the usability of an interface with disabled users. This is because elderly and disabled people are often excluded from the usability evaluation cohorts because they are considered "people with special needs" [20], instead of possible end-users of a product with divergent and alternative modalities of interaction with websites. Nevertheless, as suggested by Borsci and colleagues [21], the experience of disabled users has a great value for HCI evaluators and for their clients. Indeed, to enrich an evaluation cohort with sub-samples of disabled users could help evaluators to run a sort of stress test of an interface [21].

The main complaint of designers, as regards the involvement of disabled people in the usability evaluation, is the cost of the test for disabled users. In fact, disabled users testing usually requires more time compared with the assessment performed by people without disability. The extra-time could be due to the following reasons. First, some disabled users need to interact with a website through a set of assistive technologies and this could require conducting the test in the wild instead of a lab. Second, evaluators need to set-up an adapted protocol of assessment for people with cognitive impairment, such as dementia [7]. Nevertheless, these issues could be overcome by adopting specific strategies. For instance, experts could ask for a small sample of disabled users, who are already customers of a website, to perform at their house a set of short interactions with a website driven by scenarios. Another approach could be to ask disabled users who are novices in the use of a website, to perform at home for a week a set of tasks by controlling remotely the interaction of these users [4]. Independently from the strategies, instead of fully monitoring the usability errors performed by disabled users, experts could just request from these end-users to complete a short scale after their experience with a system to gather their overall satisfaction. The satisfaction outcomes of disabled users' cohort could be then aggregated and compared with the results of the other cohort of people without disability. Therefore, by using short scales of satisfaction evaluation, practitioners could save on costs and, with a minimal effort, report to designers the number of errors identified, the level of satisfaction experienced by users without disability, and a comparative analysis of the satisfaction with a mixed cohort of users. Thus, short scales could be powerful tools to include, at minimal cost, the opinions of disabled users in the usability assessment, in order to enhance the reliability of the assessment report for the designers.

Today, the possibility to include a larger sample of users with different kind of behaviors in the usability testing is particularly relevant to obtain a reliable assessment. In fact, in the context of ubiquitous computing people could access and interact through different mobile devices with websites, and a large set of information on public services (such as taxes, education, transport, etc.) is available online. Therefore, for the success of public services websites it is important to have an interface which is accessible to a wide range of possible users and usable in a satisfactory way.

Despite the growing involvement of disabled users in the usability analysis, there are no studies analyzing the psychometric properties of short scales of satisfaction and the use of these tools to assess the usability of website interfaces perceived by a sample of disabled users.

The aim of this paper is to propose a preliminary analysis of the use of SUS, UMUX, and UMUX-LITE with a small sample of users with and without disability. To reach this aim, we involved in a usability assessment two different cohorts (blind and sighted users), in order to observe the differences between the two samples in terms of number of errors experienced by the end-users during the navigation, and the overall scores of the questionnaires. Moreover, we compared the psychometric properties of SUS, UMUX, and UMUX-LITE when administered to blind and sighted participants in terms of reliability and scales correlation.

2 Methodology

Two evaluation cohorts composed of 10 blind-from-birth users (Age: 23.51; SD: 3.12) and 10 sighted users (Age: 27.88; SD: 5.63) were enrolled through advertisements among associations of disabled users, and among the students of the University of Perugia, in Italy. Each participant was asked to perform on the website of the Italian public train company (http://www.trenitalia.it) the following three tasks, presented as scenarios:

– Find and buy online a train ticket from "Milan – Central station" to "Rome – Termini station."
– Find online and print the location of info-points and ticket offices at the train station of Perugia.
– Use the online claim form to report a problem about a train service.

Participants were asked to verbalize aloud their problems during the navigation. In particular, sighted users were tested through a concurrent thinking aloud protocol, while blind users were tested by a partial concurrent thinking aloud [7].

After the navigation each participant filled the Italian validated version [14] of three scales, presented in a random order.

2.1 Data Analysis

For each group of participants there were descriptive statistics (mean [M], standard deviation [SD]). An independent t-test analysis was performed to test the differences between the two evaluation cohorts in terms of overall scores of the three questionnaires. Moreover, a Cronbach's α and Pearson correlation analyses were performed to analyze the psychometric properties of the scales when administered to different end-users. All analyses were performed using IBM® SPSS 22.

3 Results

3.1 Usability Problems and User Satisfaction

The two evaluation cohorts identified, separately, a total number of 29 problems: Blind users experienced 19 usability issues, while sighted users experienced only 10 issues. Of the 29 issues reported by the two cohorts, eight issues were identified by both blind and sighted users; two problems only by sighted users; and 11 only by blind users. Therefore, a sample of 21 unique usability issues was identified testing 20 end-users. As reported in Table 1, an independent t-test analysis showed that for each of the questionnaires there was a significant difference between the overall satisfaction in use experienced by blind and sighted users.

Table 1. Differences among SUS, UMUX, and UMUX-LITE administered to blind and sighted users.

Blind vs. Sighted users	Degree of Freedom	t	p
SUS	17	6.469	.001
UMUX		4.876	.001
UMUX-LITE		4.319	.001

As can be seen in Table 2, while blind users assessed the website as not usable (Grade F), sighted users judged the interface as having an adequate level of usability (Grades for C- to C). By aggregating the two evolution cohorts, the website could be judged as a product with a low level of usability (Grade F).

3.2 Psychometric Properties of Questionnaires

The Cronbach's α analysis showed that all the questionnaires are reliable when administered to both sighted and blind users (Table 3). Nevertheless, in the specific case of blind users, UMUX reliability is lower than expected (.568).

Table 2. Average score, standard deviation (SD) and average aggregated scores of the SUS, UMUX, and UMUX-LITE of blind and sighted users. For each scale the Curved Grading Scale (CGS), provided by Sauro and Lewis [16], was also used to define the grade of website usability.

	Sighted	Blind	Av. aggregated scores
SUS	67.75 (SD:20.83)	15.25 (SD:11.98)	41.5 (SD:31.6)
	Grade C	Grade F	Grade F
UMUX	62.02 (SD:17.91)	32.10 (SD:11.99)	46.27 (SD:21.21)
	Grade C -	Grade F	Grade F
UMUX-LITE	68.52 (27.48)	17.54 (14.24)	41.66 (34.27)
	Grade C	Grade F	Grade F

Table 3. Reliability of SUS, UMUX, and UMUX-LITE for both blind, and sighted users.

	Blind	Sighted
SUS	.837	.915
UMUX	.568	.898
UMUX-LITE	.907	.938

Table 4. Correlations among SUS, UMUX, and UMUX-LITE for both blind and sighted users.

Types of end-users	Scales	SUS	UMUX
Blind	SUS	1	.948**
	UMUX	.935**	1
	UMUX-LITE	.948**	.928**
Sighted	SUS	1	.890**
	UMUX	.890**	1
	UMUX-LITE	820**	.937**

**. Correlation is significant at the 0.01 level (2-tailed).

As Table 4 shows, all the questionnaires, independently from the evolution cohort, are strongly correlated ($p < .001$).

4   Discussion

Table 2 clearly shows that while sighted users judged the website as quite a usable interface (Grades from C- to C), disabled users assessed the product as not usable (Grade F). This distance between the two evaluation cohorts is perhaps due to the fact that blind users experienced 11 more problems than the cohort of sighted participants. These results indicate that a practitioner adding to an evaluation cohort a sample of disabled users may drastically change the results of the overall usability assessment, i.e., the average overall score of the scales (Table 1).

The three scales were very reliable for both the cohorts (Cronbach's $\alpha > 0.8$; Table 3), however, the UMUX showed a low reliability when administered to blind users (Cronbach's $\alpha > 0.5$). This low level of reliability of UMUX was unexpected, considering also that UMUX-LITE composed of only the positive items of UMUX – i.e., items 1 and 3 – was very reliable (Table 3). Perhaps the negative items of UMUX – i.e., items 2 and 4 – were perceived by disabled users as complex or unnecessary questions, or this effect is an artifact of the randomized presentation of the questionnaires to the participants. Finally, for both the cohorts, the three scales were strongly correlated – i.e., $p<.001$ (see Table 4).

5 Conclusion

Quick and short questionnaires could be reliably used to assess the usability of a website with blind users. All the three tools reliably capture the experience of participants with and without disability, by offering to practitioners a good set of standardized results about the usability of a website.

Although further studies are needed to clarify the reliability of UMUX when administered to disabled users, our results suggest that UMUX-LITE and SUS might be applied by practitioners as good scales of satisfaction analysis. The use of these short scales may help practitioners to involve blind participants in their evaluation cohorts and to compare the website experience of people with and without disability. In fact, practitioners with a minimal cost may administer SUS and UMUX or UMUX-LITE to a mixed sample of users, thus obtaining an extra value for their report: the divergent perspectives of the disabled users. This extra value is particularly important for websites of public administration and of those services, such as public transport, that have to be accessed by a wide range of people with different levels of functioning.

References

1. Finstad, K.: The Usability Metric for User Experience. Interacting with Computers **22**, 323–327 (2010)
2. Lewis, J.R., Sauro, J.: The Factor Structure of the System Usability Scale. In: Kurosu, M. (ed.) HCD 2009. LNCS, vol. 5619, pp. 94–103. Springer, Heidelberg (2009)
3. Lewis, J.R., Utesch, B.S., Maher, D.E.: Umux-Lite: When There's No Time for the Sus. In: Conference on Human Factors in Computing Systems: CHI '13, pp. 2099–2102 (2013)
4. Petrie, H., Hamilton, F., King, N., Pavan, P.: Remote Usability Evaluations with Disabled People. In: SIGCHI Conference on Human Factors in Computing Systems: CHI '06, pp. 1133–1141 (2006)
5. Power, C., Freire, A., Petrie, H., Swallow, D.: Guidelines Are Only Half of the Story: Accessibility Problems Encountered by Blind Users on the Web. In: Conference on Human Factors in Computing Systems: CHI '12, pp. 433 (2012)
6. Rømen, D., Svanæs, D.: Evaluating Web Site Accessibility: Validating the Wai Guidelines through Usability Testing with Disabled Users. In: 5th Nordic Conference on Human-Computer Interaction—Building Bridges: NordiCHI08, pp. 535–538 (2008)

7. Federici, S., Borsci, S., Stamerra, G.: Web Usability Evaluation with Screen Reader Users: Implementation of the Partial Concurrent Thinking Aloud Technique. Cogn. Process. **11**, 263–272 (2010)
8. ISO: Iso 9241-11:1998 Ergonomic Requirements for Office Work with Visual Display Terminals – Part 11: Guidance on Usability. CEN, Brussels, BE (1998)
9. Brooke, J.: Sus: A "Quick and Dirty" Usability Scale. In: Jordan, P.W., Thomas, B., Weerdmeester, B.A., McClelland, I.L. (eds.) Usability Evaluation in Industry, pp. 189–194. Taylor & Francis, London (1996)
10. Lewis, J.R.: Usability Testing. In: Salvendy, G. (ed.) Handbook of Human Factors and Ergonomics, pp. 1275–1316. John Wiley & Sons, New York (2006)
11. Sauro, J., Lewis, J.R.: When Designing Usability Questionnaires, Does It Hurt to Be Positive? In: Conference on Human Factors in Computing Systems: CHI '11, pp. 2215–2224 (2011)
12. Zviran, M., Glezer, C., Avni, I.: User Satisfaction from Commercial Web Sites: The Effect of Design and Use. Information & Management **43**, 157–178 (2006)
13. Bangor, A., Kortum, P.T., Miller, J.T.: An Empirical Evaluation of the System Usability Scale. International Journal of Human-Computer Interaction **24**, 574–594 (2008)
14. McLellan, S., Muddimer, A., Peres, S.C.: The Effect of Experience on System Usability Scale Ratings. Journal of Usability Studies **7**, 56–67 (2012)
15. Borsci, S., Federici, S., Lauriola, M.: On the Dimensionality of the System Usability Scale (Sus): A Test of Alternative Measurement Models. Cogn. Process. **10**, 193–197 (2009)
16. Sauro, J., Lewis, J.R.: Quantifying the User Experience: Practical Statistics for User Research. Morgan Kaufmann, Burlington (2012)
17. Lewis, J.R.: Usability: Lessons Learned … and yet to Be Learned. International Journal of Human-Computer Interaction **30**, 663–684 (2014)
18. Kortum, P.T., Bangor, A.: Usability Ratings for Everyday Products Measured with the System Usability Scale. International Journal of Human-Computer Interaction **29**, 67–76 (2012)
19. Finstad, K.: Response to Commentaries on 'The Usability Metric for User Experience'. Interacting with Computers **25**, 327–330 (2013)
20. Biswas, P., Langdon, P.: Towards an Inclusive World – a Simulation Tool to Design Interactive Electronic Systems for Elderly and Disabled Users. In: 2011 Annual SRII Global Conference, pp. 73–82 (2011)
21. Borsci, S., Kurosu, M., Federici, S., Mele, M.L.: Computer Systems Experiences of Users with and without Disabilities: An Evaluation Guide for Professionals. CRC Press, Boca Raton, FL (2013)

Automatic Deformations Detection in Internet Interfaces: ADDII

Leandro Sanchez[2] and Plinio Thomaz Aquino Jr.[1,2(✉)]

[1] Centro Universitário da FEI – Fundação Educacional Inaciana
Pe. Sabóia de Medeiros, São Bernardo do Campo, São Paulo, Brazil
plinio.aquino@fei.edu.br
[2] IPT - Instituto de Pesquisas Tecnológicas, São Paulo, Brazil
leandrosanchez@me.com

Abstract. Developers have been trying to create uniform and consistent web-pages in the different browsers available in the market. Known as Crossbrowser issue, it affects pages in different ways, on its functionalities and visually aspects and sometimes not related to the source code. Using screenshot and image comparison algorithms, this paper presents a technique for automated detection of visual deformations in web pages using a tool developed during the research called Automatic Deformations Detection in Internet Interfaces (ADDII).

Keywords: Business: interfaces in automated manufacturing · Business: visual analytics and business intelligence · Technology: intelligent and agent systems

1 Introduction

Since the beginning of the Internet and offer of different web browsers, has been a challenge to developers to keep your pages uniform and consistent between the different versions available, both in functional and visually. Much of the problem not related to the source code created by developers, but by the different implementations of browsers, which interpret and visually present the pages. About four browsers have over 70 % of market share and big companies like Microsoft are still investing on new products, as Project Spartan [1] recently announced. If we add in that count the currently available browsers on other platforms, such as smartphones and tablets, the number would be higher. Different tools have been developed and commercially available to support developers in testing your pages and applications. However, none of them is completely effective in automatically detecting visual deformations, usually leaving the checking and interpretation on developers mind. This paper presents a technique for automated detection of visual deformations in web pages using a tool developed during the research called Automatic Deformations Detection in Internet Interfaces (ADDII). The ADDII compares screenshots of pages generated in three different browsers and uses algorithms to compare type image Perceptual Hash to verify the similarity between them, indicating which browsers had a discrepancy.

In the next chapters, we will present more detailed information about the Cross browser issue, the visual algorithm's, the concept and process behind ADDII and our experiment results.

© Springer International Publishing Switzerland 2015
M. Kurosu (Ed.): Human-Computer Interaction, Part III, HCII 2015, LNCS 9171, pp. 43–53, 2015.
DOI: 10.1007/978-3-319-21006-3_5

2 Cross Browser Issue: Visual or Functional?

During the research, the compatibility issue divided into two types: Visual and Functional. The first type refers to the rendering of a page, in the interpretation of the code by web browsers, including HTML, Javascript and CSS content and present visual differences or errors that mischaracterize content. The image below illustrates the visual issue, which the center content is dislocated to right side, not following the header that is in the left position (Fig. 1).

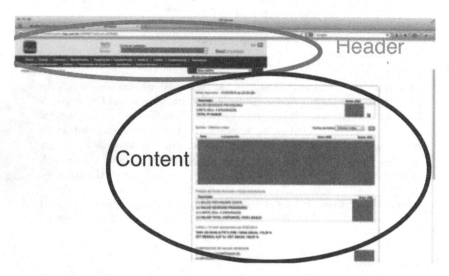

Fig. 1. Visual issue (source case: itaú internet banking, browser safari)

The second type comes to functional errors when the browser does not interpret a particular action or event correctly. Both types have common importance, however may contain different relevance depending on their use. The problem of type Visual directly affects developers who produce visual content, in which the pages created for advertising, promotion and marketing, where the inadequate presentation of a given page implies that a message not delivered to the user. The image below illustrate the functional issue, which the browser throws an error message during the execution in one of the functions (Fig. 2).

Develop applications compatible with most existing browsers is still a problem for developers, due to implementation differences in most of its components, which interpret and render the codes in different ways. Researchers Grosskurth et al. [2] presented the eight (8) components that make up the architecture of Internet browsers: User Interface; Browser Engine; Rendering Engine; Networking Subsystem; Javascript Interpreter; XML Parser Subsystem; Display Backend and Data Persistence Subsystem.

Also during the research, found that the companies that develop web browsers implement these components in different ways.

Figures 3 and 4 show two different browsers architecture. You can see the different components. The areas of User Interface, Browser Engine, Rendering Engine, Data Persistence, Networking, JavaScript Interpreter, XML (eXtensible Markup Language)

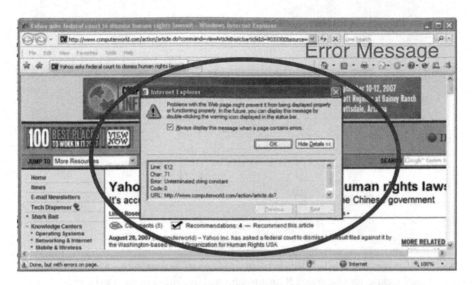

Fig. 2. Functional issue (source: computerworld (2007), browser IE 6)

Parser and Display backend have differences in their implementations. The most noticeable to the user is the user interface (User Interface), which explicitly differs between browsers. Components such as networking, because they are different, expose specific security vulnerabilities of each browser and therefore rarely the same vulnerability found is contained in all browsers. Other components have a direct influence on performance, such as *JavaScript Interpreter*. Their different implementations make a browser more efficient for execution of specific scripts on pages. It is common to find JavaScript codes that do not work in all browsers. As an example, *document.getElementById* statement, which should return the unique identifier of an object on a page in all browsers, in some versions of Internet Explorer may return unexpected values as Microsoft article [3].

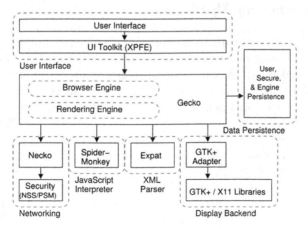

Fig. 3. Mozila architecture (source: [2] architecture and evolution of the modern web browser, p. 9).

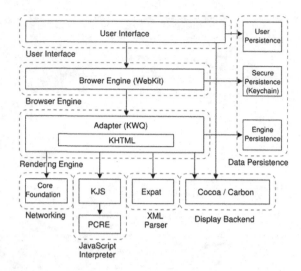

Fig. 4. Safari architecture (source: [2] architecture and evolution of the modern web browser, p. 14)

Studies continue to exist in this area, implementing different forms of check or normalize the pages, making it compatible with different browsers. The researchers Eaton et al. [4] demonstrated that the use of a tool that performs scanning in HTML (Hyper Text Markup Language) code to find invalid tags or used incorrectly, causing inconsistency in the application. Have the researchers Choudhary et al. [5] proposed the use of a tool that performs validations in the DOM (Document Object Model) structure of pages and in the analysis of images (screenshots). The researchers, Zhu et al. [6] demonstrated a technique for creating layouts, which contains a generator able to produce HTML code set for each version, and model browser.

3   Visual Comparison Algorithm's

During the research, this work tried to explore the use of image comparison algorithms, which can point the similarity between two images. Algorithms that address this issue are being developed in the areas of computer graphics and vision. Perhaps the most common algorithms are the Peak signal-to-noise ratio (PNSR) and root-mean-square error (RMSE), which are used to measure the quality of images. These algorithms can be found as library functions called *ImageMagick* [7]. An evolution of these algorithms is the Structural Similarity Image Metric (SSIM), presented by Wang et al. [8], which computes and compares the number of errors on the images to see their similarities. An implementation of this algorithm can be found in the Python-based tool called ***pyssim*** [9]. After validate these algorithms, the visual perception chosen, for its efficacy during the tests. The RMSE and PNSR algorithms were not effective to check the discrepancies and presented the results in decibels. The implementation of SSIM has values between 0 and 1, complicating the calculation to check similarity on images of different sizes. In the other hand, visual perception algorithms presented the results with numerical values that facilitate the calculation, including the number of different pixels between the two images.

There are several algorithms using Hash and its most common applications are file integrity checking. The MD5 and SHA1 algorithms have become popular on authentication systems, since the hash is unique and unchanging as a signature [10], reflecting the exact sequence of bytes. In case of any change in the bytes, the Hash will be different. These algorithms would be efficient if the scope is to validate if two images are identical, exactly same in the bytes point of view.

The Perceptual Hash allows you to check the similarity between two images, from small changes imperceptible to the human eye, including small changes of color and form.

Some researchers have been working on new algorithms and improving some existing ones over the years. Lin et al. [11] and Fridrich et al. [12] studies showed that verify the differences of two coefficients resulting from the calculation of the DCT (Discrete Cosine Transform), which is a formula used in processing digital and compression algorithms. Although they worked on different implementations, both used the DCT to calculate the Hash. Another algorithm is the SVD (Singular Value Decomposition). Kozat et al. [13] proposed an algorithm to calculate the hash using this formula. Perceptual Hash algorithms implementations are available for many different languages and platforms. For the development of ADDII, we used the algorithm written by Shepherd [14], which returns the Hamming Distance: given two strings, the Hamming distance is the lower number of replacements required to transform a string in another, or number of errors that turned on each other [15]. The Shepherd algorithm [14] was based on the article published by Krawetz [16].

The Perceptual Diff, created by Yee et al. [17] allows the comparison of two images, indicating whether they are similar or not and the number of different pixels. The comparison method used for calculating metrics of processed images, extending the VDP (Visible Differences Predictor) technique by Daly [18]. The comparison performed by the Perceptual Diff shows the differences in pixel by pixel in each image area available, taking into account the scanning angle. The algorithms and source code can be accessed through the SourceForge site *pdiff* [17].

4   ADDII: Automatic Deformations Detection in Internet Interfaces

The ADDII has four steps to perform the verification of pages. First, it loads the URL's of the pages to scanned, which should be available on web servers. The second step called *Screenshot Generator*, performs the screenshot of the images of each URL in three different browsers. The third step compares each screenshot of each URL generated in the above process, recording the result of the two algorithms implemented. Finally, the last step present the results, showing how similar is each screenshot between each other. As mentioned before, the ADDII implements two Visual comparison algorithms. Both have different metrics but with the same goal. Pointing out the similarity between two images.

4.1 Process and Components Detail

The following diagram illustrates the communication between the components created with ADDII.

Figure 5 illustrates the ADDII Architecture. The first lane shows the main process, the second the storage layer, and the interaction with the file system in the third. The lanes are also divided into three steps (columns), the first column generation screenshots, the second resizing images for the same resolution, and the third processing of the image comparison algorithms.

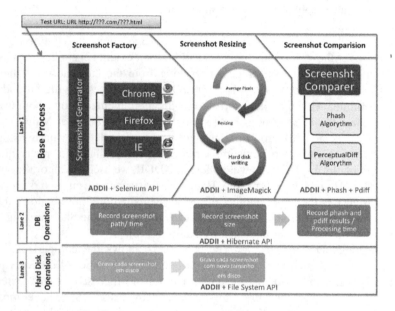

Fig. 5. Components and process (source: author)

When you run the ADDII, the first step is obtain the screenshots. This task leverage Selenium API to take screenshots. This same step stores the image in a folder in the file system and records the path in the database (lanes 2 and 3). The second step calculates and resizes the three screenshots obtained in the previous step. The third and final step, runs the two visual comparison algorithms implemented and collect the results recorded in the database.

The implementation of the above components demonstrates the modularity of the ADDII. The implementation of new browsers to obtain screenshots, through new future plugins offered by Selenium API or components developed apart is possible. New image comparison algorithms can also be added or improved in new versions.

4.2 Automatic Screenshots

To perform screenshots, ADDII utilize the Selenium Java API [19]. Selenium is an API that allows developers to perform dynamic actions on pages and sites across browsers.

It is widely used in Web Application testing automation. Selenium API requires that the browser being used is installed on the computer, the screenshots are generated directly in the browser itself. The code snippet below illustrates the Webdriver API call to perform the screenshot in Google Chrome browser.

```
public static void main ( String [ ] args ) {
/ / TODO Auto -generated method stub
  WebDriver driver = new ChromeDriver ( ) ;
  Dimension dim = new Dimension ( 1366, 768 ) ;
        driver.manage ( ) window ( ) setSize (dim ) . . ;
        driver.get ( args [ 0 ] ) ;
        try {

                File scrFile = ( ( TakesScreenshot )
driver ) getScreenshotAs ( OutputType.FILE ) . ;
                FileUtils.copyFile ( scrFile , new File (
args [ 1 ] ) ) ;
            } Catch ( IOException e1 ) {
                e1.printStackTrace ();
            }
        / / Close the browser
        driver.quit ();
```

[Code snippet from ADDII]

4.3 Visual Algorithm's Implementation

The ADDII implements two algorithms visual algorithm's. Both have different metrics but with the same goal. Pointing out the similarity between two images. The first algorithm implemented, was created by the programmer Elliot Shepherd [14], using Java language. In this work the algorithm is called pHash. The result of the algorithm is a range of values that informs how equal are two images. To perform the verification of images, it uses the DCT (Discrete Cosine Transformation) for low frequencies of the image, as used in image compressors like JPEG format. The Hamming distance algorithm is applied to calculate the difference between the Hash's. When the algorithm returns 0–10, means that the images are similar. If returning more than 10 means that the images have significant differences.

The second algorithm is called Perceptual Image Diff [17], which the binaries are distributed as free software by the GNU (General Public License). Its use is performed through the command prompt, passing the path of the two images to be verified, as the example below:

```
Perceptualdiff image1.png image2.png
```

The algorithm returns a text saying that the images are similar. In verbose mode, activated via parameter *-verbose* also returns the number of distinct pixels was found between images. During the implementation of Perceptual Image Diff, was found that the utility only compares images with similar resolution. However, the screenshots generated by Selenium API had small differences in resolution. To resolve this point, the ADDII implemented a call to *ImageMagick API*, which among its many functions allows you to resize an image to a desired resolution. To configure the most appropriate resolution, we chose a simple calculation of average pixel width and height of the three screenshots generated. The formula is:

```
The formula is:
Img1.width + Img2.width + img3.width / 3 = Average width
of screenshots
Img1.height + Img2.height + img3.height / 3 = Average
height of screenshots
```

ImageMagick using the values calculated on the above formula converts the final resolution of the screenshots. On ADDII the two algorithms are complementary. The first shows that the images are similar, the second reports the amount of distinct pixels and how different two images are.

In the next chapter will present the test scenarios for validation ad results obtained with ADDII.

5   Results

In order to validate the effectiveness of ADDII, three (3) cases were prepared, containing visual errors in at least one of the browsers. In addition, ten (10) sites also checked from the Internet, just as validation of its operation outside of a controlled environment. The definition of right or wrong in the results table was defined *pHash algorithm*, the information of pixels being informed by the additional Perceptual Diff algorithm in the analysis. For each test was selected a default browser, which is the browser where the test or site in question works correctly. The default browser shown in bold in the table below, which shows the test results.

As shown in Table 1, cases 1 and 3 showed similar results where the algorithm pHash presented a score below 10, the Mozilla Firefox and Google Chrome presented scores above 10 compared with Internet Explorer, as expected by the scenarios. Analyzing the results obtained by the *Perceptual Diff* algorithm, it was found that is consistent with results obtained by pHash, being possible to observe the large number of distinct pixels when screenshots were compared with Internet Explorer. Case 2 showed a different result than expected. The pHash algorithm assigned a score above 10 for screenshots of Mozilla Firefox and Google Chrome browsers, but it was expected a score below 10, due to the similarity of the images. Perceptual diff worked as expected, showing the similarity of screenshots browsers Mozilla Firefox and

Table 1. ADDII test cases results

Scenario	BrowserA	BrowserB	Phash score	Pdiff (pixels)	Total (pixels)	Result	Expected results
Case 1	Mozilla Firefox	Google Chrome	5	3755	636582	Ok	Ok
	Internet Explorer	Google Chrome	20	147729	636582	Error	Error
Case 2	Mozilla Firefox	Google Chrome	14	6706	807143	Error	Ok
	Internet Explorer	Google Chrome	17	20607	807143	Error	Error
Case 3	Mozilla Firefox	Google Chrome	5	39022	636582	Ok	Ok
	Internet Explorer	Google Chrome	17	348794	636582	Error	Error
Site 1	Mozilla Firefox	Google Chrome	7	66773	1169566	Ok	Ok
	Internet Explorer	Google Chrome	15	218039	1169566	Error	Error
Site 2	Mozilla Firefox	Google Chrome	6	213276	1738232	Ok	Ok
	Internet Explorer	Google Chrome	7	291147	1738232	Ok	Error
Site 3	Mozilla Firefox	Google Chrome	6	322894	2819295	Ok	Ok
	Internet Explorer	Google Chrome	14	1235330	2819295	Error	Error
Site 4	Mozilla Firefox	Google Chrome	1	88033	908424	Ok	Error
	Internet Explorer	Google Chrome	6	192627	908424	Ok	Ok
Site 5	Mozilla Firefox	Google Chrome	4	417848	1966032	Ok	Ok
	Internet Explorer	Google Chrome	27	828384	1966032	Error	Error
Site 6	Mozilla Firefox	Google Chrome	6	285333	2014163	Ok	Error
	Internet Explorer	Google Chrome	2	337863	2014163	Ok	Ok
Site 7	Mozilla Firefox	Google Chrome	2	92767	979755	Ok	Error
	Internet Explorer	Google Chrome	2	119258	979755	Ok	Ok
Site 8	Mozilla Firefox	Google Chrome	4	282375	1803528	Ok	Ok
	Internet Explorer	Google Chrome	21	1173685	1803528	Error	Error
Site 9	Mozilla Firefox	Google Chrome	13	1037731	2903274	Error	Error
	Mozilla Firefox	Internet Explorer	14	522682	2903274	Error	Ok
Site 10	Mozilla Firefox	Google Chrome	3	325485	1163376	Ok	Error
	Mozilla Firefox	Internet Explorer	4	321559	1163376	Ok	Error

Google Chrome and the high number of distinct pixels in comparison with Internet Explorer.

On the websites checking, the scenarios of Sites 1, 3, 5 and 8 showed the expected results, illustrating the problem of rendering in Internet Explorer. The scenarios of Sites 2, 4, 6, 7 and 10 showed different results than expected. This fact shows that mainly pHash algorithm was not able to identify small differences in pages such as changes in small letters and pictures or missing areas. This is due to the reduction of the image and use only low frequency in the comparison process. The Perceptual Diff was more assertive in these cases, highlighting the difference in pixels pages that showed the highest difference, which in some cases showed more than 50 % of pixels different from one browser to another, such as sites 4, 6 and 9.

The project is available for download and complete data analysis report in http://www.fei.edu.br/~plinio.aquino/ADDII/.

6 Conclusion

Based on the scenarios evaluated during the work, it was possible to prove the viability of the ADDII as a tool for visual deformations caused by the mismatch in the interpretation and rendering of HTML content. We have concluded that the goals of generating screenshots and use of algorithms for visual perception established early in the project were achieved.

The examples with low/medium difficult (medium to high differences between the screenshots) were successfully detected and represented about 50 % of total amount of tests created to identify distortions caused by the browser. When selecting a standard web browser, the user ADDII defines a base where your code has been tested, allowing comparison with other browsers, allowing different combinations.

It was also possible to observe the greater efficiency of the Perceptual Diff algorithm, which presented efficiently the non-equal pixels during the comparison. Algorithm pHash had failed in tests where the visual differences were in small areas, which makes it a not good choice for images with large viewable area. For future work, it would be interesting to further explore the Perceptual Diff algorithm, delegating to the ADDII user the task of defining the acceptable percentage of distinct pixels for a given test, allowing the user to choose the acceptable level of difference to your pages. Even was not the main reason of the research, compare the two algorithms was inevitable, adding value to the research.

The result also demonstrates the correct decision to use both algorithms in a complementary manner, as it enables the analysis of two different views.

Allow authentication pages for testing in secured pages and set the resolution of the browsers performs a test are also desirable improvements in future versions.

Acknowledgment. To FAPESP (Fundação de Amparo à Pesquisa do Estado de São Paulo) for financial support.

References

1. Project Spartan announcement. http://blogs.msdn.com/b/ie/archive/2015/01/22/project-spartan-and-the-windows-10-january-preview-build.aspx
2. Grosskurth, A., Godfrey, M.W.: Architecture and evolution of the modern web browser, 1–24 (2006)
3. MSDN GetElementById reference. http://msdn.microsoft.com/enus/library/ie/ms536437(v=vs.85).aspx
4. Eaton, C., Memon, A.M.: An empirical approach to testing web applications across diverse client platform configurations. Int. J. Web Eng. Technol. IJWET Spec. Issue Empir. Stud. Web Eng. 3(3), 227–253 (2007)
5. Choudhary, S., Versee, H., Orso, A.: WEB DIFF: automated identification of cross-browser issues in web applications. In: 2010 IEEE International Conference on Software Maintenance (ICSM) (2010)

6. Zhu, J., Liu, X., Urano, Y., Jin, Q.: A novel WYSIWYG approach for generating cross-browser web data. In: 2010 International Conference on Computational Science and Its Applications, pp. 155–164
7. IMAGEMAGICK. http://www.imagemagick.org/script/index.php
8. Wang, Z., Bovik, A.C., Sheikh, H.R., Simoncelli, E.P.: Image quality assessment: from error visibility to structural similarity. IEEE Trans. Image Process. **13**(4), 600–612 (2004)
9. PYSSIM. https://github.com/jterrace/pyssim
10. Stevens, M.: On collisions for MD5, June 2007
11. Lin, C., Chang, S.: A robust image authentication method distinguishing JPEG compression from malicious manipulation. IEEE Trans. Circ. Syst. Video Technol. **11**(2), 153–168 (2001)
12. Fridrich, J., Goljan, M.: Robust Hash Functions for Digital Watermarking Department of Electrical Engineering, SUNY Binghamton, NY 13902-6000
13. Kozat, S.S., Mihcak, K., Venkatesan, R.: Robust perceptual image hashing via matrix invariances. In: Proceedings of the IEEE Conference on Image Processing, pp. 3443–3446, October 2004
14. Shepherd, E.: Perceptual Hash Algorithm. http://pastebin.com/Pj9d8jt5
15. Hamming, R.W.: Error detecting and error correcting codes. Bell Syst. Tech. J. **29**. 147–160 (1950). http://www.caip.rutgers.edu/~bushnell/dsdwebsite/hamming.pdf
16. Krawetz, N.: A Picture's Worth ,,, Digital Image Analysis and Forensics Table of Contents, pp. 1–31 (2007)
17. Yee, H., Corley, S., Sauerwein, T., Breidenbach, J., Foster, C., Tilander, J.: Perceptual Image Diff. http://pdiff.sourceforge.net
18. Daly, S.: Visible differences predictor: an algorithm for the assessment of image fidelity. In: SPIE/IS&T 1992 Symposium, vol. 1666 (1992)
19. SELENIUM. http://seleniumhq.org/

Usability and Aesthetics: The Case of Architectural Websites

Evanthia Faliagka[2], Eleni Lalou[1], Maria Rigou[1,3(✉)], and Spiros Sirmakessis[1,2]

[1] Hellenic Open University, Parodos Aristotelous 18, 26 335 Patras, Greece
elena.lalou@gmail.com, rigou@ceid.upatras.gr,
syrma@teimes.gr
[2] Department of Computer and Informatics Engineering,
Technological Institution of Western Greece,
National Road Antirrio-Ioannina, 30020 Antirrio, Greece
efaliaga@teimes.gr
[3] Department of Computer Engineering and Informatics,
University of Patras, 26500 Rio Campus, Greece

Abstract. Modern people create, communicate and share knowledge and information through the web, but the need for usable website design is taken for granted. The ever increasing user familiarity with the web has drastically reduced user tolerance to website functionality problems. On the other hand, a requirement steadily observed by usability specialists refers to an increasing preference for the aesthetically pleasing and not the merely functional. This study aims to investigate the relation between website usability and aesthetics using the case of architectural websites and their typical users who are design experts with demanding aesthetic requirements. The study confirms that there is a close connection between aesthetics and perceived usability both when these two requirements are satisfied and when they are not.

Keywords: Usability evaluation · Aesthetics · Heuristics · Architectural websites · Questionnaires · SUS · AttrakDiff

1 Introduction

Today, the need for usable website design is taken for granted. At the same time the individual, and as a result the internet user, demonstrates an increasing preference for the aesthetically pleasing and not the merely functional; a need which is steadily being recognized by the usability specialists. The paper's scope is to investigate the relation between website usability and aesthetics. The case of architectural websites was initially chosen, since their owners and their users, who are considered design experts, have quite different aesthetic responses from those of typical web users. After going through the existing literature, where reference to the tradition of Aesthetics is rather restricted, five heuristic rules relating to basic aesthetic parameters are proposed and documented hereafter. The heuristics are based on existing aesthetic theories that have been around and validated for years and also can be used as guidelines during the

© Springer International Publishing Switzerland 2015
M. Kurosu (Ed.): Human-Computer Interaction, Part III, HCII 2015, LNCS 9171, pp. 54–64, 2015.
DOI: 10.1007/978-3-319-21006-3_6

website GUI design process. In this study, two methods were used to evaluate three indicatively chosen architectural websites: the first used heuristic evaluation that also included the five new heuristic rules and the second two questionnaires, one for general usability evaluation (SUS) and the other for evaluating website attractiveness (AttrakDiff).

The analysis of the results indicates that when the design expert user cannot identify with the aesthetics of the website, this adversely affects negatively the perceived usability (which can be considered as a hind towards "what is not beautiful is not usable"). Moreover, when the design expert user cannot identify with the aesthetics of the website, and also he/she is intensely dissatisfied by its perceived usability, this eventually leads to a negative image of the overall impression of the website. Also, the more aesthetically sensitive and critical is the eye of the user the more demands it imposes on perceived images and the visual perception of any object and that directly affects in a catalytic manner the perceived website usability.

The rest of the paper is structured as follows: the 2nd paragraph provides an introduction to the relation between aesthetics and usability and discusses the first methodological step, which refers to the architectural websites survey conducted. The 3rd paragraph presents the proposed aesthetic heuristics and the performed heuristic evaluation extended with the new rules. Paragraph 4 presents the evaluation of the three architectural websites by the architects, using the SUS and the AttrakDiff question-naires and summarizes the results, while paragraph 5 draws the main conclusions and discusses directions of future work.

2   Aesthetics and Perceived Usability

The term 'Aesthetics' addresses the overall perception of beauty or the perception of what is beauty by a single person or a group of people. Respectively, something is characterized as aesthetic when it is associated with the senses and our perception through them.

Aesthetics are mainly expressed through art and design, with design ranging from designing a city to designing the smallest everyday object. When we are working on web design, the role of aesthetics is crucial for the way a webpage is perceived. The human mind only needs 50 ms to create positive or negative impressions for a website. This is an aesthetic decision, which can influence our judgment for the whole website [1]. The conflict between form and function has long been observed in architecture and design. On the one hand, emphasizing on function stresses the importance of the object's usability and usefulness but on the other hand, emphasis on form indulges mostly the aesthetic and social needs of designers and users.

The basic principles of Human Computer Interaction emphasize in effectiveness rather than aesthetics. Generally, the criterion of aesthetic design is an integral part of the effective interaction design. The pursuit for the prominence of usability in the field of Human Computer Interaction sometimes reaches to a point that the measurement of a system's usability, determines the success in a GUI design [2]. The concepts of aesthetics and usability represent in a way two vertical dimensions of Human Computer Interaction. The aesthetics refers mostly to non-quantifiable, subjective and affected-based user system experience. On the other hand usability is usually measured by rather objective means and sets effectiveness as the most important criterion.

The marginalization of the aesthetic aspects of HCI is not a constructive position for various reasons. Firstly, it reveals a gap between the research objectives of HCI and the practice of many computer related industries on the topic of design criteria. Secondly, it ignores important needs of computer users, who are also consumers of other products and services and might also evaluate aesthetics and contemporary design in addition to usability. Thirdly studies have shown that *"the aesthetic perceptions of an interface are highly correlated with perceptions of the interface's ease of use"* [2], or in other words, *"what is beautiful is usable"*.

2.1 Architectural Websites Survey

Websites of architectural interest combine features of various website types. They aim at attracting new customers and maintaining existing ones, while posing as a kind of portfolio or monography. For the first objective it is important that these sites comply with usability principles but for the second, they must prioritize high aesthetics and free expression of creativity.

Architectural website types include:

- websites of architects or architectural offices
- websites of architectural case studies or architectural contests
- news websites with content related to architecture and design

This study focuses exclusively on the first category of websites as the main interest is set on examining the relation between aesthetics and usability in websites with users that have high demands on both features.

The first methodological step was to conduct a survey. For this purpose the Usability and Aesthetics Questionnaire (UAQ) was designed and distributed to owners of architectural websites. The UAQ comprised 26 questions grouped into five sections namely: General website info, About requirements, About usability, Usability evaluation, About Aesthetics and usability. The purpose of the questionnaire was to collect general information about the website and the way it was designed, the expected and actual users, the degree to which usability principles were applied, whether the website had been evaluated for its usability and how, the degree to which aesthetics affected the design of the website and whether aesthetics or usability had to be compromised (one to the expense of the other). For this investigation 300 websites of international renowned architects were recorded. All these websites were chosen on the basis of interesting design. A questionnaire was dispatched to 285 of the websites (15 websites did not provide a way of contacting the owner) and response was received by 55 of them. 51 % of the responses were from architects with headquarters in Europe, 13 % in Asian countries, 31 % in countries of North and South America and 5 % in Australia). The questionnaires were distributed in the period between January and February 2011.

Responses can be summarized as follows: The primary reasons for constructing and maintaining a website is attracting new customers and creating a recognizable profile in the architectural community. When designing the website the anticipated visitors were the potential new customers and the existing ones, as well as architects and designers. In practice though the majority of visitors are architects and designers followed by students in the respective fields. In all cases the architect or the group of architects had an active participation in the design process of the website. One of the most complex and interesting features of architectural websites is the presence of the architectural stigma in the website design. Also, as expected, the role of aesthetics in the design of these websites is extremely important.

3   Heuristic Evaluation Extended with Aesthetic Heuristics

3.1   Aesthetic Heuristics

Heuristic evaluation was performed by five experienced usability evaluators a number that according to [3] is adequate number for identifying around 75 % of usability problems. Initially evaluators used the typical set of Nielsen's heuristics:

1. Visibility of system status
2. Match between system and the real world
3. User control and freedom
4. Consistency and standards
5. Error prevention
6. Recognition rather than recall
7. Flexibility and efficiency of use
8. Aesthetic and minimalist design
9. Help users recognize, diagnose, and recover from errors
10. Help and documentation

Moreover evaluators were reminded of the eight more important website usability problems as identified by Nielsen and Lorangel [4] that still occur even today in many websites, despite the extensive and long use the internet. Evaluators were asked to classify those problems under the respective listed heuristic.

Briefly these commonly observed problems comprise:

- Visited links that do not change color
- Unavailability of the Back button
- Links that open new browser windows
- Pop-up windows
- Design elements that look like advertisements
- Violation of web conventions
- Vaporous content and empty hype
- Dense content and text that cannot be scanned by the eye

In addition, evaluators also used a newly introduced set of aesthetic heuristics defined as follows (their numbering continues from the core 10 heuristic rules of Nielsen):

11. *Successful use of colors*: it is a very important parameter of the overall impression and attractiveness of a website

12. *Symmetry*: it is connected to beauty and is a characteristic present essentially in every form in nature. Three basic forms of symmetry are distinguished, namely reflection symmetry, rotation symmetry and translation symmetry. Apart from its aesthetic value symmetrical forms poses some qualities that are important for design purposes, such as their ease of recognizing and recalling.

13. *Harmonic layout*: the layout of a webpage is the composition (arrangement) of its elements and the harmony of this composition refers to ratios. The golden ratio is the analogy observed quite often in nature and is considered the ideal of beauty and harmony. The omnipresent Fibonacci sequence is another example of high aesthetics, used in art, music and architecture. Using a grid for the synthesis and alignment of the elements of a composition creates a sense of order in the design.

14. *Balance*: it is of great importance in the design and the aesthetic impression of a website. Balance in a composition is analogous to balance of physical elements. A composition is balanced when the visual weight of design elements in each side in almost the same.

15. *Grouping and hierarchy*: using visual qualities such as shape, size, position and color, even hue or saturation, the partial elements of a composition can be grouped or hierarchically organized.

3.2   Architectural Web Sites and Scenarios

Two methods were combined for the usability and aesthetics evaluation of the architectural websites: (a) heuristic evaluation by experts and (b) user questionnaires. Users in this study were architects, as they are the majority of those visiting the websites of this type and due to their attitude towards aesthetics.

Both methods were applied for the evaluation referred of three selected architectural websites[1] owned by international award winning architectural firms (i.e. their studies or projects have excelled in architectural competitions, or their architects have received honors in the field of architecture). Also the selected three websites were among those that responded to the UAQ, so as to have a view of their initial attitude towards usability and a picture of their users and user needs regarding the website.

For the heuristic evaluation of the websites the experts were advised to use a full-screen browser window. They were given 3 equivalent navigation scenarios, one for each website corresponding to typical tasks visitors undertake when navigating. The aim was (by accessing various content categories and pages and while searching for specific information) to evaluate whether the website serves the needs of its indented users, as these were stated in the UAQ by the website owner. Evaluators were first asked to navigate freely through the websites and then to locate information on specific projects based on different types of information (location and progress stage or location and project award). Then they were asked to locate all awarded projects, a publication,

---

[1] The websites used in this study are the website of the Bjarke Ingels Group (BIG, www.big.dk), the website of Steven Holl Architects (www.stevenhall.com) and the website of Enric Miralles and Benedetta Tagliabue (EMBT, www.mirallestagliabue.com).

a scheduled lecture, contact information, architects working at the firm and open position, if any.

3.3   Evaluation Results

For the heuristic evaluation, the evaluators were given:

- The list of heuristics with their analysis along with a list of commonly observed website usability problems.
- The proposed navigation scenarios for each website.
- The assessment form for reporting problems, their relevance to the heuristic rules violated and their estimated severity (significance).

Evaluations were conducted by five experienced usability evaluators, one of which has studies in Architecture and another in Graphic Arts. After collecting the evaluations and analyzing the data, a single list was created for each site containing the problems and heuristic rules violations, the estimated severity of each problem identified (on a scale of 0–4), and the number of reviewers who reported the problem.

The following charts reflect the violations and the heuristics identified for all three architectural sites. We observe that the heuristic rules in which all 3 architectural sites have the most important compliance problem is "consistency and standards" (rule 4). Other commonly observed violations are: "flexibility and efficiency of use" (rule 7), the "visibility of system status" (rule 1) and "user control and freedom" (rule 3) (Figs. 1 and 2).

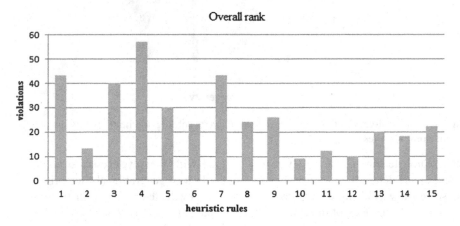

Fig. 1. Overall chart with the rules' violations in the three architectural websites

The severity of the majority of problems identified in all 3 sites was level 3 ("major problem with high priority for correction") and follow problems in level 4 ("catastrophic problems with urgent need for correction") (Fig. 3).

In the heuristic evaluation of the three sites, the problems identified, regardless the level of their severity and the priority that should be given to correct them, don't have the same degree of importance for the operation of the website. For example, the lack

Comparative study

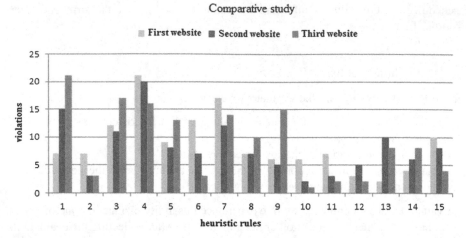

Fig. 2. Comparative char to heuristic rules' violations in the three architectural websites

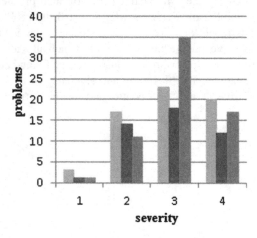

Fig. 3. Comparative chart of problems distribution according to their severity in the three architectural websites

of a search feature at the first website, is rated with the severity score of 3.5 (on average) and detected by four evaluators and the lack of geographical categorization at the same site was identified by three evaluators and evaluated with a severity score of 4 (on average). The lack of the above features (separately or in combination) is the most essential problem encountered and identified by the evaluators.

4   Architects' Questionnaire

4.1   Participants

The questionnaires were distributed to 40 architects and a separate questionnaire was designed for each one of the 3 websites. Most of the architect website visitors were architects, designers and students of respective departments, as it was derived from the UAQ. The user sample used complies with the Hassenzahl's conditions [5] for the methodological approach of studies that refer to the relationship of aesthetics and usability. This stands for both the research participants and the products evaluated, as we made a thorough selection of a homogenous sample of both the participants and the evaluated websites. The websites were selected from a broad set of candidate distinguished architectural websites, as it has been analytically described in Sect. 3.2 and the participants were architects who had participated in large-scale studies for public and private projects, architectural competitions, exhibitions, publications etc. and demonstrated an active interest in quality, aesthetics and education.

The answers collected, reached the number of 30 out of 40 for the first and the third website (70 %) and 28 out of 40 for the second one (65 %).

4.2 Questionnaire Design

The questionnaire used for this evaluation is composed of two parts. The first part is based on the System Usability Scale (SUS), developed by John Brooke, while he was working for the Digital Equipment Corporation and is known as the «easy and quick» scale [6]. SUS consists of 10 statements where users declare their degree of agreement, on a 5-value scale. Half of the statements are phrased in a positive manner and the rest in a negative one. At the end, the result is calculated as a percentage. Studies have shown that a SUS result smaller than 60 % is considered low, while a result higher than 80 % is considered very good [7].

The choice of SUS versus another questionnaire such as the Questionnaire for User Interaction Satisfaction (QUIS) adapted for the Internet, or the Computer System Usability Questionnaire (CSUQ), is due to the higher precision of this questionnaire in analyzing even small samples. As it is apparent from the research of Tullis and Stetson [8] 100 % precision can be achieved using SUS with a sample of 12 users or more, while the other questionnaires require larger samples. Also, SUS is freely available for usability evaluations, for both research and commercial purposes, provided that any published report contains a clear reference to it.

The second part of the questionnaire aims to assess aesthetics in relation to the websites' usability and for this purpose a set of questions from the AttrakDiff9 questionnaire were used [5]. AttrakDiff is designed as a tool for measuring the attractiveness of interactive products from User Interface Design GmbH and Marc Hassenzahl. With the help of opposing pairs of adjectives, users can determine exactly how they perceive the evaluated product. From these pairs of opposite adjectives derives the overall composition of the evaluated dimensions which according to Hassenzahl are:

- *Pragmatic Quality (PQ)*, which describes a product's usability. In the case of a website it shows how successfully users can achieve their goals while navigating this website.
- *Hedonic Quality – Stimulation (HQ-S)*, which describes the extent to which the website can meet one of the primordial human needs, the need to develop and progress, in terms of innovation, interest and stimulus in functions, contents, interaction and presentation style.

- *Hedonic Quality – Identity (HQ-I)*, which shows to what extent the evaluated product allows the user to match identify with it.
- *Attractiveness (ATT)*, which describes the overall value of the evaluated product based on its perceived quality.

The Hedonic and the Pragmatic Qualities are independent and contribute equally to the evaluation of the Attractiveness. The platform used for the online distribution and management of the questionnaire was SurveyGizmo 3.0 (www.surveygizmo.com), in its free version. Architects were given specific scenarios to guide them through the examination of the websites.

4.3   Discussion and Main Findings

The comparative ratings for the 3 websites evaluated by the same users in the System Usability Scale (SUS), are shown in the following chart (Fig. 4).

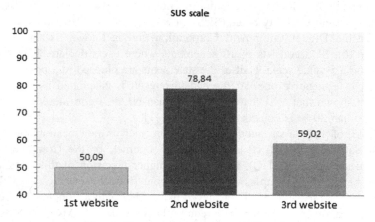

Fig. 4. Comparative ratings in SUS scale.

The SUS rating for the first website is the lowest, just 50.09 %, which as it is lower than 60 % is considered "very low". The rating of the third website is close to 60 (59.02 %), but it is still low for this scale. The highest rating was obtained the second website (78.84 %), which is close to 80 and is considered very good.

Observing the results of the questionnaires of the 3 websites, we can derive a first verification between the results of the System Usability Scale (SUS) and the results of the Pragmatic Quality of AttrakDiff. Both the usability rating of each website and the relationship between the ratings of the three websites evaluated agree. So, initially, we have verified the users' reliability and the reliability of the two types of questionnaires used.

In the comparative chart with the mean values of Hassenzahl's constructs for the 3 architectural websites evaluated (Fig. 5), we observe the following:

The first website, having the lowest rating of the Pragmatic Quality and the Hedonic Quality in terms of identity, it resulted in the lowest rating in the overall

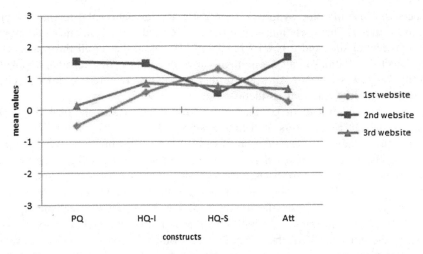

Fig. 5. Comparative chart of the mean values of the 4 Hassenzahl's constructs

perception of the website's Attractiveness, although it achieved the highest rating of the Hedonic Quality in terms of stimulation.

The second website has exactly the opposite picture of the first one in the attractiveness evaluation (AttrakDiff). It has the highest ranking in the Pragmatic and the Hedonic Quality in terms of identity, the lowest rating in the Hedonic Quality in terms of stimulation and the overall perception of the website's Attractiveness is at the highest levels of both the constructs (qualities) evaluated for the same website. It is a case where the Pragmatic Quality and the Hedonic Quality in terms of identity, influenced the final overall perceived picture of the product in a high degree despite the lack of a big stimulus in the Hedonic Quality.

The third website is an average case in comparison with the other two websites. The mean values of the constructs evaluated are steadily halfway between the highest and the lowest values of the other two websites. The very low rating in the Pragmatic Quality has little impact on the overall perception of the website's attractiveness and in this case the contribution of the Pragmatic and the Hedonic quality cannot be regarded as equal.

5   Conclusions

In the literature survey conducted in this work concerning the relationship between aesthetics and usability, it was observed that in most cases that there are references to aesthetic criteria, they are presented ad hoc without proper justification based on established aesthetic theories. In this study it was attempted to introduce a set of heuristic rules with aesthetic parameters, exploring and using widely accepted aesthetic rules and theories. These heuristics can be applied in designing the graphical interface of websites assuring its compliance with well established aesthetic principles. The proposed rules that are to be used as an extension to the core ten heuristics of Nielsen are: successful use of color, symmetry, harmonic arrangement, balance and grouping data and hierarchy. The newly introduced rules were used in the heuristic evaluation of three architectural sites and it is a remarkable observation that in all three sites evaluators detected violations to all the aesthetic heuristics. These first results are positive regarding the new set of heuristics but further research is required in order to prove their general liability and their aesthetic coverage.

Of particular interest is the correlation between the results of the usability evaluations from design expert users with high aesthetic demands and the findings of the expert usability evaluators. The opinion of architects as far as the three sites' usability is concerned is reflected in two different types of questionnaires (SUS and the first part of AttrakDiff, which refers to the Realistic Quality) and thereby the accuracy of the result was verified. What we observed considering the three reviews of AttrakDiff, is that when you ensure user satisfaction in 2 of the 3 constructs ('realistic' quality, 'hedonic' quality-identification, 'hedonic' quality-stimulus), the product attractiveness is close to the good levels of these 2 constructs. But it seems that the opposite also holds; when the two of the three constructs are very low, the product attractiveness is in the same low levels.

For the future it would also be interesting to use the same methodology (websites, questionnaires, etc.) but with a different user sample, i.e. users with typical/low aesthetic demands, non-specialized or not familiar with aesthetics, who could also be considered as potential customers of the architectural sites. This way it could be investigated whether there are differences in the perceived quality of those sites. As part of this research, we could further widen the sample both at user level but also at the size and type of the evaluated website sample.

References

1. Lindgaard, G., Fernandes, G., Dudek, C., Brown, J.: Attention web designers: you have 50 milliseconds to make a good first impression! Behav. Inf. Technol. **25**, 115–126 (2006)
2. Tractinsky, N., Katz, A.S., Ikar, D.: What is beautiful is usable. Interact. Comput. **13**, 127–145 (2000)
3. Nielsen, J.: Heuristic evaluation. In: Nielsen, J., Mack, R.L. (eds.) Usability Inspection Methods. John Wiley & Sons, New York (1994)
4. Nielsen, J., Loranger, H.: Prioritizing Web Usability. New Riders Publishing, Berkeley (2006)
5. Hassenzahl, M., Monk, A.: The inference of perceived usability from beauty. Hum. Comput. Interact. **25**(3), 235–260 (2010)
6. Brooke, J.: SUS - A quick and dirty usability scale. In: Jordan, P.W., Thomas, B., Weerdmeester, B.A., McClelland, I.L. (eds.) Usability Evaluation in Industry, pp. 189–194. Taylor & Francis, London (1996). www.itu.dk/courses/U/E2005/litteratur/sus.pdf. Accessed 14 May 2011
7. Tullis, T., Albert, B.: Measuring the User Experience: Collecting, Analyzing, and Presenting Usability Metrics. Kaufmann Publishers, an imprint of Elsevier, San Francisco (2008)
8. Tullis, T., Stetson, J.: A comparison of quesstionnaires for assessign web site usabiltiy. In: Usabilty Professionals Association Conference, Minneapolis, 7–11 June 2004. http://home.comcast.net/%7Etomtullis/publications/UPA2004TullisStetson.pdf. Accessed 11 May 2011

The Effect of Banner Location on Banner Recognition in a Turkish Government Website: An Eye Tracking Study

Hacer Güner and Yavuz İnal[(✉)]

TÜBİTAK BİLGEM Software Technologies Research Institute, Istanbul, Turkey
{hacer.guner,yavuz.inal}@tubitak.gov.tr

Abstract. This study aims to examine users' eye movement patterns and their attention to the banner of a Turkish government website. The website was redesigned as two versions in a way that the banner was located on the left (the original site) in one version and on the right in the other version. 14 university students with 9 male and 5 female participated to the study. The heat maps were examined as well as eye movement patterns while performing the given tasks. Results of the study revealed that the banner (including a picture of the head of a public institution) was not directly focused in both groups during the task completion process. Although nearly half of the participants recalled the place of the banner correctly, none of the participants remembered any information about the institution head such as name, picture or social media information.

Keywords: Banner blindness · Eye-Tracking · E-Government · Government website · Usability

1 Introduction

The creation of a website has become essential to communicate with citizens for public institutions [1, 2] in a more effective, efficient and economical way [3]. Public institutions convey information via websites in shorter time without spending extensive effort comparing with the traditional methods [4]. Government websites are mainly visited to access information about the services [5, 6], to facilitate government related transactions, and to involve in government decision making processes [6].

Government websites contain thousands of pages which enhance the interaction between citizens and the government [7] because of variety and complexity of the available public services and information [8]. Therefore, simplicity [8] and usability [9] of government websites becomes important. They have great impact on the website performance [4] and attitudes of citizens toward public institutions [1, 10].

In Turkey, e-government studies started in late 1990 s, and gained momentum with the "e-Transformation Turkey Project" which was carried out in 2003 [11]. In 2008, with the implementation of e-Government Gateway, all of the government services were standardized and centralized [11]. Nowadays, all of the public institutions in the country have their own websites providing public services and information. However, the research showed that most of these websites have serious problems on usability

© Springer International Publishing Switzerland 2015
M. Kurosu (Ed.): Human-Computer Interaction, Part III, HCII 2015, LNCS 9171, pp. 65–72, 2015.
DOI: 10.1007/978-3-319-21006-3_7

[12–14]. Due to the poor design and lack of standards on website development, users of the government websites reported to have difficulty to access information they need [15]. Therefore, government websites are supposed to meet demands and expectations of the citizens. User-centered design approach for government websites is required to be in the top priority for government agencies [16].

Considering the usability issues of websites, one of the most common problems is the redundant use of graphical elements such as pictures, photos or illustrations [17, 18]. Design of these elements are significantly influence usability of websites [19]. It is claimed that majority of the web users scan the web page without attentively reading the content and examining the images [20]). For this reason, the most of the elements in a website (i.e., images, pictures) are usually ignored by the users. Previous studies showed that while web users are seeking for specific information or performing a specific task, they generally have a tendency to skip the elements that are irrelevant to their tasks (e.g., [21, 22]). This phenomenon is called as "banner blindness"; that is, people usually tend to ignore web page elements that look like a banner or advertisement [23, 24].

Numerous studies have attempted to explain banner blindness phenomenon focusing on the advertising effect of banners and user recognition of advertisements (e.g. [22, 25–28]. However, even if graphical elements of a website are not related to advertising, users are still observed that they neglect those salient items [21]. This might be because of the fact that users ignore items which are irrelevant or less important because their main purpose on the website is to access necessary information as quickly as possible [22].

People are more interested in web page elements if they are consisting of text, faces or body parts [24]. However, previous studies about banner blindness phenomena imply that users often ignore irrelevant pictures and graphics especially when they are performing a specific task [23, 24].

Home page of most Turkish government websites consists of a picture of heads of public institutions. Those pictures generally resemble banner advertisements including the name of the heads with a link directing detailed personal information or autobiography and are one of the mostly used design components in Turkish government websites. It might be better to understand whether people perceive location and content of banners in a website. Therefore, in this study, we aimed to examine users' eye movement patterns and their attention to the banner (including a picture of the head of a public institution) of a government website in Turkey.

2   Method

2.1   Participants

14 university students participated to the study. 9 participants were male and 5 were female. The ages of the participants varied between 23 and 29. The computer use of the participants differed as 4–7 years (2 participants) and 7 years or more (12 participants). Moreover, the daily internet use of participants ranged as 1–3 h (1 participant), 4–7 h (6 participants) and 7 h or more (7 participants).

2.2 Design

The website of a Turkish Ministry was downloaded to local folder to manipulate the location of the banner corresponding to the picture of the Minister. The website is redesigned as two versions in a way that the banner was located on the left (the original website) in one version and on the right in the other version. Participants were randomly assigned into two groups (7 participants per group), each group was exposed to one of the versions. Each participant performed two tasks. The first task was to find information about a funding program for graduate students. The second task was to find the biography of a former minister on the website.

Before the experiment, participants were asked to fill out a demographic questionnaire including gender, age, education level, computer experience and daily internet usage, and a list of mostly visited commercial and governmental websites. After completing the eye tracking test, participants were asked to show position of the banner in the website in order to understand their recall performance while performing given tasks.

The study was conducted by utilizing Tobii 1750 eye tracker in a human-computer interaction laboratory in order to capture eye-tracking movements. For the accuracy of the test, participants were instructed to display normal viewing behavior without head rest, to sit up straight and not to look out of the screen. The eye-tracking data was analyzed via Tobii Studio software.

3 Results

3.1 Task Completion Time

Results of the study revealed that the mean of task completion time of first task for the participants given the banner on the right and left was 2.23 min and 2.37 min, respectively. The mean of task completion time of second task for the participants given the banner on the right and left was 0.50 min and 0.69 min, respectively. Task completion time for both groups were close to each other which might implicate that design differences between two versions of the website had almost no influence participants' task performance.

3.2 The Heat Map Visuals

The heat map visuals of home pages for both groups showed that left navigation menu and top navigation menu mostly drew attention of participants comparing the other areas on the page (Fig. 1). Participants highly focused on the navigation menus while they were performing the given tasks.

The banner (including a picture of the head of a public institution) was not directly focused in both groups; that is, the fixation on the pictures was much more scattered. However, it was observed that the amount of fixation increased more in the design involving the banner in left-hand side. This might be stemmed from its nearby location to the left and top navigation menus.

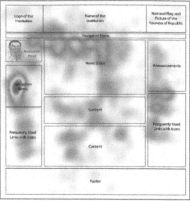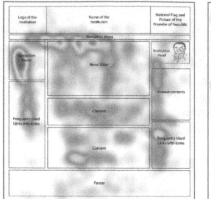

Fig. 1. The heat maps of the home pages for right aligned group and left aligned group

Task 1: Finding the information about given funding program. The first task ideally consisted of 3 steps excluding the home page. During the entire steps of the first task, no fixation was recorded upon the banner which was located on right-hand side (Figs. 2 and 3). In the first step of Task 1, there were three banner-like images at the center of the page. Each image consisted a link directing to a sub-page in the website. The first image from the left was the one that participants needed to click for the next step. As seen in the heat map visuals, although the amount of fixation decreased from unrelated image to the related one, all three images at the center of the page attracted the most attention of the participants.

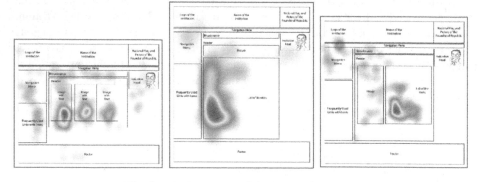

Fig. 2. The heat maps of the Task 1 (Group 1)

In the second step of the Task 1, the list of the services were provided. The name of the service that participants were looking for was in the area consisting bright red spots on the heat map. In the third step, participants found easily name of the service and clicked the link directing to the related page. Red spots on the heat map visual are seen to be clustered around that link.

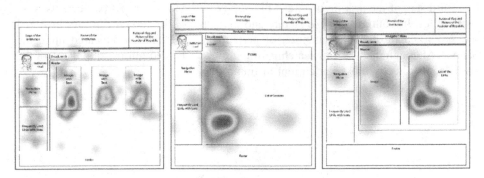

Fig. 3. The heat maps of the Task 1 (Group 2)

Examining the first two steps of the task, heat map visuals indicate that the institution head didn't take attention of the participants even though there were fixations upon other banner-like images. However, at the last step in Group 2, some fixation were appeared around the picture. Participants seemed to pay attention on upper left of the web page consisting institution logo, picture of the institution head and top navigation menu. This might be caused form the fact that all participants were asked to return home page by clicking the Home button located upper left side at the end of the task.

Task 2: Finding the biography of the given former minister. Like the first task, second task ideally consisted of 3 steps excluding home page. In the second task, finding the biography of a former minister, similar fixation patterns was recorded in both groups (Figs. 4 and 5). In the first step, participants were mainly focused on the left navigation menu and menu items at the center of the page. The right-hand side menu item below the image is the one directing to the page consisting the list of all former ministers. In the second step of the task, pictures of the former ministers were listed at the center of the page. The location with the bright red spots is the target picture and highest fixation was received on that location.

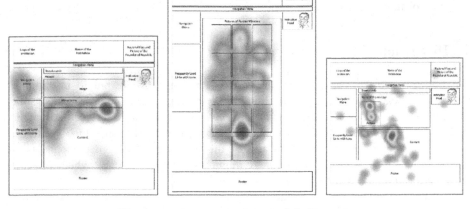

Fig. 4. The heat maps of the Task 2 (Group 1)

Third step of the task involved the biography of the minister that participants were looking for. In both groups, the picture and the name of the former minister involved red spots and most of the attention of participants. No fixation appeared upon the banner. Although the task was searching for a minister-related information, none of the participants directly looked at current institution head.

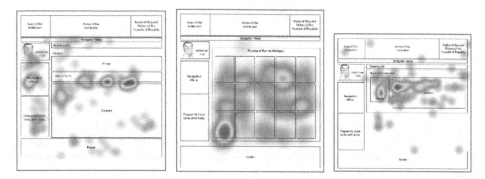

Fig. 5. The heat maps of the Task 2 (Group 2)

3.3 Recall Performance

In the first group who are given the banner on the right, 3 participants (42.86 %) recalled the place of the banner correctly, 1 participant (14.28 %) recalled the position incorrectly and 3 participants (42.86 %) were reported that they did not remember whether there was a banner or not. Similarly, in the second group who are given the banner on the left, 3 participants recalled (42.86 %) the place of the banner correctly, 3 participants (42.86 %) recalled the position incorrectly and 1 participant (14.28 %) were reported that they did not remember whether there was a banner or not. That is, the correct recall rates of the participants were the same in both groups while the incorrect recall rate was higher in the group with the banner on the left. Participants were also asked whether they remember the content of the banner. None of the participants reported that they remembered any information about the institution head such as name, picture or social media information.

4 Discussion

Government websites has become the virtual storefronts of the public institutions. Design and location of each component in government websites might need to specific attention to increase the efficiency and effectiveness of online public services. All public institutions have their own websites which consist of a picture of heads of the institution resembling banner advertisements as one of the mostly used design components in Turkish government websites. Therefore, it might be better to figure out whether people perceive location and content of such banners examining their eye movement patterns.

Results of the study showed that participants focused on the items such as menu items, which are related to given tasks at the center of the page during the task completion process. Even though participants looked at and clicked the banner-like images which might be relevant to given tasks, none of the participants paid attention on the banner including the picture of institution head. These results were congruent with the argument that [17] proposed to avoid redundant use of the graphical images at home pages because it might reduce the impact of other important components.

Institutional logo and main navigation menu were main website components that users mostly spent time and focused on [29]. Similarly, in this study, results of heat maps of home pages showed that participants mainly focused on top and left navigational menus rather than other areas on the page. This might be due to the fact that participants were motivated to complete given tasks and they were prone to neglect the irrelevant items on the page.

Eye movement patterns of participants during task completion process showed that participants didn't directly look at the banner because they might assume that the banner was irrelevant or less important. These results were consistent with the previous studies that people have a general tendency to ignore the items that are not directly related to their interest or motivation in websites [23, 24]. However, when participants were asked about the location of the banner, nearly half of the participants in both groups recall the location correctly. It might be resulted from the participants' previous experiences that most of the public institutions have websites consisting the picture of the institution head at the homepage. These results suggest that participants might remember the location of the banner although they were not directly focus on it since banner was located within their sight. However, they didn't remember any information about the institution head such as name, picture or social media information.

Findings of this study were congruent with the banner-blindness phenomena which implies that users are usually ignore the irrelevant graphical items on a web page. In order to make a deeper analysis, various types of banners may be used in government websites with large sample size for further studies.

References

1. West, D.M.: Improving Technology Utilization in Electronic Government around the World. Governance Studies at Brookings. Brookings Institution, Washington, D.C. (2008)
2. Karkin, N., Janssen, M.: Evaluating websites from a public value perspective: a review of turkish local government websites. Int. J. Inf. Manage. **34**(3), 351–363 (2013)
3. Yang, K., Rho, S.Y.: E-Government for better performance: promises, realities, and challenges. Int. J. Public Adm. **30**(11), 1197–1217 (2007)
4. Huang, C.J., Chao, M.H.: Managing WWW in public administration: uses and misuses. Gov. Inf. Quart. **18**, 357–373 (2001)
5. Thomas, J.C., Streib, G.: The new face of government: citizen-initiated contacts in the era of e-government. J. Public Adm. Res. Theor. **13**(1), 83–102 (2003)
6. Thompson, D.V., Rust, R.T., Rhoda, J.: The business value of e-government to small firms. Int. J. Serv. Ind. Manag. **16**(3), 385–407 (2005)
7. Reddick, C.G.: Citizen interaction with e-government: from the streets to servers? Gov. Inf. Quart. **22**(1), 38–57 (2005)
8. Donker-Kuijer, M.W., de Jong, M., Lentz, L.: Usable guidelines for usable websites? an analysis of five e-government heuristics. Gov. Inf. Quart. **27**(3), 254–263 (2010)

9. Youngblood, N.E., Mackiewicz, J.: A usability analysis of municipal government website home pages in alabama. Gov. Inf. Quart. **29**(4), 582–588 (2012)
10. Tolbert, C.J., Mossberger, K.: The effects of e-government on trust and confidence in government. Public Adm. Rev. **66**(3), 354–369 (2006)
11. İskender G.: Turkish e-Government Transformation: A Country Analysis Based on Efforts, Problems and Solutions. Unpublished master's thesis. Massachusetts Institute of Technology, Cambridge, Massachusetts, USA (2012)
12. Akıncı, D., Çağıltay, K.: E-devlet Web Sitelerini Kullanmak ya da Kullanamamak: Vatandaş Açısından Kullanılabilirlik Sorunları ve Önerileri (2004). www.metu.edu.tr/~kursat/TBD04-edevlet-websiteleri.doc. Accessed 24 July 2014
13. Sayıştay: Performans Denetimi Raporu: e-Devlete Geçişte Kamu Kurumları İnternet Siteleri. T.C. Sayıştay Başkanlığı, Ankara (2006)
14. İnal, Y., Özen Çinar, N., Çağıltay, K., Güngör, M.K.: Kamu İnternet Sitelerinde Yer Alan Arama Alanlarının Kullanılabilirliğinin Belirlenmesi. 8. Ulusal Yazılım Mühendisliği Sempozyumu, pp. 79–88, Güzelyurt, KKTC (2014)
15. Akman, İ., Yazici, A., Mishra, A., Arifoğlu, A.: E-Government: a global view and an empirical evaluation of some attributes of citizens. Gov. Inf. Quart. **22**(2), 239–257 (2005)
16. Bertot, J.C., Jaeger, P.T.: User-centered e-government: challenges and benefits for government web sites. Gov. Inf. Quart. **23**(2), 163–168 (2006)
17. Nielsen, J.: 113 Design Guidelines for Homepage Usability (2001). http://www.nngroup.com/articles/113-design-guidelines-homepage-usability/. Accessed 1 MArch 2015
18. Rosenfeld, L., Morville, P.: Information Architecture for the World Wide Web, 3rd edn. Oreilly, California (2006)
19. Lavie, T., Tractinsky, N.: Assessing dimensions of perceived visual aesthetics of web sites. Int. J. Hum. Comput. Stud. **60**(3), 269–298 (2004)
20. Nielsen, J.: How Users Read on the Web (1997). http://www.nngroup.com/articles/how-users-read-on-the-web/. Accessed 31 July 2014
21. Benway, J.P., Lane, D.M.: Banner Blindness: Web Searchers Often Miss "obvious" Links, Internet Technical Group. Rice University (1998)
22. Hsieh, Y.C., Chen, K.H.: How different information types affect viewer's attention on internet advertising. Comput. Hum. Behav. **27**(2), 935–945 (2011)
23. Benway, J.P.: Banner Blindness: What Searching Users Notice and Do Not Notice on the World Wide Web. Ph.D. thesis. Rice University, Houston, Texas (1999)
24. Nielsen, J.: Banner Blindness: Old and New Findings (2007). http://www.nngroup.com/articles/banner-blindness-old-and-new-findings/. Accessed 31 July 2014
25. Burke, M., Hornof, A., Nilsen, E., Gorman, N.: High-cost banner blindness: ads increase perceived workload, hinder visual search, and are forgotten. ACM Trans. Comput.-Hum. Interact. **12**(4), 423–445 (2005)
26. Çalışır, F., Karaali, D.: The impacts of banner location, banner content and navigation style on banner recognition. Comput. Hum. Behav. **24**(2), 535–543 (2008)
27. Hervet, G., Guerard, C., Tremblay, S., Chtourou, M.-S.: Is banner blindness genuine? eye tracking internet text advertising. Appl. Cogn. Psychol. **25**(5), 708–716 (2011)
28. Flores, W., Chen, V., Ross, W.H.: The effect of variations in banner ad, type of product, website context, and language of advertising on internet users' attitudes. Comput. Hum. Behav. **31**, 37–47 (2014)
29. Dahal S.: Eyes Don't Lie: Understanding Users' First Impressions on Website Design Using Eye Tracking. Master thesis. Missouri University of Science and Technology, Missouri, USA (2011)

Compatibility of Information and Interface of Universities' Multilingual Websites

Krzysztof Hankiewicz[✉]

Faculty of Engineering Management, Poznan University of Technology,
11 Strzelecka St., Poznan, Poland
krzysztof.hankiewicz@put.poznan.pl

Abstract. The article presents results of research regarding the use of Polish university websites to handle the affairs of foreign students. The study included 57 faculties in 8 universities of different size and type.

The aim of the study is to examine the way selected universities use the abilities of websites to serve foreign students. The article presents results of inspection of faculty websites of all public universities in Poznan. The results indicate that universities use the potential of websites to a limited extent. Part of the websites checked lacked even an English version, and only a few make necessary information for students in the English language sufficiently available.

Keywords: User interface · Websites · Usability · Design for diversity

1 Introduction

Due to the fact that the number of foreigners entering universities in Poland is beginning to grow, the problem of access to the same information and content for all students seems to be particularly important. The growing number of foreign students has ceased to be associated with a general increase in the number of all students at Polish universities, and with the demographic decline the proportion of foreign students is increasing. This fact should finally convince universities to put attention to better preparing information and content for foreign students on websites.

The differences between the language versions can be partially understood when the content is placed there to supplement knowledge about Poland, the region and the academic centre, or the specifics of studying in Poland, which in this regard is obvious for Polish students. On the other hand, the lack of certain information or its presentation can be surprising. It seems that a class schedule is required for all students, and the inclusion of the plan in a foreign language, which has links which lead to sites in the Polish language also does not solve the problem. In addition, the organization of the academic year may be useful not only to students, but also to candidates. The program of the same studies, regardless of the language used, should be presented in a similar form, and student scientific societies should not have to divide students into "our" or "foreign," which can be inferred from the various offers presented in the different language versions.

In addition to the above-mentioned differences is the problem of updating institutional sites. In the case of services in foreign languages, the updates are even more

© Springer International Publishing Switzerland 2015
M. Kurosu (Ed.): Human-Computer Interaction, Part III, HCII 2015, LNCS 9171, pp. 73–81, 2015.
DOI: 10.1007/978-3-319-21006-3_8

delayed. This is due to the lack of control of foreign language versions. It often happens that information is left from the previous academic years. There is also the fact that the website is completely modernized in terms of interface but content is left unchanged in foreign language versions.

In universities the management of the teaching process is done at the faculty level, as a result of their autonomy in this area. For this reason, as a rule, every faculty has a separate website or at least a part separated from the main university site. The integration of faculty websites to the main university website occurs more commonly in smaller universities. The content and layout of separate faculty websites are often set at the level of those faculties. As a result, these sites differ in both interface and functionality. For these reasons, in order to verify that students have access to the information necessary from the point of view of the education process, attention should be paid to these sites.

2 Literature Review

University websites are a platform for communication between students and the school, and they have the function of disseminating information. In the case of seeking candidates they also perform marketing functions. The form and content of university websites have an impact on the level of quality of service of candidates and students ([7, 8]). Current students, in contrast to their parents, largely acquire organizational information from websites [6]. Moreover, the level of ergonomic quality of services forms a kind of social aspect of sustainability [10]. Treating a university like any other enterprise, one of its primary objectives should be to provide [13]: efficient flow of information and avoidance of errors caused by the incompleteness of the data, which in total translates to the organization's customer satisfaction. It should be noted that websites can also be part of anti-crisis systems [1], which also indicates the need for their reliability for the multilingual student population.

In some cases, there may be a need to deliberately differentiate the different language versions for cultural reasons. Attention is drawn to this fact by Miraz, Ali and Excell [12]. In addition, they believe that the graphic elements should also be varied in each of the language versions. A diverse presentation of content can significantly condition the degree of misunderstanding, which in turn is related to the need to analyze usage patterns leading to confusion [3].

Another very important element is to provide information on websites due to the increasing proportion of people with disabilities entering universities and realizing their needs primarily through reliable information regarding adjustments provided by the institutions [5]. Currently, the estimated percentage of people with disabilities in Poland at the level of 12−14 % is strongly burdened by system error [2], but in the case of the student population it amounts to only 1 %, despite continued growth. Against the intensifying effect of demographic decline [4] universities will also be forced to expand their portfolio by courses for adults, which can also be conducted in English. Professional courses which are of great interest, such as OSH [11], already find customers willing to learn in English. This designates an additional requirement that is the ergonomic quality of services for older users [9].

3   Research

An increasing number of universities in Poland decides to open fields of study conducted in English. At the same time there is an increasing number of students who participate in selected courses in foreign exchange activities between universities in different countries. Among universities offering courses in English, public universities dominate. Therefore, the study has selected precisely these institutions. The authors conduct classes with foreign students in English in Poznan, which allows for collecting comments on the operation of websites directly from the students. To keep a reference of the obtained results to the opinion of the students, the research was conducted in universities only in Poznan. This group includes the largest universities in Poznan, as well as several smaller ones, which gives a certain cross-section of their differentiation. They represent directions of studies in the fields of humanities, sciences, environment, medicine, technical, economics, sports and arts.

Due to the fact that until now faculty sites have not been studied, only university home pages, the current study is panoramic and will continue in the future.

The scope of the present study was to check if a university possessed an English version of the faculty website, along with its contents taking into consideration the calendar of the academic year, class schedules, teachers' office hours, sample documents (including for the diploma) and interface compatibility between Polish and English versions.

The object of the study was to take advantage of the opportunities of faculty websites to support the service of students. The study was limited to elements of websites which were related to the process of studying as foreigners who do not know the Polish language and are communicating in English. Because it is assumed that the content in Polish is completely incomprehensible to this group of students, also verified were the cases of linguistically mixing the contents of the sites in two different languages. Compatibility of interfaces was assessed by comparing in pairs the language versions within each faculty.

The study included all 57 faculty websites of surveyed universities:

1. Adam Mickiewicz University
2. Poznan University of Technology
3. Poznan University of Economics
4. Poznan University of Medical Sciences
5. University of Arts in Poznan
6. Poznan University of Life Sciences
7. Eugeniusz Piasecki University of Physical Education in Poznan
8. The Ignacy Jan Paderewski Academy of Music in Poznan

The biggest university in this comparison is Adam Mickiewicz University with 15 faculties, in which nearly 50 thousand students are enrolled. The next university is Poznan University of Technology, which has 10 faculties and approximately 20 thousand students. Poznan University of Economics consists of five faculties which have over 10 thousand students. A similar number of students is studying at the Poznan University of Life Sciences. The university is divided into 8 faculties. Differently organized is Poznan University of Medical Sciences, which consists of four faculties, but the studies in English are separated, which is reflected in the recruitment procedures and two English-language versions of the website. Studying here are approximately 8 thousand students, of which a large group are foreigners studying in English. Belonging to the group of smaller universities is Eugeniusz Piasecki University of Physical Education in Poznan with 3 faculties, in which more than 4 thousand students study, as well as arts schools such as the University of Arts in Poznan and The Ignacy Jan Paderewski Academy of Music in Poznan, where the total studying are approximately 2 thousand students. The University of Arts in Poznan is divided into 7 faculties, and The Ignacy Jan Paderewski Academy of Music in Poznan into 5 faculties.

In the 8 mentioned public universities there are approximately 100 thousand students. The number of students studying in English is estimated at 3 thousand. Foreigners in this group are approximately 2 thousand people. Additionally, as part of the ERASMUS program approximately 1 thousand foreign students arrive in Poznan. Because the number of Polish students is starting to decrease, it can be expected that Poznan will become increasingly open to foreign students. To date, the percentage of foreigners in the total number of students is lower than in other European countries.

4   Results

It was decided to compile the obtained results as a percentage. The compilations contain percentages determining what percentage of the university's faculties meets the stated criterion. However, due to the diverse nature of websites, it also seems important to do a qualitative assessment. In assessing the significance of results obtained with linguistically mixed content, each case should be referred to the number of faculties with the English version of the site. When, for example, the percentage values are equal, this means that all pages in English have mixed contents. A similar situation exists in the case of interface compatibility of pages in Polish and English. A comparison could be made only in the case of finding the second version of the faculty website.

Figure 1 shows the faculties with an English webpage, as preliminary information in the study.

It is surprising that part of the group of universities, where less than half of the faculties has English language versions of the website, are the two largest universities educating students in English in several study directions and participating actively in the student exchanges.

Figure 2 presents a summary of the number of faculties where there is linguistically mixed content.

When assessing the linguistic uniformity it is assumed that if the user selects a specific language he or she should only get content in that language. Such an approach could lead to extreme, while at the same time for many universities negative results. One can guess that internal verification in universities was not as restrictive. However, the mixed content of webpages makes those who know only one language of those displayed feel lost when they do not understand the rest of their contents. The authors observed the phenomenon of mixing the contents recorded in different languages in the

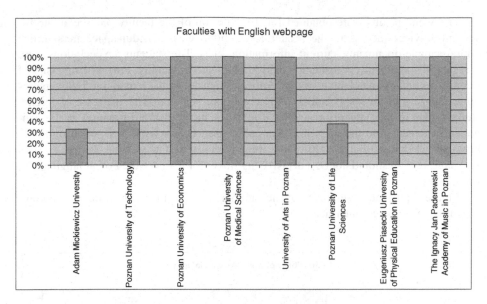

Fig. 1. Faculties with English webpage

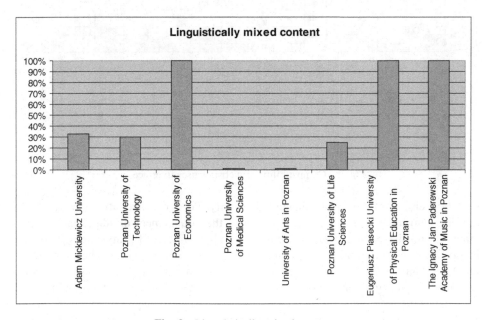

Fig. 2. Linguistically mixed content

past. Unfortunately, there is no improvement in this regard. There has even been a deterioration in this respect, when sites on a large scale began to implement content management systems. Integration of content management also leads to the integration of content and lack of separation of resources in different languages.

The worst results were obtained for the criterion of the faculty page as a site for student services (access to the academic calendar, class schedules, teachers' office hours, sample documents, current information, etc.). The students' expectations were met by only one faculty website at Adam Mickiewicz University, Poznan University of Economics and Poznan University of Medical Sciences. In the remaining 5 universities no webpage met the expectations of international students. The majority of foreign students due to lack of information in English or incomplete information in this language benefited from the help of Polish colleagues. Others used their, even rudimentary, knowledge of Polish. However, imperfections of the website in the English language version should not be a decisive argument for learning the Polish language by foreigners.

Figure 3 presents a summary of the number of departments in terms of the compatibility of websites' interface.

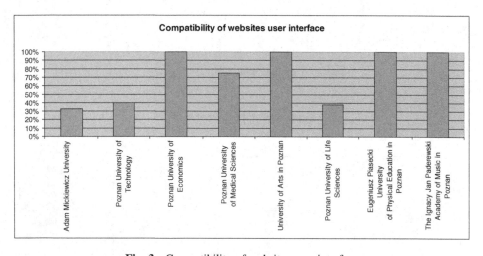

Fig. 3. Compatibility of websites user interface

The websites of Adam Mickiewicz University, Poznan University of Technology and the University of Life Sciences preserved the arrangement dividing basic information − on the main university website − and specific on faculty pages, with an independent interface and set of content, as well as varying quality. These are large reputable universities, largely available for international students. All the more shocking are the gaps in faculty web content. In many cases, no information was created about the faculty in the English language. It also happens that there is no English version of the page, but a link to the class schedule in English is between the other links of the page in Polish. The Faculty of Architecture at Poznan University of Technology used the Google translator (online) to get the English version, which gives of course a result of dubious quality. At Adam Mickiewicz University only the Faculty of English publishes the class schedule for students on the English-language website.

The University of Economics applied an integrated structure of the webpage connecting all faculties. Standing out from all, is the special service for the specialty

International Business, presented as the only one realizing a program in the English language. For this specialty there is available even a class schedule on a separate subpage of the university website. It should also be noted that in every place the selection of links to the English version leads to the main page.

An unusual case is the website of the University of Medical Sciences. This service is divided into the Polish and English versions and the English-language study programs. This is due to the specific nature of the university, where English-language classes are based on a different program of study. The last version of the webpage also has a completely different interface and structure.

The University of Physical Education and the University of Economics have bet on integrated faculty websites. The exception is the Faculty in Gorzow. In addition, class schedules for the two faculties are available in a separate part with a different interface. In this section, there is no link to the English version. Additionally, the service behaves differently depending on the browser language. Using the browser in English, mixed content - in two languages – is obtained already on the main page. When using a Polish-language browser mixed content appears only when opening links of the English version. It can be assumed that the latter situation is simply due to a lack of English counterparts of posted content.

The University of Arts also only uses the main website to service the university. In this case, a link to the English version always leads to the same page. In addition to general information about opportunities to study in English, there is no detailed, current information for students.

The website for the Academy of Music looks similar. Admittedly, it has created an English language website analogous to the Polish, but it also does not contain current information for students.

5 Conclusions

Although the assessment was based solely on university websites, still the comments of students from different countries studying in Poznan were inspirational and helped to establish the procedures and research.

Summing up the obtained results, it was noticed that most of the faculty websites is focused on Polish-speaking students, not even fulfilling the role of marketing the faculty to foreigners. Such a role is usually assigned to university home pages. This is usually done by automatically redirecting to the English-speaking university main page by clicking the link which suggests the English language, or by the total abandonment of placing such links.

The study results also indicate that universities are unlikely to improve the functionality of their web pages, and the current situation is hardly satisfactory. Faculties that have English-language versions of their site are in the minority, only a few present the necessary information to students in English. In addition, it is rare to meet website content entirely in English. Typically, the content is mixed, bilingual.

One could even argue that the teaching process in many cases could collapse without the help of Polish students studying together with foreigners.

It looks better visually when the interfaces of Polish language and English language sites are compatible. It can be assumed that it is the merit of the application of content management systems forcing such a situation.

If universities do not fully utilize the potential posed by university websites, then it will negatively affect the image of the school and will reduce the number of potential students, losing the competition with countries where the level of these services is higher.

References

1. Bajda, A., Wrażeń, M., Laskowski, D.: Diagnostics the quality of data transfer in the management of crisis situation. Electr. Rev. **87**(9A), 72–78 (2011). Sigma-Not, Poland
2. Butlewski, M.: Indirect estimation method of data for ergonomic design on the base of disability research in polish 2011 Census. In: Vink, P. (ed.) Advances in Social and Organizational Factors, pp. 454–462. CRC Press, Taylor and Francis Group, Boca Raton, London, New York (2012)
3. Butlewski, M., Jasiulewicz-Kaczmarek, M., Misztal, A., Sławińska, M.: Design methods of reducing human error in practice. In: Nowakowski, T., Młyńczak, M., Jodejko-Pietruczuk, A., Werbińska-Wojciechowska, S. (eds.) Safety and Reliability: Methodology and Applications - Proceedings of the European Safety and Reliability Conference ESREL 2014 Wrocław, pp. 1101–1106. CRC Press, London (2015)
4. Butlewski, M.: Extension of working time in Poland as a challenge for ergonomic design. Machines, Technologies, Materials, International Virtual Journal, Publisher Scientific Technical Union of Mechanical Engineering (Year VII issue), November 2013
5. Butlewski, M., Jabłońska, J.: Ergonomic model of hotel service quality for the elderly and people with disabilities. In: Occupational Safety and Hygiene II - Selected Extended and Revised Contributions from the International Symposium Occupational Safety and Hygiene, SHO, pp. 633–638 (2014)
6. Czaja, S.J., Sharit, J.: Age differences in attitudes toward computers. J. Gerontol. **53**(5), 329–340 (1998)
7. Hankiewicz, K., Prussak, W.: Assessment of higher education schools' websites in Poznan. In: Kałkowska, J. (ed.) Application of Information Technologies in Management, pp. 127–137. Poznan University of Technology, Poznan (2010)
8. Hankiewicz, K., Prussak, W.: Quality in use analysis of polish technical Universities websites. In: Hankiewicz, K. (ed.) User Interface in Contemporary Ergonomics, pp. 49–66. Poznan University of Technology, Poznan (2009)
9. Hankiewicz, Krzysztof, Butlewski, Marcin, Grzybowski, Wiesław: An ergonomic evaluation of the adaptation of polish online stores to the needs of the elderly. In: Stephanidis, Constantine, Antona, Margherita (eds.) UAHCI 2014, Part IV. LNCS, vol. 8516, pp. 26–36. Springer, Heidelberg (2014)
10. Jasiulewicz-Kaczmarek, M.: The role of ergonomics in implementation of the social aspect of sustainability, illustrated with the example of maintenance. In: Arezes, P., Baptista, J.S., Barroso, M., Carneiro, P., Lamb, P., Costa, N., Melo, R., Miguel, A.S., Perestrelo, G. (eds.) Occupational Safety and Hygiene, pp. 47–52. CRC Press, Taylor & Francis, London (2013)
11. Lis K.: Teaching ergonomics on postgraduate course. In: Marcinkowski J. (ed.) Selected problems of ergonomics education, pp. 51–62. Wydawnictwo Politechniki Poznańskiej, Poznań (2012)

12. Miraz, M.H., Ali, M., Excell, P.: Multilingual website usability analysis based on an international user survey. In: Pickingl, R., et al. (ed.) Proceedings of the Fifth International Conference on Internet Technologies and Applications (ITA 13), pp. 236–244. Glyndŵr University (2013)
13. Misztal, A., Butlewski, M.: Life Improvement at Work. Wyd. PP, Poznań (2012)

GT Journey: The Importance of Accessible Rich Data Sources to Enable Innovation

Matt Sanders[(⊠)], Russ Clark, Brian Davidson, and Siva Jayaraman

Georgia Institute of Technology, Institute for People and Technology,
75 5th St NW, Atlanta, GA 30316, USA
{msanders,russ.clark,bdavidson,jsiva}@gatech.edu

Abstract. GT Journey (gtjourney.gatech.edu) is an initiative, which empowers members of the Georgia Tech community to develop and deploy applications and services through access to resources (tools, data, services, space) and mentors with technical and domain expertise. The genesis for this initiative comes from a long history of facilitating application and service development for students by students in classroom and entrepreneurial settings. This paper reveals many of the lessons learned from this participatory design, build, and deploy initiative, which may be applicable to a variety of activities in educational, civic, and industry innovation settings.

Keywords: Civic computing · Participatory design · Open data · Development communities · Mobile computing · Hackathons · Innovation ecosystems · Devops

1 Introduction

GT Journey (gtjourney.gatech.edu) is an initiative, which empowers members of the Georgia Tech community to develop and deploy applications and services through access to resources (tools, data, services, space) and mentors with technical and domain expertise. The genesis for this initiative comes from a long history of facilitating application and service development for students by students in classroom and entrepreneurial settings. This paper reveals many of the lessons learned from this participatory design, build, and deploy initiative, which may be applicable to a variety of activities in educational, civic, and industry innovation settings [1].

The GT Journey initiative began as a collection of established projects which were created to empower members of the Georgia Tech community to create solutions for the campus; this included support for the development of mobile, web, kiosk, and desktop applications and services; creation of tools and platforms for emerging mobile and mixed reality experiences using the Argon Augmented Reality Browser [2, 3], as well as a variety of research projects which relied on operational data from the campus. The initiative leveraged the Georgia Tech Convergence Innovation Competition (CIC cic.gatech.edu) [4] by offering a dedicated Fall installation focused on campus facing solutions and experiences.

GT Journey is a production of the Georgia Tech Research Network Operations Center (RNOC) – which manages relationships with industry, civic, and academic

M. Kurosu (Ed.): Human-Computer Interaction, Part III, HCII 2015, LNCS 9171, pp. 82–91, 2015.
DOI: 10.1007/978-3-319-21006-3_9

partners in support of making the campus a living lab. This student led organization acted as the intermediary between student innovators and campus data owners. This included providing development platforms, building restful web services, building and maintaining reference applications, shepherding teams, and staffing a lab space with a wide array of resources.

The GT Journey initiative provided the necessary mandate and resources to move to a more sustainable model in support of student innovation impacting the campus experience. By offering platforms and services over an extended period of time across a diversity of data sets, the project was able to provide authentic live data for all stages of prototyping, implementation, deployment, and extended research. These resources combined with the support from Georgia Tech's President established the trust necessary for unlocking data, breaking silos, creating shared platforms and resources, building partnerships, and affirming the value of incremental design thinking through the campus as a living lab.

2 Approach

Our approach for the initiative was based on and informed by over 10 years of supporting student innovation and research with campus data; and in service to courses focused on experiential learning, conducting industry sponsored research, and stewardship of entrepreneurial innovation competitions [4]. In this section we present our observations and the key lessons learned as a result.

2.1 Validate Your Perspective

Through our work we have observed a remarkable desire from students and other motivated community members to leverage their course, competition, and independent work to improve campus experiences for themselves and other members of the community. In most cases these individuals are motivated to improve a customer experience, which they find inconvenient or inefficient. Because these individuals don't know the realities associated with the services or processes they want to improve; they often face challenges or make assumptions, which reduce their chances of success significantly. For example a recurring case involves solutions which help select a place to eat based the line length or number of tables available. Invariably the solutions proposed are done without considering that restaurants depend on queues and turnover to be viable enterprises, and therefore have a negative incentive to report this type of information, or allow it to otherwise be collected and published in real time. This lack of understanding of the realities of the service or process they wish to improve can cripple a project from the start.

Lesson 1: There is a need to coach or connect innovators so that their solutions take into account the Point of View of the different players interacting with a service or process they intend to improve, leverage, or disrupt.

Consistent with design thinking [5–8]; in our work we challenge innovators to think beyond their own needs and experiences by facilitating meetings with the operators of a service (ex: restaurant owner, bus operator, transportation manager) and surveying other types of users of a service so that they can better understand differing goals, needs, and constraints of the service.

2.2 Escape Groundhog Day

As anyone who has attended a hackathon, taught a project based course, or those in the venture capital business can tell you - there are no new ideas. There are only variations on old ideas which have either failed or which can be done differently through a new approach and with better execution. In many of our project based courses the lack of access to real data significantly contributes to execution challenges. After a few iterations of our Mobile Applications and Services course we experienced this "Groundhog day" type experience where the faces had changed, but the problems identified, the solutions proposed, and the amount of progress made was nearly the same as in previous semesters.

Lesson 2: Without access to real data, application quality will suffer and the chances for the work to have an impact are greatly reduced. The key to fostering the creation of novel and useful applications is in making rich data sets available to developers.

Over time we created platforms, which allowed students access to live campus data, required students to contribute to this platform by publishing their applications and any derivative data services they created.

2.3 Respect Data Diversity

A common mistake is to assume that because data exists, is accessible for your purposes. Among the many technical issues we have experienced unlocking campus data for use by student developers we find the following situations most prevalent:

Data Silos- data exists but is locked in a proprietary database.

No Context - the way that data is stored for its primary function is not compatible for the new use cases or services. This includes limits on data resolution or quantity.

Limited Systems - the systems where data are stored are not real-time or are not intended to be accessed by as many clients or at the transaction rate required by the new use case or service.

Multiple Systems - the data you want is spread over many systems which could have inconsistent ways of referencing the same items.

Lesson 3: Just because you can imagine or have seen data of the form necessary for an application doesn't mean that data can easily be curated or maintained.

The solutions to these challenges are varied, but they all start by developing a firm understanding of the situation and looking for sustainable opportunities to make data available. In some cases we were not able to gain access to data locked in legacy and/or proprietary systems and chose to fail fast; however, in most cases we were able to gain access to imperfect data sources and develop appropriate ways for developers to access the data without putting the primary function at risk. This included enforcing access controls on the data in some cases, as well as providing a separate service interface for application developers which would protect the primary function from rogue or aggressive activities. In other cases we worked closely with the data owner to improve upon their data collection or data services. A good example of this is our facilities data; where we were able to give access to fine grained data across multiple systems which was not possible with the collection of proprietary function-specific tools. Another good example of this was the instrumentation of bus location data collection where we were able to provide a commercial location prediction service access to our data while retaining this data for our own applications and services as well as research projects which improved the overall operation of the bus system [9, 10]. Our campus map efforts are another example of this where no fewer than 3 groups maintained 5 different databases of campus locations; each with a different set of fields, and without a common index. We were able to partner with these groups to develop a single database which could scale to everyone's needs, contained the diversity of information required by all applications, was curated and tied to authoritative campus map information. In all cases our success in gaining access to data and making it available was because we were opportunistic and circumspect in choosing targets and recognized when we could amortize our efforts, and provide value to a good partner.

2.4   Bring an Olive Branch

Beyond the technical challenges discussed above other barriers exist in the path to accessing data and evolving or leveraging data from existing services. Here are some we have experienced in our work:

Policy. privacy, risk mitigation, and/or security policies which are narrowly interpreted or crafted only for known use cases can make it difficult for data and service owners to allow access to data. In general data stewardship policies and procedures are defined around protecting data and institutional access as opposed to openly sharing and encouraging broad use by all members of the community [11]. In cases where there is ambiguity around making data accessible the process slows considerably.

Loss of Control. Even requesting access to non sensitive data can reveal fears of lack of control in what might be done or revealed by the data. This loss of editorial control (ex: defining the user interface or not allowing certain analysis) can lead decision makers to resist transparency [12]. This perceived loss of control can also be projected into the future, where the service owner sees innovation by others or supporting external access to data as limiting their opportunity to provide value (relevancy) or ability to make necessary changes to their services.

Perceived Value. If the perceived value relative to the work and risks is limited, then it is difficult to justify expending resources or extending risk. Whether it is adding a link to a web page, doing simple data entry or curation, or supporting access to data during a migration, upgrade or transition of the service; even these seemingly small amounts of work are often difficult to justify or commit to when resources are sparse or overcommitted. This is especially true for well established (and funded) services where existing service offerings are perceived to meet the needs of the community, and adding the complexity of engaging with outsiders only adds risk.

As with the data access barriers discussed above, we discovered a variety of solutions; though most centered around two lessons:

Lesson 4: without trust and value there is no basis for sharing data with developers; addressing sustainability is a key to establishing this trust with data owners.

We discuss the basis for sustainability in the next section in more detail. Our approach to these challenges in general required respect for the data stewards regardless of the barriers. While we pushed (often passionately) for access to data for campus constituents, we could not dismiss their concerns outright and worked hard to address them. This in the end informed our interactions with developers and influenced the services we provided in meaningful ways. While it is certainly possible for individual development teams to establish trust with service owners, this one-on one model is not scalable across a variety of services and applications; and more importantly it is not sustainable given the limited duration of most projects and/or engagement by members of the campus community. Our approach required that we act as intermediaries who could manage the relationships with data and service owners, support the resources used by application developers and users, and assist in transitioning applications to production or new development teams.

Because we were not focused on one team or application and had a longer timeline, we were able to build trust by accepting data in whatever form we could get it, with or without updates, and by leveraging these successes based on small initiatives, we could eventually build up to more sensitive and/or challenging data. It is worth noting that a significant number of applications and services require read-only access to data. By providing developers and application users with access to a cached read only (but updated) repository of data we were able to hurdle the barriers above in order to free data. This approach worked well with both our learning management system and our building information system, where the challenges in accessing data and/or the risks of allowing developers to write data back into the system were insurmountable and would otherwise kept this data inaccessible.

Another way we were able to build trust is by developing new & novel use cases which were not in competition with the core service but which gave the data provider some credit and association with a new technology developed by students; creating a halo effect. This was certainly the case with mixed reality applications and services [2, 3]; where the data owner didn't have the necessary resources or expertise to develop to these emerging technologies.

2.5   Sustainability Throughout

Building Strong Communities. Maintaining quality relationships with data and service owners was essential in order to maintain trust and show value, but also to provide opportunities to expand access to new data sources, discover new use cases, and to learn about transitions of services or processes. In some cases we also developed reference applications, which were of operational value to the data owner. This was the case with our utility data where we were able to provide a simple reporting capability which was previously not possible in their soloed and proprietary environment.

By far our most extensive engagement activities were focused on Developers and Designers. This was done through a diversity of efforts beginning with outreach activities in a variety of primarily project based courses and other student facing programs (Senior design and capstone projects, hackathons, and student organizations focused on entrepreneurship, application development, and innovation). We also staffed and outfitted a lab where we made development resources available to students, held Tutorials and advising sessions, and ran Competitions [4] and hackathons to encourage development in particular areas or targeting specific platforms. All of these engagement efforts were responsible for building Community - an essential element for sustaining development of the platforms and applications. These efforts relied on a large number of paid and unpaid student research assistants to conduct outreach and training, shepherd teams, maintain platforms, check-in/out resources, and in general become the domain experts acting as intermediaries between the data and service owners and the student development teams. In addition a few full time staff are employed to support this pipeline of student workers, essential in maintaining consistency as well as providing the technical and institutional oversight necessary given the data we are trusted with and the scale of operations.

Lesson 5: By placing (senior) student staff in leadership positions, we benefit from experiential learning, and consistently attract high caliber students who are highly motivated to take ownership of the applications, platforms, and lab culture. By pipelining this support we are constantly refreshing and adjusting the skillsets provided and maintaining a relevant point of view of student life.

Platforms Build Trust. We have developed and maintain platforms, which are designed to address the concerns of partners providing data or services. We are able to avoid student developed stove-pipes by requiring students to develop applications with a strict separation of front-end from back-end; such that the back-end data services are not specific to any one application or platform. We also require any new, derivative, or application specific services developed to be implemented as RESTfull web services [13] and hosted on our platform (GTdevHub). This platform provides access to data from a variety of service owners and previous student contributors, and now services unique data sets available to student developers and researchers.

Lesson 6 : Enforcing meaningful standard methods for data access and separation of back-end services from front-end applications supports sustainability.

This methodology has shown it's validity and value numerous times over the years. Perhaps the best example is our bus location API which was originally developed to support a 3rd party developer paid to provide bus arrival predictions. It was then used by dozens of student development teams in classes and competitions for a variety of mapping and tracking applications and became the back-end for a mobile web application which provides a real-time map of bus locations along with predicted arrival times. It was also used for a kiosk based web application and a Google glass live tracking application, and became the basis for a research project which was transitioned to a production service that prevents bus bunching along the route. While the back-end service has evolved over the years, it has not fractured. This not only makes sustaining the back-end code easier, it also means that the API is available for future application platforms we might not conceive of today.

Services Rise Tides. We provide three core services give application developers a trusted method for writing applications, which allow end users access to their personal information provided by data owners. One service brokers authentication and authorization in a consistent way for applications and services developed on our platforms. Another provides a cache of data where the authoritative source for the data requires some translation or cannot provide direct access to data by untrusted applications. Add to this a service, which leverages end user authentication and adds application specific access controls for individual users, which are not available in the native interfaces to data sources.

Lesson 7 : providing consistent and trusted services aided in overcoming the challenges data owners have with making data available to developers, served to "rise the tide" for developers, and made the applications more viable to end users alike.

In this model, we are establishing trust between our servers and the data source and then we are responsible for ensuring that access is only granted to those who should have access. This delegated responsibility is another example of the need for an intermediate referenced in the previous section.

Applications Need Homes. As discussed in Sect. 2.2, the churn of projects and students without a means of one team's experience informing a future team's efforts is a significant challenge for those looking to capitalize on engaging student innovators.

Fig. 1. GT mobile

Lesson 8 : by creating common application platforms we were able to retain the student work product in order to continue or learn from the work, but also provided valuable services to developers by hosting their applications on a robust and always accessible server infrastructure and facilitating immediate and iterative testing by themselves and other campus users with live data.

These attributes provided incentive for use of the platform (GT mobile) shown in Fig. 1 below, which in turn drove adoption and therefore helped with retention of the work for use by future students to improve, expand, or at least learn from the effort.

Leverage Hybrid Vigor. While our platforms had succeeded in establishing trust with data owners and provided value to developers, we continued to see the same ideas developed repeatedly. In many cases the applications addressed relevant needs and were sound prototypes; but were not feature complete and required more refinement than was possible in the context of a class, hackathon, or competition.

Lesson 9 : even with data, resources, support and platforms - to fully develop even simple applications such that they can be deployed requires significant effort and refinement.

Mobile real-time bus tracking is an example for which it was relatively straight forward to conceptualize the application and the architecture at a high level. However the user experience design, including responsiveness, visual abstractions, and supporting front end application architecture required multiple iterations and significant

Fig. 2. GT busses

work from those with a variety of skillsets. After seeing dozens of attempts, we took it upon ourselves to develop a reference application shown in Fig. 2 above, which was informed by the best ideas we had seen. The "busses" application is by far our most popular application on the platform among users, and has also provided numerous developers a needed starting point for understanding how to work with the busses API. Following this, we built a suite of reference applications were built based on past student projects, including a campus directory for people, a building directory and campus map, among others.

3   Discussion and Conclusion

The GT Journey initiative has been successful in fostering and sustaining a community around the development of applications and service improvements for the campus. The lessons learned presented in this paper provide generalized guidance relevant to those undertaking engaging data owners and disjoint or ephemeral development and design teams in the educational, civic, and industry innovation settings. In each setting the degree to which these lessons hold will depend largely on understanding and embracing the tension between producing innovative solutions and the desire for production ready services. We have benefited greatly from both the desire to provide production services, and the acceptance of "good enough" applications. This has allowed for a DevOps [14] culture where the momentum behind further development is proportional to the value perceived or demonstrated. Indeed the vast majority of applications fail or whither in this environment, but the risk and cost of supporting those failures by data and services owners is small relative to the value. By allowing the community to innovate the applications they want service owners have the opportunity to leverage innovation to gain new services in the best case, and key insights in the worse case.

Note that we did not discuss top down approaches to the barriers above. While the GT Journey Initiative was sponsored by Georgia Tech President Bud Peterson, and funded in support of the Georgia Tech strategic plan; we only leveraged this to make introductions and validate the project. Beyond this we firmly believed that a bottom up approach among stakeholders was the only way to ensure functional trust.

It is reasonable to expect that participatory and shared models will become more necessary as a number of areas of interest today mature; these including Internet of Things, Cloud and DevOps [14], and Smart Cities. In each of these there is an underlying assumption of or desire for shared services or resources and leveraging one thing for many purposes. Designing future-proof applications, architectures, and services in such a world will not be possible. Instead the need all parts of the system to be adapting to the changing needs of the rest of the system will require approaches like those presented in this paper in order to be successful.

Acknowledgments. We would like to thank our many partners on the Georgia Tech campus who have made this project possible. This includes our student innovators, the ever-dedicated RNOC lab staff, President Bud Peterson, Dr. Steve Cross, Dr. Elizabeth Mynatt, Dr. Ron Hutchins, and all of the campus partners who we have worked with to open data for student innovation on the campus.

References

1. Gandy, M., Baird, L.D., Levy, L.M., Lambeth, A., Mynatt, E., Clark, R., Sanders, M.: Midtown buzz: bridging the gap between concepts and impact in a civic computing initiative. In: M. Kurosu (ed.) Human-Computer Interaction, Part III, HCII 2015, LNCS 9171, pp. x-y. Springer, Heidelberg (2015)
2. MacIntyre, B., Hill, A., Rouzati, H., Gandy, M., Davidson, B.: The argon AR web browser and standards-based AR application environment. In: 10th IEEE International Symposium on Mixed and Augmented Reality (ISMAR), pp. 65–74 (2011)
3. Spieginer, G., MacIntyre, B., Bolter, J., Gandy, M., Lambeth, A., Levy, L., Baird, L., Mynatt, E., Clark, R., Sanders, M.: The evolution of the argon web framework through it's use authoring community-based mixed reality applications. In: Human Computer Interaction International, Los Angeles, CA (2015)
4. Clark, R., Sanders, M., Davidson, B., Jayaraman, S., DiSalvo, C.: The convergence innovation competition: helping students create innovative products and experiences via technical and business mentorship. In: M. Kurosu (ed.) Human-Computer Interaction, Part III, HCII 2015, LNCS 9171, pp. x-y. Springer, Heidelberg (2015)
5. Dix, A. (ed.): Human-Computer Interaction, 3rd edn. Pearson/Prentice-Hall, New York (2004)
6. Stickdorn, M., Schneider, J.: This is Service Design Thinking Basics, Tools, Cases. BIS Publishers, Amsterdam, The Netherlands (2011)
7. Ylipulli, J., Luusua, A., Dey, A.K.: Urban computing in theory and practice: towards a transdisciplinary approach. In: Proceedings of the 8th Nordic Conference on Human-Computer Interaction: Fun, Fast, Foundational, New York, NY, USA, pp. 658–667 (2014)
8. Bisker, S., Gross, M., Carter, D., Paulos, E., Kuznetsov, S.: Personal, public: using DIY to explore citizen-led efforts in urban computing. In: CHI 2010 Extended Abstracts on Human Factors in Computing Systems, New York, NY, USA, pp. 3547–3552 (2010)
9. Bartholdi III., J.J., Clark, R.J., Williamson, D.W., Eisenstein, D.D., Platzman, L.K.: Building a self-organizing urban bus route, pp. 66–70 (2012)
10. Christopher, B.: Bartholdi's NextBuzz Receives Innovation Award
11. Socrata, 2014 Open Data Benchmark report
12. Lathrop, D., Ruma, L.: Open Government: [Collaboration, Transparency, and Participation in Practice], 1st edn. O'Reilly; [Mass.], Beijing ; Cambridge (2007)
13. Richardson, L.: RESTful web services. O'Reilly, Farnham (2007)
14. Hüttermann, M.: DevOps for developers. Springer, New York (2012)

The Role of Quality in Websites: A Discussion Focusing on Public Versus Private Sector Organizations

Hanne Sørum(✉)

Westerdals Oslo School of Arts, Communication and Technology, Oslo, Norway
hanne.sorum@westerdals.no

Abstract. After 15 years of online experience among most organizations, we witness that increasingly more information and services are provided on the Web. Additionally, website users today are more demanding and knowledgeable compared to some years ago. High expectations and frequent use of online channels in dialogue and interaction place considerable pressure on most organizations. This paper discusses the importance of high quality websites and debates whether quality in public websites is more important compared to the private sector. The concluding remarks speculate on whether the subject of quality is more important within public sector websites, because they are serving all the citizens in provision of public information and services. Conversely, however, the quality of the website within the private sector is probably more important for creating business benefits and marketing exposure. This paper ends by providing suggestions for future research streams linked to the outcome of the present study.

Keywords: Human-Computer interaction · Website quality · eGovernment · Public sector websites · Private sector websites · User satisfaction

1 Introduction

Today we witness that most organizations, within both the public and private sector, see a window of opportunity by using Web technologies in reaching large and varied target groups, in various demographic areas around the world, or in a specific country. It is, therefore, recognized that the quality of websites is vital in the provision of online information and digital services. Compared to a decade ago, many and different types of services are available 24 h a day, without necessarily having a personal interaction with the service provider. The fact that, increasingly, information and services are made publicly available may, in many ways, create an easier and faster dialogue between the users and the service provider, and, after more than 15 years of online interactions and experiences, this applies to both the public and the private sector. Answers to questions might only be a few mouse-clicks away, and, compared to some years ago, we do not now need to use a phone or arrange a physical meeting in the search for information. Consequently, a huge amount of information and digital self-service are available online, both for the citizens and private concerns, as well as for business purposes and organizational use.

M. Kurosu (Ed.): Human-Computer Interaction, Part III, HCII 2015, LNCS 9171, pp. 92–101, 2015.
DOI: 10.1007/978-3-319-21006-3_10

Because of the ever-growing use of the Web as an important channel for communication and interaction within a wide range of business areas, we need to prepare for the future and upcoming investment. In this regard, the role of human-computer interaction (HCI) activities is vital in order to create great user experiences and successful websites that meet the users' expectations and needs in information search and task performance.

HCI can traces its roots back to the early 1980s, evolving into a subject involving design, evaluation and implementation of computer systems [1]. HCI activities can be investigated through approaches such as usability testing, with real users in a real user setting and interviews with users of a specific system [2]. The results of such testing will provide designers and developers with valuable insights and knowledge about the extent to which the users find the website (solution) easy to use, efficient and attractive.

Although many research papers investigate and highlight the importance of website quality and usability issues [e.g. 3–5], so far, there is still a lack of contributions discussing the role of quality in websites in the public versus the private sector. An analysis of eGovernment initiatives and missions indicates that it is a prerequisite to ensure user adoption, in order to serve users effectively [6, 7].

The research objective of this paper, therefore, is to discuss quality in websites and investment in HCI activities and to debate whether quality is more important in public websites compared to the private sector. This is approached from the perspective of both the user and an organization. Additionally, this paper provides a meaningful discussion grounded in prior contributions within the field of HCI and eGovernment. Although HCI research has advanced significantly and practical guidelines concerning design issues have been discussed extensively [8], examples of bad design and a lack of usability occur frequently despite the many years of online dialogue and interaction within both the public and the private sector.

The rest of the paper is structured as follows: Sect. 2 sets the agenda for this paper and provides background information concerning websites within the private and public sector, while Sect. 3 provides the research method, which consists of a literature review. Section 4 deals with the findings from the literature search, which the paper discusses in Sect. 5. In the concluding Sect. 6, the paper provides inputs and recommendations about important issues to be addressed and recognized in HCI activities, development and quality improvement of websites. Further research opportunities will also be suggested, based upon the research implications of the present study.

2 Background of the Study

In order to set the scene for the present paper, we start out by defining the two business domains emphasized in this study. According to Srivastava and Teo [9]: "Electronic government (e-government) can be broadly defined as the use of online channels for enhancing the access and delivery of any facet of government services and operations to the benefit of citizens, businesses, and other stakeholders. Electronic business (e-business), on the other hand, can be defined as the use of Internet by commercial firms for improving their business, operations and customer service." (p. 268).

These definitions are relatively similar and overlap with other definitions of the two business domains we find within the literature.

Furthermore, Srivastava and Theo [9] state that e-business research can be dived into three main streams: (1) application, implementation and adoption, (2) technological issues, and (3) impact on organizational performance, while research on eGovernment can be divided into: (1) evolution and development, (2) adoption and implementation and (3) its impact on citizens and businesses by transforming the intermediate governance and control processes. Consequently, "[i]nformation and communication technologies afford public administrations the opportunity to communicate more directly with individual members of their constituencies by offering tailored information services on-line" [10, p. 177]. As stated earlier in this paper, during the last decade the public sector has provided increasing digital content (information and services) and this trend will, most likely, only increase in the coming years. Attention must, therefore, be given to the role of HCI activities in website development and quality improvements, and the consequences of not considering this.

Within a public sector context we also find that maturity models and evaluation frameworks are used to assess e-government capabilities and use of information systems and technologies. Such models have been developed over time and can be implemented in order to rank websites that provide various types of information and digital services. These models are not framework or specific quality indicators, but they provides us with knowledge concerning the use and adoption of technologies, and stages of maturity of the level of interaction that takes place in a government-citizen context [e.g. 11].

We also witness that during the last decade governments have launched many goals and strategies related to the provision of online information and digital services, at local, national and European level. The main purpose of this is to disseminate knowledge and to have some common goals within public sector organizations in addition to increasing the overall user satisfaction in user-friendly and effective solutions.

Actions taken in this regard can, for instance, be linked to annual quality assessment and ranking of public sector websites in Norway and Denmark, for example. Based on a given set of quality criteria, hundreds of websites have, since the beginning of year 2000, been assessed annually and ranked by quality. In such evaluations, the quality in websites is mainly linked to usability issues, content of the website and accessibility requirements (WAI principles). The winners are highlighted as good practice examples within the public sector and serve as a source of inspiration to many organizations.

In this regard, we can of course discuss the use of quality criteria and the fact that real users are involved to only a small extent in such assessment as the criteria are largely based on technical measures and not actual user performance in a real user setting. However, these types of initiatives put pressure on the public sector and force the use of resources necessary for website quality development and quality improvement. As regards the private sector, organizations do not have shared goals and strategies in the same manner and therefore have more freedom to define the role of quality in their specific organization (business domain) and which quality aspects are found to be of particular importance.

Summing up, the background and inspiration for writing this paper is anchored in the widening use of the Web as a channel for communication and interaction, and the great attention websites receive today because of their endless business opportunities for an organization. The users also experience benefits of online information and services, as communication with most organizations becomes easier and more efficient. In this regard, we need to prepare for increasing investment and prioritization of resources for websites.

3   Research Method

The focus in the present paper has been website quality within the domain of public sector websites (eGovernment) and private sector websites (such as e-business websites). In order to search for relevant literature and sources, textbooks and leading academic online databases (including journals) were investigated during the research process. A number of articles were identified and are included in this paper as examples of existing knowledge and references relevant to the topic of interest.

From a wide range of articles that could be citied, a representative sample that represents the most important aspects has been chosen for the purposes of this study. The aim has been to reflect the quality aspects that are of particular interest for the two business domains (public and private sector websites), although, to a certain extent, there exists an overlap on what qualifies as quality in websites and the role of this in each of the two areas.

A discussion of findings is provided in Sect. 5, drawing upon the literature review conducted for this purpose.

4   Findings

Hereby follows the findings driven by the completed literature search, where the aim has been to debate the role and importance of website quality in the public sector versus the private sector websites.

Firstly, concerning the large degree of digitalization within the public sector, we find that traditional face-to-face interaction has, in many cases, been replaced by online communication and transaction [12]. On the whole, this also happens within the private sector, representing various business domains such as e-businesses and other types of privately-owned companies. Moreover, paper-based forms are being replaced by information exchange, which is largely digitalized. The users can in many cases accomplish transactions and make online registrations, in a simple and efficient manner, from any location with an Internet connection. In this regard, physical meetings and personal interactions have reduced in number considerably over the last decade. Consequently, we need to facilitate high quality interactions and superior user experiences on the Web [13].

Lee and Kozar [14] argue that decision makers in e-business companies have made vast investments in developing websites but not always with a clear understanding of the important aspects of quality in websites and their impact on website success. While

Zhu and Kraemer [15] state that although large investments in e-business are being made, researchers and practitioners struggle to identify the degree to which these expenditures improve the business benefits, and how to assess e-businesses initiatives in the first place.

We also witness that website quality is a widely used term and there is no single consequent and unambiguous definition. Website quality can, therefore, be classified as a multidimensional construct [16], representing various features and quality aspects of a website, which must be specified within the individual study context and/or business domain. This provides us with room for interpretation and the need to identify aspects that are of particular importance for a given website. Website quality can be associated with the scope of the website, the business model, as well as the core target group, by focusing on the users' interests, requirements and needs.

Although there is no unique understanding of website quality, Mich [17] believes that "[q]uality is a mainstream issue for Websites and Web-based systems. Analysts, designers and developers can choose from a variety of models and methods to design and evaluate quality Websites" (p. 42). Although we find that such guidelines exist, many websites and systems lack usability and user friendliness, and there is great potential for improvements to many aspects of a website, including service provision. Design principles and good practice examples are not always taken into consideration and included in the design process.

Mich [17] addresses five gaps that should be considered in evaluation and quality improvements: (1) innovation gap, (2) knowledge gap, (3) policy gap, (4) user gap and (5) communication gap. By focusing on such gaps, we can get more comprehensive knowledge and insights from various viewpoints which should in the end contribute to greater solutions and user experiences. We need to minimize such potential gaps and create a common understanding concerning the solution (website) that is under development. Various needs of the users have to be considered and taken into account. Although it is hard, and sometimes not possible, to satisfy every user, by focusing on such gaps and with different approaches, we can make good decisions grounded in right knowledge and assumptions.

In a business context we find that "Website quality is crucial for acquiring user satisfaction and e-commerce website success" [18, p. 418]. Thus, awareness of usability issues is perceived as a main contributor to success and needs to be addressed in every website. According to Heim [19]: "Usability goals provide a foundation not a prescription for design. These goals have been studied by HCI practitioners and designers, and a great deal of research has gone into studying how we can make things easy for people to understand and learn. The result for these efforts is that these goals have been defined according to design principles." (p. 228).

A website with high usability can be associated with the following characteristics: it is efficient to use, effective to use, easy to learn and remember, safe to operate, and has high utility [1]. In order to achieve business goals, users should be the most important issue and HCI activities are found to be one of the main contributors in this [e.g. 2].

In a public sector context, we find that quality within eGovernment websites is mainly associated with aspects such as content quality, usability issues and accessibility requirements. Within a private sector setting, we largely find that website aspects can be associated with aspects around product information and increased sales [e.g. 20], which are not the main concerns in public sector websites.

With public sector websites, in most cases we find a large and inhomogeneous group of users, representing various requirements and needs. The whole spectrum is represented, from extremely experienced users to those who have minimal knowledge of the use of such digital channels as websites and digital self-services. This results in the need to concentrate development not towards a very specific audience but, rather, to identify some focus points relevant to most users. Most of the effort in website development and quality improvement should, therefore, be as broad as possible, and not primarily focused on a specific audience or target group.

Porat and Tractinsky [21] suggest that issues related to usability and user satisfaction must assume considerable importance and be closely linked to enhanced task performance. It is thus vital to focus attention on issues concerning HCI activities, and the necessity to assess the quality of public websites is widely acknowledged by many researchers [22]. As a rule, public organizations enjoy an absolute monopoly on most information and services provided to the users, leading to a lack of competition. Furthermore, in the context of eGovernment, websites (including information and service provision) are funded by the government and the taxpayers' (citizens and businesses) money.

Consequently, we need to ensure that all users have equal access in our digital society, as the role played by eGovernment has evolved radically – and more information/services will be provided on the Web in the coming years. Accessibility requirements and the importance of inclusion of all type of users (with various disabilities) are also emphasized within a public sector context by, for instance, using Web Content Accessibility Guidelines (WCAG).

Moreover, according to Tan, Benbasat, & Cenfetelli [23], trust in eGovernment services is also vital for satisfaction in and use and adoption of services. The users must be able to rely on the information provided, and the digital services must be secure and trustworthy in use. We can also speculate that this is highly important in a private sector context, particularly when handling sensitive and personal information, or the transaction of money.

We can also investigate benefits driven by Web technologies and the use of websites for various purposes. Within public and private organizations we find that many benefits are overlapping and are appropriate for use in both sectors. However, Flak, Olsen, & Wolcott [24] identified two distinct approaches in eGovernment efforts; (1) cutting administration's costs and delivering services more efficiently, and (2) the desire to provide added value to the users. According to Colineau et al. [10], "Governments have, for some time, recognised the potential of the Web 2.0 to bring citizens and their government closer together by actively increasing their online presence" (p. 177). In this regard, social media such as Twitter and Facebook are also important contributors and information channels in the online dialogue between government bodies and citizens. In an e-business context, "[t]ypically, customers may spend a lot of time reviewing information and searching for products to satisfy their requirements" [20, p. 434]. Provision of customer reviews can, therefore, play a vital role in decision-making and in buying products from an e-business website, and can be seen as an important contributor in order to provide benefits.

Compared to a public sector context, economic performance and financial measures are considerations more often seen within the private sector, and in the context of selling products/services in competition within other contributors.

5 Discussion

The aim of this section is to debate whether quality in public websites is more important than in the private sector. Although prior contributions [e.g. 25] conclude that we cannot compare private and public sector websites, this paper discusses possible implications and consequences that quality might have, now that face-to-face interaction has been largely replaced by online interaction [12].

In general, provision of digital information and services gives the organizations a unique opportunity to communicate with a large group of users which is usually time-efficient and low cost compared to personal interactions and paper-based forms of communication. With the increasing use of websites for business purposes, users enjoy ease of access to information and services at all hours (24/7). This facility provides users with enormous flexibility, both in terms of freedom and monetary worth. An important aspect of this equation is website content, which, among many other characteristics, must be accurate, secure and reader-friendly. Also important is the creation of public values [26].

As the public sector lacks competitors and thus an absence of competition, when users struggle and/or are unable to find what they are looking for, they have no alternative but to send an e-mail, arrange a physical meeting with the organization or make a phone call. This would invariably result in low user satisfaction and, in the worst-case scenario, the organization would acquire a reputation of not being user-friendly. If this were to happen in a private company (e.g. within the domain of e-business), the company could lose traffic and sales, and, hence, the potential of damaging business tends to be greater. Consequently, it becomes imperative to discuss and evaluate the importance of providing high quality websites. Within public sector websites, it is common to find a large and inhomogeneous group of users, with diverse requirements and needs, while the target group in private sector websites is, generally, more homogeneous.

Only a mouse-click separates the private sector organization from its competitors, thus, if a user cannot find what they are looking for and struggles to find information/services, it is easy to give up and go to another website. Many organizations provide the same products, but the prices can vary as well as the service provided. From a user perspective, low usability and dissatisfaction can lead to frustration among the users [1]. For an organization, this can, as earlier stated, lead to loss of sales, fewer website visits and a bad reputation among the public (the target group). Thus, although many of the same issues can apply to both public websites and organizations, the consequences can be different; economic performance and the branding effect are not so vital in the monopoly situation.

The content quality in online information and service is one aspect given much attention in development and quality improvements [e.g. 2]. The content provided must be easy to read and understand, be updated, accurate and adapted to the business goals [1]. Public websites must provide a high degree of usability and focus on user-centered issues [13]. The fact that more and more information and digital services are provided online, replacing personal interaction and communication, places considerable pressure on the organizations for the provision of high quality websites.

Grounded in the findings of this study, we can also speculate on the consequences of not devoting sufficient resources and investment in website quality and HCI activities (e.g. usability testing). For the public sector, the goals and aspirations that many countries have set may not be achieved. Digitalization is not just about launching new technologies and services; it is also about having a user-centered focus and creating innovative and attractive solutions. All users should be included in the digital society and have equal access to information and services provided. This means taking into account users with special needs, such as the visually impaired and those with impaired hearing. By not satisfying users' needs and expectations, the sector also gains a bad reputation among citizens, which in turn will create dissatisfaction about public websites.

Efficiency, both for the users and the organization itself, has also been central to digitialization. This can be viewed in relation to processing times associated with applications, the quality of feedback, time saving and cost. If users find more information and services online, this will also reduce inquiries by telephone and in person. By taking into account the importance of quality, the organization can additionally attract great job applicants interested in working with technologies, development and design in public agencies.

As regards the private sector, we can speculate that poor quality can lead to reduced sales and deteriorating financial results. In many cases, the webpage is used primarily to promote and sell products and/or services. If it does not work properly, customers can switch to a competitor. As demonstrated, this may have negative consequences. As with the public sector, it will create a bad reputation among customers (users). The website is also the organization's public face and among the employees, we can speculate that this is important for being proud of the employer. Similar for both sectors are the annual web contests, where websites come up against each other. The winner will be honored as a good practical example and this contributes to marketing exposure for the individual organization (and/or the sector as a whole).

6   Conclusion

The concluding remarks speculate on whether the subject of quality in websites is more important within the public sector, considering the role of eGovernment, the lack of competition and an inhomogeneous group of users. Within the private sector, the quality of the website is probably more important in creating business benefits. Looking at efficiency and effectiveness from an organizational point of view, provision of increasing online information and services that are easy to use and useful for the users can provide both public and private sector organizations with a reduction in manual work. From a user's perspective, this may results in a faster response to inquiries, access to information and services 24 h a day, and, in general, greater satisfaction.

The present study has limitations that are worth being aware of and take into consideration in future research. A selection of references is included based on a literature review. A deeper review can lead to increased insight and knowledge related to existing research contributions. The discussion conducted is rooted only in current research and forthcoming studies could advantageously be rooted in empiricism.

As this topic is highly relevant and most likely increasingly so in the coming years, future research studies could focus on the investigation of unique and specific quality aspects important to each of the two business domains and addressing how benefits and success are relevant for both public and private sector websites. A more comprehensive discussion regarding the present topic could also be valuable in order to facilitate high quality interactions, great user experiences and benefits driven by websites in the coming decade. Consequently, collection of empirical data, within both sectors, concerning the present topic would be relevant in order to fill a gap in the research literature.

References

1. Benyon, D.: Designing Interactive Systems. Pearson Education Limited, Harlow (2014). ISBN 978-1447920113
2. Rogers, Y., Sharp, H., Preece, J.: Interaction Design: Beyond Human- Computer Interaction, 3rd edn. Wiley, Chichester (2011). ISBN 978-0470665763
3. Belanche, D., Casalo, L.V., Guinaliu, M.: Website usability, consumer satisfaction and the intention to use a website: The moderating effect of perceived risk. J. Retail. Consum. Serv. **19**, 124–132 (2012)
4. Følstad, A., Hornbæk, K.: Work-domain knowledge in usability evaluation: experiences with cooperative usability testing. J. Syst. Softw. **83**, 2019–2030 (2010)
5. Tuch, A.N., Roth, S.P., Hornbæk, K., Opwis, K., Bargas-Avila, J.A.: Is beautiful really usable? toward understanding the relation between usability, aesthetics, and affect in HCI. Comput. Hum. Behav. **28**, 1596–1607 (2012)
6. Lindgren, I., Jansson, G.: Electronic services in the public sector: a conceptual framework. Gov. Inf. Q. **30**, 163–172 (2013)
7. Shareef, M.A., Kumar, V., Kumar, U., Dwivedi, Y.K.: E-Government adoption model (GAM): differing service maturity levels. Gov. Inf. Q. **28**, 17–35 (2010)
8. Abrazhevich, S., Markopoulos, P., Rauterberg, M.: Designing internet-based payment systems: guidelines and empirical basis. Hum.-Comput. Inter. **24**, 408–443 (2009)
9. Srivastava, S.C., Teo, T.S.H.: E-Government, E-Business, and National economic performance. Commun. Assoc. Inf. Syst. (CAIS) **26**, 267–286 (2010). Article 14
10. Colineau, N., Paris, C., Linden, K.V.: Government to citizen communications: from generic to tailored document in public administration. Inf. Polity **17**, 177–193 (2012)
11. Andersen, K.V., Henriksen, H.Z.: E-government maturity models: extension of the Layne and Lee model. Gov. Inf. Q. **23**, 236–248 (2006)
12. Reddick, G.R., Turner, M.: Channel choice and public service delivery in Canada: comparing e-government to traditional service delivery. Gov. Inf. Q. **29**, 1–11 (2012)
13. Verdegem, P., Verleye, G.: User-centered E-Government in practice: a comprehensive model for measuring user satisfaction. Gov. Inf. Q. **26**, 487–497 (2009)
14. Lee, Y., Kozar, K.A.: Investigating the effect of website quality on e-business success: an analytic hierarchy process (AHP) approach. Decis. Support Syst. **42**, 1383–1401 (2006)
15. Zhu, K., Kraemer, K.L.: E-commerce metrics for net-enhanced organizations: assessing the value of e-commerce to firm performance in the manufacturing sector. Inf. Syst. Res. **13**, 275–295 (2002)

16. Kim, S., Stoel, L.: Dimensional hierarchy of retail website quality. Inf. Manag. **41**(5), 619–633 (2004)
17. Mich, L.: Evaluating website quality by addressing quality gaps: a modular process. In: 2014 IEEE International Conference on Software Science, Technology and Engineering, pp. 42–49 (2014)
18. Zhou, T., Zhang, S.: Examining the effect of e-commerce website quality on user satisfaction. In: Second International Symposium on Electronic Commerce Security, pp. 418–421 (2009)
19. Heim, S.: The Resonant Interface: HCI Foundations for Interaction Design. Pearson Education, Inc., Boston (2008). ISBN 978-0-321-37596-4
20. Leopairote, W., Surarerks, A., Prompoon, N.: Software quality in use characteristic mining from customer reviews. In: 2012 Second International Conference Digital Information and Communication Technology and it's Applications (DICTAP), pp. 434–439 (2012). doi:10.1109/DICTAP.2012.6215397
21. Porat, T., Tractinsky, N.: It's a pleasure buying here: the effects of web-store design on consumers' emotions and attitudes. Hum.-Comput. Interact. **27**, 235–276 (2012)
22. Elling, S., Lentz, L., De Jong, M., Van den Bergh, H.: Measuring the quality of governmental websites in a controlled versus an online setting with the "Website Evaluation Questionnaire". Gov. Inf. Q. **29**, 383–393 (2012)
23. Tan, C.-W., Benbasat, I., Cenfetelli, R.T.: Building citizen trust towards e-government services: do high quality websites matter? In: Proceedings of the 41 st Hawaii International Conference of System Sciences (2008)
24. Flak, L.S., Olsen, D.H., Wolcott, P.: Local e-government in Norway–current status and emerging issues. Scand. J. Inf. Syst. **17**(2), 41–84 (2005)
25. Montagna, J.M.: A framework for the assessment and analysis of electronic government proposals. Electron. Commer. Res. Appl. **4**, 204–219 (2005)
26. Karkin, N., Janssen, M.: Evaluating websites from a public value perspective: a review of Turkish local government websites. Int. J. Inf. Manage. **34**, 351–363 (2014)

How to Evaluate Investments in Website Quality Within eGovernment? Exploring the Webmaster's Perception of Benefits

Hanne Sørum[(⊠)] and Asle Fagerstrøm

Westerdals Oslo School of Arts, Communication and Technology, Oslo, Norway
{hanne.sorum, asle.fagerstrom}@westerdals.no

Abstract. For most organizations today, the website is an important channel for interacting with users. Within an eGovernment context, we find a large and inhomogeneous group of users and the quality in websites is, therefore, of particular importance. Facing this fact, many organizations spend lot of resources on development and quality improvements. In order to investigate perceptions of benefits-driven public sector websites, the present paper draws on both qualitative and quantitative data, represented by interviews and an online survey conducted among webmasters and business managers. The aim of combing qualitative and quantitative data is to provide complementary analysis. The findings show that user satisfaction is found to be the most important, followed by efficiency, effectiveness and the branding effect. The paper concludes that the website increase efficiency and effectiveness within an organization and is a great opportunity for marketing purposes, such as stimulating the branding effect. Recommendations for future research contributions are provided.

Keywords: eGovernment · Human-computer interaction · Website quality · Benefits · Public sector websites

1 Introduction

Information technology (IT) is a powerful tool for accelerating economic development and websites have evolved to become the core component of any organization, within both the public and private sectors. The use of the Web as a channel for interaction between citizens and government institutions has created new opportunities along with technological development, innovations and new trends.

According to Sandoval-Almazan and Gil-Garcia [1], "The use of information and communication technologies (ICTs) in government has significantly increased in the past decades. Countries around the world are now adopting strategies for better use of these technologies with very different objectives: greater efficiency, deeper transparency, higher service quality, and more engaged citizen participation." (p. S72). In contrast to this, we also find studies that have negative findings. According to Szkuta et al. [2]: "In the last 15 years the e-government became an important component of the public sector modernisation agenda. Yet, e-government has not lived up to expectations and did not transform the public sector. While significant progress has been made over

© Springer International Publishing Switzerland 2015
M. Kurosu (Ed.): Human-Computer Interaction, Part III, HCII 2015, LNCS 9171, pp. 102–111, 2015.
DOI: 10.1007/978-3-319-21006-3_11

the last years in terms of e-government service provision, the take-up of those services is still disappointing. As late as 2012, only 43 % of European citizens made use of e-government services, a percentage that drops off to 21 % when one looks at transactional features, i.e. submitting filled forms." (p. 558).

We find various definitions of eGovernment within the research literature. Most of the definitions concern the use of information and communications technologies, in creation of an efficient dialogue with the citizens. According to Verdegem and Verleye [3]: "One of the objectives of E-government is to make the government and its policies more efficient: providing citizens with quicker and better access to public information and the ability to use services in a more personal and cost-effective manner." (p. 488). An organization's website performs a primary function in the provision of services and online information, and acts as the fundamental channel and contributor in communication with the users. Therefore, many organizations invest lot of resources into website development and quality improvements.

Despite this considerable investment, we speculate that most organizations lack knowledge about the measurement of benefits driven by the actual website. Although there are numerous suggestions on methods of assessing the benefits of IT, this particular feature has been an area of concern for both managers and researchers [4]. We also find that this topic is widely discussed among practitioners, and there is debate about the benefits of the websites. Benefits within a public sector setting are not always that tangible and measurable, e.g. in regards to economic performance and converting rate, and therefore we need to identify measures that are appropriate and suitable for this context.

The central government, in many countries, has placed much pressure on public sector organizations with regard to provision of online information and services. In order to focus on the importance and willingness to spend time and money on website quality improvement, various initiatives have been launched during the last 15 years. One example is how Norway and Denmark, from 2000 until recently, have focused on those quality aspects that are of particular importance. Hundreds of public website are evaluated yearly and ranked by quality, the results being made publicly available and the winners highlighted as examples of best practice. The quality of websites has, consequently, received much attention during the last decade. In contrast to this, fewer measures and initiatives have been taken about the assessment of benefits driven by the use of in public sector.

This paper explores the perception of benefits of public sector websites, when almost every organization provides a website and the users are increasingly more knowledgeable and demanding. This study contributes knowledge regarding measurement of benefits perceived from a practitioner's (webmasters and business managers) point of view. An examination of prior research reveals a lack of specific studies on this topic, which makes this contribution even more relevant in filling a gap in the research literature about the perception and measurement of benefits driven by websites. Regarding practical implications, this study aims to provide the public sector and other agencies with extensive knowledge concerning the benefits of a website and the important aspects to be aware of in ongoing development and quality improvements.

The rest of the paper is structured as follows: Sect. 2 presents a literature review concerning assessment of benefits driven by the public sector website. Section 3 concerns the use of research methods in the present study while Sect. 4 presents the findings. Section 5 provides a discussion of the findings and, finally, Sect. 6 concludes and provides recommendations for subsequent research contributions.

2   Literature Review

While many public organizations invest considerably and devote countless hours of manpower in the process of quality improvement, we speculated that there still exists an overall lack of knowledge with reference to the use of benefits criteria and assessment methods. In order to justify investment in human-computer interaction (HCI), an organization should demonstrate tangible and accountable benefits for the users. In addition, public organizations should demonstrate the discernible internal organizational benefits that a website may create. Lindgaard and Millard [5] stated that investments in HCI can be translated into such benefits as increased productivity, reduced customer support, higher customer satisfaction and brand equity. Although this would be the ideal scenario, it is not the case in many organizations today.

Gupta and Jana [6] distinguish between hard and soft measures in the benefits driven by use of IT. They argue that, due to the constant interaction between public authorities and users, a combination of hard measures (e.g. cost benefits analysis, benchmarking) and soft measures (e.g. qualitative intangible measures) is more appropriate in addressing eGovernment projects.

Flak et al. [7] identified two distinct approaches for measuring benefits of IT: cutting administrative costs and providing added value for the users, while Bannister and Connolly [8] discussed public sector values in a broader sense by focusing on aspects such as respect for the citizen, transparency, integrity and honesty. Heeks [9] is more precise and detailed, classifying benefits into five categories: producing output at lower total cost; increasing output; decreasing output time; higher quality; and new outputs. These measure effectiveness and efficiency, and may generate values for both the organization itself and the users (citizens and businesses).

Because of the increasing focus on eGovernment projects worldwide, there has been increasing research into the measurement of benefits. A number of these studies test models in measuring eGovernment benefit. For example, Edrees and Mahmood [10] provide an empirical test of an adaptation of DeLone and McLean's information systems success model in the context of eGovernment. Findings showed that all factors are important for understanding eGovernment success. Rana et al. [11] used an integrated information systems success model including such constructs as system quality, information quality, service quality, perceived usefulness, perceived ease of use, perceived satisfaction, perceived risk, and behavioral intention. Results showed a strong correlation between the eight constructs, intention to use and user satisfaction.

From a stakeholder perspective, Osman et al. [12] investigated four main constructs: cost; benefit; risk and opportunity. Results from this study confirm that the framework is a useful approach for evaluating the success of e-government services from the citizens' perspective. Other studies are more focused in that they investigate a specific area within eGovernment. For example, Xinli [13] investigated the effectiveness of IT in reducing corruption in China; Arendsen et al. [14] evaluated business-to-government systems in use in the Netherlands; and Lamberti et al. [15] explored benefits sought by citizens and channel attitudes for multichannel payment services in Italy.

3 Research Method

This paper draws on both qualitative and quantitative data in order to combine different data sources pertaining to the topic of interest. The strengths of both data types give us a great opportunity to understand a complex and widely discussed issue [16]. The use of methods in this study gives a great opportunity for combining different data sources when investigating the topic of interest. Moreover, if the conclusions from each of the methods are the same, then validity of the study is strengthened [16].

Regarding the qualitative data, ten open-ended interviews were conducted among employees (webmasters and business managers) responsible for public sector websites in Norway. The qualitative interviews took place in the informant's work place. Notes were taken during the interviews and analyzed immediately afterwards. The researcher preferred not to give the respondents a text-book definition of benefits but opted instead to give the respondents the freedom to express their personal concept and understanding of the term. Consequently, the aim of the interview was to get insights from a practitioner's perspective without leading them in a certain direction. The researcher strived for a comfortable setting and informants were told the purpose of the interviews and how the data would be treated afterwards.

The informants included in the present study represent different types of public sector organizations providing online information and services to the citizens. What they had in common is that all of them are located close to Norway's capital city, Oslo, and represent large and well-known organizations with many website users on a daily basis. The questionnaire used during these interviews contained various questions about the organizations' website presentation. For the purpose of the present study, we have given special attention to the questions/answers concerning benefits of websites in order to identify trends and patterns in the findings, rather than dig into details.

Kvale [17] states that a common critique of interview studies is that the findings are not generalizable because there are too few subjects. However, the aim of this study has not been to challenge or test a theory, rather, to gain insights and knowledge about a relevant topic that, from a literature point of view, lacks references.

In addition to the interviews conducted, the present study also draws on data obtained through an online survey questionnaire involving public sector webmasters in Norway. The survey was inspired by the IS success model from DeLone and McLean [18] in the use of constructs (use of measures). This model is widely cited within information systems (IS) research [19], and for the purpose of collecting data within the public sector. In order to meet this criterion, a pilot-study and interviews was conducted (we went through the questions with experienced webmasters) before the final questionnaire was sent out to all the participants. For the number of respondents included in this paper, N = 308. For each of the questions in the questionnaire, the measurement scale ranged from "very low degree" to "very high degree." The answer alternative "not relevant" was also included as an option. In order to stick to the topic of the present paper, we have excluded the questions concerning issues other than organizational benefits.

4   Findings

Firstly, through the qualitative interviews we found that user satisfaction is the most important factor in the provision of online information and digital services. Public organizations aim to fulfill the users' requirements and needs in websites, resulting in ease in finding information and completing tasks. Although the public sector largely holds a monopoly on most information and services, we found that satisfying the users (citizens and businesses) is a vital criterion of success. Website design, content provision, services and technical issues play an important role in this. Facing the fact that the users today are increasingly more demanding, we need to create high quality interactions. Consequently, the website must facilitate great user experiences in the dialogue between citizens and the public sector.

Secondly, on the subject organizational benefits, the provision of online services reduces manual work and increase efficiency and effectiveness, by minimizing help-desk calls and reducing paperwork. Through the organizational effects driven by the website, one of the informants explained that user satisfaction and use of the website decreases the number of inquiries by phone and e-mail: "*This saves us time and effort. Answering e-mails is time-consuming, and an object is therefore to reduce the number of inquiries in the future*". Furthermore, the use of digital self-services results in more rapid feedback to the users (citizens), and from an organizational perspective there are also benefits: "*The processing time increases and provides the employees with a better overview of the information flow. We spend a lot of time on organizational changes for increasing effectiveness, and we no longer work as we used to. We need to change old routines and create new ones, as well as automating processes where possible and rather spend more time on what we cannot automate*". From this, we see that the use of Web services has a large impact and influence on the organizational performance.

Another point of discussion is whether, because of website efficiency, resources internal to the organizations can be used somewhere else. However, it is not always easy to measures the actual benefits driven by the website performance: *We want to become a transparent organization and all the time we are aware of the users. During the process we went through, due to a redesign of the website, we spent a long time discussing how to make it easy for the users. Our focus is to increase the number of digital self-services, but it is difficult to say if this will decrease the number of inquiries by phone. However, this is our goal!* While in other cases it might be easier: "*Other effects to measure may be decreasing inquiries by phone and mail, as well as the number of downloads of electronic forms and information on the website*".

In addition to effectiveness measures, the findings also reveal that it is beneficial for the employees to provide a website of great quality (including content provision and digital services). When the website appears as an internal knowledge base, the information and services provided can be used by the employees in order to solve their own tasks and by the users to achieve their (and/or the organizations') goals by visiting the website. Another advantage was pointed out: *"When a journalist calls, it is easy to refer to the website for more information"*. But, this requires well presented, relevant and updated information.

Thirdly, the findings reveal that the branding effect is an important contributor in the perception of benefits. The websites create a window of opportunity in the provision of online information and services, resulting in a more transparent and informative organization for the users. Providing a website of high quality that fulfills the user's requirements and expectations will most likely result in great marketing exposure, a good reputation among citizens, and also among employees, who can be proud of the website offered. The website can also be a channel for staff recruitment: *"The website is also important in relation to recruit staff to the municipality, for if citizens say that our website is completely hopeless and that you cannot find anything, it will not create a good reputation for the municipality as an organization and place to work"*.

Consequently, the findings in the qualitative study reveal that benefits driven by public sector websites range from, on the one hand, the website acting as a brand for the organization, in public relations and for marketing purposes, to, on the other hand, the website contributing to efficiency and effectiveness within the organization and increased productivity for the users.

In contrast to these findings, which show that satisfying the website users is perceived to be benefit number one, and that the organizations aim to provide consistently high quality information and services for the users, there is an absence of HCI activity in most organizations. Although the public sector is highly user-focused and strives to fulfill expectations and needs of citizens, real users are included to a surprisingly low extent in website development and continuous quality improvement. However, there are organizations that are great examples of user inclusion and usability testing, although the main trend among public sector organization reveals great potential for improvement, in both the frequency of testing and the use of methods in such activities.

Table 1 provides the findings from the quantitative study of the extent to which the website contributes benefits for the organization. Findings from Table 1 show that offering information and services without having a personal interaction with the users, and the reduced number of inquiries by phone, e-mail and personal visits, score high, along with organizational benefits related to more time to complete daily tasks within the organization. The website also contributes to an easier way of conveying information and services for the users and is easier to get in touch with, and have contact with, the users. In contrast to this, and to a lower extent, the website contributes to a reduction in organizational costs (e.g. staff reduction, automatic processes).

Table 1. Perception of benefits driven by public sector websites

Benefits measured	Question	Webmasters perception of benefits					
	To what degree does the website contribute benefits	Very low	Low	Medium	High	Very high degree	Not relevant
User satisfaction	...are the users perceived to be satisfied with the website in general	0.3 %	8.7 %	55.9 %	33.2 %	1.9 %	0.0 %
Efficiency and effectiveness	...more time to complete daily tasks	2.9 %	20.1 %	46.5 %	23.7 %	3.9 %	2.9 %
	...reduced number of inquiries by phone, e-mail and in person	1.3 %	12.0 %	46.1 %	33.1 %	6.5 %	1.0 %
	...reduction in organizational costs	9.1 %	40.6 %	35.4 %	9.4 %	1.6 %	3.9 %
	...offering information and services without a personal interaction	0.6 %	7.8 %	44.5 %	37.0 %	7.2 %	2.9 %
	...easier to get in contact with the users	3.2 %	21.1 %	40.3 %	27.3 %	4.9 %	3.2 %
	...more efficient communication with the users	1.6 %	12.3 %	33.4 %	40.4 %	10.7 %	1.6 %
Branding	...a great reputation for the organization	0.0 %	4.9 %	35.3 %	46.8 %	13.0 %	0.0 %

5   Discussion

The aim of combing different empirical components (both qualitative and quantitative data) has been to accomplish a complementary analysis in order to extend our knowledge and understand the topic of interest. Table 2 summarizes the qualitative and the quantitative findings provided.

Table 2. Summarizing the findings from the qualitative and quantitative study

Qualitative findings (Explorative)	Quantitative findings (Descriptive)
- User satisfaction is important for provision of online information and digital services	- Largely, the users are satisfied with the website
- The website contributes to efficiency and effectiveness within in the organization, as well as increased productivity for the users	- Largely, the website contributes to increased efficiency and effectiveness
- Branding is an important effect	- The website is important in regards to the branding effect

Firstly, in our digital community the use of IT has increased during the last decade [1], and happens to be an important contribution to the digitalization of the public sector [2]. Therefore, we need to highlight and discuss the benefits in this regard, and how the website actually contributes. The use of the Web as a channel for communication and interaction with citizens and businesses should also provide the users with better and more efficient access to public information and online services [3]. There are numerous ways to evaluate the benefits of IT [4] and different approaches can be applied. However, we can speculate that many organizations lack empirical evidence of how their website actually performs and, at first, they struggle in identifying the outcome of the benefits.

In assessing user satisfaction, the users of public information and digital services are found to be highly important and seen as the most important benefit perceived from an organizational point of view. In line with this, from the quantitative survey we find that the users are perceived to be satisfied with public sector websites when they can easily access content and digital services. Consequently, we should expect a high degree of HCI activity involved in continuous development and quality improvements, as this is found to be vital in this regard [e.g. 20, 21].

Regarding organizational impacts [see 7, 8], the findings in our study show that measures related to efficiency and effectiveness are frequently mentioned, and these benefits are mainly linked to aspects such as reduced manual work within in the organization, for instance by providing online schemes that the users can fill in online, instead of on paper. This results in more time to complete other tasks and a reduced working load. This is in line with the quantitative findings, which confirm what the website contributes to this. The website can also act as a knowledge base for both employees and external website users (e.g. citizens). This may contribute to a better flow of information (internal and external), in addition to better employee satisfaction.

Concerning the branding effect, the website can additionally stimulate public relations and marketing. Providing a website of great quality may create a good reputation for the organization (and the public sector in general) within our digital society, with increasing online information and digital services.

This study is not without limitations: the qualitative study had only ten open-ended interviews and a high degree of interpretation of the findings. However, findings from both the qualitative and quantitative study show that user satisfaction is found to be most important benefit from the webmasters' perspectives. This is followed by efficiency and effectiveness, and, finally, the branding effect. The fact that the qualitative and quantitative findings complement each other increases the validity of our study [see 16].

6   Conclusion

This study confirms that websites increase internal efficiency, which is in line with the strategies and goals launched by governments. A website contributes significantly towards facilitating daily tasks, which in turn releases resources which can then be allocated to other duties. This is often viewed as cost efficiency through staff reduction and organizational prioritization of allocation of resources. Additionally, this study highlights the branding and marketing effect as an additional benefit in increasing the reputation among users. A successful implementation of useful public electronic services bears witness to the line of thinking that users should be the prime focus and that it is essential to incorporate a public value perspective.

Upcoming research contributions could advantageously focus on how efficiency and effectiveness are perceived from a user's point of view, and what aspects of a website are particularly important to them. Moreover, it would be interesting to investigate the differences between public and private sector websites, both from a user's and an organizational point of view.

References

1. Sandoval-Almazan, R., Gil-Garcia, J.R.: Are government internet portals evolving towards more interaction, participation, and collaboration? Revisiting the rhetoric of e-government among municipalities. Gov. Inf. Q. **29**(Supplement 1), S72–S81 (2012)
2. Szkuta, K., Pizzicannella, R., Osimo, D.: Collaborative approaches to public sector innovation: a scoping study. Telecommun. Policy **38**, 558–567 (2014)
3. Verdegem, P., Verleye, G.: User-centered e-government in practice; a comprehensive model for measuring user satisfaction. Gov. Inf. Q. **26**(3), 487–497 (2009)
4. Osein-Bryson, K.-M., Ko, M.: Exploring the relationships between information technology investments and firm performance using regression splines analysis. Inf. Manag. **42**(1), 1–13 (2004)
5. Lindgaard. G., Millard. N.: The business value of HCI: how can we do better? In: Proceedings of the Conference of Human Factors in Computing Systems (CHI), Minnesota, USA (2002)
6. Gupta, M.P., Jana, D.: E-government evaluation: a framework and case study. Gov. Inf. Q. **20**, 365–387 (2003)
7. Flak, L.S., Olsen, D.H., Wolcott, P.: Local e-government in norway: current status and emerging issues. Scand. J. Inf. Syst. **17**(2), 41–84 (2005)
8. Bannister, F., Connolly, R.: ICT, public values and transformative government: a framework and programme for research. Gov. Inf. Q. **31**(1), 119–128 (2014)
9. Heeks., R.: Understanding and measuring eGovernment: international benchmarking studies. In: Workshop, E-participation and e-Government: Understanding the Present and Creating the Future, UNDESA, Budapest, Hungary (2006)
10. Edrees, M., Mahmood, A.: Measuring eGovernment systems success: an empirical study. In: Herawan, T., Deris, M.M., Abawajy, J. (eds.) Proceedings of the First International Conference on Advanced Data and Information Engineering (DaEng-2013), vol. 285, pp. 471–478. Springer, Singapore (2014)
11. Rana, N., Dwivedi, Y., Williams, M., Weerakkody, V.: Investigating success of an e-government initiative: validation of an integrated IS success model. Inf. Syst. Front. **17**, 127–142 (2015). doi:10.1007/s10796-014-9504-7
12. Osman, I.H., Anouze, A.L., Irani, Z., Al-Ayoubi, B., Lee, H., Balcı, A., Weerakkody, V.: COBRA framework to evaluate e-government services: a citizen-centric perspective. Gov. Inf. Q. **31**(2), 243–256 (2014). doi:10.1016/j.giq.2013.10.009
13. Xinli, H.: Effectiveness of information technology in reducing corruption in China. Electron. Libr. **33**(1), 52–64 (2015). doi:10.1108/EL-11-2012-0148

14. Arendsen, R., Peters, O., ter Hedde, M., Van Dijk, J.: Does e-government reduce the administrative burden of businesses? An assessment of business-to-government systems usage in the Netherlands. Gov. Inf. Q. **31**(1), 160–169 (2014). doi:10.1016/j.giq.2013.09.002

15. Lamberti, L., Benedetti, M., Chen, S.: Benefits sought by citizens and channel attitudes for multichannel payment services: evidence from Italy. Gov. Inf. Q. **31**(4), 596–609 (2014). doi:10.1016/j.giq.2014.03.002

16. Oates, B.J.: Researching Information Systems and Computing. Sage Publications Ltd., Thousand Oaks (2006)

17. Kvale, S.: Interviews: An Introduction to Qualitative Research Interviewing. Sage Publications, Thousand Oaks (1996)

18. DeLone, W.H., McLean, E.R.: The DeLone and McLean model of information systems success: a ten-year update. J. Manag. Inf. Syst. **19**(4), 9–30 (2003)

19. Prybutok, V., Zhang, X., Ryan, S.D.: Evaluating leadership, IT quality, and net benefits in an e-government environment. Inf. Manag. **45**, 143–152 (2008)

20. De Roiste, M.: Bringing in the users: the role for usability evaluation in government. Gov. Inf. Q. **30**(4), 441–449 (2013)

21. Følstad, A., Hornbæk, K.: Work-domain knowledge in usability evaluation: experiences with cooperative usability testing. J. Syst. Softw. **83**, 2019–2030 (2010)

The Evolution of the Argon Web Framework Through Its Use Creating Cultural Heritage and Community–Based Augmented Reality Applications

Gheric Speiginer[1], Blair MacIntyre[1(✉)], Jay Bolter[2], Hafez Rouzati[1],
Amy Lambeth[3], Laura Levy[3], Laurie Baird[4], Maribeth Gandy[3],
Matt Sanders[6], Brian Davidson[5], Maria Engberg[7], Russ Clark[5],
and Elizabeth Mynatt[1,4]

[1] School of Interactive Computing, Georgia Institute of Technology,
Atlanta, GA, USA
{gheric.speiginer,blair,hafez,mynatt}@gatech.edu
[2] School of Literature, Media, and Communication,
Georgia Institute of Technology, Atlanta, GA, USA
jay.bolter@lmc.gatech.edu
[3] Interactive Media Technology Center, Georgia Institute of Technology,
Atlanta, GA, USA
{amy,laura,maribeth.gandy}@imtc.gatech.edu
[4] Institute for People and Technology, Georgia Institute of Technology,
Atlanta, GA, USA
laurie.baird@ipat.gatech.edu, mynatt@gatech.edu
[5] Research Network Operations Center, Georgia Institute of Technology,
Atlanta, GA, USA
{bdavidson,russ.clark}@gatech.edu
[6] Office of Information Technology, Georgia Institute of Technology,
Atlanta, GA, USA
msanders@gatech.edu
[7] Department of Media Technology and Product Development,
Malmö University, Malmö, Sweden
maria.engberg@mah.se

Abstract. The Argon project was started to explore the creation of Augmented Reality applications with web technology. We have found this approach to be particularly useful for community-based applications. The Argon web browser has gone through two versions, informed by the work of our students and collaborators on these kinds of applications. In this paper, we highlight a number of the applications we and others have created, what we learned from them, and how our experiences creating these applications informed the design of Argon2 and the requirements for the next version, Argon3.

Keywords: Augmented reality · Web-based technology · Community computing

© Springer International Publishing Switzerland 2015
M. Kurosu (Ed.): Human-Computer Interaction, Part III, HCII 2015, LNCS 9171, pp. 112–124, 2015.
DOI: 10.1007/978-3-319-21006-3_12

1   Introduction

The Argon project (http://argon.gatech.edu) started as an industry-funded research program in 2009, aimed at understanding how web technology can be used to create mobile augmented reality (AR) applications [1], and was inspired by our previous work on the Real-World Wide Web [2] and by Spohrer's Worldboard [3]. The cornerstone of the project is the Argon iOS application, a web browser with AR capabilities. By integrating with the web, the Argon project hopes to provide AR capabilities within a mature application ecosystem, rather than focusing on creating yet-another environment for developing "AR applications".

Argon applications are based on the Web application model: each AR-enabled web application is fetched from a web server at a known URL (just as any web page or web-application), and is implemented with client-side Javascript to control the interface and communicate with remote web services. Over the years, Argon developers have implemented application prototypes across a variety of domains, and the Argon architecture has changed in response to their experiences.

In this paper, we discuss how the Argon framework evolved from Argon1 to Argon2, and the requirements we have identified for the next version (Argon3), based on the experiences of developers working with applications in the areas of community computing and cultural heritage. These domains have been a key motivator for this project from the beginning. Our work in historic sites over the years (e.g., Historic Oakland Cemetery [4] and the Auburn Avenue area of Atlanta [5]) has shown us how cultural heritage organizations often have significant amounts of pre-existing web-based content that they would like to re-purpose for an AR experience. For them, AR is exciting when used at the right moment, but much of the content (images, videos, maps) will be most useful when presented using traditional 2D display techniques. AR is one piece of a larger information system in which content will be accessed on conventional web browsers before and after visits to their sites. For similar reasons, a web-based solution is very appealing for many organizations, not just cultural heritage sites.

The key lesson we learned through the projects discussed in this paper is the value of tightly and cleanly integrating with the web ecosystem. The major difference between Argon1 and Argon2 is the format of the content that the web server delivers to the browser. In Argon1, the content is KARML [6] (a version of KML [7], the location-based XML format for Google Earth and Maps, that we extended to include AR-relevant elements). In Argon2, we change our approach and focused on cleanly integrating our tools with standard HTML5 content (with AR capabilities presented via the argon.js Javascript library). This change has had significant benefits, as we discuss throughout the paper, and in Argon3 we will continue to refine our HTML5-based approach to better leverage the web ecosystem.

2   Argon Version 1

In this section, we will give a brief overview of Argon1, describe a selection of AR applications created with it, and discuss how our experiences influenced the design of Argon2, the second version of Argon.

The first version of the Argon browser (referred to here as Argon1) has been available for iOS since February 2011. It has been used in dozens of research and class projects at Georgia Tech and elsewhere, despite modest capabilities. While Argon1 uses a standard iOS WebView for running user-created applications, we did not use HTML5 as our markup language for AR content (see [1] for architecture details). Rather, we created KARML [6] to define "channels" of AR content. With KARML, developers create AR content elements (positioned at 3D geo-locations or on simple AR markers) using the full collection of contemporary web standards (HTML5, CSS3, Javascript, etc.), using the tools, techniques, and server-side technologies they are already familiar with.

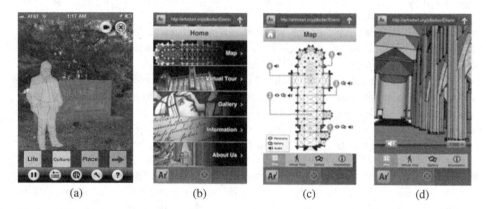

      (a)   (b)   (c)   (d)

Fig. 1. (a) The Voices of Oakland experience, showing an image of a "ghost" at a grave site on the tour. (b–d) The Lights of St. Etienne, ported to Argon2. (b) The main interface, (c) the navigational map, and (d) 3D model of the cathedral in approx. 1380 AD.

A novel capability of Argon1 (and Argon2) is that multiple channels can be displayed at once, by overlapping transparent web views. This is a first step toward an AR ecosystem where all AR content from independently-authored AR experiences is safely and simultaneously available to the user in one merged space. We will not discuss this further, as it has little impact on individual channel authors. Using multiple channels to create new kinds of user-experiences is a topic we are pursing in our future research.

2.1   Applications Built with Argon1

In this section, we highlight some projects that informed the requirements of Argon2.

The Voices of Oakland. *The Voices of Oakland* is a prototype AR tour designed to introduce visitors to the history and architecture of Oakland Cemetery, Atlanta's oldest cemetery [4]. The system was originally developed using Macromedia Director on a Windows XP laptop, but was ported to run on the iPhone3GS using Argon1. The user was able to walk among the graves and listen to the voices of historical figures interred at Oakland (voices were provided by voice actors from scripts written for the proto-type). The user was guided from grave to grave by a narrator (although Argon1 supported GPS, the prototype did not use it, but relied instead on timed directions, much like a traditional audio tour). At each grave site the user was invited choose audio segments, and could delve deeply into different categories depending on their particular interests.

The channel functioned in two modes. If the user was at the cemetery, only audio was provided. If the user was at a remote location, the channel could include pan-oramas of the cemetery to provide a virtual tour. The code therefore consisted of a screen-overlay (buttons that accessed the audio and panoramas), photo-overlays (panoramic images), and geo-located audio placemarks (where the audio was con-ceptually located for playing). The interface functionality was implemented with HTML5 and Javascript (see Fig. 1(a)). The prototype was limited to four graves and the walk between them. This prototype was created relatively quickly and demonstrated the ease with which existing content elements can be turned into an AR application using a web-based toolset.

The Lights of St. Etienne. A more ambitious tour prototype, *The Lights of Saint Etienne* was developed with the participation of students at Georgia Tech Lorraine in France. This channel served as a guided tour around the cathedral in Metz, France. The purpose was to explore a variety of different presentation modes for historical/cultural information, including interactive panoramas, still images, text, and audio. There were six main interface screens, all written in HTML5. The main interfaces were traditional 2D web content, with the AR view revealed only when appropriate.

A map indicated five sites around the cathedral the user could visit, together with the kind of information (panoramas, images, text, audio) that was available at each site. As with the Voices of Oakland, the tour did not use GPS (it was designed to be used inside the cathedral), so the user had to tell the app where she was by clicking on a map of the cathedral. An interesting feature of the tour was the use of historical panoramas at sites 1 and 2 on the map: these were pre-rendered from simple 3D models showing how the architecture of the church has changed over the period from 1207 to the Renaissance and beyond.

This prototype showed that it was relatively easy to integrate non-trivial HTML5 and Javascript into the KARML framework. The interface consisted of numerous HTML5 DOM elements, sliced images, buttons that called Javascript code for inter-active elements, and so on, just as any interactive web application would do. See Fig. 1 (b–d) for images of the Argon2 version of "The Lights of Saint Etienne", which is identical to the Argon1 version.

Campus Tour. *Campus Tour* is an augmented reality tour of Georgia Tech's campus implemented for iPad using Argon1, shown in Fig. 2(a–b). The tour gives information to users through geo-located text, pictures and videos. Our aim was to create an interactive and unique tour experience for prospective students, visitors, or anyone interested in Georgia Tech. *Campus Tour* can be viewed remotely via the use of panoramic images associated with a geospot (geo-located panorama), or using live video from the iPad's camera. The participant can select from a number of tours, see their progress, path and tour stops on a map, and delve into content that interests them.

Campus Tour is a fully dynamic web application. A server-side authoring tool allowed the content and tours to be managed from a desktop computer, and the server generated the tour application on the fly for the user. *Campus Tour* is one of most complex AR applications developed with Argon1, and proved to us that this model was useful for more than simple prototypes.

InfrastructAR. *InfrastructAR* was designed to reveal the typically hidden wireless network performance and connection information to anyone in the Georgia Tech community. Unlike other tools which visualize wireless information sensed directly from a mobile device, this application was designed to fetch and display real-time data from the wireless network management system itself. This dynamic content was rendered using HTML5 tools to visualize performance and activities of nearby wireless access points, as well as aggregate views of wireless performance in remote buildings (Fig. 3).

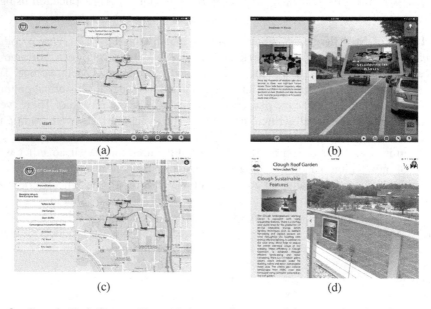

(a)   (b)

(c)   (d)

Fig. 2. Georgia Tech Campus Tour. (a) An overview map of the currently selected tour. (b) A stop on the tour, showing a mix of 2D content on the slide-in tab, and 3D content aligned with a panoramic image of the tour stop. (c–d) The second version of the tour, created in Argon2.

InfrastructAR is interesting because it uses AR to represent signals and activity in physical space that is changing dynamically, but not directly associated with a single visual object. Rather, the visualization represents the interaction between the wireless medium and any number of clients associated with the access points in a location.

Through this prototype, we came to appreciate that community applications go beyond user generated content to include community data where both operators

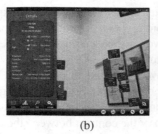
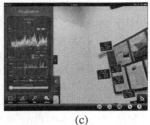

(a)   (b)   (c)

Fig. 3. InfrastructAR, an AR application designed to help the Georgia Tech community understand how the hidden WiFi infrastructure works. (a) shows the login screen based on Georgia Tech's web-based authetication system, (b) shows the details of the access point, and (c) is a real-time visualization of the network traffic flowing through that access point.

(experts) and end users are able to demystify wireless to gain a better understanding of current state and issues. Additionally, the system demonstrated how easy it was to integrate existing web services (both authentication and real-time, location-based data sources) into an Argon1 application.

2.2   Discussion of Argon1

Argon's use of the web-programming model proved to be both powerful and flexible, allowing developers to use existing web architectures for publishing AR content, ranging from static KARML files hosted on a simple web server, to dynamically generated KARML using client-side processing and AJAX communication with remote web services. Virtually any web architecture that worked for standard web content was possible to use with KARML in Argon1.

From KARML to HTML. Despite the power and flexibility afforded by a web application model, KARML proved to be awkward for most web developers to work with. The problem was not so much with KARML itself, but rather the AR-centric application model it imposed upon developers. This became a problem in each of these applications. Each had non-trivial HTML-based GUIs (including interactive charts and graphs in *InfrastructAR*), but a relatively simple AR view. Nevertheless, the entire application structure and logic had to be embedded in a KARML document, which was unintuitive for an application where AR was not the primary mode of interaction.

Also, KARML only worked in Argon1, which was problematic for two reasons. First, it made debugging extremely difficult because Argon1 content could only be viewed on a mobile device, preventing users from leveraging the increasingly sophisticated development and debugging tools available on desktop systems. Second, to build an application which worked in conventional browsers as well as Argon would have required two different application structures, one based on HTML5, and the other based on KARML, even if both versions were largely the same (except for AR features). For these reasons, we *switched to an HTML5-based approach in Argon2*.

Panoramas. Argon1 supported a panoramic-image-backgrounds feature, which was initially intended for rapid prototyping: a programmer could use panoramic images instead of live video while working on various content elements for their AR application without having to go to the site.

But panoramas soon proved valuable to experience designers, as shown in the *Lights of St. Etienne* (and the other tours), especially in light of the poor quality of the GPS and orientation sensors on mobile devices. Putting interactive panoramas in Argon made it possible to show the user the contrast between the environment she sees around her (e.g. the Cathedral as it is now) and some other condition (historical differences), without having to create fully interactive 3D models. Interactive panoramas used on a mobile device may constitute a kind of bridge between AR and VR, which is a very interesting design space that can incorporate the strengths of both these technologies.

The designers' use of panoramas drove us to *expand their capabilities* in Argon2, and to *extend this concept to other kinds of image-backgrounds* like Google Street-view.

Cross-Platform. The *Campus Tour* in particular highlighted the need for Argon content to be viewable on multiple platforms, because we wanted to embed the tour on a website to support remote visitors to the campus. Other students working with Argon expressed interest in head-worn displays, other operating systems such as Android, and in being able to run something like Argon on the desktop for debugging and authoring reasons. For these reasons, we *re-architected Argon2 to simplify porting to different platforms*.

2.3   Requirements for Argon2

The main requirements for Argon2, based on our Argon1 experience, were:

- Switch from KARML to more conventional HTML5-based web applications
- Add full 3D graphics support to allow richer content (using WebGL)
- Support natural feature tracking (using Qualcomm's Vuforia SDK)
- Add multi-device support (desktop, HMD, etc.)

3   Argon 2

Argon2 was completely rewritten with a new architecture to facilitate ease of porting to new platforms, and experimentation with different browser interfaces. The main change was a switch from one iOS WebView per channel to a single WebView with an embedded HTML5 iFrame per channel, and with the entire user-interface implemented with HTML5 in the WebView. While not a user-visible change, this made it easier to support our other requirements above.

Argon2 abandoned KARML, and instead exposed AR functionality through a Javascript library (argon.js) loaded from the HTML page. This approach allows AR web applications to be created in exactly the same way as traditional web applications, limiting the confusion created by an AR-centric application structure. This approach was also intended to allow web applications using argon.js to run on popular mobile and desktop browsers (with a more limited feature set), but unfortunately support for other browsers was never completed with Argon2.

Argon2 is built on top of Qualcomm's Vuforia computer vision SDK. Considerable effort was required to architect it in such a way that the constant stream of data into the iOS WebView does not overwhelm the system. By carefully managing data flow and batching all DOM operations for each update (to prevent extra layout and rendering operations), Argon2 web applications can run on iPhone4 or later, and all iPads with cameras (iPad2 or later), while doing both vision-based AR and geo-located AR.

All content is represented in the same 3D scene graph, unifying the content for the programmer: content following a tracked image target is attached to the camera, which is in turn located in the world via GPS and the device's built-in orientation sensors. Argon2 supported both WebGL and HTML5/CSS3 3D content. Audio is supported via Web Audio. WebGL and CSS3 content are merged in a three.js [8] scene graph. In the end, a web programmer is given a simple three.js scene graph view of the AR world, with nodes for tracked computer vision targets and geo-located locations in the world. All 2D content, interaction and web programming is done just as any mobile web app.

3.1   Applications Built with Argon2

As in the above section, here we present some applications created with Argon2 and discuss what we have learned from them about using web-technologies to create community-based AR experiences. At the end, we will outline the requirements we have for the next version of Argon (Argon3, currently under development).

A number of Argon1 applications were rewritten for Argon2. *The Lights of St. Etienne*, discussed above, was quite easy to port because all of the interface elements in HTML and Javascript could be directly reused, and the resulting interface was almost indistinguishable from the original Argon1 version. Debugging the port was made even easier because the Argon2 app (now just a single WebView) can be remotely debugged via a desktop computer, just as if it were a web page running in the Safari browser.

The second version of the *Campus Tour* ported the experience to Argon2 and improved the general user interface with an enhanced main menu allowing the user to view the route a tour takes, and see the stops along the tour visualized on a customized map within the channel instead of the native map which Argon1 provided (which showed all points of interest Argon1 knew about). From this map the user can select placemarks to "jump" to a geospot, switching into the AR experience at that location.

The biggest improvement to the *Campus Tour* was to support authoring of personalized AR experiences; students and faculty could create their own tours of the campus, showcasing Georgia Tech from their individual point of view via an associated web based authoring tool (the campus tour editor). This includes adding new points of interest or panoramic images to existing tours, or creating new tours, panoramic images, as well as points of interest with audio, video, or text content. Unfortunately, the tools attracted relatively few authors, highlighting to us the need for creating much more sophisticated authoring tools. The limited acceptance also highlighted the limitations inherent in doing AR on mobile devices. The poor quality of outdoor localization, and the limited opportunities for outdoor computer vision, made it hard for authors to create the kinds of experiences they envisioned.

Auburn Avenue. Using Argon2, we began to develop a tour of Auburn Avenue, the historical center of African-American culture in Atlanta in the twentieth century. The interface is similar to the Metz Cathedral example, although in this case the user is outside walking down an avenue. A scrolling timeline is used to indicate buildings of interest on an aerial map: these buildings are highlighted and clickable (see Fig. 4(a)). Clicking will trigger various kinds of information and interaction, including audio and historical panoramas. Vuforia-based image tracking is used to highlight details and presented information about the facade of one historical building.

The Auburn Avenue prototype is significantly more elaborate than the historic tours developed in Argon1, owing largely to the ease with which content can be authored and tested using desktop web browsers, and then integrated into the actual tour.

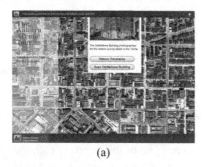 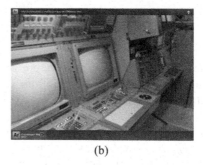

(a)   (b)

Fig. 4. (a) The Auburn Avenue map, and (b) a panorama in Neptun

Neptun. *Neptun* is based on a historic submarine that belonged to the Swedish navy, which is on exhibit in the Marine Museum in Karlskrona, Sweden [9]. The application was designed as a special companion piece to the opening of the exhibit. It is possible to go into the submarine itself; however, the confined area inside makes the visit difficult or impossible for visitors with claustrophobia or disabilities. *Neptun* offered the opportunity for a virtual visit by offering panoramic views of the upper and lower deck of the boat, along with dramatic audio narrative. On the opening day of the exhibition, iPads were available for those who wished to try this experience. By implementing the panoramas directly in three.js, the experience could be taken in a conventional web browser; the Argon2 version allowed the user to examine the whole 360 degrees of the panorama by rotating the iPad screen around herself.

This prototype showed the value of being able to move content easily between conventional desktop browsers and the Argon2 application, allowing the content to be consumed in many ways.

Midtown Buzz. Midtown Buzz (MB) (midtownbuzz.org) is a partnership between Georgia Tech and the Atlanta Midtown Alliance (MA) (www.midtownatl.com), focused on engaging urban communities through mobile innovation [10]. Since 2013, we have been collaborating with the Midtown Atlanta community with the goal of transforming the area into an innovation district, while creating a living laboratory for civic computing research. During the two years of this project we have engaged in a participatory design process with stakeholders ranging from MA staff, local start-up companies, student developer teams, and community thought leaders.

Our work culminated in the creation of some technology artifacts, including Midtown Buzz Mobile (MBM) as a gateway to a variety of applications. MBM is implemented using Argon2 and provides connections to other Georgia Tech applications that are associated with MB (e.g. Cycle Atlanta and One Bus Away) as well as to various external web resources.

MBM also includes a mixed reality storytelling experience that focuses on *personal expressive content*, aimed at creating rich community resources that are not motivated by efficiency and productivity, and are instead based on a philosophy inspired by urban computing projects [11–13]. The web-based model of Argon2 made it easy to embed mixed reality experiences inside of the application web content.

(a)   (b)   (c)

Fig. 5. The Midtown Buzz Mobile Mixed Reality Storytelling Experience. (a) An architectural rendering of a future building, (b) a video of a community author interacting with local sculpture, and (c) a map of a cycling event on Peachtree Street in Atlanta.

In MBM, key members of the community tell their stories of the Midtown neighborhood. Our prototype allows users to explore what areas will look like once new construction is complete, to get an insider's view of cycling around Midtown, all while getting a taste of the history of key locations (see Fig. 5). The site incorporates web elements in a mixed reality presentation where users can view videos, articles, photos, and other media presented over a 360-degree panorama of Midtown locations. If the user is at the locations featured, she can turn off the provided panorama image and have a true augmented reality experience overlaid on the live video feed from their device.

3.2   Discussion of Argon2

Argon2 targets experienced web developers by encapsulating AR functionality in the argon.js library, simplifying integration of third-party web services and libraries. Many of our developers used the tools they were familiar with, such as jQuery. The popular three.js rendering library was bundled with argon.js inside of the Argon2 application. (We chose three.js because it is a relatively popular library for 3d web content, with many tutorials, examples, and resources).

Tight-coupling with three.js. Our original intention for bundling three.js with argon.js was to simplify development and bypass slow download times on mobile devices, as well as avoid library incompatibilities as argon.js and three.js evolved. In practice, however, the argon.js API became tightly coupled to specific versions of three.js, which changes rapidly, meaning that developers had to be careful in making sure their applications were based on the version of three.js we included in argon.js (and did not necessarily correspond to the latest three.js documentation and examples). Due to the problems that arose because of this tight coupling and bundling, in Argon3 we plan to *decouple argon.js from any particular rendering library*, expose bindings to specific rendering libraries (such as three.js) as *separate rendering plug-ins for argon.js*, and *no longer bundle argon.js* with the Argon3 browser. The argon.js toolkit should enable web developers to leverage Argon's capabilities, and to also leverage the capabilities of other platforms and rendering libraries.

Debugging. Argon2 moved most of the core logic from native code to javascript, allowing channels running in Argon2 to be debugged via desktop Safari's remote debugging tools. Furthermore, by modularizing a channel's code such that components which depended on argon.js are only executed in the Argon browser, most of the application code could be developed and tested on the desktop browser leveraging its full debugging support. This strategy not only facilitated debugging, but also contributed to a multi-tiered design strategy: experiences could be designed to work on various devices (laptop as well as mobile) with various features, making it possible to conceive of and implement "transmedia" apps. Each of the applications discussed above (Auburn, Neptun, Midtown Buzz) leverage this strategy.

Multi-device Support. Although it was a significant goal for Argon2, we never implemented support for alternative hardware form-factors. Argon2 and argon.js were too tightly coupled to the phone/tablet form factor used by the application, making it difficult to support other platforms. In Argon3, we will *create AR abstractions and an AR framework* that allows application developers to create applications that can adapt to various hardware and software configurations without requiring the developer to create multiple versions of their application. Such a framework will also need to allow AR to be used in different ways within an application, instead of requiring applications to be "AR-first", as Argon2 does.

3.3   Requirements for Argon3

Our high level requirements for Argon3, derived from our experiences above, include:

- Decouple argon.js from specific rendering libraries
- Enhanced debugging and authoring support for AR
- Support AR/non-AR as modes of interaction
- Develop semantically meaningful abstractions for AR applications
- Multi-device support (desktop, HMD, etc.) (not implemented in Argon2)

4   Discussion and Conclusions

We are currently designing and implementing the third version of Argon, based on the lessons learned working with designers and developers who used Argon1 and Argon2 to create a wide variety of applications. We have been particularly inspired by the way Argon has allowed designers to integrate AR into community-based applications, moving both formal and informal content out into the world around them. A key insight from working with these communities is that while AR is exciting at first, it rarely ends up being the focus of the resulting applications; our job moving forward, then, is to make it as easy as possible to integrate AR content into web-based applications, and to give programmers and designers the ability to use AR in their applications in whatever way they see fit.

Acknowledgements. We would like to thank AT&T, Alcatel-Lucent and Qualcomm for their support of the Argon project, and all the students, researchers and sponsors who used (and supported those using) Argon. We have benefited from ongoing support from the GVU Center at Georgia Tech, and from the support of an NSF Graduate Research Fellowship for the first author.

References

1. MacIntyre, B., Hill, A., Rouzati, H., Gandy, M., Davidson, B.: The Argon AR Web Browser and standards-based AR application environment. In: 10th IEEE International Symposium on Mixed and Augmented Reality (ISMAR), pp. 65–74. IEEE (2011)
2. Kooper, R., MacIntyre, B.: Browsing the real-world wide web: maintaining awareness of virtual information in an AR information space. Int. J. Hum. Comput. Interact. 16(3), 425–446 (2003)
3. Spohrer, J.C.: Information in places. IBM Syst. J. 38(4), 602–628 (1999)
4. Dow, S., Lee, J., Oezbek, C., MacIntyre, B., Bolter, J.D., Gandy, M: Exploring spatial narratives and mixed reality experiences in Oakland Cemetery. In: Proceedings of the 2005 ACM SIGCHI International Conference on Advances in Computer Entertainment Technology (ACE 2005), pp. 51–60. ACM, New York (2005)
5. MacIntyre, B., Bolter, J.D., Moreno, E., Hannigan, B.: Augmented reality as a new media experience. In: IEEE/ACM International Symposium on Augmented Reality (ISAR), pp. 197–206. IEEE (2001)
6. KARML Reference. https://research.cc.gatech.edu/kharma/content/karml-reference

7. KML version 2.2. http://www.opengeospatial.org/standards/kml
8. three.js, a Javascript 3D library. https://github.com/mrdoob/three.js/
9. Marine Museum in Karlskrona, Sweden. http://www.marinmuseum.se/en/
10. Gandy, M., Baird, L.D., Levy, L.M., Lambeth, A., Mynatt, E., Clark, R., Sanders, M.: Midtown buzz: bridging the gap between concepts and impact in a civic computing initiative. In: Proceedings of Human Computer Interaction International, Los Angeles, CA, 2–7 August 2015
11. Korn, M., Back, J.: Talking it further: from feelings and memories to civic discussions in and about places. In: Proceedings of the 7th Nordic Conference on Human-Computer Interaction: Making Sense Through Design, New York, NY, USA, pp. 189–198 (2012)
12. Foth, M.: From Social Butterfly to Engaged Citizen: Urban Informatics, Social Media, Ubiquitous Computing, and Mobile Technology to Support Citizen Engagement. MIT Press, Cambridge (2011)
13. DiSalvo, C., Maki, J., Martin, N.: Mapmover: a case study of design-oriented research into collective expression and constructed publics. In: Proceedings of the SIGCHI Conference on Human Factors in Computing Systems, New York, NY, USA, pp. 1249–1252 (2007)

Historical Registry of Our Families Through Textiles

Cathy L. Starr[1], Sandra L. Bailey[1], Sheryl Brahnam[2(✉)],
and Jenifer J. Roberts[1]

[1] Fashion and Interior Design, Missouri State University, Springfield, USA
{CStarr,SBailey,JeniferRoberts}@missouriState.edu
[2] Computer Information Systems, Missouri State University, Springfield, USA
Sbrahnam@missouriState.edu

Abstract. Dress provides an insight into a person's value system, as well into the state of the socioeconomic environment of the time. The purpose of this paper is to describe the design of a mobile application and website where users of all walks-of-life can document their heritage by capturing photographs of family members' clothing throughout their lifetimes. Dress evokes memories, feelings of nostalgia, and speaks volumes about a person's personal history and heritage. This application will allow each and every person who logs on and participates to document their lives and the important role dress plays in their lives, whether they are rich and famous or not. This will enable the creation of a large archive of information representing all of the populace, not just the rich and famous, for future research based on the subjects' own words and visuals.

Keywords: Historical costume · Social media applications · Meanings of dress · Textile · Sociocultural environment

1 Introduction

In his seminal work, George P. Fox, states, *"Fashion is, has been, and will be through all ages the outward form through which the mind speaks to the universe."* [9 p. xx]. Eicher and Evenson define dress as both a product and a process that people use to distinguish themselves [1], while Kaiser, Nagasawa, & Hutton describe fashion as a social process [4]. For all intents and purpose of this paper, dress and fashion will be limited to the sense of sight, as opposed to other sensory experiences of dress, and will include make-up, hairstyles, and other body modifications, as well as individual pieces of clothing, jewelry, and accessories [2].

The purpose of this paper is to describe the design of a social media application that will document family history for people by capturing photos of a person's clothing through his or her lifetime. This application has the means to make the ordinary person as visible as their wealthy and famous counterparts. Users will upload photographs from their family archives and by taking photographs of their clothing using their phones and other digital equipment. These photographs will be uploaded to a website where they can tell stories about the meaning of their dress: for example, special occasion clothing for christenings, weddings, newborns, holidays, dances, and

© Springer International Publishing Switzerland 2015
M. Kurosu (Ed.): Human-Computer Interaction, Part III, HCII 2015, LNCS 9171, pp. 125–132, 2015.
DOI: 10.1007/978-3-319-21006-3_13

graduations. Users can also add photographs of family members and talk about their clothes and other pertinent information. This documentation will be processed through the sharing of photographs of clothing, textiles worn, and used by an individual, family member, or friend used during a specified time period. Along with sharing the photograph and noting the specified time, the website would provide documentation of the geographic location, style name (current at that specific time), specification of function for which this textile was worn or used, designation of whether this garment was handmade or purchased and where purchased and fiber content if known. This application would allow each and every person to have the opportunity to add their personal thread and tell their personal story, a virtual "Tapestry of Your Life."

How and why people choose to dress themselves has significance and is as varied and as diverse as each individual is, and in turn, the choices these same individuals make about dress affect society [6]. Dress can be an extraordinarily powerful symbolic representation of the relationship between nature, man, and his sociocultural environment, and, as such, should be studied [3, 7, 11]. A primary reason to document and study dress and fashion is to provide the students with a sense of understanding the societal expectations associated with dress, as well as to understand how and why modern fashion and dress have evolved [5, 6]. This application has the potential to retrieve and expose more information and to garner more in-depth insights into families and the specific meanings of dress to individuals and their families over the years. Historical facts, personal stories, folklore (oral history) and pictures of everyday people living during a specified timeframe will create a large database of information that has not been previously available for study.

2 Why Document Dress

Although anthropological research indicates that life histories and folklore have the potential of aiding the understanding of history and human complexities, the lack of sound methodology for this type of research results in a prolific source of knowledge being under-utilized [7]. Life histories serve as a supplemental source of data and instill the ability to infer cultural patterns [7]. Material artifacts, such as photographs, jewelry, and textiles create a small but strong sense of family and heritage. The connection to this heritage through these artifacts is brought to life by written notations, reminisced stories, and recollected memories projecting an idealized version of the time and events. According to Lillios [10], "If identified, heirlooms have the potential to provide a richer and finer-grained understanding of the human past" (p. 235). Heirlooms provide an insight into a person's value system, as well as into his or her personal preferences and style. The documentation of clothing provides insight into the artistic, economic, political, and technological environment of a specific time and how an individual reacts and lives his life affects these same environments [8].

Researchers historically have had to rely on the technology available at the time to document a former society's existence and daily movements. For example, studies focusing on prehistorical man rely on durable artifacts found at archeological digs along with available depictions of the local populace and their clothing found on artifacts [8]. As technology advanced, documentation of fashion also advanced with the dissemination of fashion being communicated using fashion dolls, fashion sketches, fashion plates, letters and diaries, as well as records of purchase or inheritance. Until the development of cameras and the more precise depictions of clothing by photograph, representations of costumes from the 18th century and earlier relied on an artist's rendition of an individual or family that could afford this luxury [8]. In other words, such portraits were rarely accurate, limited in types of dress, captive to the preferences of the artist, and limited in viewpoints of the upper classes.

Even with the advent of cameras, photography was expensive given the costs of camera, film, and development. Photographs did not become readily available for the ordinary person until recent technical developments. As a result, the fashion of the masses has not been documented nearly as well as the fashion of the wealthy, famous and notable. From the christening gown to the death shroud, certain garments hold ceremonial status and memories of times past. These garments are replete with symbolic meaning. For instance, in the West a "white" wedding gown symbolizes "purity" and is often the focus of dreams.

As often as the rich and famous are in the public eye, they actually represent a small amount of the population. Statistics indicate that in the United States, the rich form 1 % of the population, yet they capture the attention of the masses, as demonstrated by the prevalence of celebrities featured in the media [13]. Paparazzi frantically attempt to catch every moment of the rich and famous on camera, documenting fashion in all forms of life for these few, while the masses are doing most of the "living, loving, and dying," as so succinctly stated by George Bailey in the movie, *It's a Wonderful Life*. An example of the heightened attention focused on celebrities would be the documentation of the fashion of individuals like the Kardashians, famous actors, popular monarchy, or political figures like Jackie Kennedy, Princess Diana, and today Princess Kate and the young princes.

The purpose of the application "Threads of Your Life," proposed in this paper, is to reverse this trend and make visible the fashion of the masses while creating an in-depth database of information on the meanings and importance of dress for people today. Documentation of the general public and the local nobility is minimal even today compared to the documentation of the rich and famous. This results in the general public's dress being limited in visibility and a dearth of local information about the general population being available for research. Because of recent technological advancements (computers, cameras, the internet, communications technology, and social media) documenting clothing today is easier than it was historically. Technology today allows more focus on the ordinary individual, which is evidenced by the prolific posting of the extremely popular 'selfie.'

3 Social and Personal Meanings of Clothing

Dress serves as a symbolic form of language that reflects societal norms of beauty, modesty, and fashion, as well as occupational, marital, and socioeconomic status, group membership, and other social roles [4, 8, 9]. For instance, a uniform is used to establish differences as well as to depict occupation and is able to document status as evidenced with a pair of captain's bars. Throughout history, dress serves as a social prop providing a way to protect the body, cover the body to preserve modesty, decorate the body to differentiate individuals, and establish or portray status [8]. Tortura & Eubanks state that researchers agree that the primary reason for dress is decoration [8]. Even with minimal dress, prehistoric man was able to differentiate himself with scaring and other body modifications that could add a sense of mystery and fashion to one's appearance or tell stories about an individual. Researchers agree that the study of historical fashion and the meaning of dress often use core themes such as social, historical, cross-cultural, geographic, and dress as an art form. The social context includes social life, class structure, and social roles, which are aided by the knowledge of gender, age, status, identification of group membership, and ceremonial use of clothing. While the historical context is made up of politics, economics, technology and communication, the cross-cultural influences are through a process known as cultural authentication. This phenomenon is seen when designs from one culture are mixed with designs from different culture(s) creating unique designs known as a mixture. Geography plays a vital role with the human need to adapt to the natural environment and ecological conditions. Dress as an art form acts as a titillating construct that includes the relationship between costumes of a particular era, development of fine and applied arts, individual costume designers, and a revival of interest in earlier fashion styles [1, 8, 12]. For example, the wearing of a wedding ring designates marriage and acts as a symbol of status. Another example would be the wearing of a business suit to work indicating that the wearer is not a blue-collar worker and may serve as an indicator of status. Dress provides silent and symbolic cues to others.

Another source of personal choice of clothing has to do with what the German's call, Zeitgeist, meaning "the spirit of the times" [8]. Political, social and economic conditions affect a person's emotions and choices. In turn, the thoughts of people and their reactions to surrounding conditions affect the conditions of the time, leading to a common thread and trend of thought and feeling, in other words, "Zeitgeist." With reflection over the past periods of history and the change of popular dress over time, the spirit of the time becomes visible [8]. Even though these choices may be made consciously or subconsciously, when a person chooses their form of dress their choices reflect who and how they want others to perceive them [1, 8]. For example, a person dressing to go to work chooses different clothing than s/he would dressing for a favorite past time.

4 "Threads of Your Life" Application

The basic structure of "Threads of Your Life" can be described as a modification and combination of several popular social media applications, such as Facebook, Pinterest, and Ancestry.com. As illustrated in Fig. 1, this application will be similar to Pinterest in that a variety of individuals will be able to build a database filled with photographs, stories, traditions, poignant nostalgic memories, even letters and newspaper articles depicting life from the viewpoint of the local population through the sharing of their memoirs about a chosen time period, clothing style, geographical location, or accessory.

Fig. 1. Example "Tapestry of Your Life" Page, with some actual photographs and narratives produced by students.

To begin using this application, the user must first create a login ID on the website sharethethreads.com (see Fig. 2). The user must then choose whether s/he wants his or her photographs, descriptions, and personal stories to be viewed publicly or privately. The next step depends on the user, and what s/he is interested in, a specific time period, a special event, or specific dress for that event? Once the user determines the direction,

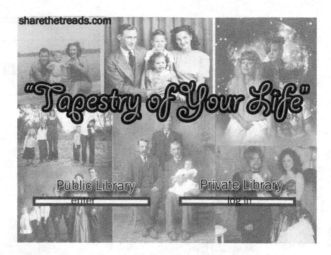

Fig. 2. Homepage

s/he chooses the category representing that interest. For example, if the user is interested in viewing other photographs and information available concerning Easter in 1970 s, s/he would first choose the correct time period and then choose Easter as the special event. From that page, s/he would then be able to read what has been published by others and to add photographs and stories of his or her own about this category.

The application is into four categories, which are available, as illustrated in Fig. 2, in a drop-down menu: time period, item, special events, and location. The time period will be identified by day/month/year or by the word "about" and the year. The dress item may be categorized as one of the following: knit top, blouse, shirt, sweater, skirt, pants, dresses, jackets, coats, shoes, foundation garments, handmade or purchased, fiber content (such as 100 % wool or 60/40 polyester/cotton). Special events are described as one of the following: Birthday, Wedding, Graduation, Death, Holidays, and Vacations with Holidays being further broken down as Valentine's Day, Easter, 4th of July, Veteran's Day, Thanksgiving, Christmas, and Hanukah. Finally, the location is identified by country, state, county/province, and city.

The proposed application will use an adaptation of Ancestry.com that allows users to search for shared "threads," much like Ancestry.com allows users to search the genealogy of their families and to look for shared connections. These "threads" consist of the four categories. For example, if a user is interested in the dress of "the people living in the Ozarks," s/he could search by geographic location. Knowing the fiber content allows users interested in the development of materials, such as wool, to research this topic (Fig. 3).

When adding a picture of dress to the application, users may choose to take a current picture or to upload an image from their computer. They will then see pop-up options to choose from, for example, public or private. Timeline will follow next with the choice of documentation by date or decade of object as close as possible. Identification of the geographic location comes next. The more complex category of item will lead to the choice of style name, specific function, whether handmade or purchased,

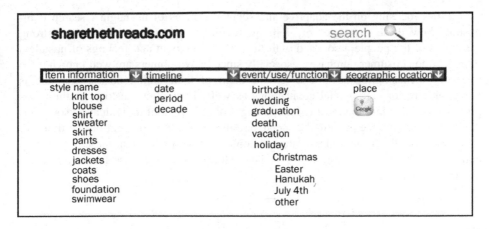

Fig. 3. Organizational Categories

and the fiber content (these may be omitted and added later by others on the system). Finally, the user will be able to add personal stories, folklore, and written documentation, such as newspaper articles or wills that discuss the event. The proposed application will also have the potential to be adapted, to evolve and to add "threads" as needed to develop a more in-depth and specific database of dress. This application has the potential to create a database focusing on ordinary people and filled with symbolism and meanings of dress.

The first users of this proposed application will be students enrolled at a Midwestern University. They will use it to complete an assignment for their History of Fashion course. This assignment is designed to promote personal investment in the assignment and the course. Each student will be asked to choose an artifact, a historical photograph of their family, and to create a connection or a memory by researching this photograph and writing a short narrative. In this narrative the student will identify who is being depicted in the photograph, the time period, and what was occurring during that time frame, along with what were the fashions being worn. Students will give feedback to help improve the website. At a later date, it is our hope to make this website available to anyone.

5 Conclusion

This application could be used as an educational tool that would grow and evolve with each person's addition of photographs and stories. This is an opportunity to make the fashion of the masses more visible and create a database full of meaningful insights and prolific visuals of ordinary people that have been living, loving, and dying behind the scenes as it were. This would make this application and website a valuable tool to be incorporated in such courses as historical fashion, costume design, product development, and a number of other courses. The material collected might even evolve into a dynamic source of inspiration for future designers.

Studies focusing on the adaptive and societal aspects of nostalgia research demonstrate how these memories of clothing, textiles, and other objects evoke strong memories of the people associated with them [3]. Sentiment and feelings of nostalgia often lead to consumer purchases, especially since baby boomers are well known to be fond of purchasing products that remind them of their childhoods. Thus there is potential here for commercial connections as well. Throughout history, clothing has provided insights into the local culture, along with glimpses of individual personalities that interacted with the natural, the social, and the artistic environment of that time [5]. It is hoped that this proposed website and application will document these histories by collecting pictures of clothing and associated stories about their use for future generations to enjoy.

References

1. Eicher and Evenson: The Visible Self. Prentice-Hall, Englewood Cliffs (2015)
2. Roach-Higgins, M., Eicher, J.: Dress and identity. Clothing Text. Res. J. **10**(4), 1–8 (1992)
3. Hamilton, J.: Mass fashion as threat in context and concept. Clothing Text. Res. J. **9**(2), 25–32 (1991)
4. Kaiser, S., Nagasawa, R., Hutton, S.: Construction of an SI theory of fashion: Part 1. ambivalence and change. Clothing Text. Res. J. **13**(3), 172–183 (1995)
5. Paoletti, J.: Does the costume and textile historian have a place in the future? Clothing Text. Res. J. **2**(2), 33–36 (1984)
6. Workman, J., Freeburg, B.: Dress and society. Fairchild Books, New York (2008)
7. Watson, L.: Understanding a life history as a subjective document: Hermeneutical and phenomenological perspectives. Ethos **4**(1), 95–131 (1976)
8. Tortora, P.G., Eubank, K.: Survey of Historic Costume, 5th edn. Fairchild Books, New York (2011)
9. Fox, George P.: Fashion: The power that influences the World. Trubner & Co., London (1871)
10. Lillios, Katina T.: Objects of memory: the ethnography and archaeology of heirlooms. J. Archaeol. Method Theory **6**(3), 235–262 (1999)
11. Matthews, V.H.: The anthropology of clothing in the Joseph narrative. J. Study Old Testament **20**(65), 25–36 (1995)
12. Miller-Spillman, K.: Introduction to dress, culture, and theory. In: Miller-Spillman, K., Reilly, A., Hunt-Hurst, P. (eds.) The Meanings of Dress, pp. 1–41. Fairchild Books, New York (2012)
13. Dunn, A.: Average America vs the one percent. Forbes, 21 March 2012. Downloaded 24 February 2015 http://www.forbes.com/sites/moneywisewomen/2012/03/21/average-america-vs-the-one-percent/

HCI in Business, Industry and Innovation

Early Prototype Assessment of a New Virtual System for Training Procedural Skills of Automotive Service Operators: LARTE Tool

Simone Borsci[1(✉)], Glyn Lawson[1], Mark Burgess[2], and Bhavna Jha[3]

[1] Human Factors Research Group, Faculty of Engineering,
The University of Nottingham, Nottingham NG7 2RD, UK
simone.borsci@gmail.com, glyn-lawson@nottingham.ac.uk
[2] Holovis International Ltd., Lutterworth, UK
mark.burgess@holovis.com
[3] Jaguar Land Rover, Abbey Road, Whitley, Coventry CV3 4LF, UK
bjhal@jaguarlandrover.com

Abstract. The consortium of the Innovate UK funded Live Augmented Reality Training Environments (LARTE) project, composed of Jaguar Land Rover (JLR), Holovis International Ltd and The University of Nottingham, developed a new concept of a 3D multiplatform training system to train the procedural skills of service maintenance operators. The LARTE tool was designed on the basis of JLR needs and desiderata. This paper presents the functionalities of the initial prototype of LARTE training system, and outcomes of an evaluation study of the usability of the product.

Keywords: Automotive · Training · Trust · Usability · Virtual reality

1 Introduction

Car manufacturers have been pioneers in the use of 3D environments for prototyping and evaluating a product's design [1], and today automakers are exploring, with growing interest, the use of virtual training solutions for training operators by investing in international research projects. Car service maintenance is considered a key topic for automotive industries, because service operators are the main interface between brand and costumers with car issues [2, 3]. Therefore, the objective of automotive industries is to invest in effective tools to enhance service operators' procedural skills. Several studies in the literature [4] outlined that virtual training has a positive impact on operators' acquisition of new skills – see for instance: techniques of welding, prototyping, object assembly etc. Nevertheless, currently only a few studies are available in the literature about virtual training of car service operators [5, 6]. Moreover, practitioners in 3D training of automotive operators are used to focus their attention on the enhancement of the interactive aspects of virtual environments only in terms of functionalities, with minimal effort in the assessment of the end-users' experience of the training system.

© Springer International Publishing Switzerland 2015
M. Kurosu (Ed.): Human-Computer Interaction, Part III, HCII 2015, LNCS 9171, pp. 135–143, 2015.
DOI: 10.1007/978-3-319-21006-3_14

As Mantovani [7] claimed the interaction experience of a 3D environment could significantly affect the trainees' interaction, thus compromising the trainees' acquisition of the content. In light of this, the usability – intended as the "extent to which a product can be used by specified users to achieve specified goals with effectiveness, efficiency and satisfaction in a specified context of use" [ISO 9241-11, 8] – is a key aspect for the success of a training application. Despite the importance of the usability of 3D environments being a well-known concept, as underlined by several authors [7, 9, 10] practitioners in the virtual reality field are used to applying a qualitative approach to usability assessment, and a large part of the studies in the field discuss the outcomes of summative evaluations – i.e., when the product is in an advanced stage of development – by presenting data obtained through qualitative and unstandardized questionnaires administrated to the end-users. Differently from the human computer interaction field, rarely do practitioners in the virtual training field discuss the approaches and methods they applied during the formative evaluation of the prototype – i.e., the phases of prototype evaluation and redesign which aim to integrate designers and end-users' mental models [11].

In this paper we will discuss a full formative evaluation paradigm applied to assess a new 3D training system for car service operators consisting of three phases. The first phase was an experts' analysis carried out by a heuristic list [12] and a four-question cognitive walkthrough [13]. The second phase was a redesign phase in which designers, in line with AGILE principles [14], solved only the most relevant interaction issues revealed by experts. The third phase consisted of a user test carried out through a scenario based analysis. In this last step, we gathered the users' errors during the interaction with the system and their satisfaction in the use through a standardized questionnaire – i.e., the System Usability Scale [SUS, see: 15]. Both the experts and the end-users interaction issues will be also modelled through estimation models, in line with the Grounded Procedure approach [i.e., GP, see: 16–18], to identify the percentage of problems identified during the evaluation test.

2 Initial Prototype

The prototype application applied in this study was developed by HoloVis international, as part of the Live Augmented Reality Training Experience project (LARTE project, TSB – 101509). LARTE software is based on the HoloVis game engine (InMo™), which enables end-users to visualise and interact with CAD data by using a number of supported devices (see Fig. 1): multi-sided CAVE, powerwall, Oculus Rift, and interactive table-top displays. For this study, LARTE system is adapted to the specific requirements and desiderata of JLR, and is used as a prototype to train car service operators on maintenance procedures. Designers developed the prototype to train in a 3D environment people who could receive an automatic step-by-step explanation of the procedure. Moreover, people could manipulate and make trials of the procedure against time limits to test their level of performance proficiency. LARTE application functions are variables to grant a degree of freedom to trainers of different industries to set up a virtual experiential activity.

Section a.   Section b.

Fig. 1. LARTE prototype experienced through Zspace (Section a.) and CAVE (Section b.)

The main five main functions of this training application can be described as follows:

- Trainers can create a training by importing a CAD object, and setting a step-by-step training video of the procedure;
- Trainers can define a set of rules and relationships among the components of the 3D objects;
- Trainees can autonomously visualize each single step of the procedure by receiving in the virtual environment verbal and textual instructions of a service procedure, through a video recorded virtual explanation of the procedure;
- Trainees can manipulate the 3D car – e.g., rotate the whole CAD, assembly, dis-assembly, rotate and move any single components of the car, zoom in and out etc.
- Each trainee's interaction can be fully recorded and observed in the 3D environment.

Finally, LARTE prototype is designed to be used through different devices, this characteristics allow operators to use during the training not only the CAVE but also portable tools, such as interactive 3D table.

2.1 Procedure

The evaluation of the LARTE prototype was carried out by using two different set of devices:

- *Not portable*: a 4-sided CAVE (VR1) with rear-projected floor (Sony VPL-FE40) with a mirror rig and 2 projectors per wall – 8 in total. The resolution of each projector was 1440 × 1050. The controller of the CAVE was a ART DTrack optical head and wand tracking. The tracking was integrated in a pair of lightweight polarized passive glasses. The system was run by 9 workstations.
- *Portable*: zSpace holographic 3D table (VR2) composed by a 24 in. (1920 × 1080) LCD monitor (tablet display) running at 120 Hz. The controller was a laser-based wired six-degree-of-freedom stylus device. The tracking was integrated in a pair of lightweight polarized passive glasses [19].

A virtual version of a Range Rover Evoque car was created to perform the usability analysis. A trainer explained to both experts and end users, for five minutes the functions of the prototype, and the use of the physical controller of the device. After the explanation experts and end-users were required to achieve the following five tasks (presented by scenarios): (i) use the controller to visualize the virtual video training; (ii) skip and rewind sections of the video training; (iii) use the control to zoom in the virtual car and remove a specific bolt; (iv) bring the removed bolt out of the car, and zoom out; (v) rotate the car and reassembly a bolt in the correct position. Five experts (2 Male; Age M.: 28.5; SD: 3.4) with at least 3 years of experience in human factors, interaction and virtual reality were asked to perform the five tasks by using both the CAVE and the zSpace. The order by which experts experienced the portable or not portable device was randomly defined. After each interaction session with a device, each expert filled the evaluation form composed of the ten classic heuristics items [12] and a four questions cognitive walkthrough [13]. Forty end users (Male: 14; Age M.: 35.89, SD: 13.11) were randomly assigned to experience the prototype by using or the CAVE or the zSPACE (i.e., 20 subjects per each device). After the interaction participants were asked to fill the SUS, composed of 10 items.

2.2 Experts' Evaluation

Experts identified 10 usability problems of interaction with LARTE tool in the CAVE, and 7 during the experience with the zSpace. In line with the GP approach, the Return of Investment model [20, 21] and the Good-Turing model probabilistic model [22, 23] were used to estimate the upper and the lower percentage of the total usability problems identified by the experts. Our analysis showed that experts identified from 92 % to 97 % of usability problems in the CAVE, and from 95 % to 98 % of problems in the zSpace. The relevance of the problems was assessed in terms of experts' agreement on the severity by using a scale from 0 to 100 (see Table 1).

Redesign After the Experts Analysis. The outcomes of the experts analysis was used to develop a list of priorities. In tune with AGILE principles, designers decided to solve, before the user test, only 10 out of 17 problems, i.e., only the issues estimated to have over 50 % relevance (see Table 1). The remained issues will be deferred and aggregated to the end-users' feedback for the further step of redesign. The redesign of the LARTE was performed in three weeks. The new version was reviewed by an external expert to assess the congruity between the outcomes of the experts' assessment and the redesign of the application. The new version of the tool, in line with indications of the experts, included revised features, such as for instance, a new and improved snap function, and new functions, such as the 'Undo/reset' control for the end-users.

2.3 User Test

The overall satisfaction in the use of LARTE tool, measured through SUS, equals 78.88 %. Participants who interacted with LARTE tool in the CAVE were more satisfied (85 %) than people who interacted with the zSpace (75 %). The t-test analysis

Table 1. Interactive problems identified by experts in the use of LARTE application experienced in the CAVE and through the zSpace, and percentage of relevance of the problems.

CAVE - Description/possible solution	Relevance
UNDO/REDO/RESET for end users	80%
Develop a menu for end users and GUI functions (Exit, Errors messages)	20%
Easy to be lost reset visualization improved a reset of visualization	20%
Develop the function by which users may swap form Movie/training to the interactive car	60%
Point and select small components is difficult improve a function that when a user is close to the target component, the pointer can highlight/Magnify/indicate the correct action	60%
Develop a way to concurrently remove an object and zoom out/in, and visual feedbacks which indicate that you are making a correct action	80%
Develop a GUI for the trainer	60%
Improve the snap tool and the highlights	60%
buttons in controller are not well organized	40%
Develop a place in which people could leave the disassembled components (virtual Basket? Table?)	40%
zSpace - Description/possible solution	**Relevance**
Develop a menu for end users and GUI functions (Exit, Errors messages), and also the UNDO/REDO/RESET	60%
rotation of objects	100%
easy to be lost reset visualization	20%
Zoom function is slow	100%
Develop a way to concurrently remove an object and zoom out/in, and visual feedbacks which indicate that you are making a correct action)	60%
Develop a place in which people could leave the disassembled components (virtual Basket? Table?)	100%
improve the snap tool functioning	40%

showed that there were no significant differences between the groups of participants who interacted with the zSpace or in the CAVE in terms of usability of LARTE tool.

The percentage of usability issues discovered by the end-users in the CAVE ranged from 87 % to 89 %, while in the zSpace end-users discovered from 86 % to 93 % of the interaction problems.

Figures 2 and 3 showed outcomes of the SUS for the CAVE and zSpace users. As reported in Fig. 2, LARTE tool in the CAVE is perceived by end-users as a little bit complex in terms of ease of use (point 2, 35 %) although users have minimal issues in learning how to use the tool functions (point 10, 32 %). The lack of a wizard on how to manipulate the interface, and use the controllers brings the end-users to say that they will need assistance to learn how to use the system (point 4, 57 %).

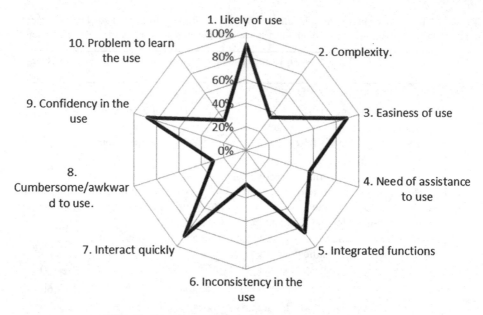

Fig. 2. Users' report about the usability of the CAVE

People who interacted with the zSpace (see Fig. 3) declared that they will need of assistance to learn how to use the LARTE system (point 4, 54 %), moreover, for these participants LARTE resulted complex (point 2, 35 %), and awkward (point 8, 33 %).

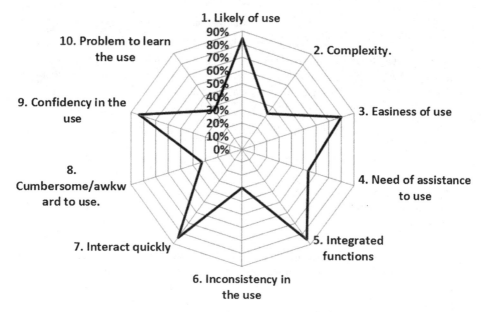

Fig. 3. Users' report about the usability of the zSpace

Nevertheless, participants experienced only minimal issues in learn how to use the tool (point 10, 36 %).

3 Discussion

The overall outcomes of the formative assessment of LARTE application showed that from the end-users' point of view this application was satisfactory. By using the standard of SUS outcomes, proposed by Sauro and Lewis [23], LARTE was usable at level B (75 %) when experienced through the zSpace, and at level A (85 %) when used in the CAVE. However, there are not significant differences in terms of number of problems experienced during the interaction with the prototype, nor in terms of satisfaction scores. Only 10 problems out of 17 are considered severe (or moderate severe) issues by experts. The remained seven issues were considered small problems that designers may solve before the first release. These 7 issues were aggregated to the indications coming from SUS, for instance, the lack of a wizard about the LARTE tool and its main functions. All the remained issues and the feedbacks of the end users will be used to define the next version of LARTE application, before the summative evaluation.

4 Conclusion

Usability assessment of 3D interactive tools is a growing topic in the community of virtual training. The use of standardised tools and reliable approaches and methods of assessment can deeply enhance the overall user experience of the 3D environments, by concurrently increasing the effectiveness of the training experienced in virtual world. This study, by proposing a framework in which AGILE and user centred design principles are mixed together to simplify the redesign of the tool, showed how classic approaches of assessment can be applied to serve the scope of gathering reliable and structured evidences to identify the lacks of a product, and to proceed or discard specific lines of design. Further usability studies are needed in virtual training fields, especially today with portable 3D tools, such as zSpace or Oculus Rift, available on the market. In fact, these portable solutions are opening up the possibility for manufacturers to train their operators with alternative devices (and comparative low costs) to classic CAVE systems.

Acknowledgements. This paper was completed as part of Live Augmented Reality Training Environments (LARTE) – 101509 project. The authors would like to acknowledge the Technology Strategy Board for funding the work.

References

1. de Gomes Sá, A., Zachmann, G.: Virtual reality as a tool for verification of assembly and maintenance processes. Comput. Graph. **23**, 389–403 (1999)

2. Dombrowski, U., Engel, C., Schulze, S.: Changes and challenges in the after sales service due to the electric mobility. In: 2011 IEEE International Conference on Service Operations, Logistics, and Informatics (SOLI), pp. 77–82 (2011)
3. Gaiardelli, P., Resta, B., Martinez, V., Pinto, R., Albores, P.: A classification model for product-service offerings. J. Clean. Prod. **66**, 507–519 (2014)
4. Malmsköld, L., Örtengren, R., Svensson, L.: Improved quality output through computer-based training: an automotive assembly field study. Hum. Factors Ergon. Manuf. Serv. Ind. **25**, 304–318 (2014)
5. Anastassova, M., Burkhardt, J.-M.: Automotive technicians' training as a community-of-practice: implications for the design of an augmented reality teaching aid. Appl. Ergon. **40**, 713–721 (2009)
6. Anastassova, M., Burkhardt, J.-M., Mégard, C., Ehanno, P.: Results from a user-centred critical incidents study for guiding future implementation of augmented reality in automotive maintenance. Int. J. Ind. Ergon. **35**, 67–77 (2005)
7. Mantovani, F.: VR learning: potential and challenges for the use of 3D environments in education and training. In: Riva, G., Galimberti, C. (eds.) Towards Cyberpsychology: Mind, Cognitions and Society in the Internet Age, pp. 207–226. IOS Press, Amsterdam (2003)
8. ISO: ISO 9241-11: 1998 Ergonomic requirements for office work with visual display terminals (VDTs) - Part 11: Guidance on usability. CEN, Brussels (1998)
9. Tichon, J., Burgess-Limerick, R.: A review of virtual reality as a medium for safety related training in mining. J. Health Saf. Res. Pract. **3**, 33–40 (2011)
10. Mantovani, F., Castelnuovo, G., Gaggioli, A., Riva, G.: Virtual reality training for health-care professionals. CyberPsychol. Behav. **6**, 389 (2003)
11. Borsci, S., Kurosu, M., Federici, S., Mele, M.L.: Computer Systems Experiences of Users with and Without Disabilities: An Evaluation Guide for Professionals. CRC Press, Boca Raton (2013)
12. Nielsen, J.: 10 Usability Heuristics for User Interface Design (1995). http://www.nngroup.com/
13. Wharton, C., Rieman, J., Lewis, C., Polson, P.: The cognitive walkthrough method: a practitioner's guide. In: Jakob, N., Robert, L.M. (eds.) Usability Inspection Methods, pp. 105–140. Wiley, New York (1994)
14. Highsmith, J.: Agile Software Development Ecosystems. Addison-Wesley Longman Publishing Co., Inc., Amsterdam (2002)
15. Brooke, J.: SUS: a "quick and dirty" usability scale. In: Jordan, P.W., Thomas, B., Weerdmeester, B.A., McClelland, I.L. (eds.) Usability Evaluation in Industry, pp. 189–194. Taylor & Francis, London (1996)
16. Borsci, S., Macredie, R.D., Barnett, J., Martin, J., Kuljis, J., Young, T.: Reviewing and extending the five-user assumption: a grounded procedure for interaction evaluation. ACM Trans. Comput. Hum. Interact. **20**, 1–23 (2013)
17. Borsci, S., Macredie, R.D., Martin, J.L., Young, T.: How many testers are needed to assure the usability of medical devices? Expert Rev. Med. Devices **11**, 513–525 (2014)
18. Borsci, S., Martin, J.L., Barnett, J.: A grounded procedure for managing data and sample size of a home medical device assessment. In: Kurosu, M. (ed.) HCII/HCI 2013, Part I. LNCS, vol. 8004, pp. 166–175. Springer, Heidelberg (2013)
19. Noor, A.K., Aras, R.: Potential of multimodal and multiuser interaction with virtual holography. Adv. Eng. Softw. **81**, 1–6 (2015)
20. Nielsen, J., Landauer, T.K.: A mathematical model of the finding of usability problems. In: Proceedings of the INTERACT 1993 and CHI 1993 Conference on Human Factors in Computing Systems, pp. 206–213. ACM, Amsterdam (1993)

21. Virzi, R.A.: Refining the test phase of usability evaluation: how many subjects is enough? Hum. Factors **34**, 457–468 (1992)
22. Lewis, J.R.: Usability: lessons learned … and yet to be learned. Int. J. Hum. Comput. Interact. **30**, 663–684 (2014)
23. Sauro, J., Lewis, J.R.: Quantifying the User Experience: Practical Statistics for User Research. Morgan Kaufmann, Burlington (2012)

The Convergence Innovation Competition: Helping Students Create Innovative Products and Experiences via Technical and Business Mentorship

Russ Clark[✉], Matt Sanders, Brian Davidson, Siva Jayaraman,
and Carl DiSalvo

Georgia Institute of Technology Institute for People and Technology,
75 5th St NW, Atlanta, GA 30316, USA
{russ.clark,msanders,bdavidson,
jsiva,carl.disalvo}@gatech.edu

Abstract. The Convergence Innovation Competition is an annual event designed to encourage innovation and entrepreneurship among students from multiple disciplines and experience levels. The competition provides a unique model for engaging industrial partners to work with students through category definition, mentoring and judging. In this paper we describe the evolution of the program over the last eight years, lessons learned and new opportunities for engaging students in a meaningful learning experience.

Keywords: Mobile computing · Student engagement · Entrepreneurship · Innovation · Hackathons · Competitions · Experiential learning

1 Introduction

The Convergence Innovation Competition (CIC) (cic.gatech.edu) is an annual event produced by the GT-RNOC and the Institute for People and Technology (IPaT). This unique competition is open to all Georgia Tech students and is run throughout the Fall and Spring semesters. Each year the categories in the CIC are defined by our industry partners who provide mentorship, judging, and category specific resources which are often available exclusively to CIC competitors. While the competition is not tied to any specific course, competitors are able to take advantage of class partnerships where lecture and lab content, guest lectures, and projects are aligned with competition categories. The student competitors are supported by the GT-RNOC research assistants who provide technical support and shepherd teams through the competition process.

Our primary goal for the CIC is to develop a sustainable model for promoting student innovation and creativity with a strong foundation in both technical sophistication and commercial viability. The program is operated by Georgia Tech faculty and staff, but the funding and other resources for the program come primarily from the industry partners who sponsor the activities and work closely with the teams each year. The students are expected to present both a working, end-to-end prototype of their idea and a business case. The CIC is not a hackfest and it is not a business plan competition,

© Springer International Publishing Switzerland 2015
M. Kurosu (Ed.): Human-Computer Interaction, Part III, HCII 2015, LNCS 9171, pp. 144–153, 2015.
DOI: 10.1007/978-3-319-21006-3_15

but it includes elements of both. The most competitive entries include a strong, validated user experience and a plan for how to attract and sustain users. The prototype implementation leverages converged services, media, networks, services, and platforms. The students who participate in the CIC go on to commercialization, other competitions, as well as internship and job opportunities strengthened by their competition experience.

This paper describes the history, key learnings and experiences of the CIC team.

2   Competitions and Hackathons

Competition are a popular tool for tapping into the talents of large numbers of people to tackle challenging problems [1]. From grand challenges like the XPrize to simple logo designs, competitions are everywhere. In the technology arena, the Hackathon has become an especially popular form of competition.

Hackathons are often touted as opportunities for rapid design and development. However in our research we have found that, by and large, the design and development is, at best, of marginal quality and value. The designs are usually reactionary rather than considered and the code is usually incomplete and often shoddy. And yet, it seems nearly every weekend there is another hackathon, more and more of them addressing another social issue. What then is the appeal of the hackathon and what are they, or what might they be, good for; especially in the domain of social issues or what we call issue-oriented hackathons?

What hackathons seem to offer is an event for building belonging [2]. First and foremost the hackathon is a social event, a place and time at which people gather. This alone has value, particularly within contemporary computing cultures. Work and play mix together at hackathons in ways that are both enjoyable and problematic: pleasurable in the play of mingling and tinkering, but questionable as a mode of speculative labor [3]. More than just belonging to a social event, the hackathon provides the opportunity for participants to perceive that they are belonging and contributing to a social cause. In that sense, we might imagine that hackathons are an opportunity to model new forms of civic engagement [2]. And yet we also need to realize that the ways in which people are participating in social causes is so structured and limited that it may just as likely present social conditions in the most naïve and reductive of ways [3].

Perhaps the best way to approach hackathons is as prototypes for what a new modes of participation might be [4]. Rather than expecting working technology from these events, or even expecting these events to build more robust and engaged communities, these events becomes testbeds for how we might want to or be able to structure new forms of technological citizenship. In this process it is important that we attend to both what works, and even more so, what does not work, what excludes, thwarts, or limits participation, what reproduces the status quo, rather than questioning it.

In designing the CIC, we have intentionally looked beyond the hackathon for a more substantive student engagement. The CIC is a longer term activity, it includes intentional support and mentorship for students, and it gives the students time to iterate on their work. From an administrative perspective, the CIC is a sustained, persistent activity for the organizing team as well as the many faculty members who are engaged across the campus.

3   CIC History

The CIC began as the IMS Research Competition in 2007 (cic.gatech.edu/2007). The initial idea was to run a student competition to find out what students could do with the emerging mobile technology known as the IP Multimedia Subsystem or IMS. The expression "searching for the killer IMS application" was often used to describe the endeavor. The first competition was co-sponsored by Cingular Wireless and Siemens, which later became ATT and Nokia-Siemens Networks. The competition idea was largely driven by the technology and the significant training and support required for students to develop applications in this new space. The sponsors made a significant investment in bringing a full IMS infrastructure to campus and making it available for students to do their development.

The competition was established in a world before the iPhone and Android and before anybody had heard of an AppStore. The state of the art development options were J2ME (Java for Mobile) and Symbian. It was very time consuming and technically challenging for students to build an application and install it on a real phone. It was nearly impossible for them to even consider commercially launching their application because the main pathway for doing so was a multi-year on-boarding process with a wireless carrier.

Because of the daunting learning curve for both the technology and the wireless business, we focused our efforts on removing barriers and reducing the challenges for students. We created a new course in Mobile Application development that was designed to teach enough of both the technology and the wireless carrier business that students could understand the constraints on developing and launching a mobile application. We also created a companion laboratory course that provided significant hands-on access and support with approximately one teaching assistant for every twenty students. Despite this effort and expense, there were still many students who were never able to get their application running on a physical device.

The first competition had four categories, defined based on the target audience for the applications. The categories were: Family, Young Adult/Teen, Business User, Campus Community. In this first year, there were twenty teams who submitted project proposals of which fifteen ultimately submitted a project. Those 15 teams included 41 students, with most teams being 2 or 3 students. The students were drawn primarily from technology majors (CS, ECE) with a few business majors.

The second year operated much the same way with mostly similar results (cic.gatech.edu/2008). The technology continued to be a steep learning curve and the participation level was about the same. One key change was in the category definitions. The user-focused categories of the first year proved to be too narrow and did not resonate with the students. The second year there were two categories simply defined as Innovation and Contextual Use. (Today we would say those are judging criteria used across the categories rather than category titles.)

By the end of the second year, the mobile applications world was dramatically changing. The introduction of the iPhone, followed by Android, and the Mobile AppStores drastically reduced both the technical and the business hurdles for creating and launching a mobile application. It became clear that the focus on IMS technology for application development was no longer necessary. It was a time of regrouping for the GT team and for our industry sponsors. For the third year, the competition was renamed the Convergence Innovation Competition, as it is still known today. The idea of convergence was motivated by the convergence of technologies (e.g. wired and wireless networks), platforms (e.g. mobile phones, tablets, TVs, cars) and users (e.g. business and personal).

In the ensuing years, the competition has grown into a twice annual event with more than 300 participants each year. While most entries include some form of a mobile application, it is no longer a requirement. The participants represent a broader student mix of majors and backgrounds. The technology hurdles are significantly lower and every project includes running prototypes, often already made available in the AppStore. The highlight of the competition is a live demo event where students present their projects to each other and to the panel of judges from across campus and from our industry partners. The industry partners are more diverse as well including technology, transportation, health care and others. For 2014 and 2015, student teams from Georgia Tech's Lorraine campus in Metz, France have also participated with a live demonstration and judging event connected via videoconference.

The competition categories have changed with the technology trends and the priorities of the different industry partners. For three years, we worked closely with a major set top box manufacturer on interactive TV technologies and had several teams developing TV-related applications. Now that "smart TVs" are commonplace in the market, that area has become less interesting for innovation. Recent years have seen "the sharing economy" appear as a popular theme with many people applying the Airbnb model to a steady stream of new application ideas.

Today, the CIC is a successful experiential learning opportunity for students to engage in real world problem solving while learning application development skills. The students are challenged to consider multiple points of view as they discover problems to be solved and possible solutions. They learn the process of ideation and are required to talk to potential users/customers to understand problems before proposing solutions or writing any code.

4 Student Teams

The students who participate in the CIC come from a mix of majors and backgrounds. While the core participation has come from our home department of Computer Science, we have worked to promote as much diversity in the teams and general lab participation as possible. We feel that this is a critical part of the learning experience and key to making the teams and their projects successful. Figure 1 shows one of the tools we have used to explain the skills mix that is required for a successful team. To promote this diversity we have explicitly called out these skills and challenged the students to

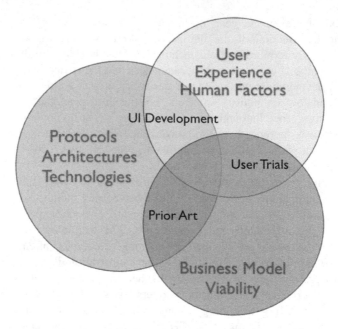

Fig. 1. Building a Team

find the expertise they need to round out their team. Historically, going all the way back to the first year, the most successful teams have followed this advice.

The CIC program is open to all current Georgia Tech students from all majors, both graduate and undergraduate. Historically, the highest participation has been from MS students from CS or related (HCI, ECE) majors. From discussions with students and alumni, we have learned that the practical nature of the projects with emphasis on industry connections has particular appeal to MS students who often have recent work experience and all of whom are actively looking for a job in the next year. We have put significant effort into attracting more undergraduate students to the program and for the last two years have seen almost equal numbers of graduate and undergraduate students involved.

One positive aspect of the student participation in the CIC has been the significant representation of female students participating in and succeeding in the program. As a Computer Science program at an engineering focused school, our programs have traditionally had extremely low (< 10 %) female enrollments. And while both the Institute and department numbers have improved in recent years, they are still disappointing. The CIC on the other hand has been very successful in engaging female students with more than 40 % representation in recent years and with multiple winning teams that were more than half female. From our experience, this is also significantly better representation than most of the hackathons with which we have been involved.

We have worked to build this team diversity over the years through several efforts. We reached out to faculty in specific areas that have been under-represented (e.g. design, business) and helped them to identify ways to integrate their regular class projects and deliverables with the CIC. In several cases those faculty have reported a noticeable improvement in the quality of their class projects after including the CIC demonstrations and judging events as part of their own semester timeline. We also hold regular tutorial sessions and open house events for the campus community on various technologies and skillsets (e.g. connected car, Google glass) and advertise the CIC as part of those events.

Over the years we have observed that the size of the team can be as important as the makeup. While we occasionally see a winning team with two members and once or twice a winning team had five or more members, the optimal team size is three or four people. Generally, a one or two person project does not have enough time to create all of the deliverables in the timeframe of one semester. With more than four members there is an increasing likelihood of friction among team members that often causes more harm than good. Whenever we've seen a successful team with more than four members, the post-mortem interviews tend to reveal that most of the work was done by a core group of three students.

While most students do not go on to commercialize their CIC entries, most do report on the benefits they have gained from the experience and how they used the CIC to help them land a job. The CIC provides students with the specific case experience of addressing a real problem, creating a real solution and having a tangible result that they can demonstrate to a would-be employer.

5   Connection to Industry

The CIC is made possible only through the generous support of our industry partners who sponsor the competition each year through financial, material, and human capital. The program was started as a unique vehicle for connecting industry with academia around a new technology. We have worked to evolve the program into a valuable model that brings value to our partners as well as Georgia Tech and our students.

The original value proposition focused on finding "the killer app" in the ideas brought forth by the students. That proved to be unrealistic for a number of reasons. First, the result of the competition is rarely a product that is ready to launch. In the cases where the participants have gone on to commercial success it has almost always taken several years, a few pivots, and maybe even a complete restart before getting there. Secondly, the sponsoring companies are rarely in a position to act on the ideas themselves and have, at least in a few cases, left the students hanging while the corporate machine tried to figure out how to move forward. In the meantime, the students graduate, get a job, and move on. In short, it does not work if the sponsor's primary objective is to identify Intellectual Property (IP) that they will acquire from the students to commercialize.

Today, we work with each industry partner to identify the most important benefits for them and then work to make those a reality. For many, there is a new technology or capability that the company has or is considering and wants to encourage people to use. For others, they are simply interested in taking the pulse of what types of trends are interesting to students. In many cases, the CIC is an important part of the recruiting program for future employees.

For the students, the benefits of the industry participation are one of the primary advantages of the CIC versus other projects or competitions. The industry input through class presentations, advising sessions, open houses and judging events provide valuable perspective to help the students understand the business space and the constraints of domain they are working in. The students learn to answer important questions like: Who is your customer? Who is using it? Who pays for it? What are the legal/licensing challenges? Who is the competition? What happens if you are successful?

The funding provided by the sponsors for the CIC supports the events and prizes but the bulk of the funding pays for the people involved whose job it is to help the students succeed. The GT-RNOC employs from ten to twenty student employees who work to keep the lab open for students, run tutorials, create sample code for new devices, and generally support the wide range of tools and technologies that are constantly appearing. With the breadth of skills required it does not work to have a few people who try to become experts on everything. Instead, there are specialists in iOS, Android, wearables, connected car interfaces, Arduino, etc. And, since presentation and business understanding are also important, we have staff with graphic design and communications skills to help students refine their presentations as well. Just as every student team needs a broad set of skills to succeed, the lab staff needs a broad set of skills to support them.

We describe the CIC ecosystem in terms of three key components: Partners, Resources and Innovation. (See Fig. 2) Our partners come industry and from across

Fig. 2. CIC Ecosystem

campus in research and academic units. Many of our partners provide direct financial support in the form of sponsorship but they also provide access, insight and guidance to the students. The resources provided for the students to support their work are extensive and include lab space, classes, workshops, devices and platforms [5]. And finally, the students are supported throughout the innovation process by mentors who guide them from ideation through customer discovery and productization.

6 Discussion and Lessons Learned

Through our experience in developing and producing the CIC we have learned many lessons about how to work with and motivate students and how to help them be successful. The CIC has changed greatly and it will no doubt continue to do so as the technologies change and the motivations and interests of both sponsors and students evolve. This section highlights some of our most important lessons learned.

6.1 Avoid Intellectual Property (IP)

The single most valuable lesson from the first two years of the competition was in how to handle IP rights for the student competitors. As part of the first year, significant cash prizes were given to the winners in exchange for the students granting "first right to commercialize" to the sponsor. This turned out to be a major issue for the students and many chose not to participate despite the financial incentive. One team even stated that they "would not give us their best idea, just their second best."

Beginning with the third year, the competition rules clearly establish that the students retain all rights to any IP they create as part of the CIC. And every year, several students will ask specifically about this issue to make sure this is the case before they will proceed. The reality is that these projects rarely generate true, patentable results. When they do, we work with the teams to file invention disclosures and prepare for patent applications. We also coach them on how to present their project and demonstrate it without disclosing the details of any patentable secrets. We encourage them to focus on getting something working and getting it in front of real users to get feedback as early as possible.

6.2 Big Prizes Are not Necessary

Our first competition included a total of $100,000 in cash prize money. The overall winning team collected $30,000. This made for great advertising and drew some large crowds to the informational events but it did not attract the right kind of student. Despite attracting large numbers of students looking for free food, this approach did not engage the most talented and dedicated people who would ultimately be successful in the competition. Since year three, we never announce the specific prizes until they are awarded at the judging event. Prizes tend to be less than $1000 in value, such as an iPad or XBox. The students we are looking for are better motivated by the opportunity to show off their ideas and to launch their project.

The other major issue with large prizes is the legal baggage associated with competition law. For the first two years the competition operated under strict rules and the students were bound by a legal contract as part of their participation. This greatly reduced our agility in responding to challenges during the course of the semester (e.g. a planned technology was not available in time) and put unnecessary limits on everything from team size to which students were eligible.

6.3   Video Presentation

The student teams are required to create a two to three minute pitch video describing their application, the problem solved, key value propositions, use cases, business case, etc. We started doing this in the mobile applications class to speed up the class presentations and scale to larger class sizes. We found that the assignment brought several key benefits for the competition as well. First, it forces the students to rehearse and refine their presentation. Second, it creates an artifact for future use in showing off the student's work. The videos from all of the winning entries for the last several years are available on the CIC website (cic.gatech.edu). This is valuable both for us and for our industry partners. The students also benefit from having a portfolio artifact to share with prospective employers.

6.4   Live Demo and Judging Event

For the first several years the judging was done online from written project reports and in closed-door presentations. The awards were then given out several days later at a separate event. The CIC now culminates with a showcase where all participating finalists set up their posters and demos in a trade-show style event. The students spend the first hour practicing their pitches with each other and the lab staff. Then, they spend about two hours demonstrating for the judges who are walking around the room, scoring each entry and voting on the winners. The winners are announced at the end of the event.

This event serves several important goals. First, it allows the students to celebrate their success with their peers and show off their work to each other and the campus community. Second, it forces the students to practice both their "elevator pitch" for their idea and their demonstration to make sure that the application really works as planned. The most successful teams are ready to hand their phone to a judge and allow them to use the application themselves. And perhaps most importantly, the judging event provides the industry partners with a phenomenal opportunity to interact with the students directly, learn about emerging trends, and identify promising talent. For the last several years, the event has been attended by several representatives from the sponsoring partners including executives that have noted to us what a unique opportunity it is for them to interact with the students.

References

1. Haller, J., Bullinger, A., Moslein, K.: Innovation Contests – Tapping Into the Wisdom of the Crowd. Bus. Inf. Syst. Eng. **3**(2), 103–106 (2011)
2. DiSalvo, C., Gregg, M., Lodato, T.: Building belonging. Interactions **21**(4), 58–61 (2014)
3. Gregg, M., DiSalvo, C.: The trouble with white hats. N. Inq. (2013)
4. Lodato, T., DiSalvo, C.: Issue-Oriented Hackathons as Material Participation. New Media and Society. Forthcoming 2015 (2015)
5. Sanders, M., Clark, R., MacIntyre, B., Davidson, B.: GTJourney: the importance of accessible rich data sources to enable innovation. Paper presented at the Human Computer Interaction International, Los Angeles, CA (2015)

Graphic Visualization of Probabilistic Traffic/Trajectory Predictions in Mobile Applications. A First Prototype and Evaluations for General Aviation Purposes

Giuseppe Frau[1,3(✉)], Francesca De Crescenzio[2],
and Damiano Taurino[3]

[1] Faculty of Engineering, Roma III University,
Via della Vasca Navale 79/81, Rome, Italy
giuseppe.frau@dblue.it
[2] Department of Industrial Engineering, University of Bologna,
Via Zamboni 33, Bologna, Italy
francesca.decrescenzio@unibo.it
[3] Deep Blue srl, Piazza Buenos Aires 20, Rome, Italy
damiano.taurino@dblue.it

Abstract. The present work describes the interactive prototype and the preliminary evaluation results of a tool dedicated to the light General Aviation pilot's community. The tool's interface has been developed through an Android tablet application and aims at supporting the pilots in the task of staying "well-clear" from the surrounding traffic by presenting them the long-term prediction of the flights. The initial results and the approach of a heuristic evaluation conducted with five experts coming from the fields of user-experience, aviation and automotive are discussed along with the improvements in the design of the user-interface focusing on the trajectory depictions.

Keywords: User-interface design · Heuristic evaluation · Light general aviation · Trajectory prediction visualization

1 Introduction

Light General Aviation (Light GA) pilots represent a little known category of users compared to the commercial ones. These pilots fly small aircraft in uncontrolled airspaces and rely on visual means to navigate and to keep themselves separated from the surrounding traffic. When navigating by visual means, Visual Flight Rules (VFR) are applied to operate the aircraft. Moreover, pilots flying under VFR conditions and in uncontrolled airspaces are not bound to submit any flight plan to any sort of authority. By contrast, in the Commercial Aviation segment, Instrumental Flight Rules (IFR) are applied and flights are operated in controlled airspaces for which formal flight plans are submitted.

Navigation and separation by visual means, however, have several limitations that may lower the safety of the flight [1]. Between 2009 and 2013, for example, EASA reported a number of 30 mid-air collisions for the Light GA segment within the

© Springer International Publishing Switzerland 2015
M. Kurosu (Ed.): Human-Computer Interaction, Part III, HCII 2015, LNCS 9171, pp. 154–164, 2015.
DOI: 10.1007/978-3-319-21006-3_16

European airspaces [2]. As a comparison, in the Commercial Aviation segment, a number of 4 mid-air collisions have been registered between 2004 and 2013 [2]. Such data solicit the need for more powerful decision support tools to provide information and interact with data that can increase the pilot situation awareness (SA). Concerning the projection component of SA a major issue is in designing tools that can effectively support pilots in taking a safe decision. In this context they rely on projections built upon their experience and their knowledge of the traffic they fly in.

The purposes of this paper are (a) to present a prototype tool dedicated to light GA pilots and developed within the ProGA[1] project aiming at improving their traffic awareness and their safety by the provision of long-term predictions of the surrounding flights, and (b) to show the initial results of the evaluation phase.

The first part of the paper is dedicated to the description of the prototype. After a general introduction is given, the concept at the base of the algorithm for the long-term trajectory prediction is briefly outlined. The following sections are devoted to the user-interface description.

Section 3 defines the method used for the evaluation along with its rationale. Finally, Sect. 4 shows the results of such approach, while conclusions are drawn in the last of the work.

Prediction Algorithm Concept. This section presents the concept on which the trajectory prediction algorithm of the ProGA system is based. This algorithm is the main source of information of the prototype evaluated in this work but it is worth to underline that its functioning has to be considered out of the scope of the evaluation.

The kinematic state (position, speed, turning rate, etc.) of an aircraft determines the so-called state-based prediction, which is obtained by plugging the kinematic state into a dynamical model of the aircraft motion. State-based predictions are reliable over a short timeframe (less than 30 s) but may prove more and more untrustworthy if casted over an increasing time interval. This behavior is in fact inherent to all kind of predictions.

The ability of casting reliable long-term predictions (2 to 5 min ahead) is an asset for ProGA because it is expected to likely increase the situational awareness and safety of the user. For this reason ProGA introduces intent-based predictions, which determine the future trajectory of the aircraft exploiting the notion of flight intent, i.e. the sequence of straight legs that the pilot has planned to fly; see [3] for further details.

Flight intents may be shared by pilots prior to takeoff or may be statistically inferred from a (local) base of knowledge describing recurring patterns and behaviors common to GA flights operating in a certain area and under specific conditions. ProGA considers those two classes of inputs, i.e. shared flight intents and inferred ones, as complementary to each other. The prediction algorithm works in fact with a subset of flight intents picked up from the union of the declared intent, if any, and the most statistically significant recurring paths. The final prediction is carried out by means of Monte Carlo simulations of the aircraft motion along the intents selected as above. The interested reader is referred to [3] for further information about the ProGA prediction algorithm.

---

[1] Probabilistic 4D Trajectories of Light General Aviation Operations www.proga.nlr.nl.

2   Prototype Description

The present section illustrates the object of evaluation of the present work, namely the user interface layer of the tablet application developed for supporting the pilot in the usage of ProGA during the in-flight phase.

The ProGA in-flight interface consists of a tablet application developed using the Android 5.0 SDK. The application is built around five main components:

- A moving map constantly centered on the own-ship position and oriented towards the own-ship speed direction;
- The own-ship and the surrounding traffic representations;
- The traffic information label;
- The global functions menu;
- The prediction visualizations.

The tablet application represents the layer for human interaction of a more articulated prototype, which consists of other two blocks, namely the traffic simulator (in which the prediction algorithm is also plugged) and the flight simulator for future tests with real pilots.

Moving Map. The moving map component represents the main view of the application. Its purpose is to provide awareness to the pilot about his/her geographic position and, at the same time, to work as a container of the surrounding traffic representation and of the predicted trajectories. The map component is provided by the Android SDK and it uses the Google Maps v2 APIs that allows the drawing of 2D primitives on the map (functionality that has been used for drawing the predicted trajectories). Figure 6 shows the main view of the application including the moving map component, the traffic representation and the global functions menu. The ProGA moving map follows the behavior of the standard moving maps to which most of the people are by now used to. As such it responds to the standard gestures such as pinch-to-zoom, pan-to-move etc.

Own-ship and Traffic Representation. All the aircraft in the map are depicted using a colored arrow with a white border. Since the background behind the arrows is dependent on the current area -hence the colors are not predictable- the white border assures a minimum level of contrast also in the situations in which the color of the arrow is similar to the color of the current background.

The aircraft positions are updated at the same frequency of the map and of the own-ship ones. Moreover, while the color of the own-ship arrow is constantly black, the traffic arrows follow a color-coding scheme that depends on two factors, namely (Table 1).

1. The difference of altitude between the own-ship and the specific aircraft;
2. The result of the "Monitor" functionality for that specific aircraft;

Traffic Information Label. While the information about the position of the surrounding traffic is naturally conveyed by the depiction on the map relatively to the own-ship one, there are a set of other information—namely the aircraft identification number, and the altitude- in which the pilot may be interested and that is displayed on demand in order to avoid cluttering on the map view.

Table 1. Color-coding schema for traffic representation

Condition	ABS(own-ship alt – aircraft alt) >= 500 ft.	ABS(own-ship alt – aircraft alt) <= 500 ft.	Dangerous
Representation	▲	▲	▲

In order to obtain these information, the pilot has to interact with the traffic arrow by a simple tap and, in this way, opening the so called Information label which consists of a floating box placed nearby the selected aircraft. Through the information label, the pilot can accomplish two goals:

1. Obtaining altitude and identification number about the selected aircraft.
2. Access to the prediction request commands: a set of buttons that allow the pilot to enquiry the system about the long-term prediction of the selected aircraft.

This double goal is reflected by the two possible modes that the information label is able to assume. In the compact mode, the label only shows the additional information of the aircraft i.e. altitude and identification number. In the expanded mode, the label size is augmented to host the prediction request buttons (Fig. 1).

The identification number of the aircraft (in these cases "NINJA34") is reported on the top left of the floating box, while the altitude (2000 feet) is on the top right. Each time the label is tapped, it switches from the compact mode to the expanded one and vice versa. The label can also be totally hidden by tapping outside of the box anywhere on the map view.

As previously mentioned, the information label also hosts the prediction request buttons. In the worst case, for requesting a prediction, the user needs to tap once on the target aircraft, then expand the label, and finally select the desired prediction time horizon. The system offers four possible time horizons for the prediction: from 2 min to 5 min with steps of 1 min. However, when the user selects a time horizon, the system doesn't merely ask for that time horizon only. A prediction request of 5 min would generate a cloud of point far enough to be isolated from the aircraft that generated it. For this reason, the system splits each request in a set of multiple requests of incremental time horizons until the target one is reached. For example a 4 min prediction request by the user generates a set of requests for predictions at 1 min, 2 min, 3 min and finally 4 min in the future. This allows the system to build an actual trajectory (or corridor) by merging the resulting data.

Prediction Visualizations. Within the developed prototype two main classes of data coming from the central system can be identified:

- Corridors data: they can be considered as the raw data produced by the system. When a prediction for a given aircraft (indicated by the pilot) is requested, the

Fig. 1. Traffic information label expanded mode

prediction algorithm produces a cloud of possible points in which that aircraft is likely to be in the future;
- Elaborated data: pilots can also enquire the system through the Hotspots tool and through the Monitor too. This two functionalities still use the same prediction capabilities but that add a processing stage to the resulting data aiming at finding more punctual information i.e. the hotpots position and the potential intruders.

The major efforts in the design and development of the visualization have been mainly directed to the first class of data. Three alternative depictions are implemented in the prototype. The following subsections explain all the depiction modes and the rationale behind them.

Note that the design of these depiction had to take into account the limitation of computing capacity in the mobile device used for the realization of the prototype. In fact, although the mobile device has been chosen inside a range of current top devices, the amount of data received and the constant need to update the whole presented scenario, still require more powerful computation resources. The following subsections illustrate the three alternative depiction modes designed for the prototype.

Particles Visualization Mode. The particles visualization is an attempt to depict the prediction results without adding any extra-processing or information layer to it. Each point inside the cloud coming from the prediction algorithm is considered as a singular entity –the particle- carrying no other information but its position. Figure 2 presents a screenshot in which a prediction of 5 min in the future for the aircraft placed on the right of the map was requested. As previously mentioned, data about 4, 3, 2 and 1 min in the future is also requested when the system is enquired; considering the full set of received data, some emergent properties can be deduced from the depiction:

- Continuity: the particles tend to naturally form a corridor if the prediction is sharp enough for the target aircraft.
- Probability Conveyance: each particle is assigned with a constant size and level of transparency [4, 5], therefore, the formed corridor tent to be more opaque when more particles overlap (even partially) at the same location, hypothetically conveying a concept of higher-probability for these parts of the corridor.

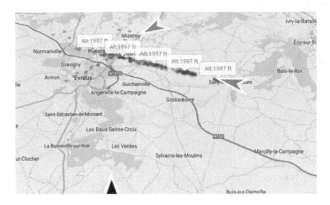

Fig. 2. Particles visualization mode

These two properties, however, are not verified in the following circumstance: the ProGA system defines a set of parameters useful to tune the algorithm behavior. The number of particles used to cast the predictions is defined by one of these parameters. A high number of particles are advisable in order to have a good quality of the results. However, when brought on a mobile device, the number of data points can't be too large due to the computational limitations. If the chosen number of particles used to cast the prediction is too low, the emerging corridor turns into a series of circular clouds of points breaking the both the described properties.

Heatmap Visualization Mode. The heatmap visualization aims at representing the natural evolution of the Particles one and it is designed to make explicit the two emergent properties of continuity and probability conveyance. In this implementation, the locations with higher probability of being occupied by the target aircraft in the selected time frame are represented with a shade of red, while as the probability lowers the hue associated tends to the color green. Hypothetically, heatmap visualizations should naturally convey the density of the data-points and at the same time provide an idea of the trajectory evolution when the uncertainty in the result is not high enough to uniformly spread the points in the different directions. Figure 3 shows a screenshot of a 5 min prediction casted for the aircraft on the right side of the image.

Connected Particles Visualization Mode Finally, the connected particles depiction aims at overcoming the limitations of the Particle one when used with a limited set of data points and at the same time is directed to provide a sharper view of the trajectory. To accomplish these objectives, this design introduces some variants to the Particle visualization mode (Fig. 4):

- Particles representation is sensibly bigger in order to have overlaps circles even when fewer particles are presented on the map.
- The particles of each prediction group are connected with the particles of the previous and the next group. For example, let's consider a situation in which a

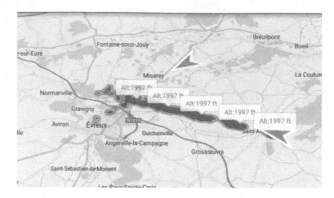

Fig. 3. Heatmap visualization mode

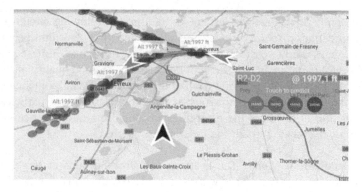

Fig. 4. Connected particles visualization mode

3 min prediction is requested. This prediction is broken in three sub-predictions of 1, 2 and finally 3 min. At this point, all the particles resulting from the 1-min. predictions get connected by a line with the respective particle of the 2 min group.

3   Evaluation Approach

In the previous sections, a prototype for the light GA pilots has been described, both under its functioning and human interaction sides. The present section illustrates the approach that has been followed in the initial evaluation of the prototype. Being the prototype on its early maturity level, the choice of the approach has been the one of the heuristic evaluation with experts [7]. However, since the application context represents a challenging factor -due to its criticalities and domain complexity-, an accurate choice of the evaluators was required. In particular the selection criteria was such to maximize the number of expertise fields within the all set of evaluators. Five experts were selected for the analysis. The fields of expertise for each evaluator are summarized in the Table 2.

Table 2. Expertise fields of the selected evaluators

Evaluator ID	Fields of expertise
Evaluator 1	Automotive, Human Factors, Aviation
Evaluator 2	Human Factors, Aviation
Evaluator 3	User-Experience, Aviation Safety, Patient Safety
Evaluator 4	User-Experience, Usability, Healthcare, Aviation
Evaluator 5	Usability, Automotive, Aviation

After being introduced to the concepts of the prototype, each evaluator has been individually asked to inspect the application, explore it and ask questions when needed. Evaluators were then asked to provide their feedbacks about the prototype. In particular feedbacks on the usability issues and on the quality of the trajectory prediction visualizations were stressed. In order to justify every found issue, the evaluators were asked to find possible consequences due to the presence of the identified issue.

The issues were, at this point, aggregated categorized and ranked. Categorization is based on which of the famous Nielsen's heuristics [6] they were found to go against. The ranking of each issue, conversely, followed a two-step process.

(a) The visibility index "V" was calculated, namely, how many evaluators detected the issue;

(b) The impact index "I" was decided on a scale between 1 and 3 where the highest value was associated to the issues directly impacting on the main user's goal, 2 was assigned to issues indirectly impacting the main goal or impacting secondary functions; finally, the value of I was assigned to all the other issues.

The final was obtained through the application of the following formula.

$$r = (I \times n) + V$$

Where n is the number of evaluators. The obtained raking has the property of giving more importance to the issues with the highest impact, and at the same time generating a local impact order based on the visibility, ergo the issues with the same impact are ordered by their visibility value.

4   Results of the Evaluation

The evaluation with the experts highlighted a number of 28 unique issues in the prototyped user interface. Each evaluator found on average 10 issues (not unique) during the review of the prototype. Looking at the unique issues, the trend shown in Fig. 5 was found to be followed in their identification, while the distribution of the issues among the not-respected Nielsen's heuristics is presented in Fig. 6.

The trend shows a growing number of overall issues that is likely to reach a plateau after the fifth expert [7], while the plateau for the important ones is reached in the very early stages of the evaluation.

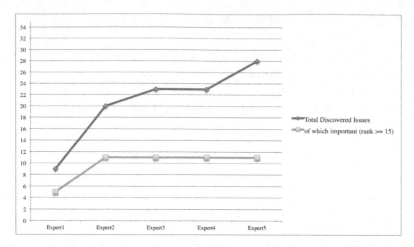

Fig. 5. Discovered issues after each expert evaluation. The upper trend shows the cumulative number of unique issues reached after the evaluation of each expert. The bottom one, instead, outlines the cumulative number of those issues considered important taking into account the original rank scale (r >= 15 on a range from 1 to 20).

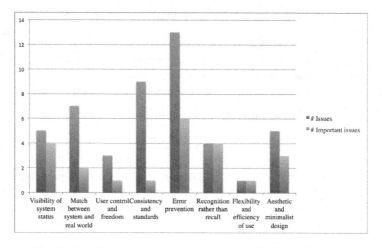

Fig. 6. Distribution of the issues among the Nielsen's heuristics

In the issues distribution mainly two aspects can be noticed: from one hand, the found issues mainly targeted the heuristic regarding *"Error prevention"*, *"Consistency and standards"*, *"Match between system and real world"*, *"Visibility of system status"* and *"Aesthetic and minimalist design"*. From the other hand, when looking at the portion of the issues considered important by the developed ranking method, a sensible flattening of some heuristics -that we can now consider as categories for the issues- can be appreciated. For instance, the *"Consistency and standards"* heuristic loses out 8 points passing from the total view to the important issues one, while categories like

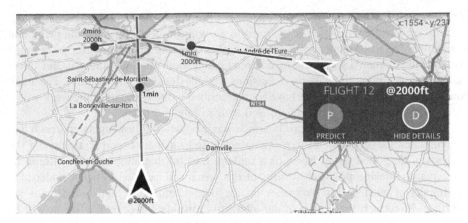

Fig. 7. Proposal of redesign

"Visibility of system status" and *"Recognition rather than recall"* do not experience such a sensible reduction.

Finally, considering output of the experts' analysis and in particular the most important issues, a redesign of the prediction visualization was produced and it is here presented (Fig. 7).

The redesign aims at solving the following identified top-issues:

(1) Intrusiveness of the prediction visualizations, causing cluttering on the screen and possible confusion with consequent disregard of the main function of the tool;
(2) Lack of the temporal dimension indication on the trajectory: causing difficulties or the even the impossibility for the user to interpret the output and possibly leading to mistakes in the decision making process;
(3) Lack of the own-ship prediction: in order to properly understand whether the surrounding traffic is going to cross the own-ship trajectory, the indication of such information must be presented for comparison purposes and it is considered a fundamental support for the main goal of the tool.

The re-design aims at solving these issues by providing a graphical notation of the time dimension, which is represented in a consistent way both on the intruder prediction and on the own-ship one. Moreover, in order to avoid cluttering, only the trajectory with highest probability is presented while the alternative ones are displayed on demand.

5 Conclusions

This work presented the prototype of a tool for GA pilots aiming at supporting the task of *"staying well clear"* from the surrounding traffic. In addition, a first heuristic evaluation was conducted.

From the design and development point of view several challenges had to be addressed: long-term prediction (from 2 to 6 min) is a difficult task when applied to light GA flights. The result of this prediction is of probabilistic nature and carries a high quantity of uncertainty, which is expected to grow as the look-ahead of the prediction goes farther. As a consequence, in order to exploit this kind of data we need to design a visualization framework capable of communicating both the potentially useful information for the pilot to make his decisions and its level of uncertainty. The main components of the user interface have been described in the first part of the work with a focus on the prediction visualizations and their rationale.

The heuristic evaluation of this interface was conducted following an approach that contemplated the selection of five evaluators based on their expertise fields and the analysis of the found issues based on a ranking method that allowed us to inform the subsequent re-design proposal. Results of this work will be used to better understand the impact of each design parameter on the overall efficiency and usability of the interface. Moreover, the design of the interactive display for general aviation will be further refined. This is one of the first attempts to introduce the visualization of uncertain data to support the human in the estimation of the projection of events in the operational environment of general aviation. Except the meteorological data, which are the uncertainty that the pilots are used to deal with, the evolution of the general aviation traffic is another component that needs to be introduced in the cockpits HCIs in order to increase the safety.

References

1. Graham, Walton, Orr, Robert H.: Separation of air traffic by visual means: an estimate of the effectiveness of the see-and-avoid doctrine. Proc. IEEE **58**(3), 337–361 (1970)
2. EASA Annual Safety Review 2013. http://easa.europa.eu/newsroom-and-events/general-publications/annual-safety-review-2013
3. Lancia, C., et al.: Traffic predictions supporting general aviation. In: Fourth SESAR Innovation Days Conference
4. Bertin, J., Berg, W.J.: Semiology of Graphics: Diagrams, Networks, Maps. University of Wisconsin, Madison (1983)
5. MacEachren, A.M., et al.: Visualizing geospatial information uncertainty: What we know and what we need to know. Cartography Geographic Inf. Sci. **32**(3), 139–160 (2005)
6. Nielsen, J.: Enhancing the explanatory power of usability heuristics. In: Proceedings of the SIGCHI Conference on Human Factors in Computing Systems. ACM (1994)
7. Nielsen, J., Rolf, M.: Heuristic evaluation of user interfaces. In: Proceedings of the SIGCHI Conference on Human Factors in Computing Systems. ACM (1990)

Building Mobile Software Ecosystems -
A Practical Approach

Steffen Hess[1(✉)], Susanne Braun[1], Johannes Feldhaus[2], Marco Hack[2],
Felix Kiefer[2], Dominik Magin[1], Matthias Naab[1], Dominik Richter[1],
Torsten Lenhart[1], and Marcus Trapp[1]

[1] Fraunhofer IESE, Kaiserslautern, Germany
{steffen.hess,susanne.braun,dominik.magin,
matthias.naab,dominik.richter,torsten.lenhart,
marcus.trapp}@iese.fraunhofer.de
[2] John Deere ETIC and ISG, Kaiserslautern, Germany
{FeldhausJohannes,HackMarco,
KieferFelix}@JohnDeere.com

Abstract. Mobile apps are gaining great importance in the world of business software. Developers' intentions are to build apps that support a specific piece of functionality with great user experience, business often needs to cover a large spectrum of functionality. The results are Mobile software ecosystems (MSE), which usually consist of a large number of apps supporting a certain type of business and combine the strengths of multiple service providers. At a first glance, developing mobile software might look simple. Doing it for business and at an ecosystem scale makes it extremely challenging in practice. Initiating an MSE means to come up with an attractive set of apps that provide adequate openness so that other companies can contribute to them and increase the value of the ecosystem for customers. This paper describes an approach to build MSEs in their initial version. This approach is based on software engineering state-of-the-art practices from requirements engineering, user experience (UX) engineering, and software architecture. The paper elaborates the specifics of MSEs and describes how they can be addressed in the approach. The approach has been applied in a large-scale industrial case study in the agricultural domain in a joint project of John Deere and Fraunhofer IESE. Within that case study, lessons learned with regard to user experience and software architecture are derived and described in detail. Practitioners setting up an MSE can avoid these pitfalls by taking our lessons learned into account.

Keywords: Mobile · App ecosystem · Practical experiences · Human-computer-interaction · Software architecture · User experience

1 Introduction

Mobile apps are gaining great importance in the world of business software. Developers' intentions are to build apps that support a specific (usually small) piece of functionality with great user experience, whereas business often needs to cover a large spectrum of functionality. Thus, there is a trend to provide multiple apps, each of them

© Springer International Publishing Switzerland 2015
M. Kurosu (Ed.): Human-Computer Interaction, Part III, HCII 2015, LNCS 9171, pp. 165–177, 2015.
DOI: 10.1007/978-3-319-21006-3_17

providing a decent amount of functionality. Therefore, companies have to develop and maintain a large number of business apps which are interconnected and still easy to use, and which share companies' look & feel. Furthermore, companies are collaborating more and more to provide added-value products and services for their users, which neither of the involved companies could provide on their own. This is directly reflected in their business software which requires the integration and alignment of their software offerings and thus their mobile business apps. The results are mobile software eco-systems (MSE), which usually consist of a large number of apps supporting a certain type of business and combine the strengths of multiple service providers. "A software ecosystem consists of the set of software solutions that enable, support and automate the activities and transactions by the actors in the associated social or business eco-system and the organizations that provide these solutions." [1].

At a first glance, developing mobile software might look simple. Doing it for business and at an ecosystem scale makes it extremely challenging in practice. Initiating an MSE means to come up with an attractive set of apps that provide adequate openness so that other companies can contribute to them and increase the value of the ecosystem for customers. Providing a great and consistent user experience across apps, platforms, devices, and form factors is really challenging. MSEs do not contain only mobile apps. For business software, a tight integration with existing IT infrastructure and potentially new backend software is necessary. Many challenges in MSEs are related to the han-dling of data: Due to their many sensors and multiple connections (e.g., WLAN, Bluetooth, NFC), mobile devices provide a lot of data sources and communication possibilities. Providing always the best possible user experience requires an excellent understanding of the domain and creative solutions. Sharing large amounts of data can be challenging, as well as sharing data among apps on the same device (e.g. on iOS), but sharing data between apps of different providers can be especially challenging as there might be the need to restrict access on a very fine-grained level.

This is only a small excerpt of aspects that in the end determine the user experience and the success of a mobile software ecosystem. In this paper, we want to describe our approach (Sect. 2) and report our lessons learned (Sect. 3) from developing an MSE that is used as an extended enterprise resource planning system running on iOS as well as on Android as a native solution. This approach has evolved from many software engineering best-practices and was refined with the learnings of multiple projects with industrial customers.

2   Approach and Application in a Case Study

In this section, we describe our development approach for setting up an MSE. Prac-titioners, which plan to initiate and develop an MSE, should work on the following four questions:

- **What is my company's maturity regarding mobile app development?**
- **What is the mobility potential of my application domain?**
- **What should our customers and users experience?**
- **What is the best technical realization?**

Before starting to develop an MSE we recommend to assess your company's maturity regarding mobile app development. Therefore, in Sect. 2.1 we describe typical maturity stages we experienced in a large number of projects with industrial partners in various application domains. Our experience shows that it is hard to decide which business processes or tasks will be supported by mobile apps and even harder which ones will not be supported. To underline this assessment of the mobility potential of an application domain we describe our mPOTENTIAL method in Sect. 2.2. As mentioned before, a great user experience is crucial for mobile business apps. Due to the larger number of apps within an MSE, each single app will not get the same attention as in a single app development scenario. To assure the expected user experience we introduce our mConcAppt method in Sect. 2.3. Each application domain and systems class has its own architectural drivers that support architectural decisions. Section 2.4 therefore introduces typical architectural drivers for MSEs.

We have applied and refined our approach in numerous projects with industrial customers in several application domains. In this paper, we specifically focus on one MSE which we developed in a large-scale case study of John Deere and Fraunhofer IESE. We illustrate aspects and specifics of the approach with examples from this case study.

Key stakeholders in the agricultural domain are operators of machines and owners or managers of farms. Additionally, there are contracting companies that offer services like harvesting to farmers and own a large set of machines and employ further operators.

Key elements in an agricultural ecosystem are operators that use machines to conduct certain field or transport operations. Machines are often equipped with so-called implements that are specific to certain operations, like a harvester implement. Managers are planning and supervising the agricultural operations and are adequately assigning machines and operators to certain operations on a specific field. Large farms own hundreds of fields, machines and employ numerous operators.

While modern agricultural machines are already equipped with proprietary displays and software, there is a trend towards using standard mobile devices for further supporting applications. Similarly, existing desktop-based planning software is also accompanied by further mobile solutions for managers. Thus, mobile devices like pads and phones are gaining more and more importance.

Additionally, smart devices add further value: iBeacons can be used to track the position of equipment, and wearables like watches and glasses allow further new interactions for operators.

All mobile apps and devices need connection and integration in order to optimally support the work on a farm. Thus, at least one backend system is necessary in order to allow data transfer and orchestration. Further other sources of information can complement an agricultural MSE: existing agricultural software systems might be included and software services like one providing weather data or map data are beneficial.

2.1   Maturity Stages Towards Mobile Software Ecosystems

The typical development stages of an MSE are illustrated in Fig. 1. In **stage 1 (first app)**, companies usually start with a first app that is individually designed and delivered in a good quality. The challenges are limited to the construction of the app user interface and local data storage – usually a company look & feel is applied in a hands-on way. Often, existing backend interfaces are simply reused for the app without mobile specific adjustments to demonstrate the feasibility. With respect to stage 1 the resulting quality is mainly based on applying a sound user centered design technique that ensures that the individual requirements are met and a good user experience is provided. Regarding the backend services, the most quality-critical aspect is whether they can deliver the right data in the right time, otherwise UX is compromised.

In **stage 2 (many single apps)**, companies deal with the existence of many single apps that are not necessarily connected and usually delivered by different development groups, business units, suppliers etc. This usually leads to potential inconsistencies with regard to all software engineering disciplines. Technically, the treatment of backend services is often uncoordinated and becomes harder with an increasing number of single apps.

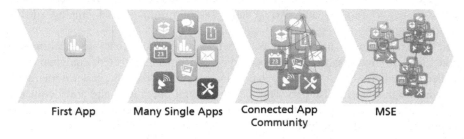

First App	Many Single Apps	Connected App Community	MSE

Fig. 1. Mobile software ecosystem development stages

In **stage 3 (connected app community)**, the rising ecosystem gains a lot of maturity by aligning the apps with a uniform UX concept and introducing consequent connections among apps, e.g. for navigation and data exchange. Technically, this step often comes with a consolidation of backend services and their consequent alignment with the needs of the mobile apps. Mostly, this means that the backend services for mobile apps are different from those serving for other purposes, like data exchange with other systems or web interfaces.

In **stage 4 (app ecosystem)**, the state of a mobile software ecosystem is reached. It goes beyond the app community by involving different organizations contributing to the app ecosystem for added overall value. It is open towards the extension with further apps and still has a focus on adequate and consistent UX, which might also mean an intended differentiation along company boundaries of the contributors. Technically, this stage requires a well-aligned communication across company boundaries and clear concepts for data exchange, which strongly increases security demands.

In the described large-scale case study, we developed an MSE that belongs to stage 4 of the ecosystem scale.

2.2 Mobility Potential Analysis

When developing an MSE the application domain provides very individual and unique constraints. It is critical to clearly understand these specifics of the application domain and the companies involved to evaluate the mobility potential.

The described case study takes place in the agricultural domain where we are facing a scenario with a focus on online/offline capability, large amounts of precise data due to precision farming techniques and very individual user requirements. Therefore, we applied a mobility potential analysis (mPOTENTIAL [2]) that consists of the following stages:

1. The **definition of goals and constraints** defines the global goal that the MSE should fulfill based on the overall company strategy. Another major outcome of this stage is that the scope and possible cooperation partners are already drafted.
2. **Identification of relevant business areas** deals with the systematic analysis and the definition of business areas that are promising from a business perspective. The result is a prioritization that supports the evolution strategy of the MSE.
3. After that, the most promising business areas are analyzed with respect to the **involved roles and business processes**. The goal is to identify possible mobile touchpoints that could be supported by an app and provide both, business benefit and user benefit.
4. The mobility potential analysis is concluded with an **ideation phase** that evolves the intial app ideas a bit further so that app ideas are basically ready to decide if the app should be part of the MSE and to determine what kind of app we are going to build.

Those four steps described above may sound simple but as they deliver valuable results and we expect MSEs to grow and get more and more complex, we assume that it is necessary to perform them continuously in order to set a basic strategy and refine this strategy throughout the development of single apps. We recommend to document the results of each step at least roughly.

Especially in the agricultural domain, the integration of different legacy farm management system backends, different kinds of machinery and mobile devices sets the context. On the one hand, this means a lot of potential for innovation, on the other hand it puts a lot of constraints on the MSE development.

In the agricultural domain, there are some specific aspects, for example, that modern machines track data such as sensor information about soil, plant, and machine conditions with a GPS positioning system and store the data every few seconds. This huge amount of data can be distributed across several farm management systems and needs to be accessed on mobile devices in the field.

The MSE has to integrate already existing mobile apps of different categories which were developed before the MSE. While our MSE focusses mainly on enterprise resource planning, other apps are closer to the agricultural machines as sources of data.

Machine-related apps in agricultural business can be distinguished between *documentation* apps like the SeedStar Mobile app by John Deere [John Deere, 2014] and *semi-machine-controlling* apps. These app types are closely related to the machine and its data. Hence a CAN to Wi-Fi access point is needed to transmit the machine information to the app. The communication between the electrical control units (ECU) and a user interface is based on CAN bus technology. The communication flow could be realized either directly between user interface devices and CAN bus or via the backend, which of course has many architectural implications, in particular also on the achievable UX.

Table 1. MSE product philosophy

Attribute A	1	2	3	4	5	Attribute B
Innovative	▓					*Classic*
Company Experience		▓				*Native Experience*
Playful				▓		*Useful*
Context Aware	▓					*Static*
Stand-Alone			▓			*Integrated*
Smart	▓					*Sluggish*
Easy of Learning		▓				*Ease of Use*
Explaining				▓		*Intelligent*

2.3   UX-Centered Mobile App Conception Method

When developing the overall UX strategy of an MSE, it is important to follow a holistic strategy to ensure a high level of consistency across all the different platforms and devices. Therefore, the starting point of UX foundation in our case study is the definition of a so called product philosophy (see Table 1). This product philosophy supports the achievement of a consistent experience as it is used continuously throughout the app development process with different team and by different stakeholders. The product philosophy of the case study shows that there is a high emphasis on innovation and providing a very unique user experience. The product philosophy is mainly used as a communication tool to substantiate decision making during the development of an MSE.

For the UX conception of single apps within the MSE we followed the mConcAppt Approach [3]. This user centered approach (see Fig. 2) allows a lightweight conception of the app performing exactly the steps that are necessary to develop apps of the MSE and to gain information to coordinate with the architectural specification. In addition to performing the app conception, decision points and activities are taken into account, which is shown in Table 2.

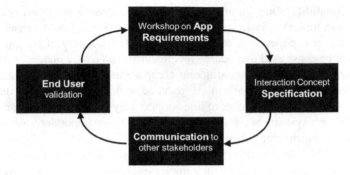

Fig. 2. mConcAppt overview

Table 2. Decision points that influence the UX of an MSE

Decision Points:
Target devices;
Linkage to the overall ecosystem product philosophy
Native vs. web
Elaboration of usage of artificial intelligence to support a positive UX
Service based app scoping
Possible reuse of user interface elements
Distribution of functionality between backend and client
Innovation and creativity
Variable vs. static user requirements
User requirements with regard to data usage
Adoption of already existing apps
Usage of ecosystem crowd functionalities
Innovation degree
Usage contexts within the MSE
Consistency

2.4 Architectural Drivers

When designing the architecture of an MSE, we often identify similar architectural drivers which can be addressed in various ways by taking different architectural decisions. The best suitable decision very often depends on the characteristics and context of the respective system. At Fraunhofer IESE, we use the Architecture-centric Engineering Solutions (ACES) [5] approach to identify the architectural drivers from all relevant stakeholders and to derive appropriate decisions and views from them. This approach is in general independent from the type of system under design. However, the specific knowledge about MSEs is in the comprehension of the architecture-specifics of this system category. Thus, we outline typical drivers and decisions we regularly observe in MSEs below.

Offline Capability: One common and important decision we often encounter is how to deal with limited or interrupted network connections. While it means definitely a much better user experience to offer the complete functionality of an app in offline mode, it has to be considered that adding this feature significantly increases complexity of synchronizing data between the different components of the app ecosystem. In the end this often leads to the tradeoff of reduced maintainability and extendibility. A compromise can be to implement offline support only for specific apps or particular features of the ecosystem, but finally it depends on the importance of the offline capability driver which approach should be taken.

Distribution of Functionality: Closely related to this is also the question where to locate specific functions respectively their implementation in the system. Here again we have a tradeoff between the limited resources on a mobile device that have to be handled carefully and the non-disruptive user experience in offline mode. For example, computing-intensive processes that need significant data from different resources should clearly reside on the backend, tailored expert systems can be integrated directly into the apps.

Selection of Synchronization Technologies: A crucial part of an MSE is also a reliable, performant and easy-to-use synchronization mechanism that takes care of the distribution of data between backend, apps and other involved components. Software architects and developers typically have to decide if they want to use a third party database replication technology or if they want to implement their own solution for this. While the latter gives the opportunity to perfectly tailor the mechanism to specific needs, such a task is very complex and costly in terms. On the other hand, even if using existing solutions results in lower effort at first, it might turn out later that they cannot fulfill the specific requirements in terms of performance and scalability, which in turn means significant additional work for adapting the solution or replacing it by another one.

Design of Data Models: Another important decision to take is how to align the data models on the different components of the system (backend, iOS apps, Android apps...). On the first glance it may seem obvious that all parts of the system should work on the same data model. However, since they are based on different technology stacks this is often very hard to achieve and also has negative impact on the tools and libraries that can be used as well as the maintainability of a specific app. On the other hand having separate platform-optimized data models on each component also has negative impact on the overall maintainability of the system and might lead to issues because of incompatibilities between the different data models.

Categorization of Data: One crucial question that typically comes up is if all data should be treated in the same way or if it should be distinguished between several types of data, especially regarding their change frequency. There is a clear trend that data gets classified in some way, e.g. master data, that changes seldom, is handled differently than data related to a concrete transaction. However, there are several approaches that differ in the number of data classes and the handling of them.

Design of APIs: An additional question that needs consideration is how to organize the APIs between the different components of the system. Backend and Apps can communicate via web services based on REST or SOAP, whereby REST is clearly state-of-the-art nowadays. However, independent of the technology, it is important to build the API in a way that it is open and extendable so that new Apps or connections to other MSEs or third party components can be realized with minimal effort.

There are many more recurring aspects that come up when designing a MSE, but because of limited space, we cannot describe them in detail here. Among these are multiple version support, internationalization, push notification concepts and data validation.

The conceptual architecture of our agricultural MSE case study consists of various elements. Farmers and their operators are the potential users of the apps. They use native apps on tablet and phone devices (iOS and Android). The system requires the availability of a central backend for data management and exchange. The backend works in a multi-tenancy way to allow efficient operation for all customers with their apps on the same backend machines. The backend is connected to external data sources, like for example a weather data provider. More detailed architectural information, with a particular focus on data, on this concrete case study can be found in [Naab et al., 2015].

3   Experiences from Building Mobile Software Ecosystems

3.1   Lessons Learned on User Experience Foundation

The following lessons learned originate from our user interface conception work during the prototyping of the described MSE. The by far most challenging task was reaching consistency with regard to UX across the different platforms and devices.

Using Product Philosophy as a Communication Tool. Using the product philosophy approach was time-consuming and unusual at the beginning, as every involved stakeholder needs to adopt this method. In the end, it was very beneficial to keep track of such a baseline that supports decision making on the interface between architecture and user experience. Many existing conflicts with regard to feature prioritization realization could be solved based on the specified philosophy. Additionally, every business stakeholder could identify himself with the philosophy as this communicates the general MSE vision on a consumable format.

Template-IOriented User Interface Conception. The usage of initial app templates for user interface conception provided a high consistency across apps of the different platforms. Reuse of design elements between smartphone and tablet was also supported. In the start-up period of the MSE, a set of user interface and interaction templates have been created and continuously maintained throughout the project. This enabled also a high amount of reusable assets during development. Nevertheless being able to provide a unique experience by having those – it was very challenging to balance between following the templates and individual solutions that provide a better UX within the single app. The following decision points accompanied us throughout the project: deciding if a template needs to be adopted; deciding in an optimal solution needs to be adopted based on an existing template; decide if an individual solution is appropriate; adopt the individual solution to the consistency requirement.

Artificial Intelligence Provides a High Potential for UX Improvement. By classifying historical user data and the application of learning algorithms in the backend a MSE can provide positive UX to the end user. In a prototype we managed to realize intelligent auto completion mechanisms based on intensive data analysis. This resulted in faster and more efficient task planning of the farmer and provided a great satisfaction in the end.

Close Alignment Between UX and Architecture Provides Unexpected Benefits. Performing joint workshops including UX experts and architects to create ideas on how UX can be improved by the reasonable usage of the data that is provided by the system provides essential benefits. This joint activity produced valuable features that would not have been identified by only applying a user-centered design approach. In the case study, we could foresee many scenarios in which we precautionary saved and analyzed data and leveraged functionalities that would not have been possible with the initial specification.

Maintenance and Integration of UX Assets. Especially with larger MSEs it gets important to think early about maintenance, integration and communication of UX assets. Changes with respect to the user interface are often expensive if they need to be done in various app instances. Therefore we recommend to use asset libraries, widgets and templates from the very beginning and ensure a sound traceability between them. In our case study we benefit a lot from having mobile developers involved into the conception phases to overcome those challenges. In addition we used if available the UI-builder within the IDE (in our case XCode) for early prototyping to show interactivity and reuse created prototypes during implementation. In general, for MSE, UX design and development need to have a tighter integration than in single app development.

Integration of Smart Devices. A sound integration of wearables (glasses, watches) and iBeacons for reasonable use cases provided a huge impact on the UX of the MSE. However, the challenge is to design the right functionality on the right device, and the design space becomes even larger when different types of smart devices are accompanying the usual mobile devices. In this case, iBeacons could be used to ensure that the right operator is driving the intended machinery.

Balance Business Goals and User Goals. Comparing to mobile development – MSE have a rather long development timespan although single apps within the MSE are realized quickly. We made good experiences with a continuous involvement of various business stakeholders and continuous user feedback. This has been very promising during the strategy phase where the scope of mobile support was set. Several innovative use cases have been provided by users and internal stakeholders (e.g., marketing, product management). Negotiating the given ideas and communicating them back and forth is a key success factor of the MSE.

3.2   Lessons Learned on Technical Foundation

The following lessons learned originate from our design and implementation work in the prototyping of the described app ecosystem. The by far most challenging task was the design and implementation of data synchronization in order to support offline mode for the apps of our ecosystem. Thus, our lessons learned mainly origin from this area. Further lessons learned with a broader focus can be found in [Naab et al., 2015].

There is No One-Size-Fits-All Solution for Data Synchronization. Even though mobile networks are still massively expanded, there may never be absolute connectivity for mobile systems. Concurrent modifications of data during offline mode inevitably lead to anomalies like e.g. lost updates. However, the criticality and the handling of those anomalies highly differ between different application domains and even between different use cases, as each use case can have completely different consistency requirements.

Although there's a lot of database replication technology around, it is a very hard task to pick the right one upfront during design phase, as they will always provide you with a compromise between availability, scalability and consistency. You will have to choose the one that serves your specific application domain and workloads best.

Designing Data Synchronization Requires Close Collaboration of Software Architects, UX Engineers and Requirements Engineers. We experienced that finding a technical solution alone is not enough. The technical solution has to support the application domain and its most important use cases in an optimal way in order to provide outstanding user experience. For example, a technical solution might be to use revision numbers in order to detect conflicting updates performed during offline mode. Clients would be notified about the conflict and would have to resolve the conflict somehow later. Nevertheless, as long as there are no good UI concepts for the presentation and resolving of conflicts this solution might be technically feasible but would result in bad usability.

Data Synchronization is Costly to Develop. From our experience designing and implementing sound synchronization is one of the most challenging tasks that software architects and developers can face. Even experienced engineers regularly fail to think ahead of all the pitfalls and imponderables. Therefore, software architects, UX engineers and requirements engineers should carefully outweigh the costs for it with the gain in user experience that brings the support for offline operations.

Keep Clients Simple with Respect to Data Synchronization. Although we do have a trend towards fat native apps, the latter should be kept simple with respect to data synchronization. If large parts of the synchronization logic like handling of concurrency anomalies, detection and resolution of conflicts is to be implemented by the clients itself, it will add an enormous amount of complexity to the app code. If multiple platforms are to be supported one will have to implement and test all or at least parts of it multiple times. Still in our experience server-side software is easier to implement, debug, quality-assure, maintain and to roll-out.

A Great Deal of Data Validation and Security Checks must be Implemented on the Client. On the other hand, clients must implement a great deal of data validation and security rule checking. If the app permits the user to write invalid data or update data he has no permission for, the app will later on not be able to synchronize back the changes made during offline mode. At the worst, the app becomes unusable due to one faulty data item that is in the change set. Thus, client-side data validation and security defects can have an enormously negative impact on the usability of the app. There are a lot of open questions on how to make the overall system more robust and fault tolerant with respect to this issue: Is it possible to discard only parts of the faulty change set? Moreover, if so, how to determine this part of the change set? If data has to be discarded, how to notify the user about this? This is not trivial, in particular as the user might have done the update some time ago during offline mode and is already in a completely different usage context then.

4 Conclusion

The given paper shows our initial approach to the development of an MSE with an emphasis on the provided UX and architectural decisions. As setting up an MSE is a very complex activity with many pitfalls, we provide our lessons learned from the application of our approach in a large scale case study within the agricultural domain.

Lessons learned from UX show that many additional aspects need to be taken into account besides the user centered conception of a single user interface. In our case study especially the usage of a product philosophy throughout the development of various apps for communication purpose derived as a best practice as well as the usage of an approach for object-oriented user interface conception. This conceptual approach has reduced the effort for conception and maintenance of apps within the MSE in a significant way.

Lessons learned on the technical foundation show that data synchronization has been a key success factor in our case study. There are many approaches available on how to tackle this challenge within MSEs and our lessons learned show that a collaboration among the stakeholders of the user interface and the software architecture overcomes many obstacles. This may sound obvious, but it has also impacts on the other lessons learned described above such as 'there is no one fits all solution' and 'data synchronization is costly to develop' as we recommend to develop a sound synchronization concept from the very beginning.

Acknowledgement. This work has been partially supported by the German Ministry of Education and Research, grant number 01IS12053.

References

1. Bosch, J.: From software product lines to software ecosystems. In: 13th International Software Product Line Conference, SPLC 2009 (2009)

2. Dörr, J., Trapp, M., Hess, S.: Mobile Prozesse: eine Chance für die Wirtschaft. Computerwoche (2014). http://www.computerwoche.de/a/mobile-prozesse-eine-chance-fuer-die-wirtschaft,2555126
3. Hess, S., Kiefer, F., Carbon, R., Maier, A.: mConcAppt – a method for the conception of mobile business applications. In: Uhler, D., Mehta, K., Wong, J.L. (eds.) MobiCASE 2012. LNICST, vol. 110, pp. 1–20. Springer, Heidelberg (2013)
4. Deere, J.: Press Release (2014)
5. Keuler, T., Knodel, J., Naab, M.: Fraunhofer ACES: Architecture-Centric Engineering Solutions. Fraunhofer IESE, IESE-Report, 079.11/E (2011)
6. Naab, M., Braun, S., Lenhart, T., Hess, S., Eitel, A., Magin, D., Carbon, R., Kiefer, F.: Why data needs more attention in architecture design - experiences from prototyping a large-scale mobile app ecosystem. In: International Working Conference on Software Architecture, WICSA 2015 (2015)

Cloud Computing: A Multi-tenant Case Study

Anindya Hossain and Farid Shirazi[✉]

Ryerson University, Toronto, Canada
{anindya.hossain, f2shiraz}@ryerson.ca

Abstract. Cloud computing has enabled businesses to infinitely scale services based on demand while reducing the total cost of ownership. Software as a service (SaaS) vendors capitalized on the scalable nature of Infrastructure as a Service (IaaS) to deploy applications without having the need for heavy upfront capital investment. This study uses a real case study from a Canadian SaaS vendor migrating from a single-tenant applications system to a single-tenant applications (MTA) system. The results of this empirical study show a decrease of a factor of 3 in setup times and a reduction in number of bugs reported and the amount of time required to fix these bugs. Despite the fact that migration from a single-tenant applications system to a multi-tenant system requires some re-engineering efforts, but the benefits of MTA far outweigh these re-engineering costs. Furthermore, migrating to MTA enables firms to focus on their core competences. The empirical results of this study show that in the long run, MTA can enable SaaS vendors to increase the quality of service, performance, service level agreement adherence, re-focus on creating innovative products, lower operational costs and earn higher profits.

Keywords: Cloud computing · Multi-tenant application · SaaS · IaaS · PaaS · ANOVA

1 Introduction

Cloud computing has truly revolutionized the IT industry in the last decade. The internet has evolved from a mere medium of communication to a medium of delivery for software, middleware platforms and hardware infrastructure. Enterprises no longer need to own their hardware to host applications, or manage and maintain software on client computers. The recent advent of cloud computing has made computing into a utility. Cloud computing has enabled businesses to infinitely scale services based on demand while reducing the total cost of ownership. Software as a service (SaaS) vendors capitalized on the scalable nature of Infrastructure as a Service (IaaS) to deploy applications without having the need for heavy upfront capital investment.

Most SaaS applications such as email and CRM applications are very standard, i.e. they all perform very similar tasks regardless of the organization using the system. Some SaaS applications need to be somewhat customized for each client. Initially, SaaS vendors started running independent application instances for each client (single-tenant applications). However, when these SaaS vendors started to scale, they ran into problems maintaining and setting up a separate instance for each client. They started developing multi-tenant applications (MTA), which can handle multiple tenants

M. Kurosu (Ed.): Human-Computer Interaction, Part III, HCII 2015, LNCS 9171, pp. 178–189, 2015.
DOI: 10.1007/978-3-319-21006-3_18

within the same application. Earlier studies confirmed that an MTA would enable firms to reduce their operating costs and reduce the number of hours spent doing maintenance. However, there was no concrete industry data to prove these theories.

Online implementation and delivery of software, more commonly known as Software as a Service (SaaS), has become more popular than ever before. Dubey and Wagle (2007) claim that SaaS vendors are significantly less profitable than traditional software vendors [1]. They speculate that this might be due to the lack of scale for SaaS. For example, WebEx, one of the largest online meeting and collaboration SaaS, has a profit margin that is almost double the SaaS industry average [1].One strategy to increase scale is to adopt a multi-tenant architecture for SaaS. In addition, multi-tenant systems are often set up in a single database to reduce the total cost of ownership [2].

Just like any other business, SaaS providers need to focus on their core competencies and continually innovate in order to be competitive in their industries. These firms have a finite set of resources and these resources need to be properly managed to maximize dynamic capabilities. In a multi-tenant environment, the software service provider runs a single instance of the application that is configured for each client (tenant). It typically runs on a single database and shares hardware resources. The goal of this research will be to demonstrate that multi-tenant setups can enable firms to focus more on their core competencies and not spend most of their resources on implementations. By focusing on their core competencies, SaaS vendors can continue to innovate and offer better products that are able to return more profit. The aim of this empirical study was to analyze the extent to which multi-tenant systems can be effective in delivering software services on-demand to various clients. To this end, we investigated two issues: a) does the setup of the multi-tenant system require less time to implement than the single-tenant system and b) is a multi-tenant setup more robust and does it require less maintenance time?

GrantStream Inc. a SaaS vendor in Canada made a strategic decision last year to move away from custom single-tenant applications towards a multi-tenant application (MTA) with a single instance of the application running on a shared database and hardware setup. Data was collected from 9 setups in legacy single-tenant applications, 9 new setups in MTA and 9 migration setups in MTA.

This case study will enable us to use real industry data to validate our research questions. The benefits and challenges of migrating to an MTA have been discussed by many researchers. However, none explored the tangible or monetary benefits of this migration. Momm and Krebbs were the first to suggest a simple cost model to evaluate MTA migration for a SaaS vendor [4]. These research findings needed to be validated using real-world data, and this case-study will enable us to validate claims made by other researchers.

2   Cloud Computing Multi-tenant Architecture

An evolution in Internet technology, cloud computing is an advancement providing users with the means to access a wide range of computing power, software and platform as a service, as well infrastructure anytime, anywhere [5]. Cloud computing enables on-demand network access to a shared pool of configurable computing resources, including servers, storage applications and services. Cloud computing services encompass the following three main layers: the hardware infrastructure (IaaS), middleware services (PaaS) and application services (SaaS). Cloud computing capabilities have enabled businesses to offer services that seem to be infinitely scalable and elastic. Subscribers of cloud services can keep their upfront costs low by adjusting their level of service based on demand. It allows companies to start small and increase incrementally with demand. Cloud computing has made IT resources into a utility that is enabling businesses to enter the markets without the need for heavy initial capital investment [6].

SaaS is a web-based software application associated with business software applications deployed and operated as a hosted service [7]. These applications typically run in the browser of a client (tenant) and can be accessed from anywhere. SaaS applications can range from a simple web mail application to a more complex CRM application [8]. They explain that SaaS vendors started allocating multiple clients on the same application to increase efficiency and reduce Total Cost of Ownership (TCO). They define multi-tenancy as: "an approach to share an application instance between multiple tenants by every tenant a dedicated 'share' of the instance, which is isolated from other shares with regard to performance and data privacy" [10:2]. SaaS providers are usually required to adhere to certain standards set out in their service level agreement (SLA). To be successful, providers need to ensure that the services are scalable on-demand, comply with SLA terms, enable customers to achieve low TCO and have low incremental costs [4]. They mention that for current SaaS providers enabling multi-tenancy is the next big evolution step; it can help them achieve a lower TCO by reducing setup and maintenance costs [4]. Bezemer and Zaidman write that multi-tenancy architecture enables service providers to reach economies of scale by sharing the same instance of the application and database. The application can be configured for each tenant, and it may appear as a custom solution to the client. In addition, multi-tenancy can enable SaaS providers to increase hardware utilization and reduce costs [9].

Multi-tenant setups can have various configurations. Pervez, Lee and Lee categorize SaaS into four maturity levels. The first level is "*custom/ad hoc*", where the SaaS application is fully customized or built for a specific client [10]. At the second level, "*Configurable*", the application is configured for a specific client, and an independent instance of the application is used for each tenant. At the third level, "*Configurable & multi-tenant efficient*", a single instance of the application is used by multiple clients and it is somewhat configured for each tenant. At the fourth level, "*Scalable, Configurable, multi-tenant-efficient*", a single instance of the application is used as in the third level, but the services are fully configurable to handle a specific business workflow. In this last level, services are also fully scalable and the focus is to meet or exceed all requirements mentioned in the SLA [10].

3 The Key Characteristics of a Multi-tenant Platform

3.1 Sharing Hardware Resources

Sharing hardware resources among multiple tenants reduces costs for the SaaS provider. Bezemer and Zaidman mention that even though server efficiency can be improved in single-tenant setups through virtualization, it imposes however, a high memory requirement for each virtual setup [11].

They explain about the different types of hardware, software combinations for a multi-tenant setup:

1. Single instance of application shared among tenants each with a separate database
2. Single instance of application with shared database, but separate Tables
3. Single instance of application with shared database and shared tables (pure multi-tenancy)

Requires High Degree of Configurability. Unlike single-tenant SaaS, multi-tenant setups cannot be completely customized since they are shared among different tenants. Therefore, it is absolutely necessary for multi-tenant software to be highly configurable. It needs to accommodate each client's settings, workflows among other [9]. They explain that in a typical single-tenant setup, updates are usually made by creating branches in the development tree, but this does not work in multi-tenant setups and configuration needs to be part of the product design itself. Other researchers propose building a workflow engine on top of a multi-tenant application instance [12]. SaaS like Email and CRM has the same workflow irrespective of which company is using the service. The service is standard across the board. However, for most SaaS, the workflow changes from client to client (tenant). As mentioned earlier, a key challenge in a multi-tenant environment was to provide a configurable setup for each tenant. Pathirage et al. propose a configurable "Workflow as a Service" (WFaaS) that will be added onto the existing multi-tenant SaaS and will allow the application to be configured for each tenant [13].

Easier Deployments. In multi-tenant setups deployments and updates can be pushed out easily as there is ideally only one instance of the program running. In some cases, a provider might have multiple instance of the application running, but it will almost always be lower than any single-tenant setups [11] Short setup times are a key requirement for SaaS clients. They expect SaaS vendors to be able to set them up in days instead of weeks or months [4]. SaaS vendors are required to agree to a Service Level Agreement which stipulates the expected setup times. If the SaaS provider cannot meet these tight deadlines, they might lose potential clients. Therefore, if multi-tenant setups can enable SaaS vendors to reduce setup time, it can lead to a competitive advantage.

3.2 Challenges of a Multi-tenant Platform

Multi-tenant setups face some challenges that are more complex than similar challenges faced in single-tenant setups. Multi-tenant setups share hardware infrastructures, databases, middleware, and the application itself. When issues arise, they cannot be contained within a certain client; they affect all clients. Bezemer and Zaidman write that the main concerns in multi-tenant setups are performance, scalability, security, downtime and maintenance. Before making the migration from a single-tenant setup to a multi-tenant setup, SaaS providers need to fully understand these complexities [11].

3.3   Cost of Migration from Single-tenant to Multi-tenant

The cost of migrating from a single-tenant to a multi-tenant setup can vary depending on the complexity of the software and its underlying architecture. Momm and Krebs developed a cost model that includes two major components: *Initial reengineering costs* and *Continuous operating costs*. They explain that any savings in operating costs will amortize the initial reengineering costs over a certain period of time, the break even period. Continuous operating costs can be calculated by evaluating fixed costs of infrastructure, middleware, maintenance, etc. They argue that introducing an additional shared resource or component in the stack saves Operating costs of (n-1) times the base costs for the shared resource [4].

Momm and Krebbs propose a simple cost model to evaluate migration to a multi-tenant architecture [4].

Months to break-even = Initial re-engineering costs / Savings in operating costs.

4   Research Approach and Theoretical Framework

Most research in this field of using single-tenant vs. multi-tenant SaaS setups is still very theoretical. There is a body of research that suggests a multi-tenant setup might be better for a large number of clients, but it does come with its own set of challenges [12]. However, none of these studies have looked at the existing SaaS industry to see how they have handled these challenges. Migrating from a single-tenant to multi-tenant setup will always require some re-engineering work as mentioned earlier, but the benefits of migration can outweigh the costs.

This research will enable SaaS vendors to decide which type of architecture better suits their strategies. Earlier studies have suggested that multi-tenant setups enable SaaS vendors to quickly set up and maintain new tenants.

GrantStream Inc. is a Canadian SaaS vendor specialized in grant management software. The company was founded in 2001 and is one of the earliest providers of SaaS in the grant management software industry. The company focuses mainly on providing services to small and medium size enterprises (SMEs). Tehrani and Shirazi argue that despite the fact that adopting new technologies helps SMEs gain a competitive advantage, it usually involves high costs. Cloud computing, as a new computing paradigm, offers many advantages to companies, especially smaller ones. Flexibility, scalability, and reduced cost are among many advantages that cloud computing offers to SMEs [14].

Before the migration to the multi-tenant setup, GrantStream was one of the few providers who provided custom SaaS applications in the grant management industry. The company felt that their ability to customize their application would give them competitive sustainability. However, the management discovered that as they spent more and more time on client setups, their core product did not receive the updates and innovations it required to differentiate it from the competition. They discovered that their product was falling behind, and to remain competitive they would need to redirect their resources towards product development rather than tenant setups.

Looking at the impact of this change in strategy within this organization will help us confirm the different theories that have been presented by earlier papers. Data from this case study might not be representative of the population, but can confirm some of the theories presented by other researchers. We will do a quantitative data analysis on tenant setup times for:

1. Single-tenant setup
2. Migrate legacy client to multi-tenant
3. New setup in multi-tenant platform

The number of hours spent are recorded by the firm and are presented during the post-project review. In addition, we will also explore the number of reported bugs in the last 12 months for that specific tenant and how many hours were spent fixing these bugs. The data analysis will help us understand how the migration from single-tenant to multi-tenant architecture affected the setup times and bug resolution time. As mentioned earlier, these are key factors in SaaS vendors' SLA terms.

4.1 Single-tenant Setup at GrantStream

As shown in Fig. 1, GrantStream's legacy setup (single-tenant) used a shared database and tables, and ran on a shared hardware setup, as well. By sharing resources, GrantStream could keep its costs fairly low since the company was founded in the early 2000 s. However, having multiple instances of the application running for each tenant made maintenance very hard. In addition, since setting up a new tenant included a custom setup, it was very time-consuming and cumbersome.

4.2 Multi-tenant Setup at GrantStream

GrantStream's multi-tenant architecture uses a single instance of the application, with an underlying shared database and tables, which runs on a shared infrastructure (see Fig. 2). GrantStream uses an IaaS service provider data center to host its SaaS system. By subscribing to this provider GrantStream can minimize costs and increase scalability without adding to operating costs. GrantStream's application needed to be re-engineered to enable it to handle multiple tenant configurations. GrantStream Inc.'s multi-tenant application has reached level 3 of the SaaS maturity model as mentioned earlier [10].

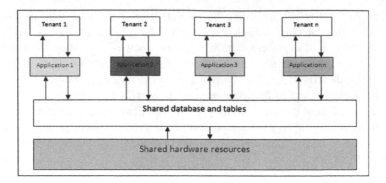

Fig. 1. Single-tenant setup at GrantStream Inc

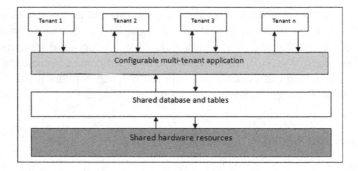

Fig. 2. Multi-tenant setup at GrantStream Inc

4.3 The Research Methodology

Data was collected for 27 client setups during the post-project reviews, and through the logged service tickets. As shown in Table 1 below, we collected number of hours to set up a tenant from post-project reviews (variable HourToSetup). We also looked at logged tickets in the last 12 months for each tenant (variable BugTickets) and the amount of time required to fix each bug (variable HoursFixBug).

Of these 27 setups, 9 were during the single-tenant phase (legacy), 9 were new setups using the multi-tenant application, and 9 were client migrations from the single-tenant to multi-tenant platform (as shown in the column, TypeOfSetup in Table 1). Setup times and hours spent on bug fixes are recorded by GrantStream during a new client implementation project. They shared the data with us for this research, but to protect the confidentiality of the clients, the names of the company's clients were not disclosed. This does not affect the results of the study.

Table 1. Data collected from GrantStream Inc.

Client name	TypeOfSetup	HourToSetup	BugTickets	HoursFixBug
BPE	1	98.58	0	0
CAN	1	79.38	1	1.5
GSC	1	117	4	2.36
SHL	1	102.7	2	1.76
MAL	1	27.65	1	0
SHU	1	77.38	0	0
STA	1	67.92	2	0
TAL	1	59	2	0.42
SLF	1	51.08	5	3.61
SH	2	57	2	1.42
AFF	2	41.72	4	0.8
ALL	2	211	4	6.5
AME	2	269	4	3.9
CPC	2	18	3	5.75
GE	2	37	1	0.33
LDC	2	63.57	4	1.2
PMV	2	128.68	0	0
SIIW	2	125.77	2	3.16
MSC	3	240.6	12	20.8
BNC	3	467.45	2	2.25
PHR	3	347.83	1	1.6
UFA	3	110	0	0
IOXM	3	113	3	0.7
IOXMR	3	178	3	1.9
ENB	3	268	2	4.5
VLE	3	195	4	3.6
HDE	3	164.65	5	9.5

Type of setup: 1 = Migration to multi-tenant, 2 = New setup in multi-tenant, 3 = New setup in single-tenant

5   Results

We completed a statistical data analysis with the data provided by GrantStream Inc. As presented earlier, researchers like [4, 11] wrote about the many benefits of migrating from the single-tenant architecture to a multi-tenant structure. However, these findings were never confirmed using empirical data. This research will try to answer two hypotheses previously mentioned: Multi-tenant clients need less time to setup and Multi-tenant setups require less time to maintain. To test these hypotheses, we collected data from 27 setups. Data was collected from 9 setups when the company was using a single-tenant setup. After the migration, we collected data from 9 new setups in a multi-tenant environment and 9 migration setups in the new platform.

Hypothesis 1: Multi-tenant Setups Require Less Time to Implement Than Single Tenant. GrantStream Inc. spent on an average almost 232 h implementing a new tenant in the single-tenant architecture of their application. After they migrated to a multi-tenant architecture, setup times dropped significantly. For new setups, they started spending close to 106 h, and for migrating old clients they spent around 76 h. However, both new setups in the legacy and multi-tenant environments have high standard deviations of 116 and 86, respectively. Compared to new setups, migration setups have a lower standard deviation of 28. New setups typically always have unknown customizations and idiosyncrasies which can cause the setup times to fluctuate more. For migration setups, the client and their setup are already known to the company and setup times are more consistent. As shown in Table 3 below, a one-way ANOVA was performed on the dataset with the *TypeOfSetup* as the independent variable. We have discovered that the *HourToSetup* has a high F of 8.5. *HourToSetup* has a high variance between groups and low variance within the group, which means that the *HourToSetup* is highly correlated with the independent variable, *TypeOfSetup*. Therefore, we can conclude that by migrating from a single-tenant to a multi-tenant architecture did reduce the number of hours required to setup a client.

As indicated in Tables 2 and 3 below, the cloud clients who migrated to a multi-tenant system experience the highest possible system performance and efficiency as measured by the number of hours spent on bugs to be fixed annually. In fact, this performance, as shown in the table, is more than 4 times higher than that for a single-tenant setup. Another important finding is that setting up a new multi-tenant system is more than 1.9 times more efficient than a single-tenant structure. The findings indicate that the cloud multi-tenant system is more efficient than the traditional single-tenant setup formats. When GrantStream Inc. was using a single-tenant application, the system needed to be customized for each client. The company could not capitalize on its learning from previous setups. After migrating to a multi-tenant architecture, there was no need to create a new custom application for each tenant. New setups were more efficient in handling different workflows of different clients. Implementation became standardized, and as a result, setup times dropped significantly.

Hypothesis 2: Multi-tenant Application Requires Less Maintenance Time. As shown in Table 2, we collected data from 27 tenants during the last 12 months to compare the number of bugs reported and the amount of time spent fixing these bugs. As previously mentioned, out of the 27 tenants, 9 are in the legacy single-tenant application, 9 were new tenants in the multi-tenant system and 9 were migrated from the single-tenant to the multi-tenant system as depicted in Table 3. Table 3 indicates also that tenants migrated to multi-tenant system had the lowest number of bugs reported with an average of 1.9 for the year. As for the two other groups, new setups in the multi-tenant system had an average of 2.7 per year and clients in the legacy platform averaged about 3.6 per year. However, for all three groups the variance ranged from 1.5 to 3.7 (shown in Table 2), which means that the number of bugs reported varied significantly from client to client and there was no significant difference between the tenants in one group compared to another. In addition, ANOVA with SetupTypes set as the independent variable indicated that the number of BugsReported had an F of 1.080 (see Table 3), which means that the number of bugs reported is not correlated with the type of architecture being used by the SaaS vendor. However, when we analyzed the amount of time it took to fix these bugs, FixBugHours, the results were significantly different. Only 1 to 2.5 h per client were spent in the group where the multi-tenant setup was used. In the legacy group, the company was spending close to 5 h per tenant per year to fix bugs reported. FixBugHours had F of 2.085 when analyzed with SetupType as the independent variable. This reduction in the number of hours spent fixing bugs can be attributed to the standard setup of a multi-tenant application instance. Bug fixes are rolled out universally and any fix is applied for all clients simultaneously. Whereas in the past each application for a client needed to be fixed individually, in multi-tenancy fixes are rolled out once and apply to all tenants. Therefore, by migrating from single-tenant architecture to a multi-tenant one, the company is saving almost 2.5 to 4 h per client per year. If a SaaS vendor has 100 clients, they would be saving almost 250 to 400 h from their operating expenses.

Table 2. Statistical Report

SetupType		HourToSetup	BugTickets	HoursFixBugs
1	Mean	75.6322	1.89	1.0722
	N	9	9	9
	Std. Deviation	27.90357	1.691	1.31238
2	Mean	105.7489	2.67	2.5622
	N	9	9	9
	Std. Deviation	86.12265	1.500	2.38821
3	Mean	231.6144	3.56	4.9833
	N	9	9	9
	Std. Deviation	116.23679	3.504	6.56049
Total	Mean	137.6652	2.70	2.8726
	N	27	27	27
	Std. Deviation	106.85945	2.415	4.26913

Table 3. Analysis of variance (ANOVA)

		Sum of Squares	df	Mean Square	F	Sig.
HourToSetup	Between Groups	123238.816	2	61619.408	8.516	.002
	Within Groups	173653.700	24	7235.571		
	Total	296892.516	26			
BugTickets	Between Groups	12.519	2	6.259	1.080	.356
	Within Groups	139.111	24	5.796		
	Total	151.630	26			
HoursFixBugs	Between Groups	70.136	2	35.068	2.085	.146
	Within Groups	403.727	24	16.822		
	Total	473.863	26			

5.1   Cost Model of Migrating to a MTA

As mentioned earlier, Momm and Krebbs proposed a simple cost model to evaluate migration to a multi-tenant architecture [4].

Months to break-even = Initial re-engineering costs/Savings in operating costs

Using the data provided above we can estimate the number of months required for a SaaS vendor to break even given these assumptions:

- Re-engineering efforts for the application cost the company $100,000
- The vendor has approximately 100 tenants
- The vendor completes 1 new tenant setup every month
- Internal development and setup cost the company $100/hour

Cost savings in doing one setup = 232 h − 76 h * $100 = $15,600

Cost savings from bug tickets = [(5 h * 100) − (3.25 h * 100 clients)]* $100 = $17,500/year

Months to break even = $100,000/[($15,600) + ($17,500/12) = 5.86 months

As shown above, a SaaS vendor can migrate to a MTA and break even fairly quickly. After the break-even period, the company will continue benefiting from costs savings. Instead of allocating much of its resources developing and maintaining customized applications, vendors can now redirect their resources towards their core competencies and focus more on developing a technological lead that will enable them to sustain a competitive advantage. As mentioned earlier, Wernerfelt recommends that firms engage their employees in stimulating jobs that create more value for the firm's products [3]. Therefore, by migrating to a multi-tenant application, SaaS vendors are not only saving on operating costs, they also have the opportunity to free up resources that can be focused on creating more innovative products and helping the firm earn higher returns.

6   Limitations and Conclusions

The software industry is constantly changing. Software vendors might find a better way to deliver their SaaS that can handle the simplicity of implementing a multi-tenant setup while maintaining the customization of single-tenant setup. The goal of this study was to investigate claims made in previous research through empirical data. This does not mean that the findings will be universal.

The data collected in this research might not be representative of the population. There have been other studies that made certain claims about multi-tenant setups, but they were never proven with empirical data. This research has tried to investigate some of those claims through data collected from a real organization. This organization has been running a single-tenant application for almost 10 years, but recently changed strategies and developed a multi-tenant application. The findings of this research might not apply to all SaaS providers. As with all technological innovations, the software industry is always changing.

In conclusion, cloud computing has truly revolutionized the IT industry. The software industry dreamed of commoditizing computing for a long time, but it did not become a reality until the last decade. The internet has enabled firms to deliver software, middleware platforms and hardware infrastructure. Enterprises no longer need to own their hardware to host applications, or manage and maintain software on client computers. Cloud computing has enabled businesses to infinitely scale services based on demand while reducing the total cost of ownership. SaaS vendors capitalized on the scalable nature of IaaS to deploy applications without having the need for heavy upfront capital investment.

References

1. Dubey, A., Wagle, D.: Delivering software as a service. The McKinsey Quarterly **6**, 1–12 (2007)
2. Aulbach, S., Grust, T., Jacobs, D., Kemper, A., Rittinger, J.: Multi-tenant databases for software as a service: schema-mapping techniques. In: Proceedings of the 2008 ACM SIGMOD International Conference on Management of Data, pp. 1195–1206. ACM, June, 2008
3. Wernerfelt, B.: A resource-based view of the firm. Strateg. Manag. J. **5**(2), 171–180 (1984)
4. Momm, C., Krebs, R.: A qualitative discussion of different approaches for implementing multi-tenant SaaS offerings. In: Software Engineering (Workshops), vol. 11 (2011)
5. Pallis, G.: Cloud computing the new frontier of internet computing. IEEE Internet Comput. **14**(5), 70–73 (2010)
6. Armbrust, M., Fox, A., Griffith, R., Joseph, A.D., Katz, R., Konwinski, A., Zaharia, M.: A view of cloud computing. Commun. ACM **53**(4), 50–58 (2010)
7. Kwok, T., Thao, N., Linh, L.: A Software as a service with multi-tenancy support for an electronic contract management application. IEEE Int. Conf. Serv. Comput. SCC **2008**, 179–186 (2008)
8. Krebs, R., Momm, C., Kounev, S.: Architectural concerns in multi-tenant SaaS applications. In: CLOSER, pp. 426–431, April, 2012
9. Bezemer, C. P., Zaidman, A., Platzbeecker, B., Hurkmans, T., & t Hart, A. (2010, September). Enabling multi-tenancy: An industrial experience report. In*Software Maintenance (ICSM), 2010 IEEE International Conference on* (pp. 1–8). IEEE
10. Pervez, Z., Lee, S., Lee, Y.K.: Multi-tenant, secure, load disseminated SaaS architecture. In: The 12th International Conference On Advanced Communication Technology (Icact), 2010, vol. 1, pp. 214–219). IEEE February, 2010
11. Bezemer, C.P., Zaidman, A.: Multi-tenant SaaS applications: maintenance dream or nightmare? In: Proceedings of the Joint ERCIM Workshop on Software Evolution (EVOL) and International Workshop on Principles of Software Evolution (IWPSE), pp. 88–92. ACM, September 2010
12. Pathirage, M., Perera, S., Kumara, I., Weerasiri, D., Sanjiva Weerawarana, S.: A scalable multi-tenant architecture for business process executions. Web Serv. Res. **9**(2), 21–41 (2012)
13. Hay, B., Nance, K., & Bishop, M. (2011, January). Storm clouds rising: security challenges for IaaS cloud computing. In System Sciences (HICSS), 2011 44th Hawaii International Conference on (pp. 1–7). IEEE
14. Tehrani, S.R., Shirazi, F.: Factors influencing the adoption of cloud computing by small and medium size enterprises (SMEs). In: Yamamoto, S. (ed.) HCI 2014, Part II. LNCS, vol. 8522, pp. 631–642. Springer, Heidelberg (2014)

On Time: Efficient and Personalized Hospital Service

So Yon Jeong and Da Young Ju[✉]

Yonsei Institute of Convergence Technology, School of Integrated Technology,
Yonsei University, Seoul, Republic of Korea
{sjeong3206,dyju}@yonsei.ac.kr

Abstract. For every kind of service, reduction of waiting time appears to be critical. Particularly, the occurrence of waiting time in a clinical environment gives patients negative impression of the clinic (or hospital). By observing the present state of hospital waiting time we suggest 'On Time', a mobile application design for when waiting time occurs. 'On Time' mobile application is efficient, personalized and patient centered hospital service that satisfies the patients by both using existing monitor service and big data.

Keywords: IT · Hospital service · Big data · Mobile application

1 Introduction

There are numerous studies that found out that waiting time is one of the primary determinants of patient satisfaction [3], [6]. Eilers (2010) have also pointed out that the speed of service is one of the major criteria to judge in medical quality care. To improve quality care, Plesk (2002) suggests a model and worksheet of 'moments of truth' to understand the level of the service. A study [5] showed that the satisfaction of patients in walk-in clinics, family practices and emergency departments also differ when it comes to waiting times. Although the aspects of satisfaction in the emergency department may be different to other [1], we researched the general medical services of a territory hospital. We selected two outpatient clinics in a tertiary hospital to collect information on actual waiting times and the method to inform patients. The patients in hospital outpatient clinic have limited information to predict waiting times although a computer monitoring system displays an ordered list of patients. In situations where patients should take multiple examinations and treatments, it makes difficult for patients to predict their waiting time. Based on the information, we developed a service system that can efficiently and personally provide hospital service to the patients using IT technology.

2 Related Work

Many studies show that hospitals are trying to increase patients' satisfaction related to waiting time. A relaxing and comfortable waiting environment such as, soothing colors, natural lighting and table lamps, can make patients think they have waited for a

M. Kurosu (Ed.): Human-Computer Interaction, Part III, HCII 2015, LNCS 9171, pp. 190–197, 2015.
DOI: 10.1007/978-3-319-21006-3_19

short amount of time [4]. The study performed by Eilers (2010) showed the dissatisfaction of patients' related to the waiting time, which was solved by an increase of same-day appointments. In our study, we focused on using data of patients in the hospital database [9] and the existing monitor service in the waiting room area. Using information technology (IT) can bring new efficient services in the hospital environment. By using healthcare IT can allow patients', give them a choice of their own in the healthcare environment [2]. The purpose of this study is to extract the actual problems that happen in the waiting environment and help patients to choose what to do with the given waiting time.

3   Patients in Clinic Environment

To understand the real situation, we observed the waiting environment, interviewing 10 patients and 3 hospital faculty members. Various problems were observed in the waiting environment such as, uncomfortable waiting room, a large number of patients and broken monitors. The only functioning only consists of simple information, such as the patients' names.

Fig. 1. Patients waiting in clinic environment

Most of the patients wait in front of the clinic area where they can hear the nurse. Through the interview, the reason they stayed close to the clinic area was to not miss there turn for treatment. The patients keep asking questions to the medical staff, making hard for them to concentrate on work. Because of these problems, the hospital provided various attractions, offering beverages and announcing the patients. However they turned out to be inefficient, increasing the necessity of system that reduces the waiting time (Figs. 1, 2 and 4).

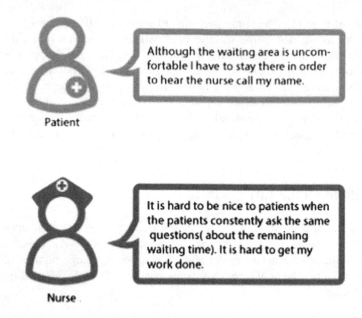

Fig. 2. Problem when waiting

4   Service System

4.1   Suitability of Smartphone

According to 2013 data, South Korea has the highest smartphone penetration rate. Because smartphone is the most typical IT technology we will only use this smartphone throughout this paper. To prove the high usability of smartphone in various age groups in South Korea, the graph in Fig. 3 proves that there are increasing rate of smartphone users in all age groups.

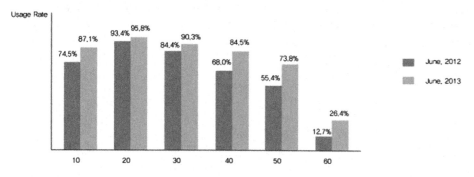

Fig. 3. Smartphone usage rate depending on age range (Source: KT economy and business research center customer data).

4.2 Application and Service Overview

'On Time' is proposed mobile application provides information that is related to healthcare and hospital. The primary function of this service is to notify the patients' waiting time in real-time, and this big data would allow patients to be more accessible on informing. Below is how to use the mobile application.

1. A patient downloads the 'On Time' medical service application and goes to the clinic.
2. When the patient registers at the relevant outpatient clinic for treatment, the nurse will send patient's information to the application database. By doing this would allow patient to check the remaining time regardless of their location.
3. When the nurse enters the patient's information, it would be shown on both application and the clinic monitor. The monitor only presents the last names and their total waiting for the patients'.

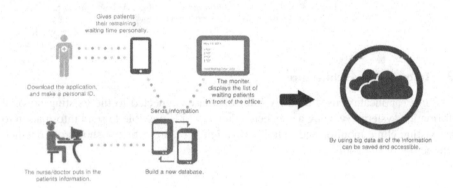

Fig. 4. Hospital service system

Patients who have chronic disease should take multiple examinations and treatments before getting medical examination from a doctor. However, they frequently are not noticed to take those steps before they consult with the doctor, increasing their time to wait in the waiting room. 'On Time' will eliminate this inconvenience by informing through the smartphone. The patients frequently forget to ask the questions to the doctors while they are consulting. 'On Time' would also have a category for these patients, sending specific questions that they would like to ask while they are waiting, making consulting time to be more valuable. My Waiting Time, Step by Step, Medical Examination Consult, and Self Examination are the main categories (Table 1).

Table 1. On time application main functions

My Waiting Time	Exposed on the main page of application. Shows the remaining waiting time individually. The time can change flexibly, adjusting to the various situations that can occur in the hospital.
Step by Step	A menu for patients who need extra examinations. Inform the multiple examinations and treatments the patient needs step by step before getting medical examination from a doctor.
Medical Examination Consult	Before getting a medical examination it is possible to enter in questions that can be answered by the doctor. It also can be used afterwards to ask additional questions that can be forgotten. Dissatisfaction of long waiting and short medical treatment with the doctor can be reduced.
Self Examination	Helps keep track of the users health daily.The application can measure data such as users bio rhythm, blood pressure and the number of steps walked.

4.3   Information Architecture

'On Time' application uses a newly built database connected to the existing hospital information system. By using a connected database it is possible to send information to the existing clinic monitor and individual patients. Figure 5 below shows the detailed architecture of the application.

4.4   Graphical User Interface (GUI)

Figure 6 shows easily accessible designated GUI of the main function. The most important function of the application'My Waiting Time' is located on the top center of the main screen. The time changes flexibly, adjusting to the various situations that can occur in the hospital. Other functions such as 'Step by Step', 'Medical Examination Consult' and 'Self Examination' are also located on the main screen of the application.

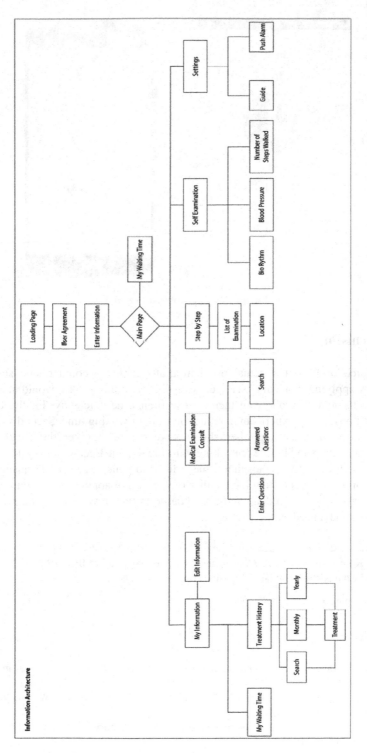

Fig. 5. On time application IA

Fig. 6. On time application GUI

5 Conclusion

This research outlined the actual problem that patients encounter, and suggests a solution by applying 'On Time' service. We expect that this service would increase the patient's satisfaction by allowing them to use their time efficiently. Firstly, they will reduce their anxiety by experiencing reduction in their waiting time. Secondly, they can be informed about what steps they should take before they see the doctor. Lastly, patients can be prepared before consulting with the doctor. Because the system is based on the research of a tertiary hospital it has a limit to generalize it to all hospitals. Our future research suggests testing the validity of the design application to actual patients, and also suggests a design that can be applicable to the universal hospital service will suggest more advanced in the future.

Acknowledgment. This research was supported by the MSIP(Ministry of Science, ICT and Future Planning), Korea, under the "IT Consilience Creative Program" (NIPA-2014-H0203-13-1002) supervised by the NIPA(National IT Industry Promotion Agency).

References

1. Bursch, B., Beezy, J.: Shaw.: emergency department satisfaction: what matters most? Ann. Emerg. Med. **22**, 92–97 (1993)
2. Daglish, D., Archer, N.: Electronic Personal Health Record Systems: A Brief Review of Privacy, Security and Architectural Issues
3. Dansky, K.H., Miles, J.: Patient satisfaction with ambulatory healthcare services: waiting time and filling time. Hosp. Health Serv. Adm. **42**, 165–177 (1997)

4. Eilers, G.: Improving patient satisfaction with waiting time. J. Am. College Health **53**, 41–48 (2010)
5. Hutchison, B., Ostbye, T., Barnsley, J., Stewart, M., Mathews, M., Campbell, M.K., Vayda, E., Harris, B.S., Torrance-Rynard, V., Tyrell, C.: Patient satisfaction and quality of care in walk-in clinics. Fam. Practices Emerg. Departments Ontario Walk-In Clinic Study Can. Med. Assoc. licensors **168**, 977–983 (2003)
6. Knudston, N.: Patient satisfaction with nurse practitioner service in a rural setting. J. Am. Assoc. Nurse Practitioners **12**, 405–412 (2000)
7. KT: Economy and business research center. cfile6.uf.tistory.com/attach/237C174452FECD26149E1D
8. Plsek, P.: Building a mind-set of service excellence, family practice management, 41–46 April 2002
9. Robertson, J., Balaam, M.: Designing for the needs of child patients in hospital settings. In: 12th International Conference on Interaction Design and Children, pp. 625–627. ACM Press, New York (2013)
10. Thompson, A.D., Yarnold, R.P., Williams, R.D., Adams, L., Stephen, Y.: Effects of actual waiting time, perceived waiting time, information delivery, and expressive quality on patient satisfaction in the emergency department. Ann. Emerg. Med. **28**, 657–665 (1996)
11. Ujjwal, A., Manglani, A., Akarte, D., Jain, A.: Healthbook-Ubiquitous Solution For Heath Services. Int. J. Eng. **2**, 965–967 (2012)
12. Unruh, K.T., Skeels, M., Civan-Hartzler, A., Pratt, W.: Transforming Clinic Environments into Information Workspaces for Patients. In: 28th SIGCHI, pp. 183–192. ACM Press, Atlanta (2010)

NAMIDA: Multiparty Conversation Based Driving Agents in Futuristic Vehicle

Nihan Karatas(✉), Soshi Yoshikawa, P. Ravindra S. De Silva,
and Michio Okada

Interaction and Communication Design Lab,
Toyohashi University of Technology, Toyohashi 441-8580, Japan
{karatas,yoshikawa}@icd.cs.tut.ac.jp, {ravi,okada}@tut.jp
http://icd.cs.tut.ac.jp/en/profile.html

Abstract. We propose socially interactive NAMIDA (Navigational Multiparty based Intelligent Driving Agents) as three friendly interfaces those sit on the dashboard inside a car. NAMIDA interfaces conduct multiparty conversation within each other to provide outside information for driver by utilising the context aware interaction. In this research, we introduce the conceptual design of NAMIDA and discuss about the superiorities of multiparty communication in the aspects of decreasing cognitive workload and increasing sociability plus enjoyable driving experience through an experiment which includes mock driving tasks by getting support from 1-NAMIDA (single) and 3-NAMIDAs (multiple) consecutively. Finally we mention about the results of the experiment which depicts that using multiparty based communication (3-NAMIDAs) could reduce the workload of driver and induced more enjoyable driving experience by increasing interaction and social bonding inside the car.

Keywords: Multiparty conversation · Context aware interaction · Conversational workload · NAMIDA

1 Introduction

While driving, a driver needs to achieve a variety of information; e.g., sightseeing places, best restaurants, the condition of roads, etc., also demands to spend enjoyable time of driving. Plenty of people prefer to use appealing mobile devices to attain useful applications to acquire mentioned information and enjoyment. Nevertheless, mobile devices are not designed to fulfil the drivers' demands inside a car, and the usage of those devices can divert driver's attention, consequently leads to accidents. Regarding to those issues, recently In Vehicle Infotainment (IVI) systems provide multitask opportunities to derive an efficient and entertaining driving as safe as possible [1]. Unfortunately common problems were identified in these systems as a workload of control menus, audio and visual feedback (looking at display), route guidance problems (always associated with designer's suggestions), reliability, lack of joy and intelligence and to give suggestions to driver. Navdy [2] is designed and developed as a transparent head up display in order to eradicate mobile phone interaction inside the car while

© Springer International Publishing Switzerland 2015
M. Kurosu (Ed.): Human-Computer Interaction, Part III, HCII 2015, LNCS 9171, pp. 198–207, 2015.
DOI: 10.1007/978-3-319-21006-3_20

providing navigation facility. By using Navdy drivers can control their smart phone through hand gestures and speech without getting in touch with the mobile device. In addition to reduce the workload and ensuring safety, considering the driver's social and emotional state is also crucial in driving. In this respect, Nissan has been implementing an assistive robot in order to present more human-like approach rather than other IVI systems [3]. Furthermore MIT created a friendly assistant AIDA which provides personalisation speciality inside the car [4]. AIDA can decide the relevant information while driving and express it at the most appropriate time with a suitable facial expression. AIDA communicates with the driver through speech coupled with expressive body movements.

All those systems use one to one communication (between a human and interface) which cannot reduce the workload sufficiently. Due to the fact that drivers still should be in an interaction with the above systems to obtain their demanded instructions while trying to focus on the road, having distraction is inevitable. It is possible to imagine a driving environment that requires less attention to be get informed and exposes social and emotional interaction with driver. At that point, applying multiparty conversation methods to an innovative driving agent interfaces in order to convey the information about outside of the car (e.g., sightseeing places, best restaurants, the condition of roads, etc.,) and providing sociability through this method can be considered.

Through multiparty conversation, the user doesn't have to participate into the conversation; instead of that user can be notified by the discussion among the other participants. Besides, whenever users want they can join into the conversation and can acquire additional information. Nakagawa [5] clarifies the advantages of multiparty conversation as (1) the conversation becomes more lively, (2) various interactive controls become possible (3) it is possible to expect the range of new applications of spoken dialog systems to widen. Furthermore, Mawari [6] has designed as an interactive social medium to boardcast information (e.g. news, etc.,). Mawari interface consists of three robots which conduct multiparty conversation to diminish the workload on the user.

In respect of reducing the workload and providing social and enjoyable environment inside a car we propose NAMIDA. NAMIDA has three intelligent social interfaces those fix on the dashboard of a futuristic vehicle and conduct multiparty conversation with respect to driver's suggestions by getting advantages of context aware interaction (e.g. suggested places in close around) facilities while providing enjoyable driving experience via establishing social bonding between the robots and the driver.

2 Concept of NAMIDA

NAMIDA interfaces conduct multiparty conversation such that the driver can obtain outside information (e.g., sightseeing places, best restaurants, etc.,) without participating in to the conversation. (Fig. 1) The multiparty conversation is fed by the outside information, which is the essence of the context-aware interaction to enlighten the driver about vicinity. Mentioned multiparty conversation includes asking questions, giving consistent answers and having discussions

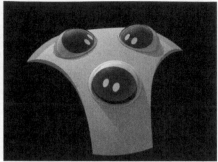

Fig. 1. The appearance of NAMIDA inside the car (*left*) and closer appearance of NAMIDA (*right*).

among the NAMIDA interfaces. While the driver having credible information from NAMIDA, he/she can make better decisions and starts to feel trust to NAMIDA. The social and emotional state based on trustfulness between two parties (driver and NAMIDA) brings more enjoyable and sociable environment inside the car. This pleasing engagement appears as a social bonding.

3   Design

We adapted to the minimal design mechanism as shown in Fig. 2. As an initial step of NAMIDA interfaces, we followed to implement an animation. The round-shape display of NAMIDA is for some facial expressions. Each NAMIDA has one degree of freedom for moving their head to right and left. All NAMIDAs sit on a common base which fits on the dashboard of the car. We used three different discernible colours (red, green, blue) for each NAMIDA's eyes and recognisable distinct roles in the conversation ((1wise (2)ignorant (3)cooperative) with varied voices to be implied that each NAMIDA has a different character. When one of them starts to talk, the other two turn their heads toward to speaker to expose the talking NAMIDA. Moreover, we used Eye Tribe in order to track the driver's eye gaze to become aware of his/her attention into road empirically.

Each NAMIDA utters its own lines according to the prepared script for a designed route. We used the Wizard Voice (ATR-Promotions) as a voice synthesis engine and Unity [13] to develop a driving simulation which consists a route of suggestible spots for driver. While getting closer to the spots, NAMIDAs start to perform multiparty conversation to give information about the place (context-aware interaction).

4   Interactive Architecture

4.1   Multiparty Conversation

One of the advantages of a multiparty conversation approach is having different personalities for each individuals to possesses their different kind of knowledge [7]. Mutlu and his colleagues [8] has explored a conversation structure,

Fig. 2. Minimal and futuristic design of multiparty based NAMIDA.

the participants' roles and the methods of shifting the roles during a multiparty-conversation. Also Goffman [9] introduced the concept of "footing" that explains the participants' roles in a conversation. Also it describes the concept of shifting roles in understanding the social interaction. It is possible to define four main roles of participants in a multiparty conversation which are speaker, address, side participants, and bystanders [10,11]. The side participant's role is waiting for the conversation to participate. However the bystander doesn't contribute to the conversation at the moment. These roles rotate/change during a conversation.

The proposed interface of NAMIDA is based on the above criteria in order to reduce the conversation workload due to shifting roles of participants during a conversation. The driver doesn't need to give an answer or respond to the conversation. Instead, another participant takes over the responsibility to continue the conversation. However there are times when the driver has to participate in the conversation. As long as the driver's role remains as a bystander, the NAMIDA interfaces interact with each other considering to the context aware interaction feature in a productive way so that, the driver can make a decision by listening the conversation. When the driver participates to the conversation then the roles are changed in to the side participant, speaker and addressee. The utterance generation of NAMIDA collaborates with symbolic display for eyes shape and basic body motions and the utterance generation architecture by utilizing the fillers, back-channel, turn-initial, etc., (Fig. 3).

4.2 Context-Aware Interaction

We designed a context-aware interaction system for NAMIDA. NAMIDA is capable of establishing interaction based on the location and it can capture those information within a certain km around from the car's current location and reveals it through a natural way in multiparty conversation. The utterance generation of NAMIDA based on modifying predetermined sentences with fillers,

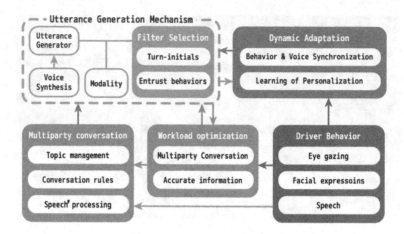

Fig. 3. Minimal and futuristic design of multiparty based NAMIDA.

back-channel, turn-initial, etc. to coordinate a productive conversation [12]. The content of the conversation (predetermined sentences) changes according to the surrounding locations. Each NAMIDA utterances their roles (according to prepared script) via a voice synthesizer to generate the conversation (in Japanese).

As an initial step, we developed a driving simulation that has several preferable destination spots to specify the locations statically for each driver. Through the context-aware interaction NAMIDAs acquaint those locations.

5   Experiment

Through our experiment, we intended to measure the workload, subjective impression (e.g. social bonding), effects of multiparty conversation, social interaction and attachment between the driver and the robots in two sessions (1-NAMIDA and 3-NAMIDA). In 1-NAMIDA interface, the participants listen to the one way conversation which consists of direct information. On the other hand, in 3-NAMIDAs interface, the participants listen to the multiparty conversation that involves asking questions, giving answers and having discussions. In both cases, the systems are using context-aware interaction. We divided our 14 participants (age range is in between 21 - 35; 3 female, 11 male) into half; while 7 participants had the experiment in the order of one NAMIDA case and three NAMIDA case, the other half had the experiment at first three NAMIDA case and then one NAMIDA case. Such a strategy is useful to acquire a counterbalance of the data, thereby reducing the effect of the sequence of trials on the results.

5.1   Experiment Set Up

In the experiments, each participant sit in a mock-in car environment and performed mock driving by watching the projected driving simulation on the wall (Fig. 4). The NAMIDA interface animations were displayed on a small screen

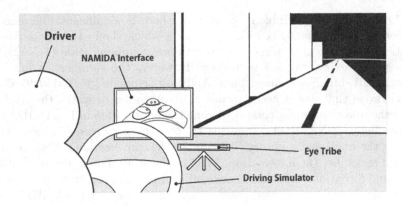

Fig. 4. The driver goes along the road while listening and understanding the contents of the nearby information through multiparty conversation.

that was placed left side of the dashboard. We arranged up two different sessions (one session for 1-NAMIDA interface, and one session for 3-NAMIDAs) for each participants. They charged to listen to the two distinct NAMIDA interfaces to wise up about the environment and remember the information to give right answers to the questions at the end of the each session. Each session took approximately 5 min. While in 1 NAMIDA session, the participants were charged to listen to the one NAMIDA interface in a one to one communication scenario; in 3-NAMIDAs session, the participants had to listen to the three NAMIDA interfaces in a multiparty conversation scenario. After each session the participants were required to evaluate 5 questions for workload and 6 questions for subjective impression which consists of social bonding. We used Driving Activity Load Index (DALI) as a subjective assessment tool in order to evaluate cognitive workload of the participants.

5.2 Driving Activity Load Index (DALI)

The DALI (Driving Activity Load Index) [14] is a revised version of the NASA-TLX [15] and adapted to the driving task. Mental workload is multidimensional and depends on the type of loading task. The basic principle of DALI is the same as the TLX. There is a scale rating procedure for six pre-defined factors, which are Effort of attention, Visual demand, Auditory demand, Temporal demand, Interference and Situational stress, (Table 1) followed by a weighting procedure in order to combine the six individual scales into a global score. However, in our study, we used five factors by excluding Interference factor, because this factor is most suitable when it is used in real driving environment.

5.3 Results

Both Workload and Interaction and Social Bonding questionnaires were scaled in a ranged of 1 - 5. For each question we applied pair-wise t-test to determine if the difference between the 1-NAMIDA and 3-NAMIDAs case is significant or not.

5.3.1 DALI Results: Table 1 shows that there is significant difference on Attention demand (p=0.033<0.05, significant) which shows that it is possible remember more content in the case of one to one communication (1-NAMIDA) due to its conveying method is directly. However, the significance in Visual (p=0.009<0.01, highly significant) and Auditory demands (p=0.0449<0.05, significant) reveal that driver needs to pay more attention to watch the road and listen to the conversation for comprehending the information in 1-NAMIDA case.

Accordingly, 3-NAMIDAs (multiparty conversation) requires less visual (watching the road) and auditory (listening to the conversation) effort to understand and remember the information (Fig. 5). The other dimensions of Temporal demand and Situation Stress have nonsignificant effect in either of the scenarios. The Global value of Dali yielded nonsignificant difference for 1-NAMIDA and 3-NAMIDA cases, because of the Temporal demand rated as higher in 3-NAMIDA case. The reason can be considered as the further conversation amount (more information) has been presented in 3-NAMIDA rather than 1-NAMIDA in the equal period of time (5 min).

Table 1. DALI factors and the mean differences for the DALI values in 1-NAMIDA and 3-NAMIDA. The endpoints for each factor is in rang 1 to 5 (1= Very Low, 2= Low, 3= Neutral, 4= High, 5= Very High)

Dimention	Endpoint	Question	Dali Values (Mean and Stand dev)		P-value
			1-NAMIDA	3-NAMIDA	
Attention demand	Low/High	How well do you remember the content of the conversations?	56.44 (8.55)	51 (28.34)	p=0.033<0.05 d.f.=13 significant
Visual demand	Low/High	Did you get tired of looking at road?	41.14 (18.72)	18.28 (9.75)	p= 0.009 <0.05 d.f.=13 significant
Auditory demand	Low/High	How much effort did you spend to understand the conversation?	34.28 (17.71)	17.5 (17.62)	p= 0.0449 <0.05 d.f.=13 significant
Temporal demand	Low/High	Did you feel time pressure to understand the conversation of the robot(s)?	19.00 (23.78)	29.81 (16.43)	p=0.145>0.05 d.f.=13 non-significant
Situation Stress	Low/High	Did you get stressed during driving?	26.66 (16.32)	25.71 (16.94)	p=0.45992>0.05 d.f.=13 non-significant
Global			35.50 (5.50)	28.46 (6.67)	p=0.224>0.05 d.f.=13 non-significant

5.3.2 Interaction and Social Bonding: The subjective impression questions which are based on interaction and social bonding (Table 2) indicates that there is significant differences on Q1, Q3 and Q6. The significance on Q1 implies that the multiparty conversation exhibits more human like approach rather than one to one communication. Also, the significance of Q3 in 3-NAMIDA case reveals to sense more animacy from multiparty conversation. Furthermore, the significance of Q6 depicts that the multiparty conversation exposes more natural way to convey the information.

On the other hand, the nonsignificant effect of Q2 can be interpret as the both system are adequate to convey the information. There is also nonsignificant difference for Q4 which means 1-NAMIDA and 3-NAMIDAs give almost the same feeling of being fellow(s) of the driver. Moreover the nonsignificant difference for Q5 indicates that both cases expose a high rated persuasiveness (Fig. 5) due to the well designed interface.

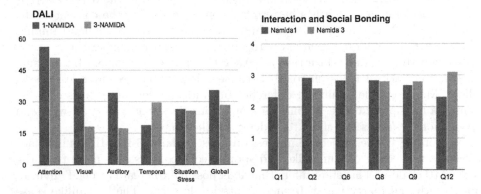

Fig. 5. Figure shows the result of Dali factors (*left*) and Interaction and Social Bonding (*right*) comparing 1-NAMIDA and 3-NAMIDAs

Table 2. Resulst of interaction and social bonding questionnaire indicates the significance state between 1-Namida and 3-Namida cases.

Code	Question	P-value	Result
Q1	Did you feel human likeness from the conversation?	p=0.000828<0.05 d.f.=13	significant
Q2	How often did you want to interact with the robot(s)?	p=0.082372>0.05 d.f.=13	non-significant
Q3	Do you feel that the robot(s) exhibited some animacy?	p=0.000944<0.05 d.f.=13	significant
Q4	Did you feel the robot(s) as friend(s)?	p=0.241561>0.05 d.f.=13	non-significant
Q5	Did you feel the robot(s) is/are persuasive?	p=0.357635>0.05 d.f.=13	non-significant
Q6	Did you feel the robot(s) conversation was spontaneous?	p=0.003853<0.05 d.f.=13	significant

5.4   Discussion and Conclusion

Overall, both cases (1-Namida and 3-Namida) there were nonsignificant differences in DALI factors of Temporal and Situation Stress demands. The reason is the both NAMIDA interfaces were capable of establishing a well-disposed social driving agents when they convey the information such that participants were not pressured to be concern about the timing and therefore experienced no fatigue or discouragement feeling. The significance in Attention demand reveals that one to one communication has better effect on remembering the content of the conversation. Yet, the highly significant difference on Virtual demand implies that driver exerts more visual effort to understand and remember the content. Consequently, we can deduce that 3-NAMIDAs can assist to avoid from visual distraction (lack of focus on road), because this approach requires less visual effort. Moreover, the significant difference on Auditory demand reveals that listening a multiparty conversation including asking questions, giving answers and discussions, requires less effort to understand the content.

According to the subjective impression questionnaire, 3-NAMIDAs interface presents the feeling of humanlike and spontaneous conversation more than the 1-NAMIDA does. This state infers that it is possible to create a social environment with multiparty based driving agents inside a car. The humanlike sense gives the feeling of the system (3-NAMIDAs) is far beyond of being just an instrument. The natural conversation manner of the multiparty conversation provides an enjoyable driving experience. In addition, the significantly highly rated animacy for 3-NAMIDAs implies that multiparty based interfaces expose more life-likeness which would be a core contribution to human-robot interaction research area. In our future work, we intend to implement a user-tracking mechanism in NAMIDA to use it in an interactive multiparty conversation to improve efficiency and sociability inside the vehicle.

Acknowledgement. Authors would like to express their gratitude to robotics designing group at Professor Michiteru Kitazaki and his Lab. This research has been supported by both Grant-in-Aid for scientific research of KIBAN-B (26280102) and Grantin-Aid for scientific research for HOUGA (24650053) from the Japan Society for the Promotion of Science (JSPS).

References

1. Integrated Computer Solutions Inc, Qt-based Automotive Software Solutions (1999). http://www.ics.com/services/ivi
2. Navdy Inc., Feels Like Driving in Future (2013). https://www.navdy.com/
3. Nissan Motor Company Ltd., PIVO: An in-car robotic assistant, In Automotto (2005)
4. Williams, K., Breazeal, C.: Reducing driver task load and promoting sociability through an Affective Intelligent Driving Agent (AIDA). In: Kotzé, P., Marsden, G., Lindgaard, G., Wesson, J., Winckler, M. (eds.) INTERACT 2013, Part IV. LNCS, vol. 8120, pp. 619–626. Springer, Heidelberg (2013)

 5. Todo, Y., Nishimura, R., Yamamoto, K., Nakagawa, S.: Development and evaluation of spoken dialog systems with one or two agents through two domains. In: Habernal, I. (ed.) TSD 2013. LNCS, vol. 8082, pp. 185–192. Springer, Heidelberg (2013)
 6. Yoshiike, Y., De Silva, P.R.S., Okada, M.: MAWARI: a social interface to reduce the workload of the conversation. In: Mutlu, B., Bartneck, C., Ham, J., Evers, V., Kanda, T. (eds.) ICSR 2011. LNCS, vol. 7072, pp. 11–20. Springer, Heidelberg (2011)
 7. Suzuki, N., Takeuchi, Y., Ishii, K., Okada, M.: Talking eye: autonomous creatures for augmented chatting. Robot. Auton. Syst. **31**, 171–184 (2000)
 8. Mutlu, B., Shiwa, T., Kanda, T., Ishiguro, H., Hagita, N.: Footing in human-robot conversations: how robots might shape participant roles using gaze cues. In: HRI 2009: Proceedings of the 4th ACM/IEEE International Conference on Human Robot Interaction, pp. 61–68. ACM, New York (2009)
 9. Goffman, E.: Footing. Semiotica **25**, 1–29 (1979)
10. Rehmann, A.J.: Handbook of Human Performance Measures and Crew: Requirements for Flightdeck Research. Ohio, Springfield, Virginia, 22161 (1995)
11. Okada, M., Kurihara, S., Nakatsu, R.: Incremental elaboration in generating and interpreting spontaneous speech. In: Proceedings of 3rd International Conference on Spoken Language Processing, pp. 103–106 (1994)
12. Sakamoto, D., Hayashi, K., Kanda, T., Shiomi, M., Koizumi, S., Ishiguro, H., Ogasawara, T., Hagita, N.: Humanoid robots as a broadcasting communication medium in open public spaces. I. J. Soc. Robot. **1**(2), 157–169 (2009)
13. Unity - PC, Mac and Linux desktop game development (2013). http://unity3d.com/
14. Pauzie, A.: A method to assess the driver mental workload: the driving activity load index (DALI). Intel. Transp. Syst. IET **2**(4), 315–322 (2008)
15. Hart, S.G., Staveland, L.E.: Development of NASA-TLX (Task Load Index): results of empirical and theoretical research. In: Hancock, P.A., Meshkati, N. (eds.) Human Mental Workload, ch. 7, pp. 139–183. Elsevier, Amsterdam (1988)

VR Processes in the Automotive Industry

Glyn Lawson[1(✉)], Davide Salanitri[1], and Brian Waterfield[2]

[1] Human Factors Research Group, Faculty of Engineering,
The University of Nottingham, Nottingham, UK
{glyn.lawson,davide.salanitri}@nottingham.ac.uk
[2] Jaguar Land Rover, Virtual Innovation Centre (VIC), Warwick, UK
bwaterfl@jaguarlandrover.com

Abstract. Virtual Reality (VR) has seen rapid developments in the past decades. Among the domains where VR has been applied, automotive has been a pioneer due to the possibility of cost and time reductions derived from the implementation of this technology. Examples of VR automotive applications include: (i) manufacturing workstation optimization; (ii) vehicle design; and (iii) assembly training. A review was conducted in order to understand opportunities and challenges in the application of VR in the automotive industry. This paper presents the review process, which encompasses interviews with stakeholders from an automotive manufacturer to understand their current processes and ambitions for VR use and a literature search of advancements in VR and empirical studies. A total of 11 stakeholders were interviewed. Recommendations are made to address the issues they reported, including: improve depth perception in VR technologies; use haptic feedback to improve manufacturing investigations; and provide virtual contexts for evaluations.

1 Introduction

Virtual Reality (VR) is defined as a 3D environment with which people are able to interact [1]. VR has seen rapid developments in the past decades, mainly due to cost reduction and an increase in the quality of both hardware and software. Thus, VR has been applied in several different fields, such as psychology, industry, medicine and training [2]. Among these domains, the automotive industry has been a pioneer of VR applications due to the possibility of cost and time reduction from the implementation of this technology [3]. Indeed, VR has been defined as one of the fundamental technologies permitting automotive firms to be competitive in this era, where time and cost reduction are essential requirements [4]. Consequentially, VR is used in several stages of the vehicle development process such as product design, modelling, simulation, manufacturing, training, testing and evaluation [4]. The following paragraphs provide some examples of VR application in the automotive industry.

Regarding manufacturing, VR has been widely applied to the extent that the term Virtual Manufacturing (VM) has been created. VM is defined as the use of virtual models or computer aided technologies in the process of developing a product [5] and has been seen as a revolutionary approach in the automotive industry, permitting firms to improve decision making and to reduce the cost of the entire manufacturing process

© Springer International Publishing Switzerland 2015
M. Kurosu (Ed.): Human-Computer Interaction, Part III, HCII 2015, LNCS 9171, pp. 208–217, 2015.
DOI: 10.1007/978-3-319-21006-3_21

[4]. Moreover, VM has been seen to enhance the capability of risk measure and control, and increase firms' effectiveness in the market [6]. As [5] stated, VM "can easily be perceived as the next generation interface, as indicated by the current trend in use of multi-media and network" (p.82).

In the field of design, VR is rapidly replacing the use of physical mock-ups to speed up the design process [7]. Indeed, the design process is not a continuous procedure, but it requires various modifications and reviews, causing a "bottleneck" effect [8]. With the application of VR this "back and forward" process is simplified and can be made without rebuilding physical mock-ups [9]. Another advantage of VR in design is the possibility of having multidisciplinary teams with people not geographically close working together [4]. For example, literature shows that the implementation of VR systems could permit a "distributed Virtual Reality" [10], where people from all around the world can contribute together in the design process at the same time, allowing a cost and time reduction and an increase of quality.

Another example of the advantages that VR has in automotive industries is in virtual prototyping (VP) defined as the use of VR to develop and design the main characteristics of a prototype. Studies show that replacing physical mocks-up with virtual prototypes reduces development time and the cost drastically [11]. This also has a great advantage in the process of decision-making, one of the most problematic situation during the developing of a product, especially in the early stages, where decisions account for as much as 70 % of the total cost of the life cycle [7, 12]. As [12] stated, VP could improve the total quality of a product.

In the field of training, the results of a review showed that Virtual and Mixed reality training has a high impact in solving problems and are preferred by the trainees [13].

Another example of how VR is implemented in the automotive industry is Virtual Assembly (VA). VA is the process where people can assemble and disassemble virtual products in a virtual environment [14] permitting the analysis of, among other things, the workers' well-being. VA has been seen as advantageous in terms of health and safety for the workers because, by allowing simulations of workspaces, it can reveal issues in the way workers perform their tasks. Another advantage of VA is the possibility to speed up the process of implementation of new design methods and tools, improve products' quality, and reduce time-to-market and cost [15]. For a complete review of the advantages of VR in the manufacturing process of a product see [4].

Jaguar Land Rover (JLR) are already using VR in their manufacturing process, and are a recognized leader in the field of VR in automotive applications. However, given the fast progress of VR technologies and recent improvements in hardware and software, and JLR's desire to continuously innovate and improve, a review was commissioned to help the firm understand the new opportunities and new challenges for virtual technologies and processes within a variety of JLR business functions. These included product development, manufacturing and service. This review has been conducted systematically and benefits from findings from research into the use of VR tools in a variety of engineering processes. The review process encompasses interviews with JLR stakeholders to understand their current processes and ambitions for VR use. These interviews guided a literature search of advancements in VR and empirical studies which formed the basis of recommendations for development in JLR.

2 Method

The method is depicted in Fig. 1. The general approach was to scope the review, then interview VR stakeholders to understand their current processes and ambitions, if any, for VR use. The results of the interviews guided a literature review on the latest advancements in VR and the most recent empirical studies to build a set of recommendations for future investments in new technology.

2.1 Participants

A total of 11 JLR employees were recruited for the interviews. The participants were recruited from a variety of engineering functions with an average of 6.8 years in their current role (SD = 6.6) and of 16.1 years at JLR (SD = 13.7). All participants were approached by the researcher based on recommendations from the Virtual Innovation Centre (VIC) at JLR of people who are currently using VR or who had expressed interest in using VR as part of their processes.

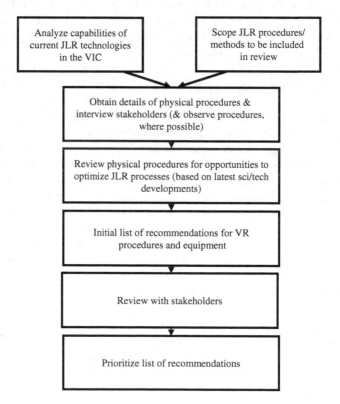

Fig. 1. Scheme of the research activities

2.2   Materials

A questionnaire was developed to understand stakeholders' roles, current processes and usage of vehicle properties, both physical and virtual. They were asked when properties were used within the vehicle development processes. Stakeholders were also asked which aspects of human interaction with the vehicle are necessary for their design and engineering activities. The questionnaire was divided into 12 topics gathered in 2 categories (Table 1).

Table 1. Division of topics and categories derived from the questionnaire

	Categories	
Topics	Physical	Virtual
	Currently used physical properties	Currently used virtual processes / properties
	Use of physical properties	Use of virtual processes / properties
	Important attributes to be demonstrated on physical properties	Important attributes for virtual properties
	Issues with physical properties	Limitations of virtual properties
	Users of physical properties	Users of virtual properties
	Comparisons of alternative design proposals	
	Comparison to competitors	

2.3   Procedure

Participants were invited to a private meeting room. They were asked to read a participant information sheet and sign a consent form. The researcher explained the purpose of the study before asking questions about VR use in a semi-structured format. The study received approval from The University of Nottingham Faculty of Engineering Ethics Committee.

3   Outcomes

The outcomes of the interviews analyses are gathered in the following Tables. Table 2 gives a general description of the information extrapolated from the interviews. Table 3 presents the recommendations derived from both the interviews analysis and literature review.

Based on the information gathered in the table above, the issues reported by the stakeholders and a detailed literature review on the latest technologies and scientific findings, a set of recommendations has been developed (Table 3).

Table 2. Summary of the information extrapolated from the interviews

Category	Topic	Summary of responses
Physical	Currently used physical properties	Respondents use a variety of properties in their current processes, including a range of prototype vehicles and adaptations to donor vehicles (i.e. modified existing production cars).
	Uses of physical properties	Physical properties are used for: evaluation of design intent with engineers, internal representations of customers and with external customers; design; communication (with engineers); and training of production line operators. A variety of properties are used throughout the physical development process.
	Important attributes to be demonstrated on physical properties	The most important attributes found were about the vehicles' appearance and components, the exterior road scene (including sound and noise), movements (such as reach and clearance) and haptic feedback.
	Issues with physical properties	The main issue regarding physical properties is the time to produce them, causing delays in reviews and evaluations. Moreover, the physical properties require space and lack modifiability. Sometimes evaluations are conducted out of context (i.e. wheel on a desk).
	Users of physical properties	The users are usually evaluators and customers
Virtual	Currently used virtual processes /properties	The three main technologies used at JLR are Cave Automatic Virtual Environment (CAVE), a dynamic simulator and a motion capture suit.
	Uses of virtual processes / properties	VR is used mainly for simulations (for vehicles architecture, overlaying vehicles, noise etc.), ergonomic evaluations, design and reviews.
	Important attributes for virtual properties /processes	Generally the same as for physical properties, although virtual properties tend to be used earlier or if there is no physical property available.

(*Continued*)

Table 2. (*Continued*)

Category	Topic	Summary of responses
	Limitations of virtual properties	In general the participants observed that there are some characteristics missing from the VR systems, such as haptic feedback, physical collision etc., some issues derive from comfort (HMD, ergo suit) and other problems came from availability.
	Users of virtual properties	All used by JLR experts.
	Comparisons of alternative design proposals	Most interviewees compare design alternatives, either alternatives for current programme or comparisons with outgoing models /competitors.
	Comparison to competitors	Done using scan data, photographs of cars, competitor benchmark data, or having properties sitting next to a representation of the design intent.

Table 3. Recommendations based on the issues addressed by stakeholders and literature review

Issues	Recommendations
Difficulties with depth perception (near distances).	Use textured background surfaces in virtual spaces [16]. Use shadows and object inter-reflections to improve depth perception Use multi-sensory (vision and haptic) feedback [17].
Lack of tool weight. Necessity to simulate the haptic feedback experienced when moving a component through a complex path. Necessity of simulation of torques and lifting weights. Need to investigate complex ergonomics tasks.	Introduce a haptic arm with force feedback for complex gross-motor tasks. This should include force feedback. The system should simulate vibration, torque and force required to lift weights [12]. A haptic system should also be developed to support Design [16].
Sound can be an important component of switch operation and assembly ergonomics. Vehicle noise was described as an important part of vehicle assessments.	3D sound should be provided [6, 17, 18]
With clash conditions, physical feedback is needed.	Develop whole-body haptic indication of collisions of human body parts in virtual environments [19].
Understanding reach is important in all processes.	Implement a system offering haptic indication of reach [20–22] .

(*Continued*)

Table 3. (*Continued*)

Issues	Recommendations
Context is required for component assessments.	Develop the CAVE to allow components to be evaluated in realistic vehicle and driving environment contexts [23].
CAVE could be useful for driver distraction work	Develop driver distraction assessment capabilities, including: ability to simulate behaviour of electrical features, eye tracking, lane deviation [24]
There are a number of issues with the current marker-based tracking system.	Investigate the use of a markless tracking system [25–27]
Need a moving road scene for subjective experience.	An exterior road scene should be displayed to users [28, 29].
Physical parts are used to assess air quality; olfactory simulation could bring assessments earlier in process.	Provide olfactory simulation [30, 31].
Garish colors in CAD can affect perception	Provide realistic colors for parts [32, 33].
There are travel issues to the site where the VR systems are situated.	Consider networked, low-end 3D VR for colleagues at other sites [10, 34, 35].
VR training could be used before people go on track or avoid stopping the line.	Use virtual reality systems for training new car assembly processes [13, 36].

4   Conclusion

Progress in VR developments affects several departments and processes of the automotive industry. In order to be competitive, a firm has to be constantly up to date with the latest innovations, which could make a fundamental difference in terms of product quality, cost and time saving, and the quality of the workplace. This review was conducted to support JLR, a leader in the use of VR in automotive applications, in remaining progressive in adapting recent technology developments and scientific discoveries.

The outcomes of the interviews with stakeholders revealed some issues in the use of both physical and VR processes. Regarding VR systems actually used at JLR, the stakeholders reported some hardware problems (e.g. weight of HMD, difficulties with the bodytracker suit), some software problems (e.g. issues with depth perception, color rendering) and other issues derived for example from the time schedule and the site where technologies have been implemented. To solve these problems the recommendations are concentrated on the enhancement of the existing technologies with new tools and new characteristics.

A limitation of this study is that only stakeholders who were existing users of VR systems were recruited to participate in the study. There may be other engineers or disciplines who could benefit from VR, but who are not aware of its capabilities or how to access it. However, the primary aim of the interviews was to guide the direction of the literature review based on the types of assessments being conducted. As many recommendations are applicable across disciplines, it is likely that these changes would benefit new users of the VIC. Moreover, recruiting a representative from every engineering discipline would have been outside the scope of this research.

Acknowledgements. The authors would like to thank Jaguar Land Rover for funding this research.

References

1. Rheingold, H.: Virtual Reality: Exploring the Brave New Technologies. Simon & Schuster Adult Publishing Group, New York (1991)
2. Slater, M.: Grand Challenges in Virtual Environments. Frontiers, p. 3 (2014)
3. Dai, F., Hopgood, F., Lucas, M., Requicha, A., Hosaka, M., Guedj, R., Bo, K., Foley, J., Hagen, P.: Virtual reality for industrial applications. Springer-Verlag New York Inc, Sesaucus (1997)
4. Mujber, T., Szecsi, T., Hashmi, M.: Virtual reality applications in manufacturing process simulation. J. Mater. Process. Technol. **155**, 1834–1838 (2004)
5. Shukla, C., Vazquez, M., Chen, F.F.: Virtual manufacturing: an overview. Comput. Ind. Eng. **31**, 79–82 (1996)
6. Lee, W., Cheung, C., Li, J.: Applications of virtual manufacturing in materials processing. J. Mater. Process. Technol. **113**, 416–423 (2001)
7. Shao, F., Robotham, A.J., Hon, K.: Development of a 1: 1 Scale True Perception Virtual Reality System for design review in automotive industry. In: 10th International Conference on Manufacturing Research ICMR 2012, published in: Advances in Manufacturing Technology – XXVI: Proceedings of the 10th International Conference on Manufacturing Research (ICMR2012), vol. 2, pp. 468 – 473 (6) (2012)
8. Fiorentino, M., De Amicis, R., Monno, G., Stork, A.: Spacedesign: a mixed reality workspace for aesthetic industrial design. In: 2002 Proceedings of the International Symposium on Mixed and Augmented Reality, ISMAR 2002, pp. 86–318. IEEE (2002)
9. Kim, C., Lee, C., Lehto, M.R., Yun, M.H.: Affective evaluation of user impressions using virtual product prototyping. Hum. Factors Ergon. Manuf. Serv. Ind. **21**, 1–13 (2011)
10. Lehner, V.D., DeFanti, T.A.: Distributed virtual reality: supporting remote collaboration in vehicle design. IEEE Comput. Graph. Appl. **17**, 13–17 (1997)
11. Kulkarni, A., Kapoor, A., Iyer, M., Kosse, V.: Virtual prototyping used as validation tool in automotive design. In: 19th International Congress on Modelling and Simulation-Sustaining Our Future: Understanding and Living with Uncertainty (2011)
12. de Sá, G.A., Zachmann, G.: Virtual reality as a tool for verification of assembly and maintenance processes. Comput. Graph. **23**, 389–403 (1999)
13. Borsci, S., Lawson, G., Broome, S.: Empirical evidence, evaluation criteria and challenges for the effectiveness of virtual and mixed reality tools for training operators of car service maintenance. Comput. Ind. **67**, 17–26 (2015)
14. Qiu, S., Fan, X., Wu, D., He, Q., Zhou, D.: Virtual human modeling for interactive assembly and disassembly operation in virtual reality environment. Int. J. Adv. Manuf. Technol. **69**, 2355–2372 (2013)

15. Jayaram, S., Connacher, H.I., Lyons, K.W.: Virtual assembly using virtual reality techniques. Comput. Aided Des. **29**, 575–584 (1997)
16. Evans, M.A.: Rapid prototyping and industrial design practice: can haptic feedback modelling provide the missing tactile link? Rapid Prototyp. J. **11**, 153–159 (2005)
17. Jayaram, S., Vance, J., Gadh, R., Jayaram, U., Srinivasan, H.: Assessment of VR technology and its applications to engineering problems. J. Comput. Inf. Sci. Eng. **1**, 72–83 (2001)
18. Slater, M., Wilbur, S.: A framework for immersive virtual environments (FIVE): Speculations on the role of presence in virtual environments. Presence Teleoperators Virtual Environ. **6**, 603–616 (1997)
19. Kim, C.E., Vance, J.M.: Collision detection and part interaction modeling to facilitate immersive virtual assembly methods. J. Comput. Inf. Sci. Eng. **4**, 83–90 (2004)
20. Barros, R.Q., Soares, M.M., Fernandes, M.G.: Ergonomic evaluation of manual force levels of the elderly in the handling of products: an analysis using virtual reality. In: Marcus, A. (ed.) DUXU 2014, Part IV. LNCS, vol. 8520, pp. 124–132. Springer, Heidelberg (2014)
21. Durlach, P.J., Fowlkes, J., Metevier, C.J.: Effect of variations in sensory feedback on performance in a virtual reaching task. Presence Teleoperators Virtual Environ. **14**, 450–462 (2005)
22. Swapp, D., Pawar, V., Loscos, C.: Interaction with co-located haptic feedback in virtual reality. Virtual Reality **10**, 24–30 (2006)
23. Maguire, M.: Context of use within usability activities. Int. J. Hum. Comput. Stud. **55**, 453–483 (2001)
24. van der Horst, R.: Occlusion as a measure for visual workload: an overview of TNO occlusion research in car driving. Appl. Ergon. **35**, 189–196 (2004)
25. Kehl, R., Gool, L.V.: Markerless tracking of complex human motions from multiple views. Comput. Vis. Image Underst. **104**, 190–209 (2006)
26. Lange, B., Rizzo, S., Chang, C.-Y., Suma, E.A., Bolas, M.: Markerless full body tracking: depth-sensing technology within virtual environments. In: The Interservice/Industry Training, Simulation & Education Conference (I/ITSEC). NTSA (2011)
27. Poppe, R.: Vision-based human motion analysis: an overview. Comput. Vis. Image Underst. **108**, 4–18 (2007)
28. Burnett, G., Lawson, G., Millen, L., Pickering, C., Webber, E.: Designing touchpad user-interfaces for right-hand drive vehicles: an investigation into where the touchpad should be located. Behav. Inf. Technol. **32**, 874–887 (2013)
29. Herriotts, P., Johnson, P.: Are you sitting comfortably? A guide to occupant packaging in automotive design. In: Gkikas, N. (ed.) Automotive Ergonomics: Driver-vehicle Interaction, pp. 17–39. CRC Press, Boca Raton (2012)
30. Matsukura, H., Yoneda, T., Ishida, H.: Smelling screen: development and evaluation of an olfactory display system for presenting a virtual odor source. IEEE Trans. Visual. Comput. Graphics **19**, 606–615 (2013)
31. Purschke, F., Schulze, M., Zimmermann, P.: Virtual reality-new methods for improving and accelerating the development process in vehicle styling and design. In: 1998 Proceedings of the Computer Graphics International, pp. 789–797. IEEE (1998)
32. Gabbard, J.L., Swan, J.E., Zedlitz, J., Winchester, W.W.: More than meets the eye: an engineering study to empirically examine the blending of real and virtual color spaces. In: 2010 IEEE Conference Virtual Reality(VR), pp. 79–86. IEEE (2010)
33. Kruijff, E., Swan II, J.E., Feiner, S.: Perceptual issues in augmented reality revisited. ISMAR **9**, 3–12 (2010)

34. Ausburn, L.J., Ausburn, F.B.: Desktop virtual reality: A powerful new technology for teaching and research in industrial teacher education. Journal of Industrial Teacher Education **41**, 33–58 (2004)
35. Sharples, S., Cobb, S., Moody, A., Wilson, J.R.: Virtual reality induced symptoms and effects (VRISE): Comparison of head mounted display (HMD), desktop and projection display systems. Displays **29**, 58–69 (2008)
36. Stone, R.: Virtual reality for interactive training: an industrial practitioners viewpoint. Int. J. Hum. Comput. Stud. **55**, 699–711 (2001)

Entrepreneurial IS Development: Why Techniques Matter and Methods Don't

Nikolaus Obwegeser[✉]

School of Business and Social Sciences, Aarhus University, Aarhus, Denmark
obweg@asb.dk

Abstract. In this article we look at the current situation of information systems development in research and mirror our findings with insights from practice. Many firms and decision makers underestimate the influence that IS development projects have on their success and competitiveness. In addition, the process of efficient development of high quality and value-creating software remains a major challenge for many organizations. After a review of general IS development approaches we draw on an analysis of the literature on method tailoring and contingency approaches in IS development in combination with qualitative empirical insights from two software development companies to posit that past research has largely focused on creating bloated, inflexible methods rather than flexible toolsets. Based on the analysis of our findings we propose an open, framework-based IS development approach that allows for the flexibility required in practice but still ensures learning processes, knowledge retention and transfer.

Keywords: IS development · Agile · Methodology · Software engineering

1 Introduction

In this article we look at the current situation of information systems development (ISD) in research and mirror our findings with insights from practice. Information systems (IS) can be the driver behind great success stories and the reason for the downfall of large companies. Nevertheless, many firms and decision makers underestimate the influence that IS development projects have on their success and competitiveness. In addition, the efficient development of high quality and value-creating software remains a major challenge for many organizations. After a review of general IS development approaches we draw on an analysis of the literature on method tailoring and contingency approaches in IS development in combination with qualitative empirical insights from two software development companies to posit that past research has largely focused on creating bloated, inflexible methods rather than flexible toolsets. Based on the analysis of our findings we propose an open, framework-based IS development approach that allows for the flexibility required in practice but still ensures learning processes, knowledge retention and transfer.

Triggered by many talks with developers and observations of ISD projects we find that, while ISD is an active field of research, academics are nevertheless largely unable to inform practitioners on practices and tools to apply in real life scenarios. Despite the

© Springer International Publishing Switzerland 2015
M. Kurosu (Ed.): Human-Computer Interaction, Part III, HCII 2015, LNCS 9171, pp. 218–225, 2015.
DOI: 10.1007/978-3-319-21006-3_22

vast amount of methods and different approaches to ISD discussed over time [1, 2], practitioners often openly report about their inability to apply theoretical, academic knowledge to practical settings, especially in the context of IT startups and SMEs. This situation might be traced back to the inherent complexities and challenges to ISD, as discussed in [3]. In this sense, we argue that there is a need for a radical re-thinking of the process of ISD, which has to start with an explorative investigation of the practices at the very core of the discipline instead of developing "yet another" normative method handbook.

In contrast to other ISD research efforts we start with a tabula-rasa, "an empty table" to provide an exploratory look at how highly entrepreneurial companies (young SMEs, start-ups) take up the challenge of ISD. This allows us to mirror the academic state-of-the-art with actual practices. We investigate two successful IT SMEs that have been founded after 2000 and have since grown steadily. Using a case study research design [4] including observation, interviews and document analysis we draw a picture of how these companies deal with methodology of IS development in practice. Case studies are especially useful in this situation because they allow us to investigate and understand the "how" and "why" behind observed behavior [5]. Both SMEs have decided on purpose not to have a formalized method but leave it greatly up to the specific project teams to decide which techniques, tools and practices are fit in the specific context, location and time. While ISD methods in large organizations with a long history of software development are often subject to path dependent decision processes that are likely to hinder innovation [6], these startups can provide unique insights and learning opportunities due to their entrepreneurial spirit and affinity to innovation.

Our findings show that while research has recently moved closer to practice, from method tailoring to flexible method combinations and contingency theories [2, 7, 8], real-life practices of SMEs are yet much more radical in the way they approach ISD projects. The project teams in the two case companies decide on a mix-and-match set of techniques that they agree on in a consensual way and re-evaluate the mix regularly to adapt it to the current state of the project. Techniques found can be based on plan-based methods like the Rational Unified Process [9] (e.g. requirement planning based on use-cases), agile methods like eXtreme Programming [10] or Scrum [11] (e.g. pair-programming, iterative prototyping). Other practices we found were partially or completely self-developed (e.g. acceptance trials by non-involved colleagues). The specific mix itself is dynamic and changes whenever the need arises. This high degree of flexibility comes with an intensive need for broad knowledge about different tech-niques and their potential combinations – in contrast to detailed knowledge or certi-fications often required for specific ISD methods and processes.

Based on our findings, we propose an open framework approach to ISD, which follows the idea of the UML and other modelling frameworks (e.g. ARIS). The framework is designed to be inclusive for all ISD related topics, e.g. coding standards, user interaction, and metrics and lists potential techniques for the respective areas. In addition, the framework holds information about possible constraints and best-practice technique combinations. Thus, practitioners are given the possibility to create ad hoc methods in a mix-and-match way, based on an informed decision process. Moreover, researchers and practitioners can add innovative techniques, combinations or practical insights to grow the knowledge base.

The remainder of this article is structured as follows. Section 2 elaborates on the methodology applied and is followed by a review of relevant literature in Sect. 3. After introducing our cases in Sect. 4 we present our findings and discussion in Sect. 5. Finally we conclude the research paper and point to future research topics.

2 Methodology

This paper builds upon an interpretive, multiple case study methodology based on qualitative data [12]. After presenting the state of the art in scientific literature on method tailoring and contingency approaches we contrast our theoretical insights with empirical data gathered from two software development companies.

Using inductive data analysis we are able to provide anecdotal evidence for our notion of a research-practice gap in IS development. A multiple case study design allows for cross-case analysis and comparison in order to generate or extend existing theory [5]. Moreover, multiple-case study research is expected to generate more robust, generalizable and testable theory than a single-case research [13].

Both case companies are SMEs according to the definition of the OECD [14], founded after 2000 and have been growing rapidly. We have chosen a qualitative research approach based on interviews and document analysis to allow for an in-depth analysis of the situation in practice. Case studies are especially valuable when studying a complex phenomenon in the practical context by means of multiple, different data collection methods in order to answer "how" and "why" questions [5].

We use interviews and document analysis in order to draw a picture of how the companies deal with methodology of IS development in practice. Mirroring real-life practices with findings from literature provides a picture of the gap that exists between theory and practice. This is in line with the claim by [7], that just as in many emerging and radically changing fields, practice is ahead of research and academia.

2.1 Selection of Case Companies

Case companies were selected among successful SME software engineering companies founded after 2000. We argue that these companies allow for better insights into the choice of ISD method since their decision processes are less framed by historically institutionalized behavior and structures. Successful companies were found by looking for continuous growth patterns in both number of employees and turnover. Both companies are mainly depending on local private and public customers and are therefore often competitors in the same market.

Table 1. Case companies

Company*	Sector	Founded	Number of employees	Interviewee
Digital Trends	ICT	2001	68	Software manager
SoftCo	ICT	2007	80	Senior developer

*Names have been changed due to confidentiality agreements.

2.2   Data Sources

Our data collection consisted primarily of interviews and analysis of ISD related documents that were provided by the companies. In addition, numerous informal talks and conversations led to the formulation of initial research hypotheses. The target informants for our interviews were software managers or senior software engineers, who were deemed to be knowledgeable about the company's choice of ISD method and the rationale behind this decision. All interviews were semi-structured and therefore partially depending on the conversational path the interviewee decided upon. All interviews and document analysis was conducted between November 2014 and February 2015. After analyzing the cases separately, we conducted a cross-case analysis to locate common themes that emerged. Our inferences are grounded on the empirical data provided by our interviews as well as the information gathered in the document analysis [15].

3   Relevant Literature

Historically, ISD has changed from small, independent experts working on specialized pieces of software to large scale software development operations. [1] provide a historical overview of ISD methods, identifying four sequential eras: pre-methodology, early methodology, methodology and post-methodology. Similarly, [2] draw a comparison between the movement from craft to industrial production of physical goods, evolving from pre-industrial to industrial and finally post-industrial making.

From the introduction of the System Development Lifecycle (SDLC), to the large scale adoption of the waterfall model [16] and heavy-weight, plan-based methods like the Rational Unified Process [9] to today's widespread use of agile methods and practices [17] as proposed in SCRUM [11] or eXtreme Programming [10]: None of the methods or method-combinations can be considered to solve all problems and complexities of ISD [3]. In addition, practitioners generally customize and adopt the formal methods according to how they see fit and need. This led to the proposal of Fitzgerald's "Method-in-Action" framework [18] of ISD, which can help to understand the multitude of influencing factors and constraint that shape a method in action, which may or may not be based on a formalized method. Reference [2] propose a contingency theory approach to method choice and tailoring. Reference [19] use a quasi-experiment to analyze the organizational challenges of enabling ambidextrous ISD processes (viz. enabling projects to use both agile and traditional methods within the same organization).

4   Case Description

In this article, we look at the current situation of ISD in research and mirror our findings with insights from practice. Being aware of fact that organizational change is often slow and follows a path-dependent logic, we have chosen not look at large scale, established companies. Our empirical data is collected from two companies in the SME sector, which have been founded after 2000 and have been growing rapidly since then. Due to the entrepreneurial atmosphere in the case companies, we were able to observe and analyze an unbiased approach to choice of ISD method. Our findings show that while the two firms pursue somewhat different approaches in the way and level they define policy and method guidelines for the development teams, they show distinct commonalities in the process of institutionalizing these processes within the organization.

5   Findings and Discussion

Our case companies provided us with detailed insights into their development environment. Both companies we investigate are software developing companies specialized on tailor-made solutions and not off-the-shelf software. In the course of our research, we were able to gather an understanding of how the organizations perceive themselves and their approach to IS development. This sometimes led to the discovery of gaps between practices that are enacted and practices as formalized. We will present both companies in detail and support our findings with anecdotal evidence from the interviews conducted. Within both companies, we could see that even in cases where only little formal requirements to the IS development process are defined, these tend to be shaped and re-defined by practitioners dynamically over and over again in a context dependent manner. Thus, any formalization of development process can be argued to be redundant, if it includes normative rules, policies, or guidelines that are interpreted context dependent.

5.1   Digital Trends

The company has been established in the early 2000 s and initially decided to start off by using SCRUM. Aside from software development, a big part of their work is related to consulting their clients in strategy, technology and project management.

As a result of constant evaluation and re-formulation of their methodological approach, Digital Trends nowadays has a very radical approach to software development methodologies. While they still consider themselves to be very close to SCRUM, the interviewee (SM) points out on many occasions that they use a different combination of tools and techniques in almost every project. Moreover, they start out with a methodological configuration (often non-formalized) at the beginning of a project which is subject to change as the project evolves. This is how they pay tribute to the truly agile nature of their work, as described by SM.

In contrast to more structured approaches to ISD, Digital Trends perceives the people as the most critical risk factors to their projects and aligns everything they do and how they do it along to this organizational context. "It's all about creating value for the customer" is what SM points out, and not about following blindly to a specific methodology.

Every decision in Digital Trends is done in a completely democratic way. While a manager can ask specific people to join a new project, it is entirely up to them to decide if they agree and see fit to their own skillset or rather opt for a different task. Within project teams, all team member decide together on what techniques can and should be applied internally (e.g. pair programming) and externally (e.g. meeting intervals with customers). This creates a high level of both trust and responsibility which fosters the individual's involvement above what is specified in work contracts or policies. According to SM, Digital Trends tries to apply this idea also with their customers, by not having (written) contractual agreements with them. Other research shows that contracts can in fact have a negative influence towards inter-personal and inter-organizational trust which leads to a people fulfilling contractual agreements but acting less benevolent [20].

Overall, the set of techniques used at Digital Trends is based partially on SCRUM, eXtreme Programming, Kanban and partially self-developed. The specific configuration for each project at a certain point in time is context dependent and can be altered by the team-members only.

5.2   SoftCo

After their foundation in 2007, SoftCo decided to adapt SCRUM to their own needs and requirements. A major criterion for SoftCo is to remain agile in all project phases, so they designed their own SCRUM based, internally formalized method called "BlueSky" (name changed).

The interviewee (SD) at SoftCo states that when developing a system, they always have three perspectives in mind: the end-user, the business requirements and the technological quality of the system. In order to achieve high levels of satisfaction on all three of these perspectives, they argue that that BlueSky allows them to remain as agile as necessary but provides basic structures to follow. To describe SoftCo's understanding of ISD methods, SD uses a quote by former US President Dwight D. Eisenhower: "Plans are nothing, planning is everything". This is to understand why they keep a model like BlueSky as a planning framework to act within, while the real planning is flexible and context-dependent.

SD points out that the simple notion of "one size fits all" methodologies will just not work in practice, so they have tailor-made approaches for their projects – based on the overall idea sketched out in BlueSky. SoftCo sees themselves as practicing a version of SCRUM that is close to the original intention of the authors - as a framework to allow for all different kinds of software developing techniques and concepts - while many companies nowadays use SCRUM in a much to formalized and by-the-book understanding.

6 Conclusion and Future Research

In this paper we point to the fact that while research on ISD methods has produced an enormous amount of literature that provides normative guidelines, what many practitioners are actually looking for is a toolbox-like collection of techniques and best practices that can be applied and combined in a mix-and-match way. Many methods - be it traditional or agile – tend to be too rigid in the way software development is approached. ISD companies nowadays often are not only engineering companies, but they have to combine skills and management support for a wide range of related tasks from strategy and technology consulting to training and education. The ISD method has to be able to fit their unique needs and dynamically adapt to changes.

Thus, we argue a framework based approach that focuses more on the level of techniques and less on the level of methods and process designs is highly valuable to practitioners. Our research is based on the findings from two case companies that allowed us insights into how entrepreneurial organizations address the problem of selecting the right ISD practices. We find that while both organizations initially aim to stick close to what literature and theory can offer them, they tend to drift away in the course of practice due to the gap between needs in practice and theoretical models. Future researchers are encouraged to pick up these ideas from the empirical base and re-consider flexible, framework-style approaches to ISD that can efficiently support practitioners in their daily work.

References

1. Avison, D., Fitzgerald, G.: Methodologies for developing information systems : a historical perspective. In: Avison, D., Elliot, S., Krogstie, J., Pries-Heje, J. (eds.) The Past Future of Information System: 1976–2006 and Beyond, pp. 27–38. Springer, Berlin (2006)
2. Austin, R.D., Devin, L.: Research commentary —weighing the benefits and costs of flexibility in making software: toward a contingency theory of the determinants of development process design. Inf. Syst. Res. 20, 462–477 (2009)
3. Brooks Jr., F.P.: No Silver Bullet—Essence and Accidents of Software Engineering. Comput. 20(4), 10 (1987). doi:10.1109/MC.1987.1663532
4. Yin, R.K.: Case Study Research: Design and Methods. SAGE Publications, Thousand Oaks (2003)
5. Benbasat, I., Goldstein, D.K., Mead, M.: The case research strategy in studies of information systems. MIS Q. 11, 369–386 (1987)
6. Patel, P., Pavitt, K.: The technological competencies of the world's largest firms: complex and path-dependent, but not much variety. Res. Policy 26, 141–156 (1997)
7. Conboy, K.: Agility from first principles: reconstructing the concept of agility in information systems development. Inf. Syst. Res. 20, 329–354 (2009)
8. Ågerfalk, P.J., Fitzgerald, B., Slaughter, S.A.: Introduction to the special issue —flexible and distributed information systems development: state of the art and research challenges. Inf. Syst. Res. 20, 317–328 (2009)
9. Rational: Rational Unified Process: Best Practices for Software Development. White paper (2001)

10. Beck, K., Andres, C.: Extreme Programming Explained. Addison-Wesley Publishing, Reading (2005)
11. Schwaber, K., Beedle, M.: Agile Software Development with Scrum. Prentice Hall, Englewood Cliffs (2001)
12. Eisenhardt, K.M.: Building theories from case study research. Acad. Manag. Rev. **14**(4), 532–550 (1989)
13. Eisenhardt, K.M., Graebner, M.E.: Theory building from cases : opportunities and challenges. Acad. Manag. J. **50**, 25–32 (2007)
14. OECD: OECD SME and Entrepreneurship Outlook: 2005 (2005)
15. Eriksson, P., Kovalainen, A.: Qualitative methods in business research. Narrative. pp. 227–243 (2008)
16. Royce, W.: Managing the development of large software systems Dr. Winston W. Rovce introduction. In: IEEE WESCON, pp. 328–338 (1970)
17. Beck, K., Beedle, M., Van Bennekum, A., Cockburn, A., Cunningham, W., Fowler, M., Grenning, J., Highsmith, J., Hunt, A., Jeffries, R., Kern, J., Marick, B., Martin, R.C., Mellor, S., Schwaber, K., Sutherland, J., Thomas, D.: Agile Manifesto. http://agilemanifesto.org/
18. Fitzgerald, B., Russo, N., Stolterman, E.: Information Systems Development: Methods in Action. McGraw Hill, New York (2002)
19. Ramasubbu, N., Bharadwaj, A., Tayi, G.: Does Software Process Ambidexterity Lead To Better Software Project Performance? (2011)
20. Woolthuis, R.K.: Trust, Contract and Relationship Development (2005)

Simulation of an Affordance-Based Human-Machine Cooperative Control Model Using an Agent-Based Simulation Approach

YeongGwang Oh, IkChan Ju, and Namhun Kim[(⊠)]

Ulsan National Institute of Science and Technology, Ulsan, Republic of Korea
nhkim@unist.ac.kr

Abstract. An automated system relies mostly on a robot, rather than a human operator. In the automated system considered in this paper, a human operator mainly verifies the product quality, where the performance of the human is affected by his or her characteristics. To present this kind of system, an ABM is better than DES to simulate the role of the human operator. This is because the human characteristics are dynamic and are affected significantly by time and environment. This paper presents a DES-ABM model which simulates the performance of a human operator in a human-machine cooperative environment. It may enable this model to be utilized for further development in controller toward the supervisory control.

Keywords: Human and robot collaboration · Affordance theory · Agent-based simulation

1 Introduction

As a manufacturing environment gets complicated, the adaptive process control in manufacturing systems focuses on improving both the manufacturing flexibility and efficiency. Automation is regarded as the driving force in strengthening productivity and efficiency [1]. However, it is almost impossible to operate a fully automated factory without human operators, not only due to economic reasons, but also due to technical shortcomings [2, 3]. In manufacturing systems, there exist tasks which should be done, or would be more efficient when done, by a human operator [4]. The optimal task allocation between human and machine is necessary to manage the combined systems effectively with dynamic human and machine interactions. Specifically, modeling and control of a human-involved semi-automated manufacturing system is a major issue in the automotive industry, because human operators play a key role for complex options and tasks in the manufacturing processes [5–7].

In human-involved manufacturing systems, a human can act as one of the most flexible system resources by performing a large variety of physical tasks ranging from material handling to complex tasks like inspections and assembly [8]. Thus, integrating humans into manufacturing systems has been considered a critical aspect in human-involved manufacturing systems modeling and control. A few modeling methods for this heterogonous system are suggested to represent interactions among the

© Springer International Publishing Switzerland 2015
M. Kurosu (Ed.): Human-Computer Interaction, Part III, HCII 2015, LNCS 9171, pp. 226–237, 2015.
DOI: 10.1007/978-3-319-21006-3_23

manufacturing resources [9, 10]. In this research, we specifically focus on an FSA (Finite State Automata) based approach classifying a human operator as a system component that can execute tasks without any physical constraints through logical process [11, 12].

A formal modeling of human-involved manufacturing system is presented [9]. The formal model used in this paper is specifically based on affordance-based Message-based Part State Graph (MPSG) which is a formal modeling methodology for control of discrete manufacturing systems [10]. The presented model incorporates a supervisory control scheme to fit into more flexible and efficient manufacturing. The implementation of the proposed manufacturing system integrates an affordance-based MPSG control model into an agent-based simulation of human and machine behaviors. The simulation result is used to make a manufacturing processes plan and control the human-machine cooperative manufacturing systems under dynamic situations.

In order to verify the affordance-based modeling and control scheme, simulation results of an existing auto-part manufacturing case with human-robot collaboration is investigated. The simulation model is planned to be implemented with hybrid modeling of DES and ABM. This is because the human characteristics are dynamic and are affected significantly by factors like time, environmental factors and operator's level of expertise. Therefore, the combined simulation model of DES and ABM is expected to mimic the human-robot collaborative manufacturing system. The productivity of the system is compared to validate the feasibility and applicability of the affordance-based modeling of human-machine cooperative systems.

The rest of this paper is organized as follows. The MABA-MABA and supervisory control are introduced in Sect. 2. The proposed implementation model of affordance based MPSG is described in Sect. 3. Section 4 illustrates the application of the implemented formal model using a simulation of the manufacturing and inspection process for plastic injection manufacturing line of automobile door, and provides an analysis of the simulation result in terms of productivity and efficiency. Section 5 presents the conclusion and scope for future works.

2 Related Work

2.1 MABA-MABA and Supervisory Control

Men Are Better At, Machines Are Better At (MABA-MABA) is provided by Fitts [13]. To design the effectiveness automated system, task allocation to human operator or automated machine is based on behavior' strength. Figure 1 shows an example of classification standard of each task.

Sheridan [3] applied the MABA-MABA theory to a task allocation of human-involved automated system. He suggested a role of human operator in auto-mated system to improve the system flexibility, and a role of an automated machine to reduce mechanical failure by operator. The study of MABA-MABA not only classifies a task allocation of human-machine, but also provides the guideline of a system operation design [4]. The supervisory control means that a human is not only taking his task in the manufacturing system, but also managing machines and the whole system

> **Men are better at:**
> - Detecting small amounts of visual, auditory, or chemical energy
> - Perceiving patterns of light or sound
> - Improvising and using flexible procedures
> - Storing information for long periods, and recalling appropriate parts
> - Reasoning inductively
> - Exercising judgment
>
> **Machines are better at:**
> - Responding quickly to control signals
> - Applying great force smoothly and precisely
> - Storing information briefly, erasing it completely
> - Reasoning deductively
> - Doing many complex operations at once

Fig. 1. The Fitts' MABA-MABA List, Abbreviated by Sheridan [3]

[14]. For example, Chef is preparing his specialty coincided with inspecting other cooks food in the restaurant; the driver is using cruise control system, while taking express way [15]. In the supervisory control, the system operator can shift efficiency process plan quickly when the process plan is exchanged by a customer. Most of current manufacturing environments are operated in terms of the supervisory control, so that the performance of the system is highly subject to the proper work allocations between manufacturing resources (e.g., human operators, machines)

2.2   Finite State Automata Representation of DES

One way of formalizing the logical behavior in discrete systems is based on theories of languages and automata. An automata theory is based on the notion that anything is possible to model with discrete states [16, 17]. This theory is an atomic mathematical model for finite state automata (FSA). Transitions of automata theory and a finite number of states is possible to model with predetermined rules. Transition functions generate transition between states. These functions of each transition determine which state to go to from a current state and a current input symbol. An FSA is a state and rule-based representing language based on well-defined rules which means an FSA is tractable [18]. A commonly FSA in practice is a deterministic finite automaton (DFA), which can be defined as a 5-tuple:

$M^{DFA} = <\Sigma, Q, q_0, \delta, F, X_p, Z_q, J, W_{pq}>$, where the definitions of the components are as follows:

- J is a juxtaposition function such that $J : X \times Z \rightarrow W_{pq}$;
- X_p is a set of affordances,
- Z_q is a set of effectivities (human capable actions),

- W_{pq} is a set of possible human actions,
- All other definitions of tuples are the same as those of $\mathbf{M^{DFA}}$

3 Modeling of Human-Involved System

3.1 Formal Modeling of an Existing Semi-automated Manufacturing System: A Door-Part Injection and Handling

The process of modeling and simulation is conducted in four steps as shown in Fig. 2: (1) the criteria of MABA-MABA in an exemplary manufacturing process were investigated, (2) the formal automata model of affordance-based MPSG was built, (3) ABM-DES simulation model is implemented, and 4) the system was verified by simulations under different condition of human performances.

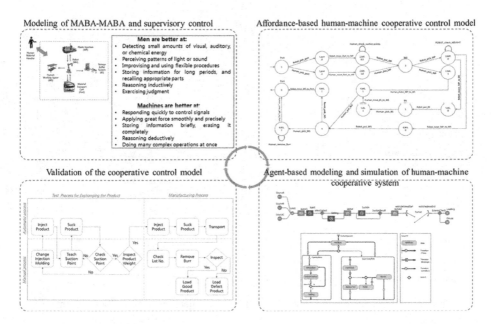

Fig. 2. Agent-based modeling of human-machine combined semi-automated manufacturing systems.

First, to represent the current process of a semi-automated manufacturing process (automobile door part injection and handling) using affordance-based MPSG, tasks and interactions need to be defined based on concepts of MABA-MABA and supervisory control as shown in Fig. 3. Identifying a key role of each task behavior in a human-involved manufacturing system starts from the analysis of the current process or a task assigned to a human. For instance, when a task is moving a rectangular box which has proper size and weight to a robot arm, this task is assigned to the robot. However, a moving route is complicated by obstacle positions, and varies according to the product option. Programming the path into the robot requires many sensors, then the necessary automation budget of the task, moving a rectangular box, is increased to operate without errors in the dynamic environment. Therefore, this task is better to a human operator than a robot.

We adopt an affordance-based MPSG presented by Kim et al., [9] as shown in Fig. 3. This formal modeling methodology distinguishes human potentially possible actions from human capable actions. In other words, a human can or cannot perform tasks due to physical limitations enforced by an environment or his/her cognitive recognition of tasks. Also, a human action is defined by the Boolean values with consideration of affordances. In their presented model, a module can generate possible transitions in terms of the MPSG that proves logical validation. Using affordance-based MPSG, the system can present a process without critical failures. The current process of the door part injection and handling system is modeled with the affordance-based MPSG (see Fig. 3) and verifies the logic and flow with a sequence diagram as shown in Fig. 4.

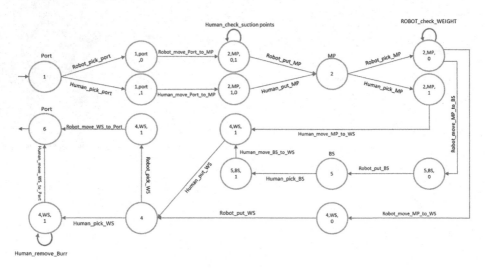

Fig. 3. Affordance-based MPSG of the door part injection and handling system

3.2   Simulation Modeling Using ABM

In regards to affordance-based MPSG, an operator is modeled as an agent instead of a machine in DES. A human operator mainly verifies the product quality after manu-facturing process, where the performance of the human is affected by its characteristics. The human characteristics are dynamic and are affected significantly by factors like time, environment, or skilled level. To simulate a human considering dynamic char-acteristics, an ABM is better than DES.

Each behavior or task of a human operator consists of a stage and transition. Each stage also can have an internal stage to make a decision via defined rules. For example, the task of an operator is to remove a burr. This task stage is involved in the Operator

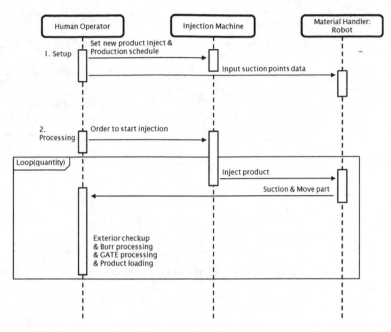

Fig. 4. The sequence diagram of the manufacturing process of the door part injection and handing [19].

Role group, and this group consists of three different stages. When the operator takes his/her task, the result of a task can be different depending on the product or other influence like fatigue or skilled level (see Fig. 5). The human operator also has supervisory role in this model. For instance, when a machine stops or the human operator finds out a problem in the process, the human operator checks the machine state and make decision whether a replace tool or repair. A dynamic characteristics of the human operator affect to decision-making. Depend on his working experience via skilled level, the human operator may repair the machine or report it based on a rule when the machine breaks down. For this reason, ABM easily presents the affordance-based MPSG. In the simulation, each operator is assumed to have a given level of skill. The skill level can be modeled as a function of the initial level of skill and total working time of the agent (experience) as shown in Fig. 5.

4   Simulation Implementation

4.1   Scenario of the Illustrative Example

The whole system process is modeled as DES, whereas each operator is modeled as an agent-based on task rules and task specifications. In this paper, plastic injection manufacturing line of an automobile door is used for simulation. The brief process is as follows: At first, raw material is injected in the injection machine. A robot arm transfers

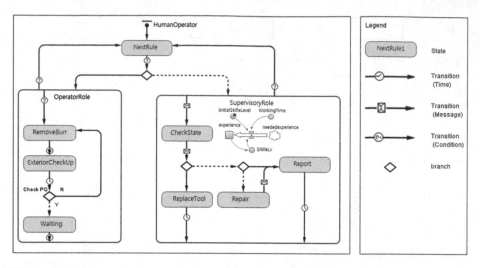

Fig. 5. State chart of a human operator in the semi-automated process of the door part manufacturing.

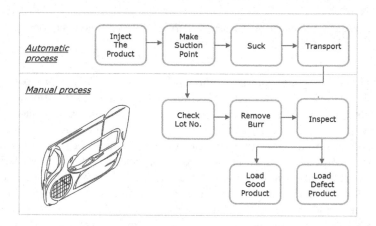

Fig. 6. Current process map of the semi-automated manufacturing system

the injected product from the machine to conveyer line. And the operator removes burrs on the product and then the operator inspects the product quality manually (see Fig. 6).

Figure 7 illustrates the simulation model of the current system. Raw material is source A, B and C. Each source is modeled as an agent and has different options like door trim size, color, or customer choice among selectable options. The setting is for machine adjust time when the source type is changed at some point. The restricted area is designated for operator tasks. Internal processes in the restricted area are similar to those shown in Fig. 5. Finally, the operator classifies and loads a product depending on the inspection standard.

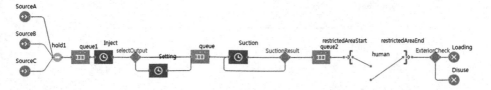

Fig. 7. Hybrid discrete event system and ABM modeling

4.2   Analysis of Simulation Results

For verifying the simulation result, the parameters of the manufacturing process are set as real data (see Table 1). The data are assumed to be the triangular distribution with mean values of actual process time. The parameter of operator's tasks is assumed as 0.95 % of which the human operator's skill level is high.

Table 1. Real process times in the manufacturing system and simulation inputs

	Process	Max. Process Time(sec)	Simulation Input(sec) (Triangular dist.)	Total Cycle Time (sec)
Set up Tasks	Injection machine	1200	(min,mean,max)	Max. 1800
	Robot arm	600		
Production Tasks	Injection	8	(6.4, 7.2, 8)	Max. 90
	Extra time for injection	22	(17.6,19.8,22)	
	Suction	10	(8,9,10)	
	Material moving	5	(4,4.5,5)	
	Human operator's tasks	15	Dependent on the operator's skill level & error rates	
	Final loading	30	(24,27,30)	

In the simulation results, the average cycle time (total time for one production) is calculated as 82.3 s (see Fig. 8). The simulation were conducted with 100 replications to analyze the variation of the data. The input parameters of the model are set with reference to the real production conditions for each manufacturing process (see Table 1). The unexpected errors occasionally cause delays on the processing times as shown in Fig. 8, it is still required to ensure realistic results of the simulation.

To show the effect of human error and operator's skill level, in the simulation the operator's skill level and error rate follows triangular distribution as follow :

$$processstime \sim Triangular(min, mean, max), \tag{1}$$

where: *mean* = required process time × *f*(operator's skill level),
min = *mean* × *error rate,* and
max = *mean* × *error rate*

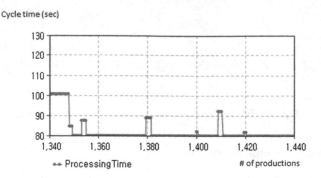

Fig. 8. Simulation test results of product time vs. the number of productions

The mean value of triangular distribution is assumed to be dependent on the operator's skill level such as that of novice, intermediate, expert cases. For the illustrative purposes, it is assumed to take 95 %, 90 %, and 85 % of the required process times for the novice, the intermediate, and the expert cases, respectively. The error rates for the cases are also assumed to have different values of min and max in the triangular distributions as shown in Fig. 9.

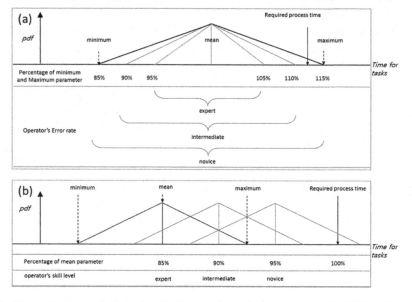

Fig. 9. The parameters of triangular distribution depend on the operator's skill level and error rate. (a) the minimum and maximum value depend on the error rate of an operator, (b) the mean value depend on the operator's skill level

The simulation results were analyzed by different error rates and the skill level assumed, by using ANOVA to illustrate how the human task variances affect the total processing time. The results show that the skill level, the error rate, and the interaction are all significant to the total process time in 95 % CI, because their p-values are all less than 0.05 (see Table 2). The error rate highly influences the process time when the operator's skill level is low, the case of novice, as shown in Fig. 10, which presents the effect of human involvement in the automated process. Thus, to identify the performance of the human-included manufacturing systems, the level of skills and error rates of the human agents should be modeled independently when the interactions among heterogeneous resources in the systems need to be considered and analyzed.

Table 2. Anova table of operator's skill level and error rate for process time

Source	DF	SS	MS	F	P
Skill level	2	3806.47	1903.24	672.39	0.00
Error rate	2	1108.98	554.49	195.90	0.00
Interaction	4	571.63	142.91	50.49	0.00
Error	891	2522.01	2.83		
Total	899	8009.09			

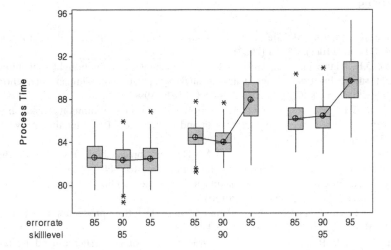

Fig. 10. Box plot of process time vs. error rate & skill level

5 Conclusion

The model presented in this paper provides a simulation implementation of an affordance-based MPSG in a real semi-automated manufacturing system. The affordance-based MPSG, the formal model methodology used in this paper, represents all possible interactions among system components in a human-involved manufacturing system. It also models human operators as components distinct from a machine or a robot. The affordance-based MPSG provides a reasonable modeling method for representing the human-involved manufacturing system. Thus, we provide the simulation and verification of the affordance-based MPSG in which an existing auto-part manufacturing system is simulated.

To make manufacturing processes plan and control the human-involved manufacturing system based on affordance-based MPSG, the simulation model combines DES and ABM. The combined simulation results of DES and ABM are implemented with real manufacturing data from a small auto part company. The simulation is modeled with the triangular distribution to obtain highly reliable data. And then, productivity and task efficiency are used for judgment of the simulation under dynamic situations, such as a different number of product types or urgent customer manufacturing orders. While the simulation model creates four types of products as an existing manufacturing system, the simulation results indicate that the minimum manufacturing time per product is four hours.

The effects of implementation of affordance-based MPSG still require further investigation with different manufacturing systems and extended environments. In addition, the affordance-based MPSG also needs to be extended to express the manufacturing process of human-machine collaboration in manufacturing systems.

References

1. Säfsten, K., Winroth, M., Stahre, J.: The content and process of automation strategies. Int. J. Prod. Econ. **110**(1), 25–38 (2007)
2. Brann, D.B., Thurman, D.A., Mitchell, C.M.: Human interaction with lights-out automation: a field study. In: Proceedings Third Annual Symposium on Human Interaction with Complex Systems, HICS 1996, pp 276–283. IEEE (1996)
3. Sheridan, T.B.: Human centered automation: oxymoron or common sense? In: IEEE International Conference on Systems, Man and Cybernetics, 1995. Intelligent Systems for the 21st Century, pp 823–828. IEEE (1995)
4. Dekker, S.W., Woods, D.D.: MABA-MABA or abracadabra? Progress on human–automation co-ordination. Cogn. Technol. Work **4**(4), 240–244 (2002)
5. Baily, M.N., Bosworth, B.P.: US manufacturing: understanding its past and its potential future. J. Econ. Perspect. **28**(1), 3–25 (2014)
6. Olhager, J.: Evolution of operations planning and control: from production to supply chains. Int. J. Prod. Res. **51**(23–24), 6836–6843 (2013)
7. Shin, D., Wysk, R.A., Rothrock, L.: Formal model of human material-handling tasks for control of manufacturing systems. IEEE Trans. Syst. Man Cybern. Part A Syst. Hum. **36**(4), 685–696 (2006)
8. Altuntas, B., Wysk, R., Rothrock, L.: Formal approach to include a human material handler in a computer-integrated manufacturing (CIM) system. Int. J. Prod. Res. **45**(9), 1953–1971 (2007)
9. Kim, N., Shin, D., Wysk, R., Rothrock, L.: Using finite state automata (FSA) for formal modelling of affordances in human-machine cooperative manufacturing systems. Int. J. Prod. Res. **48**(5), 1303–1320 (2010)
10. Smith, J., Joshi, S., Qiu, R.: Message-based part state graphs (MPSG): a formal model for shop-floor control implementation. Int. J. Prod. Res. **41**(8), 1739–1764 (2003)
11. Shin, D., Wysk, R., Rothrock, L.: A formal control-theoretic model of a human–automation interactive manufacturing system control. Int. J. Prod. Res. **44**(20), 4273–4295 (2006)

12. Shin, D., Wysk, R.A., Rothrock, L.: An investigation of a human material handler on part flow in automated manufacturing systems. IEEE Trans. Syst. Man Cybern. Part A Syst. Hum. **36**(1), 123–135 (2006)
13. Fitts, P.M.: Human engineering for an effective air-navigation and traffic-control system (1951)
14. Sheridan, T.B.: Human supervisory control. Handbook of Human Factors and Ergonomics, (4th edn), pp. 990–1015 (2012)
15. Kirlik, A., Miller, R.A., Jagacinski, R.J.: Supervisory control in a dynamic and uncertain environment: a process model of skilled human-environment interaction. IEEE Trans. Syst. Man Cybern. **23**(4), 929–952 (1993)
16. Cassandras, C.G., Lafortune, S.: Introduction to discrete event systems. Springer Science & Business Media, US (2008)
17. Zeigler, B.P., Praehofer, H., Kim, T.G.: Theory of Modeling and Simulation: Integrating Discrete Event and Continuous Complex Dynamic Systems. Academic press, Salt Lake City (2000)
18. Sipser, M.: Introduction to the Theory of Computation. Cengage Learning, Boston (2012)
19. Oh, Y., Joo, I., Lee, W., Kim, N.: Modeling and Implementation of the Affordance-based Human-Machine Collaborative System. J. Korean Inst. Ind. Eng. **41**(1), 34–42 (2015)

Cause the Trend Industry 4.0 in the Automated Industry to New Requirements on User Interfaces?

Carsten Wittenberg[✉]

Robotics and Automation, Hochschule Heilbronn – Heilbronn University,
Max-Planck-Str. 39, 74081 Heilbronn, Germany
carsten.wittenberg@hs-heilbronn.de

Abstract. Industrial automated production is a conservative domain. New information technologies find the way into this domain slowly or not at all. But in 2013 the fourth industrial revolution was announced: The so-called Industry 4.0 implicates techniques like cloud-computing and self-organizing machines. The degree of technological complexity increases. Beside the technological innovation the use context and the tasks for the users will also be changed. In the design phase the engineers have to handle the increased complexity. In the operating phase the operators and also the service and maintenance technicians have to keep the production systems running. This paper discusses the results of the research about the effects of Industry 4.0 on the different user groups and highlight selected user requirements.

Keywords: HCI in automation · Industry 4.0 · CPS · Mobile HCI · Augmented reality

1 Introduction – What Is Industry 4.0?

The domain of industrial automation is reserved and conservative to new developments in the information technology. One reason is that industrial productions systems are build to output products for a long time. A period of 20–30 years is not unusual. From this it follows that the used technology and the related spare parts has to be accessible over the period. But – is it certain that today's information technology is still available in 30 years?

A second reason is the need for information security. Only authorized persons and institutions should have access to any sensible data. But the modern information technology is based on networks and outsourced information services. How can a company make sure that sensible information is secure against unauthorized access e.g. from a third party or a competitor? How can a company make sure, that nobody can inflict damage with these data?

Nevertheless new information technologies are observed and proofed, if these technologies are suitable for the producing industry. As a result the concept of the industry 4.0 was developed and was introduced to the public in 2013.

What represents industry 4.0? After the mechanizing with water or steam power (industry 1.0, e.g. the weaving loom), the mass production with band conveyors

M. Kurosu (Ed.): Human-Computer Interaction, Part III, HCII 2015, LNCS 9171, pp. 238–245, 2015.
DOI: 10.1007/978-3-319-21006-3_24

(industry 2.0, e.g. Henry Ford's car production) and the use of electronics (industry 3.0, e.g. the programmable logic controller PLC) the level 4.0 is now reached (Fig. 1).

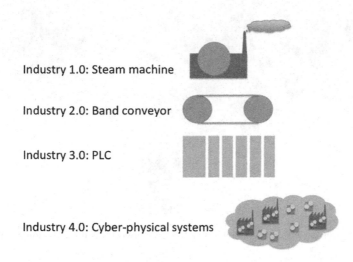

Industry 1.0: Steam machine

Industry 2.0: Band conveyor

Industry 3.0: PLC

Industry 4.0: Cyber-physical systems

Fig. 1. From Industry 1.0 to Industry 4.0

Some elements were taken from the idea of the Internet of things, some from the big data subject or the service architecture topic to shape the concept of the smart factory [1].

1.1 The Vision of Industry 4.0 – The Smart Factory

But what is the vision of Industry 4.0? What is a smart factory? The elements in a production plant become so-called cyber-physical devices that have an increased intelligence and ability to communicate compared to today's machines. With these abilities the cyber-physical systems can take a part of the planning and dispositive tasks. The machines take care about adequate supply of material, change production method to the optimal one for actual product, or figure out a new method by itself (catchword self-learning machine). The machines get social characteristics and build their own "social" networks (Fig. 2).

As one result the classical automation pyramid is change. The machines – typical located at level one (field level) – get functionalities from the upper levels, particularly from the levels 3 (MES/plant management level) and level 4 (ERP/enterprise level). Also new topics like the service-based architecture influence the systems.

At first sight it might seem that the load for the users is clearly reduced. But is this true?

1.2 The Lifecycle of Automation Systems

In the lifecycle of industrial automation systems (Fig. 3) two phases with three user groups can be pointed out:

Fig. 2. Cyber-physical systems with their own "social" network - is this still cloudy or foggy for the user?

Fig. 3. The lifecycle of automation systems

1. During the engineering phase the user group of system designer develop and design the whole production system. Different craft groups (e.g. mechanical engineers, electrical engineers, PLC software engineers etc.) work with their specific software tools sequential on the designing, configuring and building up the production systems.
2. During the operating phase two user groups play an important role:
    a. The operators supervise and control the assigned production line.
    b. The service and maintenance technicians keep the production ticking over.
3. The last phase "scrapping" is from the industry 4.0 point of view not that important.

What are the impacts of industry 4.0 for the user and for their software tools? Apparently the complexity of the procedures inside the automated productions systems is extremely raised. Beside this also economic issues and functions (based on the integration of level 3 and 4 functionality, see above) have to be considered by the designers. For example user requirements concern issues supporting the collaboration in a mixed team of special designers. Also requirements regarding the consistent data flow through all the different engineering tools become effective again – these topics were already discussed but not solved during the work on the digital factory.

Changing the focus to the operating phase the two user-roles operator and service and maintenance technicians are also confronted with changed working environments.

Due to the fact that the machines undertake more tasks from the operator the remaining operator's tasks get more and more an observing character. The operator has to monitor and supervise the automated production system. But the increased information and communication power of these systems lead to a complexity that is not understandable by classic user interfaces used actual in the industry. The operator needs support to keep the system stable in case of a fault.

The service and maintenance technician has also an altered need for information. The cyber-physical systems will have a huge diagnostic functionality. For evaluation and interpreting this new data the technician has to be supported by new user interface concepts with site-directed information access (e.g. via mobile devices combined with techniques like AR).

2 Changes for the User – New Working Conditions?

It seems clear that the entry of innovative techniques from the computer science influences the working conditions of the users. The question is in what kind of manner – and if there is a need for further support of the user.

2.1 The Engineering Phase

Unlike usual products the production plants are single-unit products. As a result the engineering and development effort play a mayor role. This can be divided in three phases: Design, manufacturing & assembly, and commissioning. In the classical way the commissioning phase in the field needs the most time.

To reduce time and effort the idea of the digital factory was developed during the last 10 years (Fig. 4). Parts of the commissioning phase should be done with simulation tools. As an advantage for the user this work is relocated from the field to the office. As a disadvantage the number of tools increases.

Also in the classical approach a huge number of tools are necessary for fulfilling the engineering tasks (Fig. 5). A major problem for the user is that these tools are disharmonious – both in their databases and in the interaction with the user [2–4]. Typically each tool has a different look & feel – different handling, different appearance, different menu structures, different keyboard layout, different shortcuts etc. In some cases the different databases lead to the manual input of the results of the prior tools.

Using the digital factory approach the number of tools increases without solving the problems of the not harmonized tools (Fig. 6).

Integrating the ideas of Industry 4.0 the number of tools still increases (Fig. 7). But the new tools have the origin not in the engineering disciplines but in the computer science. So not only the engineers have to handle the huge number of tools but also work together with colleagues from computer science domain – a new domain from the point of view of the automation society.

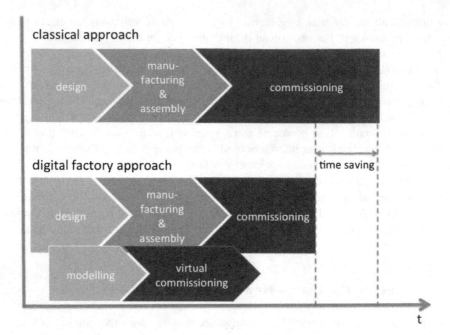

Fig. 4. Reduction of effort using the digital factory approach

Fig. 5. Typical CAx Tools in the engineering phase

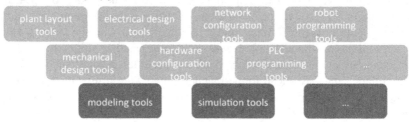

Fig. 6. Enlargement of the necessary CAx tools by the digital factory approach

Industry 4.0 approach

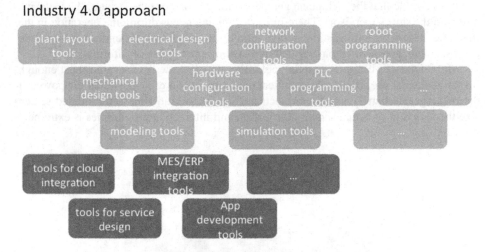

Fig. 7. Using the Industry 4.0 approach even more tools are necessary

So do we have new requirements in the engineering phase? Some are not new, but become under the Industry 4.0 focus still more important. First it has to be cleared if there are new user roles, e.g. cloud specialist for integrating the cloud system into the automated production system with its real-time and safety requirements. Based on this the interfaces between the user roles have to be analyzed and optimized.

And one of the most important point is, that the huge number of different computer-aided engineering tools have to be harmonized so support the users doing their task – including the obvious issues like an identical look and feel and the hidden issues like a common data exchange and data format (e.g. AML [5]).

2.2   The Operating Phase

Typical user groups in the operating phase are the operator supervising and controlling the plant, and the service and maintenance technician. The introduction of the Industry 4.0 topics accompanied with an increased degree of automation. That means that the complexity of the automated systems also increases – and the operators tasks have a predominant supervising character. In case of an incident or accident the irony of automation [6] become real.

The human-computer interfaces in the control rooms have to be developed based on the user-centered approach with a task- and situation-orientation. This appears correct and necessary but – because automated production plants are single-unit produced – financial issues carry weight.

The service and maintenance technician has to keep the plant running. Timely exchange of worn machine parts before the system is going down is part of the task. The technological ideas of Industry 4.0 cover also self-diagnosing machines. That means also that the disposing task moves from the shift supervisor to the Cyber-physical System.

It is possible that the technician get the working plan from the system (the factory – not from the shift supervisor). Therefor the technician needs during the operation in the field the necessary information – that requires a location-independent information access. – and also a situation-oriented and task-oriented offer of information.

Mobile devices become essential tools (Fig. 8) – if these devices are robust enough for the industrial use. Beside the technical requirements on robustness and the power of the rechargeable battery usability aspects are still important. Due to the limited screen size the selection of actual shown information and interaction possibilities is extremely relevant.

Fig. 8. Interacting via mobile devices with the Cyber-Physical System

3 Actual and Future Research at the Robotics and Automation Department at Heilbronn University

The Robotics & Automation department at Heilbronn University analyzes the use of mobile devices especially for service and maintenance technicians. Starting with applications for laptops the focus was on the augmented reality [7]. Actual the applications was ported to tablets and extended with features from computer games and interaction techniques like gesture input [8].

The next step will be the porting to data glasses to enable a *hands free, eyes free* – interaction.

In parallel the automation laboratory starts to acquire a factory in a laboratory size ("Heilbronner model factory"). This model factory can "produce" liquids and represents a real production system.

Beside research on Industry 4.0 technical aspects like including cloud servers to PLCs it is planned to perform different projects on the human-computer interaction like device-independent information visualization. The Human-robot interface to mobile robots is also a key aspect in the research activities [9].

References

1. Bauernhansl, T., ten Hompel, M., Vogel-Heuser, B.: Industrie 4.0 in Produktion, Automatisierung und Logistik (Industry 4.0 in production, automation, and logistics). Springer, Wiesbaden (2014)
2. During, A., Wittenberg, C., Berger, U.: Das Konzept eines Engineering Protals zur benuetzerzentrierten Unterstützung der Anlagenplanung (The concept of an engineering portal for the user-centred plant engineering support). In: i-com 1/2006, pp. 59 –71, April 2006
3. During, A., Komischke, T., Wittenberg, C.: Design of user oriented engineering tools in industrial automation. In: Johannsen, G. (ed.) Analysis, Design and Evaluation of Human-Machine Systems, pp. 291–295. Elsevier Science, Amsterdam (2002). ISBN: 0-08-043564-5
4. During, A., Komischke, T., Wittenberg, C.: Analysis, design and evaluation of user-centred engineering tools in industrial automation. In: Smith, M.J., Salvendy, G. (eds.) Systems, Social and Internationalization Design Aspects of Human-Computer Interaction, pp. 662–666. Lawrence Earlbaum Associates, Mahwah (2001)
5. AutomationML Consortium: Whitepaper AutomationML Part 1 – Architecture and General Requirements. AutomationML Consortium (2014)
6. Bainbridge, L.: Ironies of automation. Automatica **19**(6), 775–779 (1983)
7. Albrecht, R., Buyer, S., Qi, W., Wittenberg, C.: Einsatz von Augmented Reality Techniken im industriellen Umfeld und Entwicklung intuitiver Benutzeroberflächen (Use of Augmented Reality in industrial surroundings and development of intuitive user interfaces). In: Proceedings AALE 2011, Oldenbourg Industrieverlag (2011)
8. Buyer, S., Wittenberg, C.: AR und Webpad – nur Spielereien? (Augmented Reality and Webpad – just playing around?). In: Grundlagen und Anwendung der Mensch-Maschone-Interaktion (Foundations and Applications of Human-Machine Interaction) - Proceedings of the 10. Berliner Werkstatt Mensch-Maschine-Systeme, pp. 187–191 (2013)
9. Rixen, M.-L., Buyer, S., Heverhagen, T., Wittenberg, C.: Mobile Nutzerschnittstellen in der Automatisierungstechnik (mobile user interfaces in automation). In: Proceedings AALE 2015 (in press)

Post-Implementation ERP Success Assessment: A Conceptual Model

Fan Zhao and Eugene Hoyt[✉]

Department of Information Systems and Operations Management, Florida Gulf
Coast University, Fort Myers, USA
{fzhao,ehoyt}@fgcu.edu

Abstract. Enterprise Resource Planning (ERP) success research has been
widely studied. Models to test the success of an ERP implementation have been
developed, but most models do not adequately test all implementations success
after implementation. This literature review study introduces a new model for
testing any ERP post-implementation to determine if it was successful or not
rather than relying on other models that determine it to be a failure if it did not fit
within the model constraints.

Keywords: IS · ERP · Success · Post-implementation

1   Introduction

Businesses today are more strategic when it comes to selecting and implementing new
systems; however, the rate of successful implementations remains low even with
decades of implementation experience. There continues to be no systematic method to
evaluate the success post implementation. Most researchers point to the use of Critical
Success Factors (CSF) within the Enterprise Resource Planning (ERP) process for
testing the failure or success of a system implementation. While this is a good start, the
business community needs a better tool that can be applied across all platforms. The
need for constructing an Enterprise Resource Planning (ERP) testing model is now [1].
This model, once constructed, could be used for any enterprise resource planning
(ERP) implementation, regardless of size, complexity, scope, vendor or age of applications, to test if it was a success or not.

After nearly 75 years of applications on mainframes to Desktop environments and
with so many implementations, why are there so many failures? The disturbing
observation is the lack of conclusion on the outcome of an implementations success or
failure [2]. The focus on post implementation is the evidence of no closed loop
evaluation of success. Did we accomplish the objectives of our business case? Did we
receive the return on investment in the period we predicted? Did we gain the competitive advantage, processes, productivity expected? Were we able to accomplish the
implementation within budget, scope and time? Was the product purchased, developed
or integrated or did we need to make modifications to our own expectations on what we
expected?

© Springer International Publishing Switzerland 2015
M. Kurosu (Ed.): Human-Computer Interaction, Part III, HCII 2015, LNCS 9171, pp. 246–255, 2015.
DOI: 10.1007/978-3-319-21006-3_25

Despite the widespread research investigating ERP success and failure [3, 4], little research has empirically investigated how to evaluate ERP success. Since there are too many research studies on ERP implementation success, our research focuses on post-implementation success of ERP. While there is research on critical success factors in ERP, this empirical research focused more on relationships between critical success factors and ERP success. However, different research adopts different constructs to assess post-implementation success of ERP. There is no systematic constructs, supported by empirical studies, to evaluate post-implementation success of ERP yet. Therefore, the purpose of this article is to propose a systematic constructs to assess post-implementation success of ERP.

2 Literature Review

2.1 Information Systems (IS) Success

Plenty of research has been done on factors associated with the success of IS [6–9], notably the DeLone and McLean model (2003) which has been applied to many cases over the decade since its first publication [10, 11]. There are two versions of IS success model from DeLone and McLean. First one was developed in 1992 while the computers and Internet were not dominate in the business world. In this initial model, there are two levels, individual and organizational. They believe that system quality and information quality impact IS use and users' satisfactions, then further influence the individual behaviors, and eventually spread to organizational level.

Most studies adopt the Technology Acceptance Model (TAM) [12] to measure the system quality. However, recent researchers believe that we should use more constructs to completely represent the system quality, such as reliability, portability, user friendliness, understandability, effectiveness, maintainability, economy, and verifiability [13]. Information quality refers to the quality of system output, such as reports generated by the system. Livari [2] adopt Bailey and Pearson's construct [14] to measure information quality in six categories: completeness, precision, accuracy, reliability, currency, and format of output. IS use is typically measured in several categories, such as intent to use, which is adopted from TAM [12], frequency of use, self-reported use and actual use.

Because of the overlapping results of using all of the constructs [15], most of the studies adopt frequency of use as the dominant measure construct. However, Doll and Torkzadeh [16, 17] argue that using effects of use could be more precise than the frequency of use. Furthermore, Burton-Jones and Gallivan [18] support a measurement of using multiple perspectives across the individual and organizational levels to gain a full picture of the IS use. There are two fundamental instruments in measuring user satisfaction: End-User Computing Support (EUCS) instrument by Doll [16, 17] and User Information Satisfaction (UIS) instrument by Ives [19]. To simplify the instrument and avoid overlapping measurement of system and information quality [20], some of the researchers now prefer to use a single item to just measure overall satisfaction of the IS use (Fig. 1).

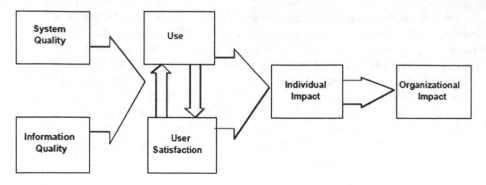

Fig. 1. The DeLone-McLean model for IS success

In 2003, DeLone and McLean updated the initial model and propose a new research model by adding several new variables and restructure the framework. With 10 more years of IT/IS experiences, now they have a clearer picture of IS. Besides information quality and system quality, service quality was added to the model as the first layer; the construct use was divided into two parts: intention to use and use because they posit in the context of IS usage, users will first have the intention to use the system before they actually use it. The relationship with user satisfaction therefore changes to a circle: after the initial use of the IS, user satisfaction will cause users' intention to use, and the more the experiences the user has with the IS, the more satisfaction generated and this relationship eventually will impact the net benefits of the organization.

Service quality is an achievement of reaching desired services level of IS for the users. SERVQUAL is adopted to measure the service quality even though some researchers criticize the instrument [10]. In the updated model, DeLone and McLean found more internal and external impacts rather than just organizational, such as work group impacts, industry impact, consumer impact, and so on. Therefore, they decide to combine all the impacts into one single category called Net Benefits (Fig. 2).

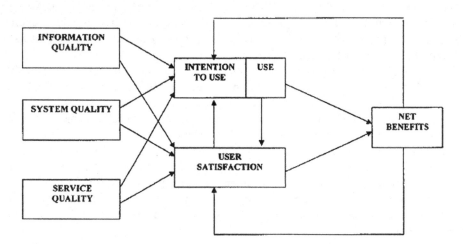

Fig. 2. The updated DeLone-McLean model for IS success

To support the DeLone-McLean Model applications, Iivari [2] conducted an empirical study to testify the model in a field study. All the relationships are found significant except two: the influence of system use on individual impact and the influence of information quality on system use.

2.2 ERP Life Cycle

ERP is unique within Information Systems (IS) because of its size. According to Capaldo and Rippa [21], there are three phases in a typical ERP life cycle: pre-implementation, implementation, and post-implementation. Pre-implementation refers to the strategic planning stage before the ERP actual project implementation, including strategic decision making, planning, system design, and system selection. Implementation phase focuses on physical processes of software and hardware installation, parameterization, database and system integration, testing, and system stabilization. Lastly, post-implementation is the stage for organizations to run and maintain the ERP systems at daily bases. The post-implementation includes six processes [22]:

- Corrective process, such as application of vendor additions and troubleshooting
- Adaptive process, such as modifications/enhancements and authorization
- Perfective process, such as system version upgrade
- Preventive process, such as administration and work-flow monitoring
- User Support process, such as help desk and user training and education
- External process, such as Coordination and administration among supplier and customers

2.3 ERP Success

To increase the efficiency and effectiveness of ERP adoptions and applications, it is necessary to study the success of ERP. However, during its life cycle, there are more than one success levels of ERP. The majority of the current studies focus on ERP implementation success. Only a few studies conducted research on ERP post-implementation success. Even in post-implementation success studies, there are two different methods, what we called Type I and Type II.

In type I method, ERP post-implementation success is studied as a dependent variable and the purpose of this type of research is to find out what are the main factors impacting the ERP post-implementation success and how to maximize the benefits of the success. Ng [23] raises a conceptual model for ERP post-implementation success. Besides the factors he adopted from DeLone-McLean Model, degree of customization, operation characteristics of the system, and three fitness variables, such as data fit, process fit, and user interface fit, are found significantly related to user satisfaction and/or system use and eventually influencing net benefits from the ERP system (Fig. 3).

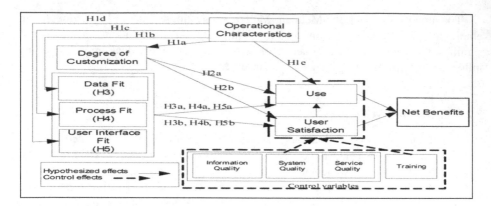

Fig. 3. A conceptual model of ERP success

From a practical development perspective, Zhu [24] proposed another research model to reveal the factors leading ERP post-implementation success. They distinguished all the factors into two levels: first order contract, including project management, system configuration, leadership involvement, organizational fit, and external support, and second order construct with technological aspect (implementation quality) and organizational aspect (organizational readiness) (Fig. 4).

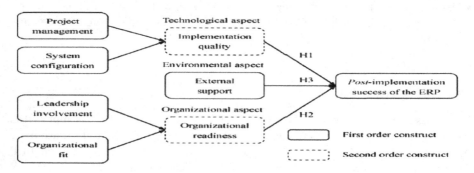

Fig. 4. Research model for ERP post-implementation success

Drawing from the leadership theory, by emphasizing organizational culture and knowledge sharing on transformational leadership, Shao [25], identified four organizational culture factors, development culture, group culture, hierarchical culture, and rational culture, which are impacted by transformational leadership, influencing ERP knowledge sharing and ERP Success (Fig. 5).

Additionally, according to the Change Management Model, AL-Ghamdi [26] proposed a research model leading to a successful ERP outcome. There were five levels in the model:

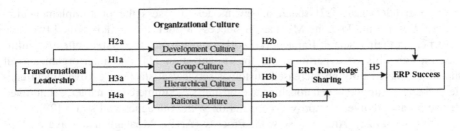

Fig. 5. Research model from Shao, et al.

- Level 1: change management environment,
- Level 2: strategies, processes, and techniques,
- Level 3: user reaction,
- Level 4: IT personnel re-skilling, user training, readiness, and introduction to new system;
- Level 5: successful system implementation (Fig. 6).

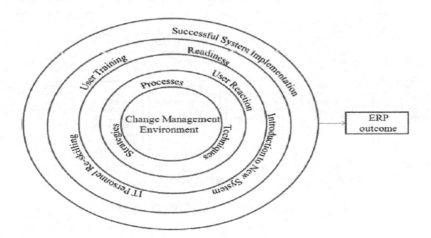

Fig. 6. Proposed change management model for successful ERP

By contrast, type II success focused on how to evaluate ERP post-implementation success. Shao [25] concluded that ERP post-implementation success should include four aspects:

- After ERP implementation, operational cost in the firm is reduced;
- After ERP implementation, sales income in the firm is increased;
- After ERP implementation, managerial decision efficiency in the firm is improved;
- After ERP implementation, customer satisfaction in the firm is enhanced.

Zare and Ravasan [27] stated a new model to assess the post-implementation success. Besides the DeLone-McLean IS Success Model, the authors added two new constructs in their research framework: workgroup impact, the system effective influence on sub-units or departments in the organization [1], and inter-organizational impact, evaluated through increased customer service/satisfaction, e-government enabler, better supplier relationships, e-business/e-commerce enabler, improved service/product delivery, improved cooperation with colleagues and so on [28].

Using the Fuzzy Analytic Network Process (ANP), Moalagh and Ravasan [29] proposed another assessment model with a middle level of managerial success, organizational success and individual success (Fig. 7).

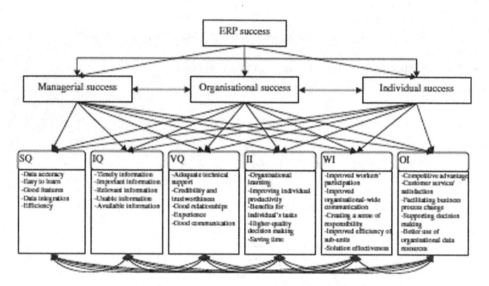

Fig. 7. ANP framework for ERP success assessment

3   Research Model

In this research model, we do not agree with the model proposed by Zare and Ravasan [27]. Even though the authors argue that inter-organizational impacts should be paid attention to when we evaluate the success, we believe that the constructs in inter-organizational impacts are overlapped by the constructs from other factors, such as service quality, organizational impact, and so on. Additionally, we also have questions with Moalagh and Ravasan's [29] model regarding to the three middle levels. The three middle level constructs are all measured by all six third level constructs, which means it's useless to have these three middle levels in the research model and without these three constructs, this research model is back to the model proposed by Ifinedo [1].

In our research model, we believe that the success of ERP post-implementation should be considered based on the original aims/purposes when organizations decide to implement the system. If the ERP achieves the original aims/purposes, we can say it is successful. Otherwise, even if it fits in the success model proposed in previous studies, we cannot say the ERP post-implementation is successful. Or, for example, based on the previous research models, the assessment shows failure of the ERP post-implementation because of the worsened supplier relationship after the ERP implementation. We cannot say the ERP post-implementation is not successful if, in the beginning, the organization did not have building a better relationship with suppliers as one of their aims/purposes for the ERP adoption (Fig. 8).

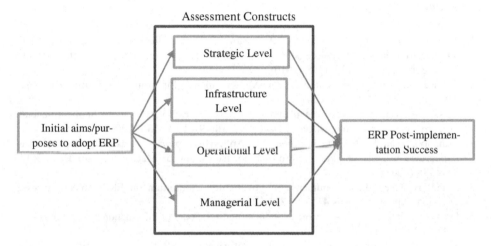

Fig. 8. Proposed research model for post-implementation assessment

Through data standardization and process integration, ERP systems have the potential to facilitate communications and coordination, enable the centralization of administrative activities, reduce IS maintenance costs and increase the ability to deploy new IS functionality [30]. Therefore, back to the original purposes of ERP adoption, we propose our research model to systematically evaluate the ERP post-implementation success:

In this model, we conceptualize the assessment into four levels consisting of the strategic level, infrastructure level, operational level, and the managerial level. In the strategic level, strategic purposes will be evaluated, such as to increase market responsiveness, sharpen the organization's competitive edge, and so on. Infrastructure level refers to IT/IS structures in the organization, such as reduce IT/IS maintenance costs, system integration, data centralization, and so on. Operational level can be evaluated through operational activities, such as adopt best practices, improve productivity, reduce operational costs, and so on. Managerial level focuses on the centralization of administrative activities, improvement of communications, effective decision making, and so on.

4 Discussion and Conclusions

This research intended to find the appropriate constructs to evaluate ERP post-implementation successes. Through the literature review process we discovered the need for a new model dealing with the ERP post-implementation success rather than the success by itself. The proposed model for testing the ERP post-implementation will offer a broader scope for testing ERP post-implementation success than previous models researched. Our study broadens the research of ERP post-implementation success thereby bringing opportunity for future research in this area.

References

1. Ifinedo, P., Rapp, B., Ifinedo, A., Sundberg, K.: Relationships among ERP post-implementation success constructs: an analysis at the organizational level. Comput. Hum. Behav. **26**(5), 1136–1148 (2010)
2. Iivari, J.: An empirical test of the DeLone-McLean model of information systems. Data Base Adv. Inf. Syst. **36**(2), 8–27 (2005)
3. Peslak, A.: Enterprise resource planning success: an exploratory study of the financial executive perspective. Ind. Manage. Data Syst. **106**(9), 1288–1303 (2006)
4. Tsai, W., Hsu, P., Cheng, J., Chen, Y.: An AHP approach to assessing the relative importance weights of ERP performance measures. Int. J. Manage. Enterp Dev. **3**(4), 351–375 (2006)
5. Wang, E., Chen, J.: The influence of governance equilibrium on ERP project success. Decision Support Systems **41**, 708–727 (2006)
6. Drury, D., Farhoomand, A.: A hierarchical structural model of information systems success. INFOR **36**(1/2), 25–40 (1998)
7. Larsen, K.: A taxonomy of antecedents of information systems success: variable analysis studies. J. Manage. Inf. Syst. **20**(2), 169–246 (2003)
8. Rai, A., Lang, S., Welker, R.: Assessing the validity of IS Success Models: an empirical test and theoretical analysis. Inf. Syst. Res. **13**(1), 50–69 (2002)
9. Sabherwal, R., Jeyaraj, A., Chowa, C.: Information system success: individual and organizational determinants. Manage. Sci. **52**(12), 1849–1864 (2006)
10. DeLone, W., McLean, E.: The DeLone and McLean model of information systems success: a ten-year update. J. Manage. Inf. Syst. **19**(4), 9–30 (2003)
11. DeLone, W., McLean, E.: Information systems success: the quest for the dependent variable. Inf. Syst. Res. **3**(1), 60–95 (1992)
12. Davis, F.D.: Perceived usefulness, perceived ease of use, and user acceptance of information technology. MIS Q. **13**(3), 318–346 (1989)
13. Rivard, S., Poirier, G., Raymond, L., Bergeron, F.: Development of a measure to assess the quality of user-developed applications. DATA BASE Adv. Inf. Syst. **28**(3), 44–58 (1997)
14. Bailey, J.E., Pearson, S.W.: Developing a tool for measuring and analyzing computer user satisfaction. Manage. Sci. **29**(5), 530–545 (1983)
15. Collopy, F.: Biases in retrospective self-reports on time use: an empirical study of computer users. Manage. Sci. **42**(5), 758–767 (1996)
16. Doll, W.J., Torkzadeh, G.: Developing a multidimensional measure of system-use in an organizational context. Inf. Manage. **33**(4), 171–185 (1998)

17. Doll, W.J., Torkzadeh, G.: The measurement of end-user computing satisfaction. MIS Q. **12** (2), 259–274 (1988)
18. Burton-Jones, A., Gallivan, M.J.: Toward a deeper understanding of system usage in organizations: a multilevel perspective. MIS Q. **31**(4), 657–680 (2007)
19. Ives, B., Olson, M.H., Baroudi, J.J.: The measurement of user information satisfaction. Commun. ACM **26**(10), 785–793 (1983)
20. Rai, A., Lang, S.S., Welker, R.B.: Assessing the validity of is success models: an empirical test and theoretical analysis. Inf. Syst. Res. **13**, 50–69 (2002)
21. Capaldo, G., Rippa, P.: A planned- oriented approach for ERP implementation strategy selection. J. Enterp. Inf. Manage. **22**(6), 642–659 (2009)
22. Nah, F., Faja, S., Cata, T.: Characteristics of ERP software maintenance: a multiple case study. J. Softw. Maint. Evol.: Res. Pract. **13**(6), 399–414 (2001)
23. Ng, C.: A case study on the impact of customization, fitness, and operational characteristics on enterprise-wide system success, user satisfaction, and system use. J. Global Inf. Manage. **21**(1), 19–41 (2013)
24. Zhu, Y., Li, Y., Wang, W., Chen, J.: What leads to post-implementation success of ERP? an empirical study of the Chinese retail industry. Int. J. Inf. Manage. **30**, 265–276 (2010)
25. Shao, Z., Feng, Y., Liu, L.: The mediating effect of organizational culture and knowledge sharing on transformational leadership and enterprise resource planning systems success: an empirical study in China. Comput. Hum. Behav. **28**, 2400–2413 (2012)
26. AL-Ghamdi, A.: Change management strategies and processes for the successful ERP system implementation: a proposed model. Int. J. Comput. Sci. Inf. Secur. **11**(2), 36–41 (2013)
27. Zare, A., Ravasan, A.: An extended framework for ERP post-implementation success assessment. Inf. Resour. Manage. J. **27**(4), 45 (2014)
28. Su, Y., Yang, C.: A structural equation model for analyzing the impact of ERP on SCM. Expert Syst. Appl. **37**(1), 456–469 (2010)
29. Moalagh, M., Zare Ravasan, A.: Developing a practical framework for assessing ERP post-implementation success using fuzzy analytic network process. Int. J. Prod. Res. **51**(4), 1236–1257 (2013)
30. Gattiker, T., Goodhue, D.: Understanding the local-level costs and benefits of ERP through organizational information processing theory. Inf. Manage. **41**, 431–443 (2004)

Societal and Cultural Impact
of Technology

Interactive Evaluation of Pragmatic Features in Spoken Journalistic Texts

Christina Alexandris[1](✉), Mario Nottas[2], and George Cambourakis[3]

[1] National University of Athens, Athens, Greece
calexandris@gs.uoa.gr
[2] Danube University Krems – National Technical University of Athens,
Athens, Greece
manottas@ilsp.gr
[3] National Technical University of Athens, Athens, Greece
gcamb@cs.ntua.gr

Abstract. The designed annotation tool intends to facilitate the evaluation of pragmatic features in spoken political and journalistic texts, in particular, interviews, live conversations in the Media and discussions in Parliament. The evaluation of pragmatic features focuses in the discourse component of spoken political and journalistic texts, in addition to implied information and connotative features. The present tool may be used by professional journalists and for training purposes, for journalists and other professionals,

Keywords: Interactive topic-tracking · Semantic relations · Discourse structure · Graphic representation · Connotative features

1 Introduction

The designed interactive annotation tool targets to function as an aid to journalists and other professionals, intending to facilitate the evaluation of pragmatic features in spoken political and journalistic texts. The proposed tool may be used to process and to evaluate spoken texts such as interviews, live conversations in the Media, as well as discussions in Parliament.

The evaluation of pragmatic features focuses in the discourse component of spoken political and journalistic texts, in addition to implied information and connotative features, available in monolingual as well as in multilingual contexts. The design of the present tool is based on data and observations provided by professional journalists.

Transcriptions from two-party or multiple party discussions of spoken journalistic texts constitute the basis of the present data. These transcriptions, performed by professional journalists, are also compared to older data transcribed from spoken journalistic texts in European Union projects. The collected data included transcriptions from projects of graduate courses for journalists, in particular, the Program M.A in Quality Journalism and Digital Technologies, Danube University at Krems, Athena-Research and Innovation Center in Information, Communication and Knowledge Technologies, Athens - Institution of Promotion of Journalism Ath.Vas. Botsi, Athens.

© Springer International Publishing Switzerland 2015
M. Kurosu (Ed.): Human-Computer Interaction, Part III, HCII 2015, LNCS 9171, pp. 259–268, 2015.
DOI: 10.1007/978 3 319-21006-3_26

Transcription and linguistic analysis was performed by two groups of 18–20 professional journalists for the academic years 2012–2013 and 2013–2014. Each journalist was assigned the evaluation of 4 interviews and performed a transcription of 15–20 min of each discussion, two in English (or any other natural language, for example, German) and two in Greek. Transcriptions from the following news broadcast networks were included in the files processed: BBC World News, CNN, AL Jazeera, Russia Today (RT) ("Crosstalk"), ZDF (Germany), ARD (Germany), available transcriptions from the German Parliament and Greek TV channels (ERT-NERIT (public television), the Parliament Channel ("Vouli"), Mega TV, SKAI TV, ALPHA). The speakers participating in the interviews or discussions were native speakers of British English or American English, German (Standard or a Dialect) and Modern Greek. English-speaking participants from countries as varied as India, Russia, Eastern Europe, the Middle East (Arab-speaking countries and Israel), Iran, Pakistan, P.R. China, Kenya and Nigeria were among the international speakers in the transcribed data.

Specifically, the professional journalists were assigned the task to transcribe interviews and two-party or multiparty discussions from national and international news networks, recording content, style and linguistic features, time assigned to each participant, turn-taking, interruptions, as well as gestures and other paralinguistic features. At the end of the analysis, the journalists provided an outline of the discourse structure of the interviews and the two-party or multiparty discussions.

2 Design and User Interaction

2.1 Overview and Design

The designed annotation tool targets (1) to provide the User-Journalist with the tracked indications of the topics handled in the interview or discussion and (2) to view the graphic pattern of the discourse structure of the interview or discussion, (3) to evaluate the discourse structure, (4) to allow the User to compare the discourse structure of conversations and interviews with similar topics or the same participants /participant and (5) to indicate the largest possible percentage of the points in the texts signalizing information with implied information and connotative features.

The interface of the annotation tool is designed to (a) to track the "local" topic discussed in a given segment of an interview or discussion or change of "local" topic in an interview or discussion and (b) annotate and highlight all the points possibly containing connotative features information, alerting the User to evaluate the parts of the text containing these expressions.

The designed tool allows the tracking of any change of topic or the same or a similar answer, as well as associations and generalizations related to the same topic. Since processing speed and the option of re-usability in multiple languages of the written and spoken political and journalistic texts constitutes a basic target of the proposed approach, strategies typically employed in the construction of Spoken Dialog Systems such as keyword processing in the form of topic detection are adapted in the present design.

Incoming texts to be processed constitute transcribed data from journalistic texts. The interactive annotation tool is designed to operate with most commercial transcription tools, some of which are available online. The designed tool may also be adapted to downloaded written texts from the internet (blogs, pdfs etc.) or scanned files from newspaper articles.

2.2   User Interaction

The steps in the interaction are initiated by the User activating the annotation tool when viewing journalistic texts online. The online journalistic texts are scanned by the proposed tool and the User is presented with an output comprising the online journalistic text with all the tracked topics, a graph of the text structure, as well as the instances of "marked" information with implied information and connotative features.

User interaction involves two fully automatic processes, one process assisted by System and one fully User-interactive process.

To help the User with the choice of local topics as a first step in the interaction, the indication of candidate topics (SELECT-TOPIC Process) is a process assisted by the System. The indication of the local topics (LOCAL-TOPIC Process) at each point in the interview or conversation is a fully User-interactive process, constituting the second step in the interaction. The SELECT-TOPIC Process is activated with the "Select Topic" command. The LOCAL-TOPIC Process may be divided into two stages, corresponding to the activation of two respective commands, "Identify Topic" and "Identify Relation" (Fig. 1).

Step in Interaction-Command	Process Activated
"Select Topic"	SELECT-TOPIC
"Identify Topic" "Identify Relation"	LOCAL-TOPIC (REP) (GEN) (ASOC) (SWITCH)
"Show Structure"	GEN-GRAPH
"Show Possible Connotative Features"	CONN-FEATURE

Fig. 1. Processes activated and respective commands

The list of the topics identified and tracked in the discussion or interview is presented to the User in chronological order.

The generation of the discourse structure (GEN-GRAPH Process) and the signalization of the points containing connotative features (CONN-FEATURE Process) are fully automatic processes. The GEN-GRAPH Process is activated with the "Show

Structure" command. The separate CONN-FEATURE Process is activated with the "Show Possible Connotative Features" command.

The generation of the discourse structure (GEN-GRAPH Process) constitutes the final step of the interaction. With the activation of "Show Structure", a graphic representation of the relation between the topics is presented, assisting the User to evaluate the flow of the conversation and the discourse structure of the discussion or interview.

2.3 The CONN-FEATURE Process: Signalizing Implied Information and Connotative Features

The signalization of "marked" information (CONN-FEATURE Process) is a fully automated process and is activated independently from the other three above-mentioned processes. The CONN-FEATURE Process signalizes all "connotatively marked" words and expressions based on the flouting of the Gricean Cooperativity Principle, especially in regard to the violation of the Maxims of Quality and Quantity [2, 4, 5].

These sets of expressions may be grouped into a finite set based on word stems or suffix type. Recognition on a word-stem or a suffix basis involves the detection of word-classes such as adjectives and adverbials or types of verbs, containing specific semantic features accessible with Wordnets and/or Selectional Restrictions [2].

Word categories whose connotative features are detected in the morphological level and whose semantic content is related to connotatively emotionally and socio-culturally "marked" elements are labelled as word groups with implicit connotative features. These word groups include the grammatical categories of verbs (or nominializations of verbs) containing semantic features (including implied connotations in language use) related to (i) mode (ii) malignant/benign action or (iii) emotional/ethical gravity, as well as nouns with suffixes producing diminutives, derivational suffixes resulting to a (ii) verbalization, (iii) an adjectivization or (iii) an additional nominalization of proper nouns (excluding derivational suffixes producing participles and actor thematic roles) [2].

3 Topic Tracking

3.1 The SELECT-TOPIC Process: Assisted Topic Selection

To assist the User in regard to the choice of topic, candidate topics consisting nouns are automatically signalized and listed with the SELECT-TOPIC Process. Pronouns and anaphoric expressions are not tracked. For the achievement of speed and efficiency, in the SELECT-TOPIC Process, the annotation module operates on keyword detection at morpheme-level or word-level. Only one topic can be set for each question or response.

Additionally, we note that selected topics may be subjected to Machine Translation. Selected topics may also be accessible as Universal Words, with the use of the Universal Networking Language (UNL) [10, 11, 13].

Finally, it should be considered that candidate topics corresponding to general subjects may receive additional signalization, also functioning as candidate topics for indicating the relation of "Generalization", presented in following sections. The topics corresponding to general subjects may be related to a sublanguage-based data base or extracted from existing resources such as specialized lexica and corpora or Wordnets. Examples of general topics are "energy", "financial crisis" or "biohazard" or a cluster of related word groups, for example, "war", "battle", "event", "incident", or "treaty", "ally" and "side" [1].

3.2   The LOCAL-TOPIC Process: Topic Identification

From the list of available nouns chosen by the System, the User chooses the topic of the question or issue addressed by the interviewer or journalist-moderator and compares it to the topic of the answer or response.

With the activation of the "Identify Topic" command, topics are defined at a local level, in respect to the question asked or issue addressed by the interviewer or moderator, allowing the content of answers, responses and reactions to be checked in respect to the question asked or issue addressed.

Topics are treated as local variables. They are defined, registered and tracked.

Within the framework of questions/issues raised and respective answers, responses or reactions, the discourse structure is observed to be in some cases compatible to turn-taking in "push-to-talk conversations" [9], where there is a strict protocol in managing the interview or discussion and turn-taking. In other cases, discourse structure and turn-taking is partially compatible to the models of Sacks et al. 1974, Wilson and Wilson 2005 [8, 12], where each participant selects self.

A basic feature of the present approach is that the expert or world knowledge of the Users-Journalists helps identify the topic of each segment of the interview or discussion and also it helps determine the relation types between topics, due to the fact that in the domain of journalistic texts these relations cannot be strictly semantic and automatic processes may result to errors.

3.3   Relation Types

In the LOCAL-TOPIC Process, with the activation of the "Identify Relation" command, the User-Journalist indicates the type of relation between the topic of the question or issue addressed with the topic of the respective response or reaction. Relations between topics may of the following types: (1) Repetition, (2) Association (3) Generalization and (4) Topic Switch.

The User determines the relation type from the available relation types related to the corresponding tags. The relation of "Repetition" between selected topics receives the "REP" tag and involves the repetition of the same word or synonym. The relation of "Association" between selected topics receives the "ASOC" tag. Association may be defined by the User's world knowledge or, if a defined sublanguage is used, the relation may be set by lexicon or Wordnet. The relation of "Generalization" between selected topics receives the "GEN" tag. We note that topics related to each other by a relation of "Generalization" can be easily defined within a sublanguage or a Wordnet. Finally, the relation of "Topic Switch" is used when the topic of a discussion or interview changes between selected topics without any evident semantic relations. The relation of "Topic Switch" receives the "SWITCH" tag.

4 The GEN-GRAPH Process: Graphic Representation

The final step of the interaction produces a graphic representation of the selected local topics in the discourse structure. The graphic representation has a "Generate Graph" and a "Generate Tree" option, since the generated structure may be depicted as a graph ("Generate Graph" option) or it may be depicted in a tree-like form, similar to a discourse tree [3, 6, 7] ("Generate Tree" option).

The generated graphic representation is based on the relations of the topics to each other, including distances from one word to another.

Distances between topics are defined as 1, 2 and 3. Distance 1 corresponds to the relation of "Repetition", Distance 2, corresponds to the relation of "Association" and Distance 3 corresponds to the relation of "Generalization".

The selected topics are attached to each other, either automatically by the System or interactively by the User, based on the set values of distances.

Depending on the type of graphic representation chosen, Distances 1, 2 and 3 are depicted as vertical lines from top to bottom, in the case of the generation of a tree-like structure, or they may be depicted as horizontal lines from left to right, in the case of the generation of a graph. The length of the lines depends on the type of distance. Thus, the shortest line corresponds to the relation of "Repetition", related to Distance 1, while Distance 2, corresponding to the relation of "Association", is represented as a longer line to the next word-node. Distance 3, corresponding to the relation of "Generaliza-tion", is represented as the longest of three types of lines to the next word-node. The longest lines corresponding to the relation of "Generalization" may be modelled to form a curve (or a slight peak) to the next word-node, if a graph is generated or a node with a larger size and characteristic indication, if a tree-like structure is generated.

The fourth type of relation, "Topic Switch", is depicted as a new, disconnected node generated to the right of the current point of the discourse structure, whether it is a tree or a graph. As separate nodes, topic switches may be connected as different branches of a tree structure, similar to discourse structures presented in tree-like forms, resembling discourse trees [3, 6, 7]. In a generated graph, topic switches may be depicted as breaks in the continuous flow of the graph.

Independently from the type of graphic representation chosen, the "Generate Graph" or the "Generate Tree" options, it should be noted that the overall shape of the generated graphic representation is dependent on the mostly occurring relation types in the discourse structure of the interview or discussion. For example, a generated graphic representation may have, in one case, many separate nodes ("Generate Tree" option) or peaks ("Generate Graph" option), in another case, a generated graphic representation may have a predominately linear structure, regardless of whether the "Generate Tree" option or the "Generate Graph" option is selected.

Furthermore, some types of linear structures may be modelled into circular structures, if the predominate relation is "Repetition" and in the graphic representation the last node is attached to the first node, corresponding to the same or a very similar (or synonymous) topic.

In the structures below, Fig. 2, corresponding to a discussion (with three participants) may be related to a predominately linear structure. On the other hand, Fig. 3, corresponding to an interview, may be related to a circular structure. In the transcribed discussions in Figs. 2 and 3, names of countries and national groups are withheld. The relation of "Generalization" is depicted in bold print.

(Respecting) laws of [National] State => [National] State => [Nationals] => [Nationals] outside [Country] => minority group ==>>	
	citizens
[>] "Nationalist"/ "Nationalism" => [country's] culture => [country's] civilization	
[>] immigrants =>	**people**
=> law-abiding household owners => [National] Law ==>>	
	violence

Fig. 2. Relations between topics generating a mostly linear structure

In Fig. 2, the topic of the conversation is "respecting laws of National State", which is, in turn, associated to "Nationals", "Nationals outside Country", a "(definition) of minority group" and "(country's) citizens" (Generalization). A topic shift occurs to the subject "Nationalist" and "Nationalism" which is, in turn, associated with the topics of a "country's culture" and a "county's civilization". A third topic shift occurs towards the subject "immigrants" that is, in turn, associated with the general topics "people" (Generalization), "law-abiding household owners", "(National) Law" and "violence" (Generalization).

On the other hand, in Fig. 3, the topic of the interview is "(country's) people" which is always reoccurring in questions and responses. Repetition is the mostly occurring relation in the predominately linear discourse structure in Fig. 3 and may be modelled into a circular structure.

In the examples in Figs. 2, 3 and 4, Distance 1 (Repetition- REP) is depicted as ">>", Distance 2 (Association- ASOC) as "=>" and Distance 3 (Generalization- GEN) is depicted as "==>>". Topic switch (SWITCH) is depicted as "[>]".

The example in Fig. 4 is a typical example resulting to the generation of a graphic representation of many separate nodes ("Generate Tree" option) or peaks ("Generate Graph" option).

| [country's] people >> [country's] people >> [country's] people >> [country's] people >> [country's] people |

Fig. 3. Relations between topics resulting to the modelling of a circular structure.

		poverty
African-American community ==>>		family
		speeches
[>]local level-=>school => children		
[>]Keystone pipeline-=> State Department		
[>]the Little Sisters of the Poor ==>>		health
[>]IRS corrupt / Benghazi ==>>		issues
		questions
[>]President of the United States ==>>		criticism
[>]President Clinton => President Bush=> (liberal) President ==>>		policies
[>]Richard Nixon- EPA- FDR=> liberal and demo-crat- liberal and conservative ==>>		country
	=>infrastructure	
	=>trillion dollars worth	
[>] basic research => innovation edge=> space => internet		
[>]seventeen trillion dollar debt=> tax code		
[>]loopholes		
[>]minimum wage ==>>		welfare
	=>nanny state	
[>]World War II==>>		middle class
[>]Veterans		

TRANSCRIPT: Full interview between President Obama and Bill O'Reilly
Published February 03, 2014. FoxNews.com
   http://www.foxnews.com/politics/2014/02/03/transcript-full-interview-between-president-obama-and-bill-oreilly/

Fig. 4. Relations between topics generating a tree-like structure with multiple branches or a graph with multiple peaks.

The example in Fig. 4, corresponding to a transcript of an available online inter-view, contains a relatively high percentage of "Generalization" relations (depicted in bold print) affecting the overall shape of the generated graphic representation.

In the example in Fig. 4, the initial topics "poverty" and "family" (Generalization) are associated with the topic "African-American community". Associated topics such as "children" and "school" are followed by multiple topic shifts to "Keystone pipeline", "State Department" and "the Little Sisters of the Poor". There is a topic shift to "health" (Generalization), a topic switch to the "IRS" and "Benghazi", both related to the topics "issues" and "questions" (Generalization). General topics such as "criticism" and "policies" are connected to multiple topic shifts concerning the topics "President of the United States" associated with the topics "President Clinton", "Richard Nixon" and "EPA", "FDR", which are, in turn, associated with "liberal and democrat", "liberal and conservative" and "country" (Generalization). The topic "country", a "Generalization" relation, is associated with "infrastructure", in turn, associated with "2 trillion dollars worth". The next topic shift concerns the topics "basic research", "innovation edge" "space", "internet" and "seventeen trillion dollar debt" which is connected to the next topic shift, "tax code" and "loopholes". Another topic shift is "minimum wage" associated with "welfare" (Generalization) and "nanny state". The last topic shift is "World War II", associated with the topic "Veterans", and connected by topic shift to the topic "middle class" (Generalization).

5 Conclusions and Further Research

The evaluation of pragmatic features in spoken political and journalistic texts is pro-posed to be assisted by an interactive annotation tool providing a graphic representation of the discourse structure and signalizing implied information and connotative features. The tool may be used to evaluate the content of interviews, live conversations in the Media and discussions in Parliament, enabling an overview of content and targeting to an objective evaluation of discourse structure and connotative elements.

The processes activated are combined with the decision-making process of the Journalist-User, allowing the combination of expert knowledge with automatic procedures.

Further research includes a full implementation of the designed tool, along with a comparison of the local topics chosen by different Users-Journalists, as well as a comparison of the effectiveness of graphic representation types, tree-like structures or graphs. Furthermore, the possibility of fully automatic topic tracking with the aid of a network or other form of resource based on a defined sublanguage is a subject of further investigation. Full implementation may provide concrete results of the proposed strategy's success level and an insight to resolving any further issues.

Acknowledgements. We wish to thank Mr. Thanasis Tsolakis, Journalist and Newscaster, who provided the basic analysis of examples presented, and the QJNT4 and QJNT5 class of graduate students of the Program M.A in Quality Journalism and Digital Technologies, Danube University at Krems, Austria.

References

1. Alexandris, C.: Accessing cause-result relation and diplomatic information in ancient "Journalistic" texts with universal words. In: Kurosu, M. (ed.) HCI 2014, Part II. LNCS, vol. 8511, pp. 351–361. Springer, Heidelberg (2014)
2. Alexandris, C.: English, German and the international "semi-professional" translator: a morphological approach to implied connotative features. J. Lang. Transl. **11**(2), 7–46 (2010). Sejong University, Korea
3. Carlson, L., Marcu, D., Okurowski, M. E.: Building a discourse-tagged corpus in the framework of rhetorical structure theory. In: Proceedings of the 2nd SIGDIAL Workshop on Discourse and Dialogue, Eurospeech 2001, Denmark, September 2001
4. Grice, H.P.: Logic and conversation. In: Cole, P., Morgan, J. (eds.) Syntax and Semantics, vol. 3. Academic Press, New York (1975)
5. Hatim, B.: Communication Across Cultures: Translation Theory and Contrastive Text Linguistics. University of Exeter, Exeter (1997)
6. Jurafsky, D., Martin, J.: Speech and Language Processing, an Introduction to Natural Language Processing, Computational Linguistics and Speech Recognition, 2nd edn. Pearson Education, Upper Saddle River (2008). Prentice Hall series in Artificial Intelligence
7. Marcu, D.: Discourse trees are good indicators of importance in text. In: Mani, I., Maybury, M. (eds.) Advances in Automatic Text Summarization, pp. 123–136. The MIT Press, Cambridge (1999)
8. Sacks, H., Schegloff, E.A., Jefferson, G.: A simplest systematics for the organization of turn-taking for conversation. Language **50**, 696–735 (1974)
9. Taboada, M.: Spontaneous and non-spontaneous turn-taking. Pragmatics **16**(2–3), 329–360 (2006)
10. Uchida, H., Zhu, M., Della Senta, T.: Universal Networking Language. The UNDL Foundation, Tokyo (2005)
11. Uchida, H., Zhu, M., Della Senta, T.: The UNLA Gift for Millennium. The United Nations University Institute of Advanced Studies UNU/IAS, Tokyo, Japan (1999)
12. Wilson, K.E.: An oscillator model of the timing of turn-taking. Psychon. Bull. Rev. **12**(6), 957–968 (2005)
13. The Universal Networking Language. http://www.undl.org

Socio-Cultural Aspects in the Design of Multilingual Banking Interfaces in the Arab Region

Sarah Alhumoud[1], Lamia Alabdulkarim[1], Nouf Almobarak[2],
and Areej Al-Wabil[2(✉)]

[1] Department of Computer Science, College of Computer and Information
Sciences, Imam Mohammed bin Saud Islamic University, Riyadh, Saudi Arabia
{sohumoud, lamia}@imamu.edu.sa
[2] Software Engineering Department, College of Computer and Information
Sciences, King Saud University, Riyadh, Saudi Arabia
{nmalmobarak, aalwabil}@ksu.edu.sa

Abstract. This paper reports on insights gained from investigating multilingual user interfaces designed for banking systems in the Arab Region. In this region, Arabic is the native language; however a plethora of expatriates reside in the region who speak different languages. Three modes of banking interactions are examined in the local context; internet banking, automatic teller machines (ATMs), and mobile banking (MB). Reflections on interaction design for the three modes of banking illuminates the culture-orientated design considerations for banking interactions and demonstrates how users, in this case bank customers, shape technological changes and influence interface design. The contribution of this research is threefold. Firstly, gain an insight into socio-cultural design requirements for banking interfaces; secondly, an exploratory survey of interface design considerations in the three modes of banking with a focus on multilingual aspects of the design; and finally, distil the findings into design recommendations for socio-cultural aspects that are relevant to the context of banking interactions in the Arab Region.

Keywords: ATM · Mobile banking · Online banking · Heuristics · Usability

1 Introduction

Banking interfaces are designed to provide a secure mode of communication for customers to access their bank accounts. Banking interfaces that reflect socio-cultural factors can provide meaningful interactions that reflect users' local context as well as providing them with social, personal, and symbolic cultural values. These aspects consequently facilitate user acceptance, and can positively influence the user experience (UX) in interacting with banking interfaces as well as the customer experience (CX) in commercial and personal banking. Users involved in banking interactions in the Arab region include native Arabic-speaking populations in addition to an expatriate community residing in these countries who predominantly speak English or French as their first language (e.g. English-speaking expatriates in the Gulf region, French-speaking

© Springer International Publishing Switzerland 2015
M. Kurosu (Ed.): Human-Computer Interaction, Part III, HCII 2015, LNCS 9171, pp. 269–280, 2015.
DOI: 10.1007/978-3-319-21006-3_27

natives and expatriates in the North African Arab region). The expatriate community often constitute more than one third of the population in some countries in the Arab region, and thus user-centered socio-cultural banking interaction design is imperative for high usability in banking interfaces and for providing good user experiences for these banking systems.

The context of this study is Saudi Arabia, where one-third of the population is non-Arabic speakers with varying proficiency in technology usage, socio-economic backgrounds, and consequently different interaction design requirements [1]. Banking systems often cater to the requirements of target user populations by offering bilingual interfaces in Arabic and English. The penetration of mobile devices in Saudi Arabia is amongst the highest in the world, with comparable adoption rates across socio-economic levels in the population [2]. Hence, examining socio-cultural aspects of design are particularly relevant to this region to gain insights into the key requirements for service and delivery of technology solutions in banking interactions. Three modes of banking are prevalent in the local context; namely, internet banking, automatic teller machines (ATMs), and mobile internet banking (MB). An examination of interaction design for the three modes of banking illuminates the history and culture-orientated design considerations for electronic banking interfaces and demonstrates how users, in this case bank customers, shape technological changes and influence interface design [3, 4].

In recent years, there has been a proliferation in research examining design consideration for Arabic Interfaces [5–7]. Banking interface design issues have been reported in the HCI literature for several decades [8, 9], and recently, specific scopes of research have emerged in ATM related literature such as accessibility for user populations with disabilities and the elderly [10]. To date, our understanding of the socio-cultural factors in the design of banking interfaces in the Arab region is limited [e.g. 11, 12]. HCI studies related to the broad scope of Internet Banking have looked at interaction and design issues in different cultures and for different user groups [13, 14]. However, the socio-cultural design considerations for Arabic banking interfaces remains to be an unexplored area of research and inadequately examined.

The contribution of this paper is threefold. Firstly, gain an insight into socio-cultural design requirements for banking interfaces; secondly, conduct an exploratory survey of interface design considerations in the three modes of banking with a focus on multilingual aspects of the design; and finally, distil the findings into design recommendations for socio-cultural aspects that are relevant to the context of banking interactions in the Arab Region.

2   Design Considerations for Banking Interactions

Designers of banking interfaces in the Arab region have not yet been able to encode cultural phenomena to the same extent as human factors (e.g. cognitive and physical) in designing devices and interfaces [7, 9]. Research has suggested that designers need to specify, analyze and integrate socio-cultural factors in the early stages of the design to understand the human factors relevant for banking interactions (e.g. [15]). Khashman and Large [5] conducted a study that considered the design characteristics of government websites in different Arab countries. Interestingly, Hofstede's culture's model was found to be inadequately reflected in the interfaces reviewed in that study [5].

Banking interfaces in the Arab region often toggle between left-to-right (LTR) and right-to-left (RTL) screen orientation in Arabic script and Latin script interfaces, and support bidirectional scripts for Arabic letters, digits and embedded charts/diagrams. Text and navigation in banking interactions cascade to the left in Arabic interfaces, and cascade to the right in English/French interfaces. Most items in the Arabic bidirectional interfaces are mirrored by comparison to the English/French versions of the interfaces. In addition to the layout of banking interfaces, directionality may affect the navigation, alignment in tables, collated images, and pop-up windows or scrolling messages. Notably, the process of producing mirrored versions of these banking interfaces is straightforward. The functionality associated with the navigation (e.g. back, next), undo and redo icons, confirm and cancel buttons, may require relocation, rather than a simple mirroring of the graphics.

In the following sub-sections, we present an overview of banking interactions offered to customers beyond branch-based banking. This includes previous research on ATM and Internet banking on web interfaces and mobile applications.

2.1   ATM-Based Banking Interactions

In recent years, researchers have examined human factors in the design and usability of ATM banking interactions. Such studies have generally focused on the design considerations of ergonomics, location, and accessibility for specific user populations such as the elderly or individuals with declining or limited abilities (e.g. visual, physical, cognitive) [10–12]. Although design recommendations have been reported for interfaces for different languages and cultural contexts [e.g. 13], little attention has comparatively been paid to design considerations for Arabic interfaces of ATM banking systems in the Arab region.

2.2   Web-Based Banking Interactions

The interest in Web-based Banking (WB), Internet Banking (IB) and E-banking has grown rapidly following the increased adoption of communication and Internet technologies. Notably, online banking started in 1995 in the United States of America, when the Presidential Savings Bank offered its customers an online service as an alternate to traditional banking [16]. A similar pattern of increased diffusion of web-based banking interactions was observed in our local region. In Saudi Arabia, the Saudi Money Agency (SAMA) has recently reported that the number of bills that have been paid using the national Electronic Bill Presentment and Payment (EBPP) system named as SADAD jumped 107 % in the period between between 2009 and 2014 [17]. An increased recognition of the importance of culture-oriented models of technology adoption is evident, as noted by a survey of Internet banking in Jordan, conducted by Siam in 2006 [18]. In this survey, it was emphasized that banks need to consider adopting Internet-based services to achieve a competitive advantage for providing customers with efficient, convenient, location-independent banking transactions [18].

2.3   Mobile Banking (MB) Interactions

With the rapid advances in communication technologies and mobile devices, using Mobile Banking (MB) has become an important alternative to branch, ATM and internet web baking for customers who are often on-the-move. A recent study has suggested that using mobile banking in the US has grown from 38 % to 42 % and reached 46 % for years 2013, 2014 and 2015 respectively [19]. In China, the rise in the number of mobile banking users has been reported from 10 % to 25 % in the timeframe between 2010 and 2011 [20]. In Saudi Arabia, with a population not exceeding 30 million, the total number of mobile subscriptions reached around 50 million with a penetration rate reaching 165.1 % in 2014 [21]. This high penetration rate was accompanied with an increased interest in providing mobile banking service from the banking sectors.

In our local context, mobile banking emerged in August 2010 with the application Samba Mobile for *Samba Financial Group* (Samba). Since then, all 12 banks in Saudi Arabia started releasing their mobile applications for both iOS and Android. The gradual diffusion of MB in Saudi Arabia is depicted in Fig. 1. Mobile banking diffusion was coupled with the high penetration rate of mobile devices and fast growing capabilities of mobile phones, which are two key drivers for MB services [22]. Other drivers include trust, ease of use and cost effectiveness. Interestingly, evidence from our exploratory study that we carried out in Saudi Arabia on banking customers suggests that 54 % of them used mobile banking as the preferred banking scheme compared to 44 % preferring to use web banking.

3   Heuristics Evaluations

The banking interfaces were inspected using Neilsen's heuristics [23]. Each system was evaluated by selecting key interfaces (such as the login screen, balance statement and transfer to an existing beneficiary) and applying the heuristics consistently across the three modes of banking. The review was conducted by the HCI team in addition to data gathered from an exploratory study for each banking interaction type with a selected sample of users from our local context. A representative sample of three banks was selected based on the popularity in the region [17]. The considered banks are Alrajhi, Riyad Bank and Alahli banks referred to as B1, B2 and B3 respectively. We present the overall heuristic evaluation and describe each banking interface's design considerations separately (Table 1).

3.1   ATM

For ATM interactions, the ergonomics and visual design of interfaces varied across the sample of banking interfaces. The location of ATMs is an important factor in design, especially in desert region in which bright sunlight impacts visibility of the interfaces in exposed locations. Banks are increasingly addressing this problem in ergonomics, location, and human factors as it directly impacts the user experience in our local context. With regards to the flow of the interfaces to meet the wide spectrum of users, consistency in flow emerged as a design issue often overlook in local interfaces. For

Table 1. Aggregate evaluation of the three types of banking interfaces, B1, B2, and B3

Heuristics	ATM Banking			Mobile Banking			Online Banking			All		
	B1	B2	B3	B1	B2	B3	B1	B2	B3	B1	B2	B3
Visibility of system status	5	2	4	5	3	3	5	2	3	5	2	3
Match with real world	5	4	4	5	4	5	5	3	1	5	4	3
User control and freedom	4	2	3	5	5	3	5	5	5	5	4	4
Consistency and standards	4	2	3	4	2	3	4	2	3	4	2	3
Error prevention	5	2	4	5	4	3	5	3	3	5	3	3
Recognition rather than recall	5	5	5	5	3	5	5	3	1	5	4	4
Flexibility and efficiency	5	3	5	5	3	4	4	3	4	5	3	4
Aesthetic/minimalist design	5	2	5	3	5	5	5	1	2	4	3	4
Error Recovery	5	2	4	5	3	3	5	4	3	5	3	3
Help and documentation	2	2	2	5	5	2	5	5	5	4	4	3
Total	**45**	**26**	**39**	**47**	**37**	**36**	**48**	**31**	**30**	**47**	**31**	**35**

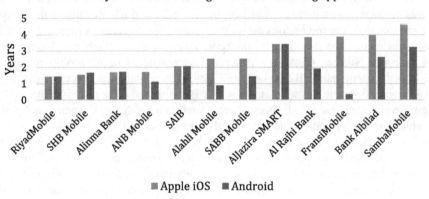

Number of years since releasing first Mobile banking application

■ Apple iOS   ■ Android

Fig. 1. Number of years since releasing first Mobile Banking application (from 2015)

example, the interface for the login was bidirectional and the language was prominently displayed for system feedback in guidance messages and in error messages. An example is shown in Fig. 2.

Error messages varied in their design from subtle cues to visually salient indicators to attract users' attention to the problem. For the main transactions in ATM interfaces, the options are often listed as icons with text-labels and in some interfaces, aligned with physical buttons located on both sides of the visual display. Information to help the user detect errors consists of indications provided during normal operations (e.g. three wrong password attempt the bank will block the user's account) [24].

Balance Inquiry is one of the options in the main menu where users check their balance. The structure and layout of the screen varied across the banking interfaces.

Arabic   English

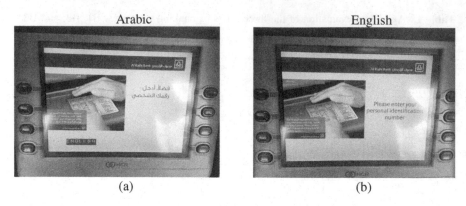

(a)   (b)

Fig. 2. Arabic and English interfaces of Alrajhi bank's ATM (B1)

Users noted that displaying more data in these transactions often hinder the sense-making process of completing the transaction. For the sub transactions in balance inquiry screen, the options listed are often related to the main option (Balance Inquiry). The readability of the text in the sub-transactions also varied across the three banking interfaces. Concerning minimalist design, B2 had higher density in the visual design and was perceived to be more cluttered compared to B1 and B3. Regarding the transfer function operation, the sub options are similar among the three banks interfaces. All the three banks require the user to enter the beneficiary Account Number or International Bank Account Number (IBAN) whether it was registered or not. With regards to visibility of system status, B2 lacked notifications in a multistep process such as the transfer transaction and balance statement. For B1, it scored higher in visibility as their design incorporates salient indicators of error such as a red X mark when compared to B3, which uses color-coded data entry fields, or color-coded subtle message.

With regards to user control, B1 fared better than the two others due to the availability of a home/escape link to previous pages on the navigation trail, whereas the other interfaces lacked this. In reviewing error prevention designs, it was noted that the multi-step process notifications were not communicated in time for users. For example, the bank statement lookup option requires authentication; however the incorrect password message is not displayed until the user proceeds to the second navigation layer. Another example is the action of withdrawing the bankcard by the machine, in which no warnings were issued to the user. The heuristic of "recognition rather recall" was sufficiently addressed in the interfaces reviewed. For flexibility and efficiency, the B2 interface was rated lower than other bank interfaces due to complexity in navigation and displaying information in dense interfaces. In aesthetics heuristics, B2 scored lower due to font selection, clutter and salience of key information. For the user control and freedom heuristics, a socio-cultural design consideration is the flexibility in selecting the language of interaction, which was sufficiently addressed in the banking interfaces. The issue with help and documentation was adequately addressed, despite the lack of options available for live user assistance (e.g. some interfaces provide customers with contact number whereas others provide a phone connection adjacent to the machine).

3.2 Web-Based Online Interfaces

For web-based online banking interfaces that we examined, the login interfaces supported both Arabic and English and the contents of the pages are similar in both languages with mirrored alignment as shown in Figs. 3 and 4.

(a)   (b)

Fig. 3. (a) Arabic and (b) English web interfaces of Alrajhi bank (B1)

Error messages in failed login attempts in banking interactions varied from one bank to another. Variation was in color, content and options presented to the customers. Interfaces of B1, B2 and B3 allowed three unsuccessful attempts, and after that account would be suspended for security reasons. Nevertheless, only one of these banks, B1 show a meaningful warning message of how many attempts the user is allowed to do before account suspension as shown in (Fig. 4).

(a)   (b)

Fig. 4. (a) Arabic and (b) English web interfaces of Riyad bank (B2)

For the main transactions in the web-based banking interfaces, the options are often listed as main menu and submenus. Visibility of system status was inconsistent across banking web interfaces. The banking system should always keep users informed about what is going on, through appropriate feedback such as warning messages, visual cues, auditory cues, within reasonable time. B1 adhered to best practices in the design of warnings (e.g. in the case of number of unsuccessful trials). It was stated clearly to users, with a salient red color, the consequence of exceeding the number of trials .

In a cultural-model of design, banking interfaces would need to speak the users' common language and avoid technical jargon, or unfamiliar phrases. In our review, we found that B1-B3 provide insufficient user control over the transactions. For example, in B2, if a user chooses to login using the English interface, the user could not change to the Arabic interface during the same session.

Inevitably, users are prone to fall in some errors while using the banking system. However, a smart system design limits the number of errors by employing different techniques. Using warning messages, meaningful icons and alerting colors are some examples. B1 uses clear warning messages for unsuccessful login with a red color that catch user attention before deactivating user account. On the other hand, B3 uses an orange color for unsuccessful login without showing how many attempts the user will have. Interestingly, B3 uses this color for different kind of messages such as confirmation messages, warning messages, and error messages. Consistency across banking interfaces designed for the same cultural context was surprisingly lacking.

Interfaces allowed different levels of customizations (e.g. B1 allowed creating a favorite menu of transactions and adding special names/tags to the beneficiary of transactions). Variations in density and navigation conventions were observed. For example, B1 contains redundant options in the main and sub-menus in the same interface on the top and on the left side, which causes confusion for the users whereas B3 uses shortcut menus for all the main headings with corresponding sub-options.

3.3 Mobile Banking Interfaces

Design considerations for mobile baking (MB) interfaces are to some extent similar to web interface requirements with some considerations specific to orientation, size and accessibility constraints. Negative space in mobile interfaces is especially relevant to support ease of navigation and interaction in various contexts of use. The two most common platforms for MB are Apple iOS and Android [25, 26].

The login interface banks B1-B3 support both Arabic and English entry points. The content of the pages are similar in both languages and mapped to the corresponding alignment. An example is shown in Fig. 5.

Interfaces for failed login using a correct user name and wrong password were examined both in English and Arabic interfaces, Fig. 6. Inconsistency was found between Arabic and English system messages of the same banking system as in B2. While B1, B2 and B3 allowed 3 unsuccessful attempts before suspending the account for security reasons, only B1 showed a warning message of how many attempts allowed before account suspension. Notably, this was the case in web interfaces of B1 as well.

For the main transactions in mobile interfaces, the options are often listed as meaningful icons selected from our local cultural context of understanding, coupled with textual labels as shown in Fig. 7 for B3.

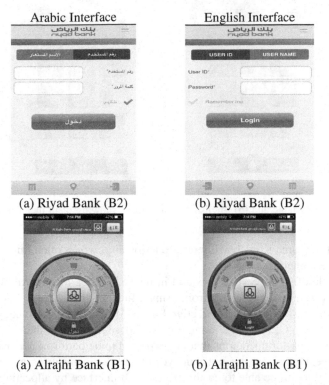

Fig. 5. Arabic and English MB interfaces of Alrajhi bank (B1) an dRiyad Bank (B2)

Fig. 6. Arabic MB interfaces for wrong password attempt in B1-B3

In our heuristics review, we noted that the MB interface design inadequately supported visibility of the system's status. For example, B1and B3 showed the cost of transfer from one account to another account, while B2 provided ambiguity in the multi-step process. The MB interfaces' language, colors and notation were found to be consistent with the socio-cultural contexts of target users. For example, B1 has meaningful and expressive icons on the main menu. However, it was noted that B3

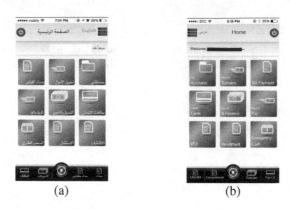

(a)   (b)

Fig. 7. (a) Arabic and (b) English MB interfaces showing main menu in bank3

used some of the same icons for different functionality, which often hinders user from adapting to new interfaces.

An example of error prevention found in many MB is a menu item being 'greyed out' or deactivated. It stops the user from using a function that shouldn't be used in that situation. In many situations, it is effective for the MB interface to do suggestions and intelligent guessing. Offering that to the user to choose from rather than having the user to memories or look for operations that are expected to be performed. For instance, B2 shows the recent bills that are not paid yet on the login menu as a user reminder. Similarly, it's good to be able to customize the MB interface by allocating a menu for frequent actions such as check balance and Pay bills to allow experienced users to perform the task without having to reach the main menu each time. MB interfaces can contain many features, and if they are all visible at the same time this can be overwhelming for a new user and would result in a crowded MB interface. Interfaces of B1, B2 and B3 varied on this feature, B2 in the login interface shows the latest transactions on the account with all details such as data, price and operation number.

4   Conclusion

This study explored the relationship between language, perceptions and beliefs of an individual's culture in banking interactions in the Arab region, a topic on which there is little previous research. In this paper, we described the wide spectrum of socio-cultural factors in the design of banking interfaces in the context of Saudi Arabia. The main objective was to shed light on the social and cultural phenomena influencing interface design in banking transactions. This was achieved by applying heuristics to a selected sample of banking interfaces and observing users in the local context. It is recommended that banking interaction designers consult extensively with banking users to help them understand the requirements of a seamless and intuitive interaction with banking interfaces and design easy-to-use and efficient systems. Future work involves developing a culture-orientated design model to assist designers of banking interfaces in the Arab region with consciously integrating culture in their design practice.

Acknowledgements. The authors extend their appreciation to the Deanship of Scientific Research at King Saud University for partially funding the work through the research group project number RGP-VPP-157.

References

1. Al-Sedrani, A., Al-Khalifa, H. S.: Design considerations for the localization of arabic e-commerce websites. In: 7th International Conference on Digital Information Management, ICDIM 2012, pp. 331–335 (2012)
2. Al-Ghaith, W., Sanzogni, L., Sandhu, K.: Factors influencing the adoption and usage of online services in saudi arabia. Electron. J. Inf. Syst. Dev. Ctries. **40**, 1–32 (2010). ISSN: 1681-4835
3. Kim, J., Moon, J.Y.: Designing towards emotional usability in customer interfaces—trustworthiness of cyber-banking system interfaces. Interact. Comput. **10**(1), 1–29 (1998)
4. Lee, Y.E., Benbasat, I.: Interface design for mobile commerce. Commun. ACM **46**(12), 48–52 (2003)
5. Khashman, N., Large, A.: Measuring cultural markers in Arabic government websites using Hofstede's cultural dimensions. Design, User Experience, and Usability. Theory, Methods, Tools and Practice, pp. 431–439. Springer, Heidelberg (2011)
6. Khashman, N., Large, A.: Arabic website design: user evaluation from a cultural perspective. In: Rau, P. (ed.) HCII 2013 and CCD 2013, Part II. LNCS, vol. 8024, pp. 424–431. Springer, Heidelberg (2013)
7. Tolba, R.: The cultural aspects of design Jordanian websites: an empirical evaluation of university, news, and government website by different user groups. Int. Arab J. Inf. Technol. **1**, 1–9 (2003)
8. Curran, K., King, D.: Investigating the Human Computer Interaction Problems with Automated Teller Machine (ATM) Navigation Menus, Computer and Information sciences, May 2008. http://www.ccsenet.org/journal/index.php/cis/article/viewFile/1908/1812
9. Al-Ashban, A., Burney, M.: Customer adoption of tele-banking technology: The case of Saudi Arabia. Int. J. Bank Mark. **19**(5), 191–201 (1983). doi:10.1108/02652320110399683
10. Adams, A.S., Thieben, K.A.: Automatic teller machines and the older population. Appl. Ergon. **22**(2), 85–90 (1991)
11. Rashed, A., Henrique, M., Santos, D.: User acceptance OTM machine: in the Arab culture. Int. J. Electron. Secur. Digit. Forensic **3**(3), 240–248 (2010). doi:10.1504/IJESDF.2010. 038286
12. El-Haddad, A.B., Almahmeed, M.A.: ATM banking behaviour in Kuwait: a consumer survey. Int. J. Bank Mark. **10**, 25–32 (1992)
13. Taohai, K., Phimoltares, S., Cooharojananone, N.: Usability comparisons of seven main functions for Automated Teller Machine (ATM) banking service of five banks in thailand. In: Proceedings of the 2010 International Conference on Computational Science and Its Applications (ICCSA 2010), pp. 176–182. IEEE Computer Society, Washington (2010)
14. Akinnuwesi, B., Uzoka, F., Obasa, A.: Enhancing automated teller machine with multi-lingual and multi-denominational software functionalities. Int. J. Electron. Financ. **7**(2), 97–114 (2013)
15. Chung, K.M., Kim, D., Na, S., Lee, D.: Usability evaluation of numeric entry tasks on keypad type and age. Int. J. Ind. Ergon. **40**(1), 97–105 (2010)
16. Banjo, A.: An investigation into the determinants of user acceptance of personalization in online banking, p. 130. Faculty of Behavioural Science, The University of Twente, Enschede, The Netherlands (2006)

17. Saudi Arabian Money Agency.: Monthly Statistical Bulletin. Saudi Arabian Money Agency, Riyadh (2014)
18. Siam, A.Z.: Role of electronic banking services on the profits of Jordanian banks. Am. J. Appl. Sci. **3**(9), 1999–2004 (2006)
19. Statista: Percentage-of-us-mobile-phone-users-who-use-mobile-banking. Statista Inc., New York (2015)
20. Statista: Users-of-mobile-banking-in-selected-countries. Statista Inc., New York (2015)
21. ICT Indicators Report End of Q1 2014, Communications and Information Technology Commission (2014)
22. m-Powering Development Initiative Report of the Working Group on m-Commerce, ITU, Geneva (2014)
23. Nielsen, J.: Usability inspection methods. In: Conference Companion on Human Factors in Computing Systems, pp. 413–414. ACM (1994)
24. Yeh, M., Jin Jo, Y., Donovan, C., Gabree, S. : Human Factors Considerations in the Design and Evaluation of Flight Deck Displays and Controls. Department of Transportation in the interest of information exchange, Washington (2013)
25. Apple: Designing for iOS (2015). https://developer.apple.com/library/ios/documentation/UserExperience/Conceptual/MobileHIG/
26. Android: Android Design Principles (2015). http://developer.android.com/design/get-started/principles.html

Prospecting HCI Challenges for Extreme Poverty Communities: Redefining and Optimizing User Experiences with Technology

Daniel Almeida Chagas[✉], Camila Loiola Brito Maia,
Elizabeth Furtado, and Carlos R. Maia de Carvalho

University of Fortaleza (Unifor), Fortaleza-CE, Brazil
{prof.daniel.chagas, camila.maia, elizabethsfur,
carlbberg}@gmail.com

Abstract. According to the United Nations (UN), 1.4 billion people live in extreme poverty conditions, about 1/5th of the planet population. Beyond the financial condition, extreme poverty is defined by the lack of access to information. This paper proposes to investigate the HCI challenges related to giving access to information for those communities, especially related to illiteracy, functional illiteracy and empowering them of technologies. Those challenges include not only the access to information, but questions about reaching the community, adapting information technology tools to their real needs, and empowering them to be not just consumers of information and systems, but also creators of new knowledge.

Keywords: Extreme poverty · Illiteracy · Oral communities · Interdisciplinary empowering

1 Introduction

The issue of poverty in the world passes through access to information. According to the United Nations, 1.4 billion people live in extreme poverty conditions, about 1/5th of the total planet population. And, beyond the financial condition, extreme poverty is also defined by the lack of access to education and information [1].

The two last points, lack of education and information access, are the ones which transform the extreme poverty problem in a vicious circle [2]. Without proper education and information, it is not possible to get a better job, or use the resources wisely, get better family agriculture, or develop innovation. Therefore, even not presented in the extreme basis of the Maslow pyramid, access to information and education are the next steps on the aid for a transformation of the community.

The reduction of extreme poverty and hunger was the first Millennium Development Goal, as set by 189 United Nations Member States in 2000 [3]. After setting a target of reducing the extreme poverty rate in half by 2015, this goal was met 5 years ahead of schedule, especially in India, China and Brazil. With the initial success, the international community, including the UN, the World Bank and the US, has set a

© Springer International Publishing Switzerland 2015
M. Kurosu (Ed.): Human-Computer Interaction, Part III, HCII 2015, LNCS 9171, pp. 281–290, 2015.
DOI: 10.1007/978-3-319-21006-3_28

target of ending extreme poverty by 2030. However, the international community focus on the issue is about the population basic needs, including food, safe drinking water, sanitation facilities, health and shelter. After an initial success, is expected to take the next step, the increase of access to education and information. In this context, some questions in Human-Computer Interaction (HCI) field rise: Is the information technology ready to reach people in extreme poverty? Åre the human computer interaction models ready to receive an illiterate user, or someone who is a functional illiterate or an oral-based? Will the information technology tools work with oral-based communities?

2 HCI Challenges

We humans have been *homo sapiens*, biologically speaking, by 200,000 years. However, it is obvious the difference between the life of a prehistoric human and a modern human. This difference is result, initially, of our tools, followed by our language, and our ability to manage the information. As more capable was the man managing his information, more evolved his society was. The information then is the great catalyst for the evolution of human society.

By expanding the information penetration ability, humanity progressed – from the spoken language to the written form, from written word to the print, from print to the telegraph, followed by radio, telephone, and culminating in the information systems based on computer networks. If the current human society is incomprehensible to a man who lived 100 years ago, this is the result of our ability to manage information, as well as collect, organize, store, retrieve, transmit and transform it. We live in the information age, in colloquial jargon.

Access to information has led individuals to educational and professional development and wellbeing, since they started developing writing skills. However, this access to information is not uniform for communities in the world, and there are often great differences between communities in the same Country [1]. Developing Countries like Brazil, India and some African countries face a dichotomy between rich communities with access to technology and information, and poor communities, such as slums, ghettos, *quilombos*[1] and workers in agricultural land. In these last communities, access to information and technologies is limited or nonexistent, and the oral communication is the standard means of exchanging information [6].

Given the importance of information to humanity, it is not surprising that the problem of information access is also political. To share information (or not share) has been a political tool for manipulation and maintenance of power by various social classes. Access to information for poor communities depends on those who are in charge.

Computer is our main current information tool, so the issue of access to information permeates the human-computer interfaces and their adopted paradigms. Access to this information occurs via interfaces, study object of HCI. The point is that these current paradigms do not include illiterate, functionally illiterate and oral communities as a whole.

---

[1] Quilombo: a Brazilian hinterland settlement founded by people of African origin. Most of the inhabitants of quilombos (called quilombolas) were escaped slaves [15].

The question that this paper wants to pass to HCI researchers is that even though public policy today wants to give access to the poor communities to information, the systems are not ready to embrace this new user.

The field of HCI consists of bridging the gap between information and human beings. One of the major challenges for the professionals that study and/or work with HCI is: How to improve the quality of life of communities with oral traditions by technological means?

HCI Challenges. The GrandHCI technical report - Grand Challenges Research in HCI in Brazil [4] - presented an expanded vision of the challenge 4 of the Grand Challenges in Computer Science Research in Brazil [5]. This challenge addresses the participative and universal access of citizens to knowledge, and recognizes the importance of HCI for research in Computer and for the development of the country. The document cited the importance of treating as target audience of digital inclusion the rural and fishermen communities, maroon and indigenous communities, settlements and invasions, public that usually does not have Internet access, and their options to stay informed are: orality, television and radio. The five challenges addressed by GrandHCI [4], attack the problems of these users with technological solutions, transversely, as described below.

Future, Smart Cities and Sustainability. The first challenge [6] addressed Sustainability, a timely topic when it comes to poor communities. Sustainability is not about environment only; it is also about the man who lives in this environment. Solutions that bring information to this man must be sustainable so that it will not impact negatively on the environment (ex.: do not print, to avoid paper consumption) and need to be realistic with the economic and materials conditions in which this population live (ex.: information via QR Code is not realistic, because this population does not have the necessary device or connection to access it).

Accessibility and Digital Inclusion. The second challenge [7] addresses the issue more directly. In addition to the people of oral tradition, the challenge includes people with special needs. For this group, the accessibility of information systems is more than a facilitator of daily life, since the technology could allow the deficiencies to be minimized or resolved.

Ubiquity, Multiple Devices and Tangibility. The third challenge [8] comments about the new and emerging forms of interaction, such as ubiquitous systems, tangible, based on brain-computer interfaces and gestures. These new forms can be adopted for human groups of oral tradition, but always with an anthropological vision of the solution. An example: the use of gestures should be adapted to the gestures already known by the user. If a gesture means anything different than the researcher expects, the researcher should rethink his use.

The tangible computing is presented as a great solution for poor communities, who are not used to the digital world today. Ubiquitous, intelligent and tangible devices may be an appropriate form of interaction for these communities.

Human Values. The challenge of human values [9] works with the reflection on the user of an artifact that does not have full awareness of the objectives and potential risks and impacts of technology. The challenge addresses issues such as ethics and privacy. In this text, researchers should draw attention to the negative feelings of the individual prior to focus on a technology that s/he cannot use it. In poor communities, technology is seen as oppressive (those who know and those who do not know) and segregating. In addition to ethical and privacy, the challenge of human values in poor communities is the self-affirmation as part of the population, with the support of information technology, extinguishing the pejorative term "marginal" (the margins of society).

Education in HCI and Labor Market. The challenge [10] highlights the need to improve the HCI curriculum recommended by SBC (Brazilian Society of Computation), mainly to form a professional focused on entrepreneurship, innovation, and finally the labor market. Dealing with the digital inclusion for such communities will require from HCI researcher unusual studies to computing, such as anthropology, sociology and psychology.

The following sections are primarily intended to raise awareness in HCI research for technological solutions that can fit (or not) to the daily life of illiterate or functionally illiterate people. Then, we present two examples of interactive devices using regional elements (image of St. Joseph against drought, and intelligent vaccination card), with other devices that can be used for digital inclusion of oral communities. At the end, we present a list of questions to drive researches through the access to information problem on extreme poverty communities.

3   Information for Life

In an exercise of meta-evaluation, someone can question the importance or validity of the information systems for oral communities. These questions fit the digital inclusion strategies adopted by public policies in Brazil. In them, the digital inclusion "force" the citizen to try to understand information systems. There are classes to demystify the computer and the Internet, making housewives seek for recipes in Internet (which do not get that taste of home food), and old people create accounts on Facebook (which will not be used again). Criticism is: access Internet for what? An analysis of this criticism is that some communities do not need to be invaded by fast and impersonal Internet connections.

The approach should be different. The vision of digital inclusion must start from an anthropocentric approach, knowing the man, their knowledge and their needs, and not try to fit the man in the contemporary digital man vision. Maybe a fishing community of subsistence does not need social networks, or e-commerce. Nevertheless, we can infer that weather information or reports of natural disasters are useful for them. As well as a farming community, that needs information on soil, rainfall, and planting techniques.

Moreover, the challenge (Accessibility and Digital Inclusion) should address not only access to information. Oral communities are also rich in information that is not in modern information systems. Beyond the preservation of culture and traditions, practical information on living, ecology, food, private practices of people can be shared with other groups.

4 Anthropology of Oral Communities and Empowerment

HCI area is the area of computing that needs to deal with social, cultural and educational issues. Addressing the digital inclusion for oral communities will require of HCI researchers the deconstruction of their knowledge, to understand the man who is not capable of reading. Concepts of screens, buttons, windows, cursor, keyboard and touchscreen, simply are no longer valid to intermediate the content and an illiterate man. It is necessary to seek new symbols and forms of interaction, known these people to build new forms of interaction.

The dialogue and understanding of this particular human allows the empowerment of content and technology [11]. Understanding how this human learns, communicates, and what is important to him makes the HCI researcher to be sensitive to issues and solutions that are out of the common thought. Technological solutions that are part of the common thought of HCI researcher, are those said universal [12], which are based on the adaptation of the system and/or content to the user. The solutions aimed at accessibility, considering, for example, the characteristics of users (their difficulty in reading, listening), the context of their use of technology (such as the platform used, weather conditions during use, etc.). The view advocated in this article requires solutions that go beyond the choices of graphics, visual, sound, gesture, etc. This is about give "power" to the users with regard to the following factors:

- Their role in the community they live in, that becomes relevant regarding knowledge that they can transmit to other communities;
- Their relationship with the technology. Here, the words "user interaction" are replaced by the words "user relationship";
- Their way to communicate. The interaction commands give rise to new solutions (as devices, artifacts) which users can express their feelings on services.

An example is the importance of popular knowledge and religiousness to the backcountry. In Ceará, as well as in all Brazilian Northeast, the drought is a constant in the life of the population. Even science has developed techniques to predict the rains, the population continues to utilize the knowledge of nature to predict whether it is time to plant or not. The *prophets of the rain* [13] use observation of clouds, wind, ants and frogs to give an opinion on the climate. The religiousness also has a connection with drought, because if it rains on March 19, day of Saint Joseph (patron of Ceará), the winter season is guaranteed. Thus, a HCI professional who is working with climate information access by the northeastern user should think beyond the creation of a website. He should think of ways to empower each citizen with technologies that allow disclose information, and also retrieve information from others, building knowledge in an accessible way for everyone.

A research project at an early stage that treats this subject is presented in the form of an interactive statue of St. Joseph, which provides important information for the small farmer. The device is proposed in a way that the farmer can understand and make use of information generated by state agencies, such as the Center of Weather Forecast and Climate Studies and the National Institute for Space Research - INPE. Powered by standard batteries, equipped with a processor that receives and decodes AM radio signals, the device is a weather station in a religious image, with total sense for that small farmer. A set of illustrations illuminated by LEDs indicate weather conditions, winds, if it is time to plant or not, date and time, and receiving data. The choice of AM radio is in function of the simplicity and low cost of the circuit, and because the wide availability of broadcast stations throughout the country. Data transmission on the AM band also has the advantage of reaching continental shortwaves. Data transmission occurs at very low speeds due to the signal quality, and is unidirectional (from the station to the user). The device can also store and play short messages of digital audio, providing details on the climatic conditions or general information to the public, such as vaccination dates, seed distribution, etc.

5   Devices for an Oral Digital Inclusion

Digital Television. Television is popularly the main way of communication in poor communities. With the advent of Interactive Digital TV, the HCI researcher can use it for the dissemination of information relevant to oral communities. The interaction with the remote control occurs using the number keys, arrow keys and the colored buttons, which allows access by people of oral tradition. However, the developer of the interactive application must have in mind the previously commented features, and thus use more pictures, shapes and audio, instead of text and computing elements, such as windows, buttons and cursors.

Radio and Digital Radio. The radio, even with over 100 years of history, is still present in the oral communities, especially those far from large urban centers. The advantages of use of radio to reach oral communities is caused by the low cost of the equipment, cost of transmission, and the far-reaching, getting to make intercontinental broadcasts when radio waves bounce off the ionosphere. The versatility of use, either with news, music or data, opens up a range of options for the researcher and developer of HCI.

The digital radio seeks to improve the audio transmission quality, also adding multimedia information transmission as the names of songs and artists, and sometimes images.

The transmission of data through radio waves is a cheap and viable option for data in small quantities because of its reach and low cost of transmission and equipment.

Mobile Digital Phones. The digital cell phone makes possible to poor communities access information and Internet. The African case M-Pesa [14] is an example of technology empowerment with simplicity, sustainability and economically viable, as it uses SMS to send small financial transactions. Adopted initially in Kenya, the solution allowed small producers and traders accept electronic payments with their mobile phones, increasing their gains, with positive effects throughout the economic chain. The adoption of SMS instead of mobile Internet-based solutions allowed rapid assimilation and adoption by poor population.

Ubiquitous and Tangible Devices. The ubiquitous devices and their distributed processing capabilities, coupled with tangible computing, are solutions that deserve research on developing ways of access to information by the less educated or illiterate. These people are not used to the virtual world, or with the HCI classical paradigms, such as windows, icons, virtual buttons and controls by mouse or touchscreen. The use of tangible objects, of real world (as opposed to virtual) to select an option, provided with feedback with colors, lights and sounds (instead of messages written on screens) can be a determining factor for a new form of digital inclusion.

An example in development, still in the early stages, is the smart vaccination card for children from poor communities. In this smart card, in addition to basic information about the development of the child, his mother could receive alerts about vaccination dates directly on the card. With a microchip and an AM wave receiver, the card decodes information provided by government agencies, and could filter that information that would be important for that child, showing the status through images and lights.

6 HCI Roadmap and Driving Questions Against Extreme Poverty

In order to facilitate the work of HCI researcher, this paper presents the Table 1 with a non-preemptive list of questions and their respective professionals. The table is divided in 3 major steps: To reach, understand, and to empower the extreme poverty community.

In summary, the reach problem includes questions about power and politics. In most cases, on extreme poverty communities, the public authorities even have control of the area, like the favelas in Brazil, or African ghettos. In some cases (as the Palestine territory), the idea of public authorities is vague. In indigenous areas, the community power structure could be complex to understand at the first time. So the HCI researcher should exercise caution when dealing with power and politics.

Understanding the community is a more common task to the HCI researcher, as the actual literature offers great methodologies and tools to analyze the users. Some areas could have better tools to understand the various layers of society. Transversal studies, using psychologists, anthropologists, sociologists and economics could leave to a better understand of those men and their relationship with information.

It becomes important to understand the complex relationship between all variables that influences the user experiences, like socio-cultural and socio-economic context, environmental, psychological and physiological issues of individuals, their actions and goals, as well as artifacts, in order to optimize them in search of a pleasant, helpful and enriching experience for these people [16]. To do so, one can (or should) make use of a mix of methodologies and techniques to collect and analyze data from these experiments, ranging from quantitative methods (on biometrics data, usage logs, etc.), with qualitative approaches (observation, interviews, etc.) [17, 18].

To empower users is a step ahead to teach them. It means to give users tools, methodologies, and information that can be used, and transformed by them along with their needs.

Table 1. Interdisciplinarity on HCI projects with extreme poverty communities

Who	Extreme Poverty Communities		
What	Reaching	Understanding	Empowering
Questions	• Who detents the power over the community? • How organized is the social structure of the community? • Does information access endanger someones power? • Does the group have any affection or confidence with other groups (teachers, doctors,etc.)? • Does the group have any rejection or afraid of other groups (politics, burocrats, etc.)? • Does any group (terrorists, drug deallers, public authorities, rival tribes, etc.) exerce any kind of violence or opressive power against the community?	• Who is this individual? • Is this individual full with her/his basic needs? • How this individual exchange information with her/his group? With other groups? • How the society interacts with this group? • Who/what is the detentor of the information on the community? • How the individuals/group economically maintain itself? • What is the information role for this individual, and for the group? • How formal the study is seen by the group? • How opressive is the tecnology for the group?	• How important is information for the individual? And for the community? • Who is the detentor of the important information for the community? • Which information the community already has? Which they didn't have? • How information is assimilated, transmited, and stored in the community? • Which information tecnology does the community already have acces? • How new technology information could be adapt, transform and used to empower new information for the group?
Professionals	Politic science Public Authorities International Aid Local places (churches, schools, etc.) NGOs	Psicology Antropology Sociology Economics	Teachers Educators Local places (churches, schools, etc.) NGOs

7 Final Consideration

The technology is often discussed as a way to reduce the individual efforts at work, and thus create free time and reduce social segregation. Nevertheless, the capitalist practice makes the technology applied to work further increase the gap between social classes. On one side are the users of digital technologies, and on the other, is the "analog" society, performing repetitive and uncreative work. Digital technologies are increasingly available, by cheapest devices or by initiatives such as the free software, however, part of the population don't seized these technologies. This population is illiterate or functional illiterate, and uses speech (oral communication) for their exchanges of information.

The HCI researchers are challenged to create forms of interaction to minimize this gap between social classes, empowering oral populations of technologies which not only access the information that are important, but generate and transmit knowledge that is useful to other communities and generate a feeling of self-affirmation and importance before the global society.

References

1. Makdissi, P., Wodon, Q.: Defining and measuring extreme poverty (2006)
2. Haydar, B.: Extreme poverty and global responsibility. Metaphilosophy **36**, 240–253 (2005)
3. United Nations: Millennium Development Goals. Goal 4: Reduce Child Mortality. http://www.un.org/millenniumgoals/childhealth.shtml
4. Baranauskas, M.C.C., de Souza, C.S., Pereira, R.: GranDIHC-BR: Prospecção De Grandes Desafios De Pesquisa Em Interação Humano-computador No Brasil. In: Companion Proceedings of the 11th Brazilian Symposium on Human Factors in Computing Systems, pp. 63–64. Brazilian Computer Society, Porto Alegre (2012)
5. de Carvalho, A.C.P.L.F., Brayner, A., Loureiro, A., Furtado, A.L., von Staa, A., de Lucena, C.J.P., de Souza, C.S., Medeiros, C.M.B., Lucchesi, C.L., e Silva, E.S., Wagner, F.R., Simon, I., Wainer, J., Maldonado, J.C., de Oliveira, J.P.M., Ribeiro, L., Velho, L., Gonçalves, M.A., Baranauskas, M.C.C., Mattoso, M., Ziviani, N., Navaux, P.O.A., da Silva Torres, R., Almeida, V.A.F., Meira, W., Jr., Kohayakawa, Y.: Grandes Desafios da Pesquisa em Computação no Brasil–2006–2016, São Paulo (2006)
6. Neris, V.P., Rodrigues, K.R., Silva, J.B.: Futuro, Cidades Inteligentes e Sustentabilidade. In: Baranauskas, M.C.C., de Souza, C.S., Pereira, R. (eds.) GranDIHC-BR — Grandes Desafios de Pesquisa em Interação Humano-Computador no Brasil, pp. 16–18. Sociedade Brasileira de Computação, Cuiabá (2012)
7. Furtado, E., Chagas, D.A., Bittencourt, I., Façanha, A.: Acessibilidade e Inclusão Digital. In: Baranauskas, M.C.C., de Souza, C.S., Pereira, R. (eds.) GranDIHC-BR — Grandes Desafios de Pesquisa em Interação Humano-Computador no Brasil, pp. 19–22. Sociedade Brasileira de Computação, Cuiabá (2012)
8. Furtado, E., Militão, G., Andrade, R., Miranda, L.C., Oliveira, K.: Ubiquidade, Múltiplos Dispositivos e Tangibilidade. In: Baranauskas, M.C.C., de Souza, C.S., Pereira, R. (eds.) GranDIHC-BR — Grandes Desafios de Pesquisa em Interação Humano-Computador no Brasil, pp. 23–26. Sociedade Brasileira de Computação (2012)

9. Maciel, C., Pereira, V., Hornung, H., Piccolo, L.G.S., Prates, R.: Valores Humanos. In: Baranauskas, M.C.C., de Souza, C.S., Pereira, R. (eds.) GranDIHC-BR — Grandes Desafios de Pesquisa em Interação Humano-Computador no Brasil, pp. 27–30. Sociedade Brasileira de Computação (2012)

10. Rosemberg, C., Boscarioli, C., Furtado, E., Silveira, M.S., Prates, R.O., Bim, S.A., Barbosa, S.D.J.: Formação em IHC e Mercado. In: Baranauskas, M.C.C., de Souza, C.S., Pereira, R. (eds.) GranDIHC-BR — Grandes Desafios de Pesquisa em Interação Humano-Computador no Brasil, pp. 31–34. Sociedade Brasileira de Computação, Cuiabá (2012)

11. Freire, P.: Pedagogy of the Oppressed, Rev edn. Penguin Group, São Paulo (1996)

12. Stephanidis, C.: User Interfaces for All. CRC Press, Mahwah (2001)

13. Pennesi, K., de Souza, C.R.B.: O encontro anual dos profetas da chuva em Quixadá, Ceará: a circulação de discursos na invençao de uma tradição. Horizontes Antropológicos. 18, 159–186 (2012)

14. Jack, W., Suri, T.: Mobile Money: The Economics of M-PESA 1, Group, pp. 1–30 (2011)

15. Anderson, R.N.: The quilombo of palmares: a new overview of a maroon state in seventeenth-century Brazil. J. Lat. Am. Stud. 28, 545–566 (1996)

16. Maia C., Carvalho, C.R.M., Furtado E., Ubiquitous technologies in education and the challenges of optimizing the user experience. In: Painel Session of Grandes Desafios de Pesquisa em Interação Humano-Computador no Brasil, IHC 2014, Foz do Iguaçu (2014)

17. Cavallin, H., Martin, W.M., Heylighen, A.: How relative absolute can be: SUMI and the impact of the nature of the task in measuring perceived software usability. AI Soc. 22(2), 227–235 (2007)

18. Schulze, K., Krömker, H.: A framework to measure user experience of interactive online products. In: Proceedings of International Conference on Methods and Techniques in Behavioral Research 2010 (2010)

Moral Biases and Decision: Impact of Information System on Moral Biases

Karim Elia Fraoua[1,2(✉)]

[1] Université Paris-Est, 77454 Marne-la-Vallée, France
[2] Equipe Dispositifs d'Information et de Communication à l'Ere Numérique
(DICEN IDF), Conservatoire National des Arts et Métiers, Paris-Est Paris-Ouest,
7339 Paris, EA, France
Fraoua@u-pem.fr

Abstract. The aim of this work, is to find a better way to understand an information system that take into consideration agent's through moral system, words, image, appeal to culture or religion, in order to correct to some biases observed in polling in France during the same-sex marriage debate. This approach will thus, in diverse and multicultural societies, provide to managers or politicians with a better definition of problems, to better predict the behavior of individuals when the efficiency of the decision taken and the possible opposition it can generate. In this way, they can build an information system capable of correcting the deviation from the expectations of agents. We could consider that this component would be the main one in decision-making during the passage of the law. We can then assess the value of this component in the calculation of expected utility as developed by Harsanyi. We can easily show that when the information system is corrected, the actors can then adhere to processes that would be in opposition to their moral principle or religious values due to the fact that in reality the lack of information has caused the appearance of this moral utility in decision-making based in principle on a single dominant component.

Keywords: Information · Harsanyi · Social representation · Central personage · Neuroscience

1 Introduction

Very recently, we see in France, despite strong adherence to the values of the republic ring fenced the equality of citizens, and despite full adherence to these values, many citizens have struggled through many means either the web 2.0, policy actions or public events against the law that allows same-sex marriage [1]. If this law was voted smoothly in many other countries, in France many people and political parties still require the removal of this law. The reason given by the majority is mostly religious or even moral. This moral bias has imposed many politicians to make decisions that go against the principle they stand for as a representative of the republic. This moral bias is greater than the expected utility predicted in the rational approach that would be normally the well-being of all.

© Springer International Publishing Switzerland 2015
M. Kurosu (Ed.): Human-Computer Interaction, Part III, HCII 2015, LNCS 9171, pp. 291–302, 2015.
DOI: 10.1007/978-3-319-21006-3_29

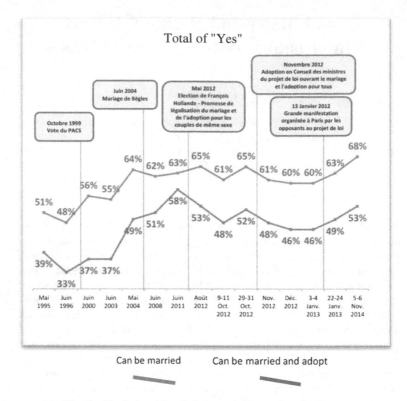

Fig. 1. Evolution of poll for same-sex marriage in France

Socrates said each of us contributes to his own happiness. Every citizen must be able to appreciate the decision elements to be considered in various social contexts which, luckily, it was not directly confronted (euthanasia, death penalty, resistance to ideological pressures, etc.). According to this basic consideration, we can see that the French citizens have now accepted maxim of Socrates. However a minority still remain opposed to the underlying issues such as adoption for this issue itself or on partisan positions. Indeed, 68 % of French are now favorable to marriage for all, and 53 % to the adoption by homosexual couples [2] (Fig. 1).

In order to comprehend these positions more clearly, it seems to us essential to understand how changing the environment or social representation in which the agent is located, can affect this agent. This could be placed on the main work on the social representation of Moscovici [3] and Abric [4] which are quite relevant to this study. Kohlberg's model [5, 6] will enable us to understand the meaning of moral and social development of an agent. Although critics are issued on this basic model, it remains satisfactory in our approach and in line with our vision of the decision-making actors in this social confrontation and to better track the game theory, including bringing our interest to know the Harsanyi approach that will consider the moral issue is closely linked to the decision, when it is not only rational [7, 8]. To bring some rational explanation to our point of view for this singular position in French polling, we will take consideration of the work of Durkheim [9]. Obviously, the French singularity can be understood from the collective consciousness in France, it makes better explanation for the stage or representation that would be dominant in France.

2 Social Representation and Moral Judgment

The concept of Moscovici's social representation [3] is significant in many ways, first by dedicating this notion as a crucial element in which an individual is enrolled in the institution, in a consensual reality and in the orientation of his communications or in his behaviors. This new form of study allows to globalize our approach to the individual by analyzing the information, values and opinions that he enjoys and coupling to external parameters which it is subjected such as norms or rules. In this way, J-C. Abric has defined the central core theory which shows that social representation is organized around a structural nucleus in connection with social representation of a society and its history [4]. This core is usually collectively shared, it defines the principle of a community as relatively stable, which gives it certain properties such as resistance to change. There are around this central core, a peripheral elements that are unstable, that evolve around the central core, which can contribute to the adaptation of representation in various social contexts, they will serve as particular interface with other social representations or other communities and can be mediators or can relay certain messages or information. Abric shows that social representation has useful functions including the membership of individuals to a given representation, a function that allows to know, to understand and explain reality. It also serves a purpose to set place of communication and social interaction, a social identity function that will preserve the specificity of social groups and keep socializing, a guidance function, which allows the production of expectations but also to decide in a particular social context and finally, a justificatory function that will be used to justify our choices and attitudes. Ultimately, a social representation allows to an agent to interpret the reality and understand new phenomena enabling their integration in socially and culturally shared mental framework, consistent with systems of values, judgments, beliefs, opinions. It also guides our behavior and our practices and interactions with others, developing a social identity, identification of the agent to one (or more) group and backup of the specificity of social groups. It finalizes our behaviors and allows to justify our attitudes in a given situation, with regard to society in general or in respect of their partners or their membership to social communities.

From above, and to understand why a person may choose a particular social representation, the information framework that he consider and therefore the decisions that he will take, we think essential to know the evolution of the individual within the organization and why it can be part of a particular representation. To permit this analysis, we link this work with the development of Kohlberg's model based on six stages grouped by two into three distinct levels [5]. The first level is that of a first-time character of the person decides according to its own interests and risks. There are two stages within the second stage, the aim is to maximize personal gain by avoiding penalties and possible retaliation. At the second level of moral development, the group is dominant and morality becomes that of the group or of a society. In stage 3, the reference group becomes the family, the network or close friends, in this spirit, loyalty, shared values, and mutual trust become the main criteria for evaluating social behavior. In stage 4, the approach is compared to the national community or to the whole society, the agent must then comply with the laws, rules and norms of a society. It is this condition that ensures the well-being of individuals. We find that in our analytical work according Harsanyi [7], it is at this stage that the "conventional" moral value or ethic is at its highest. Finally, the third level allows an agent to be in an unclear social representation in the light of stage 4, standards become blurred in many respects, the point of view of the individual puts into perspective some of them. In stage 5, the individual is capable of raising his consciousness to comment on the laws and want to change them in some cases. They accept in the name of a social contract to join the majority of a decision provided if there is no opposition between legality and morality. Finally in stage 6, the individual will also involve beyond the accepted moral values but through his the construction of his own values system on issues such as euthanasia, bioethics, as well as minority positions at the societal level, by acting on the construction of a new social contract collectively decided. Through this study, we can see that informational status is an essential condition able to change a person from one stage to another. Moreover, it is well illustrated by the statement of the following dilemma or also by the effect of accumulation of information which state that the older we get, the more reasonable (or rational) we become. In fact the context or statement will play a leading role in his reading of the situation by the agent. The formulation of the dilemma will predispose the agent's response, Sobesky [10] shows that the response of two groups of individuals is strongly influenced by the game situation or the dilemma. The decisions to break the law are very sensitive to the presence or absence of a personal interest for the protagonist of the story: stealing a drug to save his wife is easily possible… but not to save his neighbor. It appears that the involvement of the agent will affect the given answer. Indeed, the level of moral judgment is generally lower in dilemmas reported in real life, in fact, dilemmas with personal involvement induce lower judgments than those without implication [11] as if the individual involved feels less guilty from a moral point of view [11, 12] when a link to the group or social representation exists. We can consider that people who are not personally involved in a situation are more "moral" than those who are or feel close to the situation.

Several categories of so-called real-life dilemmas were listed [12], the philosophical dilemmas such the death penalty, euthanasia, anti-social dilemmas that are related to the transgression of rules such as cheating on exams, resistance to social pressures such as pressure in religious matters, lifestyle or occupational choices and finally pro social dilemmas when conflicts are inevitable between several positive motivations, for example: person's stand in relation to the divorce of their own parents, helping a friend who commits a crime, preventing their mother from taking drugs, etc. This perspective approach to social representation and Kohlberg's model [6], to better understand how the individual acquires moral and emotional values [13] and it may or may not involve them in his judgments, it also shows the consideration of the point of others view, the reciprocity phenomena, the establishment of mutual trust, especially in the case of relations between "homogeneous" agent situated on the same level and at the same stage. Durkheim has already introduced in 1898 [14] in a less formal way, the idea of collective representation and opened the way of the interface between psychology and sociology.

In fact a decision may cover several stages where the agent can be situated since it is the justification of the decision that determines actually his moral level. In this regard, Durkheim indicates that the moral of each society is directly related to the structure of the people who practice it [9]. We can conclude that often can settle a clannish state and resistance against any societal evolution. The society belief that the country's unity could be broken and that the new law may cause division and discord among the people, which was the belief for some opponents.

3 Information Impact on Kohlberg Stage

In modern information society, some agents have a fairly deep knowledge of the implementation of laws and rules. They can consider that such laws cannot be moral. It is important to note that agents easily distinguish between moral and legal, what is legal is not necessarily moral [15]. Moreover, a conclusion of this work is to consider that the opposition will be between agent obeying to Nash's approach [16] versus more Harsanyi's agents [7]. It is therefore commonplace to assume that the availability of information on the running of society can contribute to the development of responses to different dilemmas in moral judgment context. However, it is much less clear render this information more effective, even if the information is available, it must be assimilated, and we will see that the moral component can be a barrier to its acquisition, hence the crucial role of the peripheral elements in a central core social representation [4]. The central core in France was organized around religious groups who developed an information strategy, making stronger beforehand this resilience of the social representation. This evolution of the available information that lowers the "moral" component or conservative occurred through these peripheral elements often rightly involved. In fact, the information or knowledge gained on other social, cultural representations, and any real interaction with a person from another culture, may impact on individual frameworks such as sharing feelings, consideration to the needs of others....

This approach allows us to put the legal process that were established through marriage for all. The situation in France was made without the fact that the informational instruments have been totally up especially with respect to the resistant structure in which we can indicate that individuals are mostly positioned in stage 4, a stage where individuals are attached to group norms according also to Haidt's theory [17]. Durkheim explains that the correspondence between the collective consciousness and social change is a balance parameter in our society, a crisis can occur when there is a discrepancy between the moral and social or societal developments [9]. It is certain that this antagonism can generate a moral crisis and a shift between the two groups. Here we see the beginnings of the approach to game balance in the sense of Harsanyi, between a purely rational Nash's assessment and a Harsanyi's assessment that considers a moral or ethical component [18].

4 Decision and Game Theory

Rational term is closely related to the daily use of the concept of reason. Indeed, rational being means that we design things without any bias, based on our beliefs and desires and then react to our gains without violating any standards. It also involves ethical behavior. Game theory starts from a fundamental premise that clarifies the decision of a player. We consider that all agents are informed in a symmetrical way and know that other players are rational although the reality is quite different. De facto, only a rational approach, is the best action that would be logical and free of any risky behavior [19] pursuing a goal that aims to find the most intelligent solution, whatsoever the consequences, to maximize expected utility. It is therefore useful to explain expected utility, formalized by von Neumann and Morgenstern [20] and Savage [21]. It is a concept that indicates that the individual first tries to satisfy his needs by calculating all possible strategies and the results expected for each one of them by measuring the probability and expected value. However, each agent acts according to his own preferences depending on the expected result. Henceforth two concepts that are preferences and satisfaction will guide this choice. Moreover, if the result is considered inaccessible, the agent generally will change his preference which is considered as a cognitive dissonance.

The game of a prisoner's dilemma illustrates this difficulty of the choice of two agents, where the choice of each agent does not lead to a collective optimum but to individual optimization theorized by Nash [16]. In our work, we can consider that it is the state of the future society which will be at stake. If the party against the law cooperates with the supporters then I lose the state of actual society that I consider as perfect in the sense of my own social representation. We may consider the level or stage in where the agent is situated, or possibly his partition information available to it. It is a social innovation that has no observable effect which induces a risk or uncertainty. In the first and in the second case, we would act on the informational level and in the first case, as we will see later, on the concept of morality that can be considered as structural. Whatever the game to consider, like cooperative games and non-cooperative non-zero sum game, i.e. where the sum of the issues is not zero, since zero sum game are equivalent to losses of one the agent to the gain of other agent, it is complex enough to fit common social situations in a real-life situations. The situation we have here is to analyze in a rather non-cooperative structure since two clans are opposed to societal change who represents the challenge between the two "agents". In our configuration, we can consider that this is a non-zero sum game because whatever the outcome of the result, the consequences will be negative in a social point of view. The social division can appear or even a crisis can emerge in Durkheim's sense, resulting in moral values that are disconnected from the societal evolution.

The vote takes into consideration the moral issue that are evoked by Harsanyi in his approach to ethical game theory. It also takes into account rationality with an ethical conscience of the agent. If Nash's equilibrium in the prisoner's dilemma leads them to confess, the Harsanyi state that cooperation between the players will be the solution for "ethical reason", and will avoid some puzzling result as the fact that Nash equilibrium will tend to drive all agents to confess the crime even those who have not committed anything. The experimental results from the behavioral game theory [22], show that the rate of cooperation depends on two approaches, internal to the game through the value of the gains [23], the role of communication between players and here we see the role of the information system or mediation and of course the importance of peripheral agents and external logic of the game which depends on the characteristics of the players such as social origin, culture or personality, and we see here the dimension related to our previous approach through social representation of Moscovici and the belonging to a level or stage according Kohlberg makes sense. From above, the agent can be considered in a risky or uncertain environment, so the agent will uses the information as a tool to improve his knowledge or strengthen personal choice. When information is accessible and coherent, the agent will probably make a decision that will have a collective preference, if all agents are consistent to the risk. This common preference, analyzed in terms of risk, is not an individual decision but it becomes a collective construction assessed in terms of belief. This part of the analysis of the choices or the orientations of the agents was carried out a posteriori, once the law was implemented. In the first context before the law, the opposition camp was part of a process according Harsanyi with a moral component that reflected its own assessment of the situation, in respect to the classification of Kohlberg and also in the social representation in which they enrolled. The second evaluation of game theory in the evolution of choice is rather under the risky or uncertain situation in which information, through direct peripheral elements as defined by Abric, enabled the agent to remove any doubt or uncertainty in which the society would be after the law was voted [24]. Obviously nothing has changed and so we can see clearly an evolution of the state of public opinion, we can estimate that over 70 % of the French citizens are now favorable or neutral.

We can conclude in this section, that the Pareto optimal equilibrium has been reached, although it appears in radically different conditions. Indeed, Nash's equilibria is strongly influenced by the history of interactions between agents. The notion of belief plays an extremely important role and indeed if the belief agents into another equilibrium is possible, this equilibrium will be sought and achieved. The Nash equilibrium can be changed if we change the belief of agents. This Pareto-dominant equilibrium can be achieved if we are able to build a dynamic collaborative space. This is due to the existence of several possible equilibriums driven by a balance through rational and individualistic action and other equilibrium due to the cooperation between the players as long as this cooperation appear, exist and consider the collective gain is greater than the individual gain.

5 Discussion About Vote of Marriage of All in France, a Moral Effect?

To analyze further this iconoclastic position in Europe, where many countries have voted the law without incident and without social protest as in Spain or in Portugal, countries with strong Catholic culture. Nevertheless, the religious consideration, because of the separation between state and religion, still poses conceptual problems in France. Secularism is a singular fact in France. For centuries, the concept of moral was religious in nature, indeed religion and morality were not yet separated. A "feeling" of "duty" and a "good" were two elements that although quite general, apply a moral phenomena to both religious and secular moral systems, indeed the question of morality also had a singular development in the concept dictated by Durkheim: "*moral purposes are those which are intended for society. To act morally is to act for the collective interest*" [9]. We initially see a changing position after the vote. Indeed, if the society was divided between those who are supporters or indifferent to the law, and those who are against the law, they are guided by the morality that is integrated to a Harsanyi arbitration. It is certain that today the majority is no longer against including the so-called right wing parties. This leaves us with a quite complex situation to analyze where social and religious representations play a visible role in the formation of opposition groups to the law in structuring favorable agents as a community structure in order to place them in socially level within the meaning of Kohlberg at a stage 5 or 6 for supporters, and at a stage 4 for the opponents. The French population found a year after the vote, that the situation did not upset the French society, useful information has come down to the agent, his was able then to change his beliefs and join the stage 5 or 6 of Kohlberg's model. The general utility in which it was registered namely the welfare of society compared to normative concepts, biased by a moral point of view that could justify an opposite response to the rational principle of well-being.

This is a our conclusion with regard to the Harsanyi valuation approach against agents that operate according to a Nash approach. We can also conclude that the supporter of the marriage for all, also seeks the individual well-being against the old standard and wanted to change it, which is a justified perspective of Kohlberg of this agent at 5 or 6 stage. We can also conclude that the agents who were previously against marriage for all, are in "cooperative mode", as are their positions within classic societal norms and highlights the collective happiness, while supporters would promote individual happiness. In fact the position of the latter was enrolled in a cooperative mode, but the normative and moral underlying of society had to be changed in light of cultural changes. This notion of morality can not only view as philosophical or religious but must be analyzed in terms of the neuroscience concept because moral behavior requires an emotional component [25]. A study conducted by Freeman et al. showed a shift in the decision because the situation described below, is considered moral by the actors. They analyzes the bias among US physicians, they had to decide on hypothetical scenarios in which they considered deceive an insurance company was the only way for a patient to obtain the approval of a treatment or a diagnosis [26]. This emotional or sentimental feeling according to Hume, also described by the involvement of actors during a moral judgment shows that emotional closeness and thus cerebral essence. Damasio has shown that conscious or unconscious emotions are integral to the moral component and that it plays a fundamental role in our reasoning ability and such absence can lead to strange situations namely irrational [27]. Brain deterioration observed in patients treated as Elliot shows this neuroscience cause. Indeed, the prefrontal cortex is impaired in all patients with Elliot type are remarkably, this area is not responsible for the immediate response to emotional stimuli. Rather, it is the interpretation of these stimuli, which is involved in a second time. By cons, it is essential to reasoning. This demonstrates that if we are disconnected from the emotional experience, we cannot make a rational decision [28].

This emotional issue is very complex, with feeling such passion, thirst or hunger, the idea is more about the reason for less vivid and especially figment of our imagination, which can lead to imaginative bias and can also create an opposite sense, like the fact that the donation is tax deductible. If the act of donation is approved in the first time and can create a positive emotion, the fiscal privilege can generate an opposite sentiment finally. This is the first emotion that will affect our judgment. This complex situation can lead to judgment being made using the frontal and prefrontal area of our brain, the part that are designed to deal with emotion and feelings [29]. Without being able to justify, in some way, stage 4 would appeal to our frontal lobe whereas the stage 5 would be located at the prefrontal area.

If the rational decision-making involves almost all of our brain, the emotional charge is mainly localized in the amygdala, hypothalamus, insula, the ventromedial part [30], the bridges between different areas and rational emotional [31]. It is obvious that this component located in prior specific areas, seems beyond the reach of informational field, it is also the result of the legacy of the learning process, but the post-informational factors after the implementation of a law with a strong emotional charge, seems to affect the attitude of some people, however it still remains open the question in where area these information acts. Thus, we can integrate into the moral utility factor analyzed by Harsanyi, the emotional component that depends on each agent, according to his social representation and Kohlberg's level in which he is located. This emotional component will surely increase the resistance to change, or to act positively, for example on the peripheral agents of Abric's model that could be involved either personally or with relationships involved. Emotions and sentiments mechanically play a major role in the decision-making process in France, compared to the other countries that have also adopted the law:

$$U = U_r + U_{mH}$$

where $U_{mH} = U_m + U_e$ and U_m moral component (from religious or from social agreement) et U_e emotional component

The utility function that composes the moral judgments, including decentration to save a classical conception of society, is not based on pure hazard. This irrational utility component is significant in our conservative societies. An agent can fluctuate from one stage to another relatively easily as we have seen in France during the evaluation of the death penalty, including in the fringe opposed to marriage for all, or nowadays on abortion which is now widely accepted in most Western countries across Europe. The most notable exception to these trends is in the work of Jean Piaget which analyzes the impact of the environment in all its social, cultural or informational dimension. *"Socialization is by no means the result of a single causality, as the pressure of the adult social group on the child by means of family education and school education [...] rather involves the intervention of a multiplicity of different types of interactions and sometimes opposing effects"* [32].

The societal changes seen after the law was voted, including the cooperation mechanisms, seem to appear quite mechanically. Nowadays, everyone agrees with the abolition of slavery, even if it was previously accepted by most, as it is morally reprehensible from a religious point of view. The discriminatory approach keeps a negative bias on rational moral decision that considers that all individuals are equal. Moreover, the information is clearly important for these mechanisms but also through moral neuroscientist [25]. When the information system is corrected [24], the actors can then follow the process that would have been against their previous religious or moral values due to the fact that in truth, nothing stands in the lack of information that led to the emergence of the concept of moral utility in making decisions based on the principle of a single dominant component would be without this assumption only rational. However, should this information be included in a Harsanyien mind process? [8]. As already stated by Durkheim, *"means an education that prohibits any loan to the principles underlying the revealed religions, which relies exclusively on ideas, feelings and practices of individuals simply because, in a word a purely rationalist education"* [9].

This French ambiguity between the moral issue and religious and secular morality, can authorize the introduction of information to co-construct the agent's moral state that is appropriate according to the visible state and thus consequently eliminate the state of uncertainty. In fact, the opposition and resistance felt during adolescence and later in adulthood does not directly relate to the process of individual development during childhood [33]. A more likely explanation, however, is that the cognitive development of the child involves a process of building a social thought and that the roots of the opposition and resistance are already existing in childhood [34], it is certain that situate individuals in stages is a tempting approach to explain some situations, and demonstrate why some decisions are final. We have shown that under the influence of information and the reality of a situation, as in the case of anti-abortion law or the abolishing of the death penalty, the society has not changed fundamentally, individual freedoms and personal rights have been preserved, and it may be a lighting element in post-evolution of agents that explain this evolution in positive way. We can consider the population with a moral bias are in the classical Durkheim's French philosophy. The stages 5 and 6 escape to the more traditional moral approach. Nevertheless and as Durkheim said, *"the solidarity derived similarities is at its maximum when the collective consciousness exactly does our total consciousness and coincide in all respects with her, but at that moment, our individuality is null"*, from this statement, we can argue that the French confrontation is either the result of the singularity of an active and vibrant democracy conscious of other countries or in crisis compared to other nations where the law has been voted without incident.

6   Conclusion

Among many theories evoked in this work, we have seen that the post-informational process still have an important impact on those who are in resistance versus the law. This can be explained by the impact of information on lowering their moral and mainly emotional component in the utility function rather than their fatal acceptation of the law. As a proof, the acceptance of adoption which knows the same trends as the support of the same-sex marriage. The main result shows that when voting a controversial law, the government must consider post-voting process, showing that society don't knows no major upheavals, and the overall consensus is not affected by societal changes, such as the same-sex marriage or adoption, and often the shortcut of that information can lead to moral or emotional judgments, which in itself seems fairly obvious at first sight. We have shown here why and how to overcome these psychological and social obstacles, and how to avoid them in the future.

References

1. Bourret, C., Fraoua, K.E.: Religions, lobbies, media, standards and societal changes: the example of "marriage for all" in France. In: IAMCR, Dublin, 25–29 June 2013
2. http://www.atlantico.fr/decryptage/68-francais-desormais-favorables-au-mariage-pour-tous-et-53-adoption-couples-homosexuels-jerome-fourquet-1856752.html/page/0/2

3. Moscovici, S.: Notes towards a description of social representations. Eur. J. Soc. Psychol. **18**(3), 211–250 (1988)
4. Abric, J.C.: 8. L'étude expérimentale des représentations sociales. Sociol. d'Aujourd'hui **7**, 203–223 (2003)
5. Kohlberg, L.: Moral stages and moralization: the cognitive-developmental approach. In: Lickona, T. (ed.) Moral Development and Behavior: Theory, Research, and Social Issues, pp. 31–53. Holt, Rinehart & Winston, New York (1976)
6. Kohlberg, L.: Stage and sequence: the cognitive-developmental approach to socialization. In: Goslin, D.A. (ed.) Handbook of Socialization Theory and Research, pp. 347–480. Rand McNally College Publishing Company, Chicago (1969)
7. Harsanyi, J.C.: A general theory of rational behavior in game situations. Econometrica J. Econometric Soc. **34**, 613–634 (1966)
8. Harsanyi, J.C.: A new theory of equilibrium selection for games with incomplete information. Game. Econ. Behav. **10**(2), 318–332 (1995)
9. Durkheim, E.: Emile Durkheim on Morality and Society. University of Chicago Press, Chicago (1973)
10. Sobesky, W.E.: The effects of situational factors on moral judgments. Child Dev. **54**, 575–584 (1983)
11. Wark, G.R., Krebs, D.L.: Gender and dilemma differences in real-life moral judgment. Dev. Psychol. **32**, 220–230 (1996)
12. Krebs, D.L., Denton, K., Wark, G.: The forms and functions of real-life moral decision-making. J. Moral Educ. **26**(2), 131–145 (1997)
13. Martin-Juchat, F.: Penser le corps affect if comme un média. Corps **4**(1), 85–92 (2008)
14. Durkheim, É.: Représentations individuelles et représentations collectives. Revue de Métaphysique et de Morale **6**(3), 273–302 (1898)
15. Colby, A.: The Measurement of Moral Judgement. Standard Issue Scoring Manual, vol. 2. Cambridge University Press, Cambridge (1987)
16. Nash, J.F.: Equilibrium points in n-person games. Proc. Natl. Acad. Sci. **36**(1), 48–49 (1950)
17. Graham, J., Haidt, J., Rimm-Kaufman, S.E.: Ideology and intuition in moral education. Int. J. Dev. Sci. **2**(3), 269–286 (2008)
18. Lumer, C.: Introduction: The relevance of rational decision theory for ethics. Ethical Theor. Moral Pract. **13**(5), 485–496 (2010)
19. Gibbard, A.: Wise Choices, Apt Feelings: A Theory of Normative Judgment. Harvard University Press, Cambridge (1992)
20. Von Neumann, J., Morgenstern, O.: Theory of Games and Economic Behavior. Princeton University Press, Princeton (2007). (60th Anniversary Commemorative Edition)
21. Friedman, M., Savage, L.J.: The utility analysis of choices involving risk. J. Polit. Econ. **56**, 279–304 (1948)
22. Camerer, C.: Behavioral Game Theory: Experiments in Strategic Interaction. Princeton University Press, Princeton (2003)
23. Eber, N.: Le dilemme du prisonnier. La Découverte (2006)
24. Takezawa, M., Gummerum, M., Keller, M.A.: Stage for the rational tail of the emotional dog: roles of moral reasoning in group decision making. J. Econ. Psychol. **27**(1), 117–139 (2006)
25. Claverie, B., Rougier, A.: Positive emotional reactions in intracarotid sodium amytal (Wada) procedures. J. Epilepsy **7**(2), 137–143 (1994)
26. Freeman, V.G., Rathore, S.S., Weinfurt, K.P., Schulman, K.A., Sulmasy, D.P.: Lying for patients: physician deception of third-party payers. Arch. Intern. Med. **159**(19), 2263–2270 (1999)

27. Bechara, A., Damasio, A.R.: The somatic marker hypothesis: a neural theory of economic decision. Game. Econo. Behav. **52**(2), 336–372 (2005)
28. Sayegh, L., Anthony, W.P., Perrewe, P.L.: Managerial decision-making under crisis: the role of emotion in an intuitive decision process. Hum. Resour. Manage. Rev. **14**(2), 179–199 (2004)
29. Christensen, J.F., Gomila, A.: Moral dilemmas in cognitive neuroscience of moral decision-making: a principled review. Neurosci. Biobehav. Rev. **36**(4), 1249–1264 (2012)
30. Moretto, G., Làdavas, E., Mattioli, F., Di Pellegrino, G.: A psychophysiological investigation of moral judgment after ventromedial prefrontal damage. J. Cogn. Neurosci. **22**(8), 1888–1899 (2010)
31. Koenigs, M., Young, L., Adolphs, R., Tranel, D., Cushman, F., Hauser, M., Damasio, A.: Damage to the prefrontal cortex increases utilitarian moral judgements. Nature **446**(7138), 908–911 (2007)
32. Piaget, J.: The Language and Thought of the Child. Psychology Press, New York (1959)
33. Eccles, J.S.: The development of children ages 6–14. Future Child. **9**(2), 30–44 (1999)
34. Turiel, E.: The development of children's orientations toward moral, social, and personal orders: more than a sequence in development. Hum. Dev. **51**(1), 21 (2008)

Midtown Buzz: Bridging the Gap Between Concepts and Impact in a Civic Computing Initiative

Maribeth Gandy(✉), Laurie Dean Baird, Laura M. Levy,
Amy J. Lambeth, Elizabeth Mynatt, Russ Clark, and Matt Sanders

Georgia Institute of Technology, Institute for People and Technology,
75 5th St NW, 30316 Atlanta, GA, Georgia
{maribeth, laura, amy}@imtc.gatech.edu,
{mynatt, russ.clark, msanders}@gatech.edu

Abstract. Midtown Buzz is a partnership between Georgia Tech and Midtown Alliance (MA), focusing on engaging urban communities through mobile innovation. Since 2013, we have been collaborating with the Midtown Atlanta community with the goal of transforming the area into an innovation district. This approach provided us with an opportunity to utilize Midtown as a living laboratory for civic computing research. During the two years of this project we have engaged in a participatory design process with diverse stakeholders to explore the needs of people in the Midtown area, and develop new technologies and approaches to address the identified needs. In this paper we discuss the lessons learned regarding the challenges of bridging the gap between concepts and deployable systems that can create positive transformation in a community.

Keywords: Civic computing · Participatory design · Mixed reality · Mobile computing · Hackathons

1 Introduction

Midtown Buzz (MB) (midtownbuzz.org) is a partnership between Georgia Tech and Midtown Alliance (MA) (www.midtownalliance.org), a non-profit membership organization and a coalition of business and community leaders tasked with improving the quality of life for those who live, work or play in the Midtown neighborhood of Atlanta. This collaboration is focused on engaging urban communities through mobile innovation. Since 2013, we have been collaborating with the Midtown Atlanta community with the goal of transforming the area into an innovation district. This approach provided us with an opportunity to utilize Midtown as a living laboratory for civic computing research. During the two years of this project we have engaged in a participatory design process with stakeholders ranging from MA staff, local start-up companies, student developer teams, and community thought leaders to pursue a variety of activities with the goal of fostering innovation, exploring the needs of people in the Midtown area, and developing new technologies, techniques, and applications to address the identified needs.

We learned that an obstacle to civic computing, despite our myriad of activities, was taking concepts and ideas and maturing them sufficiently such that they actually

© Springer International Publishing Switzerland 2015
M. Kurosu (Ed.): Human-Computer Interaction, Part III, HCII 2015, LNCS 9171, pp. 303–313, 2015.
DOI: 10.1007/978-3-319-21006-3_30

impact the community in a positive way. In this paper we will share details on the key activities we have explored via Midtown Buzz, lessons learned, and our resulting hypotheses about what approaches can help technologists and researchers as they collaborate with community organization to bridge the chasm between good ideas and best intentions to sustainable results that provide long-term value.

1.1 Related Research and the Challenges of Civic Computing

There have been a large number of initiatives and research projects with similar goals. At the national level, Code for America (www.codeforamerica.org) connects technologists with local governments to create new solutions for civic. Cities such as Portland, Oregon [1], Pittsburgh, Pennsylvania [2], and Melbourne, Australia [3] have been the sites of collaborations between computing researchers and community organization that utilize the "neighborhood as living laboratory" [4]. And as we discuss throughout the paper, many of these projects encountered opportunities and challenges similar to those of Midtown Buzz.

Our use of participatory design as a keystone of the project is also informed by a host of related civic computing initiatives [5–10]. Many of these projects found, as we did, that the use of rich media, collected from local sources, and presented in within a "storytelling" is a promising method for to creating meaningful digital experiences for the community [11–13]. And that more significant impact can be achieved by leveraging grassroots initiatives and the "do it yourself" spirit [2]

There are many similarities between the approach and findings of the Midtown Buzz project and that of Civic Nexus [14]. Of particular relevance, was their focus on learning *how to work with organizations*, and determining *what is a "good" outcome* from such work. A major lesson we learned from the MB project was that an obstacle to creating substantive impact was, at root, due to a mismatch in expectations from the MA and GT sides of the project. We each had a different conception of what activities we should pursue and what a successful outcome would look like. For example, the MA team was eager to deploy mobile applications via "app stores" to achieve a critical mass of users while the GT team was more focused on understanding community needs and exploring the design space via prototype experiences. Similarly, in their RE-ACT project, Sabiescu et al. found a conflict of vision between the researchers and the community collaborators [13]. As Shapiro et al. explain, the failures of such participatory design projects are often not technical but social/analytic/political [15]. Throughout the two-years we have continually endeavored to educate each other regarding the language, work practices, tools, and metrics of success in our respective domains.

While we entered this process with enthusiasm and hubris, we soon learned that it was not as simple as "turning the crank" to take good ideas and convert them to a deployed application or initiative that was providing value in the community. The main challenges were two sides of the same coin: *failure to launch* and the *difficulties of sustainability*.

Throughout this work we had a variety of activities such as brainstorming charrettes, workshops, design sprints, and focus groups with diverse stakeholders. Exciting and novel ideas emerged from these activities that were meant to feed into a pipeline that would convert these ideas into impactful projects. The ecosystem of mobile applications is already robust (and for some application types, oversaturated). Therefore, we theorized that the solution was for us to identify, via ethnographic inquiry and ideation, where there were still unmet needs and then assist in the creation of technology artifacts informed by these needs. Over time, we realized that some of the conventional methods for jumpstarting implementation were not as successful as we would have hoped and that our project was stymied by a *failure to launch*. Hackathon teams, formed based on chance, struggled to work together after the event was over and startup companies fizzled due to lack of funding or the changing focus of their founders. Approachable toolkits that would allow non-technologists to create novel user experiences required extensive resources to create, iteratively develop, and to support long-term, and for outreach to attract developers. And there was an omnipresent concern that we not attempt to "compete" with commercial applications that would have considerable more resources behind them.

And thus, our other challenge was related to *sustainability*. As we attempted to turn our ideation into reality, there was a question about who would do the implementation. Our MA collaborators were eager to provide mobile experiences to the community, but did not have in-house technology expertise. There was a fear that a deployed application would quickly become irrelevant and useless without a dedicated steward to support and update the application. Similar community based technology projects such as Romani Voices [13] and Johnson and Hyysalo's social media project [5] encountered stagnation and conflict later in their projects when the researchers stepped back from active development. We realized early on that the key to a successful intervention was often rich data sets, but resources would be required to initially access the data and to make sure that its connection to our applications were properly maintained. And in some cases, a user need that kept emerging from our research (e.g. the need for real-time guidance to parking spots) would have required an entire infrastructure initiative (e.g. sensors embedded in street such as those used in the SFpark initiative, sfpark.org), rather than just the creation of mobile software. Ultimately, the problem was who should (and could) be in the business of building and maintaining applications? Working with external commercial interests is an option, but what if there is no profit associated with the service/application despite the fact that it would provide great value to the community?

As a result we re-evaluated and evolved our plan throughout the project, which is not unusual for civic computing initiatives [10]. In the following section we detail our two years of activities and describe the strategies we developed in response to these challenges.

2 Midtown Buzz Activities

In this section we will describe a subset of activities that made up the Midtown Buzz initiative to highlight lessons learned. As an overview, the entirety of Midtown Buzz activities are summarized by the following statistics Demo Days: 3, Brainstorming Sessions: 6, Developer Workshops: 3, Hackathons/Sprints: 3, Curated Data Sources: 29,Developer Tools (Argon, Beacons, Glass), "Tastemaker" Panelists: 24, Partner, Outreach: 15+, Teams Supported: 12, Community Participants: 2000+

2.1 Brainstorming

We launched this project with an initial brainstorming workshop that included ~60 participants from the community. The goal was to understand what needs and desires the residents, workers, business owners, and visitors had in the context of Midtown Atlanta. The participants were divided into groups of 10–12 that were focused on a particular domain: health and wellness, wayfinding and walking tours, or transportation and sustainability. The groups contained a scribe and a facilitator that were members of the GT team as well as participants from MA. The facilitators urged the participants to not focus on technology, but to instead think about how their experiences in Midtown could be enhanced. The groups explored novel territory with their discussions. The most promising topics that emerged could be categorized as a desire for authentic voices, the need for curation and personalization, and the potential of immersive experiences:

- *Authentic Voices.* A common theme was that, while there are already considerable resources for finding recommendations for restaurants, entertainment, and other businesses, current resources lack authentic voices and feel as though they are driven by marketers and advertising. The participants wanted to have the experience of being guided around the city by a resident who could help them discover lesser-known places. The participants wanted to be privy to the more detailed "insider" view of the community that would resonate with the visitors' current interests/needs (e.g. vegan dining, nightlife, street art, child-friendly places, etc.). Our findings are similar to those from the Virtual Town Square project, which provided a location-based interface for residents to share rich hyper-local content with each other [16].
- *Curation and Personalization.* Our participants used the word "curate" repeatedly as they described the need for a contextual lens thru which data would be filtered. They imagined rich user-generated content about the neighborhood, and the ability to vote this content up or down (similar to Reddit [17]). The voting could drive the automatic generation of "personas" that categorized the content and provided the users with a set of "lenses" with which to view the community. They wanted to personalize their "hyper local" and "authentic" experience based on these personas (e.g. a new mother getting in shape, an architecture aficionado, an avid indie music fan etc.), noting that the user might choose drastically different personas of information at different times depending on their changing interests and needs.
- *Immersive Experiences.* The participants felt that existing mobile applications are often focused on information about locations (e.g. the restaurant star rating, the location of a business, the upcoming show schedule at a venue) and do not attempt to convey the experience of visiting the area. The participants expressed the desire to access the experiential aspects of a space or community (i.e. "being there without being there"). They felt these immersive experiences could help with decision-making (e.g. which restaurant to go to, which apartment building to visit) and could entice people to visit areas in real life. They imagined augmented and virtual reality applications that would provide a far richer experience than current mobile applications.

The findings from this brainstorming defined our design philosophy going forward, a focus on allowing users to "feel like a local," accessing authentic information tailored for their current needs, presented, when possible, in more immersive ways.

2.2 Hackathons and Supporting Developers

Hackathons have become popular in recent years [8]. They can provide various benefits to the sponsor including visibility, rapid exploration of the design space, and the, often erroneous, belief that working applications will result. The competitors may participate from a desire to use their skills for an altruistic purpose, motivated by prizes, or from a desire to raise their profile in the developer community and in the eyes of the sponsors. For example, often our GT students compete in hackathons as a way of building their portfolios and getting access to potential employers. Some participants, and sponsors, imagine that the projects will persist following the competition, ideally turning into actual startup companies. However, as others have noted prototypes are not products and products are not businesses [18]. While we initially envisioned our workshops and hackathons as a relatively simple method of launching new innovation in Midtown, we soon learned that it was difficult, even with support from us, for the teams to gain traction following the event. The key findings from our hackathon activities include the need for diverse teams, the importance of focusing on ideas rather than developing software early on, and requirement for external support following the event:

- *Diverse Teams*: In both our Midtown events as well as the Convergence Innovation Competition (cic.gatech.edu) we have found that a homogenous team often struggles to take the next step to realize their vision following the event [19]. For example, a CIC team we worked with closely built an AR restaurant application to let diners view a menu through different lenses depending on their food preferences. The idea was novel and the team was strong in technical skills. However, the members lacked knowledge of user experience and interface design and they also did not have domain knowledge about the restaurant industry. They were eager to write code and to start a company around their idea, but needed considerable support from the GT team to design an application that met the needs of patrons and restaurateurs. Conversely, a later team from our "Storytelling Hackathon," had an intriguing idea that was basically a location-based acting version of karaoke. They produced a compelling concept video and seemed very motivated to bring the project to fruition. The team had formed from scratch the day of the event, and as a result they possessed differing personalities, and none of them were strong software developers. Again we tried to support them, but despite their eagerness, this lack of ability to build initial versions of a working application and their conflicting work styles stymied them. The challenge, of course, is how the planners of such an event can facilitate the creation of more diverse and effective teams.
- *Ideas Rather than Code*. Despite the importance of having a team that consists of members who understand the user experience, the domain, and possess the abilities to implement their ideas, we also found that reducing the focus on producing code during the event enhanced the creativity of the participants. Our first few workshops and hackathon events were very focused on developer tools, live data feeds, and implementation. We found the results to be bland. Our later Google Glass Design Sprint (where participants brainstormed novel uses of Google Glass) and Storytelling Hackathon (where teams were tasked with designing novel mobile applications that provided information by capturing "stories" from local residents) were all about conveying the concept and the user experience. In the Storytelling we

specifically recruited non-technical community leaders and "tastemakers" to participate along with software developers. We instructed the teams to spend their time
going into the community and collecting content (video, audio, still images) to create
a concept video that would convey what it would be like for a user to experience
their idea, rather than producing prototype code. We asked them to think about how
rich location-based information (for a wide range of applications such as wellness,
transportation, public safety, and entertainment) could be conveyed in a "storytelling" context. This was informed by the outcomes from our early brainstorming that
highlighted the need for rich content from authentic local voices. While some of the
submissions were outlandish (e.g. proposed zip lines taking visitors across the city
and a giant aquarium arching over the interstate) the results were far more exciting
and the participants far more motivated than those from our previous activities.

- *The need for support.* Early in this initiative we realized that greater impact could be
  achieved via mentoring of external developer teams rather than via the GT team
  building applications ourselves. We had also found that even motivated and skilled
  teams from our hackathons needed additional support to take the next step with their
  project idea. We recruited promising student teams from the CIC and our hackathons that had a novel idea, a potential business model, and a team interested in
  taking the project further. We found that the GT student teams often lacked HCI
  expertise. The teams focused on technologies and features and struggled when
  designing the user experience, focusing on how to produce a minimal viable
  product, and how to collect and act upon user needs. As a result we provided similar
  mentoring to a variety of teams and companies. In particular the companies ben-
  efitted from getting connected to local resources such as business owners, community organization, and economic development opportunities.

Despite all of these activities and mentoring relationships, however, we were dis-
appointed in the lack of substantive impact that was generated for Midtown as a result.
There were certainly positive outcomes. The students gained valuable experience. MA
was able to explore a wide range of user needs and possible application ideas. Awareness
about Midtown and their commitment to innovation was increased, and there were a
suite of tools and data sources (to be discussed in the next section) produced that we and
others can continue to leverage. The vision of an ecosystem of deployed applications and
startup companies testing their initial offerings in Midtown, however, was not realized.
Our experiences highlight the serious challenge that exists in bridging the gap from early
ideas and excitement to working systems in the hands of community residents.

2.3 Data Sources

Through our experiences with the Midtown Buzz projects as well as GTJourney
(gtjourney.gatech.edu) [20] we have learned that the key to fostering the creation of
novel and useful applications is in making rich data sets available to developers. As we
observed in our Midtown Buzz brainstorming, as well as in GT mobile applications
classes and student competitions (GTJourney and CIC) users often express a need for
application ideas again and again, and the obstacle is data. As an example, for a decade
or more, students at GT in various classes and competitions would attempt to build

websites and applications to track the on-campus busses. The challenge was not in identifying the user needs or creating an application; the stumbling block was that there was no way to access real-time location information for the busses. The GTJourney initiative then did the heavy lifting of working with various departments around campus to either access existing data (e.g. class location information for campus buildings) or instrument systems to collect data (e.g. trackers on the busses) that allowed the applications to be built quite easily. Therefore, in Midtown Buzz we have worked extensively with key stakeholders and data owners to identify both the technical and policy changes needed to release data, and we have created systems that provide data through APIs in a way that is scalable and protects privacy when necessary. A sample of the current data available through Midtown Buzz includes: public land use (historic buildings, open space, properties, public art), events/special deals, attractions (retail, restaurants), transportation (bike rack locations, bus/shuttle routes, EV charging stations, logged commuter data, traffic counts, parking, Zip car locations), and public services information (SeeClickFix reports, Energy Star Certified Buildings, Rainwater Cistern Tracking, Solar Energy Installations). This work allows the developer community to innovate and compete on the applications and use cases while leveraging the same data. This process resulted in a few key lessons learned:

- *Understanding the Need.* It is not intuitive to understand what it means to provide relevant and useful community and location based data as a service. The challenges include understanding the type of data that is needed (by both the end user and the developers), how it can be collected (who owns the data? How can it be accessed?), and how the service that provides it should be structured (e.g. data format, update rate, level of detail, access control etc.) to make it useful and secure.
- *Resources are Necessary.* As is discussed by Sanders et al. [20] it takes resources in both time and expertise to identify and create these services. The time element makes such efforts on a college campus difficult because students are not at the institution long enough to launch and then maintain the data sources and services so they can quickly become stale or unusable.
- *Long-term Support is Key.* And related to the need for resources is the requirement for long-term support. Developers cannot rely on a service, no matter how valuable initially, if there is not a reasonable belief that the data will be kept fresh and the services technologically up-to-date. In our experience the answer for a university is to have full-time research faculty as the keystone of the efforts, as they have the experience, work cycles, and longevity in their positions to be appropriate stewards. And to fund their participation we look to spread the cost of support (in money and time) across funded research projects, courses, and students competitions. For example elements of this project were interwoven with the Argon initiative [21, 22] Cycle Atlanta and One Bus Away research [23], GT Journey [20], and CIC [19]

2.4   The Tastemaker Panel and Storytelling

When creating urban computing solutions Kukka et al. discuss the requirement for "insider" support in understanding the social, cultural, and political contexts of the community [24]. While Sabiescu et al. leveraged in-depth interviews, focus groups, and observations with key community members to capture rich content for their "Romani Voices" [13]. Therefore, consistent with the theme of identifying "authentic voices" and collecting rich content, we approached a diverse set of interesting people with a large social media following who also have authentic knowledge and information about the Atlanta community. This "tastemaker" panel consisted of influential community members from the areas of local art, community advocacy, real estate development, foodie, local deals, photography, public media, street art, cycling, local publications, live events, local businesses, pop culture, and sports; they participated in Midtown Buzz in a variety of ways. The group participated in brainstorming workshops, collaborated with developers in the hackathons, and provided domain knowledge for our student and entrepreneur teams. They also provide the much needed hyper-local knowledge and insights to seed our own technological artifacts, the Midtown Buzz portal and prototype storytelling experience (discussed in the following section). They continue to be a resource for our civic computing initiative at GT and for MA and have proven to be one of the most impactful components of this project.

Our participatory design activities with the panel culminated in a prototype storytelling application built using our Argon framework [22] ([21] describes Argon and the MB experience in greater depth). Our goal with the storytelling approach was to focus on personal expressive content to create rich community resources that were differentiated from the type of location-based mobile applications that currently exist, which are motivated by efficiency and productivity. A philosophy inspired by related urban computing projects [11, 12, 25]).

3 Discussion and Future Work

The most significant outcome from the Midtown Buzz initiative was the discovery that the community is hungry for mobile experiences that prioritize the authenticity, experience rather than efficiency, and "local voice" of the content. Our activities also guided us into a new direction for our research, focusing on a lifecycle of content, crowd-sourced voting, automatic categorization of content into "persona" groups, and providing filtering/searching tools for users based on the concept of viewing (figuratively, but sometimes literally) a community through different lenses depending on current interests and needs. This will be the focus of our subsequent phase 2 efforts.

The major lessons learned a very much aligned with those of the Civic Nexus project [14]. The first being the need for inquiry as part of the design and the challenge in this type of project of even identifying what exactly the community partner and the researchers should be working on. Merkel et al. state about their project they "were trying to find ways that we could work together…It has been difficult to find "the project" to work on with this group." The original plan for Midtown Buzz seemed very straightforward – engage in participatory design exercises and build technology prototypes. We quickly realized that true impact on the community would not come from us building a small amount of technology to deploy, but by identifying directions for new projects, establishing community connections, and helping others to realize them [7]. We had to spend considerable time and resources working with MA to figure out what type of activities would meet their needs as well as those of the community and of our researchers. Toward this end we undertook a variety of activities such as developer workshops, hackathons, and mentoring, but as we discussed above, we learned that extracting substantive community impact from them is very difficult. In the end, the contribution of this research project is greater insight into the process of carrying out a collaborative civic computing project rather than reporting on the creation of digital artifacts that transformed a community.

The second lesson learned was related to sustainability and the technical expertise of our community partners. Merkel et al. note that their community partners had little in-house technology expertise. This meant that the partners were not able to contribute significantly to the technology process and the results were artifacts that did not meet their needs and/or systems that they could not maintain. The Civic Nexus team then explains that you must make learning about technology part of practice. Similarly, our collaborators' lack of technology knowledge meant that we struggled to manage expectations as it was not clear to them what technology ideas and timelines were realistic. There was also an ongoing question about who should be responsible for initially building apps, and what the plan for sustainability would be, especially between the stakeholders with data, MA, and the technology team. On one hand, it would seem that MA does not need to be in the business of building and supporting technology, and yet, as was found with Civic Nexus, a external research team sweeping in and creating solutions does not typically lead to long-term success. Rather a community of active stakeholders who take responsibility for long-term maintenance is needed [26]. It is these questions that led to the creation of the Argon-based mobile application and storytelling prototype. Argon is approachable for non-technologists as it is based on standard web authoring tools. This allows MA to continue to improve and expand these artifacts rather than having to let them stagnate. In Phase 2 of the project we are "stepping back" from this aspect of the project (a technique also recommended by Merkel et al.) by sharing a student who physically works at the MA offices, helping them to build more storytelling content while teaching their staff how to work with the tools.

4   Conclusion

Presently, there is considerable interest in civic computing and a belief that coupling technologists with community organizations can produce significant positive impact. However, through our research on the Midtown Buzz project we have learned that significant barriers exist that make it challenging for good intentions and innovative ideas to reach the level of maturity needed to achieve this goal.

Over the course of two years, we worked closely with the Midtown Alliance organization and various community thought leaders, residents, and business owners to explore what the next generation of mobile civic-focused applications could and should be. This process started with ethnographic inquiry and progressed to participatory design, support and collaborations with external developers, community events, tool building, and technology prototyping. While the original plan of collecting user needs and building applications proved naïve, we found that successes came from close collaborations with a diverse set of stakeholders from the "Tastemaker" panel, local entrepreneurs, and motivated groups of students. Our main lessons learned are: that current location-based applications do not provide the rich hyper-local authentic content that users desire, access to data (and persistent services that can be trusted) is key to empowering developers, hackathons and other short-term interactions with potential contributors alone are insufficient, and that an important part of a collaboration with community organization is empowering them via technology awareness, education, and accessible authoring tools.

Acknowledgments. We would like to give enthusiastic thanks to Midtown Alliance and to Shannon Powell, specifically, for funding and participating in this collaboration. We would also like to acknowledge the contributions made by our "tastemakers", student teams, startup partners, and event participants. Lastly, we would like to thank our numerous GT faculty collaborators who contributed their time, expertise, and innovative ideas to this project.

References

1. Chang, M., Jungnickel, K., Orloff, C., Shklovski, I.: Engaging the city: public interfaces as civic intermediary. In: CHI 2005 Extended Abstracts on Human Factors in Computing Systems, pp. 2109–2110, New York, NY, USA (2005)
2. Bisker, S., Gross, M., Carter, D., Paulos, E., Kuznetsov, S.: Personal, public: using DIY to explore citizen-led efforts in urban computing. In: CHI 2010 Extended Abstracts on Human Factors in Computing Systems, pp. 3547–3552, New York, NY, USA (2010)
3. Paay, J.: Where we met last time': a study of sociality in the city. In: Proceedings of the 17th Australia Conference on Computer-Human Interaction: Citizens Online: Considerations for Today and the Future, pp. 1–10, Narrabundah, Australia, Australia (2005)
4. Carroll, J.M., Rosson, M.B.: Wild at home: the neighborhood as a living laboratory for HCI. ACM Trans. Comput.-Hum. Interact. **20**(3), 16:28–16:28 (2013)
5. Johnson, M., Hyysalo, S.: Lessons for participatory designers of social media: long-term user involvement strategies in industry. In: Proceedings of the 12th Participatory Design Conference: Research Papers, vol. 1, pp. 71–80, New York, NY, USA (2012)
6. Paay, J., Kjeldskov, J., Howard, S., Dave, B.: Out on the town: a socio-physical approach to the design of a context-aware urban guide. ACM Trans. Comput.-Hum. Interact. **16**(2), 7:1–7:34 (2009)
7. Le Dantec, C.: Participation and publics: supporting community engagement. In: Proceedings of the SIGCHI Conference on Human Factors in Computing Systems, pp. 1351–1360, New York, NY, USA (2012)
8. DiSalvo, C., Clement, A., Pipek, V.: Participatory design for, with, and by communities. In: Jesper, S., Robertson, T. (eds.) International Handbook of Participatory Design, pp. 182–209. Routledge, Oxford (2012)
9. Ehn, P.: Participation in design things. In: Proceedings of the Tenth Anniversary Conference on Participatory Design 2008, pp. 92–101, Indianapolis, IN, USA (2008)
10. Fischer, G., Ostwald, J.: Seeding, evolutionary growth, and reseeding: enriching participatory design with informed participation. In: Proceedings of the Participatory Design Conference, PDC, vol. 2, pp. 135–143 (2002)
11. Korn, M., Back, J.: Talking it further: from feelings and memories to civic discussions in and about places. In: Proceedings of the 7th Nordic Conference on Human-Computer Interaction: Making Sense Through Design, pp. 189–198, New York, NY, USA (2012)

12. Foth, M.: From Social Butterfly to Engaged Citizen: Urban Informatics, Social Media, Ubiquitous Computing, and Mobile Technology to Support Citizen Engagement. MIT Press, Cambridge (2011)

13. Sabiescu, A.G., David, S., van Zyl, I., Cantoni, L.: Emerging spaces in community–based participatory design: reflections from two case studies. In: Proceedings of the 13th Participatory Design Conference Research Papers, vol. 1, pp. 1–10, New York, NY, USA

14. Merkel, C.B., Xiao, L., Farooq, U., Ganoe, C.H., Lee, R., Carroll, J.M., Rosson, M.B.: Participatory design in community computing contexts: tales from the field. In: Proceedings of the Eighth Conference on Participatory Design: Artful Integration: Interweaving Media, Materials and Practices, vol. 1, pp. 1–10, New York, NY, USA (2004)

15. Shapiro, D.: Participatory design: the will to succeed. In: Proceedings of the 4th Decennial Conference on Critical Computing: Between Sense and Sensibility, pp. 29–38, New York, NY, USA (2005)

16. Kavanaugh, A., Ahuja, A., Pérez-Quiñones, M., Tedesco, J., Madondo, K.: Encouraging civic participation through local news aggregation. In: Proceedings of the 14th Annual International Conference on Digital Government Research, pp. 172–179, New York, NY, USA (2013)

17. Adams, R.: Reddit.com: a new website makes it easier to sift the mountains of news content online - and learns what you like, The Guardian, 07 December 2005

18. Porway, J.: You can't just hack your way to social change. Harvard Business Review, 07 March 2013

19. Clark, R., Sanders, M., Davidson, B., Jayaraman, S., DiSalvo, C.: The convergence Innovation Competition: helping students create innovative products and experiences via technical and business mentorship. Presented at the Human Computer Interaction International, Los Angeles, CA (2015)

20. Sanders, M., Clark, R., MacIntyre, B., Davidson, B.: GTJourney: the importance of accessible rich data sources to enable innovation. Presented at the Human Computer Interaction International, Los Angeles, CA (2015)

21. Spieginer, G., MacIntyre, B., Bolter, J., Gandy, M., Lambeth, A., Levy, L., Baird, L., Mynatt, E., Clark, R., Sanders, M.: The evolution of the argon web framework through it's use authoring community-based mixed reality applications. Presented at the Human Computer Interaction International, Los Angeles, CA (2015)

22. MacIntyre, B., Hill, A., Rouzati, H., Gandy, M., Davidson, B.: The argon AR web browser and standards-based AR application environment. In: 2011 10th IEEE International Symposium on Mixed and Augmented Reality (ISMAR), pp. 65–74 (2011)

23. Le Dantec, C.A., Watkins, K., Clark, R., Mynatt, E.: Cycle Atlanta and OneBusAway: the key role of transportation transformation in a civic computing initiative. Presented at the Human Computer Interaction International, Los Angeles, CA (2015)

24. Kukka, H., Ylipulli, J., Luusua, A., Dey, A.K.: Urban computing in theory and practice: towards a transdisciplinary approach. In: Proceedings of the 8th Nordic Conference on Human-Computer Interaction: Fun, Fast, Foundational, pp. 658–667, New York, NY, USA (2014)

25. DiSalvo, C., Maki, J., Martin, N.: Mapmover: a case study of design-oriented research into collective expression and constructed publics. In: Proceedings of the SIGCHI Conference on Human Factors in Computing Systems, pp. 1249–1252, New York, NY, USA (2007)

26. Dearden, A., Rizvi, H.: Participatory IT design and participatory development: a comparative review. In: Proceedings of the Tenth Anniversary Conference on Participatory Design 2008, pp. 81–91, Indianapolis, IN, USA (2008)

Some Investigations of Fukushima Dai-ichi Accidents from the Viewpoints of Human Factors

Akio Gofuku[1(✉)], Hiroshi Furukawa[2], and Hiroshi Ujita[3]

[1] Graduate School of Natural Science and Technology, Okayama University,
Okayama, Japan
fukuchan@sys.okayama-u.ac.jp
[2] Faculty of Engineering, Information and Systems, University of Tsukuba,
Tsukuba, Japan
[3] The Canon Institute of Global Studies, Tokyo, Japan

Abstract. Many problems were posed in the Fukushima Dai-ichi NPS accident, including recognizing the situation in the plant, information sharing in/out of the power station, decision making, emergency response, education and training on daily basis, instrumentation/control facilities and work environment of the plant, etc. A voluntaly group in the division of Human-Machine System of Atomic Society of Japan reviewed the problems suggested in various reports from the viewpoint of human factors. This paper reports the outline of some results of the review based upon some accident reports published after the accident and the information published by the defunct Nuclear and Industrial Safety Agency. The severe situations due to the loss of all power resulted in unsuccessful operation. However, the staffs on the site seem to have taken flexible approaches based on their knowledge and experience. As for the fields of communication and information sharing, there found some problems among two groups, operation groups, or order-givers and takers. On the other hand, in the analysis of emergency response capability to the accident by several techniques, many good cases were found in individual and organizational levels, but there were bad crisis responses found in managerial or national levels.

1 Introduction

Many problems were posed in the accident happened at Fukushima Dai-ichi nuclear power station, including recognizing the situation in the plant, information sharing in/out of the power station, decision making, emergency response, education and training on daily basis, instrumentation/control facilities and work environment of the plant, etc. A voluntaly group in the division of Human-Machine System of Atomic Society of Japan reviewed the problems suggested in various reports from the viewpoint of human factors (HF: human factors to ensure safety).

By referring the documents, reports and data published, the following 6 items that are important from the viewpoint of HF are reviewed:

© Springer International Publishing Switzerland 2015
M. Kurosu (Ed.): Human-Computer Interaction, Part III, HCII 2015, LNCS 9171, pp. 314–326, 2015.
DOI: 10.1007/978-3-319-21006-3_31

(1) assessment of the plant's conditions by operators at Units 1 and 2, and a review on accident response from the viewpoint of CRM (Crew Resource Management) (until the hydrogen explosion of Unit 1 occurred);
(2) actions taken by the power station staff (recognition of operating status of the isolation condenser (IC), alternative water injection into Unit 3);
(3) challenges in terms of education and training;
(4) problems and actions to address the problems in the field of communication and information sharing;
(5) emergency response ability of the organization; and
(6) factors that inhibited from responding smoothly to the accident and plausible solutions on how to improve from the aspects of the operation of these reactors as well as from the field operation on the site.

This paper describes the outline of review results in relation to the items (1), (4) and (5).

2 Assessment of the Plant's Conditions by Operators at Units 1 and 2

2.1 How to Conduct Investigation and Examination

It is important to understand the work condition of operators in the main control room (MCR) for the assessment of grasping plant's condition by operators from the viewpoints of human factors. First, the work condition is visualized based on earthquake information and reported condition of MCR in the accident reports [1, 2]. Then, based upon the accident reports [1, 2] and information [3] published by the defunct Nuclear and Industrial Safety Agency, we examined (assumed) what picture of the plant's condition the operators grasped after the big shock by the earthquake.

There are several factors to influence the works by operators in MCR. First, there happened frequent after-shocks after the big shock resulting in disturbing the countermeasures and field inspection of the damages of facilities by the big shock. The operators inspecting the damage should postpone their works and go back to MCR under the continuous announcement of the alarm of big Tsunami. Second, because MCR is a closed space, the illumination is inevitable for human works. Flashlights are necessary for the operators in a dark MCR. Third, high radioactivity level will restrict human activities due to the necessity to wear anti-radioactivity suits and the time limitation of radiation exposure. Fourth, it is difficult for a human worker to move and make an observation outside a building in the night.

The work condition of operators is visualized for the four factors. Figure 1 shows the work condition and major events related with Unit 1 and 2 from 14:30 to 18:30 on March 11, 2015 as an example of the visualization. The figure is drawn under the following assumptions as to the influences by after-shocks, illumination condition and the light outside the building. The level of earthquake is indicated by Japan Meteorological Agency seismic intensity scale because it expresses the level of ground motion and there are many monitoring posts all over Japan. The measured level at the nearest monitoring post to Fukushima-Daiichi nuclear power station is used. The Japan Meteorological Agency explains the relations of level number in the scale and severity of ground motion as shown in Table A1 [4] of Appendix. The operators are assumed to be able to do nothing for six minutes if the intensity level by the after-shock exceeds 6. The time span is shown by black color in the figure. The operators should postpone their works for four and two minutes by the after-shocks of intensity levels 5 and 4, respectively. The operators can be supposed to continue to do their works that they are doing at a small shock below the intensity level 4. For the reference, the happening time of an after-shock of the intensity level 3 is indicated as a fine black bar. As to the illumination in the MCR, some small light sources of instrumentation indicators are assumed to exist for ten minutes after the station blackout. The time span is indicated by gray color. After the period, the MCR is assumed to be in the darkness. After putting on temporary illumination, the MCR was no longer in the darkness, but it is reported that the MCR is in the condition with insufficient illumination. Therefore, the period with temporary illumination is indicated in gray color. It is also assumed that it was not in the darkness for 30 min after the sunset and before sunrise.

As seen from Fig. 1, after-shocks frequently happened. This means that the working condition of operators was not good and they often had to postpone their works in some minutes. After the station blackout, the working condition became greatly worse. They needed flashlights to continue their works. By the station blackout, operators lost their methods to know plant condition. The sun set after two hours later. It became dark outside the building resulting in making difficulty in observing the condition of facilities from the distance. Considering the bad work condition, the operators are supposed to recognize plant condition as summarized in the next subsection.

2.2 Assessment of Units 1 and 2 Conditions Until Unit 1 was Damaged by the Hydrogen Explosion

Assessments from the occurrence of the earthquake to the onslaught of the second wave of tsunami.
In the MCR, operators precisely monitor the automatic operation and plant status through the control panel and take operation steps to shutdown the reactor in accordance with the operation manual. However, they are supposed to have had a sense of uneasiness by the frequent big after-shocks. Although the major tsunami warning was issued at 14:58, they might have not assumed such a major tsunami enough to flood the reactor building. The operators supposed that they would be able to achieve a cold shutdown in accordance with procedures specified in the operation manual if no plant component was damaged by the ground motion. They might also think that the field confirmation of the damage of plant components would continue for a long time due to frequent aftershock jolts with the major tsunami warning, However, judging from the plant parameter data over time, the operators seemed to have concluded that the main equipment and apparatus functioned well.

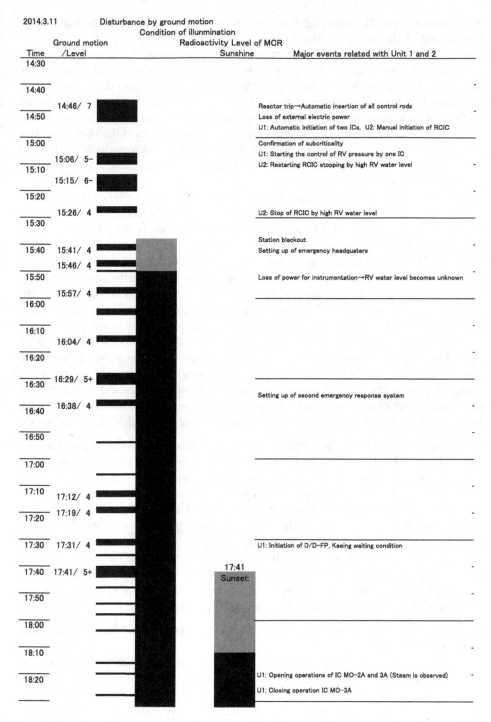

Fig. 1. Work environment of MCR operators from 14:30 to 18:30 in March 11, 2011

Assessments from the onslaught of the second wave of tsunami to temporary lighting-up of the Main Control Room.

The AC power supply was totally lost (SBO) due to the damage by the second tsunami wave at 15:32 resulting in the turning off the lighting of the MCR and main control panel. At 15:50, power supply for instruments was lost, which made the water level of the Units 1 and 2 undetectable. In the darkness, a review was made on the cause of SBO, how to restore the power source (especially, lighting of the MCR, as well as power supply of the monitoring instruments), and how to confirm the operating condition of IC (Unit 1) and Reactor Core Isolation Cooling System (RCIC) (Unit 2). Later, operators seemed to have begun studying how to inject alternative water to prepare for unexpected problems.

Judging from the happening of frequent after-shock jolts, the Emergency Preparedness Headquarters (EPH) seemed to have concluded that it would take time to restore the power source, where General Manager (GM) directed to study the alternative water injection at 17:12. Also, in the evening, the reactor water level of Unit 2 was found to be stable. This fact indirectly indicates the RCIC operation. By the identification of the extent of tsunami damage, the discussion begun on how to restore the power source by using part of Unit 2 power center with a power source car. Taking the above into account, the focus of operators' attention seemed to have shifted to how to secure water injection line for the alternative water injection and to check IC operation.

They tried to identify the IC operation in vain. Then, a review was made of procedures for the containment venting because they recognized that it would be needed depending on the future situation. Also, they worked to secure the water injection lines in the darkness in the order of Units 1 and 2. In parallel they inspected the location, etc. of field instruments based upon the drawings and entered the reactor building (R/B) to see the reactor pressure and functioning status of the main equipment.

Situations from the temporary lighting-up of the Main Control Room to the access prohibition to Unit 1 reactor building due to the increase of radiation dose.

A small generator was installed at 20:49 and temporary lighting was turned on in the MCR of Units 1 and 2. Although the temporary lighting did not serve enough illumination for smooth actions of operators, the MCR was no longer in the darkness. Temporary batteries were also connected to the monitoring instruments. They must have been relieved by obtaining the data that showed that the reactor water levels of Units 1 and 2 were above the fuel rod level meaning that the fuel rods were not exposed. As for the unknown status of IC valves, the operators were dubious if IC did function based upon the result of "opening" operation of MO-3A valve at 21:30. At 21:51, GM directed not to enter the R/B of Unit 1 due to the increase of radiation dose.

Situations from the access prohibition to Unit 1 reactor building to hydrogen explosion of Unit 1.

Probably, the cause of why the radiation levels rapidly rose was discussed. According to the data indicating the reactor water level of Unit 1 on 22 o'clock, operators may have concluded that fuel melting, if any, was only partial. Power source for control operation was expected to be restored in MCR. However, laying temporary power source lines took long time due to the evacuation by frequent after-shock jolts under the major tsunami warning. The operators focused on the confirmation of the operation status of RCIC in Unit 2. Before dawn of March 12, they obtained a proof of its functioning, and might shift their attention to how to restore the Unit 1's power source while wondering the water source.

Meanwhile, the diesel driven fire pump for water injection at Unit 1 was found to be shutdown at 1:48, and it was unable to be restarted. Facing difficulties, they seemed to have recognized that they made a step forward in the operation when they successfully started fresh water injection from fire cisterns at 5:46. They repeatedly studied venting operation procedures for pressure containment vessel (PCV), trying to collect the equipment necessary for the venting. Around 5 o'clock, they were ordered to equip themselves with the full mask, charcoal filter, and B apparatus. And the operators took shelter of the Unit 2 side due to an increase in radiation dose from the Unit 1 side. Thus, efficiency in the operations at MCR aggravated further. With the situation worsening, the operators must have believed that some of the fuel rods had exposed. The group on duty from the morning of March 11 had worked for 24 h.

In an attempt of PCV venting at a high radiation level, operators manually opened motor operated valves in the field. They also handled the air operated small valve from the MCR and tried opening operation of air operated large valves by setting up a temporary air compressor. With a decrease in the pressure of drywell, the EPH concluded that they succeeded in PCV venting. Because the operation of fresh water injection had continued during this time, emergency core cooling system, if not sufficient, may have worked to some extent. Because fresh water from the fire cistern dried up, GM directed to start seawater injection to the Unit 1 reactor at 14:54.

They managed to complete preparation for restoring the power source at around 15:30. But, a hydrogen explosion occurred in the reactor building at 15:36. This damaged cables, etc., and made all of the on-site staffs to take shelter in the important anti-seismic building.

3   Problems and Measures in Communication and Information Sharing

3.1   Objective and Method of the Study

This section aims at analyzing problems and proposing measures to cope with communication and information sharing in the case of the accident at Fukushima Dai-ichi Nuclear Power Station with the following conditions: (a) the subjects of this study are set to the MCR and EPH, because the 'sites' had a significant influence on the accident situation and the operations were restricted by time, (b) the main data used is the detailed descriptions included in the TEPCO's reports [2, 7] and the Investigation Committee on the Accidents at the Fukushima Nuclear Power Station Report [1, 6], (c) if any measures were proposed in the reports, then the validity will be evaluated in this study. If it is necessary, additional measures will be proposed as the part of this study. The following paragraphs show the analysis results in three situations: information sharing between the MCR and the EPH; within the MCR; and in the EPH.

3.2 Information Sharing Between the Main Control Room and the Emergency Preparedness Headquarters - Information Sharing Between Two Groups

Information on Unit 1 operation status and situations was not fully shared with the EPH. Figure 2 shows the process of the communication from the MCR to the EPH. Using hotlines, information of the MCR was transmitted verbally to the Power Generation Team of the EPH. The information which the team received was given orally to the Chief of Power Generation Team. Finally, the information is given to entire Headquarters using a microphone from the Chief. The information about detailed operations (e.g., valve controls) and sound they heard (e.g., generation of steam) was communicated to the entire Headquarters. The information might prove IC was functioning. However, the information opposed to it was not transmitted from the MCR to the Headquarters for some reason. The reason has not been revealed. As the result, there was a period of time that the operators in the MCR understood "IC's not functioning," while the members of the Headquarters recognized the situation as "IC's functioning" [2] (p. 323 and Appendix 8–10).

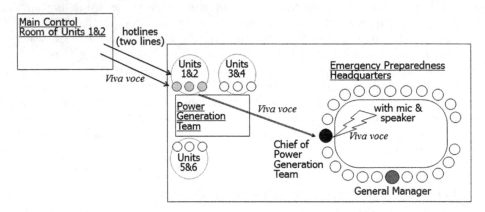

Fig. 2. Flow of information from the main control room of units 1&2 to the emergency preparedness headquarters (Source: Reference [2], Appendix 8–10, p. 2).

TEPCO proposed four measures in the report: (a) to understand the situation visually, communication form (e.g., simple diagram) should be used for communicating plant and system status, (b) the common template, e.g., dedicated sheets on white boards, should be set both in the EPH and the MCR, (c) communications should be exchanged whenever information is updated, (d) the use of these methods should be trained through disaster drills [2] (pp. 344–345 and Appendix 16–3).

In situations where old information was recorded on the template at the Headquarters, it is difficult for the members of the Headquarters to find out the operators forgot to convey new information. To address this problem, they need to compare records on the both templates. A feasible measure is using a hardware that the Headquarters can visually confirm the template in the MCR with. A software measure is stationing of staffs in charge who perform a periodical report about the information in the MCR.

It might not be feasible for them to measure and communicate everything of many items at the time of emergency. These items should be selected based upon the importance assessment. More flexible strategy may be appropriate, which ask to handle only essential information according to the situation.

3.3 Information Sharing in the Main Control Room - Information Sharing in a Working Group

The problem was that the operators in the MCR of Unit 1 failed to share the information on the operation status just before SBO. One operator testified, "Valve 3A was closed before power source was lost. I told the information to another operators" [2] (Appendix 8–10). But no similar testimony was obtained from other operators. When the control panel does not work as external memory, information that they should store in the memory rapidly increases. This easily causes a memory failure.

The measures with the block diagram and template mentioned in 3.2 can be also applicable to information sharing in a group. This may help address the problem.

3.4 Instructions and Directions at the Emergency Preparedness Headquarters - Information Sharing Between Commanders and Subordinates

At 17:12 on March 11th, the GM ordered the members of the Headquarters to make preparation of water injection by fire engines. In the reference [6] (pp. 403–404), it was reported that the instruction was not promptly accepted by the members of each function teams or groups at the Headquarters. It also pointed out that because the roles of the teams and groups are fractionated, they lack a way of thinking which is recognizing the situation in a comprehensive manner, designing their roles, and providing necessary support service.

No measure was proposed in the reports. To address this problem, it may be good to visualize the details and allocation of the tasks, and ongoing status on a white board. This allows the commanders and subordinates to clearly share the information about the task. Furthermore, if the display of the MCR can be seen from the Headquarters, it may be effectively used to develop necessary support and advice to the MCR.

3.5 Notes for Considering the Measures

For a practical use of the measures, each license holder should evaluate the effectiveness and feasibility at sites in details. One of the requirements should be satisfied is "avoiding interruption of the operator's task on the site." The first priority should be assign to achieving the control tasks in the MCR, where resources are limited. The information sharing task should be allotted to the EPH to inhibit the interruption to the task process of the operators of the MCR.

Actually it is reported that workers in charge were allocated in the Fukushima Dai-Ni and Tokai Dai-Ni Nuclear Power Plants. On the other hand, there is no such report about the case of the Fukushima Dai-ichi Nuclear Power Plant.

4 Analysis on the Emergency Response Capability by Organizations

4.1 Analysis Method

Based upon analysis methods used for various accident reports [8–10], and new methods advocated in recent years such as Resilience Engineering (RE) [11] and High Reliability Organization [12], we extracted successful and failure cases in regards to how they responded to the Accident in Fukushima Dai-ichi Nuclear Power Station, from individual via. organizational, and to the external response levels. At the analysis, based upon the report from TEPCO [6], we discuss the timeline on water injection at Unit 1, especially on the judgment to continue seawater injection.

4.2 Methods Used for the Analysis

According to the definition of RE [11], it is a strategy to control the state steady by adopting human situational awareness when the change of a system status is severe, in contrast with the concept to design a robust system against disturbance to avoid a conventional human error. Resilience (flexible and robust) refers to a capability to adjust the function, which an organization inherently has, in responding to the environment and disturbance before, amid and after it, which includes (i) studying ability, (ii) predicting ability, (iii) monitoring ability, and (iv) responding ability.

HRO [12] studied organizational capability, and refers to "honesty" (report any small indication), "prudency" (to be very careful), and "sharpness" (sharp sense about operation), at ordinary time, and then "agility" (to fully respond to problem-solving) and "flexibility" (to entrust authority to the most suitable person), at the time of emergency. High Reliability Organization is a concept to review a successful case from the standpoint of an organization, which has a common objective to alleviate accident trouble, in line with the present direction of RE.

Risk literacy (RL) is a capability to examine the background of a risk, and to understand and deal with the influence of the risk. To ensure an effective risk management of an organization, it is important for the organization or risk manager to have a risk literacy [13]. This capability includes analysis capability (collection, understanding and predictive ability), communication capability (networking and communication ability), and practice capability (response and applied ability).

4.3 Analysis Results of Organization Factors

We analyzed water injection timeline of Unit 1 from the viewpoints of RE, HRO, and RL. The analysis result is shown in the paper titled "Accident Analysis by using

Methodology of Resilience Engineering, High Reliability Organization, and Risk Literacy" written by H. Ujita for HCI 2015.

4.4 Discussion on the Accident Response Capability

A difference in accident response capability is found between individual & organizational levels, and national & industrial levels. Many successful examples of resilience were found on individual and organizational basis. The operators on the site seem to have a sense of duty, a critical mind for usual work, and an experience of accident training programs, which seemed to have worked effectively at the situation of emergency. This is what we call the significance of safety culture development. In this context, we advise that it is important to "establish study (feedback) system as an organization" on daily basis.

On the other hand, there are many flaws in crisis response of managerial and country levels. In the management division, trainings is dispensable that focus on emergency responsibility allotment, evaluation of severe situation assessment, and mode shift from normal time to emergency. Failure cases are concentrated on rare event recognition and challenges in organization culture, in the national level and industrial base. According to bounded rationality [13], they used the limited information to make a rational decision in the limited environment, which may have been a failure in the site of God. Our suggestion is that it is important to destroy bounded rationality, or to "establish the system which prioritize judgment on the site (allows violation of order). The typical example was seen in the judgment to continue seawater injection despite the order from the official residence and the headquarters. A higher priority was placed on the conclusion on the site. Also, rebuilding of the safety concept integrating unexpected responses is designed in order to eliminate errors in risk recognition.

Analyzing documents including lessons learned from the Fukushima Dai-Ni Plant accident as shown in Reference [14], the causes of such difference were due to the severity in damage and the availability of power source. In the Fukushima Dai-ni, the damage of the whole system was less than the Fukushima Dai-ichi, and the total power source was not lost. Considering the four capabilities of Resilience Engineering, the response was not greatly different between Fukushima Dai-ichi and Dai-ni Plants.

TEPCO proposed, in the accident summary newly submitted [15], in addition to the hardware measures by the Investigation Committee on the Accidents at the Fukushima Nuclear Power Station of TEPCO (Investigation Committee) [2], such means to avoid a negative chain of organization as "to improve safety awareness by the top management" and "to introduce incident-command system" for addressing the challenges of the organization suggested in this paragraph.

5 Concluding Remarks

This paper reviews some topics of the accident in Fukushima Dai-ichi Nuclear Power Station from the viewpoint of HF. First, this paper reviews how the operators had recognized the plant conditions until the hydrogen explosion of Unit 1. The operating condition of components was hard to be recognized because of the loss of functions such as control panels of the MCR, Safety Parameter Display System (SPDS), etc., which were indispensable of monitoring the situation. Also, the operation manual was no longer applicable. These severe situations resulted in unsuccessful operation. However, the staffs on the site seem to have taken flexible approaches based on their knowledge and experience. As for the fields of communication and information sharing, there found some problems among two groups, operation groups, or order-givers and takers. It is important not to prevent site/task operations in applying plausible measures for the problems. In the analysis of emergency response capability to the accident, many good cases were found in individual and organizational levels, but there were bad crisis responses found in managerial or national levels.

Based upon the review results, it will be effective to have measures to keep the power source and system function for a long duration. A system design that enables manual operation without an excessive dependence on remote control is also important.

Appendix

Table A1. Relations of level number and severity of ground motion in Japan meteorological agency seismic intensity scale

Intensity level	Influence of human activities
0	Imperceptible to people
1	Felt slightly by some people keeping quiet in buildings
2	Felt by many people keeping quiet in buildings
3	Felt by most people in buildings
4	Most people are startled Hanging objects such as lamps swing significantly Unstable ornaments may fall
5 Lower	Many people are frightened and feel the need to hold onto something stable Dishes in cupboards and items on bookshelves may fall Unsecured furniture may move, and unstable furniture may topple over
5 Upper	May people find it difficult to walk without holding onto something stable Dishes in cupboards and items on bookshelves are more likely to fall Unsecured furniture may topple over Unreinforced concrete-block walls may collapse
6 Lower	It is difficult to remain standing Many unsecured furniture moves and may topple over. Doors may become wedged shut Wall tiles and windows may sustain damage and fall In wooden houses with low earthquake resistance, tiles may fall and buildings may lean or collapse

(Continued)

Table A1. (*Continued*)

Intensity level	Influence of human activities
6 Upper	It is impossible to move without crawling. People may be thrown through the air Most unsecured furniture moves and is more likely to topple over Wooden houses with low earthquake resistance are more likely to lean or collapse Large cracks may form and large landslides and massif collapses may be seen
7	Wooden houses with low earthquake resistance are even more likely to lean or collapse Wooden houses with high earthquake resistance may lean in some cases Reinforced-concrete buildings with low earthquake resistance are more likely to collapse

References

1. Interim report by the Investigation Committee on the Accidents at the Fukushima Nuclear Power Station of Tokyo Electric Power, Study Committee (Main ver.), November 2011 (in Japanese)
2. TEPCO: Investigation Committee on the Accidents at the Fukushima Nuclear Power Station (Main ver.): (Attached documents), June 2012 (in Japanese)
3. Information from the Nuclear and Industrial Safety Agency, former organizations; TEPCO Fukushima Dai-ichi NPS, plant related parameters. http://www.nsr.go.jp/archive/nisa/earthquake/plant/2/plant-2-2303.html (in Japanese)
4. Japan Meteorological Agency, Seismic intensity scale. http://www.jma.go.jp/jma/kishou/know/shindo/
5. TEPCO: Response Immediately after Fukushima Dai-ichi and Dai-ni NPSs, June 2012 (in Japanese)
6. Investigation Committee on the Accidents at the Fukushima Nuclear Power Station of Tokyo Electric Power Company report, verification committee and final report (main-text ver.), July 2012 (in Japanese)
7. TEPCO: Accident Analysis Report by the Investigation Committee on the Accidents at the Fukushima Nuclear Power Station, Appendix 2: Response Status to the Fukushima Dai-ichi and Dai-ni Nuclear Power Stations, June 2012 (in Japanese)
8. Reason, J.: Managing the Risks of Organizational Accidents. Ashgate, Aldershot (1997)
9. Rational Concepts on Safety and Secure based upon the Risk, Operations Research, October Issue, October 2006, 646–654 Dr. Ujita (2006) (in Japanese)
10. Research on Error Management, by Quality Assurance Study Group: FY 2009 Periodical Meeting report (June 2010) (in Japanese)
11. Hollnagel, E.: Safety Culture, Safety Management, and Resilience Engineering. ATEC, International Aviation Safety Forum, Tokyo (2009)
12. Nakanishi, A.: Requirements for High Reliability Organization. Seisansei Publishing Co, Tokyo (2007). (in Japanese)
13. Hayashi, Y.: Case Studies: Introduction to Risk Literacy. Nikkei BP Publishing Co, Tokyo (2005). (in Japanese)

14. Kikuzawa, K.: Unreasonable Organization. Diamond Publishing Co, Tokai (2000). (in Japanese)
15. TEPCO: Survey and Lessons Learned from "Response to Fukushima Dai-Ni Nuclear Power Plant Accident" (Proposal); Japan Nuclear Safety Institute, December 2012 (in Japanese)

Cycle Atlanta and OneBusAway: Driving Innovation Through the Data Ecosystems of Civic Computing

Christopher A. Le Dantec[1]([⊠]), Kari E. Watkins[2], Russ Clark[3], and Elizabeth Mynatt[3]

[1] School of Literature, Media, and Communication,
Georgia Institute of Technology, Atlanta, GA, USA
ledantec@gatech.edu
[2] School of Civil and Environmental Engineering,
Georgia Institute of Technology, Atlanta, GA, USA
kari.watkins@ce.gatech.edu
[3] Institute for People and Technology, Georgia Institute of Technology,
Atlanta, GA, USA
russ.clark@oit.gatech.edu, mynatt@gatech.edu

Abstract. Smart cities and digital democracy have begun to converge around mobile computing, enabling, web services, and different operational and shared databases to create new opportunities for civic engagement for concerned citizens as well as new efficiencies for public services provided by local government. While many of these projects remain siloed to specific departments of local government, when viewed in aggregate, they begin to fill in a more complex picture of how piecemeal projects are changing the relationship between local government and the public. As an example of this change, we describe our partnership with multiple city and regional agencies in Atlanta. We discuss a pair of projects that together, aim to transform Atlanta's transportation system by more effectively connecting the public to transportation services and to the processes of infrastructure planning. The projects we present here—Cycle Atlanta and OneBusAway—are part of a larger civic computing agenda where models of digital democracy and smart cities combine to create a data ecosystem where citizens produce and consume different forms of data to enable better infrastructure planning and to enhance alternative modes of transportation.

Keywords: Digital democracy · Smart cities · Civic computing · Urban informatics

1 Introduction

Computing research into the role of technology in supporting citizens and government goes back decades [18, 19, 31, 33]. Within that legacy, researchers have looked at applying computing in different social [20, 23, 41], community [6, 29, 31], and political contexts [12, 18, 19]. Many of these earlier systems and experiments focused on the ways in which computing technology helped communities engage with each other in

© Springer International Publishing Switzerland 2015
M. Kurosu (Ed.): Human-Computer Interaction, Part III, HCII 2015, LNCS 9171, pp. 327–338, 2015.
DOI: 10.1007/978-3-319-21006-3_32

democratic discourse. These earlier systems have two main characteristics in common: first, they were based on supporting communities through strengthening social ties and building social capital to contend with local issues [13, 31]; second, they drew on a strong connection between online activity and local physical community—a critical component that Carrol argues has been ignored in more recent research [5].

In contrast to these early examples that focused on social ties and place, the past five years have seen the emergence of a new form of technology-mediated public participation where the systems are not discursive, but instead rely on sensing and data collection as the primary mode of interaction. Examples of this class of system range from platforms and systems like SeeClickFix (www.seeclickfix.com), PublicStuff (www.publicstuff.com), and Street Bump (www.streetbump.org), which each enable the public to submit data about urban conditions; to projects like Seattle in Progress (www.seattleinprogress.com) or the Atlanta Infrastructure Map (http://www.infrastructuremap.org) which present to the public data from land use offices and infrastructure planning departments. This broad category of data-based ways of integrating local government and institutions with the public relies on the production and exchange of data between the two.

In the context of Atlanta, multiple city and regional agencies have partnered with Georgia Tech to develop a robust pair of projects that aim to transform the city's transportation system by more effectively connecting the public to transportation services and the processes of infrastructure planning. The projects we present here—Cycle Atlanta and OneBusAway—are part of a larger civic computing agenda where models of digital democracy and smart cities come together to create a data ecosystem where citizens produce and consume different forms of data to enable better infrastructure planning and to enhance alternative modes of transportation.

2 App-Driven Civic Computing: Smart Cities, Smart Citizens

The move toward app- and data-driven modes of civic computing is closely tied to two larger movements: first is the emerging trends in smart cities where urban operations are driven by data generated through sensor networks [26, 39], instrumented infrastructure [8, 28] and participatory sensing [7, 32]; second, the ongoing move toward digital democracy where the internet and mobile computing create opportunities to augment face-to-face democratic processes with asynchronous means of participation [14]. These two movements complement the notion that mobile apps and data-driven practices can have a transformative effect both on the efficacy with which public policy and operations decisions are made within an urban area and on the experience that citizens have of the city as they make use of services and infrastructures. In particular, it enables new ways of participating in civic processes mediated by technology, creating new kinds of democratization in determining how those processes are accessed and enacted [15].

One domain where these different elements come together is through urban transportation, where cities and citizens desire more sustainable transportation networks. Our current auto-oriented transportation system is implicated in numerous issues of health and sustainability [37]: for example, the transportation sector accounts for 27 % of greenhouse gas end-use emissions, 43 % of which is due to the travel of passenger cars [38]; moreover, the reliance on cars compounds the ill affects of a sedentary lifestyle as the risk of obesity increases 6 % with every additional hour spent commuting in a car [10].

The deleterious consequences on personal and environmental health and the combination of the social awareness occurring within the demographic groups moving into urban centers creates an opportunity for specifically addressing issues in transportation. These opportunities combine the political will to develop attractive urban centers and to develop the technical strategies of smart city programs and new models of digital democracy and participatory planning to create a collaborative ecosystem of government, citizens, and data.

The apps that we have created in partnership with agencies in metropolitan Atlanta aim to improve access to existing transportation services and to enable new forms of participation in the public process of developing future transportation infrastructures in the city. Taken together, these projects begin to address the instrumental challenges of developing a working data ecology that supports both institutional and individual decision making through the production, exchange, and consumption of different forms of data. Importantly, this ecology is self-reinforcing where data produced and shared with other nodes in the system create feedback loops that help refine further data production, sharing, and use.

3 Civic Data Ecosystems

Cycle Atlanta and OneBusAway exemplify two critical characteristics that enable an ecosystem built around sharing data and information between cities and the public (Fig. 1). In this ecosystem, data needs to be produced and turned into information for different consumers: cyclists and transit riders produce data about the rides they take while at the same time need information to make transportation decisions;

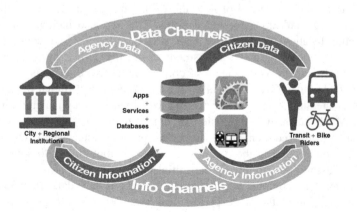

Fig. 1. Our civic data ecosystem where data production and information consumption are in constant exchange between local institutions and the public.

transportation agencies and planners need information to guide decisions on where to build new infrastructure or deploy new services while at the same time producing data about current services that can aid riders. Regardless of who consumes the data—the transit-using public or transit agencies' employees and city planners—sustainable transportation choices require data production and information sharing.

Key to the data ecosystem we are describing here is that the data neither exist purely in the hands of the public nor purely in the hands of transit agencies. Each endpoint produces data, some of which is useful as information to external consumers and some of which is useful as information in a direct feedback loop. In both cases, a feedback mechanism enables data streams to lead to information for consumption, planning, and action: Cycle Atlanta provides a new data source for the city by collecting data from cyclists who provide the city with information about the routes they do and do not take as well as issues they encountered en route (potholes, traffic signals that don't turn green, parking in bike lanes); OneBusAway enables a new data source for transit riders by aggregating data from regional transit agencies and providing users a single point of access for real-time bus and train arrival information.

These two projects create a set of opportunities to broaden access to data and to information with important implications on how decisions are made, who participates, and how that participation is translated more broadly into transit network and infrastructure changes. At the same time, these projects help shed light onto the kinds tensions and trade-offs requiring immediate negotiation between the notion of data production as a form of ground-truth measurement and data production as a form of public participation. The former is often assumed to reflect the state of the world—the location of buses and time of arrival—while the latter is bound up with issue advocacy and subjective experience.

3.1 Cycle Atlanta: Configuring Participation Through Data Collection

Cycle Atlanta (cycleatlanta.org) was launched in October 2012 and uses the geo-locative capabilities of smartphones to record and upload cycling routes. Each recorded route provides a record of how the cyclist navigated the city, including the purpose of the ride and any rider-added notes. The app also includes the ability to record specific locations with photos and text descriptions and collects optional demographic data including a self-assessment of cycling ability, cycling history, and current cycling frequency as indicators of comfort level to aid analysis.

As described above, Cycle Atlanta bridges the domains of digital democracy and smart cities by creating a platform for cyclists to influence policy making through data production. Much in the way the vision of digital democracy decouples democratic participation from the requirements of in-person participation, when cyclists record a ride, they are contributing to the planning process without having to attend a public meeting. To illustrate this, following the initial launch of the app, over 1500 cyclists have contributed (and continue to contribute) data about their daily rides through the app. In contrast, during the same period, less than 50 people turned up at public hearings related to the same project to discuss and advocate for particular bike facilities.

Asynchronous public participation enabled by the app allows more people to provide input into the planning process, solving one of the ongoing challenges in urban planning by removing the constraint of attending public meetings in order to move toward broad and substantial public participation. However, while the app lead to a difference in *quantities* of participation, it also created a difference in *kind* of participation: by recording their rides and sharing that data with city planners, Atlanta cyclists enacted a new form of civic participation accomplished through their collected data. These data are not just a metric of cycling traffic patterns, but are a form of public advocacy that changes how cyclists interact with local policy making. These changes span the individual experience and personal contribution of a single cyclist and ways in which cyclists collectively and strategically advocate for change. By turning public participation into a data-driven activity, the work to collect the data, the visibility of the collected data, and the sense-making needed with the data all need to account not just for messiness, subjectivity, and bias, but for the intentional acts of the individuals behind the data collection.

Interpreting Data Production for Planning. Since the app and the data collected were meant to be a component of, and alternative to, the public meeting, then we need to look more carefully at the patterns of use in order to respond constructively to individual contributions and aggregate trends. In a simple analysis, we looked at one key characteristic from the data set: how often users recorded rides along the same route. Using this metric, two categories were instructive for describing the patterns of use through the app: the first is what we call *casual users*—people who recorded fewer than 5 repeated rides (a repeated ride was one where the cyclist traveled the same route); the second group, *habitual users* was defined as those who recorded particular routes more than 5 times. The bulk of our app user base fell into the casual user category (88 % of the user population) but this group produced less than two-thirds of the data (64 %). In contrast, the habitual users contributed a disproportionate amount of data. Even though they were a substantial minority in the overall pool of app users (12 %), their over-representation in the data set meant routes they cared about were much more visible. This disparity was particularly exaggerated at the high end of the habitual user pool where a handful of riders were contributing 30 times more data than the casual users. When viewed in aggregate, this meant the routes preferred by specific individuals were demonstrably more visible when the data were mapped, creating an ambiguous resource for planners using the data in their analysis [22].

Data Production and Community Benefits. As a material practice, the collection of ride data by cyclists represents different ways of knowing about the city, ways that are configured by the smartphone and features of the app deployed to record rides. Recorded routes only show the road taken, not the road preferred; route choice analysis is limited to a delta between the recorded route and an optimal route model (*e.g.*, one based on geography, traffic speed and density, total distance, or proximity to existing cycling infrastructure or amenities); and differentiating between habitual users of the app and those whose use was infrequent creates incompatibilities in how popular routes are identified and interpreted.

Taking the position that data produced by cyclists in the city *leads to knowledge* to guide the development of new infrastructure imposes trade-offs about what data to excise and under what conditions. On the other hand, a starting position that the data *result from ways of knowing* about the city produces a different set of trade-offs. This shift introduces new ways to circulate the cycling route data in the ecosystem of cyclists and planners. The knowledge and advocacy represented in the data provides a resource for planners seeking to tap into local expertise and tacit knowledge and for cyclists who can share their experiences on how best to navigate the city. The app creates a kind of cycling infrastructure that is not realized through street-striping or buffered bike lanes, but through an ecosystem of data and information flows that enables new forms of action and new opportunities for shared knowledge.

3.2   OneBusAway: Configuring Participation Through Data Sharing

In contrast to the data-production focus of Cycle Atlanta, OneBusAway (http://onebusaway.org) is a set of information tools that provide access to real-time arrival predictions and other transit information for a city's bus and train network. OneBus-Away (OBA) was originally co-developed by researchers (including the co-author) at the University of Washington in an effort to bring expertise in computing and trans-portation system together in order to improve the transit system for the riding public [9]. The OBA app is available on a full range of platforms, including native applica-tions on the iPhone, Android, and Windows Phone, a website, a short-messaging service (SMS), and an Interactive Voice Recognition (IVR) system; it also drives a number of large public displays in store windows near busy transit stops.

Following the success of OBA in Puget Sound (Seattle), other regions began to express interest in replicating the program in their local community. Acting on an opportunity to link a number of geographically-diverse regions with similar goals in the area of sustainability, the OBA project has grown into a diverse nation-wide com-munity that includes representation from academia, transit agencies, industry, and independent developers. This community has supported the expansion of the project to become a multi-region platform that easily allows the integration of new cities—including Seattle, Tampa, Atlanta, and New York City [1]—and which has enabled new services like the "TextMyBus" service launched in Detroit. Altogether, OBA now serves over 400,000 unique weekly across the country.

Agency Accountability and Open Data for Developers. For real-time transit applications such as OBA to function, they must have access to data provided by the transit agencies. In some cases, transit agencies create rider information applications in-house or contract with vendors to create such applications. Over the past decade, many transit agencies have begun to publish their schedule data online for public consumption, and in recent years, this online data has transitioned to using standardized data formats such as the General Transit Feed Specification (GTFS) to allow third-party developers to create their own applications that consume the data. At the same time, agencies have also begun to include transit vehicle location and real-time station and stop arrival predictions among the data. This "open data" approach follows a national trend among public agencies in multiple sectors to improve transparency and invite broader participation in the design of citizen services. In his May 9, 2013 executive order, "Making Open and Machine Readable the New Default for Government Information", President Obama begins that "Openness in government strengthens our democracy, promotes the delivery of efficient and effective services to the public, and contributes to economic growth. As one vital benefit of open government, making information resources easy to find, accessible, and usable can fuel entrepreneurship, innovation, and scientific discovery that improves Americans' lives and contributes significantly to job creation."

As of 2012, there were no transit agencies in Georgia with open data and no source of real-time transit information (RTI) in the region, putting Atlanta behind the national trend toward providing open schedule data [43]. Unlike other cities where OBA was deployed, Atlanta did not have a large crossover between transit riders and technology advocates, therefore the transit agencies in the region had not yet been confronted with the idea of providing a higher-level of information to riders or of having third-party developers interested in working with their data. This created a number of early hurdles to overcome, including demonstrating the benefit of RTI systems to ridership, aggregating data from the regional transit system, and creating a conversation across the regional transit agencies about the importance of sharing data with the public. This last point was the most important as the status quo had been to keep transit system data private, which prevented the transit agencies from participating in a civic data ecosystem—to the detriment of area transit riders, and to the detriment of more effective management of services by the transit agencies. Concurrent with the deployment of OBA in Atlanta, MARTA, the city's core transit agency, also released an RTI app of their own, thus validating the need for better transit information in the region. OBA still serves as the regional RTI aggregator.

Changing Travel Behavior through Information. The underlying goal of OBA is to make it easier for riders to use public transportation and thereby increase rider satisfaction. As opposed to driving or cycling, transit riders are sacrificing a certain amount of control over their trip and they must trust that the vehicle will arrive and in a timely manner. Studies of transit riders using RTI have found many benefits, including increased perception of personal security and increased satisfaction with transit service [9, 11, 44]. With regard to wait times, a study of perceived and actual wait times found that riders *without* RTI, *perceived* their wait time as greater than the *measured* wait time while the perceived waiting for riders with RTI more closely matched measured time [42]. In addition, mobile RTI users in the study were observed to wait almost 2 min less per trip than those arriving using traditional schedule information.

Furthermore, Carrel *et al.* showed that riders will adapt to unreliable service by choosing alternative transit service [4]. Studies in Seattle and Tampa showed that riders self-report an increase in trips, particularly in the off-peak, a beneficial result since the transit system will have additional capacity at that point [2, 9]. Two recent studies of riders in Chicago and New York showed that real-time information can increase transit ridership by approximately 1.8–2.2 % [3, 36].

Often, one of the limitations of data returned to transit agencies from surveys is that it is not possible to track rider behavior change with any fidelity: only gross aggregate trends can be examined. We had an opportunity to address this limitation in our own project because Atlanta was one of the few cities in the US that had implemented a contactless smart card ticketing system prior to deploying RTI. This enabled us to examine changes in trip-making patterns using smart card data. In order to understand which smart card users were also real-time users, a short online survey was conducted in which respondents were asked about their use of RTI and for their unique 16-digit smart card ID number. The smart card ID number was then used to link the survey response to the corresponding smart card trip history; and this joint smart card/survey dataset allowed for a disaggregate before-after analysis of transit trips in which users of RTI were compared with non-users.

By linking these data together, transit agencies and planners in Atlanta have a new tool at their disposal to better understand how ride habits change once robust RTI options have been deployed. Even though the RTI systems in Atlanta is still relatively recent, making the impact on overall ridership more difficult to discern, the kinds of data that are present within the civic data ecosystem give Atlanta transit agencies deeper insight into how people respond to such systems so they can tailor the features and locations of their RTI systems to create opportunities for infrequent riders to consider transit alternatives.

Understanding Transit Rider Preferences and Desires. OBA, and other similar transit apps, provide information from the transit agency to the riders. However, data can also feed from one rider to another or can be used by planners and engineers working on behalf of the city and regional agencies to understand the travel patterns of riders and to gain valuable feedback directly from riders as they experience the system. One example of how transit riders can provide information to one another through such a system is Carnegie Mellon's Tiramisu Transit [35, 45]. In the absence of automated vehicle location (AVL) data to identify where transit vehicles were located in real-time, the developers created a smartphone application to allow riders to self-identify their location as they board a bus. Tiramisu also provided an option for the rider to indicate problems, positive experiences, suggestions, and other data, such as the level of fullness of the bus, which aids people with disabilities to choose the bus they want to access. Although many transit systems now have AVL, the additional crowdsourcing of data such as vehicle fullness may supplement instrumentation.

Similarly, OBA has a feature wherein a user can submit feedback that a bus or train did not arrive as predicted. Such a feature was particularly useful when King County Metro in Seattle was transitioning from one AVL system to another and errors were widespread. The precise time and location of the error is automatically reported by the system and with only a simple categorization of the error experienced, the rider can report the information. This allows the agency to take advantage of the ubiquitous presence of riders to aid in final testing of a system [11]. With a good relationship and data transfer capabilities between smartphone application developers and the transit agency, these feedback systems can go beyond just errors with the real-time information being presented to the rider to incorporate general feedback on the system as a whole, enabling riders to comment about the service or pieces of infrastructure (dirty bus, graffiti) they experience.

Within Atlanta, we are using OBA as a testbed to assess how riders would like to receive transit information, including how riders execute a frequent trip, an infrequent trip, and a new trip by seeking out information about routes, schedules and on-time arrival information. We are assessing how frequent bus or rail service must be for riders to adapt to having no schedule if RTI information is available, thus freeing agencies to operate transit services in real-time with buffers to meet a schedule. A substantial component of this work is using the transit trip planning tools and location-based smartphone applications to collect data from the rider to allow agencies to observe when and where people are trying to travel. For example, visualizations of OBA in Seattle show where riders are accessing the app [27], and with a large enough percentage of the system ridership using the app, begin to paint a picture of travel patterns throughout the day. These data can be merged with data provided by Google, transit agencies, and developers, to understand desired trips, even if those trips are not executed on transit.

4 Conclusion

As technology is used to create and mediate forms of civic engagement, we need to attend to how the affordances of those technologies support (or discourage) different kinds of democratic participation. van Dijk uses a combination of models of democracy, models of communication, and models of social interaction to begin to scaffold a robust theoretical basis for understanding digital democracy [40]. The point is that different technology interventions have different communication and interaction affordances [25], and those affordances enable or impede the *means* and the *ends* of civic computing systems designed to support the functioning of local government.

In the examples presented in this paper, the differences between a city government equipping its citizens with smartphone apps to record their bike rides, or an information sharing platform to improve the access to and quality of transportation system information both require different levels of direct and directed participation. These technologies change the nature of transparency, of fairness, and of representation through new tools for data production in public processes meant to enable citizen participation in planning policy development; they also change access to service information, making data available to improve bus system use through a more informed and better supported riding public.

In both cases, the aim is neither to blindly embrace technology as a solution for engaging in civic participation [34], nor is it to dismiss altogether the possibility for positive change when deploying mobile and social computing to mediate how we work together as communities [24]. Instead, the aim is to take deliberate steps to understand both how technology can be taken up in the hands of motivated and concerned citizens and, when that occurs, how local institutions and processes need to evolve in the face of these new civic data ecosystems.

One of the challenges in these civic data ecosystems is that the combination of data, and the agency and intent exercised through the act of their collection exist in a world where issue advocacy still normally occurs in public fora—through council meetings, neighborhood association meetings, or a range of locally developed processes that are in place to both solicit specific feedback regarding governance and urban planning [16]. Indeed, the notion of digital democracy is to augment those in-person processes with technology tools rather than replace them outright [14]. However, by shifting civic engagement from a synchronous experience of advocacy via discourse in public fora to an asynchronous experience where advocacy occurs via collected data, we dramatically change the conditions of public participation and introduce new forms of argumentation into the milieu.

Just as van Dijk enumerated how the affordances of different systems amplify and impede different democratic ends [40], the affordances of the smartphones and the particular design choices made in two transportation apps discussed here come with inherent limitations on how the public participates. By focusing exclusively on mobile interactions, these systems privilege data collection and as a consequence, impede alternate forms of providing feedback and input: if cyclists or transit riders are not participating in the civic data ecosystem then they become less visible to governing institutions and less able to act in response to new data and information flows enabled by this ecosystem.

At a minimum, addressing the challenges of broadening public involvement through data-based civic participation means engaging with the epistemic questions bound up in data as a form of participation. We need to be able to account for data production [17, 30], attending to the ways the data often convey authority divorced from the agency motivating their production [22]. Building up new practices of civic participation could be accomplished by attending to two theoretical and practical areas: first, addressing the challenge of linking individual acts of data production through person devices to forms of collective action, thereby supporting the formation of publics around a shared set of issues [20, 21]; second, examining the practices that emerge around app use and participation in digital modes of civic participation so that expectations for impact and relevancy are met with appropriate feedback mechanisms to help sustain participation over time. Ultimately, meaningful public participation is an expression of agency, of expertise, of tacit knowledge, and of individual and community identity. As we continue to develop and broaden the scope of civic data ecosystems, we need to attend to these attributes and seek productive partnerships between citizens, institutions, and the technologies upon which they increasingly rely.

References

1. Barbeau, S.J., Borning, A., Watkins, K.: OneBusAway multi-region—rapidly expanding mobile transit apps to new cities. J. Public Transp. **17**(4), 14 (2014)
2. Brakewood, C., Barbeau, S., Watkins, K.: An experiment evaluating the impacts of real-time transit information on bus riders in Tampa, Florida. Transp. Res. Part A **69**, 409–422 (2014)
3. Brakewood, C., Macfarlane, G., Watkins, K.E.: The impact of real-time information on bus ridership in New York city. Transp. Res. Part C **53**, 59–75 (2015)
4. Carrel, A., Halvorsen, A., Walker, J.L.: Passengers' perception of and behavioral adaptation to unreliability in public transportation. Transp. Res. Rec. J. Transp. Res. Board **2351**(1), 153–162 (2013)
5. Carroll, J.M., Rosson, M.B.: A trajectory for community networks. Inf. Soc. **19**(5), 381–393 (2003)
6. Carroll, J.M., Rosson, M.B.: Wild at home: the neighborhood as a living laboratory for HCI. ACM Trans. Comput. Hum. Interact. **20**(3), 1–28 (2013)

7. Doran, D., Gokhale, S., Dagnino, A.: Human sensing for smart cities. In: Proceedings of the 2013 IEEE/ACM International Conference on Advances in Social Networks Analysis and Mining, pp. 1323–1330. ACM (2013)
8. Erickson, T., Podlaseck, M., Sahu, S., Dai, J.D., Chao, T., Naphade, M.: The Dubuque water portal: evaluation of the uptake, use and impact of residential water consumption feedback. In: Proceedings of the SIGCHI Conference on Human Factors in Computing Systems, pp. 675–684. ACM (2012)
9. Ferris, B., Watkins, K., Borning, A.: OneBusAway: results from providing real-time arrival information for public transit. In: Proceedings of the SIGCHI Conference on Human Factors in Computing Systems, pp. 1807–1816 (2010)
10. Frank, L.D., Andresen, M.A., Schmid, T.L.: Obesity relationships with community design, physical activity, and time spent in cars. Am. J. Prev. Med. 27(2), 87–96 (2004)
11. Gooze, A., Watkins, K.E., Borning, A.: Benefits of real-time transit information and impacts of data accuracy on rider experience. Transp. Res. Rec. J. Transp. Res. Board 2351(1), 95–103 (2013)
12. Gordon, E., Schirra, S., Hollander, J.: Immersive planning: a conceptual model for designing public participation with new technologies. Environ. Plan. 38, 509–519 (2011)
13. Granovetter, M.S.: The strength of weak ties. Am. J. Sociol. 78(6), 1360–1380 (1973)
14. Hacker, K.L., van Dijk, J. (eds.): Digital Democracy: Issues of Theory and Practice. Sage Publications Inc., Thousand Oaks (2001)
15. Hippel, E.: Democratizing Innovation. MIT Press, Cambridge (2005)
16. Innes, J.E.: Information in communicative planning. J. Am. Plann. Assoc. 64(1), 52–63 (2007)
17. Klaebe, H., Adkins, B., Foth, M., Hearn, G.: Embedding an ecology notion in the social production of urban space. In: Foth, M. (ed.) Handbook of Research on Urban Informatics: The Practice and Promise of the Real-Time City. Information Science Reference, pp. 179–194. IGI Global, Hershey (2009)
18. Kling, R.: Automated information systems as social resources in policy making. In: ACM 1978 Proceedings of the 1978 Annual Conference, pp. 666–674. ACM (1978)
19. Kling, R.: Automated welfare client-tracking and service integration: the political economy of computing. Commun. ACM 21(6), 484–493 (1978)
20. Le Dantec, C.A.: Participation and publics: supporting community engagement. In: CHI 2012 Proceedings of SIGCHI Conference on Human Factors in Computing Systems, pp. 1351–1360 (2012)
21. Le Dantec, C.A., DiSalvo, C.F.: Infrastructuring and the formation of publics in participatory design. Soc. Stud. Sci. 43(2), 241–264 (2013)
22. Le Dantec, C.A., Asad, M., Misra, A., Watkins, K.: Planning with crowdsourced data: rhetoric and representation in transportation planning. In: CSCW 2015 (2015) (to appear)
23. Le Dantec, C.A., Farrell, R.G., Christensen, J.E., Bailey, M., Ellis, J.B., Kellogg, W.A., Edwards, W.K.: Publics in practice: ubiquitous computing at a shelter for homeless mothers. In: CHI 2011 Proceedings of the SIGCHI Conference on Human Factors in Computing Systems, ACM Request Permissions, pp. 1687–1696 (2011)
24. Morozov, E.: The Net Delusion. PublicAffairs, Philadelphia (2011)
25. Norman, D.A.: The Psychology of Everyday Things. Basic Books, New York (1988)
26. Olivares, T., Royo, F., Ortiz, A.M.: An experimental testbed for smart cities applications. In: Proceedings of the 11th ACM International Symposium on Mobility Management and Wireless Access, pp. 115–118. ACM (2013)
27. OneBusAway, ed. OneBusAway frequency of stop access over 24-hours (2011)

28. Perera, C., Zaslavsky, A., Christen, P., Georgakopoulos, D.: Sensing as a service model for smart cities supported by internet of things. Trans. Emerg. Telecommun. Technol. **25**(1), 81–93 (2014)

29. Pinkett, R., O'Bryant, R.: Building community, empowerment and self-sufficiency. Inf. Commun. Soc. **6**(2), 187–210 (2003)

30. Räsänen, M., Nyce, J.M.: The raw is cooked: data in intelligence pracitce. Sci. Technol. Human Values **38**(5), 655–677 (2013)

31. Rogers, E.M., Collins-Jarvis, L., Schmitz, J.: The PEN project in Santa Monica: interactive communication, equality, and political action. J. Am. Soc. Inf. Sci. **45**(6), 401–410 (1994)

32. Roitman, H., Mamou, J., Mehta, S., Satt, A., Subramaniam, L.V.: Harnessing the crowds for smart city sensing. In: Proceedings of the 1st International Workshop on Multimodal Crowd Sensing, pp. 17–18. ACM (2012)

33. Sackman, H.: A public philosophy for real time information systems. In: AFIPS 1968 (Fall, Part II): Proceedings of the December 9–11, 1968, Fall Joint Computer Conference, Part II, pp. 1491–1498. ACM (1968)

34. Shirky, C.: Here Comes Everybody. The Penguin Press, New York (2008)

35. Steinfeld, A., Zimmerman, J., Tomasic, A., Yoo, D., Aziz, R.D.: Mobile transit information from universal design and crowdsourcing. Transp. Res. Rec. J. Transp. Res. Board **2217**(1), 95–102 (2011)

36. Tang, L., Thakuriah, P.V.: Ridership effects of real-time bus information system: a case study in the city of Chicago. Transp. Res. Part C **22**, 146–161 (2012)

37. Transportation Research Board of the National Academies. Critical Issues in Transportation (2013)

38. US Environmental Protection Agency. Fast Facts: US Transportation Sector Greenhouse Gas Emissions, 1990–2011 (2013)

39. Vakali, A., Anthopoulos, L., Krco, S.: Smart cities data streams integration: experimenting with internet of things and social data flows. In: Proceedings of the 4th International Conference on Web Intelligence, Mining and Semantics (WIMS 2014), pp. 60:1–60:5. ACM (2014)

40. van Dijk, J.: Models of democracy and concepts of communication. In: Hacker, K.L., van Dijk, J. (eds.) Digital Democracy: Issues of Theory and Practice, pp. 30–53. Sage Publications Ltd., Thousand Oaks (2000)

41. Voida, A., Dombrowski, L., Hayes, G.R., Mazmanian, M.: Shared values/conflicting logics: working around e-government systems. In: CHI 2014 Proceedings of the 32nd Annual ACM Conference on Human Factors in Computing Systems, pp. 3583–3592 (2014)

42. Watkins, K.E., Ferris, B., Borning, A., Rutherford, G.S., Layton, D.: Where is my bus? Impact of mobile real-time information on the perceived and actual wait time of transit riders. Transp. Res. Part A **45**(8), 839–848 (2011)

43. Wong, J.: Leveraging the general transit feed specification for efficient transit analysis. Transp. Res. Rec. J. Transp. Res. Board **2338**(1), 11–19 (2013)

44. Zhang, F., Shen, Q., Clifton, K.J.: Examination of traveler responses to real-time information about bus arrivals using panel data. Transp. Res. Rec. J. Transp. Res. Board **2082**(1), 107–115 (2008)

45. Zimmerman, J., Tomasic, A., Garrod, C., Yoo, D., Hiruncharoenvate, C., Aziz, R., Thiruvengadam, N.R., Huang, Y., Steinfeld, A.: Field trial of tiramisu: crowd-sourcing bus arrival times to spur co-design. In: Proceedings of the SIGCHI Conference on Human Factors in Computing Systems, pp. 1677–1686 (2011)

Post-mortem Digital Legacy:
Possibilities in HCI

Cristiano Maciel[(✉)] and Vinicius Carvalho Pereira

Laboratório de Ambientes Virtuais Interativos (LAVI), Universidade Federal de
Mato Grosso (UFMT), Cuiabá, MT, Brazil
{crismac,viniciuscarpe}@gmail.com

Abstract. As designers and stakeholders attentive to HCI issues, it is para-
mount to understand questions such as death and post-mortem digital legacy and
how they affect systems development. This paper presents current discussions
about that topic, by presenting a brief overview of what has been produced by
the HCI community on death and digital legacy and some of the solutions
created to address those phenomena. Such solutions include adaptations to
already-existing tools, such as Facebook and its memorial profiles, as well as the
creation of new tools for the domain of death, such as social networks for dead
people's profiles. However, the implementation of those technologies demand
further studies on the differences between law systems and belief systems
regarding death and what can be considered either universal or particular in the
understanding of death. Therefore, there is an urge for more interdisciplinary
studies on this topic, so as to bring to HCI discussions different perspectives,
theories and methods that can be used in the study of death.

Keywords: Post-mortem digital legacy · Posthumous interaction · Death

1 Introduction

The birth and death of an individual within computational environments, such as the
web, are not in line with those phenomena in the real world, where different devices
and strategies are created to identify an individual throughout life in order to safeguard
his rights and legacy. So far, there are no legal means to certify the digital "birth" or
"death" of a person.

Many profiles, accounts, files etc. are daily created with technological devices, thus
requiring data management not only for lifelong purposes, but also for posthumous use.
With little legislation regarding post-mortem data, a challenge rises: the different loci,
formats and devices for storing such information [8].

In this context, a series of issues come up and point towards different researches in
the field, among which we highlight: How do users re-signify a death experience in the
digital environment, taking into account all the different stakeholders of this event (who
dies, who stays, who leaves a legacy and who inherits it)? Besides, how can designers
produce mechanisms for the user to determine his volition regarding the destination of
his digital data? However, such problems do come across human values, especially

© Springer International Publishing Switzerland 2015
M. Kurosu (Ed.): Human-Computer Interaction, Part III, HCII 2015, LNCS 9171, pp. 339–349, 2015.
DOI: 10.1007/978-3-319-21006-3_33

ethical ones, which greatly influence how researchers, designers, users and research subjects think and approach issues related to death.

Besides, developing applications with that purpose poses not only challenges to modeling death and managing data left by the deceased person, but also for designers and software engineers to deal with taboos and beliefs on death [7], which define how far they can go when designing solutions. Furthermore, in applications like digital memorials, which pay homage to the deceased, there are other concerns regarding updating and maintaining those memorials, especially when that is done by means of social networks, where different users can be connected to a memorial [21].

Designers and stakeholders, looking out for aspects of human-computer interaction (HCI), need to understand how issues about post-mortem digital legacy affect system development. We believe this is a discussion of facts and possibilities for HCI professionals and the scientific community, due to the need to design complex systems for interaction beyond the user's lifespan.

2   The Theme in Some HCI Communities

In 2012, in an initiative associated with the Special Commission of Human-Computer Interaction (SCHCI) of the Brazilian Computation Society (BCS), an open call was made to the scientific community and the country's professionals from the field, for the "GranDIHC-BR: Big HCI research challenges in Brazil", within HCI'12. At the time, researchers identified the main challenges, as presented in [1], among which we can highlight the ones related to human values, such as *Privacy in a connected world* and *Posthumous interaction and post-mortem digital legacy*. The aspects aforementioned also affect another challenge: *HCI Formation and Job Market*, once many applications regarding death and related phenomena have been developed.

Themes that associate technologies with death have called the scientific community's attention, which has been discussing them in scientific events and publications. In the 2011 and 2012 editions of ACM SIGCHI Conference on Human Factors in Computing Systems (CHI), workshops related to the theme were held. In 2010, [10] promoted at CHI the workshop "HCI at the end of life: Understanding death, dying, and the digital", so as to foster the investigation regarding the intersection of subjects related to the finitude of life (mortality, dying and death) in the scope of thanatosensitivity. For the authors, mortality is an intrinsic and permanent state throughout people's lives. Death, however, is a singular and temporally limited event. For them, the process of dying is an intermediate term, in which the individual is in a state of physiological decline (for example in case of morbid diseases and advanced age) that is imminently turned towards death, but not necessarily immediate to it. In the same year, Massimi and Baecker published paper on related themes, focusing on bereavement [13]. Those discussions stem from a previous exploratory research [11], published in the same conference.

In 2012's CHI, held in Austin/TX, the workshop *"Memento Mori: Technology Design for the End of Life"* [12] occurred, thus allowing the sharing of researches and inquiries regarding the theme among researchers from several countries. The Latin phrase *memento mori*, translated into English as "remember that you will die", gains new meanings with the development of new technologies for people who prepare for death and reflect on the destination of their legacy, including data that will be left behind for posthumous interaction. We must also mention end-of-life technologies, whose purpose is to give support to people that are getting closer to death, in order to mitigate pain and allow a positive reframing for those going through such event. In contact with researchers during that conference, a book was written and published on HCI and death [7].

In Brazil, "interaction with posthumous or post-mortem data" is among the topics of interest in CEIHC's annual event: Brazilian Symposium on Human Factors in Computing Systems (IHC). Such topic was included among the hot ones in 2012, with the arising of papers from researches regarding this content. In 2014, at IHC'14, the trail "*GranDICH-BR position papers*" has amplified the opportunity to discuss the theme, as there was a call for papers on research challenges for that community.

Notice that, although the book written by Carroll and Romano in 2011 [2] does not focus on HCI, it brings important reflections on the value of digital legacy and the relevance of discussing it in terms of computers and devices, e-mail, social websites and finance and commerce, including topics like awareness, access and wishes.

3 Some Researches in the Field

Even though there are already applications dealing with issues related to the end of life, this still remains an intimidating area, especially if we consider the taboos involving the theme [7]. As we can see, the end of life is an attractive dominion for research due to several reasons – multidisciplinary, social and cultural ones, but particularly due to the technological challenges in dealing with it.

The immortality of the individual and his information divides opinions [14]. The so-called "preservationists" defend that legacy must be left to a person's descendants; whereas "deletionists" say that internet still needs to learn how to forget. The inventory of data produced by physical and digital objects proposed by [2] is intended to emphasize that the responsibility for such data needs to be discussed in light of digital legacy and its "heirs". In simpler terms, [2] defines that a digital legacy is the sum of digital possession that you have left for others. Since the digital change continues to go on, digital possession left will become the majority of your legacy. Anyway, enthusiasts are already trying to guarantee that digital legacy is maintained alive on the internet, as can be seen from the birth of software and services industries [2] which help the user manage his "posthumous" information. Even if only briefly, the authors analyze user terms from Facebook, Gmail, Twitter, Yahoo and YouTube, regarding the treatment of post-mortem legacy. For those who use systems that do not hold responsibility for user's digital legacy, [2] suggest the adoption of a regular spreadsheet for the record of one's digital assets and its respective authentication methods, such as logins and passwords.

In 2009, [11] introduced the term "thanatosensitivity" to describe an approach that actively integrates facts about human mortality, dying and death in HCI researches and design. In that paper, initial issues are approached and they make it evident that the research and development potential of such area is big. In another study, [9] investigated grief in digital environments. In that study, we can highlight the fact that the logistics of distribution of digital assets after death is a non-considered or neglected problem among the majority of the people interviewed (79 %). The authors indicate two main reasons why the interviewees did not consider this possibility: (a) they were simply not ready to think about a will because they were too young; and (b) they see their personal computer as a functional electronic device (just like a TV) and not as a data storage device. Based on the field research results, the authors raise two ethical questions related to digital legacy: (a) the inheritance of another person's data implies a set of social commitments and ethics regarding the digital legacy; and (b) the records of technological life can be used and revisited, with new meanings, by family members of the deceased person.

Regarding virtual property in digital worlds, [6] defends that it should be treated by law as material property. In this sense, users must think in advance and state their will regarding their digital assets. Concerning the planning of design solutions for post-humous legacy in social networks, the research made with software engineers by [8] investigates the following possibilities: (a) to attribute password power to third parties, in life or in will, thus declaring the desire for posthumous interaction; (b) to have a record of one's digital legacy in other equipment or in the web, so that no login is required for access; (c) to maintain a bond with real-world institutions and documents to check whether the user really died; and (d) to provide social web applications with resources for the user to state his volition. Such possibilities allow an investigation of the needs of products (applications) and users from the point of view of developers, so as to bring more subsides to the discussion of the theme in the HCI community.

In addition, that same research with software engineers evidenced their taboos and beliefs when it comes to death [8]. Seven categories were generated contemplating implicit or explicit taboos and beliefs concerning death in the software developers' suggestions, as follows: non-profanable legacy, funeral rites, the immaterial beyond death, death as an end, death as an adversity, death as an interdiction and the space required by death.

In another research about social networks, the authors [20] carried out a series of in-depth qualitative interviews to explore issues around inheritance and post-mortem data management of Facebook accounts. They concluded "participants focused less on ownership of the data, and instead on the duties and potential conflicts associated with maintaining an account post-mortem". As a solution, the authors proposed "stewardship as an alternative to inheritance for framing post-mortem data management practices", discussing a model with interpersonal responsibilities that accompany digital assets.

For [13], HCI studies must frame death in a lifespan-oriented approach. According to different authors, there are four concepts relevant for the work in this area: life, death, the dead and mourning; and there are so far four themed areas of interest for research on the end of life: materiality, identity, temporality and ethics/methods. It is also worth mentioning that, among the design directions proposed by the authors, the "interactive technologies and systems could be designed that empower all of us, as mortals, to engage in end of life planning more readily, or to make arrangements more easily. And finally, we can consider how systems might empower people who have died to maintain a digital identity that preserves their integrity and desires in this life; or, to deliver messages for loved ones into the future."

Furthermore, it is necessary to study the most tangible aspect of post-death digital legacy: the posthumous interaction relations [7] represented by the manifestations of grief left on the internet, such as the creation of groups specifically for one person, the insertion of the word "grief" in a profile (as Brazilians often do), or even visits to posthumous profiles on the social web. In those visits, one may, for example, leave messages that express the feeling of missing the dead person as well as talk about death itself. The study proposed by Maciel and Pereira [7] seeks to understand how the internet generation deals with these interactions on social networks, in order to guide projects concerning the specificities of this type of social relation. In that study, the research was conducted with 78 adolescents of the internet generation. The interaction between systems and data from dead people or between users and dead people via system is what authors call posthumous interaction. Surprisingly, 59 % of those who are on social networks have already interacted in their network with the profile of a dead person. As the notion of death within these young users it is still being built, this issue deserves to be further investigated in light of posthumous interaction. Additionally, the possibility of interacting like that through digital memorials is another area that requires more research [21].

On the other hand, [23] affirm that, although older people should be more prone to cope with a digital inheritance, they are poorly equipped to do so. Their research aimed to understand older adults' preferences regarding digital legacy. Sourced films and artifacts were used as envisionment prompts to elicit values in a series of focus groups, with older people and in intergenerational workshops, including digital natives. As to the theoretical framework, value-sensitive design (VSD) was the main influence. The authors highlight that "older adults constitute a genuine and important 'public' and should certainly have a voice in digital legacy design. They are a group likely to be more familiar with bereavement than their younger counterparts".

By amplifying the concept of Extended Episodic Experience, [5] refers to it as the long term experience that combines multiple individual events in different spaces and times, for the understanding of digital legacy and how interaction is affected by the outlook of death. Other than pictures and messages, we have what authors consider to be an intangible legacy, such as feelings and emotions, which emerge from the interaction with other users. With the purpose of investigating Facebook users regarding their plans for the posthumous management of personal data, the authors have conducted an on-line survey and a focus group, in which the user's emotions regarding these themes could also be observed. As a result, the conclusion was that users expect that the design of applications created towards digital legacy must be based on virtues, and not only on issues such as usability and effectiveness. As virtues, the authors list moral and social impacts, which require the understanding of what it means to be a human being.

The paper by [17] aimed to answer the following question: "What should be the fate of digital footprints after our death?" The authors carried out a crowdsourced online survey with 400 participants from United States, India, Great Britain and Asia. They investigated how users want their digital footprint handled after their death, how they would like to communicate these preferences, and whom they would entrust with carrying out this part of their will. The research investigated project decisions for a digital stewardship to be offered as an online service and it was found out the participants wanted a nonprofit service. According to the authors [17], "Interestingly, responses across countries and religions were similar". As it has been stated by other researchers, people do not often think about the fate of their digital legacy. Additionally, this paper shows people want to have their accounts deleted in case a death certificate is provided.

As it can be seen, there are researches in several fields, regarding technical, legal, cultural and affective aspects related to death digital legacy and posthumous interaction, which are worth investigating. In the market, some systems and/or functionalities have been created to deal with users' death and its unfolding, as discussed in the next section.

3.1 Solutions Implemented

In order to improve the strategies that have been used in the area of post-mortem digital legacy and posthumous interaction, we must constantly analyze and question the applications available in the market.

In Brazil, Google has released "Google Inactive Accounts", which allows data management of users' accounts [7]. This functionality is available in the settings tab (www.google.com/settings) at "Account Management". This way, the user can set a digital will, by defining the destiny of his post-mortem legacy (pictures, e-mails and files associated to the user's Google account). This system offers the following management options: Supplying an alternative cellphone number and e-mail for alert; defining a deadline for the account to remain inactive; notifying contacts and sharing data; deleting the account after certain actions defined by the user have been performed.

There is a form that can be filled in on Facebook (www.facebook.com/help/contact) where one can request the deletion of a deceased person's account or its transforming into a memorial. In case of requiring the removal of a profile removal from the web, it is necessary to fill in the form and send the profile owner's death certificate. According to that form, Facebook does not forward to a third party any login information, so as to preserve its users' privacy.

Facebook has recently launched a tool that will enable the user to name someone to be contacted in case of his death, so as to take control of his account. This inheritance system will initially be used in the USA, but it is intended to be expanded to other countries. [22]. The heir will be able to: (1) accept new friend requests; (2) accept to be tagged in photos; (3) pin a post on the top of the timeline; (4) change profile photo and cover photo; and (5) download files from the account, such as photos. However, inbox messages will remain inaccessible. The inherited account will be like an additional account for the heir, but he will get no notifications from the additional one, so as not to be bothered.

Such a solution is an important advance, but there are implications that must be carefully considered, such as the peculiarities of each country's legal system and the details of the heir's responsibilities (and if they meet his desires).

In addition to that, technologies have been used in funerary rites, such as TV broadcasting of wakes and burials, as well as posts on social networks about funerary ceremonies, often posted by the deceased person's relatives. Likewise, it is worth mentioning the virtualization of memorials, through digital memorial software programs, which allow posting tributes for the dead ones, such as iHeaven (http://www.iheaven.me/) and Digital Memorial (http://www.digital-memorial.com/). As for the last one, notice that it provides QR Codes and NFC for inscriptions on gravestones, thus connecting a physical memorial to its digital counterpart.

The use of digital technologies in cemeteries is increasingly common. Cann (2013) examines QR codes and the impact of smartphone technology on tombstones and columbaria [16]. The author briefly surveys Human-Computer Interaction related to smart chip technology in the funeral industry in Japan, Korea, China, the United Kingdom and the United States, and how tombstone technology impacts the way people think about death and remember the dead, particularly in terms of religious expression.

In Brazil, such use of QR codes can be used in Consolação Cemetery, in Sao Paulo. There are totems spread throughout the graveyard, which permit the access to each grave positioning, by means of QR code. Similar tags can be found in some of the graves, especially those of famous people, which are linked to virtual memorials of the deceased. The virtual memorials are provided by MemoriAll (www.memoriall.com.br) and they present information about bios, genealogical tree, photos, videos, obituary and messages. Although this is an interesting strategy that helps finding a grave and learning about the deceased, there is a need for more interactive features in the memorials, which could allow the insertion of online contents about the honored person. Some recommendations for the development of digital memorials can be found at [21].

Furthermore, different software programs help in the managing of accounts, by sending users posthumous messages and/or passwords. In the "If I die" app (https://www.ifidie.org/), users can write a note, which is stored and sent to the destiny user in case of death. The page suggests that the note should contain passwords and instructions of what to do with the dead user's data. As to http://LegacyLocker.com, it is an example of a software program that works as a repository for accounts data, which are forwarded to the named heirs after the user's death. There are also software programs that can prolong "digital life", such as Liveson (http://liveson.org), which continues to tweet even after the user's death, based on an analysis of the user's previous tweets, so as to follow text and informational patterns used in life.

4   Research Possibilities in HCI Field

The study of after-death digital legacy brings many possibilities for investigation in HCI. Based on what has been showed, it is recommended for interested parties to take into account:

1. Pertinent issues related to research on death in digital environments

   - Fomenting methodological and epistemological interdisciplinarity with the fields of Law, Letters, Psychology, Sociology, History, Anthropology, Archeology and Librarianship, for example, so that systemic and computational issues can be discussed;

- Questioning the researchers' and designers' conceptions of mortality, to investigate how the proposition of research methods and computational solutions for the end of life may be influenced by taboos regarding death;
- Conducting studies in light of human values models, especially Value-Sensitive Design (VSD), pertinent to studies in HCI [4, 18];

2. Issues related to data management

- Questioning the persistency of users' online memory, by means of data that can't be managed in systems or under the responsibility of a third party;
- Discussing the setting of users' volition, via system, in regards to the destination of their after-death data [5, 8]. There are many ways to set users' whishes and every one of them affects posthumous interaction, thus causing reactions on users;
- Designing more "visible" terms of use and privacy, so as to allow a greater interaction between the user and his rights and obligations towards the application regarding after-death matters;
- Considering how digital footprints should be handled after death., along with issues as security and privacy of a deceased user's data [18, 19];
- Investigating the impact of digital wills automatically created by the system or manually written by the user [2], especially when it comes to succession responsibilities (rights and obligations of virtual heirs on the digital assets of the dead person, under a legal perspective);
- Considering data management in systems within each user's life cycle, from the creation of the account to the possibility of its exclusion or maintenance, i.e., designing the change of a user's status as dead or alive. Digital life lasts longer than corporeal life, and software limitations make it difficult to model such aspects on the internet;
- Observing that design strategies for digital after-death legacy differ as to the type of data (text, picture, video, audio and geolocation data...), spread in different devices and application domains;

3. Diversity of users and their views regarding death

- Ensuring the respect to cultural diversity in systems development, especially when it comes to religion matters [17, 18], especially when it comes to eschatology;
- Observing the difference between users from different digital generations [7] during design stage, by investigating how such generations react facing themes related to death in the digital environment;

4. New communication and interaction practices related to death

- Analyzing posthumous interaction and the supposed communication with the deceased via system;
- Discussing how mourners and their groups (including family, friends...) communicate about the dead person [9];
- Investigating and proposing solutions for the digital communicational practices that are disrespectful towards death;

- Studying and designing Technologies for the end of one's life, which may be used by patients at their final years;
- Studying new possibilities of interaction with dead people's data, such as the use of QR codes integrated to graves [7], digital memorials [14, 21] etc.

5 Conclusion

Even though the themes related to after-life digital legacy are a part of humans' lives, when conducting researches in this field it is necessary to have an adequate epistemological and methodological posture to approach such matter. Contrary to many HCI research fields, death and mortality are rarely likely to be studied in a laboratory [11]. Therefore, HCI researchers, through theoretical and practical studies, which are in general interdisciplinary, must feel encouraged to perform researches that include users in the design process and in the use of technologies made for this purpose, by using methods, techniques and proper instruments. Needless to say, theories from the humanities and from hard sciences must be brought together in these studies, so as to approach death and its complexities.

It is also noteworthy that different technologies have been developed to address the phenomenon of death, ranging from the adaptation of social networks to the death of its users to social networks especially developed for memorials. This is a sign that new interactive patterns are coming up, which require novel understandings of what it means to interact, either with an alive or with a dead person. Besides, technologies such as QR codes on graves establish an unprecedented bond between death representations in the physical world and in the virtual one, and that unfolds into funeral rites, bereavement expressions and mourning that blend both worlds.

Finally, one cannot disregard that discussing death and legacy entails a constant need to balance universals and local particularities, both in terms of belief systems and in terms of law. Each religion defines certain rules, prohibitions or uses that are to be adopted upon preparing to die or reacting to someone's death. Likewise, legal systems vary considerably when it comes to heritage, property and even regarding the possibility of a dead person having rights. That poses a challenge to researching and designing for death, to the extent that ethical, technical, cultural and legal issues must be considered when addressing such a complex phenomenon – the only one every single person is to experience someday.

References

1. Baranauskas, C., de Souza, C.S., Pereira, R.: I GranDIHC-BR - Grandes Desafios de Pesquisa em Interação Humano-Computador no Brasil. Relatório Técnico. Comissão Especial de Interação Humano-Computador (CEIHC) da Sociedade Brasileira de Computação (SBC), pp. 27–30 (2014)
2. Carrol, E., Romano, J.: Your Digital Afterlife: When Facebook, Flickr and Twitter are your estate, What's Your Legacy?, p. 216. New Riders Pub., Berkeley (2010)

3. Paul-Chouddhury, S.: Qual será o destino da sua alma digital? InfoExame, Ed.Abril, pp. 84–87. SP (2011)
4. Le Dantec, C.A., Poole, E.S., Wyche, S.P.: Values as lived experience: envolving value sensitive design in support of value discovery. In: CHI 2009 (2009)
5. Khalid, H., Dix, A.: Extended episodic experience in social mediating technology: our legacy. In: Meiselwitz, G. (ed.) SCSM 2014. LNCS, vol. 8531, pp. 452–461. Springer, Heidelberg (2014)
6. Lastowka, G.: Virtual Justice: The New Laws of Online Worlds. Yale University Press, London (2010)
7. Maciel, C., Pereira, V.C.: Digital Legacy and Interaction: Post-Mortem Issues. Human–Computer Interaction Series, p. 144. Springer, Switzerland (2013)
8. Maciel, C.: Issues of the social web interaction project faced with afterlife digital legacy. In: Proceedings of IHC+CLIHC 2011, pp. 3–12. ACM Press (2011)
9. Massimi, M., Baecker, R.M.: A death in the family: opportunities for designing technologies for the bereaved. In: Proceedings of CHI 2010, pp. 1821–1830. ACM Press (2010)
10. Massimi, M., Odom, W., Kirk, D., Banks, R.: HCI at the end of life: understanding death, dying, and the digital. In: Proceedings of CHI 2010 Extended Abstracts, pp. 4477–4480 (2010)
11. Massimi, M., Charise, A.: Dying, death, and mortality: towards thanatosensitivity in HCI. In: Proceedings of CHI 2009 Extended Abstracts, pp. 2459–2468 (2009)
12. Massimi, M., Moncur, W., Odom, W., Banks, R., Kirk, D.: Memento mori: technology design for the end of life. In: Proceedings of CIII 2012 Extended Abstracts, pp. 2759–2762 (2012)
13. Massimi, M., Odom, W., Banks, R., Kirk, D.. Matters of life and death: locating the end of life in lifespan-oriented HCI research. In: Proceedings of CHI 2011, pp. 987–996. ACM Press (2011)
14. Lopes, A.D., Maciel, C., Pereira, C.V.: Recomendações para o design de memórias digitais na web social. In: Proceedings of the 13th Brazilian Symposium on Human Factors in Computing Systems (IHC 2014), pp. 275–284. Sociedade Brasileira de Computação, Porto Alegre, Brazil (2014)
15. CNN: Facebook now lets you post when you're dead. CNNMoney, New York, 12 February 2015. http://money.cnn.com/2015/02/12/technology/facebook-legacy-contact/
16. Cann, C.: Tombostone technology deathscapes in Asia, the U.K. and the U.S. In: Maciel, C., Pereira, V.C. (eds.) Digital Legacy and Interaction: Post-Mortem Issues. Human–Computer Interaction Series, pp. 101–113. Springer, Switzerland (2013)
17. Grimm, C., Chiasson, S.: Survey on the fate of digital footprints after death. In: Workshop on Usable Security (USEC). Internet Society (2014)
18. Maciel, C., Pereira, V.C.: Social network users' religiosity and the design of post mortem aspects. In: Kotzé, P., Marsden, G., Lindgaard, G., Wesson, J., Winckler, M. (eds.) INTERACT 2013, Part III. LNCS, vol. 8119, pp. 640–657. Springer, Heidelberg (2013)
19. Locasto, M.E., Massimi, M., De Pasquale, P.J.: Security and privacy considerations in digital death. In: Proceedings of the 2011 Workshop on New Security Paradigms, pp. 1–10 (2011)
20. Brubaker, J.R., Dombrowski, L., Gilbert, A., Kusumakaulika, N., Hayes, G.R.: Stewarding a legacy: responsibilities and relationships in the management of post-mortem data. In: Proceedings of CHI 2014, April 26–May 1. Toronto, Canada (2014)
21. Lopes, A.D., Maciel, C., Pereira, V.C.: Virtual homage to the dead: an analysis of digital memorials in the social web. In: Proceedings of HCI International 2014, pp. 67–78. Heraklion, Crete, Greece (2014)

22. Facebook Memoralization Request. https://www.facebook.com/help/contact/305593649477238
23. Thomas, L., Briggs, P.: An older adult perspective on digital legacy. In: Proceedings of the 8th Nordic Conference on Human-Computer Interaction: Fun, Fast, Foundational (NordiCHI 2014), pp. 237–246. ACM, New York (2014)

Fukushima No. 1 Nuclear Power Plant: The Moment of "Safety Myth" Collapses

Aki Nakanishi[1], Toshio Takagi[2(✉)], Hajime Ushimaru[1],
Masato Yotsumoto[3], and Daisuke Sugihara[1]

[1] Meiji University, Tokyo, Japan
aki.nakanishi@nifty.com, ushimaru@meiji.ac.jp,
seventh.monster@gmail.com
[2] Okinawa University, Okinawa, Japan
toshio@takagi-lab.net
[3] Kanto Gakuin University, Yokohama, Japan
miyabi-4@xa2.so-net.ne.jp

Abstract. This study examines the conversations and actions of the operators and managers of the Tokyo Electric Power Company (TEPCO) on March 11, 2011, when Fukushima No. 1 nuclear power plant (1F) suffered a "severe accident" due to the Great East Japan Earthquake and the subsequent tsunami. Using the archives from TEPCO's videoconference system, we conducted a network and content analysis of discussions and steps that were taken on the cutting edge of organizational crises. Staff members at the various sites (1F operators and managers, as well as employees at Headquarters and the Offsite Center) used different vocabulary, which meant they could not build a shared organizational reality of the ongoing crisis.

1 Introduction

In this study we explored the conversations and actions that took place at Fukushima No. 1 nuclear power plant (1F), Headquarters, and the Offsite Center of the Tokyo Electric Power Company (TEPCO) after 1F suffered a "severe accident" due to the Great East Japan Earthquake and the related tsunami on March 11, 2011., Using "the videoconference system" archives[1] disclosed by TEPCO, we explain how TEPCO staff had difficulty building a common reality in the face of a drastically unfamiliar situation.

Our research methods involved network and content analysis, which proved useful under circumstances with many different actors and locations. Using these methods, at first, we review the TEPCO videoconference files and our method of analysis. Next, we explain the results of the network and content analysis. Lastly, we discuss the outcomes.

This presentation paper is excerpted from Nakanishi et al. (2014).

---

[1] http://photo.tepco.co.jp/date/2012/201210-j/121005-01j.html.
http://photo.tepco.co.jp/date/2013/201303-j/130306-01j.html.
http://photo.tepco.co.jp/date/2013/201303-j/130029-01j.html.

© Springer International Publishing Switzerland 2015
M. Kurosu (Ed.): Human-Computer Interaction, Part III, HCII 2015, LNCS 9171, pp. 350–357, 2015.
DOI: 10.1007/978-3-319-21006-3_34

2 The Analytical Framework

2.1 Data

What follows is the sequence of events triggered by the Great East Japan Earthquake, as recorded by TEPCO's videoconference system.

March 11, 2011

2:46pm	The Great East Japan Earthquake occurs.
3:35pm	The tsunami hits 1F.
3:35-41pm	1F loses all power.
9:23pm	An evacuation order is issued within a 3km circumference of 1F.

March 12, 2011

3:36pm	A hydrogen explosion damages the Unit 1 reactor building.
6:25pm	An evacuation order is issued within a 20km circumference of 1F.
10:59pm	The TEPCO videoconference system begins recording.

March 13, 2011

Before dawn	The water injection facility of the Unit 3 reactor stops functioning and the reactor pressure increases.
9:25am	Cool water is injected into Unit 3 reactor.

March 14, 2011

11:01am	A hydrogen explosion damages the Unit 3 reactor building.
1:30pm	Pressure increases in the Unit 2 reactor.
11:20pm	The nuclear fuel rod of the Unit 2 reactor is exposed, and the reactor pressure vessel vents.

March 15, 2011

5:36am	Prime Minister Kan visits TEPCO. The Nuclear Emergency Response Headquarters is established.
6:12am	A hydrogen explosion damages the Unit 4 reactor building.
11:00am	A sheltering order is issued within a 20-30km circumference of 1F.

March 16, 2011

0:02am	TEPCO's videoconference system stops recording.

For this study, we used the transcript date (about 600,000 Japanese characters) from TEPCO's videoconference system, published by the newspaper *Asahi Shimbun Company* (2012). The transcript consists of 7 scenes, which play out as follows;

Scene 1: 10:59pm, March 12
        Recording begins
Scene 2: 11:13 pm, March 12
        1F operators and managers request information on the tsunami.
Scene 3: 3:52am, March 13
        The high-pressure core water injection system of the Unit 3 reactor is stopped.
Scene 4: 5:46am, March 13
        1F operators find out that the nuclear fuel rod of the Unit 3 reactor has become
        exposing.
Scene 5: 8:57am, March 13
        The pressure in the Unit 3 reactor decreases and cool water is injected.
Scene 6: 12:41pm, March 14
        The water level in the Unit 2 reactor is low, and cooling is impossible.
Scene 7: 4:14pm, March 14
        1F operators, managers, and staff at Headquarters are confused about the vents
        of the Unit 2 reactor and inject water into it.

We chose to analyze Scene 6, which revealed an extremely dangerous situation, as the water level in the Unit 2 reactor was low and its cooling system was not under control. In such uncertain circumstances, it is necessary for the staff members of 1F, Headquarters, and the Offsite Center to make a decision. Scene 6 lasted about 30 min (12:41 pm-1:12 pm, March 14) and the personnel spoke 153 times (Headquarters: 52, 1F: 94, and the Offsite center: 7).

2.2   Research Methods

We used two research methods: (1) network analysis, and (2) content analysis. Network analysis helped clarify who spoke with whom, who was at the center of the conversation, the strength of relationships, and form of the discussion. Through this analysis, we could understand the trait of conversation in this field of research.

Next, using content analysis, we were able to explain the subject matter of each actor's speech. In the network of the conversation, we focused particularly on the question of "who says what to whom, how, and with what effect?" (Berelson 1952, p. 13). We also paid attention to the effect of location on meaning, because we studied recordings from multiple sites.

3   Results

3.1   Network Analysis

Based on the transcript of Scene 6, we used network analysis to shed light on the speakers (the nodes) and the relationships between them. We defined a structure of network links and counted the number of times when A spoke and B responded, and when no one responded to words that someone else said, we considered this autoregression.

The Actors and How Much They Spoke. First, we identified the speakers from the transcript of Scene 6 and counted the nodes and the number of times they spoke. As a result, the nodes are 16 (but unknown people at Headquarters and 1F counted with one). The nodes and locations are as follows:
<Headquarters>

- Mr. Shimizu, President of TEPCO
- Mr. Takahashi, Fellow
- Public Relations Division
- Nuclear Plant Team (the official name is unknown)
- Power Supply Distribution Division
- General Affairs Division
- Unknown People

<1F>

- Mr. Yoshida, 1F General Manager
- Power Generation Division
- Engineering Division
- Security Guard
- Information Division
- Welfare Division
- Safety Division
- Unknown People

<The Offsite Center>

- Mr. Muto, Vice President of TEPCO

Mr. Yoshida spoke 41 times, Mr. Takahashi spoke 14 times, Mr. Shimizu spoke 11 times, and Mr. Muto spoke 7 times. As for the divisions, the Power Generation Division of 1F spoke 6 times, and the Public Relations Division spoke 4 times, but some people did not mention their name or the division they belonged to; thus, we could not count all of speech whole speech by each division.

Network Structure. Next, we analyzed the network structure, with the speakers representing nodes. The results are as follows:

Mr. Yoshida, the 1F General Manager, is at the center of this network structure. He is linked to 7 other actors. The nodes representing the divisions of Public Relations, Welfare, Power Generation, and Safety are shown with autoregression loops because they shared information. For example, they said the following to all actors, *"From Public Relations, we have information just for you..."*

Mr. Muto, the Vice President, only had a few links. Even though he was one of the top-level managers, he was link fault of President Shimizu and Fellow Takahashi; Mr. Muto should have been able to make decisions about technical matters while receiving support from the Fellow. Because he was located at the Offsite Center, he could not join actively in conversations with the President and the Fellow in Headquarters. Thus, he only spoke with Mr. Yoshida and some engineers (who are grouped under "Unknown People") in order to find out technical information about the disaster (Fig. 1).

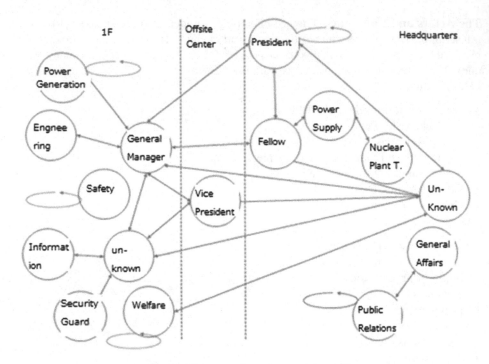

Fig. 1. The network structure of Scene 6

3.2   Content Analysis

Next, we employed content analysis to determine the kinds of words the actors were using. We concentrated especially on the difference of location, examined how frequently words appeared, and how often words were mentioned simultaneously at each site.

The Frequency of Words. Figure 2 shows the frequency of words, including a breakdown of each location in Scene 6. We only counted the times when a speaker mentioned a word multiple times, and when a synonym of a certain word appeared during the time that one person spoke.

"Unit 2 reactor" (which predicted that the water level was dropping[2] and that meltdown was occurring) was used 21 times, "request" was used 19 times, "quickly/rapidly" (which represented an urgent demand in the moment that the word was spoken) was used 17 times, "water" (which indicated the water level of nuclear reactors, and that they were being injected with water) was used 13 times, and "please" was used 12 times.

Based on location, "Unit 2 reactor" only appeared twice during conversations at Headquarters; in contrast, "request" and "please" were used numerous times there. The staff at Headquarters could not understand the conditions occurring at 1F, and tried to

---

[2] When the water level reaches the Top of Active Fuel (TAF), the fuel is exposed and the probability of meltdown increases.

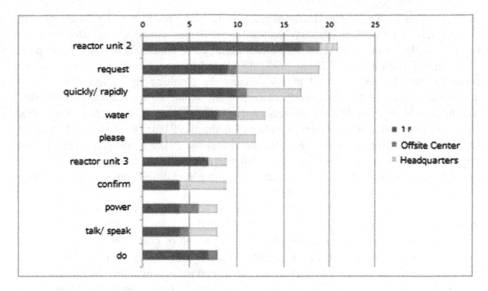

Fig. 2. The frequency of words

obtain information on the situation so they could instruct the personnel of 1F to make decisions regarding the reactors.

The Co-occurrence of Words. Next, we analyzed words to see when they appeared simultaneously and more than twice. We examined the differences between the words used in each location. Personnel at Headquarters, 1F, and the Offsite Center used distinct language when discussing key topics. "Unit 2 reactor," "quickly/rapidly," and "water" were mentioned during emergency conditions at 1F, while "please," "request," and "confirm" were used for business correspondence at Headquarters.

Regarding the words each speaker used the most, Mr. Yoshida mentioned "Unit 2 reactor," "Unit 3 reactor," and "do" when discussing accidents, whereas Mr. Shimizu mentioned "reactor manufacturer," "handling policy," and "available range" to confirm the present situation.

4 Discussion

Based on our analysis, we understood that speakers using words in conversation are difference in each location although same sever accident occurred in TEPCO. For example, 1F was located at the scene of the accident, and the staff there used words that describe immediate danger, whereas the staff at Headquarters used everyday language because they were receiving information about the catastrophe and were not directly near it. The same line of thinking applies to each speaker. Mr. Yoshida handled the situation of the Unit 2 reactor based on his previous experience dealing with the Unit 3 reactor; however, Mr. Shimizu had only experienced one set of circumstances.

According to Social Constructionism, people build realities using language and words (Gergen 1994; Burr 1995). When they use different words, it is possible for them to have a different perspective of reality than their peers. This leads us to the concept of "polyphony" (Bakhtin 1984; Boje 1995, 2008). Bakhtin analyzed the novels of Dostoyevsky and showed that "polyphony" means the "multiplicity of independent and unmerged voices and consciousness...each with equal right and its own world" (Bakhtin 1984, p. 208). We are not necessarily hearing a hero's voice, but many other kinds of voices exist, which result in reality (Takahashi 2010). The same can be said of organizations. There is not one homophonic voice, but rather a polyphonic voice, and organizations are comprised of various truths. In the field of interdiscursivity[3] (one example of interdiscursivity is conversation), multiple realities converge towards one (Broadfoot, Deetz and Anderson 2004).

In our analysis, TEPCO cannot have one reality in the response to the disaster. Rather, as with the metaphor of *Tamara*[4] (Boje 1995, 2008), we showed that different "states of emergency" occurred at each site. In situation of computer security incident response, more than one reality frequently occurs, and the personnel of the same organization are difference of speaking words in certain organization (Suzumura et al. 2011). In our study, we can explain this phenomenon in the discussions between 1F and Headquarters, and between Mr. Shimizu and Mr. Yoshida.

5   Conclusion

We studied TEPCO's videoconference system when the Great East Japan Earthquake struck on March 11, 2011, and we examined "ongoing" conversations using multilateral analysis. Staff members at Headquarters and 1F built different realities because they were facing difficult conditions and received complex information.

We scrutinized the total amount of conversations amounted to 30 min according to TEPCO's videoconference system, even though it recorded for a total of 49 h. In the future, we will expand the scope of our research and analyze the malfunctions of TEPCO in detail, as well as the relationship between conversation and power.

Acknowledgement. This work was supported by JSPS KAKENHI Grant Number 23310115 and 23530505, and Okinawa University Research Grant.

---

[3] Everyday conversation is usually casual and random, but prior discussions influence current speech, which in turn affects future discourse. Grant et al. (2004) called this phenomenon "interdiscursivity".

[4] *Tamara* is a play by John Krizanc, first performed on May 8, 1981 in Toronto, Canada. In *Tamara*, the audience fragments into small groups that chase characters from one room to the next, from one floor to the next, even going into bedrooms, kitchens, and other rooms in order to co-create the stories that interest them the most. If there are a dozen stages and a dozen storytellers, the number of story lines an audience could trace as it follows the wandering discourses of *Tamara* is a 12 factorial (Krizanc & Boje 2006, p. 70).

References

Asahi Shimbun Company: TEPCO Videoconference. Asahi Shimbun Company (2012). (in Japanese)

Takahashi, M.: Polyphony Perspective in Organization Studies. Meiji Bus. Rev. **57**(4), 99–115 (2010)

Bakhtin, M.: Problems of Dostoevsky's Poetics. University of Minnesota Press, Minneapolis (1984)

Berelson, B.: Content Analysis in Communication Research. Free Press, New York (1952)

Boje, D.M.: Stories of the storytelling organization: a postmodern analysis of disney as tamara-land. Acad. Manag. J. **38**(4), 997–1035 (1995)

Boje, D.M.: Storytelling Organizations. Sage, London (2008)

Broadfoot, K., Deetz, S., Anderson, D.: Multi-levelled, multi-method approaches in organizational discourse. In: Grant, D., Hardy, C., Oswick, C., Putnam, L. (eds.) The SAGE Handbook of Organizational Discourse, pp. 193–211. Sage Publications, London (2004)

Burr, V.: An Introduction to Social Constructionism. Routledge, London (1995)

Fairhurst, G.T., Cooren, F.: Organizational language in use: interaction analysis, conversation analysis and speech act schematics. In: Grant, D., Hardy, C., Oswick, C., Putnam, L. (eds.) The SAGE Handbook of Organizational Discourse, pp. 131–152. Sage Publications, London (2004)

Gergen, K.J.: Realities and Relationships: Soundings in Social Construction. Harvard University Press, Cambridge (1994)

Grant, D., Hardy, C., Oswick, C., Putnum, L.: Organizational discourse: exploring the field. In: Grant, D., Hardy, C., Oswick, C., Putnam, L. (eds.) The SAGE Handbook of Organizational Discourse, pp. 1–36. Sage Publications, London (2004)

Krizanc, J., Boje, D.M.: Tamara journal interview with John Krizanc. Tamara J. Crit. Organ. Inq. **5**(3), 70–77 (2006)

Nakanishi, A., Yotsumoto, M., Ushimaru, H., Sugihara, D., Takagi, T.: Analyzing discourses of the multi-location videoconference system for emergency: a case of the accident at fukushima daiichi nuclear power plant. J. Inf. Manage. **35**(1), 46–58 (2014)

Suzumura, M., Terajima, K., Nakanishi, A., Takagi, T., Yoshida, T., Hayashi, I.: Storytelling and organizational reality: a case of the computer security incident response team. In: JAMS/JAIMS International Conference on Business & Information (2011)

Accident Analysis by Using Methodology of Resilience Engineering, High Reliability Organization, and Risk Literacy

Hiroshi Ujita[✉]

The Canon Institute for Global Studies, 11F, Shin-Marunouchi Bldg.,
5-1 Marunouchi 1-Chome, Chiyoda-ku, Tokyo 100-6511, Japan
ujita.hiroshi@canon-igs.org

Abstract. The good cases of resilience response are observed in individual base and organizational base as below: The effectiveness of insight on accident cases (inundation in Madras, 9.11 terrorism-B.5.b. order) and of the risk evaluation, Decision of continuation of sea water infusion (individual base), Reflection of the experience on Chuetsu-Oki Earthquake, Improvement of seismic building which is equipped emergency power source system and air conditioning system (organizational base), Deployment of fire engines (organizational base), The effectiveness of command system in ordinal time (on-site of organizational base), and Support by cooperation companies and manufacturers (designers and site workers of organizational base). It is important to 'establish the feedback system on organization learning in ordinal time' and it means that it is important to establish the system admitting violation of order. The decision at on-site are given priority than other ones. The representative example is the decision of sea water infusion continuation which was given priority at on-site, even though the official residence and the main office of Tokyo Electric Power Company had ordered to stop the infusion.

Keywords: Resilience engineering · High reliability organization · Risk literacy · Fukushima accident · Bounded rationality · Information limitation · Context

1 Introduction

The results of Fukushima Daiichi Accident investigation with diversified characteristic have been released until now. Based upon the analyses of the investigation, the success and failure cases for emergency responses were analyzed concerning to personal-response capability, organizational-response capability, and communication ability with external organizations, and then the problems of responses were extracted. The action of sea-water infusion on Fukushima Daiichi nuclear power plant No.1 was paid attention and analyzed based on the 'Accident Analysis Report of Fukushima Nuclear Accident' [1] (Accident Report) by TEPCO, Tokyo Electric Power Company, especially focus on the decision making of continuation of pouring sea water.

© Springer International Publishing Switzerland 2015
M. Kurosu (Ed.): Human-Computer Interaction, Part III, HCII 2015, LNCS 9171, pp. 358–369, 2015.
DOI: 10.1007/978-3-319-21006-3_35

2   Bounded Rationality in Context vs. Judge by God

In the field of cognitive science and the cognitive system engineering, the human being is considered as to think and judge something reasonably along context while there is information limitation. Sometimes the decision may be judged as an error by the outside later. It is called "bounded rationality in the context" vs. "judge by God". The absurd action of the organization had been often explained in human illogicality conventionally, while the approach has recently come out to think that the human being rationality was the cause.

There are three approaches proposed from Organizational (Behavioral) Economics, business cost theory (reluctant to do), agency theory (information gap), and proprietary rights theory (selfishness). Business cost theory analyses action of opportunity principles and sunk cost, agency theory, moral hazard and adverse selection (lemon market), and proprietary rights theory, cost externality. The common supposition is "the bounded rationality and the utility maximization".

It is necessary to find the social context that the error is easy to occur, in the engineering for human beings hereafter. In other words, a way of thinking has changed in the direction to analyzing the social context that is easy to cause an error, from analyzing direct cause of the error. Because this direction is beyond the range of conventional ergonomic treating the contents of the error, it is very difficult. However, we should recognize it now, if we do not analyze an error in the viewpoint the relationship between safety and the environmental element surrounding human being, we can not to lead to measures. The measures should be matched with human rational characteristics.

Countermeasure on Business cost theory is business cost saving system which changes organizational style from group organization, via. centralization of power type organization, and to decentralization of power type organization, agency theory, agency cost reduction system based on mutual exchange of the information, and proprietary rights theory, internalization of the system externality based on proprietary rights distribution.

3   Accident Model and Error Model

As a result that the technology systems become huge, complex and sophisticated, safety issues are shifted to the problem of organization from human, and further from hardware, such socialization is occurring in every technical field. For this reason, the analytical methods, as well as type and social perceptions of error or accident, are changing with the times also. Table 1 shows trends of the accident model and error model. Human error and Domino accident model had initially appeared, are then changing to system error and Swiss cheese accident model, and recently move to safety culture degradation and the organizational accident.

A conventional accident model is the domino model, in which the causation of trouble and the error is analyzed and measures are taken. In the model, slip, lapse, and mistake are used which are the classification of the unsafe act to occur by on-site work. These are categorized as the basic error type, while violation which is intentional act violating rule has become increased recently and considered as cause of social accident.

Table 1. Accident model and Error model

Accident Model	Error Model	Analysis Method	Measure
Domino (Failure Chain)	Human Error (Individual)	Cause-Consequence Link	Encapsulation, Seek & Destroy
Swiss Cheese (Diversity Loss)	System Error (Organization)	Risk Analysis	Defense & Barrier
Organizational Accident (Fallacy of Defense in Depth)	Safety Culture Degradation	Safety Culture Check List	Monitor & Control on Organizational Culture

Design philosophy of the defense in depths has been established, and the accident to occur recently is caused by the excellence of the error of a variety of systems. The analysis of the organization blunder is necessary for the analysis by this Swiss cheese accident model in addition to conventional error analysis.

An organization accident is a problem inside the organizations, which reaches earthshaking event for the organization as a result by the accumulation of the best intentions basically. It is an act of the good will, but becomes the error. As for the organization accident, the interdependence inside of the organization or between the organizations is accumulated by fallacy in the defense in depths, and it becomes a problem of the deterioration of the safety culture in its turn. The organizational management based on the organization analyses such as behavioral sciences will be necessary for these measures.

4   The Methodology on Resilience Engineering, High Reliability Organization, and Risk Literacy

Whereas the direction which discusses the safety from the accident analysis, a new trend of analytical methods such as resilience engineering, high reliability organization, or risk literacy research, which analyze the various events by focusing on the good practices, are becoming popular.

Resilience and safety management is shown in Fig. 1. The resilience is the intrinsic ability of a system to adjust its functioning prior to, during, or following changes and disturbances, so that it can sustain required operations under both expected and unexpected conditions. A practice of Resilience Engineering/Proactive Safety Management requires that all levels of the organization are able to:

- Monitor
- Learn from past events
- Respond
- Anticipate

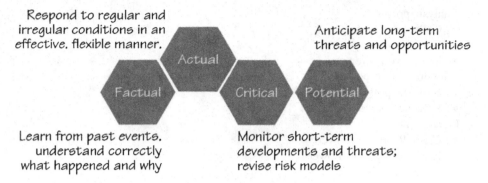

Respond to regular and
irregular conditions in an
effective. flexible manner.

Anticipate long-term
threats and opportunities

Learn from past events.
understand correctly
what happened and why

Monitor short-term
developments and threats;
revise risk models

Fig. 1. Resilience and safety management

Organizational process defined by the High Reliability Organization is shown in Fig. 2.

There are 5 powers in 2 situations.

- Preparedness for Emergency Situation in Ordinal Time:
  - Carefulness (Confirmation),
  - Honesty (Report),
  - Sensitivity (Observation),
- Emergency Response in Emergency Situation:
  - Alert (Concentration),
  - Flexibility (Response),

Ability of Risk Literacy is also defined by followings, which is largely divided to 3 powers and further classified to 8 sub-powers.

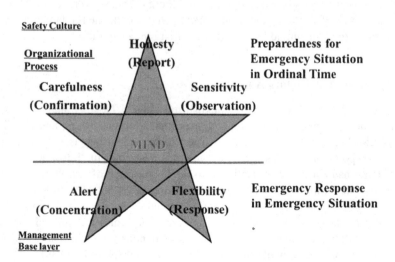

Fig. 2. High reliability organization: organizational process.

- Analysis power
  - Collection power
  - Understanding power
  - Predictive power
- Communication power
  - Network power
  - Influence power
- Practical power
  - Crisis Response Power
  - Radical Measures Power

5 The Analysis Based on Resilience Engineering, High Reliability Organization, and Risk Literacy

5.1 Chronological Analysis

The analysis for the detail of sea-water infusion to Fukushima-Daiichi No.1 has been performed. Chronological analysis was drawn up from "The main chronological analysis of Fukushima Daiichi nuclear power plant No.1 from earthquake occurrence to the next day" and "The status response relating to pouring water to Fukushima Daiichi nuclear power plant No.1", which came from the 'Accident Report'.

The chronological analysis shows that the preparation of sea-water infusion is decided and ordered concurrently with pouring freshwater, and also shows that continuation of sea-water infusion is decided as on-site judgment although an official residence and the main office of TEPCO directed to stop the infusion, in taking into consideration of the intention of official residence. The necessity of continuation of sea-water infusion was recognized consistently by on-site judgment, and these measures were taken. This means that the main office of TEPCO and the official residence violate the fundamental principle which on-site judgment should be preceded in emergency situation.

5.2 Organizational Factors Analysis

The process of sea-water infusion on Fukushima Daiichi No.1 is analyzed from the point of resilience capability, high reliability organization capability, and risk-literacy capability [2–6]. The analysis example by risk-literacy capability is shown in Table 2 from the viewpoint of risk-management, which is described in 'Introduction of Risk Literacy- Lessons Learned from Incidents' [6]. The definition of risk literacy capability which can extract communication power that is important both for ordinary time and for emergency situation is the most appropriate for analysis. The horizontal axis shows response capabilities which are suggested in each study, and the vertical axis shows each level of individual, organization and correspondence to outside. The gothic font in green means success case, while the italic font in red means failure case.

The analysis of emergency correspondence like this kind of huge accident cannot be analyzed enough using conventional framework. As a whole of one organization,

Table 2. Evaluation of response capability from the viewpoint of risk literacy: the analysis of sea water infusion process on Fukushima Daiichi No.1.

Risk literacy —— Analysis level		In Ordinal Time			In Emergency Situation			
		Analysis Power			Communication Power		Practical Power	
		Collection Power	Comprehensive Power	Predictive Power	Information Transmission Power	Influence power	Crisis Response Power	Radical Measures Power
Individual		·Damage of Tsunami	·Risk recognition of Tsunami damage	·Risk recognition of Power Loss	—	—	• Continuation of Sea water infusion	• Training for emergency
organization	on-site	·Collection of accidents: ·Jyogan- Tsunami	·Earthquake ·Tsunami ·Evaluation of influence range by PSA	Recognition of accidents damage	·Information sharing at on-site	·Command system (on-site) ·Centralized at seismic building ·Contact between Control Room & Emergency Response Room	·Infusion of fresh water and sea water ·Vent ·Prevention of damage expansion	·Preparation of seismic building and fire engines ·Command system ·AM measures ·Tsunami protection measures
	Management	·Collection of accident: Jyogan- Tsunami, JNES Tsunami PSA. Infusion at Le Blayais & Madras	·Risk misrecognition of Tsunami damage	·Risk misrecognition of Power Loss	·Information sharing between main office and on-site	·TV conference system (2F site) ·Confusion in command system between main office and on-site		·Review the education and training system
External correspondence (official residence, etc.)		·Anti- terrorism in overseas Collection of example : 9.11 terrorism- B.5.b.	·Classification of importance on accidents ·Risk misrecognition of earthquake and Tsunami	·Importance of external events ·Risk misrecognition of infrastructure damage		·Media, local government, publicity to overseas ·Confusion of command system among official residence, main office, & on-site	·Delay of initial response ·Governmental command system	·Support by vendor and cooperation company ·Support by external organizations ·Drastic measures: Structure reform (Regulation/ Electric power company)

the classifications were reviewed and revised from two points. One is that the differences in correspondence and the problems in cooperation between on-site and administration department cannot be clarified. And the other one is that communication power has two sides which are the information cooperation in ordinal time and collaboration in case of emergency situation. The analysis power and information transmission power correspond to ordinal time, and the influence power and normal time skill correspond to the case of emergency situation. In this analysis, the contact with official residence and the cooperation inside government are also included in correspond to external organizations.

6 Success and Failure Cases

From the viewpoint of Resilience Engineering, the case of success and failure are listed and analyzed.

6.1 Good Case of Resilience Response

The good cases of resilience response are observed in individual base and organizational base as below.

- The effectiveness of insight on accident cases (inundation in Madras, 9.11 terror-ism-B.5.b.) and of the risk evaluation.
  • Decision of continuation of sea water infusion (individual base)
- Reflection of the experience on Chuetsu-Oki Earthquake
  • Improvement of seismic building which is equipped emergency power source system and air conditioning system (organizational base)
  • Deployment of fire engines (organizational base)
- The effectiveness of command system in ordinal time (on-site of organizational base)
- Support by cooperation companies and manufacturers (designers and site workers of organizational base)

The reason why the good cases are occurred in on-site, the officers and workers always felt that their mission is to carry out with the sense of ownership and also with critical mind. They had trained the accident management in ordinal time, which works effectively in emergency situation, which is the just significant frame derived from the development of safety culture. It is important to 'establish the feedback system on organization learning in ordinal time'. But there were a little lack of information between control room and emergency response room, they will be able to solve by taking physical measures to clarify the circumstances at on-site. The TV conference system of Fukushima Daini nuclear power plant had worked effectively to communi-cate among on-site, the main office of TEPCO and the outside organizations. Fur-thermore using the white board for information sharing, which is the good case that the resilience works well, could prevent the confusion at on-site.

6.2 The Failure of Comprehensive Power in Organization, the Fallacy of Composition of Risk Awareness

The many failure cases are defined under national government level and nuclear industry level which are the problems of rare event awareness and of organization culture. Although everyone had same recognition for the risk of power loss and Tsu-nami, the accurate decision had not been made by national government level, just only made by individual level. The ordinal time training at on-site also work in emergency situation at the accident, while the level of administration department and government didn't work well.

- Risk misrecognition of Loss of offsite power and damage by Tsunami (national government level, industry level).
- Confusion of command system (organization base - between on-site and the main office of TEPCO).
- Confusion of command system (external correspondence base - national govern-ment level, and organization base - among official residence, regulation, and the main office of TEPCO).

The continuations of emergency training in ordinal time with assuming the severe accident progression is considered to be the effective way. As many lacks in emergency correspondence in management department and in national government level are observed, and then the emergency training is necessary in management level, in which responsibility assignment is regularly taken, the incident seriousness is evaluated, and the mode is switched from ordinal time to emergency situation.

The true nature of the problem in Japanese organization that doesn't change from when the 'Substance of Failures' [7], in which Japanese military operation failures in the World War II were analyzed, is written by Tobe, Nonaka, et. al.. Failure cause is described as standpoint of irrationality in Japanese on this book. But the problems in organization are not able to be resolved by irrationality in Japanese. It should be explained using by bounded rationality which Kikusawa advocate in 'Absurdity of Organization' [8]. His idea is that decision making which are made under limited circumstances based on limited information will end in failure from the eye of God. He also advocates destroying the bounded rationality for failure measures. It means that it is important to 'establish the system admitting violation of order in emergency situation'. The decision at on-site are given priority than other ones. The representative example is observed in the decision of sea water infusion continuation, the decision at on-site were given priority even though the official residence and the main office TEPCO had ordered to stop the infusion. Otherwise it is the failure case that occur delay of PCV vent, for time loss to get the permission of national government and local government.

6.3   Consideration on Organizational Problem

It is important to 'establish the feedback system on organization learning in ordinal time'. The continuations of emergency training in ordinal time with assuming the severe accident progression is considered to be the effective way. The emergency training is necessary in management level, in which responsibility assignment is regularly taken, the incident seriousness is evaluated, and the mode is switched from ordinal time to emergency situation.

Intrinsic qualities of Japanese organization still does not change when 'Substance of Failures' was published, while Japanese organization should be described and analyzed by using bounded rationality concept proposed by Kikusawa in 'Absurdity of Organization'. Possible countermeasures are destroying bounded rationality, that is 'Establishing the system admitting violation of order in emergency situation'.

The problems as above can be explained by "Homogeneous way of thinking" and "Concentric Camaraderie", as shown in Fig. 3, which are the hindrance on safety pursuit in Japan. 'Bottom-up decision making structure' connects to 'Absence of top management', and then becomes to 'Delay of decision making and Lack of understanding on valuing safety'. Due to the Japanese are excellent as noncommissioned officer (Soldier: Russian, Junior officer: French, Chief of staff: German, General: American), they often show their ability at emergency situation. But Japanese are short of management abilities, they often make heavy intervention or omission.

'Multilayered faction structure' appeared in "Concentric Camaraderie" makes 'Organization from Gesellschaft to Gemeinschaft', and then 'Adhesion and back-scratching' are spread in the organization. For the "Concentric Camaraderie", the

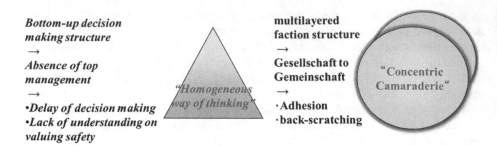

Fig. 3. "Homogeneous way of thinking" and "Concentric camaraderie", obstruction factors on safety pursuit in Japan.

feedback system in organization learning leads to the failure due to be preceded to internal logic than social common sense even in national government level or nuclear industry level.

7 Discussion

The "Privatization by National Policy" has been destroyed by large-scale disasters in Fukushima Daiichi nuclear power plants. Anyway, rare event has occurred on one occasion, measures had to be taken here after. National nuclear policies of many countries are being reexamined along with the safety evaluation. Safety design principle is "Defense in Depth" concept, which should be further reconsidered reflecting the accident causes. Usual systems focus on the forefront function, such as preventing damage, expansion mitigation, or incident prevention, while safety critical systems increases attention to back-up functions such as incident expansion mitigation or environmental effects mitigation, if it has a large enough impact on the environment. Common Mode Failure of External Initiating Event such as Earthquake or Tsunami, which is usually Rare Event, or auxiliary systems failure such as Off-site Power, EDG, Buttery, or Sea Water Cooling loss was difficult to install to Defense in Depth design, while it should be.

Rare Event is high consequence with low frequency. Low consequence with high frequency event is easy to treat by commercial reason, while it is very difficult to handle the rare event even the risk is just the same. "Unexpected event" has been used frequently, but it is the risk-benefit issues to assume or not. Tsunami Probabilistic Risk Analysis has been carried out, and safety related personnel knew the magnitude of the effect well.

Regardless of the initiating event, lack of measures to "Station blackout" is to be asked. According to the "Defense in Depth" concept reflecting Fukushima accident, we should consider three level safety functions; usual normal system, usual safety system, and newly installed emergency system including external support functions. Anyway the diversity is significantly required for not only future reactor concept but also existing plant back-fit activities.

Swiss Cheese Model proposed by Reason, J indicates operational problem other than design problem [2]. Fallacy of the defense in depth has frequently occurred

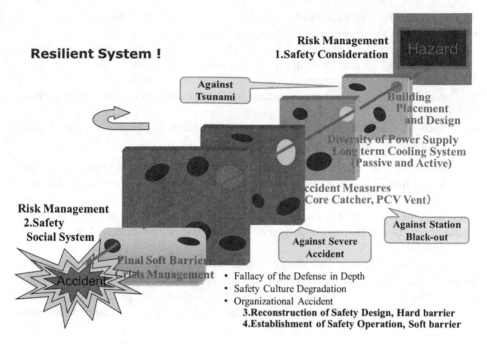

Fig. 4. Defense in depth and new safety concept

recently because plant system is safe enough as operators becomes easily not to consider system safety. And then safety culture degradation would be happened, whose incident will easily become organizational accident. Such situation requires final barrier that is Crisis Management as shown in Fig. 4.

Concept of "Soft Barrier" has been proposed here [3]. There are two types of safety barriers, one is Hard Barrier that is simply represented by Defense in Depth. The other is Soft Barrier, which maintains the hard barrier as expected condition, makes it perform as expected function. Even when the Hard Barrier does not perform its function, human activity to prevent hazardous effect and its support functions, such as manuals, rules, laws, organization, social system, etc. Soft Barrier can be further divided to two measures; one is "Software for design", such as Common mode failure treatment, Safety logic, Usability, etc. The other is "Humanware for operation", such as operator or maintenance personnel actions, Emergency Procedure, organization, management, Safety Culture, etc.

8   Conclusion

The good cases of resilience response are observed in individual base and organizational base as below.

- The effectiveness of insight on accident cases (inundation in Madras, 9.11 terrorism-B.5.b.) and of the risk evaluation.

- Decision of continuation of sea water infusion (individual base)
- Reflection of the experience on Chuetsu-Oki Earthquake.
  - Improvement of seismic building which is equipped emergency power source system and air conditioning system (organizational base)
  - Deployment of fire engines (organizational base)
- The effectiveness of command system in ordinal time (on-site of organizational base).
- Support by cooperation companies and manufacturers (designers and site workers of organizational base).

It is important to 'establish the feedback system on organization learning in ordinal time' and it means that it is important to establish the system admitting violation of order. The decision at on-site are given priority than other ones. The representative example is the decision of sea water infusion continuation which was given priority at on-site, even though the official residence and the main office TEPCO had ordered to stop the infusion.

The many failure cases are defined under national government level and nuclear industry level which are the problems of rare event awareness and of organization culture. The ordinal time training at on-site also work in emergency situation at the accident, while the level of administration department and government didn't work well.

- Risk misrecognition of Loss of offsite power and damage by Tsunami (national government level, industry level).
- Confusion of command system (organization base - between on-site and the main office of TEPCO).
- Confusion of command system (external correspondence base - national government level, and organization base - among official residence, regulation, and the main office of TEPCO).

Nuclear energy will play an important role from the necessity of mitigating climate change, as well as improve energy security. However, the Fukushima Daiichi Accident raised a new challenge of securing the safety of utilization. Following the safety design principle of "Defense in Depth", three level safety functions should be considered for the hardware. Those are, the usual normal system, usual safety system, and emergency system including external support function. On the other hand, software for design including common mode failure treatment, safety logic, and usability should be improved together with the humanware for operation including personnel actions, emergency procedure, organization, management, and safety culture.

References

1. TEPCO: Accident Analysis Report of Fukushima Nuclear Accident, June 2012
2. Reason, J.: Managing the Risks of Organizational Accidents. Ashgate, Aldersho (1997)
3. Ujita, H.: Research on Error Management, Quality Assurance Study Group 2009 Annual report, June 2010 (in Japanese)

4. Hollnagel, E.: Safety Culture, Safety Management, and Resilience Engineering, ATEC Aviation Safety Forum, November 2009
5. Weick, K.E., Sutcliffe, K.M.: Managing the Unexpected. Jossey-Bass, San Francisco (2001)
6. Lin, S.: Introduction of Risk Literacy- Lessons Learned from Incidents. NIKKEI-BP, Tokyo (2005). (in Japanese)
7. Tobe, N., et al.: Substance of Failures. DIAMOND (1984). (in Japanese)
8. Kikusawa, K.: Absurdity of Organization. DIAMOND (2000). (in Japanese)

User Studies

What Learnability Issues Do Primary Care Physicians Experience When Using CPOE?

Martina A. Clarke[1], Jeffery L. Belden[2], and Min S. Kim[1,3(✉)]

[1] Informatics Institute, University of Missouri, Columbia, MO, USA
[2] Department of Family and Community Medicine, University of Missouri, Columbia, MO, USA
[3] Department of Health Management and Informatics, University of Missouri, Columbia, MO, USA
kimms@health.missouri.edu

Abstract. *Objective:* To determine learnability gaps between expert and novice primary care physicians when using a computerized physician order entry (CPOE). *Method:* Two rounds of lab-based usability tests using video analyses with triangular method approach were conducted to analyze learnability gaps between ten novice and six expert physicians. *Results:* There was a 14 percent point increase in novice physicians' task success rate ($p = 0.29$) and an 11 percent point increase in expert physicians' task success rate between round one and round two ($p = 0.64$). There was an 8 % decrease in novice physicians' time on task between round one and round two ($p - 0.83$) and a 12 % decrease in expert physicians' time on task between round one and round two ($p = 0.47$). There was a 17 % decrease in novice physicians' mouse clicks between round one and round two ($p = 0.97$) and a 20 % decrease in expert physicians' mouse clicks between round one and round two ($p = 0.80$). There was a 5 % increase in novice physicians' mouse movements between round one and round two ($p = 0.67$) and an 8 % decrease in expert physicians' mouse movements between round one and round two ($p = 0.99$). *Conclusion:* Future directions include identifying usability issues faced by physicians when using the EHR through subtask analysis.

Keywords: Usability · Primary care · Computerized provider order entry

1 Introduction

Adverse drug events (ADEs) has incurred an additional $3.5 billion in medical costs [1]. Computerized Provider Order Entry (CPOE) was recommended by the Institute of Medicine (IOM) as a way to reduce patient harm caused by medication errors [2]. Health information technology (HIT) is being used extensively in clinical practice and more physicians are adopting CPOEs because of the financial incentives guaranteed by Centers for Medicare and Medicaid (CMS) [3]. CPOEs are as computer-aided medication and laboratory ordering system. It is mandated for any licensed healthcare professional to request laboratory, radiology, and medication orders through CPOE as a part MU stage 2 of the EHR incentive program. One major benefit to computerized medication orders is reduced medication errors created from inaccurate transcription or

© Springer International Publishing Switzerland 2015
M. Kurosu (Ed.): Human-Computer Interaction, Part III, HCII 2015, LNCS 9171, pp. 373–383, 2015.
DOI: 10.1007/978-3-319-21006-3_36

incomprehensible handwriting. On the other hand, CPOE may cause unintentional penalties, such as, increasing clinicians' workload, undesirable workflow issues, and generation of new kinds of errors [4–9]. Mediocre CPOE usability of is one of the main factor that leads to consequences, such as decreased efficiency, reduction in the quality of care given to patients, and unsatisfied clinicians [10–13]. Usability is defined in this study as how well users can maneuver a system to effectively and efficiently complete particular tasks [14]. Learnability is defined as the degree to which the system enables users to comprehend how to use the system [15]. In the literature, while there are disparities when describing usability and learnability [15–17], definitions of learnability are intensely associated with usability and proficiency [16, 18, 19]. Learnability is the length of time and effort that is needed for a user to improve proficiency with a system over a period of time and after multiple uses [20].

The objective of this study is to identify differences in learnability in terms of user performance between expert and novice primary care physicians three and seven months after resident's EHR training. Our null hypothesis is that novice and expert physicians will be more proficient with increased EHR experience. If there is no significant difference between novice and expert physicians then the performance measures identified is not based on novice physicians' inexperience with the system but that there is room for improvement in the current design of the CPOE.

2   Method

2.1   Study Design

To determine learnability gaps in use of EHR systems between expert and novice physicians, standard lab-based usability tests were conducted incorporating think aloud strategy and video analysis using Morae® (TechSmith, Okemos, MI). Twelve family medicine and four internal medicine resident physicians, completed five artificial, scenarios-based tasks. A mixed methods approach was utilized to identify the learnability gaps between the novice and expert physicians. The mixed methods approach included four types of performance measures, and qualitative debriefing session with participants. This pilot study was approved by the University of Missouri Health Sciences Institutional Review Board.

2.1.1   Organizational Setting

This study was conducted at the University of Missouri Health System (UMHS), which is a 536 bed, tertiary care academic medical hospital situated in Columbia, Missouri. In 2012, UMHS had roughly 553,300 clinic visits and employs more than 70 primary care physicians. The Department of Family and Community Medicine (FCM) oversees six clinics, while the Department of Internal Medicine (IM) manages two primary care clinics [23]. The Healthcare Information and Management Systems Society (HIMSS), a non-profit organization that rates how effectively hospitals are adopting electronic health records (EMR) in the organization, has awarded UMHS with Stage 7 of the EMR Adoption Model [24]. Specifically, UMHS has employed electronic patient charts, inspected clinical data with the use of data warehousing, and distributes health information electronically with authorized health care entities [25]. The CPOE embedded in the EHR gives physicians a safe way to electronically access and place patients' lab and medication orders, and deliver the orders to the responsible department that is processing the request. UMHS' EHR database contains all the records from the university's hospitals and clinics. Measuring learnability between expert and novice physicians in a healthcare system that uses a fully employed EHR system makes the aim of this study achievable.

2.2 Participants

There is presently no evidence-based method to quantity a user's EHR skill, therefore, novice and expert physicians were categorized based on clinical training level and number of years using the EHR. This verdict was grounded on a conversation with a knowledgeable physician champion (JLB) and two chief resident physicians from both participating departments (FCM, IM). The theory is that after one year resident physicians could achieve necessary skills to be considered an expert. Therefore, ten first year resident physicians were grouped as novice users and six second and third year resident physicians were categorized as expert users. Both FCM and IM departments offer three year residency programs. Convenience sampling methodology was utilized when selecting participants [26]. Both UMHS FCM and IM physicians were selected for the sample because, as primary care residents, they have comparable clinical responsibilities. Twelve FCM and four IM residents was a part of this study. Based on a review of the literature, ten participants were considered appropriate in explorative usability studies to discover the foremost issues to resolve in a product development cycle [27, 28]. Participation was voluntary and subjects were reimbursed for their time.

2.3 Scenario and Tasks

The scenario "a scheduled follow up visit after a hospitalization for pneumonia" was given to resident physicians in round one of the study. For round two, resident physicians received the scenario "a scheduled follow up visit after a hospitalization for heart failure." Although the residents were given two different scenarios, these two scenarios were equivalent in complexity, workflow, and functionalities used. The purpose of these scenarios were to evaluate physicians' use of the EHR that comprises of realistic inpatient and outpatient information. Five commonly completed tasks were created for both novice and expert primary care physicians to execute. These tasks met 2014 EHR certification criteria 45 CFR 170.314 for meaningful use stage 2 [20]. The tasks were also a part of the mandatory EHR training conducted at the commencement of physicians' residency. The tasks had a clear objective that physicians were able to follow without unnecessary clinical cognitive load or ambiguity, which were not a part the study's goals. The tasks were:

- Task 1: Place order for chest x-ray
- Task 2: Place order for Basic metabolic panel (BMP)
- Task 3: Change a Medication

- Task 4: Add a medication to your favorites list
- Task 5: Renew one of the existing medications

Performance Measures. Four performance measures were used to analyze user performance as follow:

1. Percent task success rate - the percentage of subtasks that participants finished successfully without any errors.
2. Time-on-task - the length of time each participant took to finish each task, starting when participants click "start task" to when "end task" is clicked.
3. Mouse clicks - the sum of clicks on the mouse taken to finish a given task.
4. Mouse movement - the length in pixels of the navigation path to finish each task.

For time on task, mouse clicks, and mouse movements, a lower value usually indicates higher performances. Higher values may portray that the participant had complications with the system when completing tasks.

Data Collection. Usability data for round one was collected between November 12, 2013 and December 19, 2013 and round two data was collected between February 12, 2014 and April 22, 2014. Round one data was collected at UMHS three months after novice resident physicians concluded their compulsory EHR training. Resident physicians were requested to take part in round two roughly three months after the date they completed round one. Usability testing took twenty minutes and was conducted using a 15 inch laptop with Windows 7 operating system. To maintain constancy and lessen unwelcome disruptions, the participant and the facilitator were the only two individuals in the conference room while the usability session took place. At the beginning of the session, the participant were advised of their rights as a participant. The participant was then given instructions to read that contained a scenario and five tasks. Think aloud strategy was used throughout the session and was recorded using Morae Recorder [30]. We encouraged participants to talk aloud and describe method of completing the tasks. Participants completed the tasks without the assistance of the facilitator who would only mediate if there were any technical difficulties. However, there were no technical difficulties and facilitator was not required to mediate. After participants completed the tasks they filled out the demographic survey. At the end of the session, a debriefing session was conducted where participants were asked to elaborate on tasks they thought were problematic. Observations of interest to the facilitator were deliberated as well.

Data Analysis. Morae Recorder was used to log audio, video, on-screen activity, as well as inputs from the keyboard and mouse. We established that there were no major EHR interface change between round one data collection and round two that may affect the results of the study. The recorded sessions were observed using Morae Manager by computing performance measures using markers to pinpoint difficulties and errors the participants faced. Video analysis took approximately 1.5 h for each 20 min recorded session. The first phase in analysis was to assess the recorded sessions and tag any tasks that were unmarked during data collection. The second step was to separate each of the five tasks into smaller tasks to compute the task success rate. The statistical test used to compare performance measures was the t-test and geometric mean [31].

3 Results

Percent Task Success Rate. Geometric mean values of percent task success rates of five tasks were compared between the expert and novice physicians across two rounds (Fig. 1) [31]. There was a 25 percent point increase in novice physicians' percent task success rate between round one and round two, but it was not statistically significant (50 %, round 1 vs. 62 %, round 2, $p = 0.67$). Similarly, expert physicians had a 41 percent point increase in percent task success rate between round one and round two, however, there was no statistically significant difference (45 %, round 1 vs. 63 %, round 2, $p = 0.58$).

To identify learnability gap, round one and round two task success of both physician groups were compared. In round one, there was no statistically significant difference in the success rate between the two physician groups (45 %, expert group vs. 50 %, novice group, $p = 0.91$) and in round two, there was no statistically significant difference in the success rate between the two physician groups (63 %, expert group vs. 62 %, novice group, $p = 0.98$). In round one, novice physicians attained lower success rates in three out of five tasks: 3 – 5 and higher success rate than expert physicians in two out of five tasks: 1 and 2. In round two, novice physicians attained lower success rates in task 1, the same success rate in two tasks: 3 and 4, and lower success rates in two tasks: 2 and 5 (Table 1).

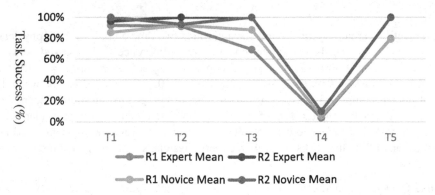

Fig. 1. Geometric mean values of percent task success rates of five tasks between the expert and novice physicians.

Time on Task (TOT). Geometric mean values of time-on-task (TOT) were compared between expert and novice physicians across two rounds Fig. 2. There was an 36 % increase in novice physicians' time on task between round one and round two, but it was not statistically significant (45 s, round 1 vs. 62 s, round 2, $p = 0.50$). There was a 24 % increase in expert physicians' time on task between round one and round two, but it was not statistically significant (37 s, round 1 vs. 45 s, round 2, $p = 0.66$).

Table 1. Demographics of 15 primary care resident physicians that participated in the usability test presented as percentages. Examined demographics include gender, age, race, and experience other than current EHR.

Demographics	Round 1				Round 2			
	Novice		Expert		Novice		Expert	
Gender								
Male	6	(60 %)	1	(17 %)	5	(63 %)	0	(0 %)
Female	4	(40 %)	5	(83 %)	3	(38 %)	4	(100 %)
Age (mean)	28 years		31 years		29 years		32 years	
Race/Ethnicity								
Black	0	(0 %)	0	(0 %)	0	(0 %)	0	(0 %)
Asian	1	(10 %)	0	(0 %)	1	(19 %)	0	(0 %)
White	9	(90 %)	6	(100 %)	7	(81 %)	4	(100 %)
American Indian/Alaskan Native	0	(0 %)	0	(0 %)	0	(0 %)	0	(0 %)
Pacific Islander	0	(0 %)	0	(0 %)	0	(0 %)	0	(0 %)
Experience other than current EHR								
None	4	(40 %)	1	(17 %)	3	(38 %)	1	(25 %)
Less than 3 months	2	(20 %)	0	(0 %)	2	(25 %)	0	(0 %)
3 months – 6 months	0	(0 %)	0	(0 %)	0	(0 %)	0	(0 %)
7 months – 1 year	1	(10 %)	1	(17 %)	1	(13 %)	1	(25 %)
Over 2 years	3	(30 %)	2	(33 %)	2	(25 %)	2	(50 %)

To identify learnability gap, round one and round two time on task for both physician groups were compared. In round one, no substantial difference was observed between the two physician groups (37 s, expert group vs. 45 s, novice group, $p = 0.45$) and similarly, in round two, no substantial difference ($p = 0.23$) was observed between the two physician groups (45 s, expert group vs. 62 s, novice group). In round one, novice physicians did not complete any of the five tasks faster than expert physicians, but completed task 4 at the same time. Similarly In round two, novice physicians did not complete any of the five tasks faster than expert physicians, but completed task 5 at the same time.

Mouse Clicks. Geometric mean values of mouse clicks were compared between the two physician groups across two rounds Fig. 3. There was a 47 % increase in novice physicians' mouse clicks between round one and round two, but it was not statistically significant (10 clicks, round 1 vs. 14 clicks, round 2, $p = 0.51$). Similarly, there was a 26 % increase in expert physicians' mouse clicks between round one and round two, but it was not statistically significant (8 clicks, round 1 vs. 11 clicks, round 2, $p = 0.67$).

To identify learnability gap, round one and round two mouse clicks for both physician groups were compared. Expert physicians completed the tasks with slightly fewer mouse clicks than novice physicians did in round one (8 clicks, expert group vs. 10 clicks, novice group, $p = 0.58$) and round two (11 clicks, expert group vs. 14 clicks,

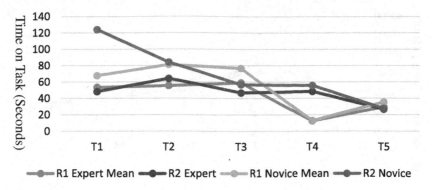

Fig. 2. Geometric mean values of time-on-task (TOT) compared between expert and novice physicians.

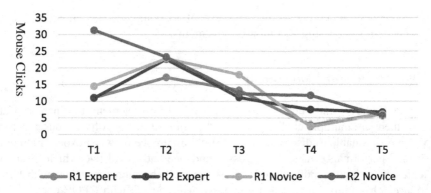

Fig. 3. Geometric mean values of mouse clicks compared between the two physician groups

novice group, $p = 0.38$). In round one, novice physicians used more mouse clicks to completed tasks 1–3, less mouse clicks to complete task 4, and the same number of clicks to complete task 5.

Mouse Movements. Geometric mean values of mouse movement, length of the navigation path to complete a given task, were compared between two physician groups across two rounds (Fig. 4). There was a 68 % increase in in novice physicians' mouse movements between round one and round two, but it was not statistically significant (8146 pixels, round 1 vs. 13,649 pixels, round 2, $p = 0.63$). There was a 28 % decrease in expert physicians' mouse movements between round one and round two, however, there was no statistically significant difference ($p = 0.64$) (8480 pixels, round 1 vs. 10,817 pixels, round 2).

To identify learnability gap, round one and round two mouse movements for both physician groups were compared. Overall, the novice physicians showed slightly longer mouse movements across the five tasks in round one (8480 pixels, expert group vs. 8146 pixels, novice group, $p = 0.59$) and round two (10,871 pixels, expert group vs. 13,649 pixels, novice group, $p = 0.34$). In round one, novice physicians used more

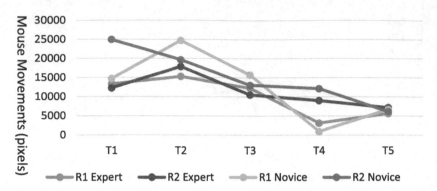

Fig. 4. Geometric mean values of mouse movement, length of the navigation path to complete a given task, compared between two physician groups.

mouse movement to complete all tasks except to complete task 4, which novice physicians completed using less mouse movements.

4 Discussion and Conclusion

While CPOEs have many benefits, such as, clinical improvement and increased efficiencies, there are multiple challenges created from insufficient software design. In our study, we were unable to discover any statistical difference between expert and novice physicians' performance measures across round one and round two which means we fail to reject the null hypothesis that physicians will be more proficient with CPOE experience. This study showed that longer exposure levels with CPOE does not correspond to being an expert, competent in using CPOEs [32]. A similar study by Kjeldskov, Skov, and Stage [12] identifying usability issues faced by novice and expert nurses studied the possibility of usability issues vanishing over time. Seven nurses completed fourteen and thirty hours of training before the first usability assessment that included seven tasks and subtasks centralized on the principal feature of the system. The same seven nurses retook the usability assessment involving the same seven tasks after fifteen months of everyday use of the system. Only two novice subjects solved all task ($p = 0.01$) while the entire expert subjects solved all seven tasks either completely or partially. Similar to the results of our study, no statistically significant difference between novice and expert nurses was found when considering only completely solved tasks (p = 0.08).

When designing CPOEs, disregarding usability issues may be partly responsible for potential human-computer interaction issues that may contribute to loss of productivity and a reduction in quality of patient care [33]. A literature review by Phansalkar et al., found that many basic human factors principles are not followed when designing clinical information systems [34]. Incorporating human-centered design, by involving users' critiques into the CPOE development process, may productively create a user-friendly system and may contribute to reducing the dissatisfaction that is associated with poor information display [35]. Designing CPOE displays that represent the pertinent information needed by physicians during clinic visits may decrease errors created by cognitive overload [36, 37]. A review written by Khajouei and Jaspers describes multiple studies expressing difficulty when searching for specific information in medication ordering systems because of inferior screen displays [32, 38]. Refining CPOE design based on information needs of clinicians in the electronic progress note by decreasing redundant information that is a part of the display and compressing the information being displayed, could address the human computer interaction problems presented in Khajouei and Jaspers' study encountered by users of the progress note [37, 39].

Limitations to This Study. This study was effective in recognizing differences in performance measures between novice and expert physicians but also contained several methodological limitations. This study was restricted to primary care physicians, a small sample size, and only involved one CPOE from one healthcare institution which conveys that results may not transferrable to other healthcare institutions and other specialties. The usability test was also conducted using a small sample of clinical tasks and may not represent other features and functions that may be used in other clinical scenarios. This study took place in a laboratory setting which does not consider distractions faced by physicians during clinical encounters. Although this study contains some methodological limitation, this is a well-controlled study that used triangular evaluation and instructions were straightforward to the physicians which permitted participants to complete the required tasks.

References

1. Committee on Identifying and Preventing Medication Errors. Preventing Medication Errors 2006, The National Academies Press, Washington, DC (2006)
2. Crossing the quality chasm: A new health system for the 21st century. National Academies Press, Washington, DC (2001)
3. Meaningful Use. Centers for Medicare and Medicaid Services (2012). http://www.cms.gov/Regulations-and-Guidance/Legislation/EHRIncentivePrograms/Meaningful_Use.html
4. Brown, N.: Driving EMR adoption: making EMRs a sustainable, profitable investment. Health Manag. Technol. **26**(5), 47–48 (2005)
5. Connolly, C.: Cedars-Sinai doctors cling to pen and paper. In: Washington Post (2005)
6. Scott, J.T., et al.: Kaiser Permanente's experience of implementing an electronic medical record: a qualitative study. BMJ **331**(7528), 1313–1316 (2005)
7. Smelcer, J., Miller-Jacobs, H., Kantrovich, L.: Usability of electronic medical records. J. Usability Stud. **4**(2), 70–84 (2009)
8. Berger, R.G., Kichak, J.P.: Computerized physician order entry: helpful or harmful? J. Am. Med. Inform. Assoc. **11**(2), 100–103 (2004)
9. Ash, J.S., Stavri, P.Z., Kuperman, G.J.: A consensus statement on considerations for a successful CPOE implementation. J. Am. Med. Inform. Assoc. **10**(3), 229–234 (2003)
10. Khajouei, R., Jaspers, M.W.: The impact of CPOE medication systems' design aspects on usability, workflow and medication orders: a systematic review. Methods Inf. Med. **49**(1), 3–19 (2010)
11. Chan, J., et al.: Usability evaluation of order sets in a computerised provider order entry system. BMJ Qual. Saf. **20**(11), 932–940 (2011)

12. Kjeldskov, J., Skov, M.B., Stage, J.: A longitudinal study of usability in health care: does time heal? Int. J. Med. Inform. **79**(6), e135–e143 (2010)
13. Neinstein, A., Cucina, R.: An analysis of the usability of inpatient insulin ordering in three computerized provider order entry systems. J. Diab. Sci. Technol. **5**(6), 1427–1436 (2011)
14. ISO 9241-11: Ergonomic Requirements for Office Work with Visual Display Terminals (VDTs): Part 11: Guidance on Usability. 1 ed. International Organization for Standardization, p. 22 (1998)
15. Systems and Software Engineering – Systems and software Quality Requirements and Evaluation (SQuaRE) – System and software quality models. International Organization for Standardization, Geneva, p. 34 (2011)
16. Elliott, G.J., Jones, E., Barker, P.: A grounded theory approach to modelling learnability of hypermedia authoring tools. Interact. Comput. **14**(5), 547–574 (2002)
17. Nielsen, J.: Usability Engineering, xiv edn, p. 358. Academic Press, Boston (1993)
18. Whiteside, J., et al.: User performance with command, menu, and iconic interfaces. In: Proceedings of the SIGCHI Conference on Human Factors in Computing Systems, pp. 185–191. ACM, San Francisco, California, USA (1985)
19. Lin, H.X., Choong, Y.-Y., Salvendy, G.: A proposed index of usability: a method for comparing the relative usability of different software systems. Behav. Inf. Technol. **16**(4–5), 267–277 (1997)
20. Tullis, T., Albert, W.: Measuring the User Experience: Collecting, Analyzing, and Presenting Usability Metrics, p. 336. Morgan Kaufmann Publishers Inc., San Francisco (2008)
21. Healthcare Reform: Impact on Physicians, in Health Capital Topics. Health Capital Consultants: HealthCapital.com, p. 3 (2011)
22. Brooke, J.: SUS-A quick and dirty usability scale. In: Jordan, P.W., et al. (eds.) Usability Evaluation in Industry, pp. 189–194. Taylor and Francis, London (1996)
23. MU 2011 Annual Report. MU Healthcare (2011). http://www.mydigitalpublication.com/publication/?i=106794. Accessed 15 April 2012
24. University Of Missouri Health Care Achieves Highest Level of Electronic Medical Record Adoption. University of Missouri Health Care News Releases (2013). http://www.muhealth.org/body.cfm?id=103&action=detail&ref=311
25. U.S. EMR Adoption Model Trends (2011). http://www.himssanalytics.org/docs/HA_EMRAM_Overview_ENG.pdf. Accessed 21 February 2014
26. Battaglia, M.: Convenience sampling. In: Lavrakas, P. (ed.) Encyclopedia of Survey Research Methods. Sage Publications Inc., Thousand Oaks (2008)
27. Barnum, C.: The magic number 5: is it enough for web testing? Inf. Des. J. **11**, 160–170 (2003)
28. Kim, M., et al.: A pilot study on usability analysis of emergency department information system by nurses. Appl. Clin. Inform. **3**, 135–153 (2012)
29. Lewis, J.R., Sauro, J.: The factor structure of the system usability scale. In: Kurosu, M. (ed.) HCD 2009. LNCS, vol. 5619, pp. 94–103. Springer, Heidelberg (2009)
30. Van Someren, M.W., Barnard, Y.F., Sandberg, J.A.: The Think Aloud Method: A Practical Guide to Modelling Cognitive Processes. Academic Press, London (1994)
31. Cordes, R.E.: The effects of running fewer subjects on time-on-task measures. Int. J. Hum.-Comput. Interact. **5**(4), 393–403 (1993)
32. Clarke, M.A., Belden, J.L., Kim, M.S.: Determining differences in user performance between expert and novice primary care doctors when using an electronic health record (EHR). J. Eval. Clin. Pract. **20**(6), 1153–1161 (2015)

33. Clarke, M.A., Steege, L.M., Moore, J.L., Belden, J.L., Koopman, R.J., Kim, M.S.: Addressing human computer interaction issues of electronic health record in clinical encounters. In: Marcus, A. (ed.) DUXU 2013, Part II. LNCS, vol. 8013, pp. 381–390. Springer, Heidelberg (2013)

34. Phansalkar, S., et al.: A review of human factors principles for the design and implementation of medication safety alerts in clinical information systems. J. Am. Med. Inform. Assoc. 17(5), 493–501 (2010)

35. Maguire, M.: Methods to support human-centred design. Int. J. Hum. Comput. Stud. 55(4), 587–634 (2001)

36. Belden, J., Grayson, R., Barnes, J.: Defining and Testing EMR Usability: Principles and Proposed Methods of EMR Usability Evaluation and Rating. Healthcare Information and Management Systems, Chicago (IL) (2009)

37. Clarke, M.A., et al.: Determining primary care physician information needs to inform ambulatory visit note display. Appl. Clin. Inform. 5(1), 169–190 (2014)

38. Khajouei, R., Jaspers, M.W.: CPOE system design aspects and their qualitative effect on usability. Stud. Health Technol. Inform. 136, 309–314 (2008)

39. Clarke, M., et al.: Creating a more readable electronic health record (EHR) model: analysis of primary care physicians' information needs. In: AMIA (2012)

40. Koopman, R.J., et al.: A diabetes dashboard and physician efficiency and accuracy in accessing data needed for high-quality diabetes care. Ann. Fam. Med. 9(5), 398–405 (2011)

Designed to Thrill: Exploring the Effects of Multimodal Feedback on Virtual World Immersion

Dimitrios Darzentas[1(✉)], Michael Brown[2], and Noirin Curran[3]

[1] Mixed Reality Lab, University of Nottingham, Nottingham, UK
`Dimitrios.Darzentas@nottingham.ac.uk`
[2] Horizon Research Institute, University of Nottingham, Nottingham, UK
`Michael.Brown@nottingham.ac.uk`
[3] Logitech, Cork, Ireland
`ncurran@logitech.com`

Abstract. The following paper presents research into the effects of multi- and uni- modal output on virtual immersion. It describes the implementation of a balanced experimental study designed to measure participant immersion in a variety of conditions and presents the resulting findings. These demonstrate the potential of primary and secondary modalities on the perception of the participants. The findings of the study can form part of the basis for a set of HCI guidelines for the creation of highly immersive digital experiences.

Keywords: Virtual worlds · Games · Immersion · Interaction · Modalities

1 Introduction

It is acknowledged that immersion, the subjective state of intense involvement in an experience [7], is a vital ingredient for numerous human-crafted experiences. From books [19, 28]; films [32, 34]; theatre [27] and games [2, 4, 17, 18, 25], immersion is recognised as being key to entertaining and engaging experiences.

In such artificial constructs the level of immersion is often determined by the quality of the work and the skill of its creation and delivery. These examples, however, rarely take advantage of the ability of extended use of sensory modalities to facilitate effective immersion. Such cases are usually limited by the form of their chosen medium. Even in cases where technology is leveraged to break the bounds of the medium, increase immersion and enrich the experience, such as with the growing and controversial domain of 3D films, they still rely on a single modality, in this case vision [35]. But virtual experiences need not be shackled by such modal limitations.

In digital experiences such as those created through virtual worlds - the domain examined in this paper - there are many varying definitions of the concepts of immersion and engagement. Some focus [25] on the engagement of learners. The authors make the important distinction that, when trying to achieve immersion, it is necessary to consider the level of engagement attained by the interactions with, and feedback from, the virtual environment but it is also important to consider the engagement that is promoted by the activities and concepts the user is involved in.

M. Kurosu (Ed.): Human-Computer Interaction, Part III, HCII 2015, LNCS 9171, pp. 384–395, 2015.
DOI: 10.1007/978-3-319-21006-3_37

Mount's interpretation [25] is applicable from the point of view of our research objective: to design and implement a digital game experience that achieves a high level of immersion and engagement, and investigate the hypothesis that unimodal and mutitimodal experiences create different levels of immersive response. Beyond the concept of an effective activity engagement, this research aims to leverage the power of multimodal interaction in achieving high levels of immersion, also by lowering the barriers to effective levels of environmental engagement because of seamless natural interfaces for input and refined multimodal output.

2 Background and Related Work

In digital experiences, engagement is a vital ingredient of immersion and there are, broadly speaking, two forms of engagement, mental and physical [10, 16]

Mental engagement is highly subjective and requires the experience to feature a context that the participant can relate to. The scenario may be one that is easily generalizable and acceptable by a variety of users. These scenarios tend to be abstract, providing little detail and relying on the immediacy of their nature, such as a base psychological need, in order to function. An example of this is fear and reflex responses such as dodging oncoming objects. Another type of mentally engaging scenario can be much more specialised or themed in order to allow an interested user to relate directly. Such cases require substantial investments, planning and design, and cater to specific user populations with thematic tastes.

Physical engagement, on the other hand, is primarily a matter of utilising interfaces that closely emulate the physical actions of the virtual scenario. Such engagement can directly promote physical immersion [30]. Examples include controllers which are physically identical to the object manipulated in the virtual world, or motion controllers and head mounted displays that achieve suspension of disbelief with regards to the physical presence and surpass the 'uncanny valley' [14, 15, 24]. The uncanny valley is a concept primarily associated with robotics and comes into play when the anthropomorphism of a robot is such that it is very similar to a human but not fully accurate. In such cases, humans experience instinctual feelings of revulsion. Similar effects can be experienced with virtual avatars and conflicts can arise when high fidelity manipulatable physical controllers do not exactly match their virtual counterparts.

Turning to human-human interaction, all of the primary senses are utilised. These feedback mechanisms are used by the human body to gather information about its condition and surroundings. More importantly, human interaction and communication is a multimodal affair. Everyday conversations go beyond the verbal and speech auditory cues. They include non-verbal elements such as: eye-contact; touch; gestures; body language and facial expressions. This both facilitates communication and delivers the visceral experience that humans are accustomed to experiencing.

Human computer interaction, however, still remains relatively limited in comparison to the richness of human interaction. There are numerous and substantial forms of multimodal input [21]. These include methods such as touch; voice; gaze; motion; gestures; and Brain-Machine-Interfaces. Inversely, output is mostly limited to visual and auditory. In contrast to the varied input methods, output is still mostly limited to screens and speakers with significant weight on the dominant visual modality [12, 31].

Research shows that auditory feedback and cues are important to human multimodal experiences. Larsson et al. (2002) tested [20] unimodal (aural only) cues and multimodal (aural and visual) cues in navigation and memory tasks in virtual environments finding that auditory information may greatly improve the experience and sometimes directly improve performance. Researchers have also investigated aural feedback in supporting orientation and navigation in virtual worlds where sound is used either as a support for the visual mode or as a substitute when no other sensory information is available. Additionally, they expand aural cues as either localisation or sonification. Localisation represents the inclusion of lifelike 3D sounds that aid in navigation and situational awareness while sonification is the use of sound to represent certain types of information. Finally, regarding somatosensory modalities, commercially available haptic feedback is usually limited to vibration. This does not always correspond to the real life feedback that the user would expect. Exceptions do exist, such as in the well-engineered and supported examples of force feedback controllers [12, 32].

Thus, motivated by the concept of immersion in crafted works across all fields of creativity and inspired by the related research, this study investigates the role of the various modalities in achieving high levels of immersion and engagement.

In terms of requirements, the design and implementation had to provide a balanced set of modal cues in order to explore the value of sensory modalities in achieving effective immersion and presence in virtual worlds. The implementation of the digital experience was evaluated by small scale pilot user tests in order to achieve as similar as possible amounts of information across the modalities. The first two modalities investigated were visual and auditory.

Regarding the game design, the implementation had to satisfy the guidelines for effective and engaging gameplay [1, 29].

3   Defining Immersion in Games

Characterising and measuring user experiences in virtual worlds are inherently difficult tasks and substantial research has been carried out to attain a level of understanding and to establish methodologies for evaluation. Concepts like immersion, have been adopted as a metric by the digital experience design and creation research communities. Research such as that of the Eindhoven University Game Experience Research Lab have postulated [17] that immersion and flow are candidates for gameplay evaluation. The nature of immersion in the context of games was further investigated in search of a concrete and applicable definition [18] and also with regard to the methods of its measurement [26].

In games, Brown and Cairns (2004) identify [4] three levels of immersion: 'engagement', 'engrossment' and 'total immersion'. 'Engagement', the lowest level, requires a user to invest "time, effort and attention" in order to learn the controls of a virtual environment. Next, 'engrossment', necessitates users becoming familiar with the environment and they must be able to experience emotional affectation by the narratives and activities involved. Finally, by overcoming barriers like empathy and

atmosphere, 'total immersion' can be experienced whereupon the users feel disconnected from reality and the passage of real world time. However, as has been noted by
others [25], the findings of Brown and Cairns are a useful classification of
engagement-based immersion but do not offer insight into the components that are
involved in each level of immersion.

Efforts to disambiguate immersion in games have led to research that attempts to
differentiate types of immersion based on the different types of information processing
of the human user instead of the degree of immersion. These include Vicarious, Action
Visceral and Mental Visceral Immersion [7], Sensory-Motoric, Cognitive and Emotional Immersion [2], Diegetic and Non-Diegetic Immersion [23], Diegetic and Situated
Immersion [33], Sensory, Challenge-Based and Imaginative Immersion [11], Mental
and Physical Immersion [31 and 5] and Perceptual and Psychological Immersion [22].

A recent, empirically grounded classification of types of immersion in games [7]
depicts immersion as having three distinct types: Vicarious Immersion, Mental Visceral
Immersion and Action Visceral Immersion. This classification emerged from an
extensive qualitative content analysis of online discussions with gamers and was
confirmed using an experimental survey-based analysis, with these types also emerging
spontaneously during the factor analysis stage of development of the IMX Questionnaire. These three types of immersion have the shared characteristic of a subjective
experience of intense involvement in a game. Vicarious Immersion occurs when the
player becomes intensely involved in a fictional world in which they may adopt the
feelings, thoughts and mannerisms of a character, and forget themselves and the real
world. In the most intense experiences of vicarious immersion, the character appears to
take on a life of its own. Action Visceral immersion occurs when the player feels a rush
of adrenaline and is swept away due to being caught-up-in-the-action of the game.
Mental Visceral Immersion involves getting deeply engaged in and excited by the
strategising and tactics of a game. It is important to note that one of the keys to
achieving immersion is the Suspension of Disbelief [8].

The different levels and types of engagement and immersion all contribute to the
experience [6]. The next sections describe a design and implementation that was motivated by these concerns that attempts to make use of the theories and findings in order to
create a digital entertainment experience that achieves high levels of immersion.

4 Technical Implementation

4.1 Rationale and Design

Bearing in mind the research surrounding immersion in virtual environments, work
began on designing a virtual digital entertainment experience that would allow for the
measurement of immersion of the participants across separate modalities and combinations thereof. The aim, was to design and implement a modular experimental setup
featuring a mentally engaging scenario and a contemporary interface that would promote high levels of physical engagement. The system output would feature output
across multiple modalities that could be isolated and combined as needed and would
provide similar amount of information to the participant.

Therefore, a study was designed featuring a simulated collision avoidance scenario as the basic gameplay premise. Specifically the participants would be introduced to a digital environment representative of a motorway and would have to avoid the oncoming traffic. This task would allow for a relatively generalizable and easy-to-relate-to context thereby allowing for mental engagement. In order to also achieve physical engagement, a natural input method was utilised: motion sensing technology. By directly mapping the mental objective of avoiding oncoming objects with a natural reflexive reaction, in this case physical movement, the suspension of disbelief was be easier to achieve and the barriers to immersion lowered.

In terms of game mechanics, the scenario and premise are quite simple, with the context and interface as the elements that promote immersion. The oncoming vehicles need to be avoided and their numbers increase as time passes. The ultimate goal of the player is to avoid the vehicles for as long as possible, an objective that becomes increasingly more difficult as the vehicles increase in number. The expected survival time of each playthrough was designed to last no more than 90 s.

4.2   Implementation Details

Physical Setup. Based on the requirement for low physical engagement barriers and the subsequent decision to use motion sensing interfaces, the setup required a considerable amount of space for the participant to be able to move unencumbered and for the interface devices to properly function. Additionally a suitable display method had to be established for the visual feedback. Initially it was planned to use a projected display in order to maximise the viewable virtual area and minimise the possibility of display limitation breaking immersion. In the process of establishing the physical setup, however, it was determined that a large screen would serve the purpose adequately and with numerous practical advantages, such as reliability and relative portability.

Software Implementation. Following the physical setup, a high fidelity implementation was necessary. For this purpose, the Unity3D engine was used to create a representation of a highway road with appropriate visual elements and a physical make-up to enhance and facilitate the gameplay. For instance, the road representation allowed for mapping of the virtual side barriers to the physical objects limiting the movement of the participants.

The moving vehicles that act as the objects to be avoided are also visible. Except in the case of the simulated fog that limits the long range visibility of the participant, thus enhancing and balancing the level of information delivered by the visual and auditory modalities.

User Interaction. As mentioned above, it was decided to utilise motion sensing interfaces in order to achieve an engaging user interaction. For this purpose, a Microsoft Kinect device was set up to map the movements of the participants on a one to one basis with their virtual avatar. Figure 1 illustrates this effect with the onscreen avatar matching the pictured volunteer's body stance, position and gesture.

Modality Balance. The balance of the provided modalities was also considered. The purpose of this was to create a digital entertainment experience that explores and utilises the effects of separate and combined modalities in achieving effective immersion.

Fig. 1. Scenario test run showing the One-to-One Motion Mapping.

The two modalities utilised were Vision and Audio. Specifically, the primary objective was to enable the implementation to be able to separate and combine the modalities creating different gameplay situations and assisting in the understanding or even determining, to some extent, the role of each modality in achieving immersion.

Therefore the amount of information that each modality delivered needed to be as similar as possible. With the Visual modality being particularly dominant in collision avoidance tasks [12, 31], the effect of fog was utilised to limit the range of this modality and bring it into line with the Auditory modality. Additionally, significant effort went into implementing a robust audio system that would accurately represent the auditory signature of the oncoming vehicles enabling the participants to determine their location using sound. For this purpose, noise cancelling headphones were used in order to isolate the participants from the physical environment and to allow them the full benefit of the virtual soundscape.

5   Study Methology

5.1   Participants

A group of 19 participants played and evaluated the game in each of the modality combinations. Participants ranged in age from late teens to mid-40 s, 4 female and 15 male. Basic background information relating to the experiment was gathered such as experience with technology and games. Especially in the latter case there was a balanced variety within the participant group as it included both self-described "gamers" and individuals with limited or no experience.

5.2   Procedure

Each participant played the game a total of 12 times, with a set of one trial run and three timed runs for each modality combination: only audio, only visual and audio/visual combined. Their stated task was to play the game by avoiding the oncoming vehicles for as long as possible. For a set of runs with both modalities enabled, the participant would experience the full breadth of the visual and auditory cues. For the visual-only set of runs, all sound would be disabled but the participant would wear noise cancelling headphones in order to maintain isolation from the physical environment. For the audio-only set of runs the participants were blindfolded and therefore their only sensory input was aural via the isolating headphones. The order in which the participants experienced the modality combinations was counterbalanced to control for order effects.

With regards to data collection, the IMX Questionnaire, a quantitative measure of immersive response [7], was completed by each participant at the end of each 4 run set, in relation to the specific modality combination just experienced. This version of the IMX consisted of 16 items with 5-point Likert scale items as responses. This version of the questionnaire measures three factors of game immersion, specifically: "General Immersion"; "Action Visceral Immersion"; and "Mental Visceral Immersion". Upon completion of all three sets, participants completed a Critical Incidence Technique [13] style questionnaire, reported their preferred modality combination for game play and a short semi-structured interview was carried out exploring participant reactions to the game. Additionally, survival times from each trial were recorded.

6   Results and Conclusions

Following the execution of the experiment, a number of findings, both qualitative and quantitate, were produced and are presented in the following sections. Additionally a number of conclusions were drawn from these findings.

6.1   Quantitative Results

Immersion. The IMX questionnaire results were scored for each mode of interaction (audio, visual or both) and game immersion (General Immersion, Action Visceral Immersion and Mental Visceral Immersion), see Fig. 2. A 3*3 repeated measured MANOVA was performed to explore the impact of output modality used on these variables. The MANOVA was found to be significant (F = 338.4, df = 16, P < 0.001).

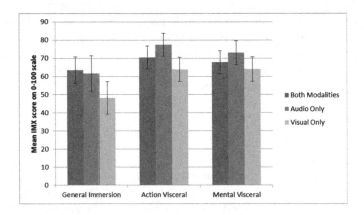

Fig. 2. Mean score and 95 % confidence intervals for IMX immersion scales.

Uni-verative testing with a Greenhouse-Geisser correction for Sphericity showed significant effects on General Immersion (F = 5.714, df = 1.943, p = 0.0076) Action Visceral (F = 7.156, df = 1.856, p < 0.0032) and Mental Visceral (F = 3.507, df = 1.806, p = 0.046).

A post hoc within subjects t-test revealed a number of significant effects as shown in Table 1.

Table 1. Post Hoc testing of modality combinations on aspects of immersion.

Measure	Modality 1	Modality 2	T	df	p
General Immersion	*Both*	*Visual only*	*3.280*	*18*	*0.004**
		Audio only	0.379	18	0.709
	Visual only	*Audio only*	*2.522*	*18*	*0.021**
Action Visceral	Both	Visual only	1.739	18	0.099
		Audio only	1.806	18	0.088
	Visual only	*Audio only*	*4.445*	*18*	*<0.001**
Mental Visceral	Both	Visual only	0.977	18	0.341
		Audio only	1.515	18	0.147
	Visual only	*Audio only*	*3.143*	*18*	*0.006**

*Significant effects at p < 0.05 highlighted.

Performance and Preference. Game play time was examined in order to explore performance differences between the modality combinations with longer play times indicating a more successful session, as illustrated in Fig. 3.

A repeated measures ANOVA and post hoc repeated measures t-test, revealed:

- a significant multivariate effect (F = 121.724, df = 2;17, p < 0.001)
- a significant difference between 'Both modalities' and 'Audio only' (T = 15.01, df = 18, p < 0.001)

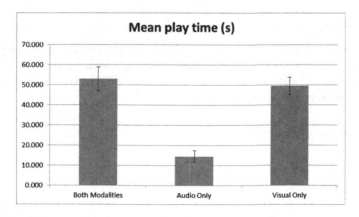

Fig. 3. Mean play time and 95 % confidence intervals for both modalities, audio only and visual only.

- a significant difference between 'Visual only and 'Audio only' (T = 11.781, df = 18, p < 0.001)
- a non-significant difference between 'Both modalities' and 'Visual only' (T = 1.129, df = 18, p = 0.274)

Despite the Audio only mode being much more difficult 4 participants reported it as their preferred mode of play with all others (15) preferring to use both modalities. None preferred the visual only mode of play.

6.2   Qualitative Results

Responses to the Critical Incidence Technique style questionnaire and interviews were collated and a thematic analysis performed, identifying three common themes: Rapid immersion, the importance of sound and engaging audio experiences.

Rapid immersion. Responses indicated that a high level of immersion was attained very quickly. This was especially noteworthy considering the very short duration of the gameplay sessions. Participants stated that they found the experience "engrossing" and "entertaining" as they would expect from a game. Familiarisation time was very brief, with the participants becoming quickly engrossed in the scenario. The users really tried to survive and felt they reacted as they would if they had been in such a situation in real life. They tried diving to the sides, turning sideways to fit between oncoming vehicles and sometimes panicking.

> *"Damn this is intense!" - Participant 2*
> *"It's going to crush my toes!" - Participant 13*

The importance of sound. Most participants agreed that the combination of the visual and aural modalities led to the best overall experience. They also stated that the visual-only version was lacking in comparison with this and felt "disconnected" and "muted". Some participants found that their attention wandered and the expectance of aural cues was "noticeable" and their absence was "disconcerting".

> *"Something was missing, I was waiting for the crunch." - Participant 17*
> *"It felt mechanical, like paying Candy Crush." - Participant 13*

Engaging audio experiences. Many shared the opinion that the audio-only version was "intense" and "thrilling" and that being deprived of their vision required them to immediately engage with the game and concentrate on survival, thus very rapidly creating an intensely immersive experience.

> *"That was absolutely terrifying! I was all there!" - Participant 6*
> *"Oh god oh god oh god..." – Participant 4*

7   Conclusions

The research objective of this study was to investigate the hypothesis that unimodal and multimodal digital experiences create different levels of immersive response.

From the above results, and keeping in mind the context and scope of the study, a number of conclusions emerge. Firstly, with regards to achieving immersion, it can be seen that the combination of natural input interfaces and relatable scenarios which are matched to the input can lead to high levels of immersion. As outlined, the sample included individuals who self-identify as gamers as well as individuals with limited exposure to games, and high levels of immersion occurred regardless of the level of familiarity with game playing. Secondly, in terms of unimodal output, the removal of the primary sense, vision in this case, had a dramatic effect, leading to intense experiences, emotions and reactions, and subsequently 'total' immersion. Conversely, the removal of a secondary sense (audio) without any context, had the exact opposite effect, with users becoming disconnected with the experience. This supports the hypothesis that unimodal and multimodal digital experiences create different levels of immersive response, also indicating that different levels of immersive response can arise depending on which output is utilised.

8 Future Work

Future work should investigate other modalities and combinations thereof. The participants commented on how they grew to expect some sort of physical feedback such as "wind disturbance from a near miss" and the "vibrations under their feet" while playing. It would be beneficial to explore these possibilities with other modalities but it would also be constructive to further refine and experiment with the visual and auditory modalities. For instance, the use of immersive displays such as the Oculus Rift DK2 [3] could further enhance immersion and therefore enhance the experience.

These technologies would also allow for the creation of a digital game experience where the suppression of specific modalities was contextualised. For example, vision could be suppressed due to fog or auditory perception suppressed due to the presence of loud environmental noises such as rain or heavy machinery. It would be interesting to determine whether the contextual suppression of the senses will affect immersion, or lack of immersion that users found in the conducted experiment. These findings could be formed into HCI guidelines for the design of immersive experiences.

Finally, future work could also take an inclusive "Design for All" stance, to determine whether the work on isolating modalities and immersion could be used to design games that can be enjoyed by players with and without sensory impairments, i.e. by all. Understanding the contribution of the various sensory modalities and their inherent power in communication information and achieving immersion, could potentially open the door to a level playing field for users of mixed abilities in cooperative and competitive contexts.

Acknowledgements. We gratefully acknowledge the support of the Horizon Centre for Doctoral Training (EPSRC Grant No. EP/G037574/1) and the RCUK Horizon Digital Economy Research Hub grant, EP/G065802/1.

References

1. Adams, E.: Fundamentals of Game Design. New Riders, Thousand Oaks (2010)
2. Björk, S., Holopainen, J.A.: Patterns In Game Design. Cengage Learning, Boston (2005)
3. Boas, Y.A.G.V. (n.d.): Overview of Virtual Reality Technologies. http://mms.ecs.soton.ac.uk/2013/papers/yavb1g12_25879847_finalpaper.pdf
4. Brown, E., Cairns, P.: A grounded investigation of game immersion. In: Extended Abstracts on Human Factors in Computing Systems, CHI EA 2004, pp. 1297–1300 (2004)
5. Carr, D.: Computer Games: Text, Narrative and Play. Polity, Cambridge, UK (2006)
6. de Castell, S., Jenson, J.: Worlds in Play: International Perspectives on Digital Games Research. Peter Lang, New York (2007)
7. Curran, N.: The psychology of immersion and development of a quantitative measure of immersive response in games. CORA Open Research Archive (2013)
8. Dede, C.: Immersive interfaces for engagement and learning. Science 323(5910), 66–69 (2009)
9. Deterding, S., Dixon, D., Khaled, R., Nacke, L.: From game design elements to gamefulness: defining 'gamification'. In: Proceedings of the MindTrek 2011, pp. 9–15. ACM (2011)
10. Dickey, M.D.: Engaging by design: how engagement strategies in popular computer and video games can inform instructional design. Educ. Tech. Res. Dev. 53(2), 67–83 (2005)
11. Ermi, L., Mäyrä, F.: Fundamental components of the gameplay experience: analysing immersion. In: DIGRA (2005)
12. Ernst, M.O., Bülthoff, H.H.: Merging the senses into a robust percept. Trends Cogn. Sci. 8(4), 162–169 (2004)
13. Flanagan, J.C.: The critical incident technique. Psychol. Bull. 51(4), 327–358 (1954)
14. Gee, F.C., Browne, W.N., Kawamura, K.: Uncanny valley revisited. In: IEEE International Workshop on Robot and Human Interactive Communication, RO-MAN 2005 (2005)
15. Geller, T.: Overcoming the Uncanny Valley. IEEE Comput. Graphics Appl. 28(4), 11–17 (2008)
16. Radu, Vasile: Application. In: Radu, Vasile (ed.) Stochastic Modeling of Thermal Fatigue Crack Growth. ACM, vol. 1, pp. 63–70. Springer, Heidelberg (2015)
17. IJsselsteijn, W., de Kort, Y., Poels, K., Jurgelionis, A., Bellotti, F.: Characterising and measuring user experiences in digital games. Proc. ACE 2, 27 (2007)
18. Jennett, C., Cox, A.L., Cairns, P., Dhoparee, S., Epps, A., Tijs, T., Walton, A.: Measuring and defining the experience of immersion in games. Int. J. Hum. Comput. Stud. 66(9), 641–661 (2008)
19. Kucklich, J.: Literary Theory and computer games. In: Proceedings of the COSIGN, pp. 51–58 (2001)
20. Larsson, P., Vastfjall, D., Kleiner, M.: Better presence and performance in virtual environments by improved binaural sound rendering. Proc. AES 22, 2002 (2002)
21. Lebedev, M.A., Nicolelis, M.A.L.: Brain–machine interfaces: past, present and future. Trends Neurosci. 29(9), 536–546 (2006)
22. Lombard, M., Ditton, T.B., Crane, D., Davis, B., Gil-Egui, G., Horvath, K., Rossman, J.: Measuring presence: a literature-based approach to the development of a standardized paper-and-pencil instrument (2000)
23. McMahan, A.: Immersion, engagement, and presence - a Method for analyzing 3-D video games. In: Wolf, M.J.P., Perron, B. (eds.) The Video Game Theory Reader, vol. 1. Routledge Chapman & amp, New York (2003)
24. Mori, M.: The uncanny valley. Energy 7(4), 33–35 (1970)

25. Mount, N.J., Chambers, C., Weaver, D., Priestnall, G.: Learner immersion engagement in the 3D virtual world: principles emerging from the DELVE project. ITALICS **8**, 40–56 (2009)
26. Nacke, L., Lindley, C.A.: Flow and immersion in first-person shooters: measuring the player's gameplay experience. In: Proceedings of the 2008 Conference on Future Play: Research, Play, Share, Future Play 2008, pp. 81–88. ACM, New York (2008)
27. Reaney, M.: Virtual reality and the theatre: immersion in virtual worlds. Digit. Creativity **10**(3), 183–188 (1999)
28. Ryan, M.-L.: Immersion vs. interactivity: virtual reality and literary theory. SubStance **28**(2), 110–137 (1999)
29. Salen, K., Zimmerman, E.: Rules of Play: Game Design Fundamentals. MIT, Cambridge (2004)
30. Sherman, W.R., Craig, A.B.: Understanding Virtual Reality Interface, Application, and Design. Morgan Kaufmann, San Francisco (2003)
31. Shimojo, S., Shams, L.: Sensory modalities are not separate modalities: plasticity and interactions. Curr. Opin. Neurobiol. **11**(4), 505–509 (2001)
32. Stapleton, C.B., Hughes, C.E.: Mixed reality and experiential movie trailers: combining emotions and immersion to innovate entertainment marketing. In: Proceedings of the SIMCHI (2005)
33. Taylor, L.N., Acknowledgments, T.P.: Video Games: Perspective, Point-of-view, and Immersion. University of Florida (2002)
34. Visch, V.T., Tan, E.S., Molenaar, D.: The emotional and cognitive effect of immersion in film viewing. Cogn. Emot. **24**(8), 1439–1445 (2010)

Survey on Risk Management Based on Information Security Psychology

Yasuko Fukuzawa[1(✉)], Masaki Samejima[2], and Hiroshi Ujita[3]

[1] Yokohama Research Laboratory, Hitachi, Ltd., Yokohama, Japan
yasuko.fukuzawa.pd@hitachi.com
[2] Graduate School of Information Science and Technology, Osaka University,
Suita, Japan
samejima@ist.osaka-u.ac.jp
[3] The Canon Institute for Global Studies, Tokyo, Japan
ujita.hiroshi@canon-igs.org

Abstract. In developing Cyber Physical Systems, such as smart grid and smart cities, risk management technologies play an important role to provide safe and secure services. In this paper, focusing on changes of recent threats represented by Social engineering, a survey shows that the information security psychology is valuable for the risk management of the Cyber Physical Systems. Through surveying, we outline the risk management framework for Cyber Physical Systems.

Keywords: Security · Cyber physical systems · Risk management · Information security psychology

1 Introduction

Cyber-Physical Systems (CPS) [17, 18], such as smart grid and smart cities, lets Control Systems cooperate with Cyber Systems strongly. CPS are integrations of computation, networking, and physical processes. Embedded computers and networks monitor and control the physical processes, with feedback loops where physical processes affect computations and vice versa.

So far, in each of control systems and information systems, a technique to manage risk has been developed, e.g. the operational techniques such as hazard analysis and threat analysis, design of security systems architecture, the abnormal detection and diagnosis technology and so on. The techniques have been already used by various systems. However, malicious actions for systems are changing. The social engineering which used the psychological weakness of the person becoming a victim increases these days. "Advanced Persistent Threat" is known as a representative attack. Therefore, a framework of risk management that paid its attention to the psychology of an assailant and the victim is demanded.

The outline of this paper is as follows. In Sect. 2, we explain the risk of Cyber Physical Systems and introduce the Committee of this field. In Sect. 3, we discuss the framework of risk management based on information security psychology. In Sect. 4,

© Springer International Publishing Switzerland 2015
M. Kurosu (Ed.): Human-Computer Interaction, Part III, HCII 2015, LNCS 9171, pp. 396–408, 2015.
DOI: 10.1007/978-3-319-21006-3_38

we give information about trend of the information security psychology. In Sect. 5 concludes the paper.

2 Trend of IT Systems and IT Risk Management

This section shows the trend of IT systems, and the need of the risk management based on Information Security Psychology.

2.1 Cyber Physical Systems and IT Risks

Cyber Physical Systems (CPS), such as smart grid and smart cities, have critical assets, so risk management technologies plays an important role on providing safe and secure services. And CPS consists of not only various devices but also various human such as operators and general users. Because human is a main factor of risks, IT risks on CPS depend on human.

Figure 1 shows a constitution model of CPS. The control object of CPS is a system of the real world to show to a retainer of Fig. 1. The information of the real world is collected with plural sensors, and that is handed by a controller through a network. The user of CPS makes the analysis of gleanings and decision making of the necessary control using a controller and inputs control contents into a controller. The control contents are handed by an actuator through a network, and the actuator controls it for the real world. Therefore it is said that CPS is a system letting real world cooperate with the cyber world as an information processing environment. Considering a smart grid as one of CPU, we collect domestic power consumption and quantity of home generation of electricity with a sensor and control the power transmission.

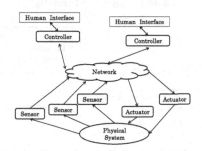

Fig. 1. Model of cyber physical system

Conventionally, there are a lot of systems controlling an object based on sensor information. However, CPS include a tight coupling of cyber world and real world, which is quite different from conventional systems. Based on the fact that consumers join as power suppliers that are unstable in a smart grid, we contribute to avoid blackout and improve the reliability. On the other hand, not only profit but also risk will happen due to the difference from the conventional systems. For example, a service stops by wrong information from the real world, which makes damage the real world. Risks of CPS also have been considered in the existing system, but the evaluation level of the risks may become larger than ever before.

The factors to decide a risk evaluation level are "Value of assets", "threats", and "Weakness (vulnerability)". Therefore, it is important how you control these factors to reduce a risk level.

In addition, a risk in CPS is different from a risk in the existing system from the viewpoint of "Value of Asset", "Threats", and "Weakness (vulnerability)". A large number of components cooperate complicatedly in CPS, which increases a risk level of CPS.

- An influence range by the attack spreads out. In other words, the value of assets is high.
- An attack point and assailants increase. For example, CPS includes not only an operator but also a general user, and the outbreak frequency of the attack increases.
- Conventionally, a vulnerable device is used in a system. This makes the system more vulnerable.

Based upon the foregoing, it is thought that the evaluation level of the risk in CPS is higher than an existing system, and sufficient risk management is necessary for CPS in the introduction.

2.2 Security and Safety

Table 1 shows a concept of "Security" and "Safety". The threat about IT System is classified into two types. One type is Safety and the other is Security [1].

Table 1. Safety and security

			Assets	
			Physical (System, Life)	Non-physical (Information, Image)
Threat	Accidental	Natural disaster (Earthquake, Flood, Thunderbolt etc.)	Safety (Reliability, Availability, Maintainability)	
		Breakdown (Hardware/Software Obstacle, Line trouble, Overload etc.)		
		Error (Data input error, Software bug, Operative mistake, False connection etc.)		
	Intentional	Illegal act of the third party (Illegal access etc.)	Security (Confidentiality, Integrity, Availability, Authenticity, Accountability, Non-repudiation, Reliability)	
		Illegal act of the persons concerned (Subsequent denial of the contract etc.)		

Safety: It is a concept against an accidental threat (danger) that is in human, organization, and resources. It mainly points to the possibility that reliability, availability, and Maintainability of the information are lost. Examples include Natural disaster (Earthquake, Flood, Thunderbolt etc.), Breakdown (Hardware/Software Obstacle, Line trouble, Overload etc.), and Error (Data input error, Software bug, Operative mistake, False connection etc.).

Security: It is a concept against an intentional threat (danger) that is in human, organization, and resources. It mainly points to the possibility of the value loss. The value is asset's Confidentiality, Integrity, Availability, Authenticity, Accountability, Non-repudiation and Reliability. Examples include Illegal act of the third party and Illegal act of the persons concerned.

"Safety" means the protection from "Human Error", and "Security" means the protection from "Human Illegal Act". Threats are often caused by human factors. Therefore as well as technical measures, it is thought that legal and ethical measures are necessary to manage the risk that a malicious user produces intentionally.

The information security psychology is positioning working on from the psychological side of the relational person (an assailant and a victim) about the risk management of the IT system [2].

2.3 Need of the Risk Management by the Information Security Psychology

In risk management, it is extremely complicated but important to consider the psychological side. So, we organized a committee for survey of risk management based on information security psychology in The Institute of Electrical Engineers of Japan. The mission of the committee is as follows:

1. Investigation into need and trend of the information security from a psychological aspect in IT systems.
2. Investigation and analyses of information security psychology, information security economics, the risk evaluation technology.
3. Consideration and proposal which are based on (1) (2) for realizing resilient system.

The following shows the risk management framework based on the information security psychology by this activity [1].

3 Risk Management Framework

This section shows the framework of the risk management based on Information Security Psychology. The framework is considered by the action of the person concerned with an IT system to clarify the positioning.

3.1 Classification of Unsecured Act

The actions of the person whom a system may plunge into an undesirable state are known to be classified like Fig. 2 [4]. As for the unsecured acts, it is classified in having intention or not.

A conventional accident model is the domino model, in which causes of troubles and errors are analyzed and measures are taken. In the model, slip, lapse, and mistake are used which are the classification of the unsafe act to occur by on-site work. These are categorized as the basic error types, while violation which is intentional act violating rule has become increased recently and considered as social accident.

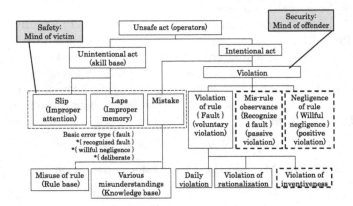

Fig. 2. Classification of unsecured act (modified Reason.J)

3.2 Model of Attack

Table 2 shows the classification of the attack model.

- Type1: Type1 is a direct attack type. This is the crime action that a system operator and an internal person and third party cause directly with malice. Type1 is human violation itself.

Table 2. Model of attacks

Direct Model	Malice	Attack
Indirect Model (Social Engineering)	Malice Vulnerability	Attack (Targeted/ Drinking fountain)
Cluster Model (Accumulation of goodwill acts becomes malice: Recognized fault, or Willful negligence)	Goodwill	Attack

- Type2: This is the indirect attack model that an assailant lets the operators such as operators cause human error. For example, there is increasing "advanced persistent threat" these days, this is so-called social engineering [3]. The assailant takes advantage of the weakness of a psychology and the action of the person becoming a victim. And a victim carries out the invasions to the facilities and a system, does the acquisition, the manipulation and the destruction of the information. For example, a link in the email text guides to the malice site that transmits a virus to PCs. The information in the PC is destroyed, and are sent to other PCs is known. As for such attack, the sender of the email pretends to be a manager and a reliable person and the distinction of a genuine article or the imitation is difficult and is hard to notice an attack. The act of the assailant is human violation, and the action of the victim is human error.

- Type3: This is a group model. It has no ill will for a personal action. However, it is taken an in total malicious action when they organize the group (willful negligence/fault of recognition). The authors analyzed the origin of an event in the use of the smart grid using Fault Tree. The event is that "Electricity consumption increased, and the administrator requested each section to save Electricity, but the member did not follow it, and, as a result, a blackout occurred" (See Fig. 3). According to the analysis, it is assumed that, "you will not need to cooperate with power saving because it is lost power and became last time" or "oneself will not need to cooperate because everybody will cooperate with power saving" causes a blackout. The psychology such as the optimistic fantasies in the group acts here. "Group thinking" consists of the following three categories [5].

- Overestimations of the group (Illusions of invulnerability creating excessive optimism and encouraging risk taking, Unquestioned belief in the morality of the group, causing members to ignore the consequences of their actions)
- Closed-Mindedness (Rationalizing warnings that might challenge the group's assumptions, Stereotyping those who are opposed to the group as weak, evil, biased, spiteful, impotent, or stupid)
- Pressure Toward Uniformity (Self-censorship of ideas that deviate from the apparent group consensus, Illusions of unanimity among group members, silence is viewed as agreement, Direct pressure to conform placed on any member who questions the group, couched in terms of "disloyalty", Mind guards : self-appointed members who shield the group from dissenting information)

The result of the analysis of Fig. 3 is explained by "Group thinking". The action of the person depends on a personal characteristic and both environment and situation. The action in the group is known to regard a different action (including the social promotion, social loafing) as the action in the one.

From the viewpoint of Information Security Psychology, a victim becomes the weakness of the system and a victim causes human error. Studies on the state of the psychology of an assailant are not sufficient, but supported by criminal psychology research in the sociology.

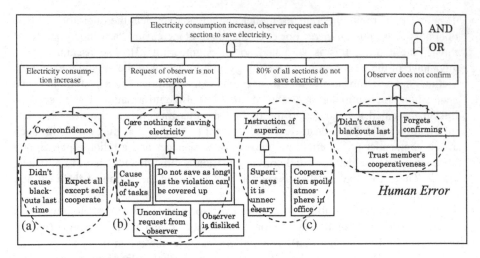

Fig. 3. Factor analysis of power failure outbreak

3.3 Situation

The action of the person depends on a personal characteristic and both environment and situation

- Position in System: An Illegal actor is the third party or the persons concerned. The case of the third party includes "outside injustice". The case of the persons concerned is "inside injustice".
- Attribute: The difference between a person in organization and a general publics are responsibility and regulation. Therefore, person in organization and general publics may do different acts on the same situation. In addition, the action in the group is known to regard a different action. For example, the collaboration performance per person in the group decreases with increase of the number of people in a group. This phenomenon is free rider or social loafing. Or work efficiency only costs because a large number of human beings perform the same work in a group. The social restraint that work efficiency decreases by social promotion and work contents or a motive produces a thing.
- Motive: Malicious mind causes "Human violation". The following is the malicious motives.

  - Intellectual play and mischief.
  - The money(profit) acquisition.
  - Political claim by hacktivist, or dissatisfaction
    And, on insider has another one.
  - Fear, uneasiness by the pressure from the neighborhood

On the Other Hand, Human Error Does not Have Motives. the Human Error Without the Intention Is Unconsciousness and Carelessness, and the Human Error with the Intention Namely the Mistake Is Misunderstood

Table 3. Injustice in IT systems

		Attribute			
		General		Organization	
		Individuals / Group		Individuals / Group	
Position in System	Persons Concerned	---		**Inside Injustice** (A) •Money •Dissatisfaction •Fear	range for CPS
	Third Party	**Outside Injustice** (B) •Money •Technical ostentation	(C) •Principles claim	**Organized Crime** (D) •National defense •Money	Motive

Table 3 shows that the classified crimes in the IT system by based on (a)-(c).

- Internal Injustice: It is a crime caused by the person in the organization. The main motive is the acquisition of money and the result, pressure from dissatisfaction or the person concerned on organization (A).
- Outside Injustice: There are two groups. One group is hacktivist whose motive is Principles claim (C). The other group's purpose is intellectual play (offender for pleasure) and money acquisition (D).
- Organized Crime: This Crime is done by various groups (including Nation and Mafia) with organized intention (D).

A national security domain is the sky, the sea, the land, the space, and Cyberspace. Defense from (C), (D) in Cyberspace is very important. However, (C), (D) have the strong will and compelling force more than feeling, and it is difficult to treat it by information security psychology. (C), (D) are out of scope in this paper.

In addition, in CPS, person in organization may be mixed with a general publics. For example, certain person is consumer of the electricity at the same time as an electricity supplier in the smart grid. Of course, this is insider.

3.4   Risk Management Framework

Figure 4 shows the framework of the risk management based on Information Security Psychology. The risks in IT System are defined by Assets, Threat, and Vulnerability in the system, then goal of risks management is the controlling them. Not only the technical aspect but also the legal side and the ethical side are necessary to prevent the malice of the user from leading to a risk. It is necessary to utilize knowledge on various human factor cultivated in psychology and criminology. In the human factor utilization, there are two important points, one is person in organization and a general publics, and the other is human error and human violation.

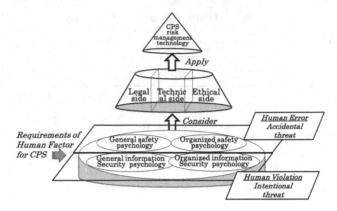

Fig. 4. Framework of the risk management based on information security psychology

4 Risk Management Based on Information Security Psychology

The information security psychology is a stage arranging a systematic theory and frame based on an individual risk on a system. Based on this, the information security psychology for the risk of the IT system is described. In addition, the future directions of the risk management are described.

4.1 Inside Injustice

"Inside Injustice" is done by an Illegal actor who is the persons concerned.

One of the works about the "Internal Injustice" is MERIT (Management and Education of Risks of Insider Threat) [6]. This models the action of the internal unjust person using "Systems Dynamics" and analyzes the characteristic tendency and factor of the internal unjust person. "Systems Dynamics" is a technique to model the behavior of systems changing dynamically such as the time.

In addition, the countermeasure of the internal injustice is considered by using the criminal psychology knowledge. Requirements of the crime establishment are that "a crime attempter" meets at "opportunity of the crime". Specifically, the "crime opportunity theory" and "crime cause theory" are used. The "crime cause theory" is a way of thinking for preventing a criminal by removing the social cause of a criminal. On the other hand, "crime opportunity theory" is thought to prevent a crime by not giving a criminal the opportunity of the crime.

"Situational Crime Prevention" is based on "crime opportunity theory" [7, 8]. In this, "The environment of the place that a crime produces" is the main factor of the crime outbreak, and the environment factor should be removed. Based on "Situational Crime Prevention", five points of view to control internal injustice are arranged. The five points of view are "Increase the Effort", "Increase the Risks", "Reduce the Rewards", "Reduce Provocations", and "Remove Excuses". In conformity with this framework, examined measure concretely for the internal crime is reported [9]. In this report, individual about attack type1, 2, or 3; is not considered. By methodology cultivated in criminology, the examination of measures is accomplished generally. In this report, it is mentioned that the measures from the legal side and the ethical side are necessary.

In addition, according to the framework of the "Situational Crime Prevention", not only the real world but also the examination that is going to apply to the field of information security is accomplished [10]. In addition, there are working papers [11] and the guidelines [12] about the injustice on internal person.

4.2 Outside Injustice

An Illegal actor is the third party is "outside injustice".

Requirements of the crime establishment are that "a crime attempter" meets at "the opportunity of the crime". However, factors to make a certain person in the whole general public "a crime attempter" are various, and it is difficult to identify it. So the removal of the factor is difficult. Therefore, for the injustice by the third party, examination from the information security psychology is not enough regardless of type difference (type1, 2, 3) in attack.

About the outside injustice by the third party, intelligence to lead to outbreak is expected in future. For example, the relationship of the action of the user who is easy to encounter the damage of PC operation and cyber attacks such as an email or the Web is studied [13].

In the situation on the victim side of attack type2, there is examination to the example bass of the social engineering. A human characteristic (reciprocation characteristics, a commitment and consistency, social proof, goodwill, authority, rarity) causing the social engineering is pointed out [2, 3].

4.3 Risk Management by Model

It is not so easy to perceive risks appropriately, *e.g.* the risk that makes a huge loss and happens rarely has a tendency of being overestimated. Modeling humans and systems allows us to manage the risks.

Considering the importance of psychological aspects of using the system, we focus on modeling humans with considering psychological factors. *Trust* [14] is one of psychological factors that have an influence on human behaviors to risks. *Trust* indicates whether a user of a system can trust the system or not. Through researches on *Trust* in areas of social science, psychology, and economics, *Trust* is regarded as a composite concept of security, reliability, availability and privacy. Even though people use the same system that has the same risk, people who trust the system with underestimating the risks. On the other hand, people who do not trust the system with overestimating the risks. This makes people use the system more carefully. In other words, *Trust* gives users a sense of security. The sense of security may make users risky operations on systems. In general, users' behaviors to a system can be modeled by users' motivation and knowledge on the system when both of motivation and knowledge are good enough to use the system. When either of motivation and knowledge is insufficient, *Trust* is a useful factor to model human behaviors.

For constructing meta-models, it is necessary to consider a risk management framework based on a standardized guideline. For example, SGIS Toolbox [15] has been proposed as a risk management framework for SG. Based on existing guidelines [16] that are related to security, SGIS Toolbox makes it possible to relate the guidelines to components of systems. Figure 5 shows a flow of using SGIS Toolbox. For developing new services that are related to SG, the guideline requires that we define use cases of the services, identify components of Zones (Market, Company, etc.), Domains (Power generation, Power Transmission, etc.), and Interoperation (Business, Function, etc.) of the use cases, and refer guideline that are related to the components. If the use cases do not satisfy requirements in the referred guideline, the use case is regarded to have risks. The requirements are based on a range of power failure, importance of information assets and so on. Because CPS is used by not only expert operators of the system but also a lot of public users, a risk management model with psychological factors plays an important role on risk management. An example of a risk is conflict of interest among public users, which is related to group psychology. In order to mitigate the risks, it is necessary to extend attack models for CPS and to use approaches of crime opportunity theory and psychological theories of crime as indicated in information security psychology. In addition, approaches from aspects of low and morals are necessary, but we should not make lows to punish seriously people that damage systems without malice. In order to prevent the public users without malice from damaging systems, instead of punishing users, activities for improving IT literacy are also effective.

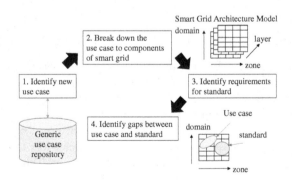

Fig. 5. Flow of using SGIS toolbox

5   Conclusion

In this paper, focusing on changes of recent threats like Social engineering, the survey shows that the information security psychology is valuable for the risk management of the Cyber Physical Systems. Through surveying, the outline of the risk management framework for Cyber Physical Systems was described.

The outline was considered the situation of the psychological side. Examination about the internal crime is advances, because its knowledge is in the field of the human error field. However, the human violation and background in the outside crime have not been analyzed yet.

Based on this result, a new committee "the information security psychology investigation for IT system management technologies" was set up in The Institute of Electrical Engineers of Japan. In this committee, the discussion is continued.

Acknowledgement. This work was supported in part by the member of the committee for survey of risk management based on information security psychology in The Institute of Electrical Engineers of Japan.

References

1. Fukuzawa, Y., Samejima, M.: An approach to risks in cyber physical systems based on information security psychology. Inst. Electr. Eng. Jpn. Trans. Electron. Inf. Syst. **134**(6), 756–759 (2014) (in Japanese)
2. Uchida, K.: Information security psychology-information security from the human and psychology sides. J. Inf. Sci. Technol. Assoc. (Johono Kagaku to Gijutsu), **62**(8), 336–341 (2012) (in Japanese)
3. Hadnagy, C.: Social Engineering : The Art of Human Hacking. Wiley, Indianapolis (2010)
4. Yuhara, N., Inagaki, T., Furukawa, Y.: Human Error and Mechanical Systems Design. Kodansha, Tokyo (2012) (in Japanese)
5. Irving, J.: Groupthink: Psychological Studies of Policy Decisions and Fiascoes. Houghton Mifflin Company, Boston (1982)
6. Cappelli, D., Desai, A.G., Moore, A.P., Shimeall, T.J., Weaver, E.A., Willke, B.J.: Management and Education of the Risk of Insider Threat (MERIT): Mitigating the Risk of Sabotage to Employers'Information, Systems, or Networks (2007). http://www.sei.cmu.edu/reports/06tn041.pdf
7. Smith, M.J., Conishi, D.B. (eds.): Theory For Practice in Situational Crime Prevention. Crime Prevention Studies, vol. 16. Criminal Justice Press, Monsey (2003)
8. Conish, D.B., Clarke, R.V.: Opportunities, precipitators and criminal decisions: a reply to wortley's critique of situational crime preventions (2003)
9. Amari, Y., Arai, S., Uchida, J.: Security Jitugen no Genten karamita Naibuyouin jiko youkuseishuhou. pp. 3–29. JNSA Press, Special Column (in Japanese)
10. Uchida, K.: Research of the application of situational crime prevention to information security (2010) (in Japanese). http://www.uchidak.com/InfoSecPsycho/20100922_uchidak01.pdf
11. Information-technology Promotion Agency, Japan: SoshikiNaibusha no Huseikoui ni yoru incident chousa (2012). http://www.ipa.go.jp/files/000014169.pdf

12. Information-technology Promotion Agency, Japan: Soshiki ni okeru NaibuFuseiBoushi guidelines (2013). http://www.ipa.go.jp/files/000027284.pdf'
13. Fujitsu Develops Industry's First Technology That Identifies Users Vulnerable to Cyber Attack Based on Behavioral and Psychological Characteristics. http://www.fujitsu.com/global/about/resources/news/press-releases/2015/0119-01.html
14. Riegelsberger, J., Sasse, M.A., McCarthy, J.D.: The mechanics of trust: a framework for research and design. Int. J. Hum. Comput. Stud. **62**, 381–422 (2005)
15. CEN-CENELEC-ETSI: Smart Grid Coordination Group Investigate standards for information security and data privacy (2012)
16. Shimada, T.: Trends in standardization of smart grid cyber security. Inst. Electr. Eng. Jpn. Trans. Electron. Inf. Syst. **133**(3), 558–561 (2013) (in Japanese)
17. Lee, E.A.: Cyber physical systems: design challenges. In: Proceedings of 2008 11th IEEE International Symposium on Object Oriented Real-Time Distributed Computing (ISORC), pp. 363–369 (2008)
18. Poovendran, R.: Cyber-physical systems: close encounters between two parallel worlds [point of view]. Proc. IEEE **98**(8), 1363–1366 (2010)

Digital Wellbeing Assessments for People Affected by Dementia

Kyle Harrington[1,2(✉)], Paul Fulton[3], Michael Brown[1,2],
James Pinchin[1], and Sarah Sharples[1,2]

[1] Horizon Digital Economy Research, University of Nottingham,
Nottingham, UK
{kyle.harrington, michael.brown,
sarah.sharples}@nottingham.ac.uk
[2] Human Factors Research Group, University of Nottingham, Nottingham, UK
james.pinchin@nottingham.ac.uk
[3] Philips Research, Cambridge, UK
paul.fulton@philips.com

Abstract. Currently there is a lack of digital tools for assessing the Wellbeing of those affected by dementia in a home environment. This paper presents an alternative to existing assessment modalities in order to facilitate large scale collection and analysis of data. This development will allow those affected to be assessed from the comfort of their own home, potentially reducing time costs and personal discomfort associated with assessment. Existing Wellbeing measures were evaluated against inclusion criteria and four tools were considered appropriate to develop into a digital application. An additional tool was also developed for quick assessment. Issues surrounding the use of technological devices for those affected by dementia are also considered. In light of these considerations an Android application was developed for Wellbeing self-assessment. Finally, the methods and approaches for user-evaluations of such technologies are explored.

Keywords: Human-centered Design · User-centered Design · Service design · Telehealth · Dementia care · Assessment · Wellbeing

1 Introduction

Assessing the Wellbeing of those affected by dementia is a research area that is becoming increasingly popular. However, there are many potential problems that need to be addressed if one is to consider seriously the possibility of developing a practical self-assessment solution. Paper-based evaluations are often time consuming and require specialists to administrate them. They are often implemented to serve as a single use evaluation and therefore cannot easily identify change over time.

© Springer International Publishing Switzerland 2015
M. Kurosu (Ed.): Human-Computer Interaction, Part III, HCII 2015, LNCS 9171, pp. 409–418, 2015.
DOI: 10.1007/978-3-319-21006-3_39

1.1 Current Practices

The importance of an effective response to dementia was highlighted by health ministers in the G8 Health summit of December 2013, who state that; "We need to provide better and more concrete measures for improving services and support for people with dementia and their carers, to improve their quality of life and wellbeing" [1]. In the UK, the needs of those who may require additional support are assessed using a Community Care Assessment which is often both time-consuming and costly. It should also be noted that Community Care Assessments vary between regions and are not designed for the purposes of continuous monitoring. Whilst there remains a great deal of optimism over current policy, there is a more general concern that those most in need may find it difficult to gain access to the relevant support [2]. Using traditional methods such as interview or pen-and-paper based approaches will become increasingly infeasible as the number of people living with dementia increases. An automated system which is able to store and automatically process such large data sets appears to be a much more preferable alternative.

It seems appropriate therefore, to develop digital tools to assess the Wellbeing of people living with dementia and their carers in order to facilitate prompt intervention for the most vulnerable. There is a general agreement on the need for people to maintain their independence and stay in their preferred home environment for as long as is possible [3], yet without adequate Wellbeing assessment it is difficult to know how people are coping and how support services could be most efficiently allocated. Developing self-assessment measures to monitor Wellbeing may prove crucial for ensuring appropriate support is provided in a timely manner and may help to promote independent living.

1.2 Defining Wellbeing

Wellbeing is an often ill-defined and ambiguous term, frequently considered synonymous with Quality of Life [4]. It is usually defined as the internal and subjective aspects of how well somebody is dealing with life in general, as opposed to Quality of Life (QoL) which also includes external and objective aspects such as housing and finance which are often beyond the immediate control of the individual. Not everyone draws such a distinction and some of the research discussed here will also include QoL studies and trials due to its pervasive reference within the literature.

Much of the research in this area is based on the work of Lawton [5] who considers QoL to be the difference between positive and negative affect as well as the congruence between desired and attained goals. Some definitions of Wellbeing include broader constructs, for instance cognitive functioning and daily living [6]. Others consider more psychological aspects such as autonomy, independence and control [7]. The most common view of Wellbeing is that it is a measure of psychological and affective states rather than cognitive capacities. However, upon examining Kitwood's definition it is clear that these aspects are not always easily delineated [7]. He suggests that the five main psychological needs that constitute Wellbeing are; comfort, attachment, inclusion, occupation and identity. Whist these aspects may seem almost entirely non-cognitive in nature, ultimately they depend upon a certain level of linguistic, attentive, and memorial capabilities. Consider for example the concept of identity, which Kitwood suggests is continuity of the self over time. This is dependent upon being able to recall past events and trace those events forward in time to the present moment. It is unlikely that such an important psychological need would easily be satisfied by an individual with severe memory impairment. Hence, despite the fact we may want to reduce the extent to which Wellbeing assessment overlaps with cognitive assessment, it is impossible even in principle to completely isolate these two distinct yet related factors.

1.3 Evaluating Wellbeing

Despite the lack of a formal consensus on a clear definition of Wellbeing there are a number of instruments available to both researcher and clinician for evaluating the Wellbeing of those affected by dementia. These instruments have been developed over the course of decades by numerous researchers and implement a variety of approaches. The most common of these are highlighted by Ready and Ott [6] and include direct measurement, proxy assessment and observational analysis. Due to the varying definitions and approaches, there are a considerable number of Wellbeing assessments. Detailed below are examples of a few popular and widely used approaches.

Dementia Care Mapping (DCM) [8] is a popular approach that is often used to assess Wellbeing and quality of life that uses a structured observational analysis. An assessor uses a six-point ordinal response format which ranges over twenty-four activity categories, and also considers staff attitude towards the service user. It is therefore most appropriate for use with moderately to severely impaired patients living away from home. Some questionnaires such as the QUALID [9] require that the main caregiver acts as a proxy rater and answers questions relating to care recipient's behaviour and mood. Each response is given a numerical value and the total assessment score is calculated by summing of all responses. It should be stated that this method is designed for individuals with severe dementia where the patient is considered unable to assess their own QoL. The QUALID questionnaire is an example of an Activity and Affect approach highlighted by Ready & Ott [6]. These are indirect ways of assessing the Wellbeing which use a proxy to rate the frequency of certain behaviors and moods exhibited by their care recipient. This approach is considered useful for assessing many people living with broad range of dementia severity. However, it should be noted that Wellbeing is by definition subjective, and therefore proxy Wellbeing assessments suffer a methodological shortfall in a way that other proxy assessments (such as Health-Related QoL) may not. It is also evidenced that carers often rate their care recipients' QoL as being lower the person in question [10].

Contrastingly, some measurements do rely on direct assessment. Usually these involve a person living with dementia being asked about various aspects of their Wellbeing in a structured interview. This method seems uniquely positioned to assess the "subjective evaluation of one's own quality of life" (pp. 356 [4]), in a way in which the other approaches do not. The BASQID is one such approach [11] and acknowledges that people with dementia are very often capable of reporting on their own experiences, unlike proxy or observational approaches which fail to take into account the views and opinions of those being assessed. Unfortunately, self-assessment measures are not appropriate for all people and no existing measure could be found that was recommended for a person with a Mini Mental-State Exam score below twelve.

2 Inclusion Criteria for Digital Assessment

In order to develop a fit for purpose, standardised digital assessment suitable for home use, it was decided that existing and well-established Wellbeing assessment tools should be integrated into a single software application as opposed to developing a completely new set of tools ex nihilo. In some circumstances it has been shown that computational assessment measures yield results indistinguishable from their paper based counterparts [12]. Further validation should be undertaken to ensure that this is the case and that the digital versions have comparable reliability and robustness.

Inclusion criteria were developed in order to decide which existing measures would be the most appropriate to digitise. The inclusion criteria are:

- Reliability
- Validity
- Brevity
- Automatability
- Simplicity

Perales et al. [13] examine methods of establishing various types of validity and reliability in relation to QoL assessments for people with dementia by collating multiple reviews of QoL instruments. They concede however, that data was not always available or consistent enough to perform a more rigorous analysis. Nevertheless, they examine various methods in which various QoL measures have been evaluated and their findings have been considered here. The validity of Wellbeing assessments is often difficult to establish. One cannot conclude with certainty that a particular assessment tool is adequately measuring Wellbeing and not a related construct. In this case, construct validity can only be approximated by comparing the assessment's items to a generally agreed upon definition of Wellbeing. Concurrent validity is also hard to establish due to the fact that there is no current Wellbeing assessment measure that is considered to be the 'Gold Standard'. Difficulties aside, Perales et al. do highlight important methods for establishing the suitability, reliability and validity of QoL scales.

Studies involving the completion rates of questionnaires were also examined order to identify which factors contribute to higher completion rates and higher quality of data. Unsurprisingly, shorter questionnaires yield higher rates of completion [14]. It has also been shown that open ended questions are less likely to be completed and would be likely to make a potential assessment much more difficult to automate. Therefore these types of assessments can be excluded for failing to meet the inclusion critera.

Two existing carer Wellbeing assessments were included for digitisation; the Satisfaction with Life Scale [15] and the Zarit Burden Interview [16]. The Satisfaction with Life Scale is a five item assessment which is designed to assess a person's global evaluation of their current life according to their own standards. It was chosen due to its short length, proven reliability, prima facie simplicity and high construct validity.

In addition, the Zarit Burden Interview was also considered appropriate to assess the Wellbeing of carers in order to evaluate how well they are coping in their role as a carer. Using two measures of Wellbeing is likely to capture a much more rounded view of how the person is coping both generally and specifically in their role as a carer.

In order to ascertain a detailed understanding of the Wellbeing of the person living with dementia, two assessments were chosen from the literature and an additional assessment was also developed.

The BASQID satisfied the inclusion criteria and was considered appropriate for inclusion in the digital toolkit. This is a direct assessment for people with dementia which aims to use brief, simple, questions in order to reduce cognitive burden. The BASQID has been validated for use with patients living with mild to moderate dementia (MMSE score 12 or above) and therefore would apply to all but the most severe cases where detailed self-assessment would not be possible.

However, it is acknowledged that some of the most afflicted would be unable to complete this assessment, especially via an Android application. For this reason a proxy assessment was also included. The QUALID instrument which seeks to discover Wellbeing through assessing the behaviours of the sufferer was chosen because it also fared well against the inclusion criteria. However, due to the concern that proxy ratings do not constitute a truly subjective evaluation, an additional tool was also developed to be used in conjunction with the QUALID. This was designed to be as simple to use as possible and consists of only one item. This is a pictorial based rating scale which simply asks the user to choose from a selection of cartoon faces which best represent their mood. It has been shown that pictorial based rating scales can produce comparable results to their text based counterparts [17]. Using a dual approach should help to mitigate some of the concerns about each individual method of operationalization.

3 Design Considerations

Developing user-interfaces for people affected by dementia presents unique design considerations. Whilst many existing and widely recognised user-interface guidelines are appropriate [18, 19] additional factors need to be considered when designing for people with cognitive impairment. Tamanini et al. highlight the importance of reducing cognitive burden for those with dementia in the design of graphical user interfaces [20]. They also suggest implementing dual user-interfaces to cater for the differing needs of people living with dementia and their carers. Other research in this area includes the work of Granata et al., who outline associated usability and accessibility problems of this population [21]. These include; scrolling, insufficient contrast, moving content and cascading navigation menus. It is thought that the layout for the application should be as clear as possible and only those elements essential to the assessment should be present. It is also thought that a high contrast colour scheme should be implemented to assist users that may have age-related visual impairments or other difficulties. Additionally questions and responses should have the option to be read aloud by the application in order to further assist in this respect and also to reinforce the questions/responses for those with attentional deficits.

The possibility of using voice recognition as an input method was also considered. It is thought that this may help increase the accessibility of the delivery system as many people living with dementia also experience poor eyesight and limited dexterity. Unfortunately, current speech recognition software is not always accurate and some of the end-users may experience problems with speech production either as a result of their dementia or other health problems. Conceivably, the speech recognition software may fail to properly comprehend their speech and thus register an incorrect response. This may not only result in a faulty or incorrect measure of Wellbeing but also cause undue stress to the user and ultimately reduce completion rates.

4 Development of a Digital Toolkit

As part of an iterative design process an Android application was developed allowing carers, clinicians and those living with dementia to easily administer and analyse the results from these five tests. With guidance from domain experts, this was developed with the Eclipse IDE using Java for Android with XML layouts for the graphics. The application contains digitised versions of the aforementioned assessment instruments, as well as home screens and a graphical representation of the assessment data. The application utilizes a high contrast colour scheme, provides appropriate cues and feedback and allows for the possibility of easily correcting errors. The home screens for each user type vary slightly in terms of the complexity and amount of data being represented and available assessments. Upon clicking a test, all users are directed to an instruction screen, which displays instructions that were taken directly from the administration manuals provided with each assessment where available.

The instructions and assessment questions are read aloud by the text-to-speech engine, and when the user makes a response it is also read aloud. Upon clicking the "submit" button their response is stored and they are taken to the next question. Haptic feedback is provided after each action to denote that the touchscreen has been pressed. After completing each assessment, users are taken to a results screen that displays their assessment score and the corresponding advice before all assessment scores are sent to a server using httppost and the JSON protocol for storage and analysis.

The carer and care recipient are presented with slightly different home screens to accommodate their different user needs. The carer's screen has access to the assessment results of both themselves and the person that they care for. It also presents more detailed information of their results over a longer time scale. On the other hand, the home screen designed for the user living with dementia shows less information and presents fewer options in order to reduce the complexity. The direct assessments for the person living with dementia are both five item response formats. The 'Quick Assessment', simply asks the user to "Click on the face that best represents how you have felt today", and presents five cartoon faces representing different moods with corresponding text underneath face. Once clicked, the application reads their response aloud using the Android text-to-speech engine and the user is given a choice to change their response before it is automatically sent to a server. The digital version of the BASQID implements the same interface with the addition of a progress bar to demonstrate progression and length of the assessment (see Fig. 1). The addition of a progress bar

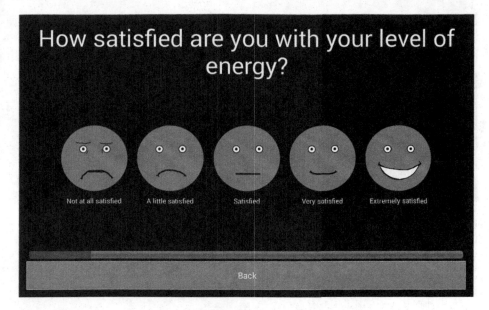

Fig. 1. Digital version of the BASQID

has been shown to significantly increase questionnaire completion rates [14]. The text underneath each face corresponds with the responses given in the BASQID.

The carer can complete a total of three questionnaires. One of these is the QUALID; a proxy rating of their care recipient. The other two evaluate their own Wellbeing; the Satisfaction with Life Scale and the Zarit Burden Interview. Both of the digital self-assessments implement a slider bar in order to show agreement or disagreement with a statement. Upon releasing the slider bar, there current response is shown on the screen and also read aloud by the text-to-speech engine. The screen also has one button to confirm their current response and another to go back to the previous question (see Fig. 2).

Unfortunately, it was not possible to implement a slider-bar interface to the digital version of the QUALID tool without significantly comprising the assessment. Instead, the QUALID interface presents users with a particular statement and shows the possible responses with large buttons.

After the completion of each assessment users are taken to a results screen which details their score, provides a bar graph representation of their results and a small description. It also suggests possible intervention methods which might be recommended for a person with that particular score.

5   Evaluating the Prototype

Currently, the prototype is undergoing an evaluation which consists of a series of focus groups constituted by carers, clinicians, researchers and other stakeholders. Initially the focus group participants are presented with the application and then asked a series of

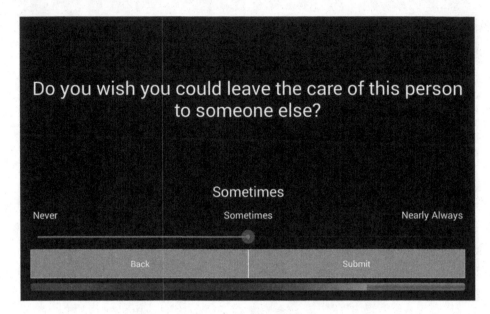

Fig. 2. Digital version of the Zarit burden interview

open ended questions pertaining to usability and appropriateness of both the assessment tools and the user interface. Once the findings of the focus groups have been analysed these insights will be taken into consideration to in order to further improve the application. Finally, it is hoped that a longitudinal study will be undertaken using people diagnosed with dementia and their carers as participants. The digital assessments could be taken in conjunction with the original assessments in order to establish the validity and reliability of the new methods. Such a study would also allow data about completion rates to be evaluated in order to further improve the application.

6   The Future of Wellbeing Monitoring

Eventually, it is thought that unobtrusive monitoring methods will one day replace digitised versions of paper and interview based assessments. Developments within this area have already been trialed regarding the early prediction of mood changes within people with bipolar disorder by detecting subtle changes in broad features and properties of speech [22]. The monitoring occurs via a smart phone application which records phone conversations. The privacy of each user is protected and the researchers only have access to the results of the computational feature extraction. Whilst this work is still in the research stage of development, initial results look promising. Results are benchmarked against standardised weekly assessments which are used to correlate the acoustic features of speech with mood. This is a major development in unobtrusive healthcare technology, and it is likely that other measures will eventually be implemented in the not too distant future. An advantage to this type of analysis is that individual differences could be taken into account using machine learning methods.

Perhaps one day these unobtrusive assessments will become more reliable, more accurate and far easier to implement than current methods. Measures such as these completely negate response bias, which is largely inescapable using any type of questionnaire of interview methods [23]. These methods could also be used to analyse a whole host of other behavioural, affective and cognitive issues facing people affected by dementia such as wandering and aggression.

7 Conclusion

Wellbeing of both the carer and care recipient, are highly correlated with the break-down of familial care and subsequent instutionalisation [24]. There is a general agreement on the need for people with dementia to maintain their independence and stay in a home environment for as long as is possible, yet without a standardised assessment for those affected it is difficult to know when and where to administer interventions. Developing digital alternatives holds the promise of facilitating more timely and appropriate intervention, potentially increasing the quality of life of those affected and simultaneously optimising the allocation of health and community care resources. Digital assessments such as these are not the deus ex machina of healthcare solutions but must instead provide a platform for all involved to monitor and communicate the needs of vulnerable people in a much more efficient and effective way.

Acknowledgements. This work was made possible thanks to Phillips Research, the University of Nottingham and the EPSRC.

References

1. G8 Dementia Summit Declaration: (2013). https://www.gov.uk/government/publications/g8-dementia-summit-agreements/g8-dementia-summit-declaration
2. World Alzheimer's Report 2013 Journey of Caring: An Analysis of Long-Term care for Dementia. http://www.alz.co.uk/research/WorldAlzheimerReport2013.pdf
3. Goldsmith, M.: Hearing the Voice of People with Dementia: Oppurtinities and Obstacles. Jessica Kingsley, London (1996)
4. Ettema, T., Droes, R., de Lange, J., Mellenbergh, G., Ribbe, M.: A review of quality of life instruments used in dementia. Qual. Life Res. **14**, 675–686 (2005)
5. Lawton, M.P.: Assessing quality of life in Alzheimer disease research. Alzheimer Dis. Assoc. Disord. **11**, 91–99 (1997)
6. Ready, R., Ott, B.: Quality of Life measures for dementia. Open Access (2003). http://www.hqlo.com/content/1/1/11
7. Kitwood, T., Bredin, K.: Towards a theory of dementia care: personhood and well-being. Ageing Soc. **12**, 269–287 (1993)
8. Brooker, D.: Dementia care mapping: a review of the research literature. Dement. Care Mapp. J. **45**(1), 11–18 (2005)
9. Weiner, M.F., Martin-Cook, K., Svetlik, D.A., Saine, K., Foster, B., Fontaine, C.S.: The quality of life in late-stage dementia (QUALID) scale. J. Am. Med. Dir. Assoc. **3**, 114–116 (2000)

10. Sands, L., Ferreira, Stewart, A.L., Brod, M., Yaffe, K.: What explains differences between dementia patients' and their caregivers' ratings of patients' quality of life? Am. J. Geriatr. Psychiatry **12**, 3 (2004)

11. Trigg, R., Skevington, S., Jones, R.: How can we best assess the quality of life of people with dementia?: the bath assessment of subjective quality of life in dementia (BASQID). Gerontologist **47**(6), 789–797 (2007)

12. Williams, J., McCord, B.: Equivalence of standard and computerized versions of the Raven progressive matrices test. Comput. Hum. Behav. **22**(5), 791–800 (2006)

13. Perales, J., Cosco, D., Stephan, B., Haro, J., Brayne, C.: Health-related quality-of-life instruments for Alzheimer's disease and mixed dementia. Int. Psychogeriatr. **25**, 691–706 (2013)

14. Galesic, M., Bosjak, M.: Effects of questionnaire length on participation and indicators or response quality in a web survey. Publ. Opin. Q. Summer **73**(2), 349 (2009)

15. Diener, E., Emmons, R.A., Larsen, R.J., Griffin, S.: The satisfaction with life scale. J. Pers. Assess. **49**, 71–75 (1985)

16. Zarit, S., Reever, K., Bach-Peterson, J.: Relatives of the impared elderly: correlates of feelings of burden. Gerontologist **20**(6), 649–655 (1980)

17. Reynolds-Keefer, L., et al.: Validity issues in the use of pictorial likert scales. Stud. Learn. Educ. Innov. Dev. **6**(3), 15–24 (2009)

18. Nielsen, J., Molich, R.: Heuristic evaluation of user interfaces. In: Proceedings of ACM CHI 1990 Conference, pp. 249–256 (1990)

19. Stone, D., Jarrett, C., Woodroffe, M., Minocha, S.: User interface design and evaluation. Morgan Kaufmann, San Francisco (2005)

20. Tamanini, C., Majeswski, M., Wiedland, A., Schehuber, C., Kamieth, F.: Graphical user interface for an elderly person with Dementia. Commun. Comput. Inf. Sci. **277**, 157–161 (2012)

21. Granata, C.M., Pino, G., Legouverneur, J., Vidal, S., Bidaud, P., Rigaud, A.S.: Robot services for elderly with cognitive impairment: testing usability of graphical user interfaces. Technol. Health Care **21**(3), 217–231 (2013)

22. Listening to Bipolar disorder: Smartphone app detects mood swings via voice analysis. http://www.engin.umich.edu/college/about/news/stories/2014/may/listening-to-bipolar-disorder-smartphone-app-detects-mood-swings-via-voice-analysis

23. Podsakoff, P., MacKenzie, S., Lee, J., Podsakoff, N.: Common method biases in behavioral research: A critical review of the literature and recommended remedies. J. Appl. Psychol. **88** (5), 879–903 (2003)

24. Hope, T., Keene, J., Gedling, K., Fairburn, C., Jacoby, R.: Predictors of institutionalization for people with dementia living at home with a carer. Int. J. Geriatr. Psychiatry **13**(10), 682–690 (1998)

Factors Influencing Online Shop Layout Preferences

Katarzyna Jach[✉] and Marcin Kuliński

Faculty of Computer Science and Management, Wrocław University
of Technology, Wrocław, Poland
{katarzyna.jach,marcin.kulinski}@pwr.edu.pl

Abstract. The usability research on web pages layout preferences of online shops consumers has been continued since 2008 on a sample of over 1,000 Polish students. This gives a possibility to observe changes in preferences, both over time as well as across the respondents' buying experience. Preferred locations of selected interface objects specific for an online shop, like a shopping cart, product image and search button were analyzed. The research showed that the main differentiating factor of preferences is the users' experience. Concurrently, the layout patterns preferred by more experienced participants were consistent with standards defined as the most frequently used placement of the objects on existing online shop web pages.

Keywords: Web usability · GUI · E-commerce · Users' preferences

1 Introduction

An online shop layout is one of the user navigation components, as it refers to the appearance and design of a website and influences the total effort of making a purchase. Reducing the search costs for a purchase, interpreted mainly as time needed to do it successfully, is a key motivation for consumers to shop online [15]. A web page design is partially responsible for the online shop ease of use, which is one of the five[1] factors affecting consumer attitude toward a retail web site [5]. Moreover, if the layout of a web site, including online shops, matches up users' expectations, it elevates the web site effectiveness by increasing orientation and reducing the time to complete a task. This was shown a.o. in the eyetracking study by Roth et al. [17].

The main purpose of the research which continues since 2008 is to investigate layout preferences of online buyers. Such analysis was inspired by Bernard's publications [1–3] about placement of web page typical elements like a title, internal and external links, the ad banner and the internal search field. A similar research, which de facto redid aforementioned studies, was done by Markum and Hall [11] and Shaikh and Lenz [18]. However, contrary to Bernard's research, in the presented study preferred locations of all the investigated items are shown on the same screen side by side, not separately, thus creating some sort of a mock-up of desired page layout. A similar approach was also applied by Roth et al. who investigated the mental model of internet

---

[1] The other four factors are: information, entertainment, trust, and currency.

© Springer International Publishing Switzerland 2015
M. Kurosu (Ed.): Human-Computer Interaction, Part III, HCII 2015, LNCS 9171, pp. 419–429, 2015.
DOI: 10.1007/978-3-319-21006-3_40

users in different web sites [16]. Due to similarity of some aspects of that research to the presented one, especially in the part related to online shops, there was the possibility of comparing results. However, it is worth to note that in the abovementioned research, in contradiction to the presented one, participants have no influence on the size of area covered by specific items.

The idea of our research was also to check the influence of some factors described in the model of the Unified Theory of Acceptance and Use of Technology (UTAUT), as proposed by Venkatesh et al. [20]. The model has four core determinants of intention and usage (performance expectancy, effort expectancy, social influence, and facilitating conditions) and four moderators of key relationships (gender, age, experience, and voluntariness of use).

In the research, the layout preferences of ten objects characteristic for online shops were analyzed as follows:

- *account log in,*
- *search,*
- *homepage link,*
- *terms of service,*
- *similar products* (i.e. other products in a given category),
- *category index* (i.e. a list of all categories),
- *shopping cart,*
- *add to shopping cart,*
- *product description,*
- *product image.*

2   Tools Description

Two purpose-built applications were used as research software for data collecting and interpreting separately. Both are intended to work over the Internet, which gives the possibility to store data in a database file and to evaluate it remotely afterwards.

2.1   Data Collecting Software

For data collecting, microSzu software was applied. The main idea of the software is to let the respondent show his or her layout preferences by placing a set of virtual cards labelled with typical online shop items like the *search* button or the *add to shopping cart* button. The program uses a metaphor of a board that mimics an area of a webpage and cards representing items under examination. The virtual cards can be placed on any of the fields of such vertically and horizontally partitioned board. In the study a partitioning grid with eight columns and six rows was used. The user can decide on the layout of objects as well as on the area covered by a single object.

MicroSzu application runs within a web browser. A subject places the cards at different fields of the board, which are preferred by him/her as the location for a given object. Technically, the investigation is done as a two-step process using two separate screens to interact with. The first one is the metric questionnaire to fulfill. The second

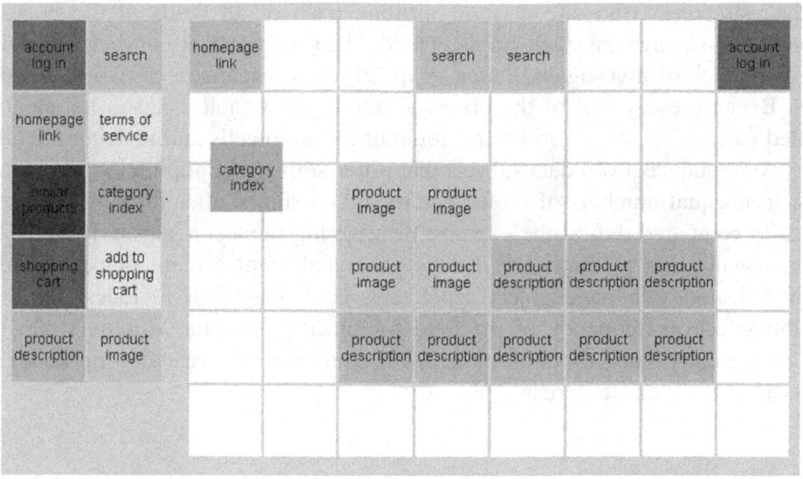

Fig. 1. The main interface of the microSzu application showing an example of the layout preferences filling-up process.

screen, presented after the questionnaire, displays the cards container situated on the left, and the board divided into fields where the cards are placed at, which occupies the main area of the screen. Additionally, some instructions are presented on the right side. The size of all visible elements automatically fits browser's window size in which application was started. For placing items the "pick & paint" method is used, which means that the subject works like in a simple paint application. A card chosen from the container with a mouse click becomes a default "painting" tool, so the user can quickly fill up a portion of the board with a specified card by repeated mouse clicks. At any moment, any card can be deleted from the board by a mouse click over an already occupied location. This fulfilling mode was chosen over the (also implemented) classical "drag & drop" method because our preliminary investigation [9] had shown it as a faster one for the majority of subjects. An example of the filling up process is illustrated on Fig. 1.

The software can be used for collecting data offline and online. A file format chosen to store data collected by the application is a variant of CSV (Comma Separated Values) standard.

2.2 Data Analyzing Software

For data analysis another application, called microVis, is used. This software was designed specifically for selecting, filtering, statistical analyzing and visualization of data from the microSzu software. More technical details about the software can be found in the paper by Kuliński et al. [10]. MicroVis enables to filter data collected by microSzu according to specified rules. Numerous filters can be applied in the same time, which allows for compound analysis. Due to the data specificity a statistical analysis is conducted on the non-parametric basis only. For comparisons of relatively huge data structures (like the way of fulfilling each of 48 fields of the board) the Pearson's Chi-square test was implemented. The significance of heterogeneity is checked for each of investigated items separately by comparison of two selected data subsets. Because every cell of the observed contingency table need to be adequately populated (see [7, 8]), an algorithm for rebinning data in cells and resizing the table is used. In consequence, even data subsets that differ strongly in population sizes (that is, these with unequal numbers of preference records assigned after filtering) still can be statistically compared, but at the expense of lowering the test's sensitivity.

The visualization of microSzu data is generated as placement density tables for each investigated web page object separately. Each table cell includes information about the selection frequency of the field for placing an item. Moreover, for better clarity of presented data, the scale of grays is used, giving a readable tip about more and less frequently chosen areas.

3   Results

The results include preferences collected by the microSzu software in the years of 2008, 2009, 2010, 2011, and 2015. The total number of subjects and analyzed records was 1016. The participants were adult Polish students of Wrocław University of Technology and Academy of Fine Arts in Wrocław. However the applied software gives the possibility to conduct data gathering over the Internet, the investigation was provided in a computer laboratory in order to keep the procedure under control. All the results were checked for consistency of the objects' selected locations. If the position of at least one object was marked in two different places (not physically connected on the board), all results from the subject were omitted. After this reduction of abnormalities, total number of 796 results was taken into account. Also, some subjects indicated single fields as preferred locations for objects, not showing the approximate size of an object, but only its rough location; still, these results were taken into account during analysis. Finally, records from 499 women and 297 men were investigated.

3.1   Experience and Voluntariness of Use

The experience moderator, as proposed in the UTAUT model, was measured by frequency of online shopping on the semantic scale ("never" – means no experience, "once a year at most", "several times a year", "once a month", and "several times a month or more"). The voluntariness of use was measured binary: if the participant have ever done online shopping, he or she showed the voluntariness of use. The impact of experience was checked between each of the groups, however, the most significant differences were found between subjects with no online buying experience and experienced participants, who buy online several times a year or more often. The significance of heterogeneity ($p < 0.05$) was confirmed for 7 of 10 investigated objects, as shown in Table 1.

Some interesting results can be observed by graphical comparisons. For the *homepage link* object, preferences of experienced subjects are more condensed and

Table 1. Chi-square test results for differences between subjects with no online buying experience (n = 303) and those who buy at least several times a year (n = 286).

Object name	p-value	Computed χ^2	d.f.
account log in	**0.020084**	22.61	11
homepage link	**0.008454**	31.12	15
Search	0.255101	22.61	19
add to shopping cart	**0.036949**	40.24	26
category index	**0.009830**	40.35	22
product image	0.989973	16.37	32
shopping cart	**5.4×10^{-10}**	81.14	18
similar products	**0.000492**	60.79	29
product description	0.651464	28.36	32
terms of service	**0.000037**	84.10	39

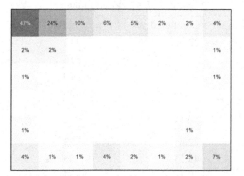 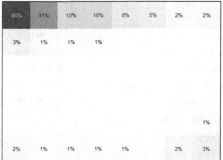

Fig. 2. The *homepage link* object: layout preferences of subjects with no online buying experience (left) and subjects who buy at least several times a year (right).

concentrated in the upper left corner (Fig. 2). This is probably caused by a higher awareness of a homepage link typical position among experienced online shop buyers. This effect shows that people prefer rather a typical, standard position of items instead of searching across the computer screen.

A similar observation can be made for other investigated items, like the *shopping cart* object (Fig. 3). Experienced buyers' preferences are more concentrated and there are considerably less unusual locations for the object, like lower left part of the screen, compared to participants with no experience. This result is very similar to the location of a shopping cart area presented in the research done by Roth et al., in which almost all participants were experienced online shoppers [16]. However, due to its specificity, this object is not so strictly connected with one particular screen region, like it was in case of the *homepage link* (see Fig. 2), therefore, even the preferences of experienced participants still show significantly more dispersion than those depicted previously. This remains consistent with the outcomes of other layout expectations investigations [3, 16, 18], where the homepage link area was most centralized among all the web interface objects under examination.

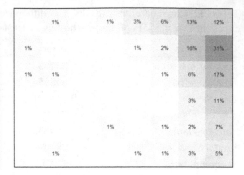

Fig. 3. The *shopping cart* object: layout preferences of subjects with no online buying experience (left) and subjects who buy at least several times a year (right).

Table 2. Chi-square test results for differences between females (n = 499) and males (n = 297)

Object name	p-value	Computed χ^2	d.f.
account log in	0.050168	22.35	13
homepage link	**0.005876**	33.75	16
Search	**0.006637**	39.02	20
add to shopping cart	0.821719	22.84	30
category index	**0.000900**	54.41	26
product image	**0.021956**	51.32	33
shopping cart	0.500708	22.33	23
similar products	0.171446	42.79	35
product description	0.706447	29.10	34
terms of service	**0.000719**	77.40	42

3.2   Gender

Generally, gender related dichotomies in layout preferences are similar to aforementioned differences related to experience (Table 2). Significant differences were stated for objects: *homepage link* (p = 0.006), *search* (p = 0.007), *category index* (p = 0.0009), *product image* (p = 0.02), and *terms of service* (p = 0.0007). Thus, the analysis of preferences related to gender and experience combined factors was conducted. Some more statistically significant differences were stated only between little experienced men and women (online shopping once a year or more seldom). For other groups of men and women with an equal level of experience, statistically significant differences were found at most for only two objects from the tested pool, and in all these cases the minimum significance level was above 0,01. This supports the hypothesis that gender dichotomies are caused probably by different frequency distributions of buying from online stores. Much higher proportion of subjects with no experience among women than among men was stated (47.2 % vs. 22.6 %, respectively). Additionally, men were the larger of the two gender groups of online buyers that buy several times a year or more often. That means that gender generally may have a little influence on layout preferences, however, in the aforesaid group of subjects with small experience, differentiations were statistically significant for the *search* (p = 0.01), *category index* (p = 0.006), *similar products* (p = 0.001), and *terms of service* object (p = 0.03).

3.3 Age

It was proved that age does not constitute a factor that differentiates preferences. Some small but statistically significant discrepancies were found by comparison of 19 and 23 year-old participants (the *account log in* object; p = 0.01 and *terms of service* object; p = 0.01). A visual interpretation confirms the little age impact on online shops layout characteristics, but this effect can be caused by our sample homogeneity, as mentioned below.

3.4 Changes Over Time

The coverage and frequency of online shopping is still growing, which can be observed in the research results as well. In the year of 2008 over 1/3 of our participants (37.3 %) was not shopping online. In 2015 this group was 12.7 % only, but some of the respondents pointed auction portals as the most often visited online shop, though it was inconsistent with the instructions given to them during the survey. Nevertheless, the rising tendency in our study is even higher than observed among Polish internet users, which was 43 % of non-shopping users in 2008 and 24 % in 2014, according to the CBOS (Public Opinion Research Center) research [4].

There were no statistically significant differences stated neither between 2008 and 2009, nor between 2010 and 2011. Between 2009 and 2010, only one significant difference was found (for the *search* object; p = 0.048). However, comparisons of data from 2010 or 2011 to 2015 show as much as five significant discrepancies (the *search*, *add to shopping cart*, *shopping cart*, *category index*, and *similar products* objects). These results are shown in Tables 3 and 4, respectively, although it is worth to note that due to a significantly smaller sample for 2015 (45 cases after removing abnormalities), the sensitivity of the applied test is lower. To confirm the results, the sample should be extended to 150–200 subjects in 2015.

For the *add to shopping cart* object (Fig. 4) it can be observed that preferences in 2015 are less spread than earlier ones and concentrated in the middle part of the screen's right side. Also, visual representations of its preferred locations for 2008, 2009 and 2010 are very similar to these presented for 2011.

An interesting result is visible for the *category index* object (Fig. 5). In 2011 and earlier this item was preferred to be close to the three screen borders, with the most distinctive concentration on the left side. In 2015 focusing on the left border is still noticeable, but the concentration is the highest in the area closer to the upper border. Additionally, the top area was pointed out by some participants. This result is very similar to the location of navigation area presented by Roth et al. [16]. Probably this tendency is caused by a rising popularity of vertical menus over time, but this observation needs further analysis.

Table 3. Chi-square test results for differences between preferences gathered in the year of 2010 (n = 157) and in 2015 (n = 45).

Object name	p-value	Computed χ^2	d.f.
account log in	0.061734	7.34	3
homepage link	0.217864	5.76	4
Search	**0.000728**	28.70	9
add to shopping cart	**0.000066**	34.76	9
category index	**0.001302**	23.67	7
product image	0.995815	4.99	16
shopping cart	**0.037000**	11.84	5
similar products	**0.001347**	35.26	14
product description	0.928768	7.15	14
terms of service	0.397065	14.73	14

Table 4. Chi-square test results for differences between preferences gathered in the year of 2011 (n = 116) and in 2015 (n = 45).

Object name	p-value	Computed χ^2	d.f.
account log in	0.534417	2.19	3
homepage link	0.458950	3.63	4
Search	**0.016325**	20.27	9
add to shopping cart	**0.033666**	18.13	9
category index	**0.024587**	16.06	7
product image	0.991723	5.62	16
shopping cart	**0.039891**	11.65	5
similar products	**0.035677**	24.89	14
product description	0.745513	10.23	14
terms of service	0.050803	23.63	14

4 Summary

According to the UTAUT model, each of the four moderators (experience, voluntariness of use, gender, age) was investigated. Venkatesh et al. stated that the influence of performance expectancy on behavioral intention is moderated by gender and age, and such the effect is stronger for younger users [20]. This observation is not supported by presented research. In our study age related discrepancies were not observed, maybe due to the age homogeneity of subjects. The differences of layout preferences found between men and women are probably caused by the experience levels variation and not by gender itself. In the investigation done by Roth et al. the expectations of web objects location were also similar for men and women, even though men declared higher frequency of internet usage and online shopping [16].

Elliot and Speck showed the negative and significant interaction between the experience of users and ease of use in the process of online shop evaluation [5].

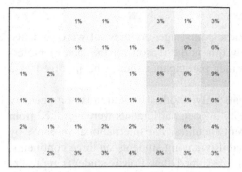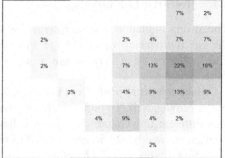

Fig. 4. The *add to shopping cart* object: layout preferences of subjects surveyed in the year of 2011 (left) and in 2015 (right).

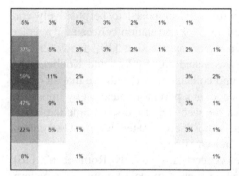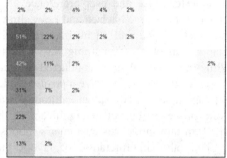

Fig. 5. The *category index* object: layout preferences of subjects surveyed in the year of 2011 (left) and in 2015 (right).

This means that for inexperienced customers, higher levels of the ease of use factor are indeed related to a more favorable evaluation of retail web sites, but the same is not necessarily guaranteed in case of experienced ones. Probably more experienced users had an occasion to interact with different online shop interfaces and therefore they feel more confident. Actually, the preferences of the most experienced users are less spread and dispersed than non-experienced ones, as our results show. Furthermore, the experienced users' preferences are more consistent with common web standards, examples of which are visible on Figs. 2 and 3.

The changes over time also showed some relation between preferences and standards (see Fig. 5). However, in this case the impact of rising experience of participants can be observed as a concentration of preferences in the most often used parts of the screen for each specific object. Similar observations were made in other follow-up surveys [9, 19]. It can be stated that, among the investigated moderators, the experience of user is a decisive one.

4.1   Research Limitations

The strong limitation was narrowing the participants' age. As they all were students, the age discrepancy was not large. Probably this is the reason for the lack of preferences differences in various age groups. Elder participants should be involved in a further research.

Since the participants were Polish students only, another limitation is homogeneity of the sample itself. To buffer the homogeneity impact, participants were recruited from two different universities and a few different faculties. An international research by Nielsen showed no differences related to usability among students on three continents, including Europe [12]. Therefore, it can be assumed that Polish students represent typical online behavior in terms of usability.

4.2   Conclusions

User performance and user preference are intuitively supposed to be positively correlated, for example Nielsen and Levy showed a strong correlation between the average task performance and an average subjective users' satisfaction [13]. However, this relation cannot be so unambiguous, which was stated e.g. by Lee and Koubek [14]. While the results of study conducted by Wu and colleagues [21] indicate that an online shop layout design may have a positive influence on a purchase intention by impacting both an emotional arousal and attitude toward the website, at the same time the layout alone proves to be not as significant as the atmosphere created with use of colors, which in turn influences customer's moods and emotions.

The other interpretation of layout preferences is given by Roth et al. [16]. According to their model, users' preferences show mental model of online shop pattern, which are the most expected by users. Nevertheless, both approaches emphasize the significant role of web site layout in total usability of web site, defined in the ISO 9241 standard as the effectiveness, efficiency and satisfaction with which specified users achieve specified goals in particular environments [6]. The layout of an online shop can influence all the main characteristics of usability by enabling a user to fulfill tasks (effectiveness), while minimizing resources needed, especially time (efficiency).

Additionally, the web site layout pattern consistent with user preferences increases the user's satisfaction. Though, according to the presented research, for increasing the overall usability of online shop it is crucial to use the layout which is in accordance with standards and users' expectations and preferences.

References

1. Bernard, M.L.: User expectations for the location of Web objects. In: Proceedings of the CHI 2001 Conference, pp. 171–172 (2001)
2. Bernard, M.L.: Developing schemas for the location of common Web objects. In: Proceedings of the Human Factors and Ergonomics Society 45th Annual Meeting, pp. 1161–1165 (2001)

3. Bernard, M.L.: Examining user expectations for the location of common e-commerce Web objects. In: Proceedings of the Human Factors and Ergonomics Society 47th Annual Meeting, pp. 1356–1360 (2003)
4. CBOS: Internauci 2014. In: Komunikat z badań 82/2014, Centralny Ośrodek Badań Społecznych (Public Opinion Research Center), Warszawa (2014)
5. Elliott, M.T., Speck, P.S.: Factors that affect attitude toward a retail Web site. J. Mark. Theor. Pract. **13**(1), 40–51 (2005)
6. PN-EN ISO 9241:11: Ergonomic Requirements for Office Work With Visual Display Terminals (VDTs) - Part 11: Guidance on Usability. International Organization for Standardization (2002)
7. Hill, T., Lewicki, P.: Statistics Methods and Applications. StatSoft, Tulsa (2007)
8. Kirkman, T.W.: Statistics to Use (1996). http://www.physics.csbsju.edu/stats/
9. Kuliński, M., Jach, K.: Investigating layout preferences of online shop buyers: a case study of a purpose-built software and its evolution. In: Rebelo, F., Soares, M.M. (eds.) Advances in Usability Evaluation, pp. 513–523. CRC Press/Taylor & Francis Group, London (2013)
10. Kuliński, M., Jach, K., Michalski, R., Grobelny, J.: Modeling online buyers' preferences related to webpages layout: methodology and preliminary results. In: Duffy, V.G. (ed.) Advances in Applied Digital Human Modeling, pp. 499–509. CRC Press/Taylor & Francis Group, London (2011)
11. Markum, J., Hall, R.H.: E-commerce Web objects: importance and expected Placement. Laboratory for Information Technology Evaluation Technical report, Missouri University of Science and Technology (2003). http://lite.mst.edu/documents/LITE-2003-02.pdf
12. Nielsen, J.: College Students (Ages 18–24) on the Web (2010). http://www.nngroup.com/articles/college-students-on-the-web/
13. Nielsen, J., Levy, J.: Measuring usability: preference vs. performance. Commun. ACM **37**(4), 66–75 (1994)
14. Lee, S., Koubek, R.J.: The effects of usability and Web design attributes on user preference for e-commerce Web sites. Comput. Ind. **61**(4), 329–341 (2010)
15. Peral Peral, B., Rodríguez-Bobada, R.J., Villarejo, R.A.F.: A study of consumer preferences for e-retailers' attributes: an application of conjoint analysis. Int. J. Manage. Sci. Inf. Technol. (IJMSIT) **I**(3), 37–67 (2012)
16. Roth, S.P., Schmutz, P., Pauwels, S.L., Bargas-Avila, J.A., Opwis, K.: Mental models for Web objects: where do users expect to find the most frequent objects in online shops, news portals, and company Web pages? Interact. Comput. **22**(2), 140–152 (2010)
17. Roth, S.P., Tuch, A.N., Mekler, E.D., Bargas-Avila, J.A., Opwis, K.: Location matters, especially for non-salient features – an eye-tracking study on the effects of Web object placement on different types of websites. Int. J. Hum Comput Stud. **71**(3), 228–235 (2013)
18. Shaikh, A.D., Lenz, K.: Where's the search? Re-examining user expectations of Web objects. Usability News **8**(1) (2006). http://psychology.wichita.edu/surl/usabilitynews/81/webobjects.asp
19. Ström, P.: Where Should the Shopping Trolley Be Placed? (2009). http://www.usabilitypartners.se/editorials/where-should-the-shopping-trolley-be-placed
20. Venkatesh, V., Morris, M.G., Davis, G.B., Davis, F.D.: User acceptance of information technology: toward a unified view. MIS Q. **27**(3), 425–478 (2003)
21. Wu, W., Lee, C., Fu, C., Wang, H.: How can online store layout design and atmosphere influence consumer shopping intention on a website? Int. J. Retail. Distrib. Manage. **42**(1), 4–24 (2014)

Playing Dice with a Digital Library: Analysis of an Artist Using a New Information Resource for Her Art Production

Heli Kautonen[1,2(✉)]

[1] Aalto University, Helsinki, Finland
heli.kautonen@helsinki.fi
[2] The National Library of Finland, Helsinki, Finland

Abstract. Artists are a lesser-known group of information resource users. Previous research on their information behavior and needs are few, and there is not enough evidence of artists' experiences of information systems in a natural context of use. This paper presents a reflective study of an artist using a new online information resource during seven intensive days for her artistic production. The resource is a digital library, which combines materials from a wide range of archives, libraries, and museums in one nation. The analysis was based on data collected during two interviews with the artist, as well as artifacts she produced during the production. The key findings were validated with a survey among a community of artists. The results indicate an impulsive and strongly associative, yet extremely goal-oriented, information usage pattern that challenges developers of the digital library service. Similar usage behavior and needs may be common among other user groups.

Keywords: Artists · User experience · Information search and retrieval · Digital library · Contextual design · Cultural-Historical Activity Theory

1 Introduction

The professional maintainers of cultural material, i.e. archives, libraries, and museums, are nowadays concerned that users should better find their treasures. Big initiatives have been carried out in the digitalization of the materials of culture and science. To provide access to the repositories of these digital materials, alongside supportive functionalities, new information resources and discovery services have been developed. The trend of the day for archives, libraries, and museums is to join their forces and build systems that pool the collections of various organizations. These new information-facilitation services can be called digital libraries [2].

Creative professionals are considered an emerging, although a less familiar, user group of digital cultural heritage. Undoubtedly, online digital repositories of archives, libraries, and museums can provide a vast source of inspiration and material for people working in the fields of, e.g., architecture, arts, design, fashion, games, and TV. Online digital libraries provide an unequalled access to these materials.

© Springer International Publishing Switzerland 2015
M. Kurosu (Ed.): Human-Computer Interaction, Part III, HCII 2015, LNCS 9171, pp. 430–440, 2015.
DOI: 10.1007/978-3-319-21006-3_41

This paper presents a reflective study of an artist using a new online information resource. The resource is a digital library, which combines materials from archives, libraries, and museums in one nation. The aim of the study was to answer the question: *What special needs does an artist have when she uses an information resource in a real work context?*

This study is based on a deep analysis of only one subject, because a rare opportunity to reflect the work of an artist in an intense real-life use case emerged. The key findings were validated with a survey among a wider community of artists.

2 Context of the Study

2.1 Artists as Users of Information Resources

Artists also have needs in their interaction with information technology. This seems to be a rare concern, since there are only a few studies focusing on the needs of this profession. Most of the research comes from the field of information and library science. There, findings and discourse have been rather consistent over the past three decades.

Gregory [4] confirms many behavior patterns that have been observed in previous studies. As long as there have been library systems, studies have shown that artists prefer browsing as a search method. Artists also seem to be rather liberal users of different resources, because their curiosity is not limited to one field, subject, or type of information. Still, images are an important material to be retrieved from libraries, bookstores, magazines, and on the Internet.

Hemming [5] has focused on art practitioners and investigated the information behavior of visual artists. Hemming found confirmation for four purposes for which artists seek information: inspiration, specific visual elements, knowledge of materials and techniques, and marketing and career guidance. He also noted the increasing use of electronic information resources among artists, and drew conclusions for the consequentially increasing use of social media.

A later study focusing on art practitioners by Mason and Robinson [12] confirmed most of the conclusions of previous studies, and pointed out that currently the Internet is often the first resource consulted by artists. Mason and Robinson also argued that communities of practice are an important source of information for artists. They saw the preference to browsing as a means to accidental discovery. They noted that artists need odd occurrences for inspiration.

A current theme of discussion in the literature is the lack of studies on artists' information behavior in a natural context of use.

2.2 Case: Digital Library for All

The information resource inspected in this paper is an online digital library, which joins together materials from several archives, libraries, and museums within one nation. The project for building the Digital Library (henceforth also DL) has been going on for over 6 years, and the service was first launched to the public in October 2013. It will reach its maturity and full user base by 2016.

The DL is meant to serve customers of all participating organizations. Since these organizations include national central agencies as well as small provincial institutions, the potential users of the DL are all Internet users in the nation. This is one of the greatest challenges for the design and development of the service.

Users and their needs have been taken into consideration from the beginning of the DL project. Being a public-funded service, resources for user-centered design and other user-oriented activities have been moderate. The advances in usability have been accomplished with effective collaboration of stakeholders and partner networks [7].

Complexity of the DL service is derived, not only from the wide user base, but also from the fact that archives', libraries', and museums' cataloguing practices differ greatly for historical reasons. Their metadata should be harmonized so that users can have simple and seamless access to data they desire [13]. Furthermore, information needs of different user groups should be considered, because they radically vary [1]. All potential user groups of the DL can hardly be studied during the development process, but it is important to pay attention to key groups, one at a time. Before the launch in 2013, users representing high-school students, university students and researchers, family historians, and visually impaired persons using a screen reader have been involved and their needs studied in user tests [9].

2.3   An Opportunity to Study an Artist's Experience

When preparations for launching the Digital Library started in autumn 2013, an unexpected opportunity to study the needs of a key user group emerged. An artist (henceforth the Artist) was employed to make a live demonstration of the DL during the launch-day festivity. In the first negotiations it was agreed that her experiences of using the DL would be reviewed, once the production was over.

The Artist is one of the pioneer urban performance artists within the nation, nowadays well recognized and award-winning. Her artwork strongly involves people and is mostly situated in public places. With her art she wishes to generate discussion about authority and responsibility, to empower citizens in their everyday environment, and to challenge the role of art and artists in modern society. The use of various media is characteristic of her work.

The core of the production was a seven-day trip abroad inspired by the DL. Throughout these days, the Artist used the DL for inspiration, for generating themes for people-involving performance activities, and for generating material for the end products. They were: a presentation to be performed at the event, a postcard to be delivered for participants at the event, and a documentary video to be used for promotional activities.

The seven-day period took place a week before the launch event of the DL. The final version of the software was to be released before this period, and the system was to function without flaws. The Artist was among first end-users of the service, and eventually the first to test the system extremely intensively, during seven full days.

This situation provided an undoubtedly unique use case, but also provided a chance to gain insight into the work processes and information needs of an artist at work. It was tempting to find out how a new information resource, i.e., the DL, integrated into the Artist's production processes and how she experienced its use.

3   Materials and Methods

3.1   Contextual Modeling of Artist's Work

One aim of the study was to inspect the DL as part of the Artist's work processes and her experiences when using the DL. The findings were expected to bring new input for the further development of the DL service.

Before the production, the Artist agreed to provide all stored notes and other types of documentation for the purposes of the study. There was no intention to disturb the natural work process, and therefore the Artist and her team initiated the means of documentation most appropriate for them. The study was retrospective in nature, since no intervention was involved in the field.

Generally, the study of a single representative of a user group cannot provide reliable or applicable information for research or development. However, a work of art is unique by definition, and is therefore a valid subject of research, particularly from an ethnographic viewpoint. In addition, the production was considered a good source of field data because it was exceptionally extensive and intensive.

The subject of the study was an art production, which started from the first meeting between the Artist and the commissioner, and ended with the DL launch event. Only activities, persons, and other elements that were in direct connection to the Artist were inspected.

Two months after the event, an exploratory interview with the Artist was conducted. Some themes and questions were derived from the Cultural-Historical Activity Theory (CHAT), which provides a framework for analyzing patterns and elements of socio-cultural activities, as well as of interaction with technology [8].

Immediately after the interview, the Artist provided access to all production-related artifacts that were still available for the study. They were: a notebook, the postcard, reference to her Pinterest account, a presentation file, and a video file (see Fig. 1).

The interview and artifacts were analyzed. Significant, contradictory, or strong expressions were distilled into descriptive notes. Modeling methods familiar from the Conceptual Design (CD) [6] process were applied.

Working models of the art production were captured using three of the CD models and drawing the diagrams of each. In this case the physical model, which aims at showing the physical layout of the work environment, was considered impossible but also useless, since the steps of the art production could have taken place anywhere.

The following models were drawn:

- A *sequence model* depicts the task of using the DL for information and material retrieval. It shows steps taken, strategies used, some intentions behind steps, breakdowns, and their interdependencies.
- A *flow model* consists of the three phases of the production: Planning, Production, and Closure. The model shows the communication and actions between the Artist and other people directly involved in the production, the role of the DL in the process, and other artifacts used or produced during the production.
- Intentionally divergent from the CD methods, a *cultural model* was drawn up using the CHAT framework and its elements. These elements were: subject, object, outcome, instruments, rules, community, and the division of labor.

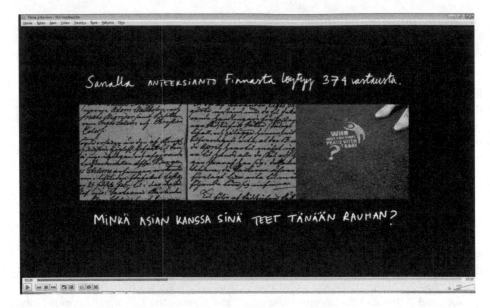

Fig. 1. A screenshot from Artist's video

- An *artifact model* shows the variety of tools and instruments the Artist used or produced in different phases of the production. The model simply shows the relation of these instruments to their main purposes: impulses and ideas, material retrieval and production, and end products.

In addition to models applied from the CD methodology, another model was drawn. Since one of the objectives of the study was to learn what Artist's experience of using the DL was like, all expressions in the interview indicating a sentiment were detected and represented in the fifth model.

- The *experience model* shows the most dominant feelings the Artist experienced during the production. Some experiences were dominant for one phase or some type of action, others occurred repeatedly or were typical for the Artist in all her art productions. (See Fig. 2.)

In order to test the validity of interpretations made and models drawn, another interview session was held with the Artist. Some corrections to the models were made and some complementary information documented.

Finally, all models were analyzed and a list of consolidated findings relevant for the design of the DL was created. The purpose of the list was to be used by the DL design team, and particularly by interaction designers for describing new features, requirements, and so called 'epics' for the agile development scheme.

The core of the study was this analysis of data from interviews and artifacts. Three interesting modes of use were distinguished for further elaboration (see chapter 4 Results).

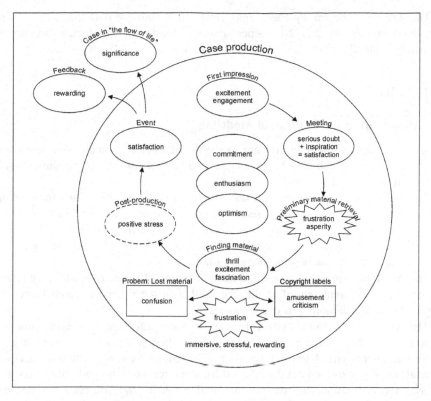

Fig. 2. The *experience model* diagram

3.2   Validation with a Survey

After collecting the results from the contextual modeling, an evaluation survey was designed and executed. The aim was not to provide statistically valid evidence, but to affirm if the detected modes of use were accurate among other professionals of art.

The survey was implemented as an online questionnaire. It consisted of questions investigating respondents' habits of accessing any kind of information resources, and their habits of using digital resources in their work. One section posed questions about erratic situations with information system, and respondents' strategies for overcoming these problems. There were three questions for background information, and 12 questions detecting artists' opinions and modes of using information resources. Respondents were also given a free word to describe their typical experience of information retrieval and usage.

The national Artists' Association helped in distributing the survey to its members. The Association is the most reliable channel to reach professional visual artists in the nation, and its registry holds information of over 2000 of them. An announcement of the online questionnaire was published in the newsletter and on the Facebook pages of the Association. The survey was open for two weeks.

The data from the survey was simply reflected against the data that was gathered from the contextual models. No deeper analysis of data was conducted, because the purpose was merely to validate the original findings.

4 Results

4.1 Results from the Contextual Modeling

Altogether 42 distinct findings concerning the Artist's behavior and expectations were listed. Only those, which may be of interest to other practitioners of human-computer interaction, are described here.

The Artist's search activities were dominantly associative. She did not focus on any particular subject and used random search terms quite often. She could jump from one idea via association to an entirely new topic. The Artist did not understand or care about the underlying metadata structures and conventions. She complained about needing help with the cataloguing logics in the libraries.

The Artist paid special attention and made meaning of the number of search results. She compared different sets of results received with the different search terms. She sought after contradictions and discrepancies.

The Artist was not too disturbed if there was some information or even some final material missing. She made associative leaps, and, when facing a restriction or an error, she took another approach to reach her goals. The Artist was most frustrated if access to material was first indicated but then denied for some reason or another. She needed the material for inspiration, for use in the final product, and for reuse in her next production.

The Artist spent hours using the information resource when working on the production. She exploited all combinations of the simple search and filtering functions, trying to find different ways to approach the material in the repository. She got deeply immersed in the production, and in the DL.

The Artist had strongly positive and only occasionally negative experiences with using the DL. Enthusiasm was her most dominant feeling. She was inspired and motivated by big questions related to such topics as humanity, existence, power, and wisdom.

Three modes of use could be recognized from these findings.

1. *Determined serendipity.* The Artist's search activities were dominantly associative but goal-oriented. She used random search terms, made associative leaps, and turned restrictions into other approaches towards her goal.
2. *Social and contextual needs.* The Artist was constantly in contact and shared her work, including retrieved materials, with other people. She needed contextual information about materials.
3. *Versatile material gathering.* The Artist saved search results and found materials in various ways. She needed the material in different formats for inspiration, for use in final products, and for reuse in her next productions.

4.2   Results from the Survey

In two weeks time 75 artists filled the online questionnaire. The web logs revealed that the announcement of the survey had attracted nearly 600 individual views. Thus, the survey covered 12,5 % of potential respondents that were reached with the announcement.

The respondents represented different fields of visual artists, and there was no demographic distortion, since there were respondents from all age groups and from different parts of the country. Only 2 respondents of 75 answered that they didn't use digital material at all. Thus, the data could be considered reliable for the purposes of the study.

A majority of respondents (46/75, 61 %) expressed to have two equal habits of searching information: they have often a clear target in mind, and they also make free associations often. Almost half of them (48/75, 64 %) use advanced search options and browsing alike. Similar tendencies could be interpreted from open-ended answers. Artists' answers to how they encounter problems indicated that they seldom give in but find different ways to overcome them. This suggests that the mode of *determined serendipity* is quite common among visual artists.

The second mode of use, *social and contextual needs,* was less obvious among survey respondents. Contextual information was considered important, since over 85 % (64/75) of respondents use digital material for gathering background information for their work. This material could be books or articles as well as images. However, less

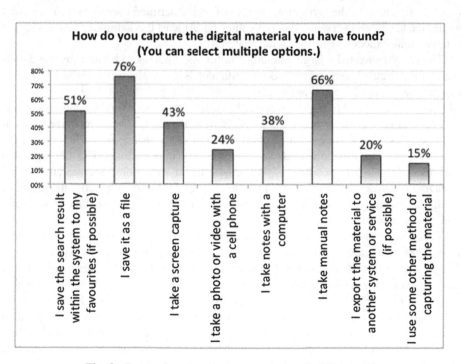

Fig. 3. Respondents' methods of capturing digital material

than third of respondents (24/75, 32 %) need the material for communication between people. Mentions of social contact were mostly in cases where respondents needed help with some technical problem.

The chart in Fig. 3 illustrates one aspect of respondents' material gathering. All respondents expressed several methods of capturing digital material after finding the search result: they save search results in the system and/or as a file, as well as take notes manually and/or by using a computer. Each method was used by at least 11 respondents (15 %). Same kind of preference for versatile methods, e.g., of problem solving, was expressed in other multiple-choice or open-ended questions. Thus, the third mode of use, *versatile material gathering,* seemed also quite common among these artists who responded to the survey.

5   Conclusions and Future Work

This study aimed at analyzing the unique case of an artist using a new information resource, i.e., a Digital Library that joins materials from archives, libraries, and museums in one nation. There has been a call to learn more of artists' information-use behavior and expectations in the natural context of use. Grounded on an ethnographic research approach, a single case was considered an opportunity, which could cast light on the role of digital information resources in artists' work processes.

However, a validation of findings among other representatives of the same profession was considered necessary. A survey that reached 75 visual artists provided some confirmation to the recognized modes of use: determined serendipity, social and contextual needs, and versatile material gathering. At least this sample of artists seemed to have similar modes of using digital material.

The study generated a large amount of notes and findings to be used by the developers of the Digital Library. The findings indicated issues in the service where it did not support user's impulsive and associative way of working. Some of the issues could be solved by redesign and reimplementation, but others raise more fundamental questions.

Previous studies have implied that artists' information-use behavior have atypical characteristics. The findings of this study were in conformance with Hemming's [5] notions: artists' information needs seem to be very idiosyncratic. The findings also confirmed Hemming's speculations that artists' prefer straightforward search options, and avoid resources that are not easy to access. Artists' reluctance to adopt the logics of the library cataloguing has also been considered notable [4], and this study gave evidence to a similar demeanor.

These types of behavior may also be common among other information resource users. There are studies showing that, nowadays, typical library patrons expect similar, Google-like logics of all their information resources [10, 11]. Artists represent the ultimate among the creative professions, but creativity is also required in other domains [14]. Therefore, information services should enable creative user behavior as a general rule, and not limit it. This is a challenge for system developers, who may need to reassess their solutions of material indexing, relevance ranking, etc. It is also a challenge for interaction designers, who should improve their ability to support creative information retrieval and interaction.

This study provided some valuable insight into a person interacting with an information resource extensively and intensively. Several findings indicated that the Artist was so immersed in the Digital Library and the material it offered that it bore some resemblance to game playing.

It was playing, like throwing dice! (The Artist).

Game playing is dominantly immersive. According to Ermi and Mäyrä [3], elements of gaming experience include sensory immersion, challenge-based immersion, and imaginative immersion. Knowing the different aspects of immersion might help designers of traditional information resources in support of a playful user experience.

The evident limitation of this study was the fact that the main findings were derived from an inspection of one user. Although the validation survey suggested verification to the core findings, the sample was small if compared to the entire population of visual artists in the nation. Therefore, no profound conclusions can be drawn from this study. Still, this study will surely help in improving the design of the Digital Library, and some ideas may be transferrable to other public digital services.

There may become an opportunity to extend this study later, if the Artist uses the Digital Library again in her art production. It would be fascinating to observe her while she works, and gain deeper insight into the way she plays with an information resource. Furthermore, it would be tempting to compare the findings of this study to research on other creative and committed professionals' information behavior – such as academic researchers. This prospect is already in the horizon, since contextual studies on researchers' expectations of the Digital Library have been initiated.

Acknowledgments. I thank the Artist, Meiju Niskala, for her enthusiasm and commitment to this project, as well as the personnel at the Artists' Association of Finland for their kind help with the survey.

References

1. Albers, M.J.: Usability of complex information systems. In: Albers, M.J., Still, B. (eds.) Evaluation of User Interaction, pp. 3–16. Taylor & Francis, Boca Raton (2011)
2. Candela, L. (ed.): The digital library reference model. DL. Org Project Deliverable (2010)
3. Ermi, L., Mäyrä, F.: Fundamental components of the gameplay experience: analysing immersion. In: Proceedings of DiGRA 2005, pp. 1–14. DiGRA (2005)
4. Gregory, T.R.: Under-served or under-surveyed: the information needs of studio art faculty in the southwestern united states. Art Documentation **26**(2), 57–66 (2007)
5. Hemming, W.: An empirical study of the information-seeking behavior of practicing visual artists. J. Documentation **65**(4), 682–703 (2009)
6. Holtzblatt, K.: Contextual design. In: Jacko, J.A. (ed.) The Human-Computer Interaction Handbook. Fundamentals, Evolving Technologies, and Emerging Applications, 3rd edn, pp. 491–513. Taylor & Francis, Boca Raton (2012)
7. Hormia-Poutanen, K., Kautonen, H., Lassila, A.: The finnish national digital library: a national service is developed in collaboration with a network of libraries, archives and museums. Insights **26**(1), 60–65 (2013)

8. Kaptelinin, V., Nardi, B.A.: Acting with technology: activity theory and interaction design. MIT, Cambridge, MA, USA (2006)
9. Kautonen, H.: Evaluating digital library's service concept and pre-launch implementation. In: Proceedings of AHFE 2014, pp. 111–122. AHFE, USA
10. Khoo, M., Hall, C.: What would 'Google' do? users' mental models of a digital library search engine. In: Zaphiris, P., Buchanan, G., Rasmussen, E., Loizides, F. (eds.) TPDL 2012. LNCS, vol. 7489, pp. 1–12. Springer, Heidelberg (2012)
11. Kress, N., Bosque, D.D., Ipri, T.: User failure to find known library items. N. Libr. World **112**(3/4), 150–170 (2010)
12. Mason, H., Robinson, L.: The information-related behaviour of emerging artists and designers. Inspiration and guidance for new practitioners. J. Documentation **67**(1), 159–180 (2011)
13. Prescott, L., Erway, R.: Single Search: The Quest for the Holy Grail. OCLC, Dublin, OH, USA (2011)
14. Shneiderman, B.: Creativity support tools: a grand challenge for HCI researchers. In: Redondo, M., et al. (eds.) Engineering the User Interface. Springer-Verlag, London, UK (2009)

The Effects of the Anthropological Race, Gender and Location of Verbal-Pictorial Stimuli on the Usability of Visual Information Conveyance

Joanna Koszela-Kulińska and Rafał Michalski$^{(\boxtimes)}$

Wrocław University of Technology, Wrocław, Poland
{joanna.koszela, rafal.michalski}@pwr.edu.pl

Abstract. The usability of information conveyance is influenced by various factors. It has already been confirmed that verbal stimuli to be more effective should be presented on the right-hand side while non-verbal stimuli on the left-hand side. The aim of this paper is to analyze the impact of three factors: the race, gender and location of the human model picture in relation to a text on people's perception of visual information promoting social campaign for tolerance. A total of 31 students from the Wrocław Academy of Art and Design took part in this study. Participants were shown a series of visual banners containing a picture of a human along with the campaign slogan. The subjective evaluation of experimental conditions was conducted by the AHP method involving pairwise comparisons. The obtained results revealed significant effects of the race, gender and the interaction between them.

Keywords: Display design · Brain lateralization · Digital signage · Ergonomics · Subjective preferences · AHP

1 Introduction

Since many years practitioners and researchers have developed and introduced techniques focused on attracting people's attention. A significant number of research works indicates that primary elements of graphical design, e.g. colors, shapes or layout may significantly impact the person's attitude towards visual information. The combination of words, symbols, and images creates a visual representation of ideas or messages and, thus, affects the comprehension and judgment of visual information conveyance.

The major objective of this investigation was to examine the influence of three factors on consumers' preferences towards graphical panels containing social message, namely: the model's race, gender and the verbal-pictorial layout. The organization of the paper is as follows. At the beginning a relevant literature review is presented. Later, the experimental design and procedure are given followed by presentation of results and their discussion.

© Springer International Publishing Switzerland 2015
M. Kurosu (Ed.): Human-Computer Interaction, Part III, HCII 2015, LNCS 9171, pp. 441–451, 2015.
DOI: 10.1007/978-3-319-21006-3_42

2 Related Literature

2.1 Anthropological Race Issues

Since early 1960's marketers have become more interested in defining a relation between consumers' behaviors and models' race in commercial advertising. Commonly raised issues concern how people of a different race/ethnicity respond to visual stimuli containing various racial cues. Past investigations were mostly focused on the anthropological race. The traditional definition refers to a person's physical appearance such as the skin, eye, and hair color, bone/jaw structure etc. Research conducted in the 1960's and 1970's on the effects of black models used in promotion materials has shown mixed findings. For example, white consumers have reacted to black models positively (Plummer and Schlinger, 1972), neutrally (Bush et al., 1974), and even negatively (Muse, 1971). Dimeo and Whittler (1991) also shown that white consumers had less favorable attitudes toward the visual stimuli when they included black rather than white models. These outcomes were opposite to those obtained by Whittler (1989) where white participants responded similarly to a picture of a white and black actor. Authors suggested that such different findings may probably depend on the social structure, customs and prejudices of the population sample.

The concept of ethnicity was incorporated in visual research in the mid-1980's. Ethnicity has a broader definition than a race and relates to such cultural factors as nationality, ancestry, language, customs and beliefs. It appeared for the first time in the investigation conducted by Deshpande et al. (1986) and concerned attitudes formation towards products in a population of Hispanic consumers with a strong ethnic identity. Numerous research revealed that visual stimuli including ethnics cues such as cultural symbols, ethnic characters, values held by a target population may positively influence on feelings and, thus, enhance for instance a purchase intention (Appiah and Yung, 2009; Deshpandé and Forehand, 2001). Some scholars use the term of race and ethnicity interchangeably e.g. Sierra et al. (2009); Fernandez et al. (2002). Butt and Run (2012) indicate that ethnicity, as a multidimensional construct, comprises the conception of race but cannot be used as a synonym.

Many recent studies take advantage of different theoretical concepts that try to explain viewers' responses to visual stimuli with racial cues. Among these, the following psychological theories may be mentioned: Distinctiveness, Identification, Social Identity Theory (SIT). Distinctiveness theory generally states that a person's distinguishing characteristics are more salient to him/her than traits that are more common in the environment. Identification theory, by contrast describes how persuasion is connected to perceptions of similarity. When people perceived a message source to be similar to them, then this source has a greater persuasive influence. Social Identity Theory provides the concept of a social identity as a way in which people assign themselves to social categories. The membership to a social group enhances the so-called self-concept which is commonly referred to as an individual's sense of self.

The abovementioned theories were applied in many studies on race/ethnicity e.g. Identification theory in Appiah (2001); Distinctiveness theory in Deshpandé and Stayman (1994), Social Identity Theory in Sierra et al. (2009).

In this study, the human typology introduced by a Polish anthropologist Jan Czekanowski was adopted. He assumes that a mankind is divided into three major varieties (commonly known as races) - white (Caucasian), black (Negroid) and yellow (Mongoloid). He distinguished them on the basis of physical characteristics concerning mainly the skin and eye color, shape and color of hair, shapes and sizes of different body regions, particularly the skull (Malinowski and Strzałko, (1985).

2.2 Gender Issues

Most of gender-related research indicates that consistently across time and countries portrayals of men and women are assigned to specific roles. According to Higgs and Milner (2004) males are perceived as voiceovers, authorities, and frequently shown as knowledgeable professionals. By contrast, females are depicted in dependent roles such as a parent, spouse, and sex object. Furthermore, research on gender imagery in television programs and advertisements suggest that female characters are more likely to be shown in home, with males rather to appear in non-domestic settings or occupational roles (Coltrane and Messineo, 2000).

Much research concerning gender issues is focused on how the content and imagery affect viewers' responses, the brand perception and hence the purchase intention or attitudes towards products. It is undoubtedly true that there are sex differences in responding to various message cues incorporated in visual information. For example, there are differences in self-confidence demonstrated by males and females. In contrary to men, women tend to perform a given task with low estimates of their ability and low expectations for achieving success (Nigro and Sleeper, 1987). According to Kempf et al. (1997) such gender-based differences in a self-confidence level may be reflected in confidence of visual information processing. The confidence is considered to be a variable on the basis of which consumers' attitudes and behaviors may be predicted. It should be understood as "the certainty with which an evaluative judgment is held". Outcomes revealed that males performed a higher confidence level depicting fictitious soft drink, than females. In practice this may signify, that females require higher advertising exposure to persuade them to purchase the product (Kempf et al., 1997).

The literature also suggests that females tend to exhibit more adverse feelings toward stereotypical role portrayal than males. According to Courtney and Whipple (1985) females generally demonstrated more favorable attitudes toward brands and products when the visual information depicted modern, liberated. The investigation conducted by Dwivedy et al. (2009) also confirmed these observations. There are, naturally many more examples of gender-based differences in responses to various visual cues. A comprehensive overview of this issue may be found in Wolin (2003).

2.3 The Role of Image-Text Layout

There is a plentiful of evidence that the organization of visual information may significantly influence the subjective evaluation of the graphical material. In the investigation which concerned magazine ads, Ellis and Miller (1981) proved that right-handers preferred the "words right – pictures left" configuration while left-handers had no overall preferences. Similar outcomes were obtained by Rettie and Brewer (2000) in the examination concerning a layout of verbal and pictorial elements of the package design. They focused only on right-handers that represent 89 % of a human population. Findings derived from both experiments are consistent with the human brain lateralization theory which states that left and right hemispheres differ in psychological functions they subserve. Right-handed people have left-hemisphere dominance for analyzing verbal information and language skills while right-hemisphere dominance for processing pictorial information. In the case of left-handed people the brain lateralization is not so obvious and, for example, language-related functions are often right-lateralized or processed bilaterally. The possibility that the stimulus placement influences the evaluation and perception of a given visual stimulus clearly derives from the neurological connection between brain's hemispheres and a human visual system. When stimulus is presented to the left side of visual field, it is sent to the right hemisphere and conversely, stimulus from the right side is sent to the left hemisphere.

According to Janiszewski (1988) the placement effect described above is considered to be a function of preattentive processing of stimuli located outside the point of focus. Therefore such stimuli are assessed at a subconscious level. In his subsequent investigation, besides the relation between the organization of the advertisement and lateralization of hemispheres processing, the influence of subconscious processing of a stimulus was additionally examined (Janiszewski, 1990). The experiment concerned the evaluation of preferences towards a brand name. The researcher pointed out that through increasing the subconscious analysis of a given stimulus also preferences towards this stimulus may be enhanced. These findings are consistent with the Matching Activation Hypothesis which states that, when hemispheres are activated differently, the less activated one processes secondary material more efficiently (Friedman and Polson, 1981). Although the lateralization of brain functions occurs in all normal human brains there is some evidence that, for instance, language differences may affect on how consumers process information about the organization of the advertising environment. In the investigation concerning consumers preferences towards packages of grocery products Hanzaee (2009) showed that in the case of right-to-left languages, verbal right - pictorial left stimulus layout may not be as effective as in the case of left-to-right languages consumers.

3   Method

3.1   Participants

A total of 34 (11 males and 23 females) white students from the Wrocław Academy of Art and Design took part in the experiment. All participants reported to be right-handed. Age of students ranged from 19 to 42 years.

3.2   Apparatus

Custom-made software was employed to conduct the experiment according to the AHP based methodology (Saaty 1980) which involves pairwise comparisons of presented stimuli. The software displayed randomly generated pairs of visual stimuli, collected the results and retrieved the subjects' hierarchy preferences. The experiments were carried out in teaching laboratories in the same lighting conditions by means of identical personal computers and monitors. Visual panels of all considered conditions were prepared by GIMP image manipulation software, version 2.8.10.

3.3   Variables and Experimental Design

The influence of three independent variables on subjects preferences were examined in this study: model's race, model's gender, and the location of verbal and non-verbal stimuli. According to the aforementioned classification of the human species, the first factor was specified at three categorical levels: black, yellow and white race. The second variable was defined at two levels: male and female. In the third one, two different types of verbal/non-verbal locations were used: the campaign slogan on the left side of model's photograph and conversely, the campaign slogan on the right side of the picture. All of the variables produced 12 variants for the AHP analysis (three races × two genders × two locations of picture vs. text). The number of pairwise comparisons amounted to 66.

A stimulus material was designed as visual panels containing a picture of a human model and the following campaign slogan ("Racism? No, thanks."). Models' photographs were taken in dormitories belonging to Wrocław University of Technology. Five unpaid volunteers agreed to use their image for the research purposes – a black male, a yellow male and female, and a white male and female. A picture of a black female was purchased and downloaded from a website http://www.shutterstock.com. Models were asked to stand upright with hands along a trunk and with a neutral facial expression. All of them were dressed in casual jeans, blouses or t-shirts. Models were photographed on a plain, neutral background. Exemplary conditions are demonstrated in Fig. 1.

The within subjects design was applied in this research, thus each subject examined all of the experimental conditions. The participants' perceptions were computed by the AHP procedure (Saaty, 1980) which produced preference weights. We also computed consistency ratios for every subject to assess the degree of comparisons validity. Specifics regarding computations of preferences' weights and consistency ratios may be found, for instance, in the paper of Grobelny and Michalski (2011) or Michalski (2011).

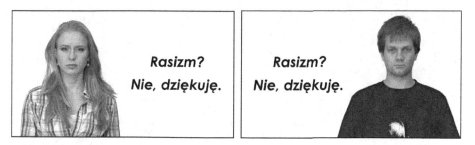

Fig. 1. Two exemplary experimental conditions. (1) left image: a female with a verbal-right – pictorial-left stimulus, and (2) right image: male with a verbal-left – pictorial-right layout.

4   Results

In the presented research the Consistency Ratios ranged from 0.012 to 0.361 with the overall mean and standard deviation of 0.111 and 0.084 respectively. Three subjects with the consistency ratio exceeding 0.2 were excluded from the further examination. Thus, priorities vectors only from 31 participants (21 females and 10 males) were taken into consideration.

The basic descriptive results obtained for these participants are given in Table 1 and illustrated in Fig. 2. One may easily notice that the highest mean preference weights

Table 1. Basic descriptive statistics for all conditions

Condition	Mean	*MSE	**CI -95 %	**CI +95 %
L_White_F	0.0657	0.0055	0.055	0.077
L_White_M	0.0692	0.0043	0.060	0.078
L_Black_F	0.0698	0.0072	0.055	0.085
L_Black_M	0.0543	0.0045	0.045	0.064
L_Yellow_F	0.1339	0.0089	0.116	0.152
L_Yellow_M	0.1006	0.0074	0.086	0.116
R_White_F	0.0678	0.0058	0.056	0.080
R_White_M	0.0685	0.0038	0.061	0.076
R_Black_F	0.0700	0.0063	0.057	0.083
R_Black_M	0.0582	0.0057	0.047	0.070
R_Yellow_F	0.1358	0.0087	0.118	0.154
R_Yellow_M	0.1062	0.0077	0.090	0.122

* MSE – Mean Standard Error, ** CI – Confidence Intervals,
L – picture on the left, R – picture on the right, F – female, M – male.

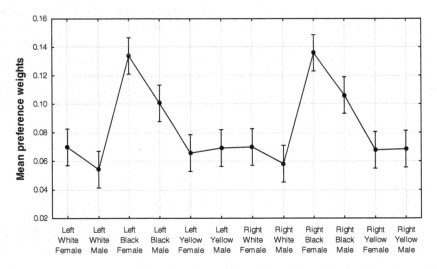

Fig. 2. Average preference weights for all experimental conditions. Vertical bars denote 0.95 confidence intervals.

have been assigned to conditions where black females were used while the smallest average values were obtained for white males.

In order to determine whether studied factors (race, gender and stimulus layout) demonstrates statistically significant influence on subjects' preferences, a three way ANOVA was applied. These results are presented in Table 2.

Among three considered factors, race and gender showed statistically meaningful influence on subjects' preferences ($p < 0.0001$ and $p = 0.000163$ respectively) while the layout was insignificant. Figure 3 suggests that advertisements with black models were the most convincing ones. The mean weight for black race, in conjunction with confidence intervals, indicates that black race may probably differ significantly from the remaining two. From the gender perspective, the discrepancy between subjects' preferences was also demonstrated. Figure 4 provides a graphical illustration of AHP weights for both sexes. Although mean weights along with confidence intervals indicates a clear trend towards female models, the difference is not as obvious as in the case of the black race.

The ANOVA analysis showed also that only race × gender interaction was statistically meaningful ($p = 0.00147$). The interaction is illustrated in Fig. 5. The data show that for white race females the preferences were much bigger than for white race

Table 2. Three-way analysis of variance results

Effect	SS	df	MS	F	p
Layout	0.0004	1	0.0004	0.33	0.56
Race	0.239	2	0.119	91	< 0.0001
Gender	0.019	1	0.019	14.5	< 0.0002
Layout × Race	0.000147	2	0.000074	0.056	0.95
Layout × Gender	0.000055	1	0.0000055	0.042	0.84
Race × Gender	0.0174	2	0.0087	6.6	0.0014
Layout × Race × Gender	0.00021	2	0.0001	0.081	0.92

*$p < 0.05$; df–degeers of freedom; SS–sum of squares; MS–mean sum of squares

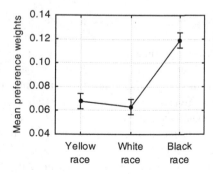

Fig. 3. Average preference weights for the race factor. $F(2, 360) = 91,042$, $p < 0.0001$. Vertical bars denote 0.95 confidence intervals.

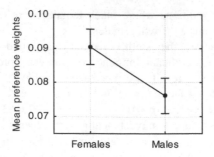

Fig. 4. Average preference weights for the gender factor. F(1, 360) = 14,5, p = 0.000163. Vertical bars denote 0.95 confidence intervals.

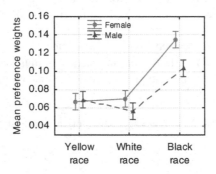

Fig. 5. Average preference weights for race and gender interaction. F(2, 360) = 6.64, p = 0,00147 Vertical bars denote 0.95 confidence intervals.

males. Similar phenomenon was observed for the black race: females were better perceived than males. However, when the yellow race is concerned, the difference between males and females does not exist.

5   Discussion and Conclusions

Scholars assume that consumers' preferences are one of the critical factors in the domain of designing efficient, effective and satisfying visual information conveyance. Many different strategies are introduced in order to attract consumers' attention and shape their behavior. Relevant literature suggests that basic elements of graphical design may influence consumers' attitudes and behaviors in a positive manner.

The aim of the current investigation was to check whether three factors, namely: model's race, model's gender and verbal-pictorial layout, affect the subjects' preferences towards social advertisement. The findings revealed that, indeed, the model's race and gender showed statistically meaningful influence. Simultaneously, subjects seemed to have no overall preferences towards visual information layout. In relation to race issues, the brief literature review showed that consumers reaction on various racial/ethnic cues differ greatly and may depend on the prejudice, education level, social structure of the population sample etc. Using different psychological theories scholars attempt to explain such a discrepancy in people's reactions. However, in this particular experiment, using one of these theories as the theoretical foundation is probably pointless. Experimental stimuli were designed as a social advertisement concerned with promoting anti-racism behaviors and the highest AHP weights were obtained for black models. This may indicate that among Polish young adults that took part in this research, the idea of racism is associated with people of the black race. Such a connection may probably results from historical conditions like: the system of racial segregation in South Africa (apartheid) or slavery.

Outcomes obtained for gender, revealed a statistically significant trend towards female models. According to research conducted by Courtney and Whipple (1985) and Dwivedy et al. (2009) females tend to exhibit more positive attitudes towards ads depicting liberated female role portrayals. Almost 70 % of participants in this experiment were females. Moreover, female banners contained a picture of young, self-confident, open-minded women, who expressed their views about an obvious social problem. Therefore, it is possible that under such circumstances female participants exhibited more favorable attitudes towards visual panels depicting female models, as they may reflect transition from a stereotyped gender role. However, it cannot be ruled out that also factors of beauty and aesthetics influenced participants' subjective evaluations. Thus, further examinations should be conducted to check whether this assumption may be correct.

There was also an interesting interaction effect observed between gender and race. Gender seemed to have an additive effect only in the case of a black race. The existing literature is insufficient to fully understand this phenomenon. Therefore, the additional research and analysis should be performed, for instance, to verify whether these outcomes may be repeated.

A further opportunity for future research involves expanding the knowledge about the impact of the constrained processing condition on consumers' attitudes and behaviors. The assumption that some conditions may temporarily inhibit cognitive capacity and thus significantly enhanced consumers' preferences is of great importance for marketing researchers and practitioners and can't be omitted in further examinations.

Acknowledgments. The work was partly financially supported by the Polish National Science Center grant no. 2011/03/B/HS4/03925.

References

Appiah, O.: Ethnic identification on adolescents' evaluations of advertisements. J. of Advertising Res. **5**, 7–22 (2001)

Appiah, O., Yung, L.: Reaching the model minority: ethnic differences in responding to culturally embedded targeted and non-targeted advertisements. J. Curr. Issues Res. Advertising **1**, 27–41 (2009)

Brewer, C., Rettie, R.: The verbal and visual components of package design. J. Prod. Brand Manage. **1**, 56–70 (2000)

Bush, R.F., Gwinner, R.F., Solomon, P.J.: White consumer sales response to black models. J. Mark. **2**, 25–29 (1974)

Butt, M.M., de Run, E.C.: Can ethnically targeted advertising work for Malay adolescents?: the moderating role of the strength of ethnic identity. Asian Acad. Manage. J. **1**, 13–39 (2012)

Coltrane, S., Messineo, M.: The perpetuation of subtle prejudice: race and gender imagery in 1990s television advertising. Sex Roles. **42**(5/6), 363–389 (2000)

Courtney, A.E., Whipple, T.W.: Female role portrayals in advertising and communication effectiveness: a review. J. Advertising **3**, 4–17 (1985)

Desphande, R., Donthu, N., Hoyer, W.D.: The intensity of ethnic affiliation: a study of the sociology of Hispanic consumption. J. Consum. Res. **2**, 214–220 (1986)

Deshpandé, R., Stayman, D.M.: A tale of two cities: distinctiveness theory and advertising effectiveness. J. Mark. Res. **1**, 57–64 (1994)

Deshpande, R., Forehand, M.: What we see make us who we are: priming ethnic self-awareness and advertising response. J. Mark. Res. **3**, 336–348 (2001)

Dimeo, J., Whittler, T.E.: Viewers' reactions to racial cues in advertising stimuli. J. Advertising Res. **6**, 37–46 (1991)

Dwivedy, A.K., Priyadarshi, P., Suar, D.: Audience response to gender role portrayals in indian advertisements. J. Creative Commun. **2**, 65–85 (2009)

Ellis, A.W., Miller, D.: Left and wrong in adverts: neuropsychological correlates of aesthetic preference. Br. J. Psychol. **2**, 225–229 (1981)

Fernandez, N., Lee, C.K.-C., Martin, B.A.S.: Using self-referencing to explain the effectiveness of ethnic minority models in advertising. Int. J. Advertising **3**, 367–379 (2002)

Friedman, A., Polson, M.C.: Hemispheres as independent resource systems: limited-capacity processing and cerebral specialization. J. Exp. Psychol.: Hum. Percept. Perform. **5**, 1031–1058 (1981)

Grobelny, J., Michalski, R.: Various approaches to a human preference analysis in a digital signage display design. Hum. Factors Ergon. Manuf. Serv. Ind. **6**, 529–542 (2011)

Hanzaee, K.H.: Verbal and pictorial stimulus of package design in right-to-left languages according to brain laterality. In: Kouwenhoven, W. (ed.) Advances in Technology, Education and Development, pp. 307–324. InTech, Rijeka (2009)

Higgs, B., Milner, L.M.: Gender sex-role portrayals in international television advertising over time: the australian experience. J. Curr. Issues Res. Advertising **2**, 81–95 (2004)

Janiszewski, C.: Preconscious processing effects: the independence of attitude formation and conscious thought. J. Consum. Res. **2**, 199–209 (1988)

Janiszewski, C.: The influence of print advertisement organization on affect toward a brand name. J. Consum. Res. **1**, 53–65 (1990)

Kempf, D.S., Laczniak, R.N., Palan, K.M.: Gender differences in information processing confidence in an advertising context: a preliminary study. Adv. Consum. Res. **1**, 443–449 (1997)

Malinowski, A., Strzałko, J.: Antropologia. Polskie Wydawnictwo Naukowe, Warszawa (1985)

Michalski, R.: Examining users' preferences towards vertical graphical toolbars in simple search and point tasks. Comput. Hum. Behav. **6**, 2308–2321 (2011)

Muse, W.V.: Product-related response to use of black models in advertising. J. Mark. Res. **1**, 107–109 (1971)

Nigro, G.N., Sleeper, L.A.: It's not who you are but who you're with: self-confidence in achievement settings. Sex roles **16**(1/2), 59–69 (1987)

Plummer, J.T., Schlinger, M.J.: Advertising in black and white. J. Mark. Res. **2**, 149–153 (1972)

Saaty, T.L.: The analytic hierarchy process. McGraw Hill, New York (1980)

Sierra, J.J., Hyman, M.R., Torres, I.M.: Using a model's apparent ethnicity to influence viewer responses to print ads: a social identity theory perspective. J. Curr. Issues Res. Advertising **2**, 41–66 (2009)

Whittler, T.E.: Viewers' processing of source and message cues in advertising stimuli. Psychol. Mark. **4**, 287–309 (1989)

Wolin, L.D.: Gender issues in advertising - an oversight synthesis of research 1970–2002. J. Advertising Res. **1**, 111–129 (2003)

Do We Differ in Our Dispositional Tendency to Perceive Virtual Agents as Animate Beings?
The Influence of User Factors in the Evaluation of Virtual Agents

Benny Liebold[(⊠)], Daniel Pietschmann, and Peter Ohler

Institute for Media Research,
Chemnitz University of Technology, Chemnitz, Germany
{benny.liebold,daniel.pietschmann,
peter.ohler}@phil.tu-chemnitz.de

Abstract. With few exceptions, the role of user factors in the evaluation of virtual agents has largely been neglected. By taking them into account properly, researchers and virtual agent developers might be able to better understand interindividual differences in virtual agent evaluations. We propose the animacy attribution tendency as a novel user factor that assesses a users individual threshold to accept virtual entities as living and animate beings. Users scoring higher in animacy attribution tendency should accept anomalies in virtual agent behavior more easily and thus provide favorable evaluations. To investigate the impact of this novel concept along with other user factors, we first developed a test to assess interindividual differences of animacy attribution and subsequently carried out an online-study, during which participants had to evaluate video recordings of different virtual agents.

Keywords: Virtual agent · Agent evaluation · Animacy · User factors

1 Introduction

While virtual agent technology advances towards more and more sophisticated patterns of social interaction, users are still reluctant in the adaptation of this new type of technology for everyday practices and react suspiciously when the virtual agents produce unexpected responses [1]. Thus, it is an important endeavor to identify factors contributing to the acceptance barrier and evaluation of virtual agents in order to address these requirements during the design process. Most research efforts focus on technological properties of virtual agents that are supposed to lead to better evaluations. Some of these features are a virtual agent's ability to produce gestures [2, 3] and authentic facial expressions [4, 5] as well as its ability to follow social motives [6]. At the same time, user factors were considered only a supplement to the technological property in question with only few exceptions [7, 8]. Yet, understanding user factors in the evaluation of virtual agents might prove a valuable asset because (1) they provide additional insight into the evaluation of a virtual agent's technological aspects and thereby (2) guide designers attention towards aspects of virtual agents that might have

© Springer International Publishing Switzerland 2015
M. Kurosu (Ed.): Human-Computer Interaction, Part III, HCII 2015, LNCS 9171, pp. 452–462, 2015.
DOI: 10.1007/978-3-319-21006-3_43

received little attention so far. As one positive exception in this context, Rosenthal-von der Pütten, Krämer, and Gratch [8] found that the predictive value of personality traits for agent evaluations even exceeded the actual behavior of the virtual agent. An important challenge in this endeavor is to identify user factors that are both stable over time and closely related to the evaluation of virtual agents. We propose that interpersonal differences in the tendency to attribute animacy to a virtual agent could serve as such a user factor.

2 User Factors in Virtual Agent Evaluation

User factors in virtual agent evaluations can be conceptualized on a continuum according to their temporal stability. Less stable user factors include variables such as prior experience and familiarity with virtual agents or new technologies in general as well as attitudes towards these technologies. A lack of prior experience with new media technologies has been found to invoke feelings of uncertainty about potential benefits and might lead to feelings of unrest about the adoption [9]. As a result, users might be less willing to engage in interactions with virtual agents (see also: technology acceptance model [10]). Additionally, inexperienced users provide evaluations with greater variance after first use, because they have no anchor for comparison. This bias can result from disappointment due to high expectancies that have not been met [11] or surprise by a virtual agents' unexpected capability. As a consequence, studies investigating virtual agent technology through biased evaluations suffer from lower than expected statistical power compromising judgments about the effectiveness of the investigated technology. Therefore, less stable user factors such as prior experience with the media technology (i.e. virtual agents) or related technologies (e.g. video games) need to be taken into account in the analysis. Yet, although beliefs about virtual agents shape the early interaction process, they can change quickly with more time spent interacting with virtual agents [9]. Thus, the increased variance in virtual agent evaluations should decrease with growing familiarity. After continued interaction with a virtual agent, the influence of less stable user factors should be negligible.

Stable user factors, on the other hand, influence user evaluations during early stages and even after extended periods of interaction. Most studies control for participant sex, which usually brings in-group and out-group favoritism effects into light [12]. However, sex tends to accumulate variance from correlated stable factors [13], when they are not controlled for. Most of those stable factors belong to the realm of personality traits. Agreeableness, conscientiousness, and neuroticism, for example, have been shown to impact usefulness-evaluations of information technology [14]. In another study, however it has been found that the predictive value of rather general traits is limited, while traits more specific to the interaction with virtual agents prove more useful [8]. In this paper, we investigate a potentially contributing factor that is responsible for the perception of a virtual agent as a living entity in the first place: the attribution of animacy.

3   Animacy Attribution Tendency

The impression of animacy can be seen as a perceptual phenomenon, during which we ascribe intention towards an entity that follows specific movement patterns [15–17]. Early work by Heider and Simmel [18] already showed, how observers of rather simplistic movements of geometric shapes infer complex narratives about the motives and actions of the supposed actors. The type of motion carried out by the geometric shapes has repeatedly been shown to have a major impact on the likelihood of animacy attributions [16, 17, 19]. Recently Santos and colleagues [15] investigated different movement parameters and their impact on animacy judgments. They concluded that interruptions of otherwise generic movements, changes of the movement direction towards other entities and interactions between entities reliably lead to a stronger animacy attribution. Thus, even simplistic cues are sufficient to elicit attributions of animacy. When an entity is assumed to be animate, users interpret the capabilities of the respective entities similarly to those of living beings [20]. Virtual agents benefit from these attributions, because even rudimentary indications of animate behavior can lead to complex assumptions about their inner processes rendering them more realistic.

Perceiving other entities as animate is a fundamental human ability [15] and is thus deeply routed within our brains recruiting neural structures with strong ties to social cognition [21]. Entities in our perceptual environment elicit momentary animacy attributions or not. Thus, animacy can be considered as a dichotomous attribution. Human observers, however, might nonetheless differ in their judgments about the animacy of a virtual entity: We know about the artificial nature of a virtual entity and are able to reflect automated reactions towards it. Accordingly, users might either tend to take any deviation from expected behavior as an indicator of the mechanistic nature of a virtual agent or willingly suspend their disbelief by giving less thought to deviant behavior. As a consequence, users might differ in their respective thresholds of perceptual cues that are required to accept virtual entities as being animate. Thus, we argue that possible interpersonal differences in the thresholds of attributing animacy might bridge occurrences in human-agent interaction, in which a virtual agent produces unexpected responses (e.g. repetitious or unrelated responses). Consequently, users with a low threshold for animacy attribution should be less sensitive to odd reactions and thus report less negative evaluation results.

4   Method

Prior research exclusively focused on the influence of behavioral properties of virtual entities on the likelihood of animacy attributions. Thus, we first needed to develop a measure for interindividual differences in animacy attribution. In a second step, we assessed the influence of various user factors on evaluations of virtual agents. We created an online questionnaire containing the newly developed measure and measures for trait empathy, three big-five personality traits, as well as sociodemographic questions. Additionally, we randomly implemented one of four recordings of social interactions with different virtual agents from the internet, for which participants had to evaluate the virtual agent and indicate their subjective impression of animacy. The online questionnaire was filled in by N = 81 students from different disciplines. Because we employed an online questionnaire during which participants had to continually focus their attention on an English video, we had to exclude 25 participants, because they reported insufficient understanding of the language (they were non-native speakers), were distracted during their participation, or reported poor internet connection. As a result we analyzed N = 56 valid data sets (age M = 23.21, SD = 2.96, female = 82,1 %).

4.1 Materials

Animacy Attribution Tendency. The behavioral cues leading to animacy attributions that are described in the literature include interrupted movement near secondary objects, approach of secondary objects, responses of secondary objects, speed change, direction change, and spatial context [15, 16, 22]. The presence of these characteristics has a strong impact on the perceived animacy and should result in firm attributions of animacy, which is only of little diagnostic value. Therefore, very subtle versions of these behavioral cues had to be employed. We created 165 stimuli depicting a black circle moving across the screen (see Fig. 1), for which we varied a broad range of movement characteristics at different intensities (see Table 1). "The stimuli were created in Adobe Flash (Adobe Systems) and presented to the participants using E-Prime 2 (Psychology Software Tools, Inc.) on PCs with 19" displays and 60 cm seating distance.
A pre-test sample of N = 48 undergraduate students (age M = 21.53, f = 76.6 %) rated the video files on a 4-point scale from "0 – not animate" to "3 – animate". Thus, participants scoring high in Animacy Attribution Tendency tend to provide higher animacy ratings than participants with lower scores. All stimuli were presented in

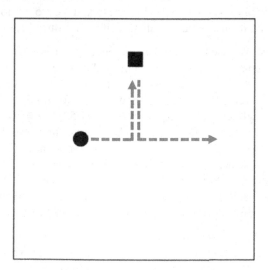

Fig. 1. In this example of the employed stimuli, the circle interrupted its linear movement by moving towards the square (arrows added for the purpose of visualization).

Table 1. Movement characteristics varied for to assess agency attribution tendency

Item number	Movement characteristic	Intensities
1–24	velocity	slow to fast
25–31	motion direction	left to right vs. right to left
32–37	movement direction left to right	0° to 45°
38–46	waiting time at screen center	200 to 3000 ms
47–55	waiting time next to second entity	200 to 3000 ms
56–71	distance to second entity	near to far
72–93	relative position to second entity	next to or away from
94–99	shape of sudden movement change towards second entity	soft to hard turn
100–122	angle of sudden change in movement direction	15° to 345°
123–138	width of a cornering movement	narrow to wide
139–142	shape of avoidance of obstacles in movement path	soft to hard turn
143–150	movement acceleration and deceleration	weak to strong
151–165	constant movement path with altering positions of second entity	–

randomized order with short breaks every few minutes. From the dataset we selected 24 items of different levels of item difficulty and different types of behavioral cues that had sufficient variance to be used as an indicator of the animacy attribution tendency.

For the sake of robustness, the data from all 81 participants of the main study were used to assess descriptive data and scale uniformity. The developed test for animacy attribution formed a highly reliable compound ($\alpha = .96$) that is normally distributed with a mean score of M = .47 (SD = .19; normed to a range from 0 to 1) and a range of 0.86 of the scale. The results remained stable with the reduced sample size.

Other User Factors. We used the empathy quotient by Baron-Cohen and Wheelwright [23] to assess trait empathy. It contains 40 items and 20 filler-items that are unrelated to empathy. Participants rated the statements on 4-point likert scales from "strongly disagree" to "strongly agree". Participants scored 1 point for mildly empathic responses and 2 points for strongly empathic responses (M = 41.52, SD = 10.38, $\alpha = .766$). The German Big-Five Inventory – Short Form by Rammstedt and John [24] assessed neuroticism (M = .58, SD = .19, $\alpha = .73$), openness to experiences (M = .76, SD = .02, $\alpha = .77$), and contentiousness (M = .62, SD = .16, $\alpha = .64$) using 7-point likert ratings from "strongly disagree" to "strongly agree" and 13 items. We additionally asked for the participants' age, sex, and prior experience with virtual agents ("How familiar are you with virtual agents?" on a scale from 0 – "not at all" to 10 "very familiar").

Agent Evaluation. We employed the Agent Persona Inventory by Baylor and Ryu [25] to assess user evaluations of the virtual agents. We used 15 items with 7-point likert-ratings of the API including the sub-scales credible ($\alpha = .76$), engaging ($\alpha = .86$), and human-like ($\alpha = .80$). Furthermore, we assessed perceived animacy for each virtual agent with a single item for which participants had to rate the agent's animacy on a scale from "0 – not animate" to "3 – animate".

4.2 Procedure

Participants were recruited via e-mail. The message contained a link to the online questionnaire. After a short explanation, they first completed the test for animacy attribution tendency. In the next part, they filled in the empathy quotient and the big-five inventory – short form. A video recording of a user interacting with a virtual agent followed the personality measures. The videos were obtained from the internet and represented different virtual agent technologies and scenarios (Obadiah & Spike, chatting, SEMAINE Project; Sgt. Star, virtual guide, ICT Virtual Human Toolkit; Lt. Rocko, virtual patient, ICT Virtual Human Toolkit). We decided to use video recordings from four different interactions to assess the importance of user factors in a more general fashion, while previous research mostly investigated direct interaction with specific agents [e.g. 8]. After watching the complete videos, participants were asked to fill in the Agent Persona Inventory and indicated their perceived level of animacy of the virtual agent. In the remainder of the questionnaire, participants were asked about the above mentioned less stable user factors and sociodemographic variables. We also included several questions to control for attention, Internet connection issues, motivation, and language comprehension.

5 Results

We first wanted to investigate the uniformity of agent evaluations across the four presented video clips. A MANOVA revealed a significant multivariate effect for video clip on the subscales of the Agent Persona Inventory, $V = 0.66$, $F(9,156) = 4.88$, $p < .001$. Although this effect should be considered with caution due to problems with multivariate normality and the assumption of homogeneity of covariance matrices, univariate ANOVAs as follow up analyses confirm this result. We found significant effects for the subscales *credible*, $F(3,52) = 11.23$, $p < .001$, $\eta_p^2 = .39$, *engaging*, $F(3,52) = 26.96$, $p < .001$, $\eta_p^2 = .61$, and *human-like*, $F(3,52) = 3.44$, $p < .05$, $\eta_p^2 = .17$. Closer inspections of the plots for each dependent variable and of post hoc comparisons indicate that these effects are a result of the very positive evaluations of Sgt. Star and to some extent of the negative evaluations of Obadiah.

Table 2 presents first-order correlations between the dependent variables and personality traits across all virtual agents. While situated animacy-judgments correlate highly with agent evaluation scales, $.42 < r < .55$, p < .01, animacy attribution tendency appears to be unrelated both to perceived animacy, $r < .01$, and agent evaluation, $r < .07$. Interestingly, we found a marginally significant[1] correlation between the animacy attribution tendency and openness to experiences, $r = -0.24$, p < .10.

---

[1] The correlation turns out to be statistically significant due to higher test power, when the complete sample (N = 81) was analyzed, $r = -.24$, $p < .05$.

Table 2. Zero-order correlations of the dependent variables and personality traits across the four virtual agents.

		1	2	3	4	5	6	7	8
1	perceived animacy	1							
2	animacy attribution tendency	−.005	1						
3	openness	−.001	−.24†	1					
4	neuroticism	.160	.111	.139	1				
5	contentiousness	−.016	−.063	−.111	−.197	1			
6	empathy quotient	−.054	.004	.458**	−.083	.102	1		
7	API − credible	.514**	.074	.071	.124	−.073	−.125	1	
8	API − engaging	.545**	−.041	−.025	.087	.014	−.206	.728**	1
9	API − humanlike	.416**	.051	.024	.077	.199	.008	.534**	.561**

Note: † p < .10, ** p < .01; N = 56

Further qualitative inspection of the correlation pattern for the different virtual agents revealed indicated heterogeneous results. Correlations between animacy attribution tendency and perceived animacy, for example, varied between − .30 and .24. Additionally, the empathy quotient and conscientiousness turned out to correlate significantly for only some of the virtual agents. Yet, the correlational differences between the virtual agents remain statistically insignificant due to low test power for the within-groups analyses (N = 17, 12, 11, 16).

To account for the significant differences in the evaluation ratings between the virtual agents, we z-standardized the evaluations within each virtual agent group. Thus, the difference between the virtual agents is removed in further analyses. Next, we carried out three multiple regression analyses, one for each subscale of the Agent Persona Inventory. Overall, the amount of explained variance was rather low. The included user factors only managed to explain sufficient variance for the engaging-subscale, $R^2_{adj.}$ = .11. The predictive power of the animacy attribution tendency was low, β < .20, n.s. However, trait empathy explained a substantial amount of variance for the factors *credible* and *engaging*. Thus, more empathic participants perceived the virtual agents as less credible and less engaging. Additionally, older participants rated the virtual agents as less engaging (see Table 3).

We again inspected individual regression analyses for each virtual agent. Despite the low statistical power, we found different patterns of significant predictors. These differences appeared to be most pronounced for the *engaging*-subscale.

6 Discussion

We sought out to assess the differential impact of interindividual differences in animacy attribution on virtual agent evaluation compared to other user factors. Generally, animacy judgments appear to be strongly related to the evaluation of virtual agents. This seems to be true only for situational judgments and not for a general tendency of animacy judgments. Yet, it should be noted that the situational judgments about the video recordings were most likely not solely based on observed movement patterns. Instead, the strong correlation between situational animacy judgments and agent

Table 3. Hierarchical regression analyses for agent evaluation

Criterion	API credible		API human-like		API engaging	
	β		β		β	
Step 1						
age	− .11		− .15		− .30	*
participant sex	.07		< .01		.06	
experience with virtual agents	.12		.07		.01	
Step 2						
age	− .09		− .15		− .31	*
participant sex	.08		<.01		.06	
experience with virtual agents	.16		.09		.03	
animacy attribution tendency	.14		.06		− .12	
Step 4						
age	− .14		−.10		− .38	**
participant sex	.10		< .01		< .01	
experience with virtual agents	.17		.11		.02	
animacy attribution tendency	.20		.09		− .08	
BFI – openness	.24		.07		.09	
BFI – neuroticism	− .05		.02		− .17	
BFI – consentiousness	− .06		.19		− .02	
Empathy Quotient	− .32	†	− .01		− .40	*
R^2 /adjusted R^2	.14	− .01	.07	− .09	.24	.11

Note: † p < .10, * p < .05, ** p < .01

evaluation could have been subject to anchoring, because the question immediately followed the Agent Personal Inventory, which assesses agent evaluation in general. Therefore, participants might have employed a wider interpretation of animacy than intended. This is also supported by the fact that agent evaluation scales tend to correlate highly as evidenced in Table 2.

Despite the fact that our scale for the animacy attribution tendency reached an exalting internal consistency of α = .96, the question remains why we could not observe a correlation with agent evaluations and situational animacy judgments. Especially the latter case raises the question, whether the scale faces issues in validity despite its high reliability. One possible explanation could lie in the nature of animacy attributions: As recognizing animacy in other entities is a basic cognitive ability [15], there might simply be no differences between individuals. However, after an analysis of animacy judgments using fMRI Santos and colleagues [21] concluded that both low- and high-level brain structures are recruited in the process. Thus, while the detection of related movement is part of low-level cognitive abilities, interindividual differences might arise at the level of social cognition in the social neural network. These differences are also reflected in the high range of scores in the test we developed. However, there might have also been other factors such as a general response bias during uncertain decisions that could be partially responsible for the variance within the sample. Lastly, because demonstration videos of virtual agent technology usually do not include unexpected behaviors, the quality of the observed behaviors might have been too high compared to a normal interaction scenario, so that interindividual differences in the threshold of animacy attribution could have played a role. At this point the relevance of interindividual differences in agency attributions for agent perception remains unclear. The marginally significant correlation with openness to experiences suggests that users seeking out interesting experiences are less likely to attribute animacy. This might be related to higher expectancies from virtual entities that are required to perceive it as an interesting experience.

The low predictive value of the other user factors in our study challenges the notion that they are an important element to fully understand agent evaluations when technological properties are manipulated. We were only able to observe effects of trait empathy on two of the three employed evaluation scales. The remaining traits from the big-five personality model had no predictive value. However, this result is in line with the argument that we need to consider personality traits that are more specific to the investigated scenario [8]. The correlational pattern of personality traits and agent evaluation could also depend on the employed measure for agent evaluation, because the Agent Persona Inventory has primarily been developed for learning scenarios with pedagogical agents. Furthermore, the diagnostic properties of the Agent Persona Inventory have not fully been explored, yet. On another note, the rather small sample size of the current study should be considered in the interpretation of the results as well as the fact that participants in our study watched videos of virtual agents rather than directly interacting with them.

In separate analyses for the different virtual agent video clips that were part of our study we found indications that the correlational pattern of user factors and agent evaluation differed depending on the displayed virtual agent. This is unexpected, because we usually assume that our findings generalize to comparable scenarios. The absent correlation between animacy attribution tendency and agent evaluation might also be a result of this inconsistency. On the other hand, studies investigating the link between user factors and agent evaluation [7, 8] so far only included one scenario. Still, the relevance of the investigated scenario for the influence of user factors should—given that this indication is confirmed by a larger sample—be high, because the use cases of current virtual agent technology are rather diverse. As a consequence, we would not be able to include a fixed set of personality inventories into user studies, but would have to identify relevant user factors in the process.

Acknowledgement. This study was partially funded by the German Research Foundation (DFG) under grant 1760 ("CrossWorlds: Connecting Virtual and Real Social Worlds"). We thank Kevin Pfeffel and Yannik Augustin for their help in the creation of the stimuli.

References

1. Kramer, M., Yaghoubzadeh, R., Kopp, S., Pitsch, K.: A conversational virtual human as autonomous assistant for elderly and cognitively impaired users? Social acceptability and design considerations. Lecture Notes in Informatics (LNI) P-220, pp. 1105–1119 (2013)

2. Bergmann, K., Kopp, S.: Increasing the expressiveness of virtual agents: autonomous generation of speech and gesture for spatial description tasks. In: Decker, K., Sichman, J., Sierra, C., Castelfranchi, C. (eds.) Proceedings of 8th international Conference on Autonomous Agents and Multiagent Systems (AAMAS 2009), pp. 361–368. IFAAMAS, Richland (2009)
3. Pelachaud, C.: Studies on gesture expressivity for a virtual agent. Speech Commun. **51**, 630–639 (2009)
4. Liebold, B., Ohler, P.: Multimodal emotion expressions of virtual agents. mimic and vocal emotion expressions and their effects on emotion recognition. In: Pun, T., Pelachaud, C., Sebe, N. (eds.) 2013 Humaine Association Conference on Affective Computing and Intelligent Interaction, ACII 2013, pp. 405–410. IEEE, Los Alamitos (2013)
5. Pelachaud, C.: Modelling multimodal expression of emotion in a virtual agent. Philos. Trans. R. Soc. Lond. B Biol. Sci. **364**, 3539–3548 (2009)
6. Schönbrodt, F.D., Asendorpf, J.B.: The challenge of constructing psychologically believable agents. J. Media Psychol. **23**, 100–107 (2011)
7. Kang, S.-H., Gratch, J., Wang, N., Watt, J.H.: Agreeable people like agreeable virtual humans. In: Prendinger, H., Lester, J.C., Ishizuka, M. (eds.) IVA 2008. LNCS (LNAI), vol. 5208, pp. 253–261. Springer, Heidelberg (2008)
8. von der Pütten, A.M., Krämer, N.C., Gratch, J.: How our personality shapes our interactions with virtual characters - implications for research and development. In: Safonova, A. (ed.) IVA 2010. LNCS, vol. 6356, pp. 208–221. Springer, Heidelberg (2010)
9. Karahana, E., Straub, D.W., Chervany, N.L.: Information technology adoption across time: A cross sectional comparison of pre-adoption and post-adoption beliefs. MIS Q. **23**, 183–213 (1999)
10. Venkatesh, V., Davis, F.D.: A theoretical extension of the technology acceptance model: four longitudinal field studies. Manage. Sci. **46**, 186–204 (2000)
11. Staples, D.S., Wong, I., Seddon, P.B.: Having expectations of information systems benefits that match received benefits: does it really matter? Inf. Manage. **40**, 115–131 (2002)
12. Guadagno, R.E., Blascovich, J., Bailenson, J.N., McCall, C.: Virtual humans and persuasion: The effects of agency and behavioral realism. Media Psychol. **10**, 1–22 (2007)
13. De Bolle, M., De Fruyt, F., McCrae, R.R., Lockenhoff, C.E., Costa, P.T., Aguilar-Vafaie, M. E., Ahn, C.K., Ahn, H.N., Alcalay, L., Allik, J., Avdeyeva, T.V., Bratko, D., Brunner-Sciarra, M., Cain, T.R., Chan, W., Chittcharat, N., Crawford, J.T., Fehr, R., Fickova, E., Gelfand, M.J., Graf, S., Gulgoz, S., Hrebickova, M., Jussim, L., Klinkosz, W., Knezevic, G., Leibovich de Figueroa, N., Lima, M.P., Martin, T.A., Marusic, I., Mastor, K. A., Nakazato, K., Nansubuga, F., Porrata, J., Puric, D., Realo, A., Reategui, N., Rolland, J. P., Schmidt, V., Sekowski, A., Shakespeare-Finch, J., Shimonaka, Y., Simonetti, F., Siuta, J., Szmigielska, B., Vanno, V., Wang, L., Yik, M., Terracciano, A.: The emergence of sex differences in personality traits in early adolescence: a cross-sectional, cross-cultural study. J. Pers. Soc. Psychol. **108**, 171–185 (2015)
14. Devaraj, S., Easley, R.F., Crant, J.M.: Research note—how does personality matter? relating the five-factor model to technology acceptance and use. Inf. Syst. Res. **19**, 93–105 (2008)
15. Santos, N.S., David, N., Bente, G., Vogeley, K.: Parametric induction of animacy experience. Conscious Cogn. **17**, 425–427 (2008)
16. Tremoulet, P.D., Feldman, J.: Perception of animacy from the motion of a single object. Perception **29**, 943–951 (2000)
17. Berry, D.S., Misovich, S.J., Kean, K.J., Baron, R.M.: Effects of disruption of structure and motion on perceptions of social causality. Pers. Soc. Psychol. Bull. **18**, 237–244 (1992)
18. Heider, F., Simmel, M.: An experimental study of apparent behavior. Am. J. Psychol. **57**, 243–259 (1944)

19. Barrett, J., Johnson, A.H.: The role of control in attributing intentional agency to inanimate objects. J. Cogn. Cult. **3**, 208–217 (2003)
20. Hoffmann, L., Krämer, N.C., Lam-chi, A., Kopp, S.: Media equation revisited: do users show polite reactions towards an embodied agent? In: Ruttkay, Z., Kipp, M., Nijholt, A., Vilhjálmsson, H.H. (eds.) IVA 2009. LNCS, vol. 5773, pp. 159–165. Springer, Heidelberg (2009)
21. Santos, N.S., Kuzmanovic, B., David, N., Rotarska-Jagiela, A., Eickhoff, S.B., Shah, J.N., Fink, G.R., Bente, G., Vogeley, K.: Animated brain: a functional neuroimaging study on animacy experience. Neuroimage. **53**, 291–302 (2010)
22. Tremoulet, P.D., Feldman, J.: The influence of spatial context and the role of intentionality in the interpretation of animacy from motion. Percept. Psychophys. **68**, 1047–1058 (2006)
23. Baron-Cohen, S., Wheelwright, S.: The empathy quotient: an investigation of adults with asperger syndrome or high functioning autism, and normal sex differences. J. Autism Dev. Disord. **34**, 163–175 (2004)
24. Rammstedt, B., John, O.P.: Kurzversion des big five inventory (BFI-K). Diagnostica **51**, 195–206 (2005)
25. Baylor, A., Ryu, J.: The API (Agent Persona Instrument) for assessing pedagogical agent persona. In: Lassner, D., McNaught, C. (eds.) Proceddings of World Conference on Educational Multimedia, Hypermedia and Telecommunications 2003, pp. 448–451. AACE, Chesapeake (2003)

Psychological Impact of Direct Communication and Indirect Communication Through a Robot

Mitsuharu Matsumoto$^{(\boxtimes)}$ and Hiroyuki Yasuda

The University of Electro-Communications, 1-5-1, Chofugaoka,
Chofu-shi, Tokyo, Japan
mitsuharu.matsumoto@ieee.org

Abstract. When we communicate with someone, we tend to send not only our intention but also our emotion. Emotion includes not only positive one but also negative one. Such negative emotion makes our communication worse in contradiction to our intention. To avoid such negative communications, we focus on indirect communication through a robot. In indirect communication through a robot, a user requests desired tasks to another user not by themselves but through a robot. If the robot is carefully designed, it is expected that users regard the robot as a client, and their emotions are directed not to the real client but to the robot. We developed a simple trash box robot and investigated psychological difference between direct communication and indirect communication through the robot. Throughout the experiments, negative emotion from the recipient was directed not to the human but to the robot via indirect communication.

1 Introduction

Although there are many communication style such as a chat, advisement, negotiation and so on, how to convey a person's intention to another person is an essential objective of communication. When we convey our intention to other persons, not only our intention but also our emotion are included in our message. The emotion does not always include positive one. It sometimes includes negative one. Such negative emotion makes our communication worse in contradiction to our intention. To avoid such negative communications, we consider indirect communication through a robot in this study. Many studies on human-robot communication have been proposed in the past. Many robots with verbal and nonverbal communication skill have been developed in the pasts to achieve natural interaction between human and robot. For example, Kobayashi et al., have proposed a multimodal communication robot and studied its psychological effect of linguistic human-robot interaction [1]. Kanda et al. have developed an autonomous humanoid-type robot named Robovie-II and evaluate psychological effect of active and passive interaction between human and robot [2]. Iwata et al. have developed a humanoid robot named TWENDY-ONE for contact based interaction between human and robot [3]. Although many studies including these studies have investigated psychological effect of human-robot

© Springer International Publishing Switzerland 2015
M. Kurosu (Ed.): Human-Computer Interaction, Part III, HCII 2015, LNCS 9171, pp. 463–470, 2015.
DOI: 10.1007/978-3-319-21006-3_44

interaction, they basically aim to develop a robot to achieve smooth human-robot interaction, and to enhance positive emotion between human and human via developed devices. There are also some devices to enhance human-human communication in engineering fields. For example, Samani et al., developed Kissenger to transmit kiss between two remotely connected people [4]. Oki et al. proposed a music box type device to express various home activity with sound and aim to enhance human-human communication in a family in a daily life [5]. As seen above, although many researchers pay attention to emotion between human and robot, and aim to enhance positive emotion in human-human interaction, few researchers pay attention to reduce negative emotion between human and human by using the robot.

In this research, we employ a robot as agency for human-human communication, and aim to divide "intention" and "emotion" to reduce negative emotion between human and human. We aim to use a robot as agency in daily life to pass the robot some troublesome problems for human-human communication.

2   Direct Communication and Indirect Communication Through a Robot

It is difficult to divide the intention and emotion as long as human communicates with each other. For example, as shown in Fig. 1, when a client asks a recipient something with some bad emotion, e.g. with anger, a recipient has some bad impression due to his/her negative emotion. As shown in Fig. 2, when a client asks a recipient, the recipient may have some bad impression to a client if the requests are bad for the recipient. When humans communicate with each other, some emotions are often attached to their intention. We next consider indirect communications through a robot, that is, employ a robot as a transmitter for human-human communication and evaluate its effect of emotion from human to human and from human to robot.

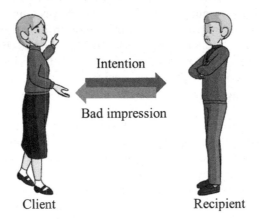

Intention

Bad impression

Client   Recipient

Fig. 1. Example of bad communication (When a client asks a recipient something, a recipient may have some bad impression.)

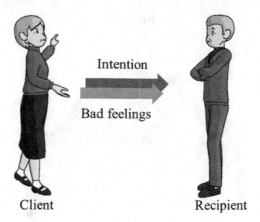

Fig. 2. Example of bad communication (When a client asks a recipient something with bad emotion, communication may become worse.)

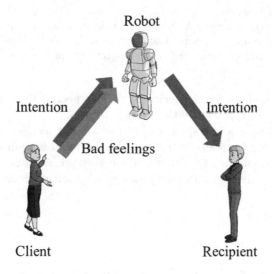

Fig. 3. Example of communication using bridge robot (When a client would like to ask a recipient something with some bad emotion, s/he asks a robot to bridge his/her intention to a recipient. The recipient does not have bad emotion regarding a client.)

Figures 3 and 4 show the concept of indirect communication through robot. In these cases, when a client would like to ask a recipient something, s/he asks a robot to bridge his/her intention to a recipient. As shown in Figs. 3 and 4, it is expected that the robot works as a kind of troubleshooter. When a client would like to ask a recipient something with some bad emotion, s/he asks a robot to bridge his/her intention to a recipient. The robot just pass the intention to the recipient, and s/he does not receive bad emotion from a client as shown in Fig. 3. As shown in Fig. 4, although the recipient may have some bad impression if the

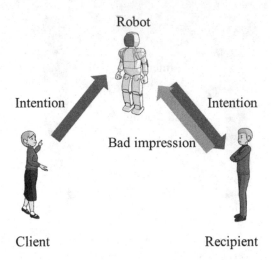

Fig. 4. Example of communication using bridge robot (When a client would like to ask a recipient something, s/he asks a robot to bridge his/her intention to a recipient. Although the recipient may have some bad impression due to the requests, it is expected that the impression is not toward the client but toward the robot.)

requests are troublesome for the recipient, it is expected that the impression is not toward the client but toward the robot.

Based on the above aspects, we aim to use a robot as agency in daily life to pass the robot some troublesome problems for human-human communication. To evaluate whether indirect communication through a robot really works, we design simple experiments and evaluate its psychological effects to users.

3 Experiments

3.1 Experimental Contents

In the experiment, we selected "dumping garbage" as a task. For the experiments, we developed a trash-box type robot as a prototype as shown in Fig. 4. A trash-box was on the wheel-base named Pioneer-III. To control Pioneer-III, we also set a notebook type computer on Pioneer-III. The robot could be controlled from a remote computer. The possible actions were "Move forward", "Move backward", "Turn clockwise" and "Turn counterclockwise". The robot also could produce a sentence "Please take garbage." The robot also had a web camera and the robot operator could observe the experimental environment in real time.

3.2 Experimental Condition

Figures 5 and 6 show the photograph of the developed robot and the experimental environment, respectively. Figure 7 shows the layout of the experimental

Fig. 5. Developed trash-box type robot

Fig. 6. Experimental environment

environment. As shown in Fig. 7, the robot was controlled by a robot operator located in the room different from the examinee. This is because we aim to show the examinee as if the robot moved autonomously. After the experiment, we asked the examinees how they felt about the robot, and all of them thought that the robot moved autonomously. The number of the examinee is four. The experimental contents is as follows:

- Scenario

1. We called the examinee to join the experiment without announcing the purpose. There were three trashes in the room as shown in Fig. 7.
2. We gave the examinee a dummy questionnaire. During this process, the coordinator went out from the room. After that, the robot moved to the examinee.

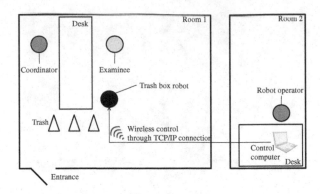

Fig. 7. Layout of experiment environment

The robot moved to the trash and said "Can you bring the garbage?" as a request. If the examinee did not respond to the robot, it said the same message a few times.

3. After the above demonstration, the coordinator came back. The robot moved to another trash and said "Can you bring the garbage?" as a request. If the examinee did not respond to the robot, it said the same message a few times.
4. After the above demonstration, the coordinator asked the examinee to pick up the trashes.
5. Next, the coordinator controlled the robot manually and made the robot say "Can you bring the garbage?" as a request.
6. Finally, the coordinator told the examinee the real purpose and asked to the examinee to answer some questionnaire. We also made the examinee take a personality test for reliability improvement.

Questionnaire contents.

Q1. We ask you the case when the coordinator was not in the room (Case 1). How did you act when the robot said "Can you take a garbage?" How did you feel about the robot and the coordinator ?

Q2: We ask you the case when the coordinator was in the room (Case 2). How did you act when the robot said "Can you take a garbage?" How did you feel about the robot and the coordinator ?

Q3: We ask you the third case. How did you act when the manually controlled robot said "Can you take a garbage?" How did you feel about the robot and the coordinator ?

Q4: We ask you the last case (Case 4). How did you act when the coordinator said "Can you take a garbage?" How did you feel about the robot and the coordinator ?

The answer's method of the questionnaire has 5-point scale. The following is grading on the answer.

-3: Unpleasant, 0: Neutral, 3: Pleasant

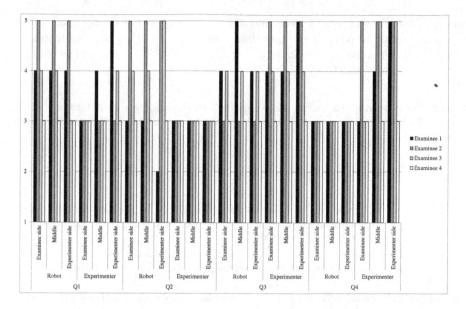

Fig. 8. Results of questionnaire in experiment

As shown in Fig. 7, we prepared three trashes, which were located on the examinee side, middle, and coordinator side, respectively. Figure 8 shows the results of the questionnaire. Although the experiment is still a primary step, we obtained some findings from the results of questionnaire.

As shown in Fig. 8, if the robot seems to move automatically, the emotion of the user was directed not to the coordinator but to the robot as we intended. The emotion of the examinees changed depending on the positional relation among trashes, the robot and humans. The examinees tended to take garbage when not only the robot but also the coordinator were in the room. When the robot seems to move manually, the examinee tended to feel unpleasant compared to direct request from the coordinator. On the other hand, if we can send a command to the robot as if the robot moved autonomously, we could use the robot as a troubleshooter and pass the robot troublesome works for human-human interaction.

4   Discussion and Conclusion

In this paper, we investigated the difference between direct communication and indirect communication through the robot. According to the experimental results, it is expected that the robot can work as an mediator to tell the recipient the client's intention. By using the robot, the recipients' emotion go not to the client but to the robot. Throughout the experiments, if we can design the robot adequately, it is expected that we can use a robot as agency in daily life to pass the robot some troublesome problems for human-human communication.

Based on the above aspects, we would like to design a robot for request, that is, an agency robot to pass the request from the client to other persons instead of a real client. We also would like to investigate how we can control the robot as if the request was just from the robot.

Acknowledgments. This work was supported by Japan Prize Foundation, Foundation for the Fusion Of Science and Technology and NS promotion foundation for science of perception.

References

1. Kobayashi, T., Fujie, S., Matsusaka, Y., Shirai, K.: Anthropo-morphic conversational robot : multimodal human interface with para-linguistic information. J. Acoust. Soc. Jp. **61**(2), 85–90 (2005)
2. Kanda, T., Ishiguro, H., Ono, T., Imai, R., Nakatsu, R.: An evaluation on interaction between humans and an autonomous robot Robovie. J. RSJ **20**(3), 315–323 (2002)
3. Iwata, H., Sugano, S.: Design of human symbiotic robot TWENDY-ONE. In: Proceedings of ICRA2009, pp. 580–586 (2009)
4. Samani, H.A., Parsani, R., Rodriguez, L.T., Saadatian, E., Dissanayake, K.H., Cheok, A.D.: Kissenger: design of a kiss transmission device. In: Proceedings of DIS2012, pp. 48–57 (2012)
5. Oki, M., Tsukada, K., Kurihara, K., Siio, I.: HomeOrgel: interactive music box for aural representation. In: Adjunct Proceedings of Ubicomp 2008, pp. 45–46 (2008)

Subjective Perception of the Background Color and Layout in the Design of Typical Graphical Control Panels

Rafał Michalski[✉] and Jerzy Grobelny

Wrocław University of Technology, Wrocław, Poland
{rafal.michalski,jerzy.grobelny}@pwr.edu.pl

Abstract. The main goal of this research is to examine the influence of various control panel background colors and geometrical layouts on users' subjective perceptions. We investigated five different colors including red, green, blue, white and grey as well as two different arrangements of the panel's informative and controlling items. In the latter case, more vertical and more horizontal layouts were investigated. Panels included typical elements and colors were selected in such a way that their perceptual differences in the CIE Lab color space are similar. A method involving pairwise comparisons was applied to compute relative preferences towards examined conditions. The outcomes generally showed significant influence of the studied effects on the subjects' subjective assessments.

Keywords: Display design · Colors · Control panels · Layout · Ergonomics · Subjective preferences · AHP

1 Introduction

The usability of various types of graphical control panel designs has been subject to investigation for many decades. It is widely known that various factors such as complexity or panel items arrangements may influence the operation efficiency and effectiveness. Reports of empirical studies along with a review of many previous investigations in this regard may be found in the works of Tullis (1981, 1983, 1988). Generally, in the literature one may find a considerable number of papers dealing with the control panel operation efficiency or effectiveness, however significantly less interest is given to the perception of the control panel designs especially with respect to their color properties. Many studies have shown that colors influence both our psychological and physiological responses. In a more general context of visual search the outcomes are to a significant extent inconsistent. For example, the results of Christ's (1975) review of 42 studies in this field published between 1952 and 1973 suggested both positive as well as negative influence of the color usage on the search performance. On the ground of general psychology, the color preferences have also been studies multiple times e.g. Granger (1955), Guilford and Smith (1959) or Helson and Lansford (1970). Since the influence of colors is very often mediated by the context in which they are applied (Schloss et al., 2012) it is very interesting whether previous

© Springer International Publishing Switzerland 2015
M. Kurosu (Ed.): Human-Computer Interaction, Part III, HCII 2015, LNCS 9171, pp. 471–479, 2015.
DOI: 10.1007/978-3-319-21006-3_45

results regarding color preferences apply in the context of graphical control panels. The second area which seems to be worth investigating in this field is concerned with the general orientation of control panel items. This aspect of the control panel design has not received much attention though there are some studies where this feature was investigated. Michalski et al. (2006) studied, among other things, the orientation effect of a graphical panels including solely digital buttons. Shih and Goonetilleke (1998) focused on horizontally and vertically arranged menu items whereas Pearson and Schaik (2003) examined menu orientation in the context of designing web pages. In this study we focus directly on the users' subjective preferences towards control panels differing in layout type (applied configuration) and various panel background colors.

2   Method

2.1   Participants

Overall, 58 student volunteers from the Wrocław University of Technology partici-pated in the study. The age of subjects ranged from 18 to 26 years with the mean of 20.8 years. The standard deviation amounted to 1.7. The sample included 29 females and the same number of men.

2.2   Apparatus

A specifically prepared for this research software application was used to carry out the research. An AHP based methodology (Saaty 1980) was implemented in this tool. Generally, according to this approach, the hierarchy of preferences is determined on the grounds of pairwise comparisons obtained from subjects taking part in the examination. The software was used for presenting appropriate pairs of graphical panels, performing necessary computations, storing the gathered data and, finally, exporting the results to a statistical package. The experiments took place in teaching laboratories in similar lighting conditions on identical personal computers and monitors.

2.3   Variables and Experimental Design

For the purposes of this research we developed a prototype of a relatively simple graphical control panel, which contains elements usually present in real life solutions. The mockup graphical panel consisted both of informative components as well as objects used for controlling the process. It may be treated as a very simplified version of the control panel used for testing the vehicle braking system effectiveness.

The research is focused on two factors. The first one involves five different graphical control panel background colors, while the second one deals with two geo-metrical layouts of panel's items. We focused on three basic colors including red, green, and blue, and additionally white and grey which are often applied in digital displays. Additionally, we controlled the perceptual differences between examined colors by selecting them in such a way that the Euclidean distance in the CIE Lab color space are almost identical. The samples of colors used in this study along with detailed specifications in RGB, HSV as well as CIE Lab color spaces are given in Table 1.

Table 1. Detailed specification of colors used in the study

Color name	Color sample	RGB	HSV	CIE lab
Red		#FFC1C1	(0, 24, 100)	(84, 23, 9)
Green		#CDD796	(69, 30, 84)	(84, -11, 30)
Blue		#AFD9E2	(191, 23, 89)	(84, -12, -9)
White		#FFFFFF	(0, 0, 100)	(100, 0, 0)
Grey		#D5D1C8	(42, 6, 84)	(84, 0, 5)

The second factor differentiated the graphical panels by the way the elements were situated on the panel. We applied two arrangements: vertical and horizontal, which are illustrated in Figs. 1 and 2 respectively. Both layouts consist of the same components.

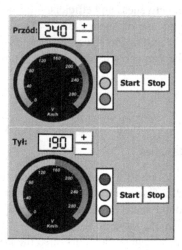

Fig. 1. Vertical version of the experimental condition with blue panel background color (Color figure online)

The combination of these two factors' levels produced ten unique experimental conditions. We employed the within subjects design, so every participant examined all of the control panel versions. Subjective perceptions of the examined graphical panel versions were measured by preference weights, determined by the AHP procedure (Saaty 1980). As a supplementary dependent variable we employed the consistency ratio which allows for assessing the inconsistency level of an individual subject's comparisons results. Details on how to compute the variables within the AHP framework are available, for instance, in the following papers Michalski (2011, 2014).

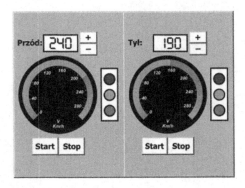

Fig. 2. Horizontal version of the control panel with blue background color (Color figure online)

2.4   Experimental Procedure

After providing the participants information about the general goal of the study and the nature of their expected contribution, they examination began. At first they entered some basic data about themselves and next the proper experiment was conducted. The subjects were to express their opinion on which version of the graphical panel would be better operated in terms of effectiveness and efficiency. Earlier, they were also informed about the possible context of use of such a panel. The control panel images were presented in pairs in random order. The left-right location of images was also determined randomly. One of the comparisons displayed by the experimental software is presented in Fig. 3.

3   Results

3.1   Basic Descriptive Statistics

The results were computed only for participants with the consistency ratio not exceeding the value of 0.25. Therefore, four subjects were excluded. Among them there were three women and one male. Basic descriptive statistical values regarding the remaining 54 persons are demonstrated in Table 2.

The results show that on average participants rated the horizontally oriented control panel with blue background color the best. On the other hand, the worst mean

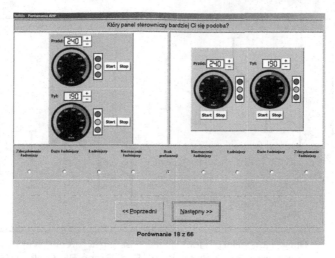

Fig. 3. An exemplary comparison presented by the experimental software

Table 2. Basic descriptive statistics for all conditions.

Condition	Min	Max	Mean	*MSE	**SD
1. H_Red	0.021	0.31	0.0994	0.0086	0.064
2. H_Green	0.029	0.29	0.1117	0.0080	0.059
3. H_Blue	0.031	0.31	0.1335	0.0093	0.068
4. H_White	0.028	0.31	0.1159	0.0097	0.071
5. H_Grey	0.027	0.25	0.1245	0.0077	0.057
6. V_Red	0.023	0.29	0.0709	0.0074	0.054
7. V_Green	0.028	0.28	0.0802	0.0073	0.054
8. V_Blue	0.025	0.27	0.0955	0.0080	0.058
9. V_White	0.020	0.22	0.0804	0.0068	0.050
10. V_Grey	0.030	0.29	0.0881	0.0071	0.052

* MSE – Mean Standard Error, ** SD – Standard Deviation,
H – horizontal layout, V – vertical layout

preference weights were obtained for the vertical version with the red background color. Analyzing the data from Table 2 and Fig. 4 one may easily notice that subjects generally better perceived horizontal layouts than their vertical counterparts. Even the worst horizontal condition with the red background color was still better than the best vertical one with the blue background color. It can also be observed that results for horizontal and vertical control panel versions exhibit a similar pattern. In other words, the perception of colors in both types of layouts seems to be comparable. The red background is the least preferred option while the blue versions are the most desired conditions both in horizontal and vertical control panel arrangements. The same situation is for the remaining colors.

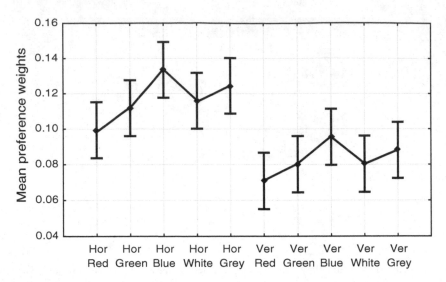

Fig. 4. Average preference weights for all experimental conditions. Vertical bars denote 0.95 confidence intervals.

3.2 Analysis of Variance

A standard two way analysis of variance was employed to formally verify if the investigated effects are statistically meaningful and whether there exists an interaction between them. The obtained ANOVA results are summarized in Table 2. They revealed that both examined factors, that is color and control panel layout significantly differentiate mean preference weights: $F(4, 530) = 3.8$, $p = 0.0047$ and $F(1, 530) = 44.7$, $p < 0.0001$ respectively. The interaction between color and layout effects occurred to be irrelevant. The mean relative preference weights for both factors are illustrated in Figs. 5 and 6.

The Fig. 5 clearly indicates that horizontal versions of the examined panels are decidedly more preferred than vertical ones. This formally supports the outcomes of the descriptive statistics analysis (Table 3).

Table 3. Two-way analysis of variance results

Effect	SS	df	MS	F	p
Color (C)	0.053	4	0.013	3.8	*0.0047
Layout (L)	0.16	1	0.16	44.7	*<0.0001
C × L	0.0016	4	0.0004	0.12	0.98
Error	1.85	530	0.0035		

*$p < 0.05$; df–degeers of freedom; SS–sum of squares;
MS–mean sum of squares

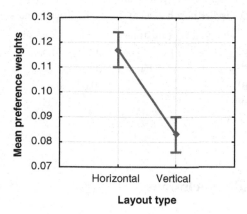

Fig. 5. Average preference weights for the layout factor. F(1, 530) = 44.7, p < 0.0001. Vertical bars denote 0.95 confidence intervals.

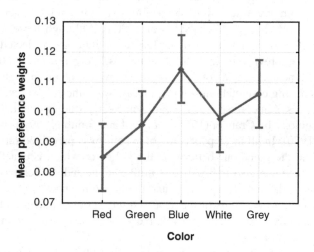

Fig. 6. Average preference weights for the Color factor. F(4, 530) = 3.8, p = 0.0047. Vertical bars denote 0.95 confidence intervals.

The Fig. 6 also confirms the observations drawn from the basic statistics presented in the previous section. The determined hierarchy of preferences towards examined control panel background colors is as follows: the best perceived is the blue then grey, white, green and finally red as the least liked color in this context.

The post hoc analysis of the color effect conducted according to LSD Fischer approach was used to further explore differences between this factor's levels. The obtained results are given in Table 4 and revealed that there were four statistically significant discrepancies between the following control panel background colors: (1) red and blue, (2) red and grey, (3) green and blue, (4) blue and white.

Table 4. LSD Fischer post hoc analysis for the Roundedness degree factor

	Red	Green	Blue	White	Grey
Red	×	0.18	*0.0003	0.11	*0.0088
Green		×	*0.021	0.78	0.20
Blue			×	*0.042	0.31
White				×	0.31
Grey					×

* p < 0.05

4 Discussion and Conclusions

The demonstrated in this study research clearly shows the significance of such factors as background color and layout on subjective users' preferences. Both investigated factors considerably differentiated relative preference weights. Horizontal arrangements were markedly better rated than vertical variants. Such results were observed in other studies dealing with the orientation factor such as Shih and Goonetilleke (1998), Pearson and Schaik (2003) or Michalski et al. (2006). Although these outcomes concerned users' performance but this study preferences might have reflected the subjects' experiences gained previously in similar situations.The color preference structures occurred to be almost identical for both types of arrangements indicating the dominance of colors having connotations with neutrality over others. The obtained structure of color preferences is in correspondence with some early studies conducted in the area of general psychology by Granger (1955), Guilford and Smith (1959) as well as Helson and Lansford (1970). In all these papers the blue color was perceived much better than the green one and the green one better than the red color which is exactly the case in our study. This outcome also indicates that unlike suggested by Schloss et al. (2012) the studied context did not change the general color preferences.

While interpreting the results of this research one should be aware of a number of limitations. The study was based on a relatively small sample of young subjects so generalizations should be made cautiously.

There may be also differences in perceiving colors by males and females, which was not verified in this paper. It future studies it would be beneficial to extend this investigation by including other colors and arrangements. It would also be interesting to compare the participants' subjective feelings with efficiency and effectiveness in operating various versions of graphical control panels.

Nevertheless the presented in this study results may be useful while designing graphical control panels and gives some insights into the nature of users preferences towards different factors of graphical control panels.

Acknowledgments. The work was partially financially supported by the Polish National Science Center grant no. 2011/03/B/ST8/06238.

References

Christ, R.E.: Review and analysis of color coding research for visual displays. Hum. Factors **17** (6), 542–570 (1975)

Granger, G.W.: An experimental study of colour preferences. J. Gen. Psychol. **52**(1), 3–20 (1955)

Guilford, J.P., Smith, P.C.: A System of color-preferences. Am. J. Psychol. **72**(4), 487–502 (1959)

Helson, H., Lansford, T.: The role of spectral energy of source and background color in the pleasantness of object colors. Appl. Opt. **9**(7), 1513–1562 (1970)

Michalski, R.: Examining users' preferences towards vertical graphical toolbars in simple search and point tasks. Comput. Hum. Behav. **27**(6), 2308–2321 (2011). doi:10.1016/j.chb.2011.07. 010

Michalski, R.: The influence of color grouping on users' visual search behavior and preferences. Displays **35**(4), 176–195 (2014). doi:10.1016/j.displa.2014.05.007

Michalski, R., Grobelny, J., Karwowski, W.: The effects of graphical interface design characteristics on human–computer interaction task efficiency. Int. J. Ind. Ergon. **36**(11), 959–977 (2006). doi:10.1016/j.ergon.2006.06.013

Pearson, R., Schaik, P.: The effect of spatial layout of and link color in web pages on performance in a visual search task and an interactive search task. Int. J. Hum Comput Stud. **59**, 327–353 (2003)

Saaty, T.L.: The analytic hierarchy process. McGraw-Hill, New York (1980)

Schloss, K.B., Strauss, E.D., Palmer, S.E.: Object color preferences. Color Res. Appl. **38**(6), 393–411 (2012)

Shih, H.M., Goonetilleke, R.S.: Effectiveness of menu orientation in Chinese. Hum. Factors **40**, 569–576 (1998)

Tullis, T.S.: An evaluation of alphanumeric, graphic and color information displays. Hum. Factors **23**(5), 541–550 (1981)

Tullis, T.S.: The formatting of alphanumeric displays: a review and analysis. Hum. Factors **25**(6), 657–682 (1983)

Tullis, T.S.: Screen design. In: Helander, M. (ed.) Handbook of Human-Computer Interaction, pp. 377–411. North Holland/Elsevier, Amsterdam (1988)

A User Interface Usability Evaluation of the Electronic Ballot Box Used in the 2014 Brazilian Election

Mauro C. Pichiliani[1](✉) and Talita C.P. Britto[2]

[1] Department of Computer Science, Instituto Tecnológico de Aeronáutica,
São José Dos Campos, Brazil
pichilia@ita.br
[2] Department of Computer Science, Federal University of São Carlos,
São Carlos, Brazil
talita.cpb@gmail.com

Abstract. Electronic ballot boxes are becoming one of the main instruments used to represent and reinforce democracy in modern world electoral processes. Most recent research focuses on security, confidentiality and trust requirements. Few of those works target ergonomics, usability, and accessibility of the user interface (UI) and interaction elements issues. We present an empirical evaluation based on usability heuristics and accessibility guidelines assessed from the UI elements presented to voters during their interaction with the electronic ballot box used in the 2014 national Brazilian election. We show that there are many recommendations and design suggestions that can reduce voter's confusion, decrease the number of typing errors, and increase the accessibility for voters with special needs.

Keywords: Brazilian election · Electronic ballot box · User interface · Usability · Interaction · Accessibility · Evaluation · Redesign

1 Introduction

In 1996, the national election process in Brazil became electronic, i.e. all the voters used an electronic ballot box to cast their votes for their favorite candidates to fulfill public offices. The use of an electronic ballot presented many advantages over the traditional system including fast voting count, increased security against frauds, visualization of candidate information, confirmation actions, and faster voting time.

The system went through many changes over the years, but its UI design and interaction elements remained basically the same since the 2004 election. In October 2014, Brazil had its fifth national election for five public offices: a federal president, a state governor, one state senator, and two state congress members. Official statistics report that roughly 115 million people with different literacy levels, ages, technology skills, or disabilities voted in this election. Voters' educational diversity and the fact that a decade passed since the last usability study of the electronic ballot box motivates a new analysis of the ballot box interaction aspects to identify which problems were resolved, which ones persisted, and any new issues.

M. Kurosu (Ed.): Human-Computer Interaction, Part III, HCII 2015, LNCS 9171, pp. 480–491, 2015.
DOI: 10.1007/978-3-319-21006-3_46

The goal of this paper is to evaluate the usability and accessibility of the user interface and its interaction elements of the electronic ballot boxes used in the 2014 Brazilian national election. The evaluation was based on a UI inspection technique with usability and accessibility heuristics that critique the elements presented to voters during their interaction with the system. Initially, we found aspects that do not comply with current best practices and recommendations for a UI suitable for a large and diverse voter's population. Therefore, we suggested aesthetic and functional modifications for the UI and interaction elements that can produce better user experiences while still preserving security, privacy, and confidentiality features found on the system.

The rest of the paper is organized as follows: Sect. 2 reviews the related work on electronic ballot systems for election processes. Section 3 presents the details of the device employed by voters. Section 4 discusses the methodology applied to evaluate the usability and accessibility of the user interface and its interaction elements found on the electronic ballot boxes used on the 2014 Brazilian election. Section 5 presents the results and the findings of the study and Sect. 6 provides a redesign proposal and suggestions to improve the UI of the system. Finally, Sect. 7 presents the conclusions and future work.

2 Related Work

The adoption of an electronic system to support voting processes represents a challenge in many countries. From the system usage perspective, the benefits include a decrease in the number of frauds, faster process to collect and analyze the data, and reduced logistics and material costs. However, the challenges to maintain the confidence and trust in the process are the main concern that needs to be addressed.

Security, privacy, transparency, and confidentially requirements receive the main efforts in the conceptualization, design, and construction of most electronic voting systems. As a consequence, few resources have been directed to improve usability, accessibility and ergonomic aspects concerning how the users interact with the device employed to collect the votes.

Previous work [8, 9] in the HCI area address general and specific aspects of ergonomics and overall system usage focusing on UI elements and interaction. Traditionally, these approaches focus on common operational scenarios that do not share the unique constrains, users, and characteristics of national election processes such as large and diverse group of users, the mandatory use of the system, and lack of external help. To fill this gap, [10] developed electoral ergonomic criteria focused on voting machines user experience and reported its application in the Brazilian electronic ballot box, presenting relevant results. However, the most recent results are based on the 2005 version of the device and were published almost a decade ago.

In this work we focus our research efforts on the analysis of the system components used in the 2014 Brazilian election. Specifically, we address usability and accessibility aspects of the electronic ballot box. The details of the 2014 electronic ballot box are described in the next section.

Focusing on particular interaction aspects of electronic ballot boxes, previous research has already explored some ergonomics aspects of older device models [4] and more recently the UI [6, 10]. These works provide suggestions adopted by the Federal Supreme Court (FSC), the institution responsible for the election process, leading to improvements on the usability of the device and on the overall election process.

Some of the problems reported include legibility and color contrast issues, lack of visual feedback when finishing vote modules, difficult to understand the CONFIRMA (confirm) button by visually impaired or elderly people, lack of delimitation of vote modules, difficult to understand the correction of a vote through the CORRIGE (correct) button and issues related to content organization on the vote confirmation screen.

This work aims to complement the recommendations and suggestions presented in the literature by analyzing the system with a different perspective based on recent HCI concerns, discussing new issues and problems that still persist, and suggesting design modifications based on our findings.

3   The Brazilian Electronic Electoral Process

The usage of an electronic ballot box in Brazil began at the end of 1990 and it is one the world's first completely automated national election [6]. The benefits of the system reduced the amount of frauds such as replacement of ballot boxes, vote alteration, bias, and coercion to vote for a candidate or political party. Although there was many attempts to fraud the electronic system, Lima [6] reports that the implementation was robust enough to avoid manipulation of votes.

In the 2002 elections, the electronic system led to a new record number of voters, candidates, and vote options. Voters had to choose representatives for six public offices in the first round, including national president candidates. The second round, held a few weeks later, asked which of two candidates should occupy the president office.

From 2002 to 2014 there were few modifications and adjustments of the system. The main changes included the insertion and posterior removal of an external paper printer, the change of the manufacturer, and minor software and hardware changes such as processor and memory upgrades and separation of the user interface to choose senators.

The electronic ballot boxes employed in the two rounds of the 2014 election were a mix of several models used in previous elections, but the most common was the UE2013 manufactured in 2013. It has custom built hardware and software provided by the Procomp Company, a local subsidiary of the hardware manufacture Diebold Incorporated.

According to [5] the UE2013 model hardware specification included a 1,10 GHZ Atom processor, 512 MB of DDR2 SDRAM memory, and a VGA color monitor with a 46 degree inclination from the voter perspective. The keyboard had the 0 to 9 keys and buttons to confirm the number (CONFIRMA), to reset the current vote module (CORRIGE), and to choose to abdicate the vote (BRANCO) meaning that the vote goes to the candidate that has the most votes for a specific public office. All buttons have braille marks for accessibility and the voter could nullify its choice by inserting an invalid number for the candidate and confirming it. The cabinet size was 15.3 cm (height) x 42.0 cm (width) x 27.9 cm (depth), and contained an internal battery with ten hours autonomy. There were also two slots for memory cards that stored the operational system and the election data. Figure 1 shows the front view of the UE2013 electronic ballot box.

Fig. 1. Front view of the UE2013 electronic ballot box model

On October 5th, 2014 Brazil had the first round of the national election that asked the population to choose representatives for five public offices: a federal president, a state governor, one state senator, and two state congressman or congresswoman. The second round of the election happened on October 26th and voters chosen one of two candidates to be the president of the country.

Voting in Brazil is mandatory from the age 18 to 70 and optional from the ages 16 to 17 and beyond 70. According to official statistics [2], the overall election process had 142 million registered voters, 6 million more than the previous 2010's president election and roughly 71 % of the country's population, which make the electronic ballot box one of the most used computing systems in the country. Voters used 429 thousand electronic ballot boxes over 27 states to choose among 26 thousand political candidates to fulfill more than 1,600 public offices. From these 142 million voters, about 115 million effectively voted while 27 million absented.

4 Evaluation Methodology

We used a heuristic evaluation, a usability inspection method performed by expert evaluators to identify problems in an interface, to evaluate the usability of the Electronic Ballot Box. The evaluators examined the compliance of the interface according to usability heuristics, which are principles to design an easy to use interface [7].

We used this technique because of its simplicity and effectiveness in identifying problems in a user interface. The heuristic approach was also used to evaluate the interface accessibility because a system should be easy to be used by all people regardless of age, technology skill, social context, or disability.

As the physical electronic ballot box was not available to the authors to perform the evaluation, the official online simulator provided by FSC for voting training [1] was used instead. The simulator presents a skeuomorphic design faithful to the physical design and has identical features: the users can vote, correct their vote, vote blank or nullify the vote (Fig. 2). The simulator offers a list of fictional candidates and their numbers for each political office.

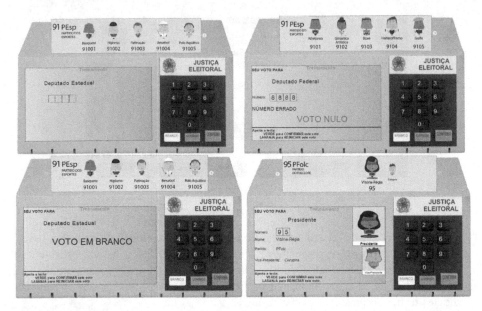

Fig. 2. Different screens of the online simulator, from top left to bottom right: start screen of a vote module, null vote, blank vote, president vote screen.

The scope of our evaluation was to cover: (i) usability of the software interface, including aesthetical design, information grouping, messages, error handling, consistency and clarity of information; (ii) accessibility of the software interface, including contrast and legibility; and (iii) layout and accessibility aspects of the physical buttons, since they are part of the interaction context. Thus, we did not perform ergonomic evaluation nor inspections related specifically to security, even if they are related to usability. The evaluation process was developed using a checklist that combined Michel's usability heuristics for electronic ballot boxes [10] and some accessibility guidelines for software applications from the Accessibility Management Platform [12]. The combination resulted in the following criteria, heuristic, and evidences presented in Table 1.

5   Results

The authors acted as the evaluators and applicants of the heuristics presented in Sect. 4 and used them to check the compliance of the ballot box with user experience aspects. This evaluation does not override an evaluation with voters, which may capture more problems than the ones reported in this paper. However, relevant aspects could be identified through the heuristic evaluation.

5.1   Usability Problems

Applying some of the usability heuristics for voting machines proposed by [10], we found the following list of issues regarding the ease of use:

Table 1. Evaluation heuristics based on [10] and [12]

Scope	Heuristic	Evidence
Voting machine usability	Compatibility with knowledge of computers and other technological tools	Users shouldn't be assumed to know how to operate computers to vote
	User friendly and reinforced guidance	Clear and detailed information, precise labels and instructions
	Clear delimitation of vote modules	Display clear information concerning the start and the end of a vote module
	Local and global feedback control	General summary of what was done, give opportunity to cancel everything and restart the votes
	Attention focusing	Information display and entry devices should be placed as close as possible to concentrate attention
	Intuitive errors correction	Allow to correct actions and cancel one or all votes before leaving electoral poll
	Compatibility with voters objective	Users shouldn't have to discover by themselves any possibility of vote
	Modal flexibility	Presentation should consider different kind of visual forms, sound, touch (Braille) and even haptic display
	Special legibility	Functions to enhance legibility for people with low vision or elderly
	Electoral language	Use terms that are common to users and that contextualize them of actions
Accessibility	Applications shall not disrupt or disable accessibility features	Assistive technology should not cause interference on system functions
	Non-animation mode for people who cannot see or understand animation	When animation is displayed, the information shall be displayable in at least one non-animated presentation mode at the option of the user
	Color coding shall not be used as the only means of conveying information	Information must be displayed in formats that do not require the user to note or distinguish specific colors

5.1.1 Compatibility with Knowledge of Computers and Other Technological Tools

The start screen of each vote module does not present instructions neither help information regarding the task to be performed, such as "*Enter the candidate number or the party number using the keyboard on the right*". Instructions may be useful not only for voters with low technology skills, but also for a broader range of users since the ballot box is a device used once every two years. As a consequence, some voters, i.e. elderly people, may need help to remember how to interact with the system.

5.1.2   User Friendly and Reinforced Guidance

Presenting help information on the start screen of the vote modules, as explained in the previous heuristic, is also a strategy to reinforce guidance by showing a redundant textual instruction explaining the interface.

5.1.3   Clear Delimitation of Vote Modules

The 2014 elections were the first elections that used the electronic ballot box to present a progress bar after the final screen with the goal to provide feedback of the voting recording process. However, the progress bar with the 0 to 100 % range may not correspond to the process status that records the votes. The authors experienced the progress bar jumping from 50 % to 100 % and instantly switching to the final screen ("FIM"). If the voter did not perceive the 100 % status, the percentage may be confused with statistical votes, as informally related to the authors by voters. The loading screen is a suitable pattern, but its visual representation should not be related to amount of completion as in loading wheels.

Since complete voting session has many modules, voters need to type, check and confirm their choices for five political offices. Voting steps, using a wizard pattern, provide voting session status visibility and guide the voters through the process.

5.1.4   Local and Global Feedback Control

Voters can cancel the current vote module but they can't review their choices at the end and return to previous steps. Returning options to previous vote modules can prevent wrong or invalid votes. Nonetheless, it can increase the voting time.

5.1.5   Attention Focusing

The input fields for candidates' number have a thin border with a discrete flashing caret on the active field, which may be difficult to notice due to screen color contrast. The active field should present a thicker border and/or a caret above the number.

The layout of the confirmation screen presents the candidate and its surrogates images far away from their names, making it difficult to associate the name with the image and possibly delaying the voting process. Candidates must be identified immediately by voters, considering that the ideal time for each vote session is about 1 min [11]. People with low literacy levels, low technology skill, and elderly may take more time to associate distant information, thus spending more time in the voting booth.

5.1.6   Intuitive Errors Correction

For each vote module, the correct button erases the whole screen and does not allow correction by steps (last digit), requiring the voter to start typing all the candidates' numbers again. We recommend that the CORRIGE (correct) button erase only the last digit pressed.

5.1.7   Compatibility with Voters' Objective

There are no clear instructions on how to perform a vote for a party, blank, or null until the user enters a condition of those votes, i.e. typing a whole invalid number (null vote) or an invalid candidate number with valid party number (party vote). Information about these possibilities may be placed discretely on the bottom of the start screen of each vote module.

5.1.8   Modal Flexibility

Visual impaired voters had access to ballot boxes with audio, but this option is not available for the illiterate. Although the candidates have pictures, those have low resolution and there are no pictures or icons for the political parties, in case of party vote, or blank/null vote. Additionally, there were not any accessibility features for users with hearing impairment.

5.1.9   Special Legibility

As presented above in *Attention focusing*, the border delimiting the candidate number has low contrast and the caret of the active digit should be more prominent to be easily identified.

Candidates' images have low resolution due to the monochromatic pictures chosen, thus identifying the proper candidate is difficult. The position of the ballot box on the voting booth makes the display far from the head and eyes of voters, which combined with the screen color contrast, aggravate this usability issue.

5.1.10   Electoral Language

There is no explanation of the party vote (*voto de legenda*) expression when voters type only the number of the party or enter an invalid candidate number with a valid party number. Concise information should be provided on the interface for users who are not familiar with the party vote.

5.2   Accessibility Problems

As the electronic ballot box does not allow the use of assistive technology, it addresses an important issue related to the accessibility of the electronic ballot box: the lack of resources to enhance accessibility for different user needs. Regarding UI aspects, we found the following accessibility issues:

5.2.1   Applications Shall not Override User Selected Contrast and Color Selections

The ballot box does not offer high contrast function. As its legibility is not enough, it should offer a function, perhaps enabled by the poll workers, to switch the screen colors to high contrast mode upon voter request. This will benefit people with visual impairment and elderly.

5.2.2   Non-Animation Mode for People Who Cannot See or Understand Animation

The ballot box do not present animations, i.e. there is no transition from the start screen of the vote modules to the vote confirmation screen that is shown after voters type at least two numbers. A discrete transition, such as fade in, should be displayed to enhance usability and to not interfere with the accessibility.

5.2.3   Color Coding Shall not Be Used as the Only Means of Conveying Information

The text on the bottom of vote screen says: *"Press the key: GREEN to CONFIRM this vote; ORANGE to RESTART this vote"*, which may cause confusion for people with color blindness. A possible change could be: *"Press the key: CONFIRM (GREEN) to CONFIRM this vote; CORRECT (ORANGE) to RESTART this vote"*, thus maintaining the colors and using name of the buttons as primary information.

5.3   Discussions and Comparison with Previous Works

One of the problems reported in previous research [10] is that people needed to adapt from a paper-based to a computer-based process that was not similar in terms of flow and function. Nowadays this problem is mitigated and most people began voting using only computer-based process. However, the massive use of the ballot box raised accessibility issues that were not considered before.

Voter demographics can be extrapolated from the data provided by [2, 3], which state that Brazil has 45 million people with some disability (visual, hearing, cognitive or neuronal) and that 7 million of registered voters are illiterate along with 17 million that can read and write but do not have formal education. This wide user context should be considered to provide a device and user interface that is easy to use and accessible for this diverse audience. The problems we identified in previous sections were concerned with this context of use.

From the Brazilian's scenario of user diversity, the following problems still persists in the electronic ballot box design: low color contrast between foreground and background, absence of a final screen to confirm votes, possibility to return to previous modules to correct the vote, content organization, and issues that affect illiterate, elderly or people with disabilities.

Some improvements were made in the last decade on layout and functionalities. In the 2014 elections, the noticeable change was the fact that voters with visual impairment had access to ballot boxes with audio to hear what was being typed. Headphones are available to those who choose to use this function and keep vote secrecy.

6   Redesign Proposal and Suggestions

The outputs of the heuristic evaluation allows the identification of critical issues that need to be fixed to improve the ease of use and universal access, as presented on Sect. 5. Figure 3 presents mockups of the modified UI screens with new elements and content arrangement.

The redesign proposal suggests UI, functional, and interaction modifications covering most of the usability and accessibility problems identified. Figure 3a present a mockup of a vote module start screen with modifications on the input fields that make candidate numbers more prominent, inclusion of reinforce guidance above the input fields, instructions about party and blank vote types and the wizard steps at the screen bottom. The instructions say *"Press the BLANK key to vote blank for this office; To vote for the party, type the party's two numbers and press the CONFIRM key (GREEN)"*.

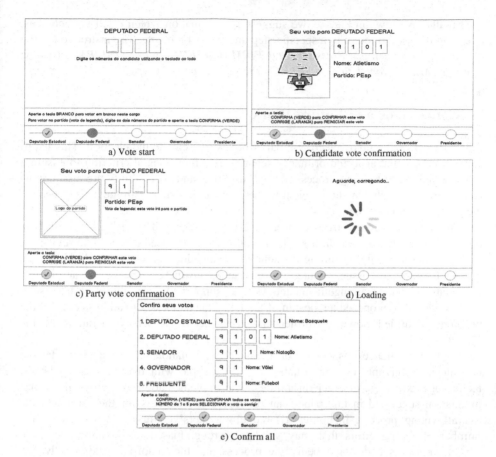

Fig. 3. Modified mockup screens: a) Start screen of the vote module for state congressman/congresswoman; b) Confirmation screen with new content arrangement; c) Confirmation screen for party vote; d) Intermediate loading screen between vote modules; and e) Final screen to confirm all votes or to correct a vote.

Figure 3b shows the modified vote confirmation screen with content rearranged to group candidate's information to facilitate the association between candidate photo, name, and number. We also suggest the modification of the bottom screen's instructions to not link button colors to actions by changing its text to "*Press the key: CONFIRM (GREEN) to CONFIRM this vote; CORRECT (ORANGE) to RESTART this vote*".

Figure 3c presents the confirmation screen for party vote, including the party logo and the following explanation above the party's name: "*Party vote: this vote will be held to the party*".

At Fig. 3d we present a new intermediate screen between vote modules based on the last screen with the progress bar replaced by a loading wheel without percentage numbers that can confuse voters.

Finally, as shown in Fig. 3e, we suggest a confirmation screen of all vote choices, allowing the user to return to a specific step and correct the vote. The instruction at the bottom of the screen is: *"Press the CONFIRM (GREEN) key to CONFIRM all votes; Press NUMBER from 1 to 5 to SELECT the vote to be corrected"*.

7 Conclusions and Future Work

Since 1996 Brazil employ electronic ballot boxes to facilitate the election. This led to several studies that analyzed primarily security as a fundamental criterion to ensure a reliable and trustful voting process, though usability and accessibility are also important to provide a reliable and efficient process, since they deal with the active agent of the electoral process: the voters.

The latest researches covering user experience aspects of the Brazilian electronic ballot box were performed almost a decade ago, which inspired this work to revisit the usability and accessibility through a heuristic evaluation approach, highlighting persistent barriers and issues related to guidance, instruction messages, ambiguous information, content arrangement, and lack of support to accessibility and assistive technologies. We proposed a redesign of the UI of the ballot box to address most of the problems identified; however, further studies are needed to achieve a full accessible system.

Significant changes, especially on the vote confirmation screen, are important to provide a design that can be equally used by people with diverse literacy levels, technology skills, age or other disabilities. The implementation of the design recommendation suggested in this paper can provide many benefits for the users and the overall voting process, including: (i) reducing voters' confusion; (ii) decrease the number of typing errors that may generate wrong, biased, or invalid votes; and (iii) make voters understand better the process and their choices. Additionally, the design suggestions can facilitate the accessibility for voters with special needs such as color blindness.

A bias that needs to be considered when implementing a redesign for the electronic ballot box UI is the impact of the changes in the voting process, such as the addition of screens or the significant changes made on content arrangement. Thus, the next step of this work is to test and validate the solutions proposed with real users.

References

1. Brazilian Election Simulator: (2015). http://www.tse.jus.br/eleicoes/eleicoes-2014/simula dor-de-votacao/simulador-eleicao-2014
2. Brazilian Election Statistics: (2015). http://www.tse.jus.br/eleicoes/estatisticas/estatisticas-eleitorais-2014-eleitorado
3. Brazilian Institute of Geography and Statistics: 2010 Census (2015). http://censo2010.ibge.gov.br/

4. Couto, I.C.: Ergonomic evaluation with voters of the electronic ballot interfaces used in the 1996 Brazilian municipal elections. Master of Science Dissertation, Federal University of Santa Catarina (1999)
5. Electronic Ballot Box model UE2013: (2015). http://www.tre-sc.jus.br/site/eleicoes/urna-eletronica/modelos/urna-2013/index.html
6. Lima, S.L.S.: Cognitive ergonomic and the interaction people computer: the ergonomic analysis of the electronic ballot box (2002) and of the extern printing module. Master of Science Dissertation, Federal University of Santa Catarina (2003)
7. Nielsen, J.: Finding usability problems through heuristic evaluation. In: proceedings of ACM CHI 1992 Conference, pp. 373–380 (1992)
8. Nielsen, J., Molich, R.: Heuristic evaluation of user interfaces. In: proceedings of ACM CHI 1990 Conference, pp. 249–256 (1990)
9. Monk, A., Wright, P., Haber, J., Davenport, L.: Improving Your Human-Computer Interface: A Practical Technique. Prentice Hall, New York (1993)
10. Michael, G., Cybis, W., Brangier, É.: Electoral ergonomic guidelines to solve the interference of new technologies and the dangers of their broader use in computerized voting. In: Proceedings of the 7th European Conference on e-Government, pp. 337–348 (2007)
11. Missing 13 days: average voting time in 2014 will be 1 minute and 14 seconds (2015). http://www.tse.jus.br/noticias-tse/2014/Setembro/faltam-13-dias-tempo-medio-de-votacao-do-eleitor-em-2014-sera-de-1-minuto-e-14-segundos
12. Web Accessibility Best Practices: (2015). https://www.webaccessibility.com/best_practices.php?standard_id=1000705

Instantaneous Human-Computer Interactions: Button Causes and Screen Effects

Kjetil Raaen[1,2,3]($\boxtimes$) and Ragnhild Eg[1]

[1] Westerdals - Oslo School of Arts, Communication and Technology, Oslo, Norway
raakje@westerdals.no
[2] Simula Research Laboratory, Bærum, Norway
[3] University of Oslo, Oslo, Norway

Abstract. Many human-computer interactions are highly time-dependent, which means that an effect should follow a cause without delay. In this work, we explore how much time can pass between a cause and its effect without jeopardising the subjective perception of instantaneity. We ran two experiments that involve the same simple interaction: A click of a button causes a spinning disc to change its direction of rotation, following a variable delay. In our *adjustment experiment*, we asked participants to adjust the delay directly, but without numerical references, using repeated attempts to achieve a value as close to zero as possible. In the *discrimination task*, participants made judgements on whether the single rotation change happened immediately following the button-click, or after a delay. The derived thresholds revealed a marked difference between the two experimental approaches, participants could adjust delays down to a median of 40 ms, whereas the discrimination mid-point corresponded to 148 ms. This difference could possibly be an artefact of separate strategies adapted by participants for the two tasks. Alternatively, repeated presentations may make people more sensitive to delays, or provide them with additional information to base their judgements on. In either case, we have found that humans are capable of perceiving very short temporal delays, and these empirical results provide useful guidelines for future designs of time-critical interactions.

1 Introduction

Several of our work and after-work hours are spent typing and clicking with keys and buttons to tell a machine what to show on a screen. Sometimes, we don't pay much attention to the swiftness of the visual presentation; yet at times, we want the input to lead to instant results. However, due to screen refresh intervals, buffering and sometimes network stalls, our actions are not always immediately followed by the expected outcomes. The extent and acceptability of an outcome delay is highly context-dependent. In human-computer interactions, the *responsiveness* of a system can vary from a few milliseconds to a few seconds. Seow separates between four categories of responsiveness [1], labelling the slowest interactions *flow* and *continuous*; both of these exceed one second. Somewhat faster are *immediate* responses, which range from half a second to one second,

© Springer International Publishing Switzerland 2015
M. Kurosu (Ed.): Human-Computer Interaction, Part III, HCII 2015, LNCS 9171, pp. 492–502, 2015.
DOI: 10.1007/978-3-319-21006-3_47

and the fastest are termed *instantaneous*. The latter category is recommended for graphical controls and other interactions that mimic the physical world, but the thresholds are only estimated to be between 100 and 200 ms. While delays shorter than 100 ms may be imperceptible, they can still affect user performance, for instance through increased stress levels [2]. This work sets out to establish empirical values for how fast an outcome must follow an input in order for a user to perceive it as *instantaneous*.

1.1   Interaction Delays and Sensory Processes

Humans are very adept at handling and acting on objects, facilitated by both the motoric and the visual systems, along with other inputs. Sense of agency refers to the experience of being the direct cause of an event, and this term encompasses the expected delays that follow many actions [3]. Indeed, one study found that participants maintained the sense of agency from a joystick controlling the movements of an image for intervals as long as 700 ms [4]. This type of delay can approximate those found that follow real physical events, where consequences are stalled by the time taken to traverse a distance. However, many human-computer interactions involve series of inputs and outputs and these require far more speedy reactions. Whether typing in text, shooting at moving targets, or moving a cursor across the screen, most users expect instantaneous responses from the system. The higher demands for this type of human-computer interaction is emphasised by the findings of an experiment that compare the temporal boundaries for the sense of agency and the sense of simultaneity [5]. Participants were asked to push a button and watch for a visual flash, then make a judgement on the simultaneity of the events, or on the event serving as the agent. On average, the button-push was perceived as the agent as long as the visual flash did not lag by more than ≈400 ms; conversely, the two events were judged as simultaneous, at greater than chance rates, when the flash delay stayed below ≈250 ms [5]. In fast-paced game scenarios, similar delays become noticeable to players around 100 ms, and these can be detrimental to the gaming experience [6,7]. Furthermore, mouse actions that require pointing and dragging have been found to be even more sensitive to temporal delays [8]. Still, humans are capable of adapting to fairly long temporal delays (235 ms) between movements of a mouse and movements on a screen, although this becomes increasingly difficult as the visual task speeds up [9].

Clearly, instantaneous and simultaneous are not synonymous with zero delay, a computational impossibility. Yet, these and similar human-computer interactions place strong demands for speedy responses on a system. Moreover, studies on multisensory and sensorimotor processes have demonstrated that the human perceptual system is adaptable and quite capable of compensating for short temporal offsets between corresponding signals [5,10–12]. In our quest to find out exactly how much visual lag the perceptual system can compensate for following a motoric input, we have run a series of behavioural experiments on motor-visual delays. Our initial investigations involved direct delay adjustments using a jog-shuttle, with the corresponding visual event presented as disc that flashed on or off on a screen [13]. This approach allowed participants to repeatedly test and adjust the delay by turning the wheel and clicking the button of the jog-shuttle. Results from this experiment revealed that people vary greatly in their sensitivity to this type of delay, but the established median threshold was still far lower than expected at 39 ms. Adding system limitations to this value, our first investigation concluded that humans are on average capable of perceiving motor-visual delays as short as 51–90 ms.

1.2 Discrimination and Adjustment of Delays

This study continues our investigations into human sensitivity to motor-visual delays. It addresses the question on the appropriateness of our initial experimental approach and puts it back to back with a more traditional approach. Hence, we compare thresholds derived from two distinct methodologies, aiming for a more expansive range of data to generalise from. Because our first paradigm [13] allows participants some leeway to get results lower than they can actually perceive, we selected an isolated experimental task that relies on subjective discrimination and a binomial response selection. The simultaneity judgement task is a common methdology in multisensory research [5,10,12], and like the name implies, it involves a judgement call on the simultaneity of two signals. In our version of this task, participants are asked to discriminate between a motoric input and a visual output and make a judgement on whether the output followed immediately or whether it was delayed. Our comparison of delay thresholds established from two different methodologies thus forms the basis for an ongoing discussion around the use of less traditional experimental methods. Furthermore, we build on our earlier experiment where the motoric input, the button-click, resulted in the appearance or disappearance of a black disc [13]. Thus, we extend our work by adding dynamics to the previously static presentation. In the two current experiments, the visual presentation is made up of a black disc that rotates continuously at a steady pace. Moreover, bearing in mind that fast visual presentations can affect performance on these types of tasks [9], we include two speeds of rotation. By doing so, we explore whether the speed of motion can influence not only performance, but also the sensitivity to motor-visual delays.

2   Method

We explored subjective sensitivity to temporal delays between motor inputs and visual outputs in two repeated-measures experiments. The first experiment applied the described adjustment task, extending on our earlier work by replacing the static visual stimulus with a rotating disc. The second experiment encompassed the same visual presentation, but introduced a variation of the more common simultaneity judgement task [5,10,12], hereafter referred to as the *discrimination task*. We ran the two experiments over one session in a computer lab at Westerdals, with the order of presentation counterbalanced across our 10 female and 41 male participants (aged between 19 and 33 years).

Fig. 1. Illustration of the experimental set-up.

We aimed to keep conditions as comparable as possible across the experiments, allowing for a direct comparison between the two methodologies. We therefore used the same visual stimulus throughout, simply a black disc moving in a continuous circle. The experiments ran on MacBook Pro computers with 15.4″ monitors and participants' adjustments and responses were registered using Griffin click+spin USB controllers[1]. These are simple controllers called *jog-shuttles*, comprised of a big click button that also serves a rotating wheel. In both experiments, the button served as a trigger to change the direction of the disc's rotation, as portrayed in Fig. 1. The disc rotated either slowly or quickly (0.2 or 1 revolution/s), with the speed of rotation varying randomly from trial to trial; the initial direction of rotation was also randomised across trials.

2.1   Adjustment Experiment

For the adjustment experiment, each trial commenced with an initial delay (100, 200, 300, or 400 ms). Participants were instructed to push the button on the jog-shuttle to change the direction of rotation and turn the wheel to adjust the delay between their push and the visual change. Due to the lack of reference points, participants were always unaware of the physical value of the delay; however, a clock-face served as a visual cue for the full range of delays. The task involved repeated adjustments and tests of the motor-visual delay, using the jog-shuttle, until the visual presentation was perceived to follow the motoric input instantaneously. Participants were allowed to spend as long as they wanted on each trial, but they had to make a minimum of ten button-clicks before proceeding to the next trial. Each trial therefore involved a series of wheel rotations and button-clicks before reaching the point of no delay, in a sequence illustrated in Fig. 2. With four levels of initial delay, two levels of rotation speed and two levels

---

[1] http://store.griffintechnology.com/powermate.

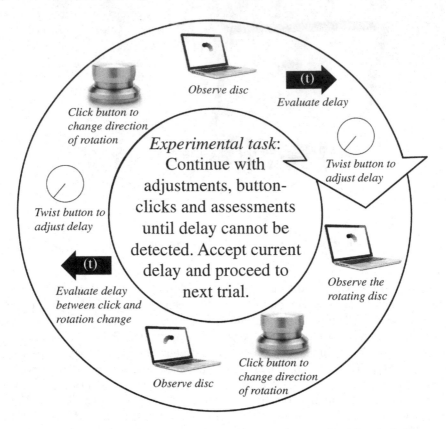

Fig. 2. Circular timeline illustrating the experimental procedure for the adjustment experiment. The experiment starts with an initial push of the button and a delayed change in rotation direction and it continues for as long as it takes the participant to adjust the delay down to an imperceptible level.

of rotation direction, along with two repetitions of all conditions, the full adjustment experiment included 32 trials and took approximately 10 min to complete.

2.2 Discrimination Experiment

In the discrimination experiment, each trial involved a single button-click with a corresponding change in the direction of rotation. The delay between the click and the directional change varied randomly between 11 pre-established values (0, 20, 40, 60, 80, 100, 140, 180, 220, 260, and 300 ms). We asked participants to click button and pay close attention to the visual change. They were thereafter prompted for a judgement on the simultaneity of the motor and the visual events. Participants provided their responses by turning the wheel left or right to choose either the "immediate" or the "delayed" response options. We included four repetitions of all delay, direction and speed conditions, making a total of 176 experimental trials. With the short trial presentations, the experiment duration was on average 12 min.

2.3   Limitations

Our methodologies carry with them a few limitations. Even without system or network lags, computers will always introduce some delay in any interaction. These values are largely disregarded in the literature because they cannot be controlled in an experimental set-up. Although a computer's internal system does not have the functionality to calculate the total duration between user input and screen output, we have applied an external set-up to measure this delay. Using a light sensor on the screen and an extra connector to the button, we performed 10 measurements and obtained an average input-output delay of 51 ms, this procedure is described in more detail in [14]. We report all scores and thresholds without adding this delay, in order to allow for comparisons with earlier studies in the field. However, this number should be kept in mind for a better representation of the human ability to detect motor-visual delays. Moreover, adding this delay to our results also improves the ground for comparison with findings from studies that make use of purpose-built experiment hardware.

3   Results

We initially treated data from the two experiments separately. For every factor and delay level, we calculated each participant's mean and then derived the 50th percentile threshold from their individual distributions. This statistical approach did result in thresholds that exceeded the presented delay values, but only for a few individuals who likely have high tolerance to these types of delay. Furthermore, we took the precaution of checking for outliers based on the discrimination task distributions. For the vast majority of participants, the rate of "immediate" responses decreased as delays increased. However, one participant's scores were discarded because the rate of "immediate" responses increased alongside the delay values, yielding a negative threshold value.

3.1   Adjustment Task

We ran two Wilcoxon signed rank-sum tests to investigate potential variations in delay sensitivity between the two initial disc rotation directions and the two disc rotation speeds, we also ran a Friedman test to explore differences due to the initial delay values. None of the tests revealed significant differences between the conditions. Following this, we collapsed scores across presentation modes and established the overall median threshold for adjusted delays to 40 ms. The 25th, 50th and 75th percentile thresholds are presented as an empirical cumulative distribution in Fig. 3. With our motivation to evaluate the appropriateness of two distinct experimental methodologies, we also established the mode value for delay adjustments from the density plot presented in Fig. 5a. From this distribution, we found that the mode falls around 30 ms, a lower value than the median threshold. Furthermore, we observed an asymmetrical distribution, where the majority of scores centered around the mode, but a long tail of delay scores extended close to 400 ms.

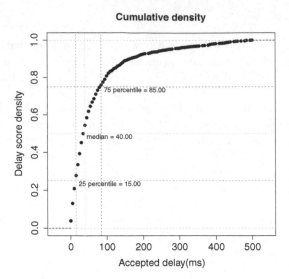

Fig. 3. Individual adjusted delay scores plotted as an empirical cumulative density distribution. The x-axis shows participants' final accepted delay score and the y-axis corresponds to the proportion of scores that fall within defined range.

3.2 Discrimination Task

For the discrimination scores, we derived a best-fit logistic regression model, see Fig. 4. Running another two Wilcoxon signed rank-sum tests, we found no significant differences between the rotation directions and the rotation speeds. Hence, we collapsed scores across presentation modes and established the discrimination threshold from the mid-point between "immediate" and "delayed" responses, at 148 ms. As before, we established the mode value for the discrimination mid-points from their density plot, which is illustrated in Fig. 5b. Again the mode yielded a lower value than the median, this time it approximated 121 ms. The distribution showed a wide dispersion of scores around the mode, along with a long tail that ran to the end of the experimental range of 500 ms.

3.3 Comparison of Experimental Methodologies

Running a Wilcoxon signed rank-sum test, we settled that the striking difference between the mid-point thresholds established from the two methodologies is statistically significant (W(49) = 1871, p < 0.001). While the median for the adjusted delay scores came to 40 ms, the corresponding median for discrimination mid-points was more than 100 ms higher at 148 ms. The same difference was evident for the mode values, established at 30 ms and 121 ms, respectively. Furthermore, scores varied greatly across participants in both experiments. Yet, the wider dispersion of the density plot for discrimination mid-points suggests more individual variation for this task compared to the adjustment task.

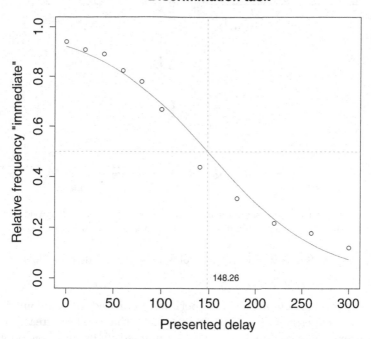

Fig. 4. The best-fitting logistic regression line with the proportion of participants' "immediate" responses plotted as a function of presented motor-visual delays.

4   Discussion

In this work, we have addressed the question on human sensitivity to motor-visual delays. This question has been considered by others before us, in the broad context of human-computer interactions [1], but also for fundemental multisensory processes [4,5,11] and for game-specific scenarios [6,7]. We followed up this body of work with a study that explored isolated motor-visual interactions, focusing on the lower range of delay values. We set out to extend on our ongoing innvestigations by introducing dynamic visual stimuli. Furthermore, we sought to assess the generalisibility of results from our adjustment experiment.

In contrast to the higher ranges of motor-visual delays explored by others on this topic [1,4,9], we found that humans are capable of perceiving delays shorter than 100 ms. The thresholds derived from our adjustment experiment indicate that approximately half of the motor-visual adjustments yielded values equal to or below 40 ms, while a quarter of adjustment values fell around or below 15 ms. Keeping in mind that delays related to internal processes are often overlooked, we emphasise that these thresholds are under-estimates of the true delay. By adding the measured system delay to our results (outlined in Sect. 2.3), we include all known sources of delay. Thus we present our most representative thresholds, the 25th, 50th and 75th percentiles at 66 ms, 91 ms and 136 ms.

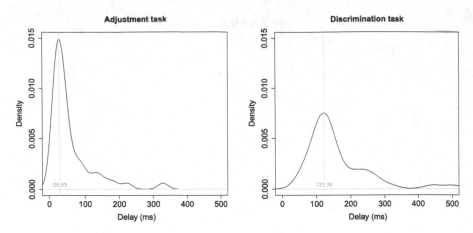

(a) Density plot of each participant's median accepted delay in the adjustment task.

(b) Density plot of each participant's midpoint in the discrimination task.

Fig. 5. Subjective delay thresholds presented as density plots

From our comparison of the two experimental procedures, we found that the discrimination experiment's mid-point was more than 100 ms greater than the adjustment experiment's median. With this marked difference, how do we deem which one is more representative of human delay sensitivity? The answer may lie in the context. A short delay can be difficult to perceive with just a single presentation, whereas repeated exposures provide several temporal reference points. Moreover, the discrimination task calls for a simple decision on the precense or absence of delay, whereas the adjustment task rests on the premise that there is a delay present and this should be adjusted down. Hence, the adjustment task dictates engagement from participants and it provides ample opportunity to move past points of uncertainty. On the other hand, the repetitive nature of the adjustment task could also allow participants to adapt a personal strategy to minimise the accepted delay. We observed examples of participants clicking the button quickly and steadily, making the disc bounce back and forth, so they could more easily judge the delay following the click. Relatedly, the repeated adjustments could give way for accepted delay values that fall below the subjective detection thresholds. If a participant manages to find two detection thresholds, one on either side of point zero, they could theoretically turn the wheel midway between the thresholds and accept a value very close to zero. Nevertheless, even when assuming that all pariticpants have adopted such a strategy, the extended range of delay values still fall below the discrimination threshold [13].

Furthermore, the adjustment experiment demonstrates internal validity from the constancy of the derived thresholds. We ran the first experiment with a static visual presentation and a 20 ms temporal resolution on the adjustment wheel. This time we introduced a moving visual presentation and we increased the temporal resolution for adjustments, before we ran the experiment on a new group of participants. Despite the changes, the 25th, 50th and 75th percentiles are virtually identical across the two adjustment experiments. Although there is no ground for a similar comparison for the discrimination experiment, the density plots in Fig. 5 show a wider dispersion of subjective thresholds. Accordingly, the task of judging immediacy and delay had our participants accept higher delay values than they could adjust for, and they made their judgements with less consistency. As before, this outcome may be an artefact of strategies adopted by participants. Despite this note of warning, we find it remarkable that several of our participants are capable of manually tuning the motor-visual delays down to values below 100 ms, and do so repeatedly and congruously.

Many human-computer interactions involve more than a single, delayed output. Ongoing tasks that are carried out using a computer tend to involve series of inputs and outputs, similar to our adjustment task. Arguably, the adjustment experiment may be more representative of the scenarios we are interested in. However, what we perceive may not necessarily affect how we perform. In order to understand how motor-visual delays influence not only the conscious experience, but also the interaction itself, we need to evaluate the ability to compensate for delays when performing a task. Thus, we plan to apply the derived range of subjective thresholds, which covers a fairly large sample's sensitiviy to motor-visual delays, to the study of performance on motor-visual tasks. In so doing, we aim to shed more light on which experimental approach provides the most representative estimate of motor-visual temporal sensitivity, and we hope to find out whether perceptible and imperceptible delays can affect performance.

5   Concluding Remarks and Future Work

This study presents findings on human sensitivity to delays between a button-click and a visual presentation, which show that repeated motor-visual interactions can make inherent delays more noticeable. Our results also demonstrate that the dynamics of a visual presentation has little impact on the perceived delay that precedes it. Instead, variations are far greater between individuals. The most sensitive of our participants contributed to establish the 25th percentile at 15 ms, or 66 ms when adding internal system delays. Considering that the median also falls below 100 ms, these outcomes speak in favour of designing interactive systems with very fast responses. Ideally, no user should be able to notice delays during interactions with a computer and the presented thresholds highlight the challenge of meeting these demands.

So far, our investigations have focused on universal thresholds for motor-visual delay sensitivity. Our work shows that this sensitivity varies greatly between individuals, and we wish to explore potential factors that could influence the subjective perception of temporal delays. In particular, we plan to look into earlier encounters with highly time-dependent processes, such as gaming and musical experience. Additionally, some of the work on motor-visual delay addresses the relevant scenarios directly; for instance, the work of Claypool and colleagues focus on delay in real games [6]. Conversely, we commenced our investigations with simple and isolated motor-visual interactions. In this work, we have extended on our earlier study and added dynamics to the previously static visual presentation. This had very little influence on the derived thresholds for the delay adjustment task. The final step in our on-going work will be to apply motor-visual delays to an interactive task, a simple game, to explore whether task performance is affected by barely noticeable delays.

References

1. Seow, S.C.: Designing and Engineering Time. Addison-Wesley, Boston (2008)
2. Chen, K.-T., Lei, C.-L.: Are all games equally cloud-gaming-friendly? An electromyographic approach. In: Proceedings of the 11th Annual Workshop on Network and Systems Support for Games (NetGames), pp. 1–6, November 2012
3. Haggard, P., Chambon, V.: Sense of agency. Curr. Biol. **22**(10), R390–R392 (2012)
4. Ebert, J.P., Wegner, D.M.: Time warp: authorship shapes the perceived timing of actions and events. Conscious. Cogn. **19**(1), 481–489 (2010)
5. Rohde, M., Scheller, M., Ernst, M.O.: Effects can precede their cause in the sense of agency. Neuropsychologia **65**, 191–196 (2014)
6. Claypool, M., Claypool, K.: Latency and player interaction in online games. Commun. ACM **49**(11), 40–45 (2006)
7. Dick, M., Wellnitz, O., Wolf, L.: Analysis of factors affecting players' performance and perception in multiplayer games. In: Proceedings of the 4th ACM SIGCOMM Workshop on Network and System Support for Games (NetGames), New York, pp. 1–7 (2005)
8. Jota, R., Ng, A., Dietz, P., Wigdor, D.: How fast is fast enough? A study of the effects of latency in direct-touch pointing tasks. In: Proceedings of the SIGCHI Conference on Human Factors in Computing Systems, Paris, pp. 2291–2300 (2013)
9. Cunningham, D.W., Billock, V.A., Tsou, B.H.: Sensorimotor adaptation to violations of temporal contiguity. Psychol. Sci. **12**(6), 532–535 (2001)
10. Fujisaki, W., Nishida, S.: Audio-tactile superiority over visuo-tactile and audio-visual combinations in the temporal resolution of synchrony perception. Exp. Brain Res. **198**(2–3), 245–259 (2009)
11. Heron, J., Hanson, J.V.M., Whitaker, D.: Effect before cause: supramodal recalibration of sensorimotor timing. PLoS ONE **4**(11), e7681 (2009)
12. Occelli, V., Spence, C., Zampini, M.: Audiotactile interactions in temporal perception. Psychon. Bull. Rev. **18**(3), 429–454 (2011)
13. Raaen, K., Eg, R., Griwodz, C.: Can gamers detect cloud delay? In: Proceedings of the 13th Annual Workshop on Network and Systems Support for Games (NetGames), Nagoya, vol. 200 (2014)
14. Raaen, K., Petlund, A.: How Much Delay Is There Really in Current Games? In: ACM MMsysz, pp. 2–5 (2015)

How Do Japanese People Return a Greeting with a Bow?

Mamiko Sakata[1(✉)], Noriko Suzuki[2], Kana Shirai[1], Haruka Shoda[1,3],
Michiya Yamamoto[4], and Takeshi Sugio[1]

[1] Graduate School of Culture and Information Science, Doshisha University,
Kyoto, Japan
msakata@mail.doshisha.ac.jp
[2] Faculty of Business Administration, Tezukayama University, Nara, Japan
[3] Japan Society for the Promotion of Science, Tokyo, Japan
[4] School of Science and Technology, Kwansei Gakuin University, 1-3 Tatara
Miyakodani, Kyotanabe City 6100394, Japan

Abstract. The greeting is one of the most familiar communicative behaviors in
everyday life. In this study, we clarified the features of spontaneous greeting
interactions by focusing on the timing of bows and utterances. In particular, we
focused on how the response changes with the timing of the greeting. In the
experiment, we performed simulated interviews and analyzed spontaneous
greetings before and after the interview. Our experiment showed that the
responses did not change with the interviewer's bows and utterances. It also
revealed that there was a routine response pattern, appropriate for the people
(i.e., greeters) involved.

Keywords: Greeting behavior · Spontaneous bowing · Timing structure

1 Introduction

The greeting is one of the most familiar communicative behaviors in everyday life.
Identifying the rules and trends seen in greetings can offer important basic resources for
understanding face-to-face interactions.

Yamamoto et al. (2004) looked at the timing between "bows" and "utterances"
when Japanese people meet and greet each other and showed that bows preceded
utterances. Through experiments, Kobayashi et al. (2013) showed the most comfortable
utterance timing when responding to a greeting. In our daily greeting behavior, the
people involved in greeting interactions seem to share the timing patterns considered
appropriate for them.

In the past, studies on greeting behavior were conducted using robots, CG characters, etc. by making them bow (Yamamoto et al. 2004, Shibata et al. 2014) or by
using an audio-response system (Kobayashi et al. 2013), often rigorously controlling
the greeting condition. Yamamoto et al. (2006) actually measured bows by Japanese
people and quantified their behavioral characteristics. However, they examined
"extrinsic bows" by giving advance directions to the subjects. These earlier studies,

© Springer International Publishing Switzerland 2015
M. Kurosu (Ed.): Human-Computer Interaction, Part III, HCII 2015, LNCS 9171, pp. 503–513, 2015.
DOI: 10.1007/978-3-319-21006-3_48

therefore, eliminated errors but cannot be said to represent the "spontaneous bowing" behavior that Japanese people do in their daily life.

Our study, on the other hand, examined spontaneous greetings by the people responding to an initial greeting. Generally speaking, Japanese people's greetings involve both vocal utterances and bowing (Tanaka 1989). In our study, we divided the greeting behaviors into "bows" and "utterances" and analyzed the timing of their occurrence. In particular, we focused on quantifying the changes in the respondent's behavior according to the greeting patterns of the initiator, i.e., greeting generation patterns such as a bow followed by an utterance, an utterance followed by a bow, and a simultaneous occurrence of a bow and utterance. The purpose of our study is to examine the characteristic aspects of greeting behavior.

2   Experiment Overview

2.1   Experiment Procedure

This study sheds light on the spontaneous greetings by responding subjects, looking at how they are generated in different greeting patterns where the bow and utterance timings vary. We conducted a simulated interview experiment (Fig. 1). The pre-assigned interviewer (a woman) first greeted the subject by saying, "*Yoroshiku onegai shimasu.* (Thank you for participating in our experiment.)" After the interview, she greeted the subject by saying, "*Arigato gozaimashita.* (Thank you for your cooperation.)" The interviewer used the following three timing patterns in her bows and utterances:

Fig. 1. Interview experiment

- Bow first: The interviewer greets the subject by first greeting with a bow, followed by an utterance.
- Utterance first: The interviewer utters the greeting first, followed by a bow.
- Simultaneous bow and utterance: The interviewer greets the subject by simultaneous bow and utterance

The interviewer wore the same clothing throughout the experiment. She was instructed to "Start the utterance after completely finishing the bow" in the Bow First pattern, and to "Start bowing after completely finishing the utterance" in the Utterance

First pattern. The interviewer practiced her patterns about 20 times in advance so that her behavior would be uniform throughout the experiment.

We measured and quantitatively analyzed the spontaneous greetings by the responders (subjects) as well as the timing of their behaviors.

2.2 The Subjects of Our Experiment

The subjects of our experiment were thirty university students (15 male and 15 female students, mean = 20.0, SD = 1.50) meeting each other for the first time. We assigned five male and five female students to each of the experimental conditions.

2.3 Procedure

After the subjects were briefed on the experiment procedure in an anteroom, they were asked to sign an agreement for participation in our experiment. Then each subject was led into the experiment room and to a chair. When the subject entered the experiment room, the interviewer waited, standing at the back of the room. The interviewer and the subject stood facing each other, at a distance of 115 *cm*.

After the interviewer's greeting "*Yoroshiku onegai shimasu*", they both sat down and conducted a simulated interview for five minutes. After the interview, both stood up and, following the interviewer's parting greeting, "*Arigato gozaimashita*," the subject left the experiment room. The interviewer used one of the greeting patterns shown in Sect. 2.1. Each subject's response to the interviewer's greeting was recorded by motion capture and wireless microphone.

2.4 Data Extraction

We obtained the characteristic bowing behavior data by using an optical motion capture system. We placed reflective markers on three body parts (Fig. 2): the top of the head, neck (seventh cervical vertebra), and lower back (sacral bone). We obtained time-series (fps = 120) 3D coordinates of these markers.

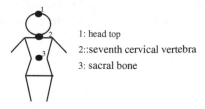

1: head top
2::seventh cervical vertebra
3: sacral bone

Fig. 2. Position of reflective markers

2.5   Analytical Indicator of Bows

From the 3D coordinates we obtained by motion capture, we extracted different types of data: Bow Length, Bow Bending Angle, Delayed Bow Time and Delayed Utterance Time for every greeting condition.

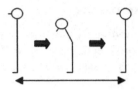

Fig. 3. Bow length

- Bow Length
  The "Bow Length" is defined as the time lapse between the responding subject starting to lower his/her head in a bow and returning the head to the original position, i.e., the end of the bow (Fig. 3).
- Bow Bending Angle
  The angle (θ) of maximum bow of the responding subject from the original position, i.e., standing straight (Fig. 4).

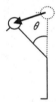

Fig. 4. Bow bending angle

- Delayed Bow Time
  The time lag between the bow start by the interviewer and the responding subject is defined as the "Delayed Bow Time" (Fig. 5). We measured the exact time lapse between the interviewer's bow start time and the responding subject's bow start time.

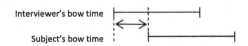

Fig. 5. Delayed bow time

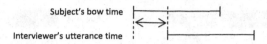

Fig. 6. Delayed utterance time

- Delayed Utterance Time
  The length of time between the interviewer's utterance start and the subject's bow
  start is defined as the "Delayed Utterance Time" (Fig. 6).
  Table 1 shows the basic statistics of Bow Length and Bow Bending Angle of the
  interviewer. The result of the paired t-test did not show any significant difference in
  the Bow Length and Bow Bending Angle ($p < .05$). Therefore, it was determined
  that the interviewer's bows were properly controlled.

Table 1. Basic statistics for the interviewer's bows

	Before - After	*Mean*	*SD*
Bow length	Before	1408.267	207.959
	After	1447.200	135.390
Bow bending angle	Before	31.204	6.110
	After	33.275	9.788

3 Results

We will now describe the results of our experiment conducted. That data include the
three greeting patterns by the interviewer, their respective responses by the responding
subjects and the characteristic features of the bows. Our experiment did not show any
gender differences; therefore, gender difference is not discussed in this study report.

3.1 Response Greeting Patterns

Our experiment revealed that all of the study subjects spontaneously greeted the
interviewer, before and after the interview, and that all of these greetings involved both
bows and utterances. First, we classified the order of the response greetings: A bow
followed by an utterance; an utterance followed by a bow; and a bow and an utterance
occurring simultaneously.

When a subject's response greeting pattern was the same as that of the interviewer,
this response pattern was determined to be "matching". When the subject's response
greeting pattern was different from that of the interviewer, this response patterns was
determined to be "unmatching" (Fig. 7). In order to examine different rates of
"matching" and "unmatching" patterns before and after the interview, we conducted a
Fisher's exact test. The result showed that there was a difference in the greeting
conditions both before and after the interview (before the interview: $p < .01$, after the
interview: $p < .001$). Similar trends were shown before and after the interview. About

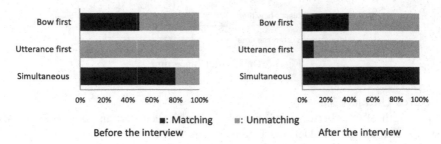

Fig. 7. Response greeting patterns

half of the subjects showed the matching "bow" and "utterance" generating order as that of the interviewer, both before and after the interview.

Table 2 shows the response greetings before and after the interview. When the interviewer bowed first, close to a half of the responding subjects also bowed first, before uttering a greeting. The remaining half of the responding subjects generated both a bow and utterance simultaneously. On the other hand, when the interviewer greeted the subject with an utterance first followed by a bow, the majority of the responding subjects generated both a bow and utterance simultaneously. Similarly, when the interviewer started her greeting with a simultaneous bow and utterance, the majority of the responding subjects also responded with a simultaneous bow and utterance.

Table 2. Cross table of order of greeting behavior (3) × matching trend (2)

		Before the interview			After the interview		
		Matching	Unmatching	Sum	Matching	Unmatching	Sum
Bow first	N	5	5	10	4	6	10
	Expected value	4.333	5.667	10	5.000	5.000	10
Utterance first	N	0	10	10	1	9	10
	Expected value	4.333	5.667	10	5.000	5.000	10
Simultaneous	N	8	2	10	10	0	10
	Expected value	4.333	5.667	10	5.000	5.000	10
Sum	N	13	17	30	15	15	30
	Expected value	13.000	17.000	30	15.000	15.000	30

From the above results, it was clear that the "bow" and "utterance" generating pattern of the responding subject did not always match that of the interviewer. In particular, because the generating pattern tended to match that of the interviewer when she greeted both with a "bow" and "utterance," everyday greetings are known to consist of "bows (bowing behavior)" and "utterances (greeting)". It was also shown that when the interviewer started either the "bow" or "utterance" before the other action, the subject's responses did not match that of the interviewer. In particular, because the interviewer's "bow first" behavior tended to generate a matching response, we can say that the subject's greetings tend to be affected more by the physical movement.

3.2 Quantifying the Response Greeting

The preceding section revealed how the responding subjects generated bows and utterances according to the different greeting patterns of the interviewer. In this section, the present authors looked at the "bowing action" to see how it changed with the three different greeting patterns of the interviewer.

In order to examine if the bowing action changes with the different greeting conditions of the interviewer, we conducted two - way factorial analyses of variance with "before- and after-interview" (2) and "greeting conditions" (3) being used as dependent variables of the bow analytical index shown in Sect. 2.5.

As regards to the Bow Length and Bow Bending Angle, the main effects were seen significantly before and after the interview (F (1, 27) = 25.616, p < .001, F (1, 27) = 30.094, p < .001). In both cases, for each parameter, the main effect of the greeting condition and two- way interaction were not significant. It was shown that the response bows were longer and deeper after the interview than before the interview, regardless of the interviewer's greeting pattern (Figs. 8 and 9). The mean Bow Length of the responding subject was 1233 ms before the interview. It was 1575 ms after the interview, thus showing that the bow time was longer by about 300 ms. The mean Bow Bending Angle was 47 ° before the interview but was 52 ° after the interview, showing that the bow became deeper by 5 °.

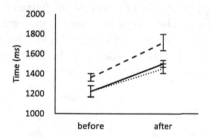

Fig. 8. Result of bow length

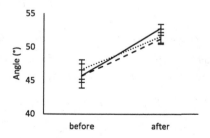

Fig. 9. Result of bow bending angle

We observed the significant main effect of the greeting condition for the Delayed Bow Time (F (2, 27) = 16.66, $p < .05$). The main effect and interaction, however, were not observed before and after the interview. The result of multiple comparison showed that there were significant differences between "utterance first and simultaneous bow and utterance" ($p < .05$) and between "utterance first and bow first" ($p < .05$). As for the greeting patterns of "bow first" and "simultaneous bow and utterance", we found that the responding subject's bows started about 600 ms after the interviewer's bow start. On the other hand, under the "utterance first" condition, the responding subject started the responding bow before the interviewer began bowing (Fig. 10).

From the above, it was shown that the responding subject's bowing timing was affected by the greeting generating order of the interviewer.

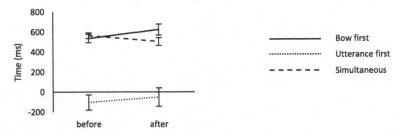

Fig. 10. Result of delayed bow time

3.3   Response Greeting Timing Structure

In order to find what prompts the subject's bow, we examined the Bow Delay Time and the Delayed Utterance Time. The Bow Delay means the time lag between the interviewer's bow start and the responding subject's bow start. The Delayed Utterance Time means the time lag between the start of utterances by the interviewer and the subject. Figure 11 shows the mean values of these indices.

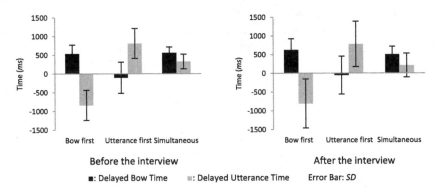

Fig. 11. The mean values of delay time

Figure 11 shows that under the "bow first" condition the Delayed Utterance Time are negative values, indicating that the subjects started bowing before the interviewer's utterance. This means that the subject used the interviewer's bow as the starting point. In the case of the "utterance first" condition, the Delayed Bow Time is in the negative range, indicating that the subjects used the interviewer's utterance as the starting point. Under the "simultaneous bow and utterance" condition, both are possibilities. Subjects' behavior deviation is smaller when the standard deviation is lower. It was considered that the subjects used the interviewer's bows as the starting point.

Under the "bow first" and "simultaneous bow and utterance" conditions when the interviewer's bow was the starting point, the subjects were shown to start their bows about 500–600 ms after the interviewer's bow. However, under the "utterance first" condition, the subjects were shown to start bowing about 800 ms after the interviewer's bow start.

From these results, the subjects returned bows prompted by the interviewer's bow under the "bow first" and "simultaneous bow and utterance" conditions, in which the interviewer started the bow before uttering the greeting. It was shown that the subjects' bowing timing varied with the interviewer's greeting condition, i.e., "utterance first" or "bow first".

4 Discussion

4.1 Bow and Utterance Timing

The results of our experiment revealed that the responding subject spontaneously returned a greeting under all experimental conditions, however, not always using the same pattern as the interviewer. It also revealed that the simultaneous generation of a bow and utterance was the most frequent pattern. Kinemuchi et al. (2014) showed that the greeting speed of the responding subject changed with that of the interviewer. However, our experiment showed that the responding subject's bow-and-utterance generation pattern was not necessarily matched with that of the interviewer. Only when the interviewer bowed first, about a half of the responding subjects bowed accordingly. This indicates that the responding subjects start bowing even if the interviewer does not say anything. This seems to reflect the Japanese greeting manner of "silently bowing to each other". In business and as social etiquette, "An utterance followed by a bow" is considered proper. Our study, however, barely showed this kind of greeting pattern.

As stated at the beginning of this paper, greetings by Japanese people involve utterances and bows (Tanaka 1989). In our experiment, all subjects greeted with both an utterance and a bow. This spontaneous daily greeting pattern, therefore, consists of both visual (body movement) and auditory (utterance) elements. In particular, our experiment showed that in both the "bow first" and "simultaneous bow and utterance" greeting patterns, bows were always involved, thus showing that it is a very important body movement in the Japanese-style greeting.

4.2 The Characteristics of Spontaneous Bows

Our experiment showed that the length and depth of the responding subjects' bows were not affected by the interviewer's greeting pattern. Regardless of the differences in the interviewer's bow and utterance timing, the responding subjects maintained certain bow length and depth. Due to the fact that the bows tended to be longer and deeper after the interview, greetings appeared more sincere after the interview than before it. These observations suggest that bow lengths and depths considered appropriate for different occasions are shared as part of the cultural norm.

When the interviewer greeted with the "bow first" or "simultaneous bow and utterance" patterns, the responding subject started the bow approximately 600 ms after the start of the interviewer's bow. Kobayashi et al. (2013) showed that the most agreeable utterance timing was 600 ms when responding vocally. Nagaoka et al. (2005) also showed that the speaker's timing latency of 600 ms sounded most natural and agreeable. This is the time lapse between the end of the utterance by the interviewer and the start of the utterance by the responding subject. With our experiment, on the other hand, the most agreeable physical responding time was also 600 ms, just like the vocal response, measured from the interviewer's bow start. In the case of vocal interactions, the utterance started after a lapse of 600 ms after the end of the interviewer's greeting. In the case of physical interactions, the responding subject started their greeting 600 ms after the bow start by the interviewer.

Here are the reason we obtained the above results. In the case of vocal interactions, the responder ("responding subject" in our experiment) must listen to and understand the utterance of the initiator ("interviewer" in our experiment) before responding vocally. The end of the initiator's utterance is thought to prompt a vocal response 600 ms later. In the case of physical interactions, the behavior gives out visual information which can be understood instantly, allowing a response before the initiator finishes her action. Thus, the bow start by the initiator must have prompted a response 600 ms later. However, if the initiator started an utterance before a bow, it was also shown that the response bow was started about 800 ms later, without waiting for the start of utterance by the initiator.

From the above results, the responder's bows are generated as prompted by the initiator's bow or utterance. When the initiator bowed at the start of the greeting, the responder also bowed. However, when the initiator uttered at the start of the greeting, the responder returned a bow after a certain time lapse. Therefore, the initiator's bowing action is considered to strongly affect the responder's bowing action.

5   Conclusion

This study examined spontaneously generated greeting patterns, quantified how the responding subjects' greeting patterns changed with the bow-and-utterance greeting patterns of the interviewer, and discussed their characteristics. The results of our experiment showed that the greeting patterns did not necessarily go along with that of the interviewer. It also showed that the formal greeting pattern of "utterance first followed by a bow" was rarely practiced. The "simultaneous bow and utterance" was the most common greeting pattern. As for the response timing, it was learned that it was generated with a clue from the start of the greeting by the interviewer. This study was significant in clearly showing the features of one of the most usual means of communication, i.e., the greeting behavior. By building realistic human models based on human behavior, studies like ours are expected to help develop support tools for better communication.

References

Kinemuchi, K., Yamamoto, T.: Synchronization between rhythm of body movement and prosodic information in greeting. Correspondences Hum. Interface **16**(3), 247–252 (2014). (in Japanese)

Kobayashi, H., Omura, T., Yamamoto, T.: Generation of proper utterance timing for dialogue system. Rep. Hum. Interface Soc. **15**(9), 23–28 (2013). (in Japanese)

Nagaoka, C., Komori, M., Nakamura, T., Draguna, M.: Effect of receptive listening om the congruence of speakers' response latencies in dialogues. Psychol. Rep. **97**, 265–274 (2005)

Shibata, H., Takahashi, J., Gyoba, J.: Subjective impressions of bowing actions and their appropriateness in specific social contexts. Japan. J. Psychol. **85**(6), 571–578 (2014). (in Japanese)

Tanaka, H.: An analysis of how teaching bowing brings about changes in the bowing movement. J. Shohoku Coll. **10**, 39–50 (1989). (in Japanese)

Yamamoto, M., Watanabe, T.: Time lag effects of utterance to communicative actions on human-robot greeting interaction. J. Hum. Interface Soc. **6**(3), 87–94 (2004). (in Japanese)

Yamamoto, M., Watanabe, T.: Timing control effects of utterance to communicative actions on CG character-human greeting interaction. Proc. of IEEE RO-MAN **2006**, 629–634 (2006)

An Experimental Study on the Effect of Repeated Exposure of Facial Caricature on Memory Representation of a Model's Face

Yoshimasa Tawatsuji[1(✉)], Yuki Iizuka[2], and Tatsunori Matsui[3]

[1] Graduate School of Human Sciences, Waseda University, Saitama, Japan
wats-kkoerverfay@akane.waseda.jp
[2] Department of Human Sciences, Waseda University, Saitama, Japan
y.i.hshi.abul009@gmail.com
[3] Faculty of Human Sciences, Waseda University, Saitama, Japan
matsui-t@waseda.jp

Abstract. Why does human can identify a facial caricature with its model's face? We hypothesize that a facial caricature has an effect on a person's memory representation of the model's face to get closer into the facial caricature itself, which causes a person to evoke the feeling of similarity between the model's face and its facial caricature. In this point, we conducted the experiment to verify whether the continuous exposure of a facial caricature changes participants' memory representation and whether the exposure also evokes participants' feeling of similarity between them.

Keywords: Face recognition · Facial caricature · Facial similarity

1 Introduction

Face recognition system is important for social animals, of course for human, to live up in their communities. This system enables us to process face fast and to distinguish one face from another based on a slight difference of appearances. From this, human strictly responds to a slight difference between a face and another. On the other hand, interestingly, facial caricature simply depicted of a face is also identifiable. A facial caricature simplified a face, which can cause an observer to identify it with various faces (related to inverse problem) ("simplified" means its imprecise line and lack of color or shade, compared to the photographic face). In addition to this, in the dairy life scene, it is often experienced that a facial caricature is identified without being informed who is depicted. In this study, "identification" in observing a facial caricature is referred to as "to evoke a feeling of similarity" between a facial caricature and its model's face.

Enomoto et al. pointed out that identification is resulted from two types of factors; one was a factor of physical similarity and the other was a factor of mental similarity [1]. Former is, for example, in case of twins, and later is in case of one's look-alike or a facial caricature.

Several studies dealing with facial caricature have developed the system of how a well-identifiable facial caricature can be generated automatically as the input of a

© Springer International Publishing Switzerland 2015
M. Kurosu (Ed.): Human-Computer Interaction, Part III, HCII 2015, LNCS 9171, pp. 514–524, 2015.
DOI: 10.1007/978-3-319-21006-3_49

model's face [2]. On the other hand, we focus on how human identifies the facial caricature with its model's face. This identification should be based on how similar it is with his/her memory representation of the model's face. One interesting topic is "Why human feels similar between a facial caricature and its modeled person's face." Our hypothesis is that (1) a facial caricature influences on the memory representation of a face, which causes the memory representation of face to get similar to the facial caricature, and is that (2) this transformation evokes a person to feel similarity between a facial caricature and its model's face.

2 Experimental Method

The experiment was conducted to verify two hypotheses: (1) facial caricatures can affect the memory representation to get similar to the facial caricature, (2) this effect causes a person to feel similarity between facial caricature and its modeled person's face. According to Hiraoka et al. [3], a facial caricature that a participant draws reflects the memory representation of the participant as to the model's face (This was called "Reproduction task"). Thus, analyzing the difference among facial caricatures which a participant draws can reveal the transformation of the memory representation. But in this study, the software different from the previous work [3] was used.

2.1 Stimuli

The model face of a person used in the experiment was expected to be unfamiliar and distinctive for the participants. Nishitani et al. investigated how distinctive or attractive human evaluated towards an average face according to the number of samples used in making the average face [4]. The results indicated that the evaluation of its distinctiveness and attractiveness towards the average face made from more than 10 faces are almost same in each other. Therefore, not so many samples are required to make an average face. In this study, an average face from 9 samples (Age: Average 22.9, SD 8.09) was made for the experiment. In addition to this, the average face was transformed into a face with distinctiveness. Figure 1 shows the average face and the transformed face. To make the average face and the transformed face, software "FaceTool" and its extended tools (ref. "http://nae-lab.org/project/face/IPA/" and "http://nae-lab.org/project/face/HeikinTool/") was used.

Secondly, the facial caricature of the transformed face was made. The transformed face was illustrated into facial caricatures by a pro-illustrator. Figure 2 shows the facial caricature used in the experiment. The pro-illustrator was required to draw four kinds of facial caricatures; pro-illustrator was asked to draw intentionally (1) eye-exaggerated, (2) nose-exaggerated, (3) mouth-exaggerated facial caricature, or (4) drew a facial caricature without any order. In these facial caricatures, mouth-exaggerated facial caricature was used to investigate in whether the memory representation of the participants were affected by the exposure of facial caricature.

Fig. 1. Average face and its transformed face

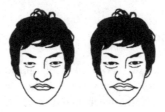

Fig. 2. Left shows the facial caricature which the pro-illustrator freely drew without any order. Right shows the facial caricature used in the experiment. This facial caricature was drawn with its mouth exaggerated. (*Note*: the eyes were also exaggerated to be balanced in its components.).

2.2   Procedure

In this experiment, participants were asked to remember a face (referred to as "*target face*"), and draw a facial caricature of the target face. The experiment was conducted two times per participant, where the participant was shown a different type of interferer face. One of interferer face was facial caricature (Condition "FC") and the other was portrait (Condition "P") for the first experiment. The duration of each condition was at least 1 week and counterbalance was taken into consideration.

For each condition, participants were required to draw a facial caricature three times. The flow of the experiment is shown as Fig. 3. At first, participants were required to observe a target face and required to draw a facial caricature of the face, and then, the participants were asked to answer three questions about the facial caricature which they drew; (i) "*How much could you represent his facial features (such as size of facial parts or location of them)?*" (ii) "*How much could you represent his image (such as his character or impression)?*" and (iii) "*How much could you totally represent him both in his facial feature and in his image?*" The participants were asked to score these questions by 7 point scales. 1 denotes "not very well" and 7 denotes "very well." From here, this questionnaire is called "SEC" (Self Evaluation of his/her Facial Caricature").

At the second step, they were required to observe the facial caricature which a pro-illustrator had drawn (referred to as "*interferer* face") for 10, 20, or 30 s. Importantly, the instruction for participants to observe to this interferer face was strictly carefully conducted so as for them not to consciously refer to it in the consequent steps of illustrating facial caricatures. In particular, this caricature was introduced to participants as merely "an illustration" (not a facial caricature and of course not informed who had been depicted), and they were strongly required to draw the target face. After this exposure to the interferer, participants were asked to score how similar "the illustration" was with the target face by 7 point scales (1 denotes "very dissimilar", and 7 denote "very similar"). After answering the questionnaire, they were asked to draw a facial caricature of the target face. At the third step, the participants were required to step on the same procedure with the second one. After all experiment was over, participants were asked to answer the questionnaire. This questionnaire had five questions: (i) *"Which part of the face did you focus on in drawing the facial carica-tures?"* (ii) *"Did you refer to the illustration in representing your facial image of the target face?"* (iii) *"Inform me of what was difficult for you to represent your facial image of the target face?"* (iv) *"Inform me of what was easy for you to represent your facial image of the target face?"* and (v) *"If you have any comments or feedback, please describe here."*

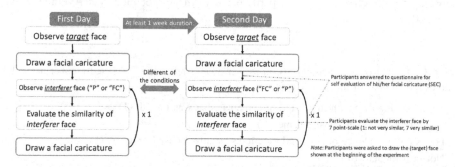

Fig. 3. The flow of the experiment. Each participant was asked to draw a facial caricature for the three times in each condition (Condition "FC" (Facial caricature as an interferer face) and Condition "P" (Portrait as an interferer face)).

2.3   Subjects and Apparatus

There were 10 participants (Age: Average 21.9, SD 0.89) and 9 was male. In the experiment, participants were required to make facial caricatures. They were required to draw a facial caricature with the software "charapeal" (http://www.nigaoe-e.com/) installed to the Windows XP PC. Sitting 60 ~ 80 cm away from the monitor, participants did the drawing and answered to the questionnaire.

Brief questionnaire before the experiment was conducted in order to clarify their characteristics of how they remembered the face and to measure if they were good or bad at remembering a face. Questionnaire was consist of four questions: (i) *"Where are you from?"*(Required the prefecture where they were born or grown up), (ii) *"Have you ever drawn a facial caricature?"* (1. Never, 2. I have for a few time ever, 3. I have for a few time in mouth, and 4. I draw every day), (iii) *"Are you good at remembering the other's face?"*(1. Very bad, 2. Bad, 3. Good, and 4. Very good) and (iv) *"When you remember the other's face, how do you do that? Please describe."* And after these, the target face and additional questionnaire were presented: (v) *"Do you know him?"* (1. I don't know, 2. I have ever seen before, 3. I know his name but I don't know his characteristic, 4. I know both his name and his characteristics), (vi) *"Are you attracted to his face?"* (answer by 7 point scales (1 denotes "dislike", and 7 denote "like"))

3   Results

3.1   Subject's Characteristics and the Unfamiliarity of the Target Face

The brief questionnaire before the experiment shows the participants' characteristics. The results of Question (ii) show that five participants had never drawn a facial caricature and another five had a few time ever, which indicated a low tendency of participants' experiences for drawing a facial caricature ever. In addition to this, according to Question (iii), participants tended not to be good at remembering other's face (average = 2.00, SD = 0.67). And Question (iv) revealed each tendency to remember the face. Table 1 summarizes how participants remember other's face. All but one participant didn't know him (one participant answered to have ever seen him before). The attractiveness of the participants to the target face was Average = 2.4, SD = 1.07.

Table 1.   The list of how participants remember other's face. The bracketed number in the list denotes the number of the participants.

1. Memorize him/her with the image of contents what was talked. (1)
2. Accord the face with his/her name. (2)
3. Focus on the balance of eyes and mouth, especially focused on eyes. (1)
4. Not in particular. (6)

3.2   Analysis of SEC

In this section is the results described as to the self-evaluation of participants' facial caricature (SEC) conducted after drawing a facial caricature. Figure 4 shows the results of the question (iii) of SEC "*How much could you totally represent him both in his facial feature and in his image?*" in the condition of "FC" and of "P" respectively. For few participants in the experiment for the efficient statistical analysis, qualitative analysis based on the increase or decrease of the derivation of the scoring was conducted. In the condition of "FC," all but one participant scored lower or no differently

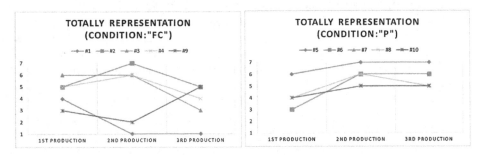

Fig. 4.   Transition of how much participants could represent a total impression of the target face on the first day (Left: Condition "FC", Right: Condition "P").

in the 3rd trial compared with in the 1st trial. On the contrary, in the condition of "P," all participants scored higher in the 3rd trial than in the 1st trial. Especially, in the condition "P," the scoring of the question (iii) of SEC tends to get gradually higher.

3.3 Qualitative Analysis for Transformation of the Shape of Facial Caricatures

In the experiment, participants were required to draw a facial caricature of the target face shown at the beginning of the experiment. Therefore, each facial caricature drawn by a participant were expected to be almost same in its shape. Nonetheless, if the shape was transformed, our hypothesis could be supported. Figure 5 shows the outputs of a participant through the experiments (condition FC).

Fig. 5. Facial caricatures that a participant drew in the condition "FC". The left shows the first, the center the second, and the right third representation in the experiment.

To analyze the transformation of the shapes of facial caricatures, the degree of the transformation should be defined. Therefore, each output of a facial caricature is superimposed and it is examined how each part of a face (eye, nose, mouth and outline of face) changes among the trials. For the analysis for the degree of the derivation, we defined the measurement as follows: Δx_i^{eyes}, Δx_i^{nose}, Δx_i^{mouth} and $\Delta x_i^{location}$ ($i = 2, 3$) were defined respectively as a degree of the derivation of the shape of eye, nose, mouth and location of the parts of facial components. Here, the derivation meant how closer it was affected by the interferer face, compared with the first drawing. From these variables, we defined E as the degree of effect of the interferer face on the memory representation as follow equation.

$$E_i = \Delta x_i^{eyes} + \Delta x_i^{nose} + \Delta x_i^{mouth} + \Delta x_i^{location} \tag{1}$$

The range of each variable is defined as follows. As E is automatically fixed whenever the other variables are fixed for the equcation (1), variable Δx_i^{eyes}, Δx_i^{nose}, Δx_i^{mouth} and $\Delta x_i^{location}$ are defined. These variables were set 2 as a standard score, and as a definition, if each shape of the facial part was the closer to the interferer face compared with the first drawing, the corresponded variable was added 1 (scored as 3).

On the contrary, if each shape of the part was the farther, the corresponded variable was reduced 1 (scored as 1). In addition to this, the interferer face was chosen which was exaggerated in its eyes and mouth. Therefore, in particular for the exposure in the condition "FC", if either eyes or mouth was more exaggerated, the corresponded variable was added more 1. And if the shape of the nose and location was the extremely closer to the interferer face, the corresponded variable was added more 1. Under these criterions, E was subjectively given, and all variables could be a value whose range was from 1 to 4, so that E was allowed to be from 4 to 16.

Outputs of drawn facial caricatures were compared with each other. Figure 6 shows a samples of superimposed facial caricatures which a participant produced, where left-side indicates the 1st day's representation and right-side the 2nd day's. The black line shows the representation for the first drawing, blue line shows the representation for the second drawing, and red line shows the representation for the third drawing. The participant was, for the 1st day, shown the facial caricature as the interferer face (Condition "FC").

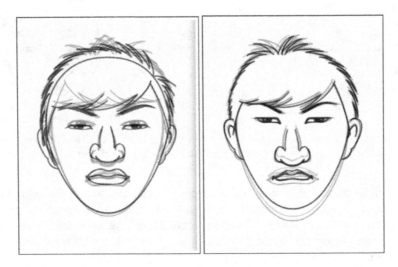

Fig. 6. Superimposed outputs drawn by a participants (Left: On the first day drawing. In this case, the condition was "FC," Right: On the second day drawing. The condition was "P").

Here is described the results of analysis for the participant of Fig. 6 in detail. Firstly, the results of first day drawing is described. The outputs are also shown as Fig. 5. These output faces are remarkable in that eyes were exaggerated compared with the first drawing, hair style changed at each trial and at the third drawing was used the mouth of the corner of which was turned down. E_2 was calculated 9 as $\Delta x_2^{eyes} = 2$, $\Delta x_2^{nose} = 2$, $\Delta x_2^{mouth} = 2$ and $\Delta x_2^{location} = 3$. Likewise, E_3 was calculated 10 as $\Delta x_3^{eyes} = 3$, $\Delta x_3^{nose} = 2$, $\Delta x_2^{mouth} = 2$ and $\Delta x_2^{location} = 3$. In the next, the result is descripted of analysis for the second day of the participant (Condition "P"). It was remarkable in that the chin was gradually larger, and the shape of the nose changed both from the first to the second drawing and from the second to the third drawing.

Table 2 indicates the results of calculating E_2 and E_3 for each participant. E in the standard point was 8, as all variables were 2. Therefore, that E got more than 8 score could reflect that it had been affected by the interferer face. This is shown at the columns gray-colored in Table 2.

Table 2. The results of E_2 and E_3 for each participant, and the results of the questionnaire as to whether the interferer face was referred or not. Grayed columns indicate where the output got the closer to the interferer face.

#	E_2	E_3	If the interferer face was referred to or not
1	9	10	Yes, I referred to it.
2	9	10	I referred to it at the second time. In particular, eyebrows, the shape of eyes, size of nose, shape and size of mouth and the location of these were referred to.
3	7	9	On the first day, I did not refer to it because it seems not to be similar. On the second day, I referred to it as it looked like well. It was helpful to grab the location of the facial parts. At last, I think that I represented the illustration rather than the photograph.
4	9	10	Yes, I referred to it.
5	7	7	Yes, I referred to it.
6	8	8	As it was difficult for me to represent the shape of eyebrows, I referred to the eyebrows of the illustration.
7	8	8	No, but I referred to the hair parting when the more alike one was shown.
8	13	10	Yes, I referred to it.
9	8	8	On the first day, I did not refer to it because I thought that it didn't look like. On the second day, I did refer to it very much.
10	6	9	Yes, I referred to it.

3.4 Transition for Similarity Feeling Through the Trials

How the feelings of similarity had changed through the exposure of an interferer face was examined by the questionnaire which the participants answered after observing the interferer face. Figure 7 shows the scores which the participants kept on how similar they felt between the target face and the interferer face. Blue bar "similarity 1" indicates their feeling of similarity reported after observing the interferer face for the first time, and red bar "similarity 2" indicates one reported after the second observation of the interferer face.

On the first day, 60 % of the scores of similarity, which participants belonging to the condition "FC" had marked, increased through the trial, while all of participants belonging to the condition "P" marked the score of similarity gradually lower or not differently. On the other hand, on the second day, almost all participants marked high score of similarity, none of whose score of similarity decreased, except for one participant #7. The derivation of the score between the days was larger in the condition "FC" than in the condition "P."

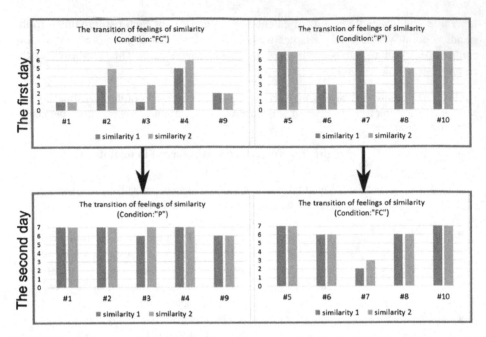

Fig. 7. The transition of feelings of similarity from the first day to the second day. (Up: the transition of feelings of similarity on the first day, Down: the transition of feelings of similarity on the second day).

4   Discussion

To extract the features of the memory representation of the face, the reproduction task with the software [3] was adopted. And the transformation of the outputs of the facial caricature were analyzed and it was suggested that observing the interferer face effected on the shapes of the facial caricatures drawn by more than 50 % of participants to be closer to the interferer face. This transformation is possible to indicate that the memory representation got closer to the interferer face. In addition, the results suggested that there should be the difference between the effect which the two types of the interferer faces, "facial caricature" and "portrait," had on the human memory representation of a face.

4.1   First Day Transition of Feeling of the Similarity

On the first day, the participants tended to score, in terms of the similarity between the target face and the interferer face, higher at the interferer face of the condition "P" than at that of the condition "FC." One possibility that the interferer face of the condition "FC" was not felt similar with the target face was that the interferer face was intentionally exaggerated on its mouth and eyes. That is to say, the intentional exaggeration did not match to the memory representation of the target face which had been immediately made when seeing it. Another explanation can be provided that the portrait was so well depicted that participants could easily identify it.

However, while the participants belonging to the condition "FC" tended to do higher and higher, those belonging to the condition "P" tended to score the similarity of the interferer face lower and lower through the trials. As to the former tendency of the similarity increase in the condition "FC," the four participants included in this condition were given high E through the trials. Thus, there can be the relationships between the transformation of memory representation and the feeling of similarity between the target face and the interferer face.

For the former tendency of the similarity decrease in the condition "P," the participants in the condition "P" evaluated their total representation of the target face better and better through the trials, and otherwise, those in the condition "FC" tended to evaluate worse. This enhance of total representation in the condition "P" was given by the satisfaction of the reproduction through self-making, and these feelings could provide the participants the critical viewpoints for the portrait.

4.2 The High Score of Similarity in Condition FC on Second Day

It is remarkable that the results on the second day experiment show that the similarity feeling were very high, regardless of the condition. Especially, in the condition "FC," the difference between the results of each day were salient. In the condition "P," the participants were provided much more detailed information as interferer face that was really alike than provided one in the first day. In addition to this, the interferer face presented before as the facial caricature were intentionally exaggerated in some parts, which were much less similar than the interferer as the portrait. Therefore, the gap of the similarity could directly work and it might enhance the similarity feeling.

On the other hand, in the condition "FC" the similarity feeling also increased though the interferer face were much more dissimilar than in the condition "P." According to one experiment (Experiment 2 in the paper) of Rhodes et al. [5], the participants were asked to rate score in terms of "goodness of likeness" (used as "recognizability") at a veridical drawings, caricature and anticaricature[1] of a face unfamiliar for them, comparing with the photograph(s). In the result, the veridical drawings were judged as better likeness than the others. Therefore, it was suggested that unfamiliar faces could not be suitable for testing "the caricature hypothesis" because the advantage of caricatures required the long-term memory representation, not short-time one.

Likewise, in our experiment, as the target face in the experiment were also unfamiliar for the participants except for one, they might feel dissimilar to the facial caricature with the target face (This can be corresponded with the first day similar feeling of the participant in condition "FC"). And, the participants in the condition "P" on the first day, observed the portrait as the interferer face, which caused them in the situation where was like their continuous exposure to the target face. Thus, their long-term memory representation about the interferer face was equivalent with that about the target face, and they got more familiar with the target face, and this

---

[1] Anticaricature is a kind of facial caricature that the face is transformed closer to the norm face. With the mathematical description, as a caricature is defined as "the model's face" (MF) (1 + "a proportion of exaggerating" (E)), its anticaricature can be defined as MF (1 − E).

familiarity could be related with the enhance of the similar feeling of the participants belonging to the condition of "FC" on the second day.

5 Conclusion and Future Work

In this study, we analyzed the transition of shapes of facial caricatures which participants had drawn, to clarify how the memory representation of the target face was influenced by the interferer. The results indicated the memory representation could be affected to get similar to a facial caricature.

There are several tasks that should be taken into consideration. First, the way to make a facial caricature was not same among the pro-illustrator and the participants. In particular, the participants should make a facial caricature under the limitation of usage of the facial parts. Therefore, the facial caricature made by the participants were qualitatively different from one by the pro-illustrator. Secondly, the measurement quantitatively indicating how similar the facial representation got closer to the interferer face was required. And at last, there should be information of the characteristics of the model's person ("he seems kind." or "he is short-tempered.") taken into consideration.

References

1. Enomoto, M., Ohya, J., Kurumisawa, J.: Study of a Caricatured Portrait Generate System Which Can Categorize and Describe Facial Feature, Technical report of IEICE, MVE, vol. 105, no. 683, pp. 19–24 (2006)
2. Nakasu, T., Naemura, T., Harashima, H.: Applying Various Artists' Style of Exaggeration to a Facial Caricature Drawing System with an Interactive Genetic Algorithm. J. Inst. Image Inf. Telev. Eng. **63**(9), 1241–1251 (2006)
3. Hiraoka, N., Yoshikawa, S.: Using a cartoon portrait composition task to investigate facial representation: Comparison of familiar and unfamiliar faces, Technical report of IEICE, PRMU, vol. 105, no. 534, pp. 93–98 (2006)
4. Nishitani, M., Yoshikawa, S., Akamatsu, S.: Characteristics of average faces: Analysis of distinctiveness, attractiveness and memory performance, Technical report of IEICE, HCS, vol. 98, no. 503, pp. 23–30 (1999)
5. Rhodes, G., Brennan, S., Carey, S.: Identification and ratings of caricatures: implications for mental representations of faces. Cogn. Psychol. **19**(4), 473–497 (1987)

An Experimental Study on Visual Search Factors of Information Features in a Task Monitoring Interface

Xiaoli Wu[1,2(✉)], Chengqi Xue[2], and Feng Zhou[1]

[1] College of Mechanical and Electrical Engineering, Hohai University,
Changzhou 213022, China
wuxlhhu@163.com
[2] School of Mechanical Engineering, Southeast University,
Nanjing 211189, China

Abstract. This paper carries out an experimental study on eye movement tracking when performing different visual searching tasks on a task monitoring interface, from the perspective of psychometrics. Behavior and physiological reaction data have been obtained through experiments - firstly in a scenario where no visual searching task is requested, and secondly within three separate tasks where the subjects are asked to search for enemy information, threat information and data information, respectively. Eye movement data indexes in nine areas of the task monitoring interface have been analyzed for each task based on a division of the different task monitoring areas. The experiments demonstrate that the search path followed by subjects on the task monitoring interface show significantly different subject reaction times and eye movements when undergoing each different task, as the search path is influenced by task-driven cognitive information processing and information search time. Fixation duration, duration count and visit count also show significant differences in each different monitor area; there-fore information features distributed in the radar sub-interface can be easily captured, which have been proven to be related to task-driven automatic capture. In-formation position and features such as colors, shapes and sizes have a significant impact on visual searches as they can easily cause problems with information omission, misreading and mis-judgment, missing/ignoring data etc. when under-going each different task. The paper concludes that monitoring tasks and the individual information features within in an interface have a great influence on the visual search, which will guide further research on design of information features in task monitoring interfaces.

Keywords: Task monitoring · Visual search · Information features · Factors · Information interface

© Springer International Publishing Switzerland 2015
M. Kurosu (Ed.): Human-Computer Interaction, Part III, HCII 2015, LNCS 9171, pp. 525–536, 2015.
DOI: 10.1007/978-3-319-21006-3_50

1 Introduction

Monitor task information is the major resource for pilots to learn about the flight status data, task information as well as threat and security state information. Pilots must grasp distinct, real and complete information of combat situation, so that to have the initiative to the battlefield in hands. Thus, it is clear that the display of information about the battlefield situation is extremely significant. The information display regarding to automatic combat identification system has been studied [1]. This paper discussed how these two groups of forms, uniforms and helmets, be presented to conduct the identification of combat information as well as the information analysis with combination of information reliability. After obtaining the reliable simulated data, there was found that the display formats of mesh chart and integrated data are more adaptive for combat information identification. The researchers have studied the identification performances of the colors, positions and shapes of different symbols and texts, and have obtained a series of valuable results [2–4]. The layout design of fighter radar situation-interface has been evaluated experimentally and has been analyzed through an objective evaluation technology of eye's tracker [5, 6]. They also have selected a special scheme of rational layout optimization through the evaluation by eye's moving data indexes. The researchers simulated the general operation sequence of enemy attack task in avionics system to conduct interface design [7–9]. The researchers have studied the influence of complex digital interfaces on color and shape codes to explore the identification performances under different time pressures [10].

Feature analysis research includes studies seeking to identify and observe movement and fixation of the eyes. Studies have found that if subjects gaze at one particular feature of a visual information interface for a relatively long time, then more information features can be extracted from subjects in comparison with saccadic eye movements. Yarbus [11] proposed that the more information a feature carried, the longer the eyes rested on it. Therefore, searching tasks on visual information interfaces depend not only on the nature of the physical stimuli (color, shape and location of information, etc.), but also contain information on higher cognitive processes such as attention and intention. Eye tracking can therefore be used to explain the cognitive process underlying visual searches.

The opinion has been held that the occurrence of attention capture basically depends on the significance level of the feature one stimulus relative to other stimuli [12, 13]. Then higher the featured significance level of a stimulus that higher the possibility of its generating attention captures. Through experimental observation, the researchers have found that the first factor is the quantity of icons, which influence to the user's visual search, the second is the target boundary, and the last one is the quality and resolution of icons [14, 15]. Patrick has applied the experimental paradigm of visual delay search task to comparatively study of the binding experiment of colors, positions as well as colors and positions [16]. These two experiments validated that word gap is a necessary and sufficient condition for visual interference derived from context. The researchers have employed the brightness and flash as the way of highlighting to study the symbol's shapes and colors, and testified to the influence of this on search time [17].

2   Objective

In order to analyze different information features in a task monitoring interface, such as information layout, information display, task type and potential problems in information extraction, the experimental paradigm of feature analysis and eye tracking technology are applied to study the factors involved during visual searches for information. The experiment focuses on the attention processing feature of human eyes when searching for information, based on the condition that the task monitoring interface displays complex information features. It is designed to check if there is any difference in eye movement indexes for different tasks and information areas, and to explore the relative differences between different searches in different information areas.

3   Methods

3.1   Material

This experiment uses a task monitoring interface of an aircraft, which is composed of four sub-interfaces - a flight data display, a horizontal position display, a radar display and weapons mount. The task monitoring interface carries a great deal of information which was considered in the experiment design, including many icons with different meanings, information represented by different graphs, a variety of data expressions, symbols at various positions, various status updates and also many abbreviations in capital letters. An excellent pilot must possess both professional flight skills and flight experience before he can master such extensive information and store this in his long-term memory as professional knowledge. This experiment uses a real task monitoring interface as the visual search material for eye tracking, and displays the same information interface when subjects are undergoing different tasks.

3.2   Design

This experiment was conducted by adopting two-factor (4 tasks × 9 areas) within the experiment design. Specifically, the tasks are divided into task 1, task 2, task 3 and an independent variable for where no task is set for the subject, based on the main tasks of an operator of the monitoring process. Different tasks to be performed by subjects are as follows:

1. No specified task: random observations of the monitoring interface.
2. Task 1: search for all symbols representing an aircraft (regardless of size) and remember their colors and positions.
3. Task 2: search for information representing threats, both symbols and numbers, and remember their features.
4. Task 3: view different data elements and attempt to identify how many different expressions there are, such as different colors, character sizes, emphasis formats, etc.

The task monitoring interface of complex navigation warfare information is divided into nine different areas according to different information features.

1. Information bar: Left- and right-hand upper information bars are respectively marked as INFO 1 and INFO 2;
2. Sub-interface: The four sub-interfaces - flight data display, horizontal position display, radar display and weapons mount - are respectively marked as INFO 3, INFO 4, INFO 5 and INFO 6;
3. Sub-interface status information bars: The corresponding status information bars of flight data, horizontal position display and weapons mount are respectively marked as INFO 7, INFO 8 and INFO 9.

3.3   Apparatus and Procedure

The experiment was conducted in the eye's movement tracking laboratory of HHU (Hohai University). The Switzerland-made Tobii1X120 eye tracker with a sample frequency of 120 HZ and gaze location precision of 0.5 degrees was adopted. The computer with a display pixels of 1280×1024 (pix), a color quality of 32-bit, a and a head movement range of $30 \times 16 \times 20$ cm was accepted. The sight-line gaze location data of the system were delayed to 3 ms and possessed an ideal gaze and instantaneous display. The system took samples from the eyeballs of subjects every 20 ms to investigate and collect the data of subjects' eyeball movement.

Subjects were firstly asked to view pictures and read text on the task monitoring interface, with the material background introduced by a specially-assigned person to ensure that subjects were familiar with the navigation system environment. When the experiment began, subjects were invited to check the information interface at random under the "no task" scenario for 6,000 ms. The visual search task then commenced and task 1, task 2 and task 3 were performed sequentially. The subjects were asked to press the space bar once they had completed all tasks, and were also requested to complete a questionnaire after each task had been performed. It took about 30 min for each subject to finish the entire experiment.

4   Result and Discussion

The Tobii1X120 eye tracker recorded the eye movement of subjects while searching for information, and the Tobii Studio Version 3.1.0 software collected relevant data related to the output search path, fixation duration, saccade counts, saccadic incubation period, etc. Based on the collection rate of eye tracking data, information from eight subjects were exported for statistical analysis with SPSS, which excluded two subjects whose collection rates were both less than 70 % (42 % and 26 %).

4.1   Fixation and Saccade

The fixation and saccadic process of subjects when searching for information can be illustrated using the data visualization software Tobii Studio Version 3.1.0. As shown in Fig. 1, random observation by subjects displays an intense fixation and saccade pattern when not performing any specific task. Although subjects observe at random,

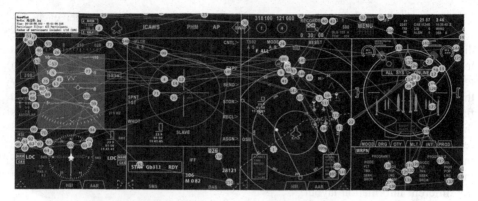

Fig. 1. Fixation and saccade of no task

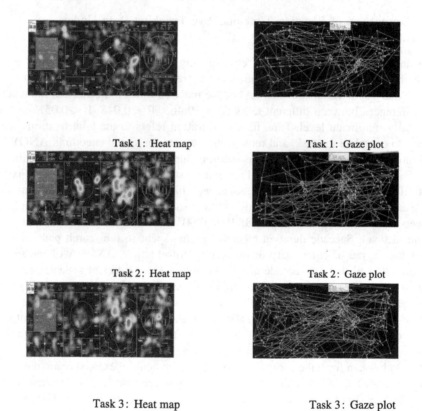

Task 1: Heat map	Task 1: Gaze plot
Task 2: Heat map	Task 2: Gaze plot
Task 3: Heat map	Task 3: Gaze plot

Fig. 2. Fixation and saccade of three tasks

more fixations are gathered in a certain area in Fig. 1. The length of the saccadic path also shows that subjects have checked the information back and forth, up and down repeatedly.

The fixation and saccadic process shows a significant difference under each different task. As shown in Fig. 2, the areas where fixations are gathered are quite different. Task 1 requires subjects to search for aircraft symbols, so they focus on icon information related to aircrafts. Task 2 requires subjects to search for information representing threats, so they search for colors, shapes and data to identify if there is any threat. It shows that visual attention moves in accordance with threat correlation and fixations gather frequently at positions where an enemy aircraft is found. It indicates that subjects are undergoing a process of under-standing and identification. Task 3 requires subjects to search for specific data information. A large amount of data information is distributed in different ways at different positions in the task monitoring interface. Saccade counts in task 3 are much higher than in task 1 and task 2 because of the different information layout.

4.2 Comparison of Reaction Time and Eye Tracking Data Under Different Tasks

Mean and SD of reaction time and eye tracking data under each different task are shown in Table 1. The reaction time index represents the speed of the information search. Analysis of variance (ANOVA) of the reaction times indicates that the reaction time differences between different tasks ($F = 19.463$, $P = 0.048$, $P < 0.05$) reaches a statistically significant level. Total fixation duration refers to the total fixation time in minutes to complete the task, and represents the time for visual encoding. ANOVA of the fixation durations shows that the fixation duration differences between different tasks ($F = 55.687$, $P = 0.005$, $P < 0.01$) reaches a statistically significant level. Fixation count refers to the effectiveness of the saccade, which reflects the relative difficulties of target searching. ANOVA of the fixation counts showed that fixation count differences between different tasks ($F = 54.918$, $P = 0.005$, $P < 0.01$) reaches a statistically significant level. Saccade duration means the time spent in the search path, and represents the degree of complexity of processing information. ANOVA of the saccade durations showed that the saccade duration differences of different tasks ($F = 55.907$, $P = 0.005$, $P < 0.01$) reached a statistically significant level. Saccade count index refers to pre-search efficiency. ANOVA of the saccade counts indicates that the main effect of different tasks ($F = 55.698$, $P = 0.005$, $P < 0.01$) reaches a statistically signif-icant level. From above, it can be concluded that all different tasks have a statis-tically significant effect on visual cognition of the information search.

As can be seen from the comparison of eye movement indexes, saccade duration is far longer than fixation duration and saccade counts are also far greater than fixation counts. The search efficiency of the interface information can be compared based on the fixation/saccade ratio and the ratio of time between cognitive in-formation processing and information searches. Based on calculation using the formula:

Ratio = time for cognitive information processing (f)/time for information search (s), both the ratio of total fixation duration to saccade duration and the ratio of average fixation duration to saccade duration for each time can be obtained. ANOVA of two types of fixation/saccade ratios indicated that the main effect of different tasks ($F = 792.817$, $P = 0.001$, $P < 0.01$) reaches a statistically significant level.

Table 1. Mean and SD of reaction time and eye tracking data under different tasks

	RT(ms)		Total fixation duration (ms)		Fixation count(n)		saccade duration(ms)		saccade count (n)	
	M	SD	M	SD	M	SD	M	SD	M	SD
No task	–	–	5435.75	5868.98	47.13	38.83	42108.13	6540.77	370.75	41.71
Task 1	29949.38	12749.72	2847.38	2326.12	24.50	13.94	22598.88	11330.33	196.63	68.50
Task 2	45356.75	32579.52	3736.88	3183.25	32.75	18.73	29990.75	15157.98	254.00	113.73
Task 3	67027.38	36417.68	4590.25	4772.31	40.50	32.03	39542.63	13643.28	324.63	125.45

Note: Reaction time under random observation ("no task") is set as 6,000 ms, and thus has not been included in the table.

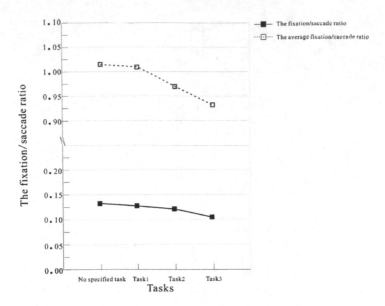

Fig. 3. Fixation/saccade ratio

As shown in Fig. 3, the results show that the fixation/saccade ratio is quite different from the average fixation/saccade ratio at each time point. For the average fixation/saccade ratio for each time point, both the ratios of random observation and task 1 are greater than 1, and those of task 2 and task 3 are also close to 1 (0.967 and 0.931 respectively). The total fixation/saccade ratio is below 0.13. It is difficult to explain the information layout in the task monitoring interface based on the value of search efficiency. For further research, it is necessary to divide the task monitoring interface into different areas and analyze eye movement data in each of these different information areas.

4.3   Comparison of Eye Tracking Data in Different Monitor Area

Total Fixation Duration. The nine divisions in the monitor task interface are called AOIs (Areas of Interest) in software Tobii Studio, namely, areas of interest for the subjects. Total fixation duration refers to the subject gazing time when performing each different task. ANOVA of the reaction time in the monitor area indicates that the main effect of different areas (F = 7.939, P = 0.045, p < 0.05) reaches a statistically significant level. As shown in Fig. 4, the monitor areas 1 and 2 are in the upper information bars, and fixation duration on the right-hand side is significantly more than on the left-hand side. Monitor areas 3, 4, 5 and 6 represent sub-interfaces of light data display, horizontal position display, radar situation and weapons mount respectively. It shows that fixation duration on the radar situation interface is significantly higher than on any other area. Monitor areas 7, 8 and 9 represent the corresponding status information bars of flight data, horizontal position display and weapons mount respectively. Since there is less information in the horizontal position display interface, the fixation duration is also

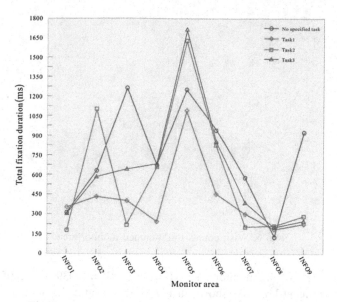

Fig. 4. Total fixation duration in difference monitor area

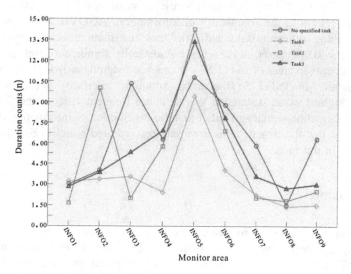

Fig. 5. Duration counts in difference monitor area

relatively short. No obvious change of fixation duration has been found for different tasks. Figure 4 shows that the fixation duration on task 1 is generally shorter than on other tasks, which indicates that the task of searching for aircraft icons is easy to perform.

Duration counts. Duration count refers to the total number of fixations, representing the number of times that subjects search for task information and perform cognitive pro-cessing. ANOVA of the monitor area when undergoing different tasks indicates

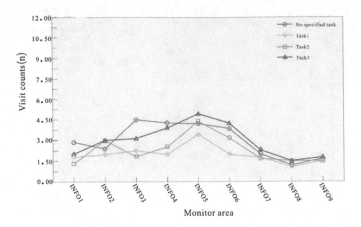

Fig. 6. Visit counts in difference monitor area

that the main effect of the monitor areas (F = 7.786, P = 0.039, p < 0.05) reached a statistically significant level. As shown in Fig. 5, the trend of duration counts in nine different monitor areas is basically consistent with total fixation duration.

Visit counts. Visit count refers to the process of subjects repeatedly searching for a target, which relates to the complexity of information. ANOVA of the monitor area when undergoing different tasks indicates that the main effect of monitor areas (F = 9.033, P = 0.004, p < 0.01) reaches a statistically significant level. As shown in Fig. 6, visit counts in areas of INFO 3, 4, 5 and 6 are significantly higher than in other areas, especially in INFO 5 (the radar situation interface) whose visit count reached the highest value. It suggests that there are frequent visits to the INFO 5 area during the information search and either that the distribution of information in this area is intensive, or that the target in this area requires repeated searches because of weak identification in this area.

5   Conclusion

1. The search path followed by subjects on the task monitoring interface show significantly different subject reaction times and eye movements when undergoing each different task, as the search path is influenced by task-driven cognitive in-formation processing and information search time.
2. Fixation duration, duration count and visit count also show significant differences in each different monitor area; therefore information features distrib-uted in the radar sub-interface can be easily captured, which have been proven to be related to task-driven automatic capture.
3. Information position and features such as colors, shapes and sizes have a significant impact on visual searches as they can easily cause problems with in-formation omission, misreading and misjudgment, missing/ignoring data etc. when undergoing each different task.

The paper concludes that monitoring tasks and the individual information fea-tures within in an interface have a great influence on the visual search, which will guide further research on design of information features in task monitoring in-terfaces.

Acknowledgment. This work was supported by science and technology projects of Chang-zhou (CJ20140033), the Project of Philosophy and Social Science Research in Colleges and Universities in Jiangsu Province (2014SJD065, 2013SJD760027), Fundamental Research Funds for the Central Universities (Grant No. 2013B10214), the National Nature Science Foundation of China (Grant No. 71471037,71271053).

References

1. Neyedli, H.F., Hollands, J.G., Jamieson, G.A.: Beyond identity: Incorporating system reliability information into an automated combat indentification system. Hum. Factors: J Hum. Factors Ergon. Soc. **53**(4), 338–355 (2011)
2. Damin, Z., Yinxue, Y.: Encoding of aircraft cockpit display interface. J. Nanjing Univ. Aeronaut. Astronaut. **41**(4), 466–469 (2009). (in Chinese)
3. Lei, Z., Damin, Z.: Color matching of aircraft interface design. J. Beijing Univ. Aeronaut. Astronaut. **35**(8), 1001–1004 (2009). (in Chinese)
4. Lei, Z., Damin, Z.: Text and position coding of human-machine display inter-face. J. Beijing Univ. Aeronaut. Astronaut. **37**(2), 185–188 (2011). (in chinese)
5. Haiyan, W., Ting, B., Chengqi, X.: Layout design of display interface for a new generation fighter. Electro-Mech. Eng. **27**(4), 57–61 (2011). (in Chinese)
6. Haiyan, W., Ting, B., Chengqi, X.: Experimental evaluation of fighter's interface layout based on eye tracking. Electro-Mech. Eng. **27**(6), 50–53 (2011). (in chinese)
7. WU, X., Chengqi, X., Haiyan, W.: E-C mapping model based on human computer interaction interface of complex system. J. Mech. Eng. **50**(11), 206–212 (2014)
8. Wu, X., Xue, C., Niu, Y., Tang, W.: Study on eye movements of information omission/misjudgment in radar situation-interface. In: Harris, D. (ed.) EPCE 2014. LNCS, vol. 8532, pp. 407–418. Springer, Heidelberg (2014)
9. Wu, X., Xue, C., Feng, Z.: Misperception model-based analytic method of visual interface design factors. In: Harris, D. (ed.) EPCE 2014. LNCS, vol. 8532, pp. 284–292. Springer, Heidelberg (2014)
10. Jing, L., Chengqi, X., Haiyan, W.: Information encoding in human-computer interface on the equilibrium of time pressure. J. Comput. Aided Des. Comput. Graph. **25**(7), 1022–1028 (2013). (in Chinese)
11. Yarbus, A.: L.Eye movements and vision. Plenum, New York (1967)
12. Theeuwes, J., Burger, R.: Attentional control during visual search the effect of irrelevant singletons. J. Exp. Psychol. Hum. Percept. Perform. **24**, 1342–1353 (1998)
13. Theeuwes, J.: Top-down search strategies cannot override attentional capture. Psychon. Bull. Rev. **11**(1), 65–70 (2004)
14. Fleetwood, M.D., Byrne, M.D.: Modeling icon search in ACT-R/PM. Cogn. Syst. Res. **3**, 25–33 (2002)
15. Fleetwood, M.D., Byrne, M.D.: Modeling the visual search of displays: a revised ACT-R/PM model of icon search based on eye-tracking and experimental data. Hum. Comput. Inter. **21**(2), 153–197 (2006)

16. Monnier, P.: Redundant coding assessed in a visual search task. Displays **24**(1), 49–55 (2003)
17. Van Orden, K.F., Divita, J., Shim, M.J.: Redundant use of luminance and flashing with shape and color as highlighting codes in symbolic displays. Hum. Factors **35**, 195–204 (1993)

Health Information Tailoring and Data Privacy in a Smart Watch as a Preventive Health Tool

Qualitative Study of Users' Perceptions and Attitudes

HongSuk Yoon[1], Dong-Hee Shin[2(✉)], and Hyup Kim[3]

[1] Department of Interaction Science, Sungkyunkwan University,
Seoul, Republic of Korea
yoonhs9@skku.edu
[2] Professor at Interaction Science, Sungkyunkwan University,
Seoul 110-745, Republic of Korea
dshin@skku.edu
[3] Interaction Science, Sungkyunkwan University,
Seoul 110-745, Republic of Korea
henryskim@naver.com

Abstract. Wearable technologies, especially smart watches are recently becoming popular and their health-related functions are well recognized. They can be effective to deliver health information to users, because they are able to track their activities. Whereas there is a privacy concern that users' personal health data could be misused according to be monitored their physical conditions via the smart watch, In this light of importance, this qualitative study explores the perceptions of smart watches as preventive health tools with 2 subjects: information tailoring and data privacy. This study used multiple methods: online survey, focus group interview and in-depth interview. A total of 12 users including power users and non-power users from Korea participated in a survey, 3 focus group sessions and post interviews. Three main themes emerged: (1) useful high-tech toy, (2) needs of hybrid tailoring service and (3) unnecessary anxiety vs. vague fear. Finally implications and limitations are discussed.

Keywords: Customization · Data privacy · Health informatics · Information tailoring · Personalization · Power user · Smart watch · Wearable device

1 Introduction

The rapid expanding of mobile devices, including smart phones and tablet computers, has significantly changed our lifestyle in recent years; the ways in which we can access, acquire, and share information have become increasingly mobile. More importantly, mobile devices have further evolved from portable to wearable technology such as smart watches (Samsung Galaxy Gear, Sony Smartwatch) and smart glasses (Google Glass). Wearable devices are especially effective in delivering health-related information because they are literally attached to users' body and able to monitor users' physical conditions (heart rate), which subsequently increases user awareness and

© Springer International Publishing Switzerland 2015
M. Kurosu (Ed.): Human-Computer Interaction, Part III, HCII 2015, LNCS 9171, pp. 537–548, 2015.
DOI: 10.1007/978-3-319-21006-3_51

Table 1. Participant Characteristics

Participants	Age	Gender	Usage experience of smart watch	Power user index	Preference for information tailoring
1	30	Male	O	6.71	Both
2	21	Female	X	2	Personalization
3	39	Female	X	2.43	Both
4	41	Male	O	6	Personalization
5	28	Male	X	2.43	Customization
6	27	Female	X	5.23	Personalization
7	32	Male	X	5.43	Customization
8	29	Male	X	6.43	Customization
9	26	Female	O	2.71	Customization
10	32	Male	O	7	Both
11	30	Female	O	6.43	Personalization
12	34	Female	O	6.43	Personalization

acceptance of preventive health information [1]. In other words, it is to stay connected more closely to users' body unlike smartphone.

There are increasing needs of health information largely. First of all, users prefer to be notified of the accurate environmental conditions. For example, Seoul Air Quality Information Center provides the service of air quality massage from October 2013. The service allows users to customize the each information following kinds of air pollution (yellow dust, fine dust and ozone) and level of notification (forecast, watch, warning and emergency warning). Second emphasis is being placed on providing not only actual care but health information that functions as preventive measures [2]. As new mobile devices and services offer more and more tailoring interface, it is important for researchers to understand these trends and effects in terms of human-computer interaction (Table 1).

On the contrary, concerns for privacy are concurrently increasing according to monitor and collect personal health information and data via their smart watches using embedded sensors. Information tailoring always has generated information privacy issue inevitably, because it entails sacrificing some private information. Recently data privacy issue beyond information privacy has presented according to treat vast amount of data, namely Big Data, and work of human data interaction [3]. More seriously, users' biometric data tend to be collected by oblivious and passive ways, because individuals are not be able to aware of every signals emitted as various health data. In this light of importance, we need to understand not only providing of preventive measures using wearable devices, but also many complex and subtle privacy concerns surrounding use of personal health data.

Therefore, it is both theoretically and practically critical to explore users' perceptions and attitudes on smart watches as preventive health tools with emphasis on 2 sides: health information tailoring and data privacy. We aimed to obtain both quantitative and qualitative data to generate 3 research questions on how users aware these issues. As such a purpose, this qualitative study intends: (1) to explicate distinct difference of awareness and attitude on the health information tailoring, namely personalization and customization, via their smart watches by classifying power users and non-power users (2) to identify significant difference of awareness of data privacy concern according to power users and non-power users in delivering health contents via a wearable device, especially the smart watch.

2   Literature Review

2.1   Emergence of a Smart Watch as Preventive Health Tools

A smart watch is a wearable computer on the wrist (a wrist watch computer) with functionality of personal information access and notification [4]. Several smart watches have been developed starting from 2000 such as the IBM Linux Watch with no sensors like PDA (Personal Digital Assistant) on the wrist. Microsoft also released their smart watch (SPOT, Smart Personal Object Technology) from 2004 offering personalized information such as weather and news [5]. Although these devices remain a very small portion of information technology industry until now, the smart watches have been getting lots of attention from 2013, as giant companies like Samsung and Sony have released their products using touch screen linked to their smartphone (Galaxy Gear, SmartWatch). According to the research of Consumer Electronics Association (CEA), global smart watch market will grow to 1.5 million shipments during 2014, and sales of smart watches are predicted to grow exponentially, selling 44 million units globally by 2016.

Smart watches have been introduced to users as a preventive health tool recently. Many major ICT companies such as Samsung, Microsoft and Apple have all announced their watches focusing fitness related functions at 2014. Samsung released their new smart watch line (Gear Fit) including personalized fitness manager application providing real time information and results of user's workout. Microsoft created a wrist worn fitness watch (Band) connected to their clouding service (Microsoft Health) and analyzes the tracking data for personalized fitness goals to text messages [6]. Apple also introduced their smart watch (iWatch) at September 2014 with emphasizing the device's capability as a health monitoring watch. Apple has been partnered with many health care industries to get ready for their first wearable device [7].

It has strong emphasis on health related functions because it is attached and fitted to users' wrist like a traditional wrist watch. In other words, it is to stay connected more closely to users' body than any other devices like smartphone and tablet pc in terms of physical side. Furthermore, it is able to track and collect users' physical data such as movement, location, skin temperature, and even heart rate using embedded sensors beyond the functionality of general smartphone. Taking advantage of the fact that this technology is constantly worn on the wrist, most of smart watches (Pebble, Basis band) which were released from small companies offer personalized health information like tracking data of heart rate, number of steps, calories burned, sleep and perspiration [8].

However, little is known about how users access and acquire their health information on the wearable devices and potential users aware these functions. As such a thing, it is valuable to explore qualitatively the perceptions pertaining to engaging with health contents in context of wearable devices, especially smart watches, which can be described by addressing the following research question.

– Research Question 1: For smart watch users and potential users, what are their perspectives and views of wearable technology, especially the smart watches as preventive health tools?

2.2   Health Information Tailoring

Much of the literature on health communication has conducted researches on health information tailoring. 'Tailoring' defined as some of methods for creating communications in which individualized information is used for their receivers, with the expectation that this individualization will enhance effects of these communication and thereby promote desired changes [9]. A meta-analytic review of 57 studies on health communication found that tailored health information produce positive effect on health behavior changes in response to their messages [10].

Information can be tailored in two ways through digital media: personalization and customization. Personalization is system-initiated, such that the system (computer, website, application) tracks and identifies individual users' needs, interests, knowledge, and goals [11]. Personalization collects data either by directly asking users for their name, gender, date of birth and geographical location or by indirectly observing and tracking user behaviors (web history, log data) [12]. Most of these services are automatic and hence require no direct user involvement. In sum, personalization is a system-initiated ways of tailoring. In contrast, customization is a highly user-driven process of information tailoring [13]. It emphasizes user control and involvement, placing users in the driver seat and allowing them to initiate their interaction with the system [14]. In sum, users have a relatively passive role in personalization, whereas in customization, they serve as active organizers of the information [15]. By extension, these different types of information tailoring are likely to have significant psychological effects on user awareness and attitude toward the conveyed health information, we are also able to classify according to users' tendency and pattern of technology usage.

Users who prefer to customization have been classified as "power users or early adopters." Power users spend much time on using various gadgets offered by various technologies [16] and tend to have a precise control over their interaction with digital functions including new features. They also prefer to control their interaction with technology as much as possible [17]. Therefore, power users tend to have strong self-efficacy and clear outcome expectation [12]. In contrast, non-power users lack the interest in adopting new technologies. They tend to avoid taking a charge in controlling the device due to the lack of self-efficacy. They would rather not select among options and spend their time controlling interface.

Some studies found that customization is more effective to promote positive effect on healthy behavior than personalization in a digital world. For example, participants who customize their own avatars show a higher tendency for self-preservation [18]. In addition, customization provides users with a strong sense of user and personal agency, according to the agency model [14]. It allows them to highly personal choices and active participation in the customization service more than personalization, and trigger sense of control and involvement. This self-schema enhances their self-determination, self-efficacy and autonomy in an online environment, especially customizable interfaces [19].

By extension, users who acquire customized health information via their smart watch are likely to have a more positive attitude toward the information than those who receive personalized health information. Therefore, these different types of users are likely to have distinctive awareness and attitude on tailored health information, which can be investigated by addressing the following research questions.

- Research Question 2: For both power users and non-power users, is there distinct difference of awareness and attitude on the health information tailoring (personalization vs. customization) via their smart watches?

2.3   Data Privacy

Many empirical privacy researches in the field of social science have focused the effect of privacy concerns and dealt with the construct of privacy concerns related behavior and attitude variables. Some previous studies treated willingness to share personal information from personalized service [20], and used level of information disclosure attitude as their privacy related variables [21].

Privacy is one of the most sensitive and complex topic because of the inconsistencies in defining and measuring privacy and also because the important relationships depend more on perceptions than on rational assessments [22]. Studies in the field of Information Systems (IS) have considered to information privacy as one of the most salient issue in information and technology based services like online shopping and transaction [23]. Privacy concerns were defined as concerns reflecting individuals' general worries about disclosure of personal information in many studies of IS [24]. But the concept of privacy concern recently is much more understandable in specific situation and context compared to general worries and concerns for privacy [25]. In other words, contextual privacy concerns need to distinct to general concerns about personal information and must be studied in each domains.

Information tailoring service like both personalization and customization are sacrificed some of the personal information necessarily, because the vendors should collect the personal data to provide their service and users have to put out their information and data. It is impossible to get without loss of privacy since users need to offer their preferences when they use the internet personalization services [20]. Following tailoring technology gradually invades to our digital life, some users certainly have much more worried about the amount of personal information that the system would collect and utilize automatically. These privacy concerns affected negatively to online consumers in transaction although the consumers were interested in e-commerce services. The most important problem is that way of tracking is performed in oblivion ways without the awareness and control of the users [26]. This effect is more unobtrusive to non-power users who lack the expertise and interest in adopting new technologies than power users who have a strong self-efficacy and motivation using features [12]. In other words, users who prefer customization service are shown to better protection and aware of their privacy than personalization, whereas non-power users may be oblivious to their disclosure problem. As such, privacy concern related to online users' ability to control their conditions by acquiring their personal information and data [27].

Given the concerns for information privacy documented in the literature, users who participate to customize their health information and data are more likely to have a higher privacy protection and positive evaluation of health contents than non-power users. Therefore, these different types of users are likely to have distinctive perception and attitude on data privacy protection and concern, which can be examined by the following research question.

- Research Question 3: For both power users and non-power users, what are the significant difference of perception and attitude on concern for health data privacy related to their smart watches?

3   Methods

This study was conducted multiple methods of quantitative and qualitative data collection combining pre online survey, focus groups interviews and post in-depth interviews. The researchers analyzed the data of survey and transcripts of interviews by using QSR International (NVivo 10) with simple counting method [28] to conduct content and discourse analysis.

The participants were recruited from online communities for the smart watch users in South Korea and a large private university in Seoul, Korea. Preliminary online survey was used to make sure the participants' basic attributes related to technology, health and privacy issues during the recruiting process. In total, 12 participants (6 males, 6 females) were interviewed and ranged in age from 21 to 41 years, with a mean age of 31 years (SD = 5.74). Each participant gave written informed consent to participate before the interviews.

3.1   Pre online Survey

This study was used by pre online survey to make sure index of power user, e-health literacy and concern for privacy before the main interviews. The participants were asked to respond to the questionnaire by marking on a 7 point Likert scale (1 = "strongly disagree", 7 = "not at all"). In order to measure power user scale ($\alpha = 0.87$), 6 items are adopted from the previous study [17]. The items are included such as "I love exploring the features that any technological gadget has to offer," "Using any technological device comes easy to me," and "Using information technology gives me greater control over my work environment."

The aim of the pre online survey was to make adequate interview questions regarding health information tailoring and data privacy issue via smart watches and classify the users according to their self-reported index. All collected data was stored to Microsoft Excel file format and analysed by PASW Statistics 18.

3.2 Focus Groups Interviews

This study was conducted the 3 sessions of focus groups interviews with 4 participants each in February 2015. Each session was offered in an atmosphere of freedom by the researchers and a moderator. Each interview was lasted about 90–100 min and all procedures were audiotaped and transcribed by the researcher. All questions and answered were totally opened and the participants were asked to talk about their views and personal experiences related to using smart watch. All participants including power users asked to wear the smart watch (Sony, SmartWatch2) during the interview and freely browse the health contents via there smart watch for 5 min.

The main goal of the focus groups interview was to identify the perspectives, awareness, attitudes, perceptions and intrinsic motivation of users with respect to using a smart watch as a preventive health tool, with emphasis on health information tailoring and concern for data privacy.

3.3 Post In-depth Interviews

Our researchers undertook additional in-depth interviews personally through online chatting service (Kakao Talk) lasted about 15-20 min. We prepared new questions and asked to answer additional personal experience for discussing changed views and needs after online survey and focus groups interviews in depth.

4 Results

The researchers analyzed the results of online survey and the transcripts of 2 interviews for emerging themes regarding the smart watch as preventive health tools with health information tailoring and data privacy concern. Three main themes emerged: (1) useful high-tech toy, (2) needs of hybrid tailoring service and (3) unnecessary anxiety vs. vague fear. The characteristics of participants are as below.

4.1 Useful High-Tech Toy

There were significant two sides of perspective to using the smart watch as a preventive health tool: useful health kit but a toy of a wrist watch. Most participants (10/12) reported the potential value of the smart watches as for managing physical conditions daily. All of them mentioned usefulness and convenience of these health related functions to check their activity and conditions. As one participant said it:

- It is surprisingly tiny and also wearable easily unlike other digital devices… It may be my personal assistant who manages my health conditions daily and automatically… It has a potential value to access, collect and manage my physical data conveniently (participant 12).

However, most participants (11/12) also expressed their worrying about health related functions. They raise various questions for inaccuracy, untrustworthiness and possibility of generalization. Some participants pointed these:

- They (smart watches) are just funny and attractive accessories yet... I still do not believe their accuracy of digital sensors. It has a many errors collecting physical data because of their technical problems (participant 8).
- It will be attractive but not main device like smart phone... I have a doubt that the device can collect real data and show complex statistical health information... their small screen often makes me face (participant 9).

In sum, most participants mentioned that they have a positive view of using smart watches as preventive health tools, but at the same time they expressed that the smart watch is just wearable high tech toy not a medical device for actual health care.

4.2 Needs of Hybrid Tailoring Service

According to our analysis of survey and interviews, there was no significant difference between power users (6/12) who showed power user index over 6 and non-power users (4/12) who recorded the index under 3 in terms of information tailoring. Half of users (3/6) who showed high index of power users prefer to use personalization service than customization. Likewise, half of non-power users (2/4) reported to use customization not personalization on the internet. In addition, some users (3/12) identified that they prefer both ways of tailoring depending on the service. So we reclassified users with their self-reported preference of using the information tailoring service as three types: personalization, customization and both.

Some users (5/12) who only prefer to personalization service said that they would still use personalization in health information tailoring via their smart watch. They expressed ease of use, annoying from a lot of information, fatigue of digital information and reducing the time. Some of them (4/5) noted that they have a plan for using customization in their smart watch if the device could collect sensitive biometric data such as iris and fingerprint beyond their activity.

- I have used movie recommendation service and I feel much great tailoring... Sometimes I am very tired of much useless visual information and it makes me really annoying, stressful... I prefer to get my every information automatically because I have no much time to get all information (participant 11).
- I will participate to organize and put my information actively although it is annoying to me... I will have to manage directly my valuable private data like health record... I think the information provider need to consider way of tailoring according to characteristics of data not economic interests (participant 2).

On the contrary, some users (4/12) who select customization reported that they will definitely use this way of health information tailoring through their smart watch. They expressed unsatisfactory experience and untrustworthiness of system, strong needs of accurate information and enjoyment of engaging with process. Two of these participants pointed out it:

- It (personalization) was not enough to meet sensitive consumers... We need to provide our detail preference to get high-quality information... Automatic tailoring system cannot satisfy detailed demands, it just provide superficial contents, not personal (participant 10).

- I enjoy the participating to match my preference from A to Z... I feel better to get accurate information although it spends some time to use (participant 9).

Half of them (2/4) also expressed the needs of mixed tailoring service in the second interview. They wanted to get both insightful information and convenience. They also reported that they have used many personalization services actually without awareness. A few participants (3/12) who enjoy both services mentioned that there is no significant difference between personalization and customization. Two participants argued that hybrid way of tailoring is the advanced service and will be the adequate way in context of health information via smart watch. These opinions are as below:

- We are exposed to a lot of personalized services as mobile devices... Actually I have no choice but to use some services because we have to login... The system has provided me with some information automatically and maybe health data will be collected in the same way if users would not aware their data (participant 5).
- I do not think two way of tailoring is different. This is a single procedure to provide personal information... Mixed way is a much superior service... I am willing to provide any data to get deep info if there is a special family history... We need also compulsory ways to prevent unexpected health problems (participant 10).

4.3   Unnecessary Anxiety Vs. Vague Fear

The researchers classified as power users (6/12) who recorded power user index over 6 scales and non-power users (4/12) who showed same index under 3. There is a distinct difference of perception about concern for health data privacy via there smart watches between power users and non-power users. However, this analysis showed different results instead of the previous studies and findings [14, 18, 19]. Power users reported various level of their concern for data privacy, but non-power users expressed rather deep concern and strong interest about their health data privacy.

Half of power users (3/6) mentioned that concern for health data privacy is an unnecessary anxiety. They focused on positive health related functions and chances to use physical data personally. Some participants said it:

- Bio data without process and analysis is just digital signals... worry about health data is useless concern like fear... The most important thing is to construct safe firewall and develop advanced security system not worry (participant 10).
- Any digital records and data have a bad side to exposure... but the advantages are much bigger than this negative side... new wearable technology including the smart watch will give us opportunities from check our conditions to prevent disease easily... privacy issue will be covered by these (participant 1).
- Privacy problems of course will be occurred... I have felt much dissatisfaction at managing my health record. Even now I cannot access it easily although it is mine, my basic right... It can be innovative turning point by having the right of managing my health data on my own as smart watch collects the data (participant 12).

But to the contrary, all of non-power users (4/12) said that they have strong concern for exposing their personal information including health data. The results are totally opposite effects compared to our literature review which founded non-power users have lower protection of online privacy than power users [27]. The 4 participants expressed their some motivation and experience of general privacy issue, untrustworthiness of security system, importance of life and body.

- Health data are related to our life and body directly... I cannot imagine that my health data will be used for other purpose in spite of myself... I strongly give my concern about collecting my any health data automatically even my devices (participant 2).
- I heard a lot of problems, victims of online hacking like their bank account, ID from some media... I felt much fear to use internet services and cannot trust the security anymore increasingly whenever I heard these... Smart watch also collects data and submits to others to provide information, so it is not area of my wrist but others I could not know (participant 9).
- I am concerned that my personal information is open all the time... but I have no special solution to keep my information in online. This worry is more serious in mobile environment... electronic health record system arouse my attention especially health application of wearable device (participant 3).

5   Discussion

Our qualitative research indents to explore the user perceptions of a smart watch as a preventive health tool with focus on 2 subjects: health information tailoring and data privacy. The results of this study showed that there are 2 sides of perspective of a smart watch as a preventive health tool: useful health kit but a toy of a wrist watch. In addition, the study indicates that there is no significant breakpoint between power users and non-power users according to their preference of 2 ways of information tailoring. Finally, we found that concern for health data privacy was divided into useless worry and vague fear according to the difference between power users and non-power users. Our findings will offer theoretical and practical insights for information providers, UX designers, and HCI scholars who are interested in the role of smart watches as emerging preventive health tools.

The current study has several limitations. Firstly, we relied on survey and interview accounts instead of observation of actual using. Naturalistic observations which are able to check users' actual behavior would be necessary for further verification of power users' index. Secondly, our interviews were conducted to a small number of participants. We need to conduct additional interviews to more random sample of participants. Finally we have concerns for generalizability. It is hard to generalize our findings to other contexts because the data were only collected from the limited demographic participants in Seoul, South Korea.

In the future, we will focus on improving the methodological tasks to identify users' intrinsic motivation and actual behavior in context of the smart watch. In doing so, the future study would be used observational or experimental method with a larger sample and wider population to obtain more generalizable founding. Additional qualitative researches are needed to design innovative information tailoring services for promoting users to engage with health contents on the wearable technology.

Acknowledgments. This research was supported by the Ministry of Education, South Korea, under the Brain Korea 21 Plus Project (Grant No. 10Z20130000013).

References

1. Patrick, K., Griswold, W.G., Raab, F., Intille, S.S.: Health and the mobile phone. Am. J. Prev. Med. **35**(2), 177–181 (2008)
2. Fotheringham, M.J., Owies, D., Leslie, E., Owen, N.: Interactive health communication in preventive medicine: Internet-based strategies in teaching and research. Am. J. Prev. Med. **19**(2), 113–120 (2000)
3. Haddadi, H., Mortier, R., McAuley, D., Crowcroft, J.: Human-data interaction. Technical report, University of Cambridge, Computer Laboratory (2013)
4. Raghunath, M.T., Narayanaswami, C.: User interfaces for applications on a wrist watch. Pers. Ubiquit. Comput. **6**(1), 17–30 (2002)
5. Bonino, D., Corno, F., De Russis, L.: dwatch: A personal wrist watch for smart environments. Procedia Comput. Sci. **10**, 300–307 (2012)
6. Microsoft Jumps into Growing Market for Wearable Fitness Technology. The New York Times, http://www.nytimes.com/2014/10/30/business/microsoft-jumps-into-the-growing-market-for-wearable-fitness-technology.html?_r=1
7. Success of Apple's iWatch May Rely on Health Care Partnerships. The New York Times, http://www.nytimes.com/2014/09/08/technology/can-apple-build-a-cool-and-convenient-iwatch.html
8. A Growing Role in Health Care for Smartwatches. The New York Times, http://www.nytimes.com/2014/01/21/fashion/a-growing-role-in-health-care-for-smartwatches.html?_r=1
9. Hawkins, R.P., Kreuter, M., Resnicow, K., Fishbein, M., Dijkstra, A.: Understanding tailoring in communicating about health. Health Educ. Res. **23**(3), 454–466 (2008)
10. Noar, S.M., Benac, C.N., Harris, M.S.: Does tailoring matter? Meta-analytic review of tailored print health behavior change interventions. Psychol. Bull. **133**(4), 673–693 (2007)
11. Serino, C.M., Furner, C.P., Smatt, C.: Making it personal: how personalization affects trust over time. In: Proceedings 38th Annual Hawaii International Conference on System Sciences, pp. 170a–170a. IEEE (2005)
12. Sundar, S.S., Marathe, S.S.: Personalization versus customization: the importance of agency, privacy, and power usage. Hum. Commun. Res. **36**(3), 298–322 (2010)
13. Personalization is over-rated. Jakob Nielsen's Alertbox, http://www.nngroup.com/articles/personalization-is-over-rated
14. Sunder, S.S.: Self as Source: Agency and Customization in Interactive Media. Routledge, New York (2008)
15. Treiblmaier, H., Madlberger, M., Knotzer, N., Pollach, I.: Evaluating personalization and customization from an ethical point of view: an empirical study. In: Proceedings 37th Annual Hawaii International Conference on System Sciences, pp. 1–10. IEEE (2004)
16. Bhargava, H.K., Feng, J.: America online's internet access service: how to deter unwanted customers. Electron. Commer. Res. Appl. **4**(1), 35–48 (2005)

17. Marathe, S.S., Sundar, S. S., Bijvank, M.N., van Vugt, H., Veldhuis, J.: Who are these power users anyway? Building a psychological profile. In: Proceedings 57th Annual Conference of the International Communication Association (2007)
18. Kim, Y., Sundar, S.S.: Visualizing ideal self vs. actual self through avatars: Impact on preventive health outcomes. Comput. Hum. Behav. **28**(4), 1356–1364 (2012)
19. Sundar, S.S., Bellur, S., Jia, H.: Motivational technologies: a theoretical framework for designing preventive health applications. Springer, Berlin Heidelberg (2012)
20. Chellappa, R.K., Sin, R.G.: Personalization versus privacy: An empirical examination of the online consumer's dilemma. Inf. Technol. Manage. **6**(2–3), 181–202 (2005)
21. Joinson, A.N., Reips, U.D., Buchanan, T., Schofield, C.B.P.: Privacy, trust, and self-disclosure online. Hum. Comput. Interact. **25**(1), 1–24 (2010)
22. Xu, H., Dinev, T., Smith, J., Hart, P.: Information privacy concerns: linking individual perceptions with institutional privacy assurances. J. Assoc. Inf. Syst. **12**(12), 798–824 (2011)
23. Miyazaki, A.D., Fernandez, A.: Consumer perceptions of privacy and security risks for online shopping. J. Consum. Aff. **35**(1), 27–44 (2001)
24. Malhotra, N.K., Kim, S.S., Agarwal, J.: Internet users' information privacy concerns (IUIPC): the construct, the scale, and a causal model. Inf. Syst. Res. **15**(4), 336–355 (2004)
25. Solove, D.J.: A taxonomy of privacy. University of Pennsylvania law review (2006)
26. Ho, S.Y.: The attraction of internet personalization to web users. Electron. Markets. **16**(1), 41–50 (2006)
27. Metzger, M.J.: Making sense of credibility on the web: models for evaluating online information and recommendations for future research. J. Am. Soc. Inform. Sci. Technol. **58** (13), 2078–2091 (2007)
28. Seale, C.: The Quality of Qualitative Research: Introducing qualitative methods. Sage, London (1999)

A Study of the Interactive Application in Aquarium Exhibit

Linye Zhang[(✉)] and Young Mi Choi

Georgia Institute of Technology, Atlanta, USA
zly0305@gmail.com, christina.choi@gatech.edu

Abstract. Mobile technology is becoming increasingly widespread in museums, and many institutions have already developed applications that can be downloaded on mobile phones. The use of mobile technology is a new communication between museum and visitors yet there are few mobile apps for Aquariums even though there is an enormous amount of information available to visitors. Mobile apps are a powerful educational environment for inspiring and supporting children and adults interested in nature. They potentially may be used commonly due to increasing use of wireless networks for dissemination of media. The aim of this study is help visitors get information and interact with marine animals in the aquarium via a mobile app. Data collected from observations, surveys and tests with 259 visitors to exhibits in the Georgia are discussed in this study. The results will provide insights and guidelines for using mobile technology to interact in other museums.

Keywords: Aquarium · Interaction · Usability · Mobile app

1 Introduction

Nowadays, a smart phone is one of the most common personal belongings. Equipped with a computer and many sensors, smart phones are able to run various useful applications [1]. Common usage and the ability to utilize wireless data networks [2], smart phones allow both communication and the ability to obtain information immediately.

Smart phones and other mobile devices have recently been widely applied to education [3]. Since they are highly portable, they have been used in both animal watching and museum visiting [4] in order to enhance and support a visitors' experience.

Museums, especially natural museums, have played an import role in education. Extensive exhibits and valuable collections provide powerful educational environments which inspire and support the inquiry of children and adults interested in science and nature [5]. Museums are also one of the few out of school environments where the public can be exposed to and learn about the world. In order to provide knowledge to visitors effectively, many museums have begun to provide educational learning experiences through media, gaming, and Web-based platforms.

© Springer International Publishing Switzerland 2015
M. Kurosu (Ed.): Human-Computer Interaction, Part III, HCII 2015, LNCS 9171, pp. 549–559, 2015.
DOI: 10.1007/978-3-319-21006-3_52

This paper introduces a mobile app intended for use by aquarium visitors. In the aquarium, there are many marine animals in one or more exhibits. The app is designed to provide information that visitor may want to know about the various exhibits and enables visitor interaction with marine animals.

2 Background

Museums are a unique environment for learning. They provide a rich environment for the experience of nature which is not usual in many people's daily lives [6]. Some studies of the 1990s have demonstrated that students enjoy visits to museums and that visits increased interest and enjoyment in nature. These visits can provide valuable learning outcomes that persist over time for both students as well as adults [7–10]. Museum learning has been closely associated with adult education due to their inter-active nature [11].

Visiting and enjoying a museum is not only in the sense of what is inside a museum but also what we can learn from the museum. For example a visitor may see penguins at an aquarium but just by seeing will not learn about where they live, how they live or how their lives may be connected to ours. Ideally these environments allow visitors to explore their own interests, provide interactive spaces for learning and encourage in depth exploration of current or relevant topics [12]. Research has shown that museum visits do not always provide these opportunities [13–15]. Mobile, digital technologies may help improve these environments so that they can become more effective places for learning [16].

Mobile technology has been increasing in popularity resulting in the development of a wide variety of applications for many different platforms [17]. There have been 1.5 million mobile apps, 500,000 tablet apps and over 60 billion mobile apps downloaded [18]. This represents a great opportunity for institutions to connect with a growing number of customers [19].

An early design example is an Electronic Guidebook of the Exploratorium in San Francisco. It started with the idea of creating a pocket travel guide for visitors to add personal notes [20]. The possibility to transfer texts, images, sounds and video through the mobile devices was used to provide information about displays, which also encouraged visitors to extend their relationship between their activities and the exhibits [21]. In 2005 Nancy Proctor listed 101 handheld and wireless cultural tour projects. The number has rapidly increased since it moved into museums and includes games, storytelling, and other means of actively engaging visitors [22]. In 2007, Stephen Weil invited visitors to create their own meaning from the collections for museum, encouraging existing audiences to interact in new ways, as well as reaching out to new audiences. In this process, museums have been experimenting with different strategies and practices [23]. Since 2009, the release of museum-related applications for mobile phones were designed for Apple's iPhone. Many museums have released iPhone Apps such as the Van Gogh Museum, the British Museum and the National Gallery in London.

The number of mobile applications are rapidly increasing because allow users download content before visiting the museum and extend preview experience; they help eliminate interface issues as people are accustomed to their own mobile device's environment, and can reduce maintenance costs allowing investment in content development [17].

This study focuses on the design of a mobile app for the Penguin Exhibit at the Georgia Aquarium, which houses more than 100,000 animals [24]. The Penguin Exhibit is located in Cold Water Quest habitat and is one of the last habitats seen by guests within the larger exhibit. A daylight simulator in the exhibit matches the seasonal light cycles of the penguins' natural habitat [24]. However, there was little information about individual penguins within the exhibit and it was hard for visitors to interact with penguins. The design of a mobile app for this exhibit was a convenient, low cost way to enhance visitors' experience.

3 Objective

The objective in this study is to help visitors get information and interact with penguins in the aquarium by using a mobile app. Two fundamental question guide this study: What informational should be shown to visitors? What is the best way to enable visitors interact with marine animals?

Visitors can learn general information about penguins from the current exhibit. However, there was hardly any information about individual penguins within the exhibit. Visitors, both adults and children, tried many different ways to make penguins pay attention to them since attempting to take pictures with the penguins in the exhibit is popular. These attempts were generally unsuccessful and some attempts could negatively impact the penguins.

The aim of the mobile app is to provide a convenient way to help users get information easily and quickly. It also needed to provide users an innovative way to interact with penguins and enable satisfactory pictures quickly in a way that does not negatively impact the penguins.

4 Method

This study included three phases: visitor observation, survey and user testing. The goal of phase 1 was to identify the main barriers in the exhibit. The goal of Phase 2 was to identify user requirements for a mobile app to provide information and interaction with the penguins. An app was designed based on these results and tested with visitors in Phase 3.

4.1 Phase 1 - Observation

In this phase visitors to the exhibit were simply observed and their activities in the exhibit were compiled. Visitors were observed on both weekend and weekdays because the makeup of visitors are different between weekends and weekdays. For example, some student groups visit the aquarium on weekdays and most family groups visit on weekends. When the participant entered the penguin exhibit, the time was recorded, the age group of the visitor and the number of group members were captured. Activities visitors performed in the exhibit were timed and their movements were sketched on an exhibit map.

The Penguin Exhibit observations included four parts: visitor information, activity performed, time spent for each activity and movement through the exhibit. Visitor information recorded visitor's age group, whether they come with group and group numbers. This section collected data about how visitors came to the exhibit, alone or with a group; which type of visitors most often came to the exhibit. Activities included things such as: Did they move around exhibit? Whether they tried to interact with penguins? Whether they took photos or videos for penguins? How long did visitors spend on each activity? This data allowed identification of the most popular activities and any potential barriers to performing those activities at the exhibit. The movement map sketched how visitors moved through the exhibit.

4.2   Phase 2 - Survey

Phase 2 included two surveys: a Penguin Information Survey (Survey 1) and Taking Pictures with Penguin Survey (Survey 2). Sixty visitors aged over 18 were randomly selected to participate in the survey. Half (30 participants) completed survey 1 and half (30 participants) completed survey 2. Visitors were chosen randomly to participate. After consenting to participate, the purpose of the study was explained and the surveys were administered.

Survey 1 asked six questions about penguin information do determine what kinds of information the app would need to provide. The question asked about what information they want to know about the penguins; how they want to get those information; what they would be willing to do to get the information; whether they want to know about individual penguins and what information they want to get about individual penguins. Survey 2 focused on taking pictures with penguins. It included seven questions, such as whether they want to take pictures with penguin; what kind of pictures they want to take; how they take pictures and what they will do for those pictures.

The last question in both surveys was whether they would be willing to download an app if the app provide these functions

4.3   Phase 3 - App Testing

Phase 3 focused on testing the app that was designed based on the data from the first two phases. Thirty subjects aged over 18 participated in this phase. The purpose of the app and functions provided were explained to participants in this phase after which they were allowed to use it themselves within the exhibit. Once finished in the exhibit, a survey about the appearance and function of the app was completed.

The survey had ten questions. The questions about the app's appearance included questions about the interface, readability and layout/looks. The questions about the apps functionality asked about whether it included all of the needed functions, if functions were easy to find and use and if language support was adequate.

5 Results

5.1 Phase 1

Population. Figure 1 shows that 254 visitors, 98 % of them went to penguin exhibit in group. 50 % of visitors were adults but most of them came with children or infants.

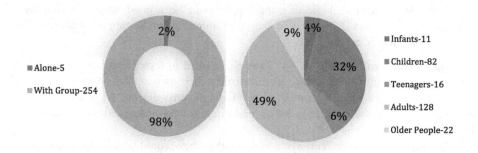

Fig. 1. Observed population at phase#1

Activity. Visitors participated in two main activities when they went to the Penguin Exhibit: taking photos and interacting with penguins. More than half visitors took photos for penguins or their friends and family. Taking pictures caused visitors to spend more time at the exhibit because few penguins paid attention to the camera and visitors moved around a lot in order to get a picture that they liked.

58 % visitors interacted with penguins. Many hit the glass and yelled at the penguins to try to get the penguins pay attention to them. These actions can frighten the penguins and cause potentially cause damage to the glass. Some visitors tried to communicate with penguins by waving their hands, talking to penguins and making funny faces. Many visitors attempt to play with the penguins. Most attempts were not effective although shiny things such as watches, flashlights, light sticks and shiny ribbons might get a penguin's attention.

The two main barriers identified were barriers to education and interaction.

Education. Nearly half of the visitors to the penguin exhibit were children and teenagers. Education was an important factor for visitors. However, there was no information about individual penguins around the exhibit and staff were often busy directing traffic, leaving little time to provide information to visitors.

Interaction. Visitors wanted to take pictures of penguins but the current exhibit does not provide immersive and locations designed for optimal pictures. Penguins didn't pay attention to cameras or interact with visitors, leading to some negative ways to draw penguins' attention to them.

5.2   Phase 2

Penguin Information. More than a half of the visitors wanted to know about penguin behavior and where they come from. They were interested in what penguins do day to day and how they grow up. More than 60 % people wanted to know individual penguin information, especially a penguin's age, personality and behavior.

40 % people preferred to get the information from the signage around the exhibit. This could be from a kiosk or information hoard. 53 % wanted to be able to get information from their smart devices indicating that app would be a good way to provide the information to visitors. Most people were not interested in saving or sharing information about individual penguins.

Taking Pictures with penguin. 83 % people wanted to take pictures with penguins. Of this 83 %, 88 % wanted to take pictures using their own device. More than an half wanted to be able to their pictures online. Though most did not want to share only information about the penguins, 84 % participants were interested in knowing the information.

The last question in the surveys asked whether they would be willing to download and use an app. More than 60 % (Fig. 2) indicated that they would download an app. 35 % participants would download it for taking pictures with penguins, others would download it for obtaining information about the penguins.

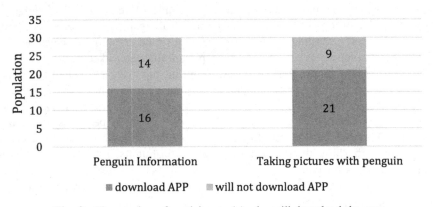

Fig. 2. The number of participants (n) who will download the app

5.3   Phase 3

An application was designed based on the initial phases. Figure 3 shows a mockup sketch of the app. 30 participants tested the app and then provided feedback via a survey.

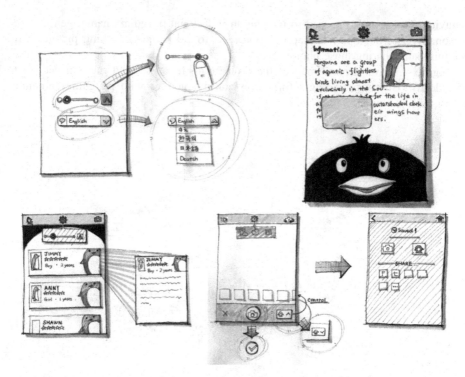

Fig. 3. Mockup app sketch

The first section of the surveys asked about app's appearance. 28 participants liked the blue background. Only two participants preferred a white background. Out of the 30 participants, 19 of them preferred white text with the rest preferring black. For the font style, all the participants liked the Arial Regular that was used and the penguin speaker. 17 participants found the icon size to be good, 5 wanted bigger icons and 8 wanted smaller icons.

For the app function section, all the participants needed English, 7 people needed Chinese, and 3 needed Korean. 100 % of participants wanted the app to including penguin information. 13 of them wanted the ability to get information from scanning a code and 18 participants thought that the ability to take a picture within the app was necessary. More than a half preferred the ability to change the font size by themselves while using the app. All the participants indicated that they were able to easily use the all of the provided functions. When asked about how they wanted to download the app, 11 wanted to do this via scanning a QR code and 16 wanted to download it from an app store.

6 Discussion

Phase 2 collected data about what information visitors wanted to get and what functionality they needed in an app. The app needed to provide information about: where are the penguins come from, how the penguins evolved, the species of a penguin and behavior. The app also needed to include an individual penguin's name, gender, age, personality and behavior. The app also needed to aid people in taking pictures with penguins and sharing those photos.

Figure 4 shows a mind map of the three main functions that the app needed to provide to visitors: providing information, taking pictures with penguins and interacting with penguins.

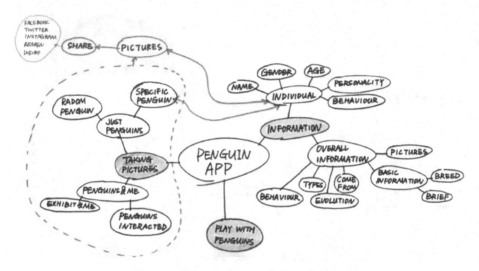

Fig. 4. Mind map (The app's three function)

When user first opens the app they are prompted to choose the language (via text or voice prompt) and set a default font size. The main homepage is shown after the setup which shows three choices: Penguin Information, Find the Penguin and Take Pictures. Penguin Information includes two part: general penguin introduction and information about individual penguins. There has a Penguin Bot icon on the bottom of the information pages. Penguin Bot will read the word to user. User can touch to Penguin Bot to turn off the sound. Find the Penguin provide individual penguin information. By using the app to scan the penguins, users will get the specified penguin information which they scanned. The Take Pictures function is used take pictures. When selected, the flash on the phone lights up to help to get a penguin's attention and attempt to draw them closer to the phone. This function also provides a feature called penguin frame, which can composite a picture with different people. It allows sharing of the picture online and access to the penguin's information in the picture. Figure 5 shows a flow chart of the functions provided by the app.

Fig. 5. Function flow chart

The mobile app employs a blue background color matching the aquarium's main color. The font color is white as preferred by most users. The app provided six languages (Fig. 6).

Fig. 6. UI design

7   Conclusions

The development of this mobile app for an aquarium exhibit generated positive results on visitor's experience. It was able to provide information about the target marine animals (penguins) and aided in interaction with the animals both of which helped to improve visitors' experience by utilizing a mode of interaction (a device app) which is common and familiar to many. The app was able to deliver existing information through a new medium and that information to be updated easily. This study represents just the initial stages in design of an aquarium application. Further investigation and refinement of the interface, functionality and/or use of additional technologies may be needed.

Even from initial results, mobile apps that can meet visitor expectations have a potential to become a successful and important part of the visitor. A similar approach to identifying visitor needs/expectations may be applied to other aquarium exhibits or other environments such as museums. Mobile apps can encourage a transition from a passive model of visitor engagement to an engagement featuring interactive, collaborative and learning.

References

1. Jaegeol, Y.: Design of the recommendation module for context aware VOD museum guide android App. Int. J. Softw. Eng. Appl. **7**(2), 273 (2013)
2. Caverly, D.C.: Techtalk: how technology has changed developmental education. J. Dev. Educ. **27**, 38–39 (2003)
3. Tatar, D., Roschelle, J., Vahey, P., Penuel, W.R.: Handhelds go to school. IEEE Comput. **36** (9), 58–65 (2003)
4. Hsi, S.: A Study of user experiences mediated by nomadic web content in a museum. J. Comput. Assist. Learn. **19**, 308–319 (2003)
5. Steiner, M., Crowley, K.: The natural history museum: taking on a learning agenda. Curator **56**(2), 267–272 (2013). doi:10.1111/cura.12024
6. Falk, J.: The director's cut: toward an improved understanding of learning from museums. Sci. Educ. **88**(1), 83–96 (2004)
7. Anderson, D.: The development of science concepts emergent from science museum and post-visit activity experiences: students' construction of knowledge. Unpublished Doctor of Philosophy thesis. Queensland University of Technology, Brisbane, Australia (1999)
8. Anderson, D.: An analysis of the importance of informal and formal science learning contexts to each other: an overview perspective. In: Proceedings of the Learning Science in Informal Contexts Conference, Questacon, Canberra, ACT, Australia, August 1998
9. Ayres, R., Melear, C.T.: Increased learning of physical science concepts via multimedia exhibit compared to hands-on exhibit in a science museum. Paper presented at the Annual Meeting of the National Association for Research in Science Teaching, San Diego, CA (April 1998)
10. Ramey-Gassert, L., Walberg III, H.J., Walberg, H.J.: Reexamining connections: museums as science learning environments. Sci. Educ. **78**(4), 345–363 (1994)
11. Monk, D.F.: John dewey and adult learning in museums. Adult Learn. **24**(2), 63–71 (2013)
12. Bell, P., Lewenstein, B., Shouse, A., Feder, M.: Learning Science in Informal Environments: People, Places, and Pursuits. National Academies Press, Washington, DC (2009)
13. Griffin, J.: Research on students and museums: looking more closely at the students in school groups. Sci. Educ. **88**(11), 59–70 (2004)
14. Tal, T., Morag, O.: School visits to natural history museums: teaching or enriching? J. Res. Sci. Educ. **44**(5), 747–769 (2007)
15. Rennie, L., Johnston, D.: The nature of learning and its implications for research on learning from museums. Sci. Educ. **88**(1), 4–16 (2004)
16. Vartiainen, H., Enkenberg, J.: Learning from and with museum objects: design perspectives, environment, and emerging learning systems. Educ. Technol. Res. Dev. **61**(5), 841–862 (2013). doi:10.1007/s11423-013-9311-8
17. Carillo, E., Rodriguez-Echavarria, K., Arnold, D., Chikama, M., Kadobayashi, R., Shimojo, S.: Making history alive and interactive: designing an iPhone app to present the summer war of Osaka Byōbu. In: 2010 16Th International Conference on Virtual Systems and Multimedia, VSMM 2010, (2010 16th International Conference on Virtual Systems and Multimedia, VSMM 2010), pp. 365–368. doi:10.1109/VSMM.2010.5665932 (2010)
18. School of Management Del Politecnico di Milano, Mercati Digitali Consumer e Nuova Internet, Smau Milan 2012 Conference, Milan, 17–19 October (2012)
19. Palumbo, F.F., Dominici, G.G., Basile, G.G.: Designing a mobile app for museums according to the drivers of visitor satisfaction. In: Raguz, I.V., Roushdy, M. (eds.) Recent Advances in Business Management and Marketing, pp. 159–166. WSEAS Press, USA (2013)

20. Hsi, S.S., Milrad, M.M., Kinshuk, U.H.: The electronic guidebook: astudy of user experiences using mobile web content in a museum setting (2002). doi:10.1109/WMTE. 2002.1039220
21. Economou, M.: Promising beginnings? Evaluating museum mobile phone apps, 31 March 2010. http://www.idc.ul.ie/techmuseums11/paper/paper8.pdf. Accessed 13 October 2014
22. Proctor, N.: Off base or On Target? Pros and Cons of wireless and location aware applications in the museums. In: Trant, J., Bearman, D. (eds) ICHIM (International Cultural Heritage Informatics Meeting) (2005)
23. Weil, S.: From being about something to being for somebody the ongoing transformation of the American museum. In: Sandel, R., Janes, R. (eds.) Museum Management and Marketing, pp. 30–48. Routledge, London (2007)
24. Georgia Aquarium: October 2014. http://www.georgiaaquarium.org/. Accessed 13 October 2014

Author Index

Printed in the United States
By Bookmasters